W9-DAE-559

# THE LIFE OF THOMAS HARDY

Thomas Hardy, aged 80

# THE LIFE OF
# THOMAS HARDY
## 1840-1928

COMPILED LARGELY
FROM CONTEMPORARY NOTES, LETTERS,
DIARIES, AND BIOGRAPHICAL MEMORANDA,
AS WELL AS FROM ORAL INFORMATION
IN CONVERSATIONS EXTENDING
OVER MANY YEARS

BY

FLORENCE EMILY HARDY

ARCHON BOOKS
Hamden, Connecticut
1970

PRINTED IN GREAT BRITAIN

This volume brings together for the first time *The Early Life of Thomas Hardy, 1840–1891*, and *The Later Years of Thomas Hardy, 1892–1928*, which were originally published in 1928 and 1930 respectively and have been out of print for several years.

# PREFATORY NOTE TO 'THE EARLY LIFE'

MR. HARDY's feeling for a long time was that he would not care to have his life written at all. And though often asked to record his recollections he would say that he 'had not sufficient admiration for himself' to do so. But later, having observed many erroneous and grotesque statements advanced as his experiences, and a so-called 'Life' published as authoritative, his hand was forced, and he agreed to my strong request that the facts of his career should be set down for use in the event of its proving necessary to print them.

To this end he put on paper headings of chapters, etc., and, in especial, memories of his early days whenever they came into his mind, also communicating many particulars by word of mouth from time to time. In addition a great help has been given by the dated observations which he made in pocket-books, during the years of his novel-writing, apparently with the idea that if one followed the trade of fiction one must take notes, rather than from natural tendency, for when he ceased fiction and resumed the writing of verses he left off note-taking except to a very limited extent.

The opinions quoted from these pocket-books and fugitive papers are often to be understood as his passing thoughts only, temporarily jotted there for consideration, and not as permanent conclusions — a fact of which we are reminded by his frequent remarks on the tentative character of his theories.

As such memoranda were not written with any view to their being printed, at least as they stood, and hence are often abrupt, a few words of explanation have been given occasionally.

It may be added that in the book generally Mr. Hardy's own reminiscent phrases have been used or approximated to whenever they could be remembered or were written down at the time of their expression *viva voce*. On this point great trouble has been taken to secure exactness.

Some incidents of his country experiences herein recorded may be considered as trivial, or as not strictly appertaining to a personal biography, but they have been included from a sense that they embody customs and manners of old West-of-England life that have now entirely passed away.

F. E. H.

# CONTENTS

## PART I

### EARLY LIFE AND ARCHITECTURE

## PART II

### NOVELS — TO ILLNESS

## PART III

### ILLNESS, NOVELS, AND ITALY

# CONTENTS

## PART VII

### 'TIME'S LAUGHINGSTOCKS', 'SATIRES OF CIRCUMSTANCE', AND 'MOMENTS OF VISION'

## PART VIII

### LIFE'S DECLINE

# ILLUSTRATIONS

# PART I

## EARLY LIFE AND ARCHITECTURE

Thomas Hardy's Birthplace
*From a drawing made by him*

# CHAPTER I

# BIRTH AND BOYHOOD

1840–1855 : *Aet.* 1–15

*June* 2, 1840. It was in a lonely and silent spot between woodland and heathland that Thomas Hardy was born, about eight o'clock on Tuesday morning the 2nd of June 1840, the place of his birth being the seven-roomed rambling house that stands easternmost of the few scattered dwellings called Higher Bockhampton, in the parish of Stinsford, Dorset. The domiciles were quaint, brass-knockered, and green-shuttered then, some with green garden-doors and white balls on the posts, and mainly occupied by lifeholders of substantial footing like the Hardys themselves. In the years of his infancy, or shortly preceding it, the personages tenanting these few houses included two retired military officers, one old navy lieutenant, a small farmer and tranter, a relieving officer and registrar, and an old militiaman, whose wife was the monthly nurse that assisted Thomas Hardy into the world. These being mostly elderly people, the place was at one time nicknamed 'Veterans' Valley'. It was also dubbed 'Cherry Alley', the lane or street leading through it being planted with an avenue of cherry-trees. But the lifeholds fell into hand, and the quaint residences with their trees, clipped hedges, orchards, white gatepost-balls, the naval officer's masts and weather-cocks, have now perished every one, and have been replaced by labourers' brick cottages and other new farm-buildings, a convenient pump occupying the site of the mossy well and bucket. The Hardy homestead, too, is weather-worn and reduced, having comprised, in addition to the house, two gardens (one of them part orchard), a horse-paddock, and sand-and-gravel pits, afterwards exhausted and overgrown : also stabling and like buildings since removed ; while the leaves and mould washed down by rains from the plantation have risen high against the back wall of the house, that was formerly covered with ivy. The wide, brilliantly white chimney-corner, in his child-time such a feature of the sitting-room, is also gone.

Some Wordsworthian lines — the earliest discoverable of young
Hardy's attempts in verse — give with obvious and naïve fidelity the
appearance of the paternal homestead at a date nearly half a century
before the birth of their writer, when his grandparents settled there,
after his great-grandfather had built for their residence the first house
in the valley.[1]

The family, on Hardy's paternal side, like all the Hardys of the
south-west, derived from the Jersey le Hardys who had sailed across

[1] The poem, written between 1857 and 1860, runs as follows :

### DOMICILIUM

It faces west, and round the back and sides
High beeches, bending, hang a veil of boughs,
And sweep against the roof.  Wild honeysucks
Climb on the walls, and seem to sprout a wish
(If we may fancy wish of trees and plants)
To overtop the apple-trees hard by.

Red roses, lilacs, variegated box
Are there in plenty, and such hardy flowers
As flourish best untrained.  Adjoining these
Are herbs and esculents ; and farther still
A field ; then cottages with trees, and last
The distant hills and sky.

Behind, the scene is wilder.  Heath and furze
Are everything that seems to grow and thrive
Upon the uneven ground.  A stunted thorn
Stands here and there, indeed ; and from a pit
An oak uprises, springing from a seed
Dropped by some bird a hundred years ago.

                              In days bygone —
Long gone — my father's mother, who is now
Blest with the blest, would take me out to walk.
At such a time I once inquired of her
How looked the spot when first she settled here.
The answer I remember.  'Fifty years
Have passed since then, my child, and change has marked
The face of all things.  Yonder garden-plots
And orchards were uncultivated slopes
O'ergrown with bramble bushes, furze and thorn :
That road a narrow path shut in by ferns,
Which, almost trees, obscured the passer-by.

'Our house stood quite alone, and those tall firs
And beeches were not planted.  Snakes and efts
Swarmed in the summer days, and nightly bats
Would fly about our bedrooms.  Heathcroppers
Lived on the hills, and were our only friends ;
So wild it was when first we settled here.'

to Dorset for centuries — the coasts being just opposite.   Hardy
often thought he would like to restore the 'le' to his name, and call
himself 'Thomas le Hardy'; but he never did so.   The Dorset Hardys
were traditionally said to descend in particular from a Clement le
Hardy, Baily of Jersey, whose son John settled hereabouts in the
fifteenth century, having probably landed at Wareham, then a port.
They all had the characteristics of an old family of spent social energies,
that were revealed even in the Thomas Hardy of this memoir (as in
his father and grandfather), who never cared to take advantage of
the many worldly opportunities that his popularity and esteem as an
author afforded him.   They had dwelt for many generations in or
near the valley of the River Froom or Frome, which extends inland
from Wareham, occupying various properties whose sites lay scattered
about from Woolcombe, Toller-Welme, and Up-Sydling (near the
higher course of the river), down the stream to Dorchester, Weymouth, and onward to Wareham, where the Froom flows into Poole
Harbour.   It was a family whose diverse Dorset sections included the
Elizabethan Thomas Hardy who endowed the Dorchester Grammar
School, the Thomas Hardy captain of the *Victory* at Trafalgar,
Thomas Hardy an influential burgess of Wareham, Thomas Hardy
of Chaldon, and others of local note, the tablet commemorating the
first-mentioned being still in St. Peter's Church, Dorchester, though
shifted from its original position in the 'Hardy Chapel', the inscription
running as follows :

TO THE MEMORYE OF
THOMAS HARDY OF MELCOMBE REGIS IN THE COUNTY OF
DORSETT, ESQUIER, WHOE ENDOWED THIS BORROUGHE
WTH A YEARELY REVENEW OF 50*l.*; AND APPOYNTED OUT
OF IT, TO BE EMPLOYED FOR YE BETTER MAYNTENANCE OF
A PREACHER, 20*l.*; A SCHOOLEMASTER, TWENTY POUNDES;
AN HUISHER, TWENTY NOBLES; THE ALMES WOMEN FIVE
MARKS.   THE BAYLIVES AND BURGISSES OF DORCHESTER, IN
TESTIMONY OF THEIR GRATITUDE, AND TO COMMEND TO
POSTERITY AN EXAMPLE SO WORTHY OF IMITATION, HATH
ERECTED THIS MONUMENT.
HE DYED THE 15 OF OCTOBER, ANNO DO: 1599.

But at the birth of the subject of this biography the family had
declined, so far as its Dorset representatives were concerned, from
whatever importance it once might have been able to claim there ;
and at his father's death the latter was, it is believed, the only landowner of the name in the county, his property being, besides the

acre-and-half lifehold at Bockhampton, a small freehold farm at Tal-bothays, with some houses there, and about a dozen freehold cottages and a brick-yard-and-kiln elsewhere. The Talbothays farm was a small outlying property standing detached in a ring fence, its possessors in the reign of Henry VIII having been Talbots, from a seventeenth-century daughter of whom Hardy borrowed the name of Avis or Avice in *The Well-Beloved*.

On the maternal side he was Anglo-Saxon, being descended from the Chiles, Childs, or Childses (who gave their name to the villages of Child-Okeford, Chilfrome, Childhay, etc.), the Swetmans, and other families of northwest Dorset that were small proprietors of lands there in the reign of Charles the First (see Hutchins' *History of Dorset*): and also from the Hanns or Hands of the Pidele Valley, Dorset, and earlier of the Vale of Blackmore. (In the parish register of Affpuddle the spelling is Hann.) The Swetmans and the Childses seem to have been involved in the Monmouth rising, and one of the former to have been brought before Jeffreys, 'for being absent from home att the tyme of the Rebellion'. As his name does not appear in the lists of those executed he was probably transported, and this con-nection with Monmouth's adventures and misfortunes seems to have helped to becloud the family prospects of the maternal line of Hardy's ancestry, if they had ever been bright.

Several traditions survived in the Swetman family concerning the Rebellion. An indubitably true one was that after the Battle of Sedge-moor two of the Swetman daughters — Grace and Leonarde — were beset in their house by some of the victorious soldiery, and only escaped violation by slipping from the upper rooms down the back stairs into the orchard. It is said that Hardy's great-grandmother could remember them as very old women. Part of the house, now in the possession of the Earl of Ilchester, and divided into two cottages, is still standing with its old Elizabethan windows; but the hall and open oak staircase have disappeared, and also the Ham-Hill stone chimneys. The spot is called 'Townsend'.

Another tradition, of more doubtful authenticity, is that to which the short story by Hardy called *The Duke's Reappearance* approxi-mates. Certainly a mysterious man did come to Swetman after the battle, but it was generally understood that he was one of Monmouth's defeated officers.

Thomas Hardy's maternal grandmother Elizabeth,[1] or Betty, was

---

[1] [She married George Hand (or Hadd). Her daughter Jemima used the former spelling.]

the daughter of one of those Swetmans by his wife Maria Childs, sister of the Christopher Childs who married into the Cave family, became a mining engineer in Cornwall, and founded the *West Briton* newspaper, his portrait being painted when he was about eighty by Sir Charles Eastlake. The traditions about Betty, Maria's daughter, were that she was tall, handsome, had thirty gowns, was an omnivorous reader, and one who owned a stock of books of exceptional extent for a yeoman's daughter living in a remote place.[1]

She knew the writings of Addison, Steele, and others of the *Spectator* group almost by heart, was familiar with Richardson and Fielding, and, of course, with such standard works as *Paradise Lost* and *The Pilgrim's Progress*. From the old medical books in her possession she doctored half the village, her sheet-anchor being Culpepper's *Herbal* and *Dispensary*; and if ever there was any doubt as to the position of particular graves in the churchyard, the parson, sexton, and relatives applied to her as an unerring authority.

But alas for her fortunes ! Her bright intelligence in a literary direction did not serve her in domestic life. After her mother's death she clandestinely married a young man of whom her father strongly disapproved. The sturdy yeoman, apparently a severe and unyielding parent, never forgave her, and never would see her again. His unbending temper is illustrated by the only anecdote known of him. A fortune-telling gipsy had encamped on the edge of one of his fields, and on a Sunday morning he went to order her away. Finding her obdurate he said : 'If you don't take yourself off I'll have you burnt as a witch !' She pulled his handkerchief from his pocket, and threw it into her fire, saying, 'If that burn I burn'. The flames curled up round the handkerchief, which was his best, of India silk, but it did not burn, and she handed it back to him intact. The tale goes that he was so impressed by her magic that he left her alone.

Not so long after the death of this stern father of Elizabeth's — Hardy's maternal great-grandfather — her husband also died, leaving her with several children, the youngest only a few months old. Her father, though in comfortable circumstances, had bequeathed her nothing, and she was at her wit's end to maintain herself and her family, if ever widow was. Among Elizabeth's children there was

[1] A curious reminiscence by her daughter bears testimony to her rather striking features. She was crossing the fields with the latter as a child, a few years after Waterloo, when a gentleman shouted after her : 'A relation of Wellington's ? You must be ! That nose !' He excitedly followed them till they were frightened, jumping over stiles till they reached home. He was found to be an officer who had fought under Wellington, and had been wounded in the head, so that he was at times deranged.

one, a girl, of unusual ability and judgment, and an energy that might have carried her to incalculable issues. This was the child Jemima, the mother of Thomas Hardy. By reason of her parent's bereavement and consequent poverty under the burden of a young family, Jemima saw during girlhood and young womanhood some very stressful experiences of which she could never speak in her maturer years without pain, though she appears to have mollified her troubles by reading every book she could lay hands on. Moreover she turned her manual activities to whatever came in her way; grew to be exceptionally skilled in, among other things, 'tambouring' gloves; also was good at mantua-making, and excellent in the oddly dissimilar occupation of cookery. She resolved to be a cook in a London club-house; but her plans in this direction were ended by her meeting her future husband, and being married to him at the age of five-and-twenty.

He carried on an old-established building and master-masoning business (the designation of 'builder', denoting a manager of and contractor for all trades, was then unknown in the country districts). It was occasionally extensive, demanding from twelve to fifteen men, but frequently smaller; and the partner with whom she had thrown in her lot, though in substantial circumstances and unexceptionable in every other way, did not possess the art ofenri ching himself by business. Moreover he was devoted to church music, and secondarily to mundane, of the country-dance, hornpipe, and early waltz description, as had been his father, and was his brother also. It may be mentioned that an ancestral Thomas Hardy, living in Dorchester in 1724, was a subscriber to 'Thirty Select Anthems in Score', by Dr. W. Croft, organist of the Chapel Royal and Westminster Abbey, which seems to show that the family were interested in church music at an early date.

Jemima's husband's father, our subject's grandfather (the first Thomas of three in succession), when a young man living at Puddle-town before the year 1800, had expressed his strong musical bias by playing the violoncello in the church of that parish. He had somewhat improvidently married at one-and-twenty, whereupon his father John had set him up in business by purchasing a piece of land at Bock-hampton in the adjoining parish of Stinsford, and building a house for him there. On removing with his wife in 1801 to this home provided by his father John, Thomas Hardy the First (of these Stinsford Hardys) found the church music there in a deplorable con-dition, it being conducted from the gallery by a solitary old man with an oboe. He immediately set himself, with the easy-going vicar's hearty concurrence, to improve it, and got together some instrumentalists, himself taking the bass-viol as before, which he played in the gallery of Stinsford Church at two services every Sunday from 1801 or 1802 till his death in 1837, being joined later by his two sons, who, with other reinforcement, continued playing till about 1842, the period of performance by the three Hardys thus covering inclusively a little under forty years.

It was, and is, an interesting old church of various styles from Transition-Norman to late Perpendicular. In its vaults lie many members of the Grey and Pitt families, the latter collaterally related to the famous Prime Minister ; there also lies the actor and dramatist William O'Brien with his wife Lady Susan, daughter of the first Earl of Ilchester, whose secret marriage in 1764 with the handsome Irish comedian whom Garrick had discovered and brought to Drury Lane caused such scandal in aristocratic circles. 'Even a footman were preferable' wrote Walpole. 'I could not have believed that Lady Susan would have stooped so low.'

Though in these modern days the 'stooping' might have been viewed inversely — for O'Brien, besides being *jeune premier* at Drury, was an accomplished and well-read man, whose presentations of the gay Lothario in Rowe's *Fair Penitent*, Brisk in *The Double Dealer*, Sir Harry Wildair in *The Constant Couple*, Archer in *The Beaux' Stratagem*, Sir Andrew Aguecheek, the Prince in *Henry the Fourth*, and many other leading parts, made him highly popular, and whose own plays were of considerable merit. His marriage annihilated a promising career, for his wife's father would not hear of his remaining on the stage. The coincidence that both young Hardy's grandmothers had seen and admired O'Brien, that he was one of the Stinsford congregation for many years, that young Thomas's great-grandfather and grandfather had known him well, and that the latter as the local builder had constructed the vault for him and his wife (according to the builder's old Day-books still in existence his workmen drank nineteen quarts of beer over the job) ; had been asked by her to 'make it just large enough for our two selves only', had placed them in it, and erected their monument, lent the occupants of the little vault in the chancel a romantic interest in the boy's mind at an early age.

In this church (see the annexed plan, which is reproduced from a drawing made by Hardy many years ago under the supervision of his father) the Hardys became well known as violinists, Thomas the

Second, the poet and novelist's father aforesaid, after his early boyhood as chorister beginning as a youth with the 'counter' viol, and later taking on the tenor and treble.

They were considered among the best church-players in the neighbourhood, accident having helped their natural bent. This was the fact that in 1822, shortly after the death of the old vicar Mr. Floyer, the Rev. Edward Murray, a connection of the Earl of Ilchester, who was the patron of the living, was presented to it. Mr. Murray was an ardent musician and performer on the violin himself, and the two younger Hardys and sometimes their father used to practise two or three times a week with him in his study at Stinsford House, where he lived instead of at the Vicarage.

Thus it was that the Hardy instrumentalists, though never more than four, maintained an easy superiority over the larger bodies in parishes near. For while Puddletown west-gallery, for instance, could boast of eight players, and Maiden Newton of nine, these included wood-wind and leather — that is to say, clarionets and serpents — which were apt to be a little too sonorous, even strident, when zealously blown. But the few and well-practised violists of Stinsford were never unduly emphatic, according to tradition.

Elaborate Canticle services, such as the noted 'Jackson in F', and in 'E flat' — popular in the West of England, possibly because Jackson had been an Exeter man — Pope's Ode, and anthems with portentous repetitions and 'mountainous fugues', were carried through by the performers every Sunday, with what real success is not known, but to their own great satisfaction and the hearty approval of the musical vicar.

In their psalmody they adhered strictly to Tate-and-Brady — upon whom, in truth, the modern hymn-book has been no great improvement — such tunes as the 'Old Hundredth', 'New Sabbath', 'Devizes', 'Wilton', 'Lydia', and 'Cambridge New' being their staple ones; while 'Barthélémon' and 'Tallis' were played to Ken's Morning and Evening Hymns respectively every Sunday throughout the year: a practice now obsolete, but a great stimulus to congregational singing.

As if the superintendence of the Stinsford choir were not enough distraction from business for Thomas Hardy the First, he would go whenever opportunity served and assist other choirs by performing with his violoncello in the galleries of their parish churches, mostly to the high contentment of the congregations. Although Thomas the Third had not come into the world soon enough to know his grand-

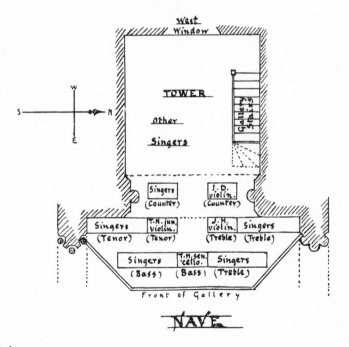

STINSFORD CHURCH.

Plan of West Gallery – circa 1835, Shewing Positions of Choir.

Explanation

| | | |
|---|---|---|
| T.H. sen. | Tho. Hardy | b. 1778. d. 1837. |
| T.H. jun. | Tho. Hardy | b. 1811. d. 1892. |
| J.H. | James Hardy | b. 1805. d. 188–. |
| J.D. | James Dart | b. 181–. d. 187–. |

father in person, there is no doubt that the description by Fairway in
*The Return of the Native* of the bowing of Thomasin's father, when
lending his services to the choir of Kingsbere, is a humorous exaggeration of the traditions concerning Thomas Hardy the First's musical
triumphs as locum-tenens.

In addition it may be mentioned that he had been a volunteer till
the end of the war, and lay in Weymouth with his company from
time to time, waiting for Bonaparte who never came.

Conducting the church choir all the year round involved carol-
playing and singing at Christmas, which Thomas Hardy the Second
loved as much as did his father. In addition to the ordinary practice,
the work of preparing and copying carols a month of evenings beforehand was not light, and incidental expenses were appreciable. The
parish being a large and scattered one, it was the custom of Thomas
Hardy the First to assemble the rather perfunctory rank-and-file of
the choir at his house; and this necessitated suppers, and suppers
demanded (in those days) plenty of liquor. This was especially the
case on Christmas Eve itself, when the rule was to go to the northern
part of the parish and play at every house before supper; then to
return to Bockhampton and sit over the meal till twelve o'clock,
during which interval a good deal was consumed at the Hardys'
expense, the choir being mainly poor men and hungry. They then
started for the other parts of the parish, and did not get home till all
was finished at about six in the morning, the performers themselves
feeling 'no more than malkins'[1] in church next day, as they used to
declare. The practice was kept up by Thomas Hardy the Second,
much as described in *Under the Greenwood Tree or The Mellstock
Quire*, though its author, Thomas Hardy the Third, invented the
personages, incidents, manners, etc., never having seen or heard the
choir as such, they ending their office when he was about a year old.
He was accustomed to say that on this account he had rather burlesqued
them, the story not so adequately reflecting as he could have wished
in later years the poetry and romance that coloured their time-honoured
observances.

This preoccupation of the Hardys with the music of the parish
church and less solemn assemblies did not, to say the least, assist their
building business, and it was somewhat of a relief to Thomas Hardy
the Second's young wife — though musical herself to a degree —
when ecclesiastical changes after the death of Thomas Hardy the First,
including the cession of the living by Murray, led to her husband's

---

[1] *Malkin*, a damp rag for swabbing out an oven.

abandoning in 1841 or 1842 all connection with the choir. The First Thomas's death having been quite unexpected, inasmuch as he was playing in the church one Sunday, and brought in for burial on the next, there could be no such quiring over his grave as he had performed over the graves of so many, owing to the remaining players being chief mourners. And thus ended his devoted musical services to Stinsford Church, in which he had occupied the middle seat of the gallery with his bass-viol on Sundays for a period of thirty-five years — to no worldly profit; far the reverse, indeed.

After his death the building and masoning business also saw changes, being carried on by his widow, her sons assisting — an unsatisfactory arrangement which ultimately led to the division of the goodwill between the brothers.

The second Thomas Hardy, the author's father, was a man who in his prime could be, and was, called handsome. To the courtesy of his manners there was much testimony among the local county-ladies with whom he came in contact as a builder. All the Dorset Hardys have more or less a family likeness (of which the Admiral may be considered the middle type), and the present one was a good specimen. He was about five feet nine in height, of good figure, with dark Vandyke-brown hair, and a beard which he wore cut back all round in the custom of his date; with teeth that were white and regular to nearly the last years of his life, and blue eyes that never faded grey; a quick step, and a habit of bearing his head a little to one side as he walked. He carried no stick or umbrella till past middle life, and was altogether an open-air liver, and a great walker always. He was good, too, when young, at hornpipes and jigs, and other folk-dances, performing them with all the old movements of leg-crossing and hop, to the delight of the children, till warned by his wife that this fast perishing style might tend to teach them what it was not quite necessary they should be familiar with, the more genteel 'country-dance' having superseded the former.

Mrs. Hardy once described him to her son as he was when she first set eyes on him in the now removed west gallery of Stinsford Church, appearing to her more travelled glance (she had lived for a time in London, Weymouth, and other towns) and somewhat satirical vision, 'rather amusingly old-fashioned, in spite of being decidedly good-looking — wearing the blue swallow-tailed coat with gilt embossed buttons then customary, a red and black flowered waistcoat, Wellington boots, and French-blue trousers'. The sonnet which follows expresses her first view of him.

## A CHURCH ROMANCE

### (MELLSTOCK, *circa* 1836)

She turned in the high pew, until her sight
Swept the west gallery, and caught its row
Of music-men with viol, book, and bow
Against the sinking, sad tower-window light.

She turned again ; and in her pride's despite
One strenuous viol's inspirer seemed to throw
A message from his string to her below,
Which said : 'I claim thee as my own forthright !'

Thus their hearts' bond began, in due time signed,
And long years thence, when Age had scared Romance,
At some old attitude of his or glance
That gallery-scene would break upon her mind,
With him as minstrel, ardent, young, and trim,
Bowing 'New Sabbath' or 'Mount Ephraim'.

Mrs. Hardy herself was rather below the middle height with
chestnut hair and grey eyes, and a trim and upright figure. Her
movement also in walking being buoyant through life, strangers approaching her from behind imagined themselves, even when she was
nearly seventy, about to overtake quite a young woman. The Roman
nose and countenance inherited from her mother would better have
suited a taller build. Like her mother, too, she read omnivorously.
She sang songs of the date, such as the then popular Haynes Bayly's
'Isle of Beauty', and 'Gaily the Troubadour'; also 'Why are you
wandering here, I pray ?' and 'Jeannette and Jeannot'. The children
had a quaint old piano for their practice, over which she would sigh
because she could not play it herself.

Thomas Hardy the Third, their eldest child of a family of four
(and the only one of the four who married, so that he had no blood-
nephew or niece), showed not the physique of his father. Had it not
been for the common sense of the estimable woman who attended as
monthly nurse, he might never have walked the earth. At his birth he
was thrown aside as dead till rescued by her as she exclaimed to the
surgeon, 'Dead ! Stop a minute : he's alive enough, sure !'

Of his infancy nothing has been handed down save the curious
fact that on his mother's returning from out-of-doors one hot afternoon, to him asleep in his cradle, she found a large snake curled up

upon his breast, comfortably asleep like himself. It had crept into the house from the heath hard by, where there were many.

Though healthy he was fragile, and precocious to a degree, being able to read almost before he could walk, and to tune a violin when of quite tender years. He was of ecstatic temperament, extraordinarily sensitive to music, and among the endless jigs, hornpipes, reels, waltzes, and country-dances that his father played of an evening in his early married years, and to which the boy danced a *pas seul* in the middle of the room, there were three or four that always moved the child to tears, though he strenuously tried to hide them. Among the airs (though he did not know their names at that time) were, by the way, 'Enrico' (popular in the Regency), 'The Fairy Dance', 'Miss Macleod of Ayr' (an old Scotch tune to which Burns may have danced), and a melody named 'My Fancy-Lad' or 'Johnny's gone to sea'. This peculiarity in himself troubled the mind of 'Tommy' as he was called, and set him wondering at a phenomenon to which he ventured not to confess. He used to say in later life that, like Calantha in Ford's *Broken Heart*, he danced on at these times to conceal his weeping. He was not over four years of age at this date.

One or two more characteristics of his personality at this childhood-time can be recounted. In those days the staircase at Bockhampton (later removed) had its walls coloured Venetian red by his father, and was so situated that the evening sun shone into it, adding to its colour a great intensity for a quarter of an hour or more. Tommy used to wait for this chromatic effect, and, sitting alone there, would recite to himself 'And now another day is gone' from Dr. Watts's Hymns, with great fervency, though perhaps not for any religious reason, but from a sense that the scene suited the lines.

It is not therefore to be wondered at that a boy of this sort should have a dramatic sense of the church services, and on wet Sunday mornings should wrap himself in a tablecloth, and read the Morning Prayer standing in a chair, his cousin playing the clerk with loud Amens, and his grandmother representing the congregation. The sermon which followed was simply a patchwork of the sentences used by the vicar. Everybody said that Tommy would have to be a parson, being obviously no good for any practical pursuit; which remark caused his mother many misgivings.

One event of this date or a little later stood out, he used to say, more distinctly than any. He was lying on his back in the sun, thinking how useless he was, and covered his face with his straw hat. The sun's rays streamed through the interstices of the straw, the lining having disappeared.  Reflecting on his experiences of the world so far as he had got, he came to the conclusion that he did not wish to grow up.  Other boys were always talking of when they would be men ; he did not want at all to be a man, or to possess things, but to remain as he was, in the same spot, and to know no more people than he already knew (about half a dozen).  Yet this early evidence of that lack of social ambition which followed him through life was shown when he was in perfect health and happy circumstances.

Afterwards he told his mother of his conclusions on existence, thinking she would enter into his views.  But to his great surprise she was very much hurt, which was natural enough considering she had been near death's door in bringing him forth.  And she never forgot what he had said, a source of much regret to him in after years.

When but little older he was puzzled by what seemed to him a resemblance between two marches of totally opposite sentiments — 'See the conquering hero comes' and 'The Dead March in *Saul*'. Some dozen years were to pass before he discovered that they were by the same composer.

It may be added here that this sensitiveness to melody, though he was no skilled musician, remained with him through life.


## 1848.  First School

Until his fifth or sixth year his parents hardly supposed he would survive to grow up, but at eight he was thought strong enough to go to the village school, to learn the rudiments before being sent further afield ; and by a curious coincidence he was the first pupil to enter the new school-building, arriving on the day of opening, and awaiting tremulously and alone, in the empty room, the formal entry of the other scholars two-and-two with the schoolmaster and mistress from the temporary premises near.  The school is still standing much in its original condition.

Here he worked at Walkingame's Arithmetic and at geography, in both of which he excelled, though his handwriting was indifferent. About this time his mother gave him Dryden's *Virgil*, Johnson's *Rasselas*, and *Paul and Virginia*.  He also found in a closet *A History of the Wars* — a periodical dealing with the war with Napoleon, which his grandfather had subscribed to at the time, having been himself a volunteer.  The torn pages of these contemporary numbers with their melodramatic prints of serried ranks, crossed bayonets, huge knapsacks, and dead bodies, were the first to set him on the train of ideas that led to *The Trumpet-Major* and *The Dynasts*.

## A JOURNEY

The boy Thomas's first experience of travel was when, at eight or nine years old, his mother took him with her — 'for protection', as she used to say — being then an attractive and still young woman — on a visit to her sister in Hertfordshire. As the visit lasted three weeks or a month he was sent while there to a private school, which appears to have been somewhat on the Squeers model. Since, however, he was only a day-scholar this did not affect him much, though he was mercilessly tyrannized over by the bigger boys whom he could beat hollow in arithmetic and geography.

Their return from this visit was marked by an experience which became of interest in the light of after events. The Great Northern Railway to London was then only in process of construction, and it was necessary to go thither by coach from Hertfordshire in order to take the train at Waterloo Station for Dorchester. Mrs. Hardy had not been to London since she had lived there for some months twelve years earlier. The coaching-inn was The Cross-Keys, St. John Street, Clerkenwell, and here mother and boy put up for the night. It was the inn at which Shelley and Mary Godwin had been accustomed to meet at week-ends not two-score years before, and was at this time unaltered from its state during the lovers' romantic experiences there — the oval stone staircase, the skylight, and the hotel entrance being untouched. As Mrs. Hardy and her little boy took a room rather high up the staircase for economy, and the poet had probably done so for the same reason, there is a possibility that it may have been the same as that occupied by our most marvellous lyrist.

They stayed but a short time in London, but long enough for him to see and remember some of the streets, the Pantheon, then a fashionable pantechnicon, Cumberland Gate into Hyde Park, which then could boast of no Marble Arch, and the pandemonium of Smithfield, with its mud, curses, and cries of ill-treated animals. Also, that when passing through the city on the way up, they stopped at the point now called Swiss Cottage, and looked back at the *outside* of London creeping towards them across green fields.

## 1849-1850

By another year he was judged to be strong enough to walk further than to the village school, and after some postponements he was sent to a Dorchester day-school, whose headmaster his mother had learnt to be an exceptionally able man, and a good teacher of Latin, which was quite enough to lead her to waive the fact that the school was Nonconformist, though she had no nonconforming tendencies whatever.

It is somewhat curious, and shows the honour with which the school was conducted, that the boy did not know till he had been there several months that it was a Nonconformist school, a large number, probably a majority, of the boys coming like himself from Church-of-England homes, having been attracted thither by the reputation of the said master ; though Thomas used to wonder why the familiar but rather boring Church Catechism had vanished — or rather all of it except the Ten Commandments, in which the pupils were made proficient once a week. However, though nominally unorthodox during the week Thomas was kept strictly at church on Sundays as usual, till he knew the Morning and Evening Services by heart including the rubrics, as well as large portions of the New Version of the Psalms. The aspect of that time to him is clearly indicated in the verses 'Afternoon Service at Mellstock', included in *Moments of Vision*.

The removal of the boy from Bockhampton school seriously wounded the lady of the manor who had erected it, though she must have guessed that he had only been sent there till sturdy enough to go further. To his mother this came as an unpleasant misunderstanding. While not wishing to be uncivil she had, naturally, not consulted the other at all in taking him away, considering his interests solely, the Hardys being comparatively independent of the manor, as their house and the adjoining land were a family lifehold, and the estate-work forming only part of Mr. Hardy's business. That the school to which he was removed was not a Church-of-England one was another rock of offence to this too sensitive lady, though, as has been stated, it was an accident as unwished by the boy's mother as by the squire's wife. The latter had just built a model school at her own expense and, though it was but small, had provided it with a well-trained master and mistress ; had made it her hobby, till it was far superior to an ordinary village school. Moreover under her dignity lay a tender heart, and having no children of her own she had grown passionately fond of Tommy almost from his infancy — he is said to have been an attractive little fellow at this time — whom she had been accustomed to take into her lap and kiss until he was quite a big child. He quite reciprocated her fondness.

Shortly before or after the boy's removal the estate-building work was taken out of the hands of Tommy's father, who went further afield to replace it, soon obtaining a mansion to enlarge, and other contracts, and thus not suffering much from his loss of business in the immediate vicinity of his home. He would have left the parish altogether, the house his grandfather John had built for his father Thomas the First, as stated, being awkwardly small and ill-arranged, and the spot inconvenient for a builder. But as the rambling dwelling, field, and sandpits attached were his for life, he remained.

Thomas Hardy the youngest, however, secretly mourned the loss of his friend the landowner's wife, to whom he had grown more attached than he cared to own. In fact, though he was only nine or ten and she must have been nearly forty, his feeling for her was almost that of a lover. He had been wont to make drawings of animals in water-colours for her, and to sing to her, one of his songs being 'I've journeyed over many lands, I've sailed on every sea', which was comical enough considering the extent of his travels. He so much longed to see her that he jumped at the offer of a young woman of the village to take him to a harvest-supper at which he knew she would be present, one of the farms on the estate being carried on by the landowner himself as a hobby, with the aid of a bailiff — much to his pecuniary loss as it turned out. The young woman, a small farmer's daughter, called for young Thomas on the afternoon of the festivity. Together they went off, his mother being away from home, though they left word where he had gone. The 'Supper', an early meal at that date, probably about four o'clock, was over by the time they reached the barn, and tea was going on, after which there was singing and dancing, some non-commissioned officers having been invited from the barracks by the Squire as partners for the girls. The Squire showed himself by no means strait-laced in this respect. What his wife thought is not recorded. It may be remarked in passing that here probably began Thomas's extensive acquaintance with soldiers of the old uniforms and long service, which was to serve him in good stead when he came to write *The Trumpet-Major* and *The Dynasts*.

Presently the manor-lady, her husband, and a house-party arrived to lead off some dances. As soon as she saw little Thomas — who had no business whatever there — she came up to him and said reproachfully:

'O Tommy, how is this ?  I thought you had deserted me !'

Tommy assured her through his tears that he had not deserted her, and never would desert her : and then the dance went on.  He being wildly fond of dancing, she gave him for a partner a little niece of hers about his own age staying at her house, who had come with her. The manor-house party remained for a few figures and then left, but Tommy perforce stayed on, being afraid to go home without the strapping young woman his companion, who was dancing with the soldiers.  There he wearily waited for her till three in the morning, having eaten and drunk nothing since one o'clock on the previous day, through his fear of asking the merry-makers for food.  What the estate owner's tender wife would have given him had she but known of his hunger and thirst, and how carefully have sent him home had she been aware of his dilemma !  A reproof from both his parents when Tommy reached home ended the day's adventure.  It was the only harvest-supper and dance that he ever saw, save one that he dropped into by chance years after.

In spite of his lover-like promise of fidelity to her ladyship, the two never met again till he was a young man of twenty-two, and she quite an elderly woman ; though it was not his fault, her husband selling the estate shortly after and occupying a house in London.

It may be worthy of note that this harvest-home was among the last at which the old traditional ballads were sung, the railway having been extended to Dorchester just then, and the orally transmitted ditties of centuries being slain at a stroke by the London comic songs that were introduced.  The particular ballad which he remembered hearing that night from the lips of the farm-women was that one variously called 'The Outlandish Knight', 'May Colvine', 'The Western Tragedy', etc.  He could recall to old age the scene of the young women in their light gowns sitting on a bench against the wall in the barn, and leaning against each other as they warbled the Dorset version of the ballad, which differed a little from the northern :

> 'Lie there, lie there, thou false-hearted man,
>     Lie there instead o' me ;
> For six pretty maidens thou hast a-drown'd here,
>     But the seventh hath drown-ed thee !'

> .     .     .     .     .

> 'O tell no more, my pretty par-rot,
>     Lay not the blame on me ;
> And your cage shall be made o' the glittering gold,
>     Wi' a door o' the white ivo-rie !'

The question of moving from the parish, above alluded to, and taking more commodious premises nearer to or in the town, again arose with the Hardys — was, indeed, always arising. An opportunity to develop her husband's business which a more convenient centre would have afforded him had been long in Mrs. Hardy's perception, and she thought he should seek it for the sake of his growing family. It must be admitted that a lonely spot between a heath and a wood, the search for which by messengers and other people of affairs often became wearisomely tedious to them, was almost unreasonable as a place for carrying on the building trade. But Thomas Hardy the Second had not the tradesman's soul. Instead of waylaying possible needers of brick and stone in the market-place or elsewhere, he liked going alone into the woods or on the heath, where, with a telescope inherited from some collateral ancestor who had been captain of a merchant craft, he would stay peering into the distance by the half-hour; or, in the hot weather, lying on a bank of thyme or camomile with the grasshoppers leaping over him. Among his son's other childish memories were those of seeing men in the stocks, corn-law agitations, mail-coaches, road-waggons, tinder-boxes, and candle-snuffing. When still a small boy he was taken by his father to witness the burning in effigy of the Pope and Cardinal Wiseman in the old Roman Amphitheatre at Dorchester during the No-Popery Riots. The sight to young Hardy was most lurid, and he never forgot it; and when the cowl of one of the monks in the ghastly procession blew aside and revealed the features of one of his father's workmen his bewilderment was great.

His earliest recollection was of receiving from his father the gift of a small accordion. He knew that he was but four years old at this time, as his name and the date were written by his father upon the toy: Thomas Hardy. 1844.

Another memory, some two or three years later, is connected with the Corn Law Agitation. The boy had a little wooden sword, which his father had made for him, and this he dipped into the blood of a pig which had just been killed, and brandished it as he walked about the garden exclaiming: 'Free Trade or blood!'

A member of his family recalled, even after an interval of sixty years, the innocent glee with which the young Thomas and his mother would set off on various expeditions. They were excellent companions, having each a keen sense of humour and a love of adventure. Hardy would tell of one prank when he and his mother put on fantastic garb, pulling cabbage-nets over their faces to disguise themselves. Thus oddly dressed they walked across the heath to visit a sister of Mrs. Hardy, living at Puddletown, whose amazement was great when she set eyes upon these strange visitors at her door.

It was natural that with the imitativeness of a boy he should at an early age have attempted to perform on the violin, and under his father's instruction was soon able to tweedle from notation some hundreds of jigs and country-dances that he found in his father's and grandfather's old books. From tuning fiddles as a boy he went on as a youth in his teens to keep his mother's old table-piano in tune whenever he had the time, and was worried by 'The Wolf' in a musical octave, which he thought a defect in his own ear.

One other experience of his boyhood may be mentioned which, though comical in itself, gave him much mental distress. This was at church when listening to the sermon. Some mischievous movement of his mind set him imagining that the vicar was preaching mockingly, and he began trying to trace a humorous twitch in the corners of Mr. S——'s mouth, as if he could hardly keep a serious countenance. Once having imagined this the impish boy found to his consternation that he could not dismiss the idea. Like Sterne in the pulpit, the vicar seemed to be 'always tottering on the verge of laughter', and hence against his will Thomas could scarcely control his merriment, till it became a positive discomfort to him.

By good fortune the report that the schoolmaster was an able teacher turned out to be true — and finding that he had an apt pupil who galloped unconcernedly over the ordinary school lessons, he either agreed to Hardy's parents' proposal, or proposed himself, that he should teach the boy Latin immediately, Latin being considered an extra.

### 1852

So at twelve years of age young Thomas was started on the old Eton grammar and readings in Eutropius and Caesar. Though extraordinarily quick in acquisition he was undoubtedly rather an idle schoolboy; and in respect of the grammar, having, like so many thousands of schoolboys before him, been worried by the 'Propria quae maribus', he devised a plan for saving himself trouble in learning the genders by colouring the nouns in three tints respectively; but whether he profited much by his plan is not known. Once, many years after, he deplored to a friend, a classical scholar and Fellow of his college, that he had been taught from the venerable Etonian 'Introduction to the Latin Tongue', and not from the celebrated new

Latin primer which came out later. His friend said grimly : 'The old one was just as good as the new.'

But despite the classics and his general bookishness he loved adventures with the fiddle, both now and far on towards young manhood, though it was strange that his mother, a 'progressive' woman, ambitious on his account though not her own, did not object to these performances. Possibly it was from a feeling that they would help to teach him what life was. His father, however, objected to them strongly, though as he himself had not been averse to them when young he could hardly do other than wink at them. So little Thomas played sometimes at village weddings, at one of which the bride, all in white, kissed him in her intense pleasure at the dance ; once at a New Year's Eve party in the house of the tailor who had breeched him ; also in farmers' parlours ; and on another occasion at a homestead where he was stopped by his hostess clutching his bow-arm at the end of a three-quarter-hour's unbroken footing to his notes by twelve tireless couples in the favourite country-dance of 'The New-Rigged Ship'. The matron had done it lest he should 'burst a blood-vessel', fearing the sustained exertion to be too much for a boy of thirteen or fourteen.

He had always been told by his mother that he must on no account take any payment for these services as fiddler, but on one occasion temptation was too strong. A hatful of pennies was collected, amounting to four or five shillings, and Thomas had that morning seen in a shop in Dorchester a copy of *The Boys' Own Book* which could be bought with about this sum. He accepted the money and soon owned the coveted volume. His mother shook her head over the transaction, and refused to see any merit in a book which was chiefly about games. This volume was carefully kept, and remained in his library to the end of his life.

Among the queer occurrences accompanying these merry minstrellings may be described one that happened when he was coming home with his father at three in the morning from a gentleman-farmer's house where he had been second violin to his senior's first for six or seven hours, his father for some reason having had a generous wish to oblige the entertainers to the full. It was bitterly cold, and the moon glistened bright upon the encrusted snow, amid which they saw motionless in the hedge what appeared to be a white human figure without a head. The boy, being very tired, with finger-tips tingling from pressing the strings, was for passing the ghastly sight quickly, but the elder went up to the object, which proved to be a very tall thin man in a long white smock-frock, leaning against the bank in a drunken stupor, his head hanging forward so low that at a distance he had seemed to have no head at all. Hardy senior, seeing the danger of leaving the man where he might be frozen to death, awoke him after much exertion, and they supported him to a cottage near, where he lived, and pushed him in through the door, their ears being greeted as they left with a stream of abuse from the man's wife, which was also vented upon her unfortunate husband, whom she promptly knocked down. Hardy's father remarked that it might have been as well to leave him where he was, to take his chance of being frozen to death.

At this age Thomas also loved reading Dumas *père's* romances, which he did in an English translation, and Shakespeare's tragedies for the plots only, not thinking much of *Hamlet* because the ghost did not play his part up to the end as he ought to have done.

## 1853–1854

A year or two later his accomplished schoolmaster opened a more advanced school called an Academy, where boarders were taken. His abilities had in fact attracted the notice of parents and guardians, and but for an affection of the chest which compelled him later to give up teaching he would no doubt have been heard of further afield. (His son, it may be observed, became a well-known science-master at South Kensington.) Hardy followed him to the new school — the grammar school founded by his namesake being reported to be indifferent just then — and remained there all the rest of his school life, thus continuing his Latin under the same teacher, and winning the prize of Beza's Latin Testament for his progress in the tongue — a little pocket edition which he often carried with him in after years. His course of instruction also included elementary drawing, advanced arithmetic, geometry, and algebra, in which he was fairly good, always saying that he found a certain poetry in the rule for the extraction of the cube-root, owing to its rhythm, and in some of the 'Miscellaneous Questions' of Walkingame. In applied mathematics he worked completely through Tate's *Mechanics* and Nesbitt's *Mensuration*.

Hardy was popular — too popular almost — with his schoolfellows, for their friendship at times became burdensome. He loved being alone, but often, to his concealed discomfort, some of the other boys would volunteer to accompany him on his homeward journey to Bockhampton.  How much this irked him he recalled long years after.  He tried also to avoid being touched by his playmates.  One lad, with more insight than the rest, discovered the fact: 'Hardy, how is it that you do not like us to touch you?'  This peculiarity never left him, and to the end of his life he disliked even the most friendly hand being laid on his arm or his shoulder.  Probably no one else ever observed this.

One day at this time Hardy, then a boy of fourteen, fell madly in love with a pretty girl who passed him on horseback near the South Walk, Dorchester, as he came out of school hard by, and for some unaccountable reason smiled at him.  She was a total stranger.  Next day he saw her with an old gentleman, probably her father.  He wandered about miserably, looking for her through several days, and caught sight of her once again — this time riding with a young man.  Then she disappeared for ever.  He told other boys in confidence, who sympathized, but could do nothing, though some boarders watched for her on his behalf.  He was more than a week getting over this desperate attachment.

At fifteen he was sent to receive French lessons from a lady who was the French governess at the school attended by his sister, and began the study of German from a periodical in which he had become deeply interested, entitled *The Popular Educator*, published by that genius in home-education, John Cassell.  Hardy's mother had begun to buy the publications of that firm for her son, and he himself continued their purchase whenever he had any pocket-money.

And it was about this date that he formed one of a trio of youths (the vicar's sons being the other two) who taught in the Sunday School of the parish, where as a pupil in his class he had a dairymaid four years older than himself, who afterwards appeared in *Tess of the d'Urbervilles* as Marian — one of the few portraits from life in his works.  This pink and plump damsel had a marvellous power of memorizing whole chapters in the Bible, and would repeat to him by heart in class, to his boredom, the long gospels before Easter without missing a word, and with evident delight in her facility ; though she was by no means a model of virtue in her love-affairs.

Somewhat later, though it may as well be mentioned here among other such trivialities, he lost his heart for a few days to a young girl who had come from Windsor just after he had been reading Ainsworth's *Windsor Castle*.  But she disappointed him on his finding that she took no interest in Herne the Hunter or Anne Boleyn.  In this kind there was another young girl, a gamekeeper's pretty daughter, who won Hardy's boyish admiration because of her beautiful bay-red hair. But she despised him, as being two or three years her junior, and married early. He celebrated her later on as 'Lizbie Browne'. Yet another attachment, somewhat later, which went deeper, was to a farmer's daughter named Louisa. There were more probably. They all appear, however, to have been quite fugitive, except perhaps the one for Louisa.

He believed that his attachment to this damsel was reciprocated, for on one occasion when he was walking home from Dorchester he beheld her sauntering down the lane as if to meet him. He longed to speak to her, but bashfulness overcame him, and he passed on with a murmured 'Good evening', while poor Louisa had no word to say.

Later he heard that she had gone to Weymouth to a boarding school for young ladies, and thither he went, Sunday after Sunday, until he discovered the church which the maiden of his affections attended with her fellow-scholars. But, alas, all that resulted from these efforts was a shy smile from Louisa.

That the vision remained may be gathered from a poem 'Louisa in the Lane' written not many months before his death. Louisa lies under a nameless mound in 'Mellstock' churchyard. That 'Good evening' was the only word that passed between them.

# CHAPTER II

# STUDENT AND ARCHITECT

1856–1862 : *Aet.* 16–21

AT sixteen, though he had just begun to be interested in French and the Latin classics, the question arose of a profession or business. His father as a builder had carried out the designs of, and so become associated with, Mr. John Hicks, an architect and church-restorer originally in practice in Bristol and now in Dorchester. Having seen Thomas Hardy junior when his father conjointly with another builder was executing Mr. Hicks's restoration of, it is believed, Woodsford Castle, and tested him by inviting him to assist at a survey, Hicks wished to have him as a pupil, offering to take him for somewhat less than the usual premium, payable in the middle of a term of three years. As the father was a ready-money man, Mrs. Hardy suggested to the architect a substantial abatement for paying down the whole premium at the beginning of the term, and to this Mr. Hicks, who was not a ready-money man, agreed. Hardy was a born bookworm, that and that alone was unchanging in him; he had sometimes, too, wished to enter the Church; but he cheerfully agreed to go to Mr. Hicks's.

## JULY 1856

The architect's office was at 39 South Street, Dorchester, now part of a Temperance Hotel, though the room in which Hardy used to draw is unchanged. On arriving he found there a pupil of twenty-one, who was at the end of his term and was just leaving; also a pupil in the first year of his articles, a year or more older than himself, who had been well educated at a good school in or near London, and who, having a liking for the classical tongues, regretted his recent necessity of breaking off his studies to take up architecture. They began later to read together, and during the ensuing two or three years often gave more time to books than to drawing. Hicks, too, was exceptionally well educated for an ordinary country architect. The son of a Gloucestershire rector, who had been a good classical scholar, he had read some Greek, and had a smattering of Hebrew (probably taught him by his father) ; though, rather oddly, he was less at home with Latin. He was a kindly-natured man, almost jovial, and allowed the two youths some leisure for other than architectural study, though much of Hardy's reading in the ensuing years was done between five and eight in the morning before he left home for the office. In the long summer days he would even rise at four and begin. In these circumstances he got through a moderately good number of the usual classical pages — several books of the *Aeneid,* some Horace and Ovid, etc. ; and in fact grew so familiar with his authors that in his walks to and from the town he often caught himself soliloquizing in Latin on his various projects. He also took up Greek, which he had not learnt at school, getting on with some books of the *Iliad.* He once said that nearly all his readings in the last-named work had been done in the morning before breakfast.

Hicks was ahead of them in Greek, though they could beat him in Latin, and he used to ridicule their construings, often when these were more correct than his own. When cornered and proved wrong he would take shelter behind the excuse that his school-days were longer ago than theirs.

At this time the Rev. William Barnes, the Dorset poet and philologist, was keeping school next door. Knowing him to be an authority upon grammar Hardy would often run in to ask Barnes to decide some knotty point in dispute between him and his fellow-pupil. Hardy used to assert in later years that upon almost every occasion the verdict was given in his favour.

An unusual incident occurred during his pupillage at Hicks's which, though it had nothing to do with his own life, was dramatic enough to have mention. One summer morning at Bockhampton, just before he sat down to breakfast, he remembered that a man was to be hanged at eight o'clock at Dorchester. He took up the big brass telescope that had been handed on in the family, and hastened to a hill on the heath a quarter of a mile from the house, whence he looked towards the town. The sun behind his back shone straight on the white stone façade of the gaol, the gallows upon it, and the form of the murderer in white fustian, the executioner and officials in dark clothing and the crowd below being invisible at this distance of nearly three miles. At the moment of his placing the glass to his eye the white figure dropped downwards, and the faint note of the town clock struck eight.

The whole thing had been so sudden that the glass nearly fell from Hardy's hands. He seemed alone on the heath with the hanged man, and crept homeward wishing he had not been so curious. It was the second and last execution he witnessed, the first having been that of a woman two or three years earlier, when he stood close to the gallows.

It had so happened that Bastow, the other pupil (who, strangely enough for an architect mostly occupied with church-work, had been bred a Baptist), became very doctrinal during this time ; he said he was going to be baptized, and in fact was baptized shortly after. He so impressed young Hardy with his earnestness and the necessity of doing likewise that, though the junior pupil had been brought up in High Church principles, he almost felt that he ought to be baptized again as an adult. He went to the vicar of his parish and stated the case. The vicar, an Oxford man, seemed bewildered, and said that the only book he possessed that might help Hardy was Hooker's *Ecclesiastical Polity*, which he lent his inquirer. Finding that this learned work did not help much in the peculiar circumstances, Hardy went to the curate of another parish with whom he was acquainted. But all that the curate had was a handbook on the Sacraments of an elementary kind.

However, he got hold of as many books and notes on Paedobaptism as he could, and though he was appalled at the feebleness of the arguments for infant christening (assuming that New Testament practice must be followed) he incontinently determined to 'stick to his own side', as he considered the Church to be, at some costs of conscience. The clash of polemics between the two pupils in the office sometimes reached such a pitch of clamour that the architect's wife would send down a message from the drawing-room, which was on the first floor over, imploring them not to make so much noise. To add to the heat, two of the Dorchester Baptist minister's sons, friends of Bastow, hard-headed Scotch youths fresh from Aberdeen University, good classics, who could rattle off at a moment's notice the Greek original of any passage in the New Testament, joined in the controversy. But though Hardy thus found himself in the position of one against three, he fought on with his back to the wall as it were — working at night at the Greek Testament to confute his opponents, and for this purpose getting a new text, Griesbach's, that he had seen advertised as the most correct, instead of his old one, and conceding to his serious-minded disputants as much as he thought a Churchman fairly could concede — namely, that he would limit his Greek reading to the New Testament in future, giving up the heathen authors, and would show his broad-mindedness by attending a prayer-meeting in the chapel-vestry.

At half-past six on a hot August evening he entered the chapel for the meeting. Not a soul was in the building, and he waited in the dreary little vestry till the hour of appointment had passed by nearly half an hour, the yellow sun shining in on the drab paint through the skylight, through which also came the faint notes of a brass band. Just as he was about to leave at a quarter-past seven, Bastow and the minister's sons tumbled breathlessly in, apologizing for their lateness. Cooke's then popular circus had entered the town at the moment of the prayer-meeting, and they had all dismissed the engagement for a while, and remained for the spectacle. Hardy had known the circus entry was going to take place ; but he had kept his appointment faithfully. How the meeting ended Hardy had forgotten when he related the experience.

His convictions on the necessity of adult baptism gradually wore out of him. Though he was younger than his companions he seems to have possessed a breadth of mind which they lacked ; and while perceiving that there was not a shred of evidence for infant baptism in the New Testament, he saw that Christianity did not hang on temporary details that expediency might modify, and that the practice of an isolated few in the early ages could not be binding on its multitudes in differing circumstances, when it had grown to be the religion of continents.

Nevertheless it would be unjust to the Baptist minister Perkins and his argumentative family to omit from these gleanings out of the past Hardy's remarks on their finer qualities. They formed an austere and frugal household, and won his admiration by their thoroughness and strenuousness. He often visited them, and one of the sons about his own age, not insistent on Baptist doctrines like his two brethren, was a great friend of Hardy's till his death of consumption a year or two after. It was through these Scotch people that Thomas Hardy first became impressed with the necessity for 'plain living and high thinking', which stood him in such good stead in later years. Among the few portraits of actual persons in Hardy's novels, that of the Baptist minister in *A Laodicean* is one — being a recognizable drawing of Perkins the father as he appeared to Hardy at this time, though the incidents are invented.

To return to the architect's pupils. The Greek Testament had been now taken up by both of them — though it had necessitated the younger's learning a new dialect — and Homer and Virgil were thrown aside (a misfortune to Hardy, who was just getting pleasure from these). In pursuing this study it became an occasional practice for the youths to take out their Testaments into the fields and sit on a gate reading them. The gate of the enclosure in Kingston Maurward eweleaze, now the cricket-ground, was the scene of some of the readings. They were brought to an end by the expiry of Bastow's term of four years as a pupil, and his departure for the office of a London architect, which, it may be mentioned, he shortly afterwards left to start in practice on his own account in Tasmania.

## 1860–1861

With the departure of Bastow, Hardy's duties grew more exacting, and though, in consideration of his immaturity, the term of his pupillage had been lengthened by between one and two years, a time had arrived at which it became necessary that he should give more attention to practical architecture than he had hitherto done. Church 'restoration' was at this time in full cry in Dorsetshire and the neighbouring counties, and young Hardy found himself making many surveys, measurements, and sketches of old churches with a view to such changes. Much beautiful ancient Gothic, as well as Jacobean and Georgian work, he was passively instrumental in destroying or in altering beyond identification; a matter for his deep regret in later years.

Despite the greater demands of architecture upon his attention it appears that Hardy kept up his classics for some time after the departure of his fellow-pupil for Tasmania; since, in an old letter of Bastow's, replying to Hardy from Hobart Town in May 1861, the emigrant says:

'Really you are a plodding chap to have got through such a lot of Homer and all the rest. I am not a bit farther than I was in Dorchester; indeed, I think I have scarcely touched a book — Greek, I mean — since. I see you are trying all you can to cut me out!'

The allusion to Homer seems to show that after his earnest Baptist-senior's departure, and the weakening of his influence, Hardy, like St. Augustine, lapsed from the Greek New Testament back again to pagan writers, though he was rather impulsive than 'plodding' in his studies, his strength lying in a power of keeping going in most disheartening circumstances.

Owing to the accident of his being an architect's pupil in a county-town of assizes and aldermen, which had advanced to railways and telegraphs and daily London papers ; yet not living there, but walking in every day from a world of shepherds and ploughmen in a hamlet three miles off, where modern improvements were still regarded as wonders, he saw rustic and borough doings in a juxtaposition peculiarly close.  To these externals may be added the peculiarities of his inner life, which might almost have been called academic — a triple existence unusual for a young man — what he used to call, in looking back, a life twisted of three strands — the professional life, the scholar's life, and the rustic life, combined in the twenty-four hours of one day, as it was with him through these years.  He would be reading the *Iliad*, the *Aeneid*, or the Greek Testament from six to eight in the morning, would work at Gothic architecture all day, and then in the evening rush off with his fiddle under his arm, sometimes in the company of his father as first violin and uncle as 'cellist, to play country-dances, reels, and hornpipes at an agriculturist's wedding, christening, or Christmas party in a remote dwelling among the fallow fields, not returning sometimes till nearly dawn, the Hardys still being traditionally string-bandsmen available on such occasions, and having the added recommendation of charging nothing for their services, which was a firm principle with them, the entertainers being mostly acquaintances ; though the tireless zeal of young couples in the dance often rendered the Hardys' act of friendship anything but an enjoyment to themselves.  But young Hardy's physical vigour was now much greater than it had been when he was a child, and it enabled him, like a conjuror at a fair, to keep in the air the three balls of architecture, scholarship, and dance-fiddling, without ill effects, the fiddling being of course not daily, like the other two.

His immaturity, above alluded to, was greater than is common for his years, and it may be mentioned here that a clue to much of his character and action throughout his life is afforded by his lateness of development in virility, while mentally precocious.  He himself said humorously in later times that he was a child till he was sixteen, a youth till he was five-and-twenty, and a young man till he was nearly fifty.  Whether this was intrinsic, or owed anything to his having lived in a remote spot in early life, is an open question.

During the years of architectural pupillage Hardy had two other literary friends in Dorchester.  One was Hooper Tolbort, orphan nephew of one of the partners in a firm of mechanical engineers, who had an extraordinary facility in the acquisition of languages.  He was a pupil of the Rev. W. Barnes, and was preparing for the Indian Civil Service.  The other was Horace Moule of Queens' College, Cambridge, just then beginning practice as author and reviewer. Walks in the fields with each of these friends biassed Thomas Hardy still further in the direction of books, two works among those he met with impressing him much — the newly published *Essays and Reviews* by 'The Seven against Christ', as the authors were nicknamed ; and Walter Bagehot's *Estimates* (afterwards called *Literary Studies*). He began writing verses, and also a few prose articles, which do not appear to have been printed anywhere. The first effusion of his to see the light of print was an anonymous skit in a Dorchester paper on the disappearance of the Alms-House clock, which then as now stood on a bracket in South Street, the paragraph being in the form of a plaintive letter from the ghost of the clock. (It had been neglected, after having been taken down to be cleaned.) As the author was supposed to be an alderman of influence the clock was immediately replaced. He would never have been known to be Hardy but for the conspiracy of a post-office clerk, who watched the handwriting of letters posted till he had spotted the culprit. After this followed the descriptive verses 'Domicilium', and accounts of church-restorations carried out by Hicks, which Hardy prepared for the grateful reporter of the *Dorset Chronicle*.

It seems he had also set to work on the *Agamemnon* or the *Oedipus*; but on his inquiring of Moule — who was a fine Greek scholar and was always ready to act the tutor in any classical difficulty — if he ought not to go on reading some Greek plays, Moule's reluctant opinion was that if Hardy really had (as his father had insisted, and as indeed was reasonable, since he never as yet had earned a farthing in his life) to make an income in some way by architecture in 1862, it would be hardly worth while for him to read Aeschylus or Sophocles in 1859–61. He had secretly wished that Moule would advise him to go on with Greek plays, in spite of the serious damage it might do his architecture ; but he felt bound to listen to reason and prudence. So, as much Greek as he had got he had to be content with, the language being almost dropped from that date ; for though he did take up one or two of the dramatists again some years later, it was in a fragmentary way only. Nevertheless his substantial knowledge of them was not small.

It may be permissible to ponder whether Hardy's career might not have been altogether different if Moule's opinion had been the contrary one, and he had advised going on with Greek plays. The younger man would hardly have resisted the suggestion, and might have risked the consequences, so strong was his bias that way. The upshot might have been his abandonment of architecture for a University career, his father never absolutely refusing to advance him money in a good cause. Having every instinct of a scholar he might have ended his life as a Don of whom it could be said that

>He settled *Hoti's* business,
>Properly based *Oun*.

But this was not to be, and it was possibly better so.

One other Dorchester young man, who has been cursorily mentioned — the pupil of Hicks's whose time had expired shortly after Hardy's arrival, and who then departed permanently from the West of England — may be again given a word for the single thing about him that had attracted the fresh-comer — his one or two trips to London during their passing acquaintance, and his return thence whistling quadrilles and other popular music, with accounts of his dancing experiences at the Argyle Rooms and Cremorne, both then in full swing. Hardy would relate that one quadrille in particular his precursor Fippard could whistle faultlessly, and while giving it would caper about the office to an imaginary dance-figure, embracing an imaginary Cremorne or Argyle *danseuse*. The fascinating quadrille remained with Hardy all his life, but he never could identify it. Being some six years the junior of this comet-like young man, Hardy was treated by him with the superciliousness such a boy usually gets from such seniority, and with the other's departure from Dorchester he passed quite out of Hardy's knowledge.

CHAPTER III

# WORK IN LONDON

1862–1867 : *Aet.* 21–27

## A New Start

On Thursday, April 17, 1862, Thomas Hardy started alone for London, to pursue the art and science of architecture on more advanced lines. He had for some time left Bockhampton as a permanent resident, living, except at weekends, in Dorchester, either with Hicks or at lodgings ; though he often sojourned at Bockhampton later on.

The Great Exhibition of that year was about to be opened, and this perhaps influenced him in the choice of a date for his migration. His only previous journey to the capital had been made with his mother in 1848 or 1849, when they passed through it on the way to and back from Hertfordshire, on a visit to a relative, as mentioned earlier. With prudent forethought he bought a return ticket for the journey, so that he might be able to travel back to Dorchester did he reach the end of his resources. After six months he threw away the unused half.

Hardy used to relate humorously that on the afternoon of his arrival he called to inquire for lodgings at a house where was employed a bachelor some ten years older than himself, whose cousin Hardy had known. This acquaintance, looking him up and down, was sceptical about his establishing himself in London. 'Wait till you have walked the streets a few weeks', he said satirically, 'and your elbows begin to shine, and the hems of your trousers get frayed, as if nibbled by rats ! Only practical men are wanted here.' Hardy began to wish he had thought less of the Greek Testament and more of iron girders.

However, he had at least two letters of introduction in his pocket — one from a gushing lady to Mr. Benjamin Ferrey, F.R.I.B.A., of Trinity Place, Charing Cross, an architect who had been a pupil of the elder Pugin's, was connected with the West of England, and had designed a Dorset mansion of which Hardy's father had been one of the builders, carrying out the work to that gentleman's complete satisfaction.  But, as usually happens, this sheet-anchor was less trustworthy than had been expected.  Mr. Ferrey was civil to the young man, remembered his father, promised every assistance ; and there the matter ended.

The other introduction was to Mr. John Norton of Old Bond Street, also an architect in full practice.  Mr. Norton was a Bristol man, a pupil of Ferrey's, and a friend of Hicks of Dorchester, by reason, it is believed, of their joint association with Bristol.  Anyhow, Norton received young Thomas Hardy with great kindness, and, his friendship coming at the nick of time when it was needed, he proved himself one of the best helps Hardy ever had.  The generous architect told him that he must on no account be doing nothing in London (Hardy looked quite a pink-faced youth even now), and arranged that he should come daily and make drawings in his office for a merely nominal renumeration whilst looking further about town.  As Mr. Norton was in no real need of assistance the proposal was most considerate of him.

### LAST WEEK IN APRIL 1862

Here was indeed as good a thing as could have happened.  It was an anchorage, and Hardy never forgot it.  Strangely enough, on his arriving on the following Monday to begin, Mr. Norton informed him that a friend whom he had met at the Institute of British Architects had asked him if he knew of a young Gothic draughtsman who could restore and design churches and rectory-houses.  He had strongly recommended Hardy, and packed him off at once to call on Mr. Arthur Blomfield, the friend in question.

Blomfield was a son of the recently deceased Dr. Blomfield, Bishop of London ;  a Rugbeian, a graduate of Trinity College, Cambridge, where he had been a great boating man ; and a well-known church-designer and restorer, whose architectural pupillage had been under Philip C. Hardwicke.  Hardy found him in, a lithe, brisk man of thirty-three, with whom Hardy was to keep up a friendship for near on forty years.  Arrangements were made, and on the following Monday, May 5, he began work as an assistant-architect in Mr. Blomfield's drawing-office — at that time at 8 St. Martin's Place, in rooms also used by the Alpine Club.  This was another linking coincidence with aftertimes, for Leslie Stephen, an ardent climber and a member of the Club, was a visitor to these rooms, though ten years were to elapse before Hardy got to know him, and to be mentally influenced by him so deeply. In the following autumn or winter, however, more commodious and lighter drawing-offices were taken at 8 Adelphi Terrace, first floor ; which Blomfield continued to occupy during the remaining five years that Hardy worked with him. Shortly after his entry there Hardy had an experience which might have been serious :

'*March* 10. Went into the streets in the evening to see the illuminations on the occasion of the P. of Wales's marriage. By the fortunate accident of beginning my walk at the city end of the route I had left the neighbourhood of the Mansion House before the great mass of people got there, but I had enough to do to hold my own at the bottom of Bond Street, where my waistcoat buttons were torn off and my ribs bent in before I could get into a doorway. Molsey and Paris [two pupils of Ferrey's, friends of Hardy's] were in the Mansion House crush, having started from the West End, like most of the spectators. Six people were killed close to them, and they did not expect to get out alive.'

In a letter written many years after to an inquirer who was interested in his association with Adelphi Terrace, Hardy states :

'I sat there drawing, inside the easternmost window of the front room on the first floor above the ground floor, occasionally varying the experience by idling on the balcony. I saw from there the Embankment and Charing-Cross Bridge built, and of course used to think of Garrick and Johnson. The rooms contained at that date fine Adam mantelpieces in white marble, on which we used to sketch caricatures in pencil.'

It may be added that the ground-floor rooms of this 8 Adelphi Terrace were occupied by the Reform League during Hardy's stay overhead, and that Swinburne in one of his letters speaks of a correspondence with the League about this date. 'The Reform League,' he says, 'a body of extreme reformers not now extant I believe, but of some note and power for a time, solicited me to sit in Parliament — as representative of more advanced democratic or republican opinions than were represented there.' Swinburne consulted Mazzini, who dissuaded him from consenting. The heads of the League were familiar personages to Blomfield's pupils, who, as became Tory and Churchy young men, indulged in satire at the League's expense, letting down ironical bits of paper on the heads of members, and once coming nearly to loggerheads with the worthy resident secretary, Mr. George Howell — to whom they had to apologize for their exasperating conduct — all this being unknown to Mr. Blomfield himself.

The following letters were written to his sister, Miss Mary Hardy, during 1862 and 1863, the first year that Hardy was at St. Martin's Place and Adelphi Terrace.

'KILBURN, 17 *August* 1862.
'9 P.M.

'MY DEAR MARY

'"After the fire a still small voice" — I have just come from the evening service at St. Mary's Kilburn and this verse, which I always notice, was in the 1st Lesson.

'This Ch. of St. Mary is rather to my taste and they sing most of the tunes in the Salisbury hymn book there.

'H. M. M. was up the week before last. We went to a Roman Catholic Chapel on the Thurday evening. It was a very impressive service. The Chapel was built by Pugin. Afterwards we took a cab to the old Hummums, an hotel near Covent Garden where we had supper. He may come and settle permanently in London in a few months, but is not certain yet.

'E— was up last week. I had a half day at the Exhibition with him. He is now living at home, looking out for a situation. I do not think he will get into anything yet.

'I have not been to a theatre since you were here. I generally run down to the Exhibition for an hour in the evening two or three times a week; after I come out I go to the reading room of the Kensington Musuem.

'It has been pouring with rain all the day and last night, such a disappointment for thousands of Londoners, whose only holiday is Sunday.

'I should like to have a look at the old Cathedral, etc., in about a month or so. The autumn seems the proper season for seeing Salisbury. Do you ever go to St. Thomas's ? Be careful about getting cold again and do not go out in evenings.

'P. S. is reading extracts from Ruskin's "Modern Painters" to me which accounts for the wretched composition of this epistle as I am obliged to make comments etc. on what he reads.

'Ever yours,
'T. H.'

'KILBURN, 19*th February*.

'MY DEAR MARY:

'I don't fancy that 'tis so very long since I wrote and the Saturdays [*Saturday Reviews*] have been sent regularly but I really intended to write this week.

'You see that we have moved, so for the future my address will be as on the other side. We have not recovered from the confusion yet, and our drawings and papers are nohow.

'The new office is a capital place. It is on the first floor and on a terrace that overlooks the river. We can see from our window right across the Thames, and on a clear day every bridge is visible. Everybody says that we have a beautiful place.

'To-day has been wretched. It was almost pitch dark in the middle of the day, and everything visible appeared of the colour of brown paper or pea-soup.

'There is a great deal of preparation for the approaching wedding. The Princess is to arrive on the 7th March and the wedding will be on the 10th. On her landing at Gravesend she will be received by the Prince, the Mayor, Mayoress, etc. They will then go by train to the Bricklayers' Arms station, and then in procession over London Bridge, along Fleet Street, Strand, Charing Cross, Pall Mall, Piccadilly, through Hyde Park, and up the Edgware Road to Paddington Station — thence to Windsor. The windows along the route are full of notices that seats to view the procession are to be let. There will be an illumination the evening of the 10th.

'I went to Richmond yesterday to see Lee. He is better but is going to Kent for a short time before coming back to the office.

'I have not heard anything about the Essay yet. The name of the successful competitor will be known in about a fortnight. I am now very busy getting up a design for a country mansion for which a small prize is offered — £3 the best and £2 the second best. It has to be sent in by the 27th March.

'I am glad you have got a drawing prize, but you don't say what. I think you have done very well altogether. Tell me about the organ and how the Sundays go off — I am uncommonly interested. How is your friend the blind man etc., School, clergyman etc. *Say how you are*, don't forget. I am quite well. Horace Moule has been ill. So has H. A. as I daresay you know. Has she written yet? I sent a valentine to Harry and Kate to please them. Harry wrote me a letter, and Kate printed one and sent — rather a curiosity in its way.

'I sent Mrs. Rolls photographs and she sent me a paper and letter.

She says that Parsons is postmaster in place of Lock who has resigned.

'I tried the Underground Railway one day — Everything is excellently arranged.

'Do you think to run up Easter? If so, you must not mind being left alone all day — but you know your way about.

'T. S. has commenced the sketch of our house for you. He says it will soon be finished.

'Is Katie coming up to live with you and when is Mother coming?

'Ever your affectionate
'TOM'

'8 ADELPHI TERRACE,
'19 *Dec.* 1863.

'MY DEAR MARY,

'I was beginning to think you had given up writing altogether, when your letter came. Certainly try to get as long a time as you can Christmas.

'I am glad you have been to Oxford again. It must be a jolly place. I shall try to get down there some time or other. You have no right to say you are not connected with art. Everybody is to a certain extent; the only difference between a professor and an amateur being that the former has the (often disagreeable) necessity of making it his means of earning bread and cheese — and thus often rendering what is a pleasure to other people a "bore" to himself.

'About Thackeray. You must read something of his. He is considered to be the greatest novelist of the day — looking at novel writing of the highest kind as a perfect and truthful representation of actual life — which is no doubt the proper view to take. Hence, because his novels stand so high as works of Art or Truth, they often have anything but an elevating tendency, and on that account are particularly unfitted for young people — from their very truthfulness. People say that it is beyond Mr. Thackeray to paint a perfect man or woman — a great fault if novels are intended to instruct, but just the opposite if they are to be considered merely as Pictures. *Vanity Fair* is considered one of his best.

'I expect to go home about Tuesday or Wednesday after Xmas and then shall find you there of course — We must have a "bit of a lark."

'Ever affectionately
'TOM.

'I am able to write 40 words a minute. The average rate of a speaker is from 100, to 120 and occasionally 140; so I have much more to do yet.'

During the first few months of Hardy's life in London he had not forgotten to pay a call on the lady of his earliest passion as a child, who had been so tender towards him in those days, and had used to take him in her arms. She and her husband were now living in Bruton Street. The butler who opened the door was, he recalled, the same one who had been with the family at Kingston Maurward all those years ago, and looked little altered. But the lady of his dreams — alas! To her, too, the meeting must have been no less painful than pleasant: she was plainly embarrassed at having in her presence a young man of over twenty-one, who was very much of a handful in comparison with the rosy-cheeked, innocent little boy she had almost expected 'Tommy' to remain. One interview was not quite sufficient to wear off the stiffness resulting from such changed conditions, though, warming up, she asked him to come again. But getting immersed in London life, he did not respond to her invitation, showing that the fickleness was his alone. But they occasionally corresponded, as will be seen.

It may be hardly necessary to record, since he somewhere describes it himself, that the metropolis into which he had plunged at this date differed greatly from the London of even a short time after. It was the London of Dickens and Thackeray, and Evans's supper-rooms were still in existence in an underground hall in Covent Garden, which Hardy once at least visited. The Cider Cellars and the Coal Hole were still flourishing, with 'Judge and Jury' mock trials, 'Baron Nicholson' or his successor being judge. And Dr. Donovan the phrenologist gauged heads in the Strand, informing Hardy that his would lead him to no good.

The ladies talked about by the architects' pupils and other young men into whose society Hardy was thrown were Cora Pearl, 'Skittles', Agnes Willoughby, Adah Isaacs Menken, and others successively, of whom they professed to know many romantic and *risqué* details but really knew nothing at all; another of their romantic interests that Hardy recalled being, a little later, the legend of the moorhen dive of Lady Florence Paget into Marshall & Snelgrove's shop away from Mr. Chaplin, her *fiancé*, and her emergence at the other door into the arms of Lord Hastings, and marriage with him — a sensational piece of news with which they came in breathless the week it happened.

Hungerford Market was still in being where the Charing Cross Station now stands, and Hardy occasionally lunched at a 'coffee house' there. He also lunched or dined at Bertolini's with some pupils of Ferrey's, the architect who had known his father and been the pupil of Pugin. This restaurant in St. Martin's Street, Leicester Square, called Newton House, had been the residence and observatory of Sir Isaac Newton, and later the home of the Burneys, who were visited there by Johnson, Reynolds, etc., and the stone floors were still sanded as in former days. A few years after Hardy frequented it Swinburne used to dine there as a member of the 'Cannibal Club'. Tennyson is also stated to have often dined at Bertolini's. To Hardy's great regret this building of many associations was pulled down in later years.

On his way to Adelphi Terrace he used to take some short cut near Seven Dials, passing daily the liquor saloons of Alec Keene and Tom King (?) in West Street (now demolished), and Nat Langham at the top of St. Martin's Lane, when he could sometimes discern the forms of those famous prize-fighters behind their respective bars.

There was no Thames Embankment. Temple Bar still stood in its place, and the huge block of buildings known as the Law Courts was not erected. Holborn Hill was still a steep and noisy thorough-fare which almost broke the legs of the slipping horses, and Skinner Street ran close by, with presumably Godwin's house yet standing in it, at which Shelley first set eyes on Mary. No bridge across Ludgate Hill disfigured St. Paul's and the whole neighbourhood. The South Kensington Museum was housed in iron sheds nicknamed the 'Brompton Boilers', which Hardy used to frequent this year to obtain materials for an Essay he sent in to the Royal Institute of British Architects; it was awarded the prize in the following spring. The Underground Railway was just in its infancy, and omnibus conductors leaving 'Kilburn Gate', near which Hardy lived awhile, cried, 'Any more passengers for London?' The list of such changes might be infinitely extended.

Charles Kean and his wife were still performing Shakespeare at the Princess's Theatre, and Buckstone was at the Haymarket in the new play of *The American Cousin*, in which he played the name-part. At most of the theatres about nine o'clock there was a noise of tramp-ling feet, and the audience whispered, 'Half-price coming in'. The play paused for a few moments, and when all was quiet went on again.

Balls were constant at Willis's Rooms, earlier Almack's, and in

1862 Hardy danced at these rooms, or at Almack's as he preferred to call the place, realizing its historic character. He used to recount that inoqɪ se old days, the pretty Lancers and Caledonians were still footed there to the original charming tunes, which brought out the beauty of the figures as no later tunes did, and every movement was a correct quadrille step and gesture. For those dances had not at that date degenerated to a waltzing step, to be followed by galloping romps to uproarious pieces.

Cremorne and the Argyle he also sought, remembering the jaunty senior-pupil at Hicks's who had used to haunt those gallant resorts. But he did not dance there much himself, if at all, and the fascinating quadrille-tune has vanished like a ghost, though he went one day to second-hand music shops, and also to the British Museum, and hunted over a lot of such music in a search for it. Allusions to these experiences occur in more than one of his poems, 'Reminiscences of a Dancing Man' in particular ; and they were largely drawn upon, so he once remarked, in the destroyed novel *The Poor Man and the Lady* — of which later on.

In a corresponding fit of musical enthusiasm he also bought an old fiddle at this time, with which he practised at his lodgings, with another man there who performed on the piano, pieces from the romantic Italian operas of Covent Garden and Her Majesty's, the latter being then also an opera house, which places they used to frequent two or three times a week ; not, except on rare occasions, in the best parts of the houses, as will be well imagined, but in the half-crown amphitheatre.

The foreign operas in vogue were those of Rossini, Donizetti, Verdi, Meyerbeer, Bellini: and thus Hardy became familiar with such singers as Mario (Grisi had just departed), Tietjens, Nilsson, Patti (just come), Giuglini, Parepa, and others of the date. An English Opera Company was also in existence, and Hardy patriotically supported it by going often to operas by Balfe, Wallace, and others. Here he had the painful experience of hearing the gradual breakdown of the once fine voice of William Harrison, who, with Miss Louisa Pyne, had established the company and endeavoured to keep such opera going. Hardy was heard to assert that, as it were in defiance of fate, Harrison would sing night after night his favourite songs, such as 'Let me like a soldier fall' in *Maritana*, and, particularly, 'When other lips' in *The Bohemian Girl*, wherein his complete failure towards the last attempts would move a sensitive listener to tears : he thought Harrison's courage in struggling on, hoping against hope, might probably cause him to be remembered longer than his greatest success.

## AT BLOMFIELD'S

Mr. Blomfield (afterwards Sir Arthur) being the son of a late Bishop of London, was considered a right and proper man for supervising the removal of human bodies in cases where railways had obtained a faculty for making cuttings through the city churchyards, so that it should be done decently and in order. A case occurred in which this function on the Bishop's behalf was considered to be duly carried out. But afterwards Mr. Blomfield came to Hardy and informed him with a look of concern that he had just returned from visiting the site on which all the removed bodies were said by the company to be reinterred; but there appeared to be nothing deposited, the surface of the ground lying quite level as before. Also that there were rumours of mysterious full bags of something that rattled, and cartage to bone-mills. He much feared that he had not exercised a sufficiently sharp supervision, and that the railway company had got over him somehow. 'I believe these people are all ground up!' said Blomfield grimly.

Soon there was to occur a similar proceeding on a much larger scale by another company; the carrying of a cutting by the Midland Railway through Old St. Pancras Churchyard, which would necessitate the removal of many hundreds of coffins, and bones in huge quantities. In this business Mr. Blomfield was to represent the Bishop as before. The architect said that now there should be no mistake about his thoroughly carrying out the superintendence. Accordingly, he set a clerk-of-works in the churchyard, who was never to leave during working hours; and as the removals were effected by night, and the clerk-of-works might be lax or late, he deputed Hardy to go on evenings at uncertain hours, to see that the clerk-of-works was performing his duties; while Hardy's chief himself was to drop in at unexpected moments during the week, presumably to see that neither his assistant nor the clerk-of-works was a defaulter.

The plan succeeded excellently, and throughout the late autumn and early winter (of probably the year 1865 or thereabouts) Hardy attended at the churchyard — each evening between five and six, as well as sometimes at other hours. There after nightfall, within a high hoarding that could not be overlooked, and by the light of flare-lamps, the exhumation went on continuously of the coffins that had been uncovered during the day, new coffins being provided for those that came apart in lifting, and for loose skeletons; and those that held together being carried to the new ground on a board merely; Hardy supervising these mournful processions when present, with what thoughts may be imagined, and Blomfield sometimes meeting him there. In one coffin that fell apart was a skeleton and two skulls. He used to tell that when, after some fifteen years of separation, he met Arthur Blomfield again and their friendship was fully renewed, among the latter's first words were: 'Do you remember how we found the man with two heads at St. Pancras?'

It may conceivably have been some rumour of the possibility of this lamentable upheaval of Old St. Pancras Churchyard by the railway company in the near future which had led Sir Percy, the son of Mary Shelley, to remove the bodies of her parents therefrom to St. Peter's, Bournemouth, where she had been buried in 1851, and where they now lie beside her, though few people seem to know that such an illustrious group is in the churchyard.

Hardy used to tell some amusing stories of his chief, a genuine humorist like his father the bishop. Among other strange ways in which he and his pupils, including Hardy, used to get on with their architecture was by singing glees and catches at intervals during office hours. Having always been musically inclined and, as has been stated, a fiddler of countless jigs and reels in his boyhood, Hardy could sing at sight with moderate accuracy from notation, though his voice was not strong. Hence Blomfield welcomed him in the office choir, where he himself took the bass, the rest waiting till he had 'got his low E'. Hardy also, at Blomfield's request, sang in the church-choir at the opening of the organ at St. Matthias' Church, Richmond, where Blomfield took a bass part, one of his pupils being organist. But in the office the alto part was the difficulty, and Blomfield would say: 'If you meet an alto anywhere in the Strand, Hardy, ask him to come in and join us'.

Among other things, the architect related that one day before he (Hardy) came, a Punch-and-Judy show performed outside the office in St. Martin's Place. Presently the housekeeper, a woman London-bred, came running upstairs exclaiming, 'Why, Mr. Arthur, I declare there's a man inside! And I never knew it before!'

On an occasion when a builder had called on business, Hardy being present and some pupils, Blomfield airily said to the builder: 'Well, Mr. T——, what can I do for you? What will you take this morning — sherry or port?' Though it was only between 10 and 11 Mr. T—— reflected earnestly and said, 'Port, sir, if you please'.

As they naturally had no wine or any other liquor at the offices, Blomfield was comically disconcerted at the worthy builder's seriousness, but was as good as his word, and the office-boy was secretly dispatched to the Strand to buy a bottle of port, and to the housekeeper to borrow a glass.

Grotesque incidents that seldom happened to other people seemed to happen to Blomfield. One day he and Hardy went together to some slum near Soho to survey the site for a new building. The inspection made their boots muddy, and on the way back Blomfield suggested they should have them cleaned, as two bootblacks had come up pointing significantly. When Hardy and he had placed themselves Blomfield asked the second why he did not proceed with his brushing, like the first. ''Cause he's got no blacking nor brush', said the first. 'What good is he then ?' asked Blomfield. 'I've cracked my blacking-bottle, and it goes dry ; so I pay him a penny a day to spit for me.'

However, matters were graver sometimes. Hardy remembered how one morning he arrived at the Terrace to find Blomfield standing with his back to the fireplace, and with a very anxious face. The architect said slowly without any preface, 'Hardy, that tower has fallen'. His eyes were fixed on the opposite wall where was the drawing of a new church just then finished. It was a serious matter, especially as some years earlier another well-known architect had been sentenced to a year's imprisonment for manslaughter, one of his new erections having fallen and killed some people. Fortunately no one was killed in the present case, and the designer was quite exonerated by having the tower rebuilt stone by stone as it had been before, and so proving the construction to be unimpeachable, for there it has stood ever since without a crack. What had caused the fall was always a mystery.

This used to remind Hardy of another church-tower story. Mr. Hicks, with whom he served his pupillage, once told him that at the beginning of his practice he built a church-tower near Bristol, and on a night just after its erection he dreamt that on approaching it he saw a huge crack in its west wall from the parapet downwards. He was so disturbed that next morning he mounted his horse ; it was before railways, and architects often then rode on horseback to the supervision of their buildings ; and trotting off to the village the tower rose into his view. There was the crack in its face exactly as he had beheld it in his dream.

Having somewhat settled down with Blomfield, but feeling that architectural drawing in which the actual designing had no great part

was monotonous and mechanical; having besides little inclination
for pushing his way into influential sets which would help him to
start a practice of his own, Hardy's tastes reverted to the literary
pursuits that he had been compelled to abandon in 1861, and had not
resumed except to write the Prize Architectural Essay before mentioned. By as early as the end of 1863 he had recommenced to read
a great deal, with a growing tendency towards poetry. But he was
forced to consider ways and means, and it was suggested to him that
he might combine literature with architecture by becoming an art-
critic for the press, particularly in the province of architectural art.
It is probable that he might easily have carried this out, reviewers
with a speciality being then, and possibly now, in demand. His
preparations for such a course were, however, quickly abandoned,
and by 1865 he had begun to write verses, and by 1866 to send his
productions to magazines. That these were rejected by editors, and
that he paid such respect to their judgment as scarcely ever to send
out a MS. twice, was in one feature fortunate for him, since in years
long after he was able to examine those poems of which he kept
copies, and by the mere change of a few words or the rewriting of a
line or two to make them quite worthy of publication. Such of them
as are dated in these years were all written in his lodgings at 16 Westbourne Park Villas. He also began turning the Book of Ecclesiastes
into Spenserian stanzas, but finding the original unmatchable abandoned
the task.

As another outcome of the same drift of mind, he used to deliver
short addresses or talks on poets and poetry to Blomfield's pupils and
assistants on afternoons when there was not much to be done, or at
all events when not much was done. There is no tradition of what
Blomfield thought of this method of passing office hours instead of
making architectural plans.

The only thing he got published at the time was, so far as is
known, a trifle in *Chambers's Journal* in 1865 entitled 'How I built
myself a house', written to amuse the pupils of Blomfield. It may
have been the acceptance of this *jeu d'esprit* that turned his mind in
the direction of prose; yet he made such notes as the following:

'*April*, 1865. The form on the canvas which immortalizes the
painter is but the last of a series of tentative and abandoned sketches
each of which contained some particular feature nearer perfection
than any part of the finished product.'

'Public opinion is of the nature of a woman.'

'There is not that regular gradation among womankind that there is among men.  You may meet with 999 exactly alike, and then the thousandth — not a little better, but far above them.  Practically therefore it is useless for a man to seek after this thousandth to make her his.'

'*May.*  How often we see a vital truth flung about carelessly wrapt in a commonplace subject, without the slightest conception on the speaker's part that his words contain an unsmelted treasure.'

'In architecture, men who are clever in details are bunglers in generalities.  So it is in everything whatsoever.'

'More conducive to success in life than the desire for much knowledge is the being satisfied with ignorance on irrelevant subjects.'

'The world does not despise us ; it only neglects us.'

Whether or no, he did not seriously take up prose till two or three years later, when he was practically compelled to try his hand on it by finding himself perilously near coming to the ground between the two stools of architecture and literature.

Subsequent historic events brought back to his mind that this year he went with Blomfield to New Windsor, to the laying of the Memorial-stone of a church there by the Crown Princess of Germany (the English Princess Royal).  She was accompanied by her husband the Crown Prince, afterwards the Emperor Frederick.  'Blomfield handed her the trowel, and during the ceremony she got her glove daubed with the mortar.  In her distress she handed the trowel back to him with an impatient whisper of "Take it, take it !"'

Here is another note of his relating to this time :

'*July* 2 (1865).  Worked at J. H. Newman's *Apologia*, which we have all been talking about lately.  A great desire to be convinced by him, because Moule likes him so much.  Style charming, and his logic really human, being based not on syllogisms but on converging probabilities.  Only — and here comes the fatal catastrophe — there is no first link to his excellent chain of reasoning, and down you come headlong. . . . Read some Horace ; also *Childe Harold* and *Lalla Rookh* till ½ past 12.'

However, as yet he did not by any means abandon verse, which he wrote constantly, but kept private, through the years 1866 and most of 1867, resolving to send no more to magazines whose editors probably did not know good poetry from bad, and forming meanwhile the quixotic opinion that, as in verse was concentrated the essence of all imaginative and emotional literature, to read verse and nothing else was the shortest way to the fountain-head of such, for one who had not a great deal of spare time. And in fact for nearly or quite two years he did not read a word of prose except such as came under his eye in the daily newspapers and weekly reviews. Thus his reading naturally covered a fairly large tract of English poetry, and it may be mentioned, as showing that he had some views of his own, that he preferred Scott the poet to Scott the novelist, and never ceased to regret that the author of 'the most Homeric poem in the English language — *Marmion*' — should later have declined on prose fiction.

He was not so keenly anxious to get into print as many young men are ; in this indifference, as in some qualities of his verse, curiously resembling Donne. The Horatian exhortation that he had come across in his reading — to keep his own compositions back till the ninth year — had made a deep impression on him. *Nescit vox missa reverti* ; and by retaining his poems, and destroying those he thought irremediably bad — though he afterwards fancied he had destroyed too many — he may have been saved from the annoyance of seeing his early crude effusions crop up in later life.

At the same time there can be no doubt that some closer association with living poets and the poetry of the moment would have afforded Hardy considerable stimulus and help. But his unfortunate shyness — or rather aloofness, for he was not shy in the ordinary sense — served him badly at this period of his life. During part of his residence at Westbourne Park Villas he was living within half a mile of Swinburne, and hardly more than a stone's throw from Browning, to whom introductions would not have been difficult through literary friends of Blomfield's. He might have obtained at least encouragement from these, and, if he cared, possibly have floated off some of his poems in a small volume. But such a proceeding as trying to know these contemporaries seems never to have crossed his mind.

During his residence in London he had entered himself at King's College for the French classes, where he studied the tongue through a term or two under Professor Stiévenard, never having taken it up seriously since in his boyhood he had worked at exercises under a governess. He used to say that Stiévenard was the most charming Frenchman he ever met, as well as being a fine teacher. Hardy's mind had, however, become at this date so deeply immersed in the practice and study of English poetry that he gave but a perfunctory attention to his French readings.

'*March* 11. The woman at a first interview will know as much of the man as he will know of her on the wedding morning ; whilst she will know as little of him then as he knew of her when they first shook hands. Her knowledge will have come upon her like a flood, and have as gradually soaked away.'

'*June* 2. My 25th birthday. Not very cheerful. Feel as if I had lived a long time and done very little.

'Walked about by moonlight in the evening. Wondered what woman, if any, I should be thinking about in five years' time.'

'*July* 9. The greatest and most majestic being on the face of the earth will accept pleasure from the most insignificant.'

'*July* 19. Patience is the union of moral courage with physical cowardice.'

'*End of July*. The dull period in the life of an event is when it ceases to be news and has not begun to be history.'

'*August*. The anguish of a defeat is most severely felt when we look upon weak ones who have believed us invincible and have made preparations for our victory.'

'*Aug.* 23. The poetry of a scene varies with the minds of the perceivers. Indeed, it does not lie in the scene at all.'

About this time Hardy nourished a scheme of a highly visionary character. He perceived from the impossibility of getting his verses accepted by magazines that he could not live by poetry, and (rather strangely) thought that architecture and poetry — particularly architecture in London — would not work well together. So he formed the idea of combining poetry and the Church — towards which he had long had a leaning — and wrote to a friend in Cambridge for particulars as to matriculation at that University, which with his late classical reading would have been easy for him. He knew that what money he could not muster himself for keeping terms his father would lend him for a few years, his idea being that of a curacy in a country village. This fell through less because of its difficulty than from a conscientious feeling, after some theological study, that he could hardly take the step with honour while holding the views which on examination he found himself to hold. And so he allowed the curious scheme to drift out of sight, though not till after he had begun to practise orthodoxy. For example :

'*July* 5. Sunday. To Westminster Abbey morning service. Stayed to the Sacrament. A very odd experience, amid a crowd of strangers.'

Among other incidents of his life in London during these years was also one that he used to recall with interest, when writing *The Dynasts* — his hearing Palmerston speak in the House of Commons a short time before his death, Palmerston having been War Secretary

during the decisive hostilities with Napoleon embodied in the Third
Part of Hardy's Epic-Drama, a personal conjunction which brought
its writer face to face not only with actual participants in the great
struggle — as was the case with his numerous acquaintance of rank-
and-file who had fought in the Peninsula and at Waterloo — but with
one who had contributed to direct the affairs of that war.   The only
note on the fact that can be found is the following :

'*Oct.* 18 [1865].   Wet evening.   At Regent Circus, coming home
saw the announcement of the death of Ld. Palmerston, whom I heard
speak in the House of Commons a year or two ago.'

'*Oct.* 27.   To Westminster Abbey with Mr. Heaton and Lee.
Took up a position in the triforium, from which spot I saw Ld.
Palmerston lowered into the grave.   Purcell's service.   Dead March
in *Saul*.'

The following letter to his sister describes the ceremony :

'*Saturday, Oct.* 28. 1865.'

'MY DEAR MARY

'I sent *Barchester Towers* by B. P., and you are probably by this
time acquainted with Eleanor Bold, etc.   This novel is considered
the best of Trollope's.

'Yesterday Lord Palmerston was buried — the Prime Minister.
I and the Lees got tickets through a friend of a friend of Mr. B's, and
we went of course.   Our tickets admitted to the triforium, or monks'

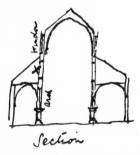

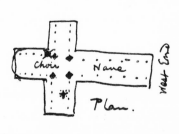

walk, of Westminster Abbey, and we got from there a complete view
of the ceremony.   You will know wh. part of the Abbey I mean if
you think of Salisbury Cathedral and of the row of small arches over
the large arches, wh. throw open the space between the roof of the
aisles and the vaulting.

'Where I have put the ✗ in the Section is where I stood ;   over
the ⊗ on the Plan.   The mark ✳ shows where the grave is, between

L.T.H—E

Pitt's and Fox's and close by Canning's. All the Cabinet Ministers were there as pall bearers. The burial service was Purcell's. The opening sentences "I am the resurrection, etc" were sung to Croft's music. Beethoven's Funeral March was played as they went from the choir to the vault, and the Dead March in *Saul* was played at the close. I think I was never so much impressed with a ceremony in my life before, and I wd. not have missed it for anything. The Prince of Wales and Duke of Cambridge were present.

'Ld. John Russell, or Earl Russell as he is now, is to be Prime Minister in Pam's place. Only fancy, Ld. P. has been connected with the govt. off and on for the last 60 years, and that he was contemporaneous with Pitt, Fox, Sheridan, Burke, etc. I mean to say his life overlapped theirs so to speak. I sent father a newspaper containing an account of his life, and today one with an account of the funeral. As you are not a politician I didn't send you one, but these things interest him.

'If you can get *Pelham*, read it when you want something. Do not hurry over *Barchester*, for I have enough to do. I think Wells is the place intended. Will it be a good thing or will it be awkward for you if H. A. and I come down for Xmas day and the next?

'I am rather glad that hot close weather is gone and the bracing air come again. I think I told you I had joined the French class at King's College.

'Ever sincerely.

'T. H.'

'A tall man went to see Chang the Chinese Giant, and on his offering to pay, the doorkeeper said "Not at all Sir, we don't take money from the *profession*!" at least so *Punch* says.'

Through this winter the following note continually occurs: 'Read some more Horace'.

His interest in painting led him to devote for many months, on every day that the National Gallery was open, twenty minutes after lunch to an inspection of the masters hung there, confining his attention to a single master on each visit, and forbidding his eyes to stray to any other. He went there from sheer liking, and not with any practical object; but he used to recommend the plan to young people, telling them that they would insensibly acquire a greater insight into schools and styles by this means than from any guide-books to the painters' works and manners.

During Phelps's series of Shakespeare plays at Drury Lane Hardy followed up every one, his companion being one of Blomfield's pupils. They used to carry a good edition of the play with them, and be amongst the first of the pit crowd, holding the book edgewise on the barrier in front (which in those days was close to the orchestra) during the performance — a severe enough test for the actors, if they noticed the two enthusiasts. He always said that Phelps never received his due as a Shakespearean actor — particularly as Falstaff.

He also frequented the later readings by Charles Dickens at the Hanover Square Rooms, and oratorios at Exeter Hall.

### SUMMER 1867

Adelphi Terrace, as everybody knows, faces the river, and in the heat of summer, while Hardy was there, the stench from the mud at low water increased, the Metropolitan main-drainage system not having been yet constructed. Whether from the effects of this smell upon a constitution that had grown up in a pure country atmosphere (as he himself supposed), or because he had been accustomed to shut himself up in his rooms at Westbourne Park Villas every evening from six to twelve, reading incessantly, instead of getting out for air after the day's confinement, Hardy's health had become much weakened. He used to say that on sitting down to begin drawing in the morning he had scarcely physical power left him to hold the pencil and square. When he visited his friends in Dorset they were shocked at the pallor which sheeted a countenance formerly ruddy with health. His languor increased month by month. Blomfield, who must have been inconvenienced by it, suggested to Hardy that he should go into the country for a time to regain vigour. Hardy was beginning to feel that he would rather go into the country altogether. He constitutionally shrank from the business of social advancement, caring for life as an emotion rather than for life as a science of climbing, in which respect he was quizzed by his acquaintance for his lack of ambition. However, Blomfield thought that to stay permanently in the country would be a mistake, advising him to return to London by the following October at latest.

An opportunity of trying the experiment, at any rate, was afforded by the arrival of a communication from Mr. Hicks, his old instructor in architecture, asking if he could recommend him any good assistant accustomed to church-restoration, as he was hampered by frequently suffering from gout. Hardy wrote that he would go himself, and at the latter part of July (1867) went down to Dorchester, leaving most of his books and other belongings behind him at Westbourne Park, which included such of his poems in manuscript as he had thought worth keeping.  Of these the only ones not ultimately destroyed were consigned to darkness till between thirty and forty years after, when they were printed — mainly in *Wessex Poems*, though several, that had been overlooked at first, appeared in later volumes.  Among the earliest were 'Amabel', 'Hap', 'In Vision I Roamed', 'At a Bridal', 'Postponement', 'A Confession to a Friend', 'Neutral Tones', 'Her Dilemma', 'Revulsion', 'Her Reproach', 'The Ruined Maid', 'Heiress and Architect', and four sonnets called 'She, to Him' (part of a much larger number which perished).  Some had been sent to magazines, one sonnet that he rather liked, which began 'Many a one has loved as much as I', having been lost, the editor never returning it and Hardy having kept no copy.  But most had never been sent anywhere.

It should be mentioned that several months before leaving London he had formed an idea of writing plays in blank verse — and had planned to try the stage as a supernumerary for six or twelve months, to acquire technical skill in their construction — going so far as to make use of an introduction to Mark Lemon, the then editor of *Punch*, and an ardent amateur-actor, for his opinion on this point.  Nothing, however, came of the idea beyond the call on the genial editor, and on Mr. Coe, the stage-manager at the Haymarket under Buckstone's lesseeship, with whom he had a conversation.  The former rather damped the young man's ardour by reminding him that the elder Mathews had said that he would not let a dog of his go on the stage, and that he himself, much as he personally liked the art of acting, would rather see a daughter of his in her grave than on the boards of a theatre.  In fact almost the first moment of his sight of stage realities disinclined him to push further in that direction ; and his only actual contact with the stage at this time was his appearance at Covent Garden as a nondescript in the pantomime of 'The Forty Thieves', and in a representation of the Oxford and Cambridge boat-race — this having come about through the accident of the smith who did the ironwork for the pantomime being the man who executed some of Blomfield's designs for church metal-work, and who made crucifixes and harlequin-traps with equal imperturbability.  More than forty years were to elapse before Hardy trod the same boards again — this time at rehearsals of the Italian Opera by Baron Frédéric d'Erlanger, founded on *Tess of the d'Urbervilles*.

'*End of Dec.* 1865. To insects the twelvemonth has been an epoch, to leaves a life, to tweeting birds a generation, to man a year.'

## NOTES OF 1866–67

'A certain man: He creeps away to a meeting with his own sensations.'

'He feels himself shrink into nothing when contemplating other people's *means* of working. When he looks upon their *ends* he expands with triumph.'

'There is no more painful lesson to be learnt by a man of capacious mind than that of excluding general knowledge for particular.'

'The defects of a class are more perceptible to the class immediately below it than to itself.'

'*June* 6. Went to Hatfield. Changed since my early visit. A youth thought the altered highway had always run as it did. Pied rabbits in the Park, descendants of those I knew. The once children are quite old inhabitants. I regretted that the beautiful sunset did not occur in a place of no reminiscences, that I might have enjoyed it without their tinge.'

'*June* 19. A widely appreciative mind mostly fails to achieve a great work from pure far-sightedness. The very clearness with which he discerns remote possibilities is, from its nature, scarcely ever co-existent with the microscopic vision demanded for tracing the narrow path that leads to them.'

'*July* 13. A man's grief has a touch of the ludicrous unless it is so keen as to be awful.'

'*Feb.* 18. Remember that Evil dies as well as Good.'

'*April* 29. Had the teachings of experience grown cumulatively with the age of the world we should have been ere now as great as God.'

# CHAPTER IV

# BETWEEN ARCHITECTURE AND LITERATURE

1867–1870 : *Aet.* 27–30

## END OF SUMMER 1867

A FEW weeks in the country — where he returned to his former custom of walking to the Dorchester architect's office from his mother's house every day — completely restored him. He easily fell into the routine that he had followed before, though, with between five and six years superadded of experience as a young man at large in London, it was with very different ideas of things.

Among the churches for restoration or rebuilding that Hicks had in hand, or in prospect, was one which should be named here — that of the parish of St. Juliot in Cornwall — for which remote spot Mr. Hicks set out one day to report upon the said building, shortly after Hardy had gone back to help him. Hardy noticed the romantic name of the church and parish — but had no idea of the meaning it would have for him in aftertime.

An effect among others of his return to the country was to take him out of the fitful yet mechanical and monotonous existence that befalls many a young man in London lodgings. Almost suddenly he became more practical, and queried of himself definitely how to achieve some tangible result from his desultory yet strenuous labours at literature during the previous four years. He considered that he knew fairly well both West-country life in its less explored recesses and the life of an isolated student cast upon the billows of London with no protection but his brains — the young man of whom it may be said more truly than perhaps of any, that 'save his own soul he hath no star'. The two contrasting experiences seemed to afford him abundant materials out of which to evolve a striking socialistic novel — not that he mentally defined it as such, for the word had probably never, or scarcely ever, been heard of at that date.

So down he sat in one of the intervals of his attendances at Mr.

Hicks's drawing-office (which were not regular), and, abandoning verse as a waste of labour — though he had resumed it awhile on arriving in the country — he began the novel the title of which is here written as it was at first intended to be :

THE POOR MAN AND THE LADY

A STORY WITH NO PLOT

*Containing some original verses*

This, however, he plainly did not like, for it was ultimately abridged to

THE POOR MAN AND THE LADY

By the POOR MAN

And the narrative was proceeded with till, in October of this year (1867), he paid a flying visit to London to fetch his books and other impedimenta.

Thus it happened that under the stress of necessity he had set about a kind of literature in which he had hitherto taken but little interest — prose fiction ; so little indeed, that at one of the brief literary lectures, or speeches, he had occasionally delivered to Blomfield's pupils in a spare half-hour of an afternoon, he had expressed to their astonishment an indifference to a popular novelist's fame.

1868.   JANUARY 16 AND ONWARDS

We find from an entry in a note-book that on this date he began to make a fair copy of the projected story, so that all of it must have been written out roughly during the five preceding months in the intervals of his architectural work for Hicks. In the February following a memorandum shows that he composed a lyric entitled 'A Departure by Train', which has disappeared. In April he was reading Browning and Thackeray ; also taking down the exact sound of the song of the nightingale — the latter showing that he must have been living in sylvan shades at his parents', or at least sleeping there, at the time, where nightingales sang within a yard of the bedroom windows in those days, though they do not now.

On June 9 he enters, 'Finished copying MS.', and on the 17th is recorded at some length the outline of a narrative poem on the Battle of the Nile. It was never finished, but it shows that the war with Napoleon was even then in his mind as material for poetry of some sort.

On July 1 he writes down — in all likelihood after a time of mental depression over his work and prospects :

'Cures for despair :

'To read Wordsworth's "Resolution and Independence".

„    „    Stuart Mill's "Individuality" (in *Liberty*).

„    „    Carlyle's "Jean Paul Richter".'

On July 17 he writes : 'Perhaps I can do a volume of poems consisting of the *other side* of common emotions'. What this means is not quite clear.

On July 25 he posted the MS. of *The Poor Man and the Lady* to Mr. Alexander Macmillan, and now being free of it, lent some more help to Mr. Hicks in his drawings for church-restorations, reading the Seventh Book of the *Aeneid* between whiles.

'*August* 12. A reply from Macmillan on the MS.'

The letter was a very long and interesting one, and is printed in full in the *Letters of Alexander Macmillan*. The well-known publisher begins by stating that he had read the novel 'with care, and with much interest and admiration, but feeling at the same time that it has what seem to me drawbacks fatal to its success, and what I think, judging the writer from the book itself, you would feel even more strongly, to its truthfulness and justice'.

He then went into particulars of criticism. 'The utter heartlessness of *all* the conversation you give in drawing-rooms and ballrooms about the working-classes has some ground of truth, I fear, and might justly be scourged as you aim at doing ; but your chastisement would fall harmless from its very excess. Will's speech to the working men is full of wisdom. . . .

'Much of the writing seems to me admirable. The scene in Rotten Row is full of power and insight. . . . You see I am writing to you as a writer who seems to me, at least potentially, of considerable mark, of power and purpose. If this is your first book I think you ought to go on. May I ask if it is, and — you are not a lady, so perhaps you will forgive the question — are you young ?

'I have shown your MS. to one friend, whose judgment coincides with my own.'

The opinion of the friend — who was Mr. John Morley — was enclosed. He said that the book was 'A very curious and original performance : the opening pictures of the Christmas-eve in the

tranter's house are really of good quality : much of the writing is
strong and fresh'.  But he added as to its faults that 'the thing hangs
too loosely together', and that some of the scenes were wildly extra-
vagant, 'so that they read like some clever lad's dream'.  He wound
up by saying, 'If the man is young he has stuff and purpose in him'.

It was perhaps not usual for a first haphazard attempt at fiction
to receive such close attention from so experienced a publisher as
Mr. Macmillan, and so real a man of letters as Mr. Morley.  However,
Hardy seems to have done little in the matter during the autumn,
beyond rewriting some of the pages ; but in December he paid a
flying visit to London, and saw Mr. Macmillan.

The substance of the interview was that though *The Poor Man
and the Lady*, if printed, might create a considerable curiosity, it was
a class of book which Macmillan himself could not publish ; but if
Hardy were bent on issuing it he would probably have no difficulty
in doing so through another firm, such as that of Chapman and Hall.
The young man, it is assumed, was so bent, for Mr. Macmillan gave
him an introduction to Mr. Frederick Chapman, and Hardy called on
the latter with the MS. under his arm.  He makes a note on December
8 that he had been to see Chapman, adding : 'I fear the interview
was an unfortunate one'.  He returned to Dorchester, leaving the
MS. in Mr. Chapman's hands, and this brought the year to an unsatisfactory close — so far as it affected Hardy's desire to get into print
as the author of a three-volume novel, since he could not do so as a
poet without paying for publication.

In the midst of these attempts at authorship, and the intermittent
preparation of architectural drawings, Hardy found time to read a
good many books.  The only reference discoverable includes various
plays of Shakespeare, Walpole's *Letters to Sir Horace Mann* in six
volumes, Thackeray, Macaulay, Walt Whitman, Virgil's *Aeneid* (of
which he never wearied), and other books during his interval of leisure.

The following note, amongst others, occurs in his pocket-book
this autumn :

'The village sermon.  If it was very bad the parish concluded
that he [the vicar] wrote it himself ; if very good, that his wife wrote
it ; if middling, that he bought it, so that they could have a nap
without offending him.'  What parish this refers to is unknown.

There is also another note, some days later :

'How people will laugh in the midst of a misery !  Some would
soon get to whistle in Hell.'

## 1869

Presumably it was the uncertainty of his position between architecture and literature, and a vague sense of ominousness at getting no reply (so far as can be ascertained) from Messrs. Chapman and Hall, that led Hardy to London again during the January of the new year.

Suggestions that he should try his hand at articles in reviews were made to him by Mr. Macmillan, and also by the critic of his manuscript, Mr. Morley, with whom he got acquainted about this time, Morley offering him an introduction to the editor of *The Saturday Review*. But Hardy was not so much in want of a means of subsistence — having always his father's house to fall back upon in addition to architectural jobs which were offered him readily by Blomfield and other London architects — as of a clear call to him which course in life to take — the course he loved, and which was his natural instinct, that of letters, or the course all practical wisdom dictated, that of architecture.

He stayed on in London lodgings, studying pictures at the South Kensington Museum and other places, and reading desultorily, till at last a letter did arrive from Chapman and Hall. On his calling at their address in Piccadilly Chapman was in the back part of the shop, and on Hardy's joining him said with nonchalance, ignoring Hardy's business, 'You see that old man talking to my clerk? He's Thomas Carlyle.' Hardy turned and saw leaning on one elbow at the clerk's desk an aged figure in an inverness cape and slouched hat. 'Have a good look at him,' continued Chapman. 'You'll be glad I pointed him out to you some day.' Hardy was rather surprised that Chapman did not think enough of Thomas Carlyle to attend to his wants in person, but said nothing.

The publisher stated they could not purchase the MS. outright, but that they would publish it if he would guarantee a small sum against loss — say £20. The offer on the whole was fair and reasonable : Hardy agreed to the guarantee, Chapman promised to put the book in hand and to send a memorandum of his undertaking to publish it ; and Hardy shortly after left London, expecting proof-sheets soon to be forwarded.

As they did not come he may have written to inquire about them ; anyhow Messrs. Chapman suddenly asked him in a note if he would call on them and meet 'the gentleman who read your manuscript' — whose opinion they would like him to have.

He went in March, by appointment as to the day and hour, it is believed, not knowing that the 'gentleman' was George Meredith. He was shown into a back room of the publishing offices (opposite Sackville Street, and where Prince's Restaurant now stands); and before him, in the dusty and untidy apartment, piled with books and papers, was a handsome man in a frock-coat — 'buttoned at the waist, but loose above' — no other than Meredith in person, his ample dark-brown beard, wavy locks, and somewhat dramatic manner lending him a striking appearance to the younger man's eye, who even then did not know his name.

Meredith had the manuscript in his hand, and began lecturing Hardy upon it in a sonorous voice. No record was kept by the latter of their conversation, but the gist of it he remembered very well. It was that the firm were willing to publish the novel as agreed, but that he, the speaker, strongly advised its author not to 'nail his colours to the mast' so definitely in a first book, if he wished to do anything practical in literature; for if he printed so pronounced a thing he would be attacked on all sides by the conventional reviewers, and his future injured. The story was, in fact, a sweeping dramatic satire of the squirearchy and nobility, London society, the vulgarity of the middle class, modern Christianity, church-restoration, and political and domestic morals in general, the author's views, in fact, being obviously those of a young man with a passion for reforming the world — those of many a young man before and after him; the tendency of the writing being socialistic, not to say revolutionary; yet not argumentatively so, the style having the affected simplicity of Defoe's (which had long attracted Hardy, as it did Stevenson, years later, to imitation of it). This naïve realism in circumstantial details that were pure inventions was so well assumed that both Macmillan and Morley had been perhaps a little, or more than a little, deceived by its seeming actuality; to Hardy's surprise, when he thought the matter over in later years, that his inexperienced imagination should have created figments that could win credence from such experienced heads.

The satire was obviously pushed too far — as sometimes in Swift and Defoe themselves — and portions of the book, apparently taken in earnest by both his readers, had no foundation either in Hardy's beliefs or his experience. One instance he could remember was a chapter in which, with every circumstantial detail, he described in the first person his introduction to the kept mistress of an architect who 'took in washing' (as it was called in the profession) — that is, worked at his own office for other architects — the said mistress adding to her lover's income by designing for him the pulpits, altars, reredoses, texts, holy vessels, crucifixes, and other ecclesiastical furniture which were handed on to him by the nominal architects who employed her protector — the lady herself being a dancer at a music-hall when not engaged in designing Christian emblems — all told so plausibly as to seem actual proof of the degeneracy of the age.

Whatever might have been the case with the other two, Meredith was not taken in by the affected simplicity of the narrative, and that was obviously why he warned his young acquaintance that the press would be about his ears like hornets if he published his manuscript. For though the novel might have been accepted calmly enough by the reviewers and public in these days, in genteel mid-Victorian 1869 it would no doubt have incurred, as Meredith judged, severe strictures which might have handicapped a young writer for a long time. It may be added that the most important scenes were laid in London, of which city Hardy had just had between five and six years' constant and varied experience — as only a young man at large in the metropolis can get it — knowing every street and alley west of St. Paul's like a born Londoner, which he was often supposed to be ; an experience quite ignored by the reviewers of his later books, who, if he only touched on London in his pages, promptly reminded him not to write of a place he was unacquainted with, but to get back to his sheepfolds.

The upshot of this interview was that Hardy took away the MS. with him to decide on a course.

Meredith had added that Hardy could rewrite the story, softening it down considerably ; or what would be much better, put it away altogether for the present, and attempt a novel with a purely artistic purpose, giving it a more complicated 'plot' than was attempted with *The Poor Man and the Lady*.

Thus it happened that a first and probably very crude manuscript by an unknown young man, who had no connection with the press, or with literary circles, was read by a most experienced publisher, and by two authors among the most eminent in letters of their time. Also that they had been interested to more than an average degree in his work, as was shown by their wish to see him, and their voluntary bestowal of good counsel. Except the writer himself, these three seem to have been the only ones whose eyes ever scanned the MS.

It was surprising enough to Hardy to find that, in the opinion of such experienced critics, he had written so aggressive and even dangerous a work (Mr. Macmillan had said it 'meant mischief') almost without knowing it, for his mind had been given in the main to poetry and other forms of pure literature. What he did with the MS. is uncertain, and he could not precisely remember in after years, though he found a few unimportant leaves of it — now also gone. He fancied that he may have sent it to some other publisher just as it stood, to get another opinion before finally deciding its fate, which publisher may have thought it too risky also. What happened in respect of new writing was that he took Meredith's advice too literally, and set about constructing the eminently 'sensational' plot of *Desperate Remedies*, of which anon.

Meanwhile, during his stay in London in the winter, Hardy heard news of the death at Dorchester of Mr. John Hicks, whose pupil he had been, and whom he had lately assisted; and at the end of April received a request from Mr. G. R. Crickmay, an architect of Weymouth, who had purchased Mr. Hicks's practice, to aid him in carrying out the church-restorations that Hicks had begun, or undertaken to begin. Hardy called on Mr. Crickmay, who appeared not to have studied Gothic architecture specially, if at all, but was an amiable, straight-dealing man; and Hardy assented to help him finish the churches. Probably thinking of his book, he agreed for a fortnight only in the first place, though Mr. Crickmay had asked for a longer time.

During May Hardy continued to prepare for Crickmay, in Hicks's old Dorchester office, the church-drawings he had already made some progress with; and the arrangement proved eminently satisfactory, as is evident, Mr. Crickmay proposing to enlist Hardy's services for three months certain at his Weymouth office, the church-work left unfinished by Hicks turning out to be more than had been anticipated It is to be gathered that Hardy considered this brief occupation would afford, at any rate, breathing-time while he should ruminate on what it was best to do about the writing of the novels, and he closed with Crickmay for a term which was afterwards still further lengthened by unforeseen circumstances.

He used to remember that after coming away from the interview with Crickmay with much lightness of heart at having shelved further thought about himself for at least three months, he stood opposite the Burdon Hotel on the Esplanade, facing the beautiful sunlit bay, and listened to the Town band's performance of a set of charming new waltzes by Johann Strauss. He inquired their name, and found that it was the 'Morgenblätter'. The verses 'At a Seaside Town' must refer in their background to this place at this time and a little onward, though the gist of them can be fancy only.

He now became regularly resident at Weymouth, and took lodgings there, rowing in the bay almost every evening of this summer, and bathing at seven in the morning either on the pebble-beach towards Preston, or diving off from a boat. Being — like Swinburne — a swimmer, he would lie a long time on his back on the surface of the waves, rising and falling with the tide in the warmth of the morning sun. He used to tell that, after the enervation of London, this tonic existence by the sea seemed ideal, and that physically he went back ten years in his age almost as by the touch of an enchanter's wand.

In August or September a new assistant came to Mr. Crickmay's drawing-offices, who was afterwards sketched in *Desperate Remedies* as 'Edward Springrove' — and in November this young man persuaded Hardy to join a quadrille class in the town, which was a source of much amusement to them both. Dancing was still an art in those days, though Hardy remarked once that he found the young ladies of Weymouth heavier on the arm than their London sisters. By the time that winter drew on he had finished all the drawings for church-restoration that had been placed in his hands, but he remained at his Weymouth lodgings, working at the MS. of *Desperate Remedies*, the melodramatic novel, quite below the level of *The Poor Man and the Lady*, which was the unfortunate consequence of Meredith's advice to 'write a story with a plot'.

## A DEVELOPMENT

So 1869 passed, and at the beginning of February in the year following Hardy gave up his rooms at Weymouth and returned to his rural home to be able to concentrate more particularly on the MS. than he could do in a lively town and as a member of a dancing-class where a good deal of flirtation went on, the so-called 'class' being, in fact, a gay gathering for dances and love-making by adepts of both sexes. The poem entitled 'The Dawn after the Dance', and dated 'Weymouth, 1869', is supposed, though without proof, to have some bearing on these dances.

He had not been in the seclusion of his mother's house more than a week when he received the following letter from Mr. Crickmay, which, as it led to unexpected emotional developments, it may be worth while to give verbatim :

'Weymouth,
'11th February, 1870.

'Dear Sir :

'Can you go into Cornwall for me, to take a plan and particulars of a church I am about to rebuild there ? It must be done early next week, and I should be glad to see you on Monday morning. — Yours truly,
'G. R. Crickmay.'

This was the church of St. Juliot, near Boscastle, of which Hardy had vaguely heard in Mr. John Hicks's time as being likely to turn up for manipulation, and had been struck by its romantic sound. Despite the somewhat urgent summons he declined the job, the moment being inconvenient with the new novel in hand. But receiving a more persuasive request from Crickmay later, and having finished the MS. of *Desperate Remedies* (except the three or four final chapters) by the beginning of March, he agreed to go on the errand.

Sending off, therefore, on the previous Saturday the copy of his second novel to Mr. Alexander Macmillan, whom he now regarded as a friend, he set out on Monday, March 7, for the remote parish mentioned, in a county he had never entered, though it was not distant. It was a journey of seeming unimportance, and was reluctantly undertaken, yet it turned out to have lifelong consequences for him. The restoration of this church was, moreover, the work which brought to a close Hardy's labours in Gothic architecture, though he did not know it at the time.

Though the distance was not great the way was tedious, there being few railways in Cornwall at this date. Rising at four in the morning, and starting by starlight from his country retreat, armed with sketch-book, measuring-tape, and rule, he did not reach Launceston till four in the afternoon, where he hired a conveyance for the additional sixteen or seventeen miles' distance by the Boscastle road towards the north coast, and the spot with the charming name — the dilapidated church, parish, and residence of the Rev. Caddell Holder, M.A. Oxon.

It was a cloudy evening at the end of a fine day, with a dry breeze blowing ; and leaving the Boscastle highway by a by-road to the left he reached St. Juliot Rectory, by which time it was quite dark. His arrival and entry can best be described in the words of the lady whom he met that night for the first time, and who later on became his wife. Long afterwards she wrote down her 'Recollections', which are given in the following pages in full so far as they relate to her husband, these making up the whole of the second half of her manuscript, the first half being entirely concerned with other members of her family and herself before she knew him.

She was born at 10 York Street, Plymouth, and baptized at St. Andrew's Church, being the younger daughter of Mr. J. Attersoll Gifford, a solicitor. She had grown up in a house close to the Hoe, which she used to call 'the playground of her childhood'. She would relate how, to her terror at first, she was daily dipped as a little girl in the pools under the Hoe; and on its cliffs — very much more rugged than now — had had her youthful adventures, one of which, leaving her clinging to a crag, would have cost her her life but for the timely aid of a kind boatman. Her education was carried on at a school for young ladies also overlooking the Hoe's green slopes, where, to use her own words, 'military drills took place on frequent mornings, and then our dear instructress drew down the blinds'. At nineteen she removed from Plymouth with her parents.

Thomas Hardy, aged 30, *c.* 1870

Emma Lavinia Gifford, 1870
(afterwards Mrs. Thomas Hardy)

# CHAPTER V

# ST. JULIOT

1870 : *Aet.* 29–30

THE LATTER PART OF MRS. (EMMA LAVINIA) HARDY'S MS., FOUND AFTER HER DEATH, AND ENTITLED 'SOME RECOLLECTIONS'

[The words in square brackets are added
to make the allusions intelligible]

'MY only sister married the Rev. Caddell Holder, son of a Judge of Barbadoes, where he was born : he often spoke of his beautiful home there, with oranges growing by his bedroom window. At Trinity College, Oxford, he was a "gentleman-commoner" (this is now abolished), where so far as he could discover his only privilege [from the distinction] was being allowed to walk upon the grass and wear a gold-tasselled cap, he used to say. He was rector of St. Juliot, North Cornwall, where I [first] knew him ; and it was there that my husband made my acquaintance, which afterwards proved a romance in full for us. . . .

'[He was] a man older than herself by many years, and somewhat delicate because of his West Indian birth ; he was, however, energetic, and a very Boanerges in his preaching, which style was greatly relished by the simple folk of his scattered parish. In those days clergymen were [often] very lax in their duties, but he was quite exact and faithful, and [after I went to live there with my sister] we were marshalled off in regular staff style to the services. On Sundays they were two only, and the choir *nil* — the whole being carried out by the parson, his wife, myself, and the clerk. The congregation were mostly silent, or merely murmuring occasionally. The duty, however, was only arduous on Sundays.

'They were married from our home, and immediately after went to his — and I went with them — to the said St. Juliot Rectory. My sister required my help, for it was a difficult parish, from neglect by a former incumbent, whose wife, however, had done as much as she could, even to ringing the bell for service.

'At this date [of writing, *i.e.* 1911] it seems as if all had been arranged in orderly sequence for me, link after link occurring in a chain of movements to bring me to the point where my own fortunes came on.

'St. Juliot is a romantic spot indeed of North Cornwall. It was sixteen miles away from a station then, [and a place] where the belief in witchcraft was carried out in actual practice among the primitive inhabitants. Traditions and strange gossipings [were] the common talk . . . indulged in by those isolated natives [of a parish] where newspapers rarely penetrated, or [were] thrown aside for local news; where new books rarely came, or strangers, and where hard labour upon the stony soil made a cold, often ill-natured, working class; yet with some good traits and fine exceptions. Our neighbours beyond the hamlets were nine miles off, or most of them.

'When we arrived at the Rectory there was a great gathering and welcome from the parishioners, and a tremendous fusilade of salutes, cheering, and bell-ringing — quite a hubbub to welcome the Rector home with his new wife. Then these welcomers (all men and nearly all young) came into the hall to drink the healths of bridegroom and bride, and a speech was made by the foremost young farmer and duly replied to by my brother-in-law. . . . It proved indeed an eventful day for me, for my future was bound up in that day in a way which I could not foresee.

'The whole parish seemed delighted with the event and the prospect of having things in better order after the long neglect. . . . Riding about on my Fanny [her pony] I enjoyed the place immensely, and helped my sister in the house affairs, visiting the parish folk, and playing the harmonium on Sundays. . . .

'It was a very poor parish; the church had been a long while out of repair for want of funds; the Patron lived abroad: in contrast with these days of frequent services [and attendance] it was unfrequented, the Sunday congregation in the morning not large, not much larger in the evenings [afternoons]. No week-day services were held. The tower went on cracking from year to year, and the bells remained in the little north transept [to which they had been removed for safety], their mouths open upward. The carved benchends rotted more and more, the ivy hung gaily from the roof timbers, and the birds and the bats had a good time up there unmolested; no one seemed to care. The Architect continued delaying and delaying to come or send his head man to begin operations, though my sister was active in the matter, both Patron and Architect getting urgent appeals from her, till the former decided at last to commence.

'It was the period of Church restoration, most churches being dilapidated more or less. My life now began. . . .

'Scarcely any author and his wife could have had a much more romantic meeting, with its unusual circumstances in bringing them together from two different, though neighbouring counties to this one at this very remote spot, with a beautiful sea-coast, and the wild Atlantic Ocean rolling in with its magnificent waves and spray, its white gulls, and black choughs and grey puffins, its cliffs and rocks and gorgeous sunsettings, sparkling redness in a track widening from the horizon to the shore. All this should be seen in the winter to be truly appreciated. No summer visitors can have a true idea of its power to awaken heart and soul. [It was] an unforgettable experience to me, scampering up and down the hills on my beloved mare alone, wanting no protection, the rain going down my back often, and my hair floating on the wind.

'I wore a soft deep dark coloured brown habit longer than to my heels, (as worn then), which had to be caught up to one side when walking, and thrown over the left arm gracefully and carefully, and this to be practised during the riding instruction — all of which my father [had] taught me with great pleasure and pride in my appearance and aptitude. I also wore a brown felt hat turned up at the sides. Fanny and I were one creature, and very happy. She was a lovely brown colour too, stopping where she liked, to drink or munch, I often getting off sketching and gathering flowers. The villagers stopped to gaze when I rushed down the hills, and a butterman laid down his basket once to exclaim loudly. No one except myself dared to ride in such fashion.

'Sometimes I left Fanny, and clambered down to the rocks and seal-caves. Sometimes I visited a favourite in the scattered parish. . . .

'When it was known that the Church-restoration was to be gone on with, the whole village was alive about it. Mr. Crickmay of Weymouth undertook it — Mr. Hicks, the first architect consulted, having died in the interval. The [assistant-architect] of his office was to come on a certain day. The letter that brought this intelligence interested the whole house, and afterwards, later in the day, the whole parish too; it seemed almost wonderful that a fixed date should at last be given and the work set in hand, after so many years of waiting, of difficulties, and delays, since back in the time of the previous incumbent. All were delighted. I had myself worked hard for my brother-in-law, collecting small sums from time to time and selling water-colour sketches I had painted, and saving household expenses in order that the historic old church might be rebuilt — there being no landed proprietor, no "equals" in the parish (as the rector often explained plaintively). So we were all ready to see the fruition of our endeavours, that is, my sister's and mine particularly.

'I must confess to a curiosity started by the coming event as to what the Architect would be like; seeing few strangers we had a vivid interest in every one who came : a strange clergyman, an occasional *locum-tenens*, a school-inspector, a stray missionary, or school-lecturer — all were welcome, including this architect to put us to rights at once.

'It was a lovely Monday evening in March [1870], after a wild winter, that we were on the *qui-vive* for the stranger,[1] who would have a tedious journey, his home being two counties off by the route necessitated changing trains many times, and waiting at stations, a sort of cross-jump journey like a chess-knight's move. The only damp to our gladness was the sudden laying up of my brother-in-law by gout, and he who was the chief person could not be present on the arrival of our guest. The dinner-cloth was laid ; my sister had gone to her husband who required her constant attention. At that very moment the front-door bell rang, and the architect was ushered in. I had to receive him alone, and felt a curious uneasy embarrassment at receiving anyone, especially so necessary a person as the architect. I was immediately arrested by his familiar appearance, as if I had seen him in a dream — his slightly different accent, his soft voice ; also I noticed a blue paper sticking out of his pocket. I was explaining who I was, as I saw that he took me for the parson's daughter or wife, when my sister appeared, to my great relief, and he went up to Mr. Holder's room with her.

'So I met my husband. I thought him much older than he was. He had a beard, and a rather shabby greatcoat, and had quite a business appearance. Afterwards he seemed younger, and by daylight especially so. . . . The blue paper proved to be the MS. of a poem, and not a plan of the church, he informed me, to my surprise.

'After this our first meeting there had to be many visits to the church, and these visits, of deep interest to both, merged in those of

---

[1] The verses entitled 'A Man was drawing near to Me' obviously relate to this arrival. But in them Hardy assumes that she was not thinking about his coming, though from this diary one gathers that she was ; which seems to show that when writing them he had either not read her reminiscence of the evening as printed above, or had forgotten it.

further acquaintance and affection, to end in marriage, but not till after four years.

'At first, though I was interested in him, the church-matters were paramount, and in due time I laid the foundation stone one morning [for the aisle and tower that were to be rebuilt] ; with a bottle containing a record of the proceedings, the school-children attending. I plastered it well, the foreman said. Mr. Holder made a speech to the young ones to remember the event and speak of it to their descendants — just as if it had been a matter of world-wide interest. I wonder if they do remember it, and me.

'The work went rapidly on under the direction of the Architect, who had stayed on his first visit rather longer than intended. We showed him some of the neighbourhood, some clergymen and their wives came to visit us: we were all much pleased at the beginning. Mr. Holder got well again. The Patron of the living, who lived in Antigua, wrote to inquire about it; an account was duly sent, and he replied that he was coming to see it if he could, and would certainly be at the opening.

'My Architect came two or three times a year from that time to visit me. I rode my pretty mare Fanny and he walked by my side, and I showed him some [more] of the neighbourhood — the cliffs, along the roads, and through the scattered hamlets, sometimes gazing down at the solemn small shores below, where the seals lived, coming out of great deep caverns very occasionally. We sketched and talked of books ; often we walked to Boscastle Harbour down the beautiful Vallency Valley where we had to jump over stones and climb over a low wall by rough steps, or get through a narrow pathway, to come out on great wide spaces suddenly, with a sparkling little brook going the same way, in which we once lost a tiny picnic-tumbler, and there it is to this day no doubt between two of the boulders.[1]

'Sometimes we all drove to Tintagel, and Trebarwith Strand where donkeys [word illegible] employed to carry seaweed to the farmers ; Strangles Beach also, Bossiney, Bude, and other places on the coast. Lovely drives they were, with sea-views all along at intervals, and very dawdling enjoyable slow ones ; sometimes to visit a neighbouring clergyman and his family. We grew much interested in each other. I found him a perfectly new subject of study and delight and he found a "mine" in me he said. He was quite unlike any other person who came to see us, for they were slow of speech and ideas.

'In the intervals of his visits we corresponded, and I studied, and sketched, and drove my brother-in-law and sister to the nearest market-

[1] This incident was versified by Hardy afterwards, and entitled 'Under the Waterfall'.

town, Camelford, nine miles off, or to Launceston to see my cousins. The man-servant taught me to jump hurdles on Fanny, but Fanny, though not at all objecting, got a little lame, so we stopped jumping.

'I like to think of those details and small events, and am fancying some other people may like to have them.

'It was a pleasant time, though there were difficulties in the parish. I have never liked the Cornish working-orders as I do Devonshire folk; their so-called admirable independence of character was most disagreeable to live with, and usually amounted to absence of kindly interest in others, though it was unnoticeable by casual acquaintance. . . . Nevertheless their nature had a glamour about it — that of an old-world romantic expression; and then sometimes there came to one's cognizance in the hamlets a dear heart-whole person.

'So the days went on between the visits. The church-opening was somewhat impressive, the element of unusualness being more conspicuous however by the immense numbers of people outside waiting for it to be over and the lunch to begin, than the many attentive and admiring parishioners within, collected imperatively by the rector's wife and himself. Mr. Holder was in a good state of health and spirits; my sister was very important. The patron of the living, the Rev. Richard Rawle, [who owned land in the parish, and was about this time consecrated as Bishop of Trinidad] was present; but no architect came on that brilliant occasion.[1] He appeared, however, on the same scene from time to time afterwards.

'I had two pleasant changes — one to stay at Bath with an old friend of the family; and when my chosen came there too, by her kindness, we had together an interesting time. And I went as country cousin to my brother in London, and was duly astonished, which gave him even more pleasure than it did me.

'After a little time I copied a good deal of manuscript, which went to and fro by post, and I was very proud and happy doing this — which I did in the privacy of my own room, where I also read and wrote the letters.

'The rarity of the visits made them highly delightful to both; we talked much of plots, possible scenes, tales and poetry, and of his own work. He came either from Dorset or London, driving from Launceston station eighteen [sixteen and a half] miles off.

'The day we were married was a perfect September day — the 17th of the month — 1874, — not of brilliant sunshine, but wearing a soft sunny luminousness; just as it should be.

[1] Neither Hardy nor Crickmay was able to attend, for some unknown reason.

'I have had various experiences, interesting some, sad others, since that lovely day, but all showing that an Unseen Power of great benevolence directs my ways ; I have some philosophy, and mysticism, and an ardent belief in Christianity and the life beyond this present one, all which makes any existence curiously interesting. As one watches *happenings* (and even if should occur unhappy happenings), outward circumstances are of less importance if Christ is our highest ideal. A strange unearthly brilliance shines around our path, penetrating and dispersing difficulties with its warmth and glow.

'E. L. HARDY.
'MAX GATE. *January 4th,* 1911.'[1]

This transcript from the first Mrs. Hardy's 'Recollections' (of the existence of which he was unaware till after her death) has carried us onward four years further than the date of Thomas Hardy's arrival in Cornwall on that evening of March 1870. He himself entered in a memorandum-book a few rough notes of his visit, and from these we are able to glean vaguely his impressions of the experience.

It is apparent that he was soon, if not immediately, struck by the nature and appearance of the lady who received him. She was so *living,* he used to say. Though her features were not regular her complexion at this date was perfect in hue, her figure and movement graceful, and her corn-coloured hair abundant in its coils.

It may be mentioned here that the story *A Pair of Blue Eyes* (which Hardy himself classes among his Romances and Fantasies — as if to suggest its visionary nature) has been considered to show a picture of his own personality as the architect on this visit. But in addition to Hardy's own testimony there is proof that this is not the case, he having ever been shy of putting his personal characteristics into his novels. The Adonis depicted was known to be both in appearance and temperament an idealization of a pupil whom Hardy found at Mr. John Hicks's on his return there temporarily from London ; a nephew of that architect, and exactly of the age attributed to Stephen Smith. He is represented as altogether more youthful and sanguine in nature than Hardy, a thoughtful man of twenty-nine, with years of London buffeting and architectural and literary experiences, was at this time. Many of his verses with which readers have since grown familiar in *Wessex Poems* had already been written. Stephen Smith's father was a mason in Hardy's father's employ, combined with one near Boscastle, while Smith's ingenious mode of being

---

[1] It will be seen later that she died the year after this was written.

tutored in Latin was based on a story Hardy had from Holder, as that of a man he had known. Its practicability is, however, doubtful. Henry Knight the reviewer, Elfride's second lover, was really much more like Thomas Hardy as described in his future wife's diary just given ; while the event of the young man arriving as a town-stranger at a village with which he was quite familiar, and the catastrophe that ensued when his familiarity with it was discovered, was an experience of an uncle of his, of which the dramatic possibilities had long arrested him. His own wooing in the 'Delectable Duchy' ran, in fact, without a hitch from beginning to end, and with encouragement from all parties concerned.

But the whole story, except as to the lonely drive across the hills towards the coast, the architectural detail, and a few other external scenes and incidents, is so at variance with any possible facts as to be quite misleading, Hardy's wilful purpose in his early novels until *Far from the Madding Crowd* appeared, if not later, having been to mystify the reader as to their locality, origin, and authorship by various interchanges and inventions, probably owing at first to his doubt if he would pursue the craft, and his sense of the shadow that would fall on an architect who had failed as a novelist. He modified the landscape, and called the Rectory a vicarage in early editions, showing a church with the sea visible from it, which was not true of St. Juliot. The character and appearance of Elfride have points in common with those of Mrs. Hardy in quite young womanhood, a few years before Hardy met her (though her eyes would have been described as deep grey, not as blue) ; moreover, like Elfride, the moment she was on a horse she was part of the animal. But this is all that can be asserted, the plot of the story being one that he had thought of and written down long before he knew her.

What he says about the visit is laconic and hurried, but interesting enough to be given here :

'*March* 7. The dreary yet poetical drive over the hills. Arrived at St. Juliot Rectory between 6 and 7. Received by young lady in brown (Miss Gifford, the rector's sister-in-law). Mr. Holder gout. Saw Mrs. Holder. The meal. Talk. To Mr. Holder's room. Returned downstairs. Music.

'*March* 8. Austere grey view of hills from bedroom window. A funeral. Man tolled the bell (which stood inverted on the ground in the neglected transept) by lifting the clapper and letting it fall against the side. Five bells stood thus in a row (having been taken down from the cracked tower for safety). Staying there drawing and measuring all day, with intervals for meals at rectory.

'*March* 9. Drove with Mrs. Holder and Miss Gifford to Boscastle, and on to Tintagel and Penpethy slate-quarries, with a view to the church roofing. Mr. Symons accompanied us to the quarries. Mr. Symons did not think himself a native; he was only born there. Now Mrs. Symons *was* a native; her family had been there 500 years. Talked about Douglas Cook coming home [the first editor of the *Saturday Review*, whom the Holders had known; buried on the hill above Tintagel]. . . . Music in the evening. The two ladies sang duets, including "The Elfin Call", "Let us dance on the sands", etc. . . . Miss Gifford said that a man asked her for "a drop o' that that isn't gin, please, Miss". He meant hollands, which they kept at the Rectory, as he knew.

'*March* 10. Went with E. L. G. to Beeny Cliff. She on horse-back. . . . On the cliff. . . . "The tender grace of a day", etc. The run down to the edge. The coming home.

'In the afternoon I walked to Boscastle, Mrs. H. and E. L. G. accompanying me three-quarters of the way: the overshot mill: E. provokingly reading as she walked; evening in garden; music later in evening.

'*March* 11. Dawn. Adieu. E. L. G. had struck a light six times in her anxiety to call the servants early enough for me. The journey home. Photo of Bishop of Exeter (for Mrs. Holder). . . .'

The poem entitled 'At the Word "Farewell"' seems to refer either to this or the following visit; and the one called 'When I set out for Lyonnesse' refers certainly to this first visit, it having been his custom to apply the name 'Lyonnesse' to the whole of Cornwall. The latter poem, it may be mentioned, was hailed by a distant voice from the West of America as his sweetest lyric, an opinion from which he himself did not dissent.

'*March* 12. (Sat.) Went to Weymouth. Mr. Crickmay's account £6 : 10 : 9.'

On April 5, having resumed lodgings at Weymouth, to proceed, probably, with the detailed drawings for the restoration of St. Juliot Church by the light of the survey and measurements he had made, Hardy received a letter from the Messrs. Macmillan declining to publish *Desperate Remedies*, the MS. of which they returned, on the ground (it is conjectured) of their disapproval of the incidents. By this time it seemed to have dawned upon him that the Macmillan publishing-house was not in the way of issuing novels of a sensational kind : and accordingly he packed up the MS. again and posted it to the Messrs. Tinsley, a firm to which he was a stranger, but which did publish such novels. Why he did not send it to Messrs. Chapman and Hall, with whom he had now a slight link, and whose reader, George Meredith, had recommended him to write what Hardy understood to be a story of this kind, is inexplicable. Possibly it was from an adventurous feeling that he would like the story to be judged on its own merits by a house which had no knowledge of how it came into existence ; possibly from inexperience. Anyhow it was a mistake from which he suffered, for there is no doubt that Meredith would have taken an interest in a book he had, or was supposed to have, instigated ; and would have offered some suggestions on how to make a better use of the good material at the back of the book. However, to Tinsley's it had gone, and on May 6 Tinsley wrote, stating the terms on which he would publish it, if Hardy would complete the remaining three or four chapters of which a *précis* only had been sent.

About the second week in May, and possibly as a result of the correspondence, Hardy left Mr. Crickmay (whose church-designing he appears to have airily used as something of a stop-gap when his own literary enterprises hung fire) and on the following Monday, the 16th, he started again for London — sadly, as he said, for he had left his heart in Cornwall.

'*May* 18. Royal Academy. No. 118. "Death of Ney", by Gérôme. The presence of Death makes the picture great.

'No. 985. "Jerusalem", by the same. The *shadows only* of the three crucified ones are seen. A fine conception.'

He seems to have passed the days in Town desultorily and dreamily — mostly visiting museums and picture-galleries, and it is not clear what he was waiting for there. In his leisure he seems to have written the 'Ditty' in *Wessex Poems*, inscribed with Miss Gifford's initials. In May he was reading Comte. Crossing Hyde Park one morning in June he saw the announcement of Dickens's death. He was welcomed by Mr. Blomfield, to whom he lent help in finishing some drawings. Being acquainted with another well-known Gothic architect, Mr. Raphael Brandon, Hardy assisted him also for a few weeks, though not continuously.

Brandon was a man who interested him much. In collaboration with his brother David he had published, several years before, the *Analysis of Gothic Architecture* in two quarto volumes, and an extra volume on the *Open Timber Roofs of the Middle Ages*. Both these works were familiar to Hardy, having been quite text-books for architects' pupils till latterly, when the absorbing interest given to French Gothic had caused them to be superseded by the works of Norman Shaw, Nesfield, and Viollet-le-Duc. Brandon, however, was convinced that the development of modern English architecture should be based on English Gothic and not on French, as was shown in his well-known design for the Catholic Apostolic Church in Gordon Square; and that his opinion was the true one was proved in the sequel, notwithstanding that the more fashionable architects, including Arthur Blomfield, were heart and soul of the other opinion at this date. It may have been partly on this account, partly because he was a 'literary architect' — a person always suspect in the profession in those days, Hardy used to say — that Brandon's practice had latterly declined, and he had drifted into a backwater, spending much time in strange projects and hopes, one of these being a scheme for unifying railway-fares on the principle of letter-postage. Hardy was in something of a similar backwater himself — so far as there could be similarity in the circumstances of a man of twenty-nine and a man of sixty, and the old-world out-of-the-way corner of Clement's Inn where Brandon's offices were situate made his weeks with Brandon still more attractive to him, Knight's chambers in *A Pair of Blue Eyes* being drawn from Brandon's. Whilst the latter attended to his scheme for railway-travel, Hardy attended off and on to Brandon's architecture, which had fallen behindhand. Sometimes Hardy helped him also in the details of his scheme; though, having proved to himself its utter futility, he felt in an awkward dilemma; whether to show Brandon its futility and offend him, or to go against his own conscience by indulging him in the hobby.

However, the summer was passed in this way, and his friend Horace Moule, the reviewer and leader-writer, being also in London, the time was pleasant enough. Nothing seems to have been done about the novel, of which the MS., representing about seven-eighths of the whole, was apparently still lying at Tinsley's. He kept up a regular correspondence with 'the young lady in brown' who had attracted him at St. Juliot Rectory, and sent books to her, reading himself among other works Shakespeare and general poetry as usual, the Bible, Alison's *Europe*, and *Mohammed and Mohammedanism* by Bosworth Smith, his friend in later years; though it does not appear that he wrote any verses.

'*June* 30. What the world is saying, and what the world is thinking: It is the man who bases his action upon what the world is thinking, no matter what it may be saying, who rises to the top.

'It is not by rushing straight towards fame that men come up with her, but by so adapting the direction of their path to hers that at some point ahead the two must inevitably intersect.'

On July 15 war was declared by France against Prussia — a cause of much excitement to Brandon, who during the early weeks of the struggle would go into the Strand for every edition of the afternoon papers as they came out, and bring them in and read them to Hardy, who grew as excited as he ; though probably the younger man did not realize that, should England have become involved in the Continental strife, he might have been among the first to be called upon to serve, outside the regular Army. All he seems to have done was to go to a service at Chelsea Hospital and look at the tattered banners mended with netting, and talk to the old asthmatic and crippled men, many of whom in the hospital at that date had fought at Waterloo, and some in the Peninsula.

On August 6 occurred the Battle of Wörth : and on the 8th, in keeping with a promise given on his previous visit, he severed his temporary connection with Brandon and left for Cornwall.

Here, as he said, he found the 'young lady in brown' of the previous winter — at that time thickly muffled from the wind — to have become metamorphosed into a young lady in summer blue, which suited her fair complexion far better ; and the visit was a most happy one. His hosts drove him to various picturesque points on the wild and rugged coast near the Rectory, among others to King Arthur's Castle, Tintagel, which he now saw for the first time ; and where, owing to their lingering too long among the ruins, they found themselves locked in, only narrowly escaping being imprisoned there for the night by much signalling with their handkerchiefs to cottagers in the valley. The lingering might have been considered prophetic, seeing that, after it had been smouldering in his mind for between forty and fifty years, he constructed *The Famous Tragedy of the Queen of Cornwall* from the legends connected with that romantic spot. Why he did not do it sooner, while she was still living who knew the scene so well, and had frequently painted it, it is impossible to say.

H. M. Moule, who by this date knew of the vague understanding between the pair, sent them from time to time such of the daily and weekly papers as contained his leading articles on the war. Concerning such wars Hardy entered in his notebook : 'Quicquid delirant reges, plectuntur Achivi!' On the day that the bloody battle of Gravelotte was fought they were reading Tennyson in the grounds of the rectory. It was at this time and spot that Hardy was struck by the incident of the old horse harrowing the arable field in the valley below, which, when in far later years it was recalled to him by a still bloodier war, he made into the little poem of three verses entitled 'In Time of "the Breaking of Nations"'. Several of the pieces — as is obvious — grouped as 'Poems of 1912-13' in the same volume with *Satires of Circumstance*, and three in *Moments of Vision*, namely, 'The Figure in the Scene', 'Why did I sketch', and 'It never looks like Summer now', with doubtless many others, are known to be also memories of the present and later sojourns here in this vague romantic land of 'Lyonnesse'.

It was at this time, too, that he saw the last of St. Juliot Church in its original condition of picturesque neglect, the local builder laying hands on it shortly after, and razing to the ground the tower and the north aisle (which had hitherto been the nave), and the transept. Hardy much regretted the obliteration in this manner of the church's history, and, too, that he should be instrumental in such obliteration, the building as he had first set eyes on it having been so associated with what was romantic in his life. Yet his instrumentality was involuntary, the decision to alter and diminish its area having been come to before he arrived on the scene. What else could be done with the dilapidated structure was difficult to say if it had to be retained for use. The old walls of the former nave, dating from Norman or even earlier times, might possibly have been preserved. A north door, much like a Saxon one, was inadvertently destroyed, but Hardy made a drawing of it which is preserved in the present church, with his drawings of the highly carved seat-ends and other details that have disappeared. Fortunately the old south aisle was kept intact, with its arcade, the aisle now being adapted for a nave.

It was at this church that occurred his humorous experience of the builder's view of the old chancel-screen. Hardy had made a careful drawing of it, with its decayed tracery, posts, and gilding, marking thereon where sundry patchings and scarfings were to be applied. Reaching the building one day he found a new and highly varnished travesty of the old screen standing in its place. 'Well, Mr. Hardy,' replied the builder in answer to his astonished inquiries, 'I said to myself, I won't stand on a pound or two while I'm about it, and I'll give 'em a new screen instead of that patched-up old thing.'

PART II

NOVELS — TO ILLNESS

CHAPTER VI

# FIRST THREE BOOKS

1870–1873 : *Aet.* 30–33

HE must when in London have obtained from Tinsley the MS. of *Desperate Remedies* ; for during the autumn of this year 1870 there were passing between him and Miss Gifford chapters of the story for her to make a fair copy of, the original MS. having been interlined and altered, so that it may have suffered, he thought, in the eyes of a publisher's reader by being difficult to read. He meanwhile wrote the three or four remaining chapters, and the novel — this time finished — was packed off to Tinsley in December. However, a minute fact seems to suggest that Hardy was far from being in bright spirits about this book and his future at this time. On the margin of his copy of *Hamlet* the following passage is marked with the date, 'December 15, 1870' :

'Thou wouldst not think how ill all's here about my heart : but it is no matter!'

Tinsley wrote his terms again, which for some unaccountable reason were worse now than they had been in the first place, an advance of £75 being demanded ; and the following is a transcript of Hardy's letter to the publisher on these points, at the end of December :

'I believe I am right in understanding your terms thus — that if the gross receipts reach the costs of publishing I shall receive the £75 back again, and if they are more than the costs I shall have £75, added to half the receipts beyond the costs (*i.e.*, assuming the expenditure to be £100, and the receipts £200, I should have returned to me £75 + £50 = £125).

'Will you be good enough to say, too, if the sum includes advertising to the customary extent, and about how long after my paying the money the book would appear.'

This adventurous arrangement by the would-be author, who at that date had only £123 in the world, beyond what he might have obtained from his father — which was not much — and who was virtually if not distinctly engaged to be married to a girl with no

83

money except in reversion after the death of relatives, was actually carried out by him in the January following (1871): when, being in London again, he paid the £75 over to Tinsley in Bank of England notes (rather, as it seemed, to Tinsley's astonishment, Hardy said) and retired to Dorset to correct the proofs, filling up leisure moments not by anything practical, but by writing down such snatches of the old country ballads as he could hear from aged people. On the 25th March the book was published anonymously in three volumes; and on the 30th he again went to his Weymouth lodgings to lend Mr. Crickmay more help in his church-restorations.

On April 1 *Desperate Remedies* received a striking review in the *Athenæum* as being a powerful novel, and on April 13 an even better notice in the *Morning Post* as being an eminent success. But, alas, on the 22nd the *Spectator* brought down its heaviest-leaded pastoral staff on the prematurely happy volumes, the reason for this violence being mainly the author's daring to suppose it possible that an unmarried lady owning an estate could have an illegitimate child.

'This is an absolutely anonymous story', began the review: 'no assumption of a *nom-de-plume* which might, at some future time, disgrace the family name, and still more the Christian name, of a repentant and remorseful novelist — and very right too. By all means let him bury the secret in the profoundest depths of his own heart, out of reach, if possible, of his own consciousness. The law is hardly just which prevents Tinsley Brothers from concealing their participation also.'

When Moule, whom Hardy had not consulted on the venture, read the reception of the novel by the *Spectator* he wrote a brief line to Hardy bidding him not to mind the slating. After its first impact, which was with good reason staggering, it does not seem to have worried Hardy much or at any rate for long (though one of the personalities insinuated by the reviewer, in clumsy humour, that the novel must have been 'a desperate remedy for an emaciated purse', may well have been galling enough). And indeed about this time he noted down: 'Strictly, we should resent wrongs, be placid at justice, and grateful for favours. But I know one who is placid at a wrong, and would be grateful for simple justice; while a favour, if he ever gained one, would turn his brain.' He remembered, for long years after, how he had read this review as he sat on a stile leading to the eweleaze he had to cross on his way home to Bockhampton. The bitterness of that moment was never forgotten; at the time he wished that he were dead.

But that humorous observation was not seriously disturbed in him is shown by what he entered immediately after :

'*End of April.* At the dairy. The dog looks as if he were glad that he is a dog. The cows look at him with a melancholy expression, as though they were sorry they are cows, and have to be milked, and to show too much dignity to roll in the mulch as he does. . . . The dairymaid flings her feet about the dairy floor in walking, as if they were mops.'

Anyhow, in May he enjoyed another visit to Cornwall. But in returning therefrom the day after his birthday in June he received a fresh buffet from circumstance in seeing at Exeter Station *Desperate Remedies* in Messrs. Smith and Son's surplus catalogue for sale at 2*s.* 6*d.* the three volumes, and thought the *Spectator* had snuffed out the book, as it probably had done.

Although this was a serious matter for a beginner who had ventured on the novel £75 out of the £123 he posesssed, one reason for the mitigation of his trouble may well have been that the powerfully, not to say wildly, melodramatic situations had been concocted in a style which was quite against his natural grain, through too crude an interpretation of George Meredith's advice. It was a sort of thing he had never contemplated writing, till, finding himself in a corner, it seemed necessary to attract public attention at all hazards. What Meredith would have thought of the result of his teaching was not ascertained. Yet there was nothing in the book — admittedly an extremely clever novel — to call for such castigation, which, oddly enough, rather stultified itself by certain concessions on the nameless author's ability. Moreover he was surprised some time later by a letter from the reviewer, a stranger — whether dictated by pricks of conscience, an uneasy suspicion that he had mistaken his man, or otherwise, is unknown — showing some regret for his violence. Hardy replied to the letter — tardily and curtly enough at first, it is true — but as it dawned upon him that the harm had been done him not through malice but honest wrongheadedness he ceased to harbour resentment, and became acquainted with his critic, the *Spectator* reviewing him later with much generosity.

During June and July he marked time, as it were, by doing some more Gothic drawings for Crickmay, though in no very grand spirits, if we may judge from a marginal mark with the date 'July 1871' in his Shakespeare, opposite the passage in *Macbeth* :

> Things at their worst will cease, or else climb upward
> To what they were before.

Later in the summer he finished the short and quite rustic story entitled
*Under the Greenwood Tree. A Rural Painting of the Dutch School* —
the execution of which had arisen from a remark of Mr. John Morley's
on *The Poor Man and the Lady*, that the country scenes in the latter
were the best in the book, the 'tranter' of *The Poor Man and the Lady*
being reintroduced.

The pages of this idyll — at first intended to be called *The Mellstock Quire* but altered to *Under the Greenwood Tree* because titles
from poetry were in fashion just then — were dispatched to the
Messrs. Macmillan some time the same autumn, and in due course
Hardy received from them a letter which, events having rendered
him sensitive, he read to mean that the firm did not wish to have
anything to do with his 'Rural Painting of the Dutch School',
although they said that 'they felt strongly inclined to avail themselves
of his offer of it'; hence he wrote to them to return the MS. This
was an unfortunate misunderstanding. It was not till its acceptance
and issue by another publishing-house the year after that he discovered
they had never declined it, and indeed would have been quite willing
to print it a little later on.

They had taken the trouble to enclose when writing about the
tale the opinion of the 'accomplished critic' to whom they had submitted it, the chief points of which may be quoted here :

'The work in this story is extremely careful, natural, and delicate,
and the writer deserves more than common credit for the pains which
he has taken with his style, and with the harmony of his construction
and treatment. It is a simple and uneventful sketch of a rural court-
ship, with a climax of real delicacy of idea. . . . I don't prophesy a
large market for it, because the work is so delicate as not to hit every
taste by any means. But it is good work, and would please people
whose taste was not ruined by novels of exaggerated action or forced
ingenuity. . . . The writer would do well to shut his ears to the
fooleries of critics, which his letter to you proves that he does not do.'

However, deeming their reply on the question of publishing the
tale to be ambiguous at least, he got it back, threw the MS. into a box
with his old poems, being quite sick of all such, and began to think
about other ways and means. He consulted Miss Gifford by letter,
declaring that he had banished novel-writing for ever, and was going
on with architecture henceforward. But she, with no great opportunity
of reasoning on the matter, yet, as Hardy used to think and say —
truly or not — with that rapid instinct which serves women in such
good stead, and may almost be called preternatural vision, wrote

back instantly her desire that he should adhere to authorship, which she felt sure would be his true vocation. From the very fact that she wished thus, and set herself aside altogether — architecture being obviously the quick way to an income for marrying on — he was impelled to consider her interests more than his own. Unlike the case of Browning and Elizabeth Barrett, no letters between the couple are extant, to show the fluctuation of their minds on this vital matter. But what happened was that Hardy applied himself to architectural work during the winter 1871–72 more steadily than he ever had done in his life before, and in the spring of the latter year again set out for London, determined to stifle his constitutional tendency to care for life only as an emotion and not as a scientific game, and fully bent on sticking to the profession which had been the choice of his parents for him rather than his own ; but with a faint dream at the back of his mind that he might perhaps write verses as an occasional hobby.

The years 1872 and 1873 were pre-eminently years of unexpectedness. Having engaged to give some help to Mr. T. Roger Smith, a well-known London architect and Professor of Architecture at the Royal Institute of British Architects, he speedily found himself on his arrival in the first-named year assisting Professor Smith in designing schools for the London School Board, which had then lately come into existence, public competition between architects for such designs being arranged by the Board from time to time. Hardy had no sooner settled down to do his best in this business than he met in the middle of a crossing by Trafalgar Square his friend Moule, whom he had not seen for a long time. Moule, a scholar and critic of perfect taste, firmly believed in Hardy's potentialities as a writer, and said he hoped he still kept a hand on the pen ; but Hardy seems to have declared that he had thrown up authorship at last and for all. Moule was grieved at this, but merely advised him not to give up writing altogether, since, supposing anything were to happen to his eyes from the fine architectural drawing, literature would be a resource for him ; he could dictate a book, article, or poem, but not a geometrical design. This, Hardy used to say, was essentially all that passed between them ; but by a strange coincidence Moule's words were brought back to his mind one morning shortly after by his seeing, for the first time in his life, what seemed like floating specks on the white drawing-paper before him.

For some reason or other at this date — a year after its publication — he wrote to his publishers to render an account of their

transactions over *Desperate Remedies*, which he had once before requested, but had not been very curious upon ; for though the *Saturday
Review* had brought the volumes to life after their slaughter by the
*Spectator*, he quite supposed he had lost on the venture both his time
and his money.  By return of post Tinsley Brothers rendered the
account, showing that they had printed 500 copies of the novel in
three volumes, and sold 370, and enclosing a cheque for £60, as being
all that was returnable to him out of the £75 paid as guarantee —
after the costs and the receipts were balanced, no part of the receipts
being due to him.

From these figures Hardy, who did not examine them closely,
found that after all he had only lost his labour and £15 in money —
and was much gratified thereby.

Quite soon after, while reading in the Strand a poster of the
Italian Opera, a heavy hand was laid on his shoulder, and turning he
saw Tinsley himself, who asked when Hardy was going to let him
have another novel.

Hardy, with thoughts of the balance-sheet, drily told him never.

'Wot, now!' said Tinsley.  'Haven't you anything written?'

Hardy remarked that he had written a short story some time
before, but didn't know what had become of the MS., and did not
care.  He also had outlined one for three volumes ; but had abandoned
it.  He was now doing better things, and attending to his profession
of architect.

'Damned if that isn't what I thought you wos!' exclaimed Mr.
Tinsley.  'Well, now, can't you get that story, and show it to me?'

Hardy would not promise, reminding the publisher that the
account he had rendered for the other book was not likely to tempt
him to publish a second.

''Pon my soul, Mr. Hardy,' said Tinsley, 'you wouldn't have got
another man in London to print it!  Oh, be hanged if you would!
'twas a blood-curdling story!  Now please try to find that new manuscript and let me see it.'

Hardy could not at first recollect what he had done with the MS.,
but recalling at last he wrote to his parents at home, telling them
where to search for it, and to forward it to him.

When, the first week in April, *Under the Greenwood Tree* arrived
Hardy sent it on to Tinsley without looking at it, saying he would
have nothing to do with any publishing accounts.  This probably
was the reason why Tinsley offered him £30 for the copyright,
which Hardy accepted.  It should be added that Tinsley afterwards

sent him £10 extra, and quite voluntarily, being, he said, half the amount he had obtained from Tauchnitz for the Continental copyright, of which transaction Hardy had known nothing.

Hardy's indifference in selling *Under the Greenwood Tree* for a trifle could not have been because he still had altogether other aims than the literature of fiction, as had been the case in the previous winter; for he casually mentioned to Tinsley that he thought of going on with the three-volume novel before alluded to. Moule's words on keeping a hand on the pen, and the specks in his eyes while drawing, may have influenced him in this harking back.

In the early part of May he was correcting the proofs of the rural story. It was mostly done late at night, at Westbourne Park, where he was again living, the day being occupied with the competition-drawings for Board schools in the various London districts — and some occasional evenings in preparing drawings for Blomfield, with whom Hardy was in frequent and friendly touch — though he told Blomfield at that time nothing about his adventures as a novel-writer.

*Under the Greenwood Tree* was published about the last week in May (1872) and met with a very kindly and gentle reception, being reviewed in the *Athenæum* as a book which could induce people 'to give up valuable time to see a marriage accomplished in its pages', and in the *Pall Mall Gazette* as a story of much freshness and originality.

As its author was at Bedford Chambers in Bedford Street — Professor Smith's offices — every day, and the office of the publishers was only a street or two further along the Strand, he was not infrequently encountering Tinsley, who one day asked him — the book continuing to receive good notices — for how much he would write a story for *Tinsley's Magazine*, to run a twelvemonth, the question being probably prompted by this tone of the press towards *Under the Greenwood Tree*.

Hardy reflected on the outlined novel he had abandoned — considered that he could do it in six months — but 'to guard against temptation' (as he put it) multiplied by two the utmost he could expect to make at architecture in the time, and told his inquirer the sum.

'All right, all right, Mr. Hardy — very reasonable,' said the friendly publisher, smacking Hardy's shoulder. 'Now come along into the office here, and we'll sign the agreement, and the job will be off our minds.'

Hardy, however, for some reason or other was growing wary, and said he would call next day. During the afternoon he went to a law-bookseller, bought *Copinger on Copyright*, the only book on the subject he could meet with, and sat up half the night studying it. Next day he called on Tinsley, and said he would write the story for the sum mentioned, it being understood that the amount paid was for the magazine-issue solely, after which publication all rights were to return to the author.

'Well, I'm damned!' Tinsley said, with a grim laugh. 'Who the devil have you been talking to, Mr. Hardy, if I may ask, since I saw you yesterday?'

Hardy said 'Nobody'. (Which was true, though only literally.)

'Well, but — Now, Mr. Hardy, you are hard, very hard upon me! However, I do like your writings: and if you'll throw in the three-volume edition of the novel with the magazine rights I'll agree.'

Hardy assented to this, having, as he used to say, some liking for Tinsley's keen sense of humour even when it went against himself; and the business was settled shortly after, the author agreeing to be ready with the first monthly part of his story for the magazine soon enough to give an artist time to prepare an illustration for it, and enable it to be printed in the September number, which in the case of this periodical came out on August 15.

It was now the 24th July, and walking back towards Professor Roger Smith's chambers Hardy began to feel that he had done rather a rash thing. He knew but vaguely the value of a three-volume edition, and as to the story, he had, as already mentioned, thought of a possible one some time before, roughly noted down the opening chapters and general outline, and then abandoned it with the rest of his literary schemes. He had never written a serial narrative and had no journalistic experience; and he was pledged to the Board-school drawings for at least another week, when they were to be sent in to the Committee. Nevertheless, having promised Tinsley, he resolved to stick to his promise, and on the 27th July agreed by letter.

Apparently without saying anything of his new commitment, he informed the genial Professor of Architecture that he thought he would take a holiday in August, when there would be little more of a pressing nature to do for that year; and going home to Westbourne Park wrote between then and midnight the first chapter or two of *A Pair of Blue Eyes*. Even though he may have thought over and roughly set down the beginning of the romance, the writing it out connectedly must have been done very rapidly, despite the physical enervation that London always brought upon him. (It may be noticed that he gave the youth who appears first in the novel the sur-name of the Professor of Architecture he had been assisting.) At

The Mellstock Quire
or
Under the Greenwood Tree

A rural painting of the Dutch School.

Part I. Winter.

Chapter I

Mellstock Lane.

To dwellers in a wood, almost every species of tree has its voice as well as its feature. At the passing of the breeze the fir-trees sob & moan no less distinctly than they rock: the holly whistles as it battles with itself: the ash hisses amid its quivering: the beech rustles as its flat boughs rise & fall. And winter, which modifies the notes of such trees as shed their leaves, does not destroy their individuality.

On a cold & starry Christmas-eve not less than a generation ago a man was passing along a lane in the darkness of a plantation that whispered thus distinctively to his intelligence. All the evidences of his nature were those afforded by the spirit of his footsteps, which succeeded each other lightly & quickly, & by the liveliness of his voice as he sang in a rural cadence.
"— With the rose & the lily
And the daffodowndilly,
The lads & the lasses a-sheep-shearing go."

Under the Greenwood Tree
First page of the MS.

any rate the MS. of the first number, with something over, was ready for the illustrator in an incredibly quick time. Thereupon, though he had shaped nothing of what the later chapters were to be like, he dismissed the subject as Sheridan dismissed a bill he had backed, and on August 7 went on board the *Avoca*, of the Irish Mail Packet Company (a boat which, by the way, went to the bottom shortly after) at London Bridge, to proceed to Cornwall by water.

In Cornwall he paid a visit to some friends — Captain and Mrs. Serjeant, of St. Benet's Abbey, who owned valuable china-clay works near, which were just then being developed ; drove to St. Juliot, and met there among other visitors Miss d'Arville, a delightful old lady from Bath, who had a canary that fainted and fell to the bottom of the cage whenever a cat came into the room, or the picture of a cat was shown it. He walked to Tintagel Castle and sketched there a stone altar, having an Early-English ornamentation on its edge ; which altar in after years he could never find ; and in the intervals of this and other excursions went on with his MS., having naturally enough received an urgent letter for more copy from the publisher. He returned to London by way of Bath, where he left Miss d'Arville, who had accompanied him thus far.

He could not, however, get on with his novel in London, and late in September went down to the seclusion of Dorset to set about it more thoroughly. On this day *Under the Greenwood Tree* was reviewed by Moule in the *Saturday*. The *Spectator*, however, which had so mauled *Desperate Remedies*, took little notice of the book.

An entry in the diary at this time was : 'Sept. 30. Posted MS. of *A Pair of Blue Eyes* to Tinsley up to Page 163.'

Before the date was reached he had received a letter from Professor Roger Smith, informing him that another of the six Board-school competitions for which Hardy had helped him to prepare designs had been successful, and suggesting that he had 'been at grass' long enough, and would be welcomed back on any more liberal terms, if he felt dissatisfied.

This architectural success, for which he would have given much had it come sooner, was now merely provoking. However, Hardy confessed to the surprised and amused Smith what he had been doing, and was still occupied with ; and thus was severed, to his great regret, an extremely pleasant if short professional connection with an able and amiable man ; though their friendship was not broken, being renewed from time to time, and continued till the death of the elder of them.

Till the end of the year he was at Bockhampton finishing *A Pair of Blue Eyes*, the action of which, as is known, proceeds on the coast near 'Lyonnesse' — not far from King Arthur's Castle at Tintagel. Its scene, he said, would have been clearly indicated by calling the romance *Elfride of Lyonnesse*, but for a wish to avoid drawing attention to the neighbouring St. Juliot while his friends were living there. After a flying visit to the Rectory, he remained on through the spring at his mother's ; and it may be mentioned here that while staying at this place or at the Rectory or possibly in London, Hardy received an account of the death of 'the Tranter', after whom the character in *Under the Greenwood Tree* had been called, though it was not a portrait, nor was the fictitious tranter's kinship to the other musicians based on fact. He had been the many years' neighbour of the Hardys, and did the haulage of building materials for Hardy's father, of whom he also rented a field for his horses. The scene of his last moments was detailed in a letter to Hardy by one present at his death-bedside :

'He was quite in his senses, but not able to speak. A dark purple stain began in his leg that was injured many years ago by his waggon going over it ; the stain ran up it about as fast as a fly walks. It ran up his body in the same way till, arriving level with his fingers, it began in them, and went on up his arms, up his neck and face, to the top of his head, when he breathed his last. Then a pure white began at his foot, and went upwards at the same rate, and in the same way, and he became as white throughout as he had been purple a minute before.'

In this connection it may be interesting to add that the actual name of the shoemaker 'Robert Penny' in the same story was Robert Reason. He, like the Tranter and the Tranter's wife, is buried in Stinsford Churchyard near the tombs of the Hardys, though his name is almost illegible. Hardy once said he would much have preferred to use the real name, as being better suited to the character, but thought at the time of writing that there were possible relatives who might be hurt by the use of it, though he afterwards found there were none. The only real name in the story is that of 'Voss', who brought the hot mead and viands to the choir on their rounds. It can still be read on a headstone, also quite near to where the Hardys lie. It will be remembered that these headstones are alluded to in the poem entitled 'The Dead Quire' —

> There Dewy lay by the gaunt yew tree,
> There Reuben and Michael, a pace behind,
> And Bowman with his family
> By the wall that the ivies bind.

Old Dewy has been called a portrait of Hardy's grandfather, but this was not the case; he died three years before the birth of the story-teller, almost in his prime, and long ere reaching the supposed age of William Dewy. There was, in fact, no family portrait in the tale.

*A Pair of Blue Eyes* was published in three volumes the latter part of May.

'*May* 5. "Maniel" [Immanuel] Riggs found dead. [A shepherd Hardy knew.] A curious man, who used to moisten his lips between every two or three words.'

'*June* 9, 1873. To London. Went to French Plays. Saw Brasseur, etc.'

'*June* 15. Met H. M. Moule at the Golden Cross Hotel. Dined with him at the British Hotel. Moule then left for Ipswich on his duties as Poor Law Inspector.'

'*June* 16–20. About London with my brother Henry.'

'*June* 20. By evening train to Cambridge. Stayed in College — Queens' — Went out with H. M. M. after dinner. A magnificent evening: sun over "the Backs".'

'Next morning went with H. M. M. to King's Chapel early. M. opened the great West doors to show the interior vista: we got upon the roof, where we could see Ely Cathedral gleaming in the distant sunlight. A never-to-be-forgotten morning. H. M. M. saw me off for London. His last smile.'

From London Hardy travelled on to Bath, arriving late at night and putting up at 8 Great Stanhope Street, where lodgings had been obtained for him by his warm-hearted friend Miss d'Arville, whom Miss Gifford was then visiting. The following dates are from the intermittent diary Hardy kept in these years.

'*June* 23. Excursions about Bath and Bristol with the ladies.'

'*June* 28. To Clifton with Miss Gifford.' — Where they were surprised by accidentally seeing in a newsagent's shop a commendatory review of *A Pair of Blue Eyes* in the *Spectator*.'

'*June* 30. About Bath alone. . . . Bath has a rural complexion on an urban substance. . . .'

'*July* 1. A day's trip with Miss G. To Chepstow, the Wye, the Wynd Cliff, which we climbed, and Tintern, where we repeated some of Wordsworth's lines thereon.

'At Tintern, silence is part of the pile. Destroy that, and you take a limb from an organism. . . . A wooded slope visible from every unmullioned window. But compare the age of the building with that of the marble hills from which it was drawn! . . .'

Here may be stated, in relation to the above words on the age of the hills, that this shortcoming of the most ancient architecture by comparison with geology was a consideration that frequently troubled Hardy's mind when measuring and drawing old Norman and other early buildings, just as it had been troubled by 'The Wolf' in his musical tuning, and by the thought that Greek literature had been at the mercy of dialects.

'*July* 2.  Bath to Dorchester.'

# CHAPTER VII

# 'FAR FROM THE MADDING CROWD', MARRIAGE, AND ANOTHER NOVEL

### 1873–1876 : *Aet.* 33–36

SOME half-year before this, in December 1872, Hardy had received at Bockhampton a letter from Leslie Stephen, the editor of the *Cornhill* — by that time well known as a man of letters, *Saturday* reviewer, and Alpine climber — asking for a serial story for his magazine. He had lately read *Under the Greenwood Tree*, and thought 'the descriptions admirable'. It was 'long since he had received more pleasure from a new writer', and it had occurred to him that such writing would probably please the readers of the *Cornhill Magazine* as much as it had pleased him.

Hardy had replied that he feared the date at which he could write a story for the *Cornhill* would be too late for Mr. Stephen's purpose, since he already had on hand a succeeding novel (*i.e. A Pair of Blue Eyes*), which was arranged for; but that the next after should be at Mr. Stephen's disposal. He had thought of making it a pastoral tale with the title of *Far from the Madding Crowd* — and that the chief characters would probably be a young woman-farmer, a shepherd, and a sergeant of cavalry. That was all he had done. Mr. Stephen had rejoined that he was sorry he could not expect a story from Hardy at an earlier date; that he did not, however, mean to fix any particular time; that the idea of the story attracted him; also the proposed title; and that he would like Hardy to call and talk it over when he came to Town. There the matter had been left. Now Hardy set about the pastoral tale, the success of *A Pair of Blue Eyes* meanwhile surpassing his expectations, the influential *Saturday Review* pronouncing it to be the most artistically constructed of the novels of its time — a quality which, by the bye, would carry little recommendation in these days of loose construction and indifference to organic homogeneity.

But Hardy did not call on Stephen just then.

It was, indeed, by the merest chance that he had ever got the *Cornhill* letter at all. The postal arrangements in Dorset were still so primitive at this date that the only delivery of letters at Hardy's father's house was by the hand of some friendly neighbour who had come from the next village, and Stephen's request for a story had been picked up in the mud of the lane by a labouring man, the school children to whom it had been entrusted having dropped it on the way.

While thus in the seclusion of Bockhampton, writing *Far from the Madding Crowd*, we find him on September 21, walking to Woodbury-Hill Fair, approximately described in the novel as 'Green-hill Fair'. On the 24th he was shocked at hearing of the tragic death of his friend Horace Moule, from whom he had parted cheerfully at Cambridge in June. The body was brought to be buried at Ford-ington, Dorchester, and Hardy attended the funeral. It was a matter of keen regret to him now, and for a long time after, that Moule and the woman to whom Hardy was warmly attached had never set eyes on each other; and that she could never make Moule's acquaintance, or be his friend.

On the 30th of September he sent to Leslie Stephen at his request as much of the MS. of *Far from the Madding Crowd* as was written — apparently between two and three monthly parts, though some of it only in rough outline — and a few days after a letter came from Stephen stating that the story suited him admirably as far as it had gone, and that though as a rule it was desirable to see the whole of a novel before definitely accepting it, under the circumstances he decided to accept it at once.

So Hardy went on writing *Far from the Madding Crowd* — some-times indoors, sometimes out — when he would occasionally find himself without a scrap of paper at the very moment that he felt volumes. In such circumstances he would use large dead leaves, white chips left by the wood-cutters, or pieces of stone or slate that came to hand. He used to say that when he carried a pocket-book his mind was barren as the Sahara.

This autumn Hardy assisted at his father's cider-making — a proceeding he had always enjoyed from childhood — the apples being from huge old trees that have now long perished. It was the last time he ever took part in a work whose sweet smells and oozings in the crisp autumn air can never be forgotten by those who have had a hand in it.

Memorandum by T. H. :

'Met J. D., one of the old Mellstock fiddlers — who kept me talking interminably : a man who speaks neither truth nor lies, but a sort of Not Proven compound which is very relishable. Told me of Jack ——, who spent all the money he had — sixpence — at the Oak Inn, took his sixpence out of the till when the landlady's back was turned, and spent it over again ; then stole it again, and again spent it, till he had had a real skinful. "Was too honest to take any money but his own", said J. D.' (Some of J. D.'s characterisitics appear in 'the Tranter' of *Under the Greenwood Tree*.)

At the end of October an unexpected note from the *Cornhill* editor asked if, supposing he were to start *Far from the Madding Crowd* in the January number (which would be out the third week in December) instead of the spring, as intended, Hardy could keep in front of the printers with his copy. He learnt afterwards that what had happened was that the MS. of a novel which the editor had arranged to begin in his pages in January had been lost in the post, according, at any rate, to its author's account. Hardy thought January not too soon for him, and that he could keep the printers going. Terms were consequently arranged with the publishers and proofs of the first number sent forthwith, Hardy incidentally expressing with regard to any illustrations, in a letter of October 1873, 'a hope that the rustics, although *quaint*, may be made to appear intelligent, and not boorish at all' ; adding in a later letter : 'In reference to the illustrations, I have sketched in my note-book during the past summer a few correct outlines of smockfrocks, gaiters, sheep-crooks, rick-"staddles", a sheep-washing pool, one of the old-fashioned malt-houses, and some other out-of-the-way things that might have to be shown. These I could send you if they would be of any use to the artist, but if he is a sensitive man and you think he would rather not be interfered with, I would not do so.'

No response had been made to this, and he was not quite clear whether, after all, Leslie Stephen had finally decided to begin so soon, when, returning from Cornwall on a fine December noontide (being New Year's Eve 1873–74), he opened on Plymouth Hoe a copy of the *Cornhill* that he had bought at the station, and there to his surprise saw his story placed at the beginning of the magazine, with a striking illustration, the artist being — also to his surprise — not a man but a woman, Miss Helen Paterson. He had only expected, from the undistinguished rank of the characters in the tale, that it would be put at the end, and possibly without a picture. Why this had come without warning to him was owing to the accident of his being away from his permanent address for several days, and nothing having been forwarded. It can be imagined how delighted Miss Gifford was to receive the first number of the story, whose nature he had kept from her to give her a pleasant surprise, and to find that her desire of a literary course for Hardy was in fair way of being justified.

In the first week of January 1874 the story was noticed in a marked degree by the *Spectator*, and a guess hazarded that it might be from the pen of George Eliot — why, the author could never understand, since, so far as he had read that great thinker — one of the greatest living, he thought, though not a born storyteller by any means — she had never touched the life of the fields : her country-people having seemed to him, too, more like small townsfolk than rustics ; and as evidencing a woman's wit cast in country dialogue rather than real country humour, which he regarded as rather of the Shakespeare and Fielding sort. However, he conjectured, as a possible reason for the flattering guess, that he had latterly been reading Comte's *Positive Philosophy*, and writings of that school, some of whose expressions had thus passed into his vocabulary, expressions which were also common to George Eliot. Leslie Stephen wrote :

'I am glad to congratulate you on the reception of your first number. Besides the gentle *Spectator*, which thinks that you must be George Eliot because you know the names of the stars, several good judges have spoken to me warmly of the *Madding Crowd*. Moreover the *Spectator*, though flighty in its head, has really a good deal of critical feeling. I always like to be praised by it — and indeed by other people! . . . The story comes out very well, I think, and I have no criticism to make.'

Respecting the public interest in the opening of the story, in later days Miss Thackeray informed him, with some of her father's humour, that to inquiries with which she was besieged on the sex of the author, and requests to be given an introduction to him or her, she would reply : '*It* lives in the country, and I could not very well introduce you to *it* in Town.'

A passage may be quoted here from Mr. F. W. Maitland's *Life of Leslie Stephen* (to which Hardy contributed half a chapter or so, on Stephen as editor) which affords a humorous illustration of the difficulties of 'serial' writing in Victorian days. Stephen had written to say that the seduction of Fanny Robin must be treated in 'a gingerly fashion', adding that it was owing to an 'excessive prudery of which I am ashamed'.

'I wondered what had so suddenly caused, in one who had seemed anything but a prude, the "excessive prudery" alluded to. But I did not learn till I saw him in April. Then he told me that an unexpected Grundian cloud, though no bigger than a man's hand as yet, had appeared on our serene horizon. Three respectable ladies and subscribers, representing he knew not how many more, had written to upbraid him for an improper passage in a page of the story which had already been published.

'I was struck mute, till I said, "Well, if you value the opinion of such people, why didn't you think of them beforehand, and strike out the passage?" — "I ought to have, since it is their opinion, whether I value it or no", he said with a half groan. "But it didn't occur to me that there was anything to object to!" I reminded him that though three objectors who disliked the passage, or pretended to, might write their disapproval, three hundred who possibly approved of it would not take the trouble to write, and hence he might have a false impression of the public as a body. "Yes ; I agree. Still I suppose I ought to have foreseen these gentry, and have omitted it," he murmured.

'It may be added here, to finish with this detail (though it anticipates dates), that when the novel came out in volume form *The Times* quoted in a commendatory review the very passage that had offended. As soon as I met him, I said, "You see what *The Times* says about that paragraph ; and you cannot say that *The Times* is not respectable." He was smoking and answered tardily : "No, I can't say that *The Times* is not respectable." I then urged that if he had omitted the sentences, as he had wished he had done, I should never have taken the trouble to restore them in the reprint, and *The Times* could not have quoted them with approbation. I suppose my manner was slightly triumphant ; at any rate, he said, "I spoke as an editor, not as a man. You have no more consciousness of these things than a child."'

To go back for a moment. Having attracted so much attention Hardy now again withdrew into retreat at Bockhampton to get ahead with the novel, which was in a lamentably unadvanced condition, writing to Stephen, when requesting that the proofs might be sent to that hermitage : 'I have decided to finish it here, which is within a walk of the district in which the incidents are supposed to occur. I find it a great advantage to be actually among the people described at the time of describing them.'

However, that he did not care much for a reputation as a novelist in lieu of being able to follow the pursuit of poetry — now for ever hindered, as it seemed — becomes obvious from a remark written to Mr. Stephen about this time :

'The truth is that I am willing, and indeed anxious, to give up any points which may be desirable in a story when read as a whole, for the sake of others which shall please those who read it in numbers. Perhaps I may have higher aims some day, and be a great stickler for the proper artistic balance of the completed work, but for the present circumstances lead me to wish merely to be considered a good hand at a serial.'

The fact was that at this date he was bent on carrying out later in the year an intention beside which a high repute as an artistic novelist loomed even less importantly than in ordinary — an intention to be presently mentioned.

He found he had drifted anew into a position he had vowed after his past experience he would in future keep clear of — that of having unfinished on his hands a novel of which the beginning was already before the public, and so having to write against time.  He wrote so rapidly in fact that by February he was able to send the editor an instalment of copy sufficient for two or three months further, and another instalment in April.

On a visit to London in the winter Hardy had made the personal acquaintance of Leslie Stephen, the man whose philosophy was to influence his own for many years, indeed, more than that of any other contemporary, and received a welcome in his household, which was renewed from time to time, whereby he became acquainted with Mrs. Stephen and her sister Miss Thackeray.  He also made acquaintance with Mr. G. Murray Smith, the publisher, and his family in April.  At dinner there in May he met his skilful illustrator, Miss Helen Paterson, and gave her a few points ; Mr. Frederick Greenwood ; and Mrs. Procter, wife and soon after widow of 'Barry Cornwall' the poet.  The enormous acquaintance of Mrs. Procter with past celebrities was astonishing, and her humour in relating anecdotes of them charmed Hardy.  She used to tell him that sometimes after avowing to Americans her acquaintance with a long list of famous bygone people, she had been compelled to deny knowledge of certain others she had equally well known, to re-establish her listener's wavering faith in her veracity.

Back again in Dorsetshire he continued his application to the story, and by July had written it all, the last few chapters having been done at a gallop, for a reason to be told directly.  In the middle of the month he resumed residence in London, where he hurriedly corrected the concluding pages and posted the end of the MS. to the editor early in August.

The next month Thomas Hardy and Miss Emma Lavinia Gifford were married at St. Peter's, Elgin Avenue, Paddington, by her uncle Dr. E. Hamilton Gifford, Canon of Worcester, and afterwards Archdeacon of London. In the November following *Far from the Madding Crowd* was published in two volumes, with the illustrations by Miss Helen Paterson, who by an odd coincidence had also thought fit to marry William Allingham during the progress of the story. It may be said in passing that the development of the chapters month by month had brought these lines from Mrs. Procter:

'You would be gratified to know what a shock the marriage of Bathsheba was. I resembled Mr. Boldwood — and to deceive such an old novel-reader as myself is a triumph. We are always looking out for traps, and scent a long way off a surprise. . . .

'I hear that you are coming to live in stony-hearted London. Our great fault is that we are all alike. . . . We press so closely against each other that any small shoots are cut off at once, and the young tree grows in shape like the old one.'

When the book appeared complete the author and his wife, after a short visit to the Continent — their first Continental days having been spent at Rouen — had temporarily gone to live at Surbiton, and remained there for a considerable time without nearly realizing the full extent of the interest that had been excited among the reading public by the novel, which unsophistication was only partially removed by their seeing with unusual frequency, during their journeys to and from London, ladies carrying about copies of it with Mudie's label on the covers.

Meanwhile Mr. George Smith, head of the firm of Smith and Elder — a man of wide experience, who had brought Charlotte Brontë before the reading public, and who became a disinterested friend of Hardy's — suggested to him that he should if possible get back the copyright of *Under the Greenwood Tree*, which he had sold to Tinsley Brothers for £30. Tinsley at first replied that he would not return it for any sum : then that he would sell it for £300. Hardy offered half, which offer Tinsley did not respond to, and there the matter dropped.

Among the curious consequences of the popularity of *Far from the Madding Crowd* was a letter from the lady he had so admired as a child, when she was the *grande dame* of the parish in which he was

born. He had seen her only once since — at her town-house in
Bruton Street as aforesaid. But it should be stated in justice to her
that her writing was not merely a rekindled interest on account of
his book's popularity, for she had written to him in his obscurity,
before he had published a line, asking him to come and see her, and
addressing him as her dear Tommy, as when he was a small boy,
apologizing for doing so on the ground that she could not help it.
She was now quite an elderly lady, but by signing her letter 'Julia
Augusta' she revived throbs of tender feeling in him, and brought
back to his memory the thrilling 'frou-frou' of her four grey silk
flounces when she had used to bend over him, and when they brushed
against the font as she entered church on Sundays. He replied, but,
as it appears, did not go to see her.

Meanwhile the more tangible result of the demand for *Far from
the Madding Crowd* was an immediate request from the editor and
publishers of the *Cornhill* for another story, which should begin as
early as possible in 1875.

This was the means of urging Hardy into the unfortunate course
of hurrying forward a further production before he was aware of
what there had been of value in his previous one : before learning,
that is, not only what had attracted the public, but what was of true
and genuine substance on which to build a career as a writer with a
real literary message. For mere popularity he cared little, as little as
he did for large payments ; but having now to live by the pen — or,
as he would quote, 'to keep base life afoot' — he had to consider
popularity. This request for more of his writing not only from the
*Cornhill* but from other quarters coincided with quizzing personal
gossip, among other paragraphs being one that novel-writing was
coming to a pretty pass, the author of *Lorna Doone* having avowed
himself a market-gardener, and the author of *Far from the Madding
Crowd* having been discovered to be a house-decorator (!). Criticism
like this influenced him to put aside a woodland story he had thought
of (which later took shape in *The Woodlanders*), and make a plunge
in a new and untried direction. He was aware of the pecuniary value
of a reputation for a speciality ; and as above stated, the acquisition
of something like a regular income had become important. Yet he
had not the slightest intention of writing for ever about sheepfarming,
as the reading public was apparently expecting him to do, and as, in
fact, they presently resented his not doing. Hence, to the consternation of his editor and publishers, in March he sent up as a response to
their requests the beginning of a tale called *The Hand of Ethelberta*

— *A Comedy in Chapters* which had nothing whatever in common with anything he had written before.

In March he went to the Oxford and Cambridge Boat-Race, and entered rooms taken in Newton Road, Westbourne Grove, a light being thrown on the domestic and practical side of his life at this time by the following :

'NEWTON ROAD, WESTBOURNE GROVE,
*March* 19, 1875.

'Messrs Townly and Bonniwell,
Surbiton.

'Gentlemen : Please to warehouse the cases and boxes sent herewith, and numbered as follows :

'No. 1. Size 3 ft. 6 ins. × 2 ft. 6 ins. × 2 ft. 2 ins., containing linen and books.

'No. 2. Size 2 ft. 0 ins. × 1 ft. 9 ins × 1 ft. 7½ ins. containing books.

'No. 3. Size 2 ft. 0 ins. × 1 ft. 4 ins. × 1 ft. 2 ins. containing books.

'No. 4. Size 1 ft. 5 ins. × 1 ft. 0 ins. × 1 ft. 0 ins. containing sundries.

'A receipt for same will oblige'.

Their entire worldly goods were contained in this small compass.

The next three months were spent at the address given above, where they followed an ordinary round of museum, theatre, and concert-going, with some dining-out, in keeping with what he had written earlier to Mr. George Smith : 'We are coming to Town for three months on account of Ethelberta, some London scenes occurring in her chequered career which I want to do as vigorously as possible — having already visited Rouen and Paris with the same object, other adventures of hers taking place there.' He also asked Smith's advice on a German translation of *Far from the Madding Crowd*, which had been asked for.

The *Comedy in Chapters*, despite its departure from a path desired by his new-found readers, and to some extent desired by himself, was accepted for the magazine. The beginning appeared in the *Cornhill* for May, when Hardy had at last the satisfaction of proving, amid the general disappointment at the lack of sheep and shepherds, that he did not mean to imitate anybody, whatever the satisfaction might have been worth. The sub-title did not appear in the magazine, Mr. Stephen having written in respect of it :

'I am sorry to have to bother you about a trifle! I fully approved of your suggestion for adding to "Ethelberta's Hand" the descriptive title "A Comedy in Chapters". I find however from other people that it gives rather an unfortunate idea. They understand by Comedy something of the farce description, and expect you to be funny after the fashion of Mr. ——, or some professional joker. This, of course, is stupid; but then, advertisements are meant for stupid people. The question is, unluckily, not what they ought to feel but what they do feel. . . . I think, therefore, that if you have no strong reason to the contrary it will be better to drop the second title for the present. When the book is reprinted it can of course appear, because then the illusion would be immediately dispelled.'

One reflection about himself at this date sometimes made Hardy uneasy. He perceived that he was 'up against' the position of having to carry on his life not as an emotion, but as a scientific game; that he was committed by circumstances to novel-writing as a regular trade, as much as he had formerly been to architecture; and that hence he would, he deemed, have to look for material in manners — in ordinary social and fashionable life as other novelists did. Yet he took no interest in manners, but in the substance of life only. So far what he had written had not been novels at all, as usually understood — that is pictures of modern customs and observances — and might not long sustain the interest of the circulating library subscriber who cared mainly for those things. On the other hand, to go about to dinners and clubs and crushes as a business was not much to his mind. Yet that was necessary meat and drink to the popular author. Not that he was unsociable, but events and long habit had accustomed him to solitary living. So it was also with his wife, of whom he wrote later, in the poem entitled 'A Dream or No':

> Lonely I found her,
> The sea-birds around her,
> And other than nigh things uncaring to know.

He mentioned this doubt of himself one day to Miss Thackeray, who confirmed his gloomy misgivings by saying with surprise: 'Certainly; a novelist must necessarily like society!'

Another incident which added to his dubiety was the arrival of a letter from Coventry Patmore, a total stranger to him, expressing the view that *A Pair of Blue Eyes* was in its nature not a conception for prose, and that he 'regretted at almost every page that such unequalled beauty and power should not have assured themselves the immortality which would have been impressed upon them by the form of verse'. Hardy was much struck by this opinion from Patmore. However, finding himself committed to prose, he renewed his consideration of a prose style, as it is evident from the following note :

'Read again Addison, Macaulay, Newman, Sterne, Defoe, Lamb, Gibbon, Burke, *Times* leaders, etc., in a study of style. Am more and more confirmed in an idea I have long held, as a matter of common sense, long before I thought of any old aphorism bearing on the subject : "Ars est celare artem". The whole secret of a living style and the difference between it and a dead style, lies in not having too much style — being, in fact, a little careless, or rather seeming to be, here and there. It brings wonderful life into the writing :

> 'A sweet disorder in the dress . . .
> A careless shoe-string, in whose tie
> I see a wild civility,
> Do more bewitch me than when art
> Is too precise in every part.

'Otherwise your style is like worn half-pence — all the fresh images rounded off by rubbing, and no crispness or movement at all.

'It is, of course, simply a carrying into prose the knowledge I have acquired in poetry — that inexact rhymes and rhythms now and then are far more pleasing than correct ones.'

About the time at which the Hardys were leaving Surbiton for Newton Road occurred an incident, which can best be described by quoting Hardy's own account of it as printed in Mr. F. W. Maitland's *Life of Leslie Stephen* :

'One day (March 23, 1875) I received from Stephen a mysterious note asking me to call in the evening, as late as I liked. I went, and found him alone, wandering up and down his library in slippers ; his tall thin figure wrapt in a heath-coloured dressing-gown. After a few remarks on our magazine arrangements he said he wanted me to witness his signature to what, for a moment, I thought was his will ; but it turned out to be a deed renunciatory of holy-orders under the act of 1870. He said grimly that he was really a reverend gentleman still, little as he might look it, and that he thought it was as well to cut himself adrift of a calling for which, to say the least, he had always been utterly unfit. The deed was executed with due formality. Our conversation then turned upon theologies decayed and defunct, the origin of things, the constitution of matter, the unreality of time and kindred subjects. He told me that he had "wasted" much time on systems of religion and metaphysics, and that the new theory of vortex rings had "a staggering fascination" for him.'

On this description the editor of the *Life*, Mr. Maitland, remarks : 'This scene — I need not say it — is well drawn. A tall thin figure wrapt in a heath-coloured dressing-gown was what one saw if one climbed to that Stylites study at dead of night.'

In May Hardy formed one of a deputation to Mr. Disraeli in support of a motion for a Select Committee to inquire into the state of Copyright Law ; and on Waterloo Day he and his wife went to Chelsea Hospital — it being the 60th anniversary of the battle — and made acquaintance with the Waterloo men still surviving there. Hardy would tell that one of these — a delightful old campaigner named John Bentley whom he knew to the last — put his arm round Mrs. Hardy's waist, and interlarded his discourse with 'my dear young woman', while he described to her his experiences of that memorable day, one rather incisive touch in his tale to her being that through the haze of smoke all that could be discerned was 'anything that shined', such as bayonets, helmets, and swords. The wet eve of the battle, when they slept in the rain with nothing over them, he spoke of as 'last night', as if he were speaking on the actual day. Another experience he related to her was a love-affair. While quartered in Brussels he had a sweetheart. When ordered to advance to Waterloo her friends offered to hide him if he would desert, as the French were sure to win. He refused, urging the oath he had taken ; but he felt strongly tempted, as she was very fond of him, and he of her. She begged him to write, if he lived through the campaign, and to be sure to get a Belgian or Frenchman to direct the letter, or it might not find her. After the battle, and when he was in Paris he did write, and received an answer, saying she would come to Paris and meet him on Christmas Day at 3 o'clock. His regiment had received orders to march before that time, and at Christmas he was — Mrs. Hardy forgot where. But he thought of her, and wondered if she came. 'Yes, you see, 'twas God's will we should meet no more', said Bentley, speaking of her with peculiar tenderness.

In this same month of 1875, it may be interesting to note, occurs the first mention in Hardy's memoranda of the idea of an epic on the war with Napoleon — carried out so many years later in *The Dynasts*. This earliest note runs as follows :

'Mem : A Ballad of the Hundred Days. Then another of Moscow. Others of earlier campaigns — forming altogether an Iliad of Europe from 1789 to 1815.'

That Hardy, however, was endeavouring to live practically at this time, as well as imaginatively, is shown by an entry immediately following :

'House at Childe-Okeford, Dorset. To be sold by auction June 10' ; and by his starting on the 22nd for a day or two in Dorsetshire house-hunting, first visiting Shaftesbury, where he found a cottage for £25 a year, that did not, however, suit ; thence to Blandford, and thence to Wimborne, where on arrival he entered the Minster at ten at night, having seen a light within, and sat in a stall listening to the organist practising, while the rays from the musician's solitary candle streamed across the arcades. This incident seems to have inclined him to Wimborne ; but he did not go there yet.

In July the couple went to Bournemouth, and thence by steamer to Swanage, where they found lodgings at the house of an invalided captain of smacks and ketches ; and Hardy, suspending his house-hunting, settled down there for the autumn and winter to finish *The Hand of Ethelberta*.

While completing it he published in the *Gentleman's Magazine* a ballad he had written nine or ten years earlier during his time with Blomfield, called 'The Fire at Tranter Sweatley's' (and in some editions 'The Bride-night Fire') — which, as with his other verses, he had been unable to get into print at the date of its composition by the rather perfunctory efforts he made.

'*Nov.* 28. I sit under a tree, and feel alone : I think of certain insects around me as magnified by the microscope : creatures like elephants, flying dragons, etc. And I feel I am by no means alone.

'29. He has read well who has learnt that there is more to read outside books than in them.'

Their landlord, the 'captain', used to tell them, as sailors will, strange stories of his sea-farings ; mostly smuggling stories — one of them Hardy always remembered because of its odd development. The narrator was in a fishing-boat going to meet a French lugger half-Channel-over, to receive spirit-tubs and land them. He and his mates were some nine miles off Portland, which was the limit allowed, when they were sighted by the revenue-cutter. Seeing the cutter coming up, they said 'We must act as if we were fishing for mackerel'. But they had no bait, and the ruse would be discovered. They snapped up the stems of their tobacco-pipes, and unfastening the hook from a line they had with them slipped on the bits of tobacco-pipe above the shank. The officers came — saw them fishing, and merely observing that they were a long way from shore, and dubiously asking why, and being innocently told because the fish were there, left them. Then, as if the bait had been genuine, to their surprise, on pulling up the sham line they began to haul in mackerel. The fish had made their deception truth.

Masters also told them that when persons are drowned in a high sea in the West (or Deadman's) Bay, 'the sea undresses them' — mauling off their clothes and leaving them naked.

While here at Swanage they walked daily on the cliffs and shore, Hardy noting thereon :

'Evening. Just after sunset. Sitting with E. on a stone under the wall before the Refreshment Cottage. The sounds are two, and only two. On the left Durlstone Head roaring high and low, like a giant asleep. On the right a thrush. Above the bird hangs the new moon, and a steady planet.'

In the same winter of 1875 an article appeared in the *Revue des Deux Mondes* on *Far from the Madding Crowd* entitled 'Le roman pastoral en Angleterre'.

*Ethelberta* was finished in the January of the next year (1876) and the MS. dispatched. Pending the appearance of the story in volumes the twain removed in March to lodgings at Yeovil to facilitate their search for a little dwelling. Here they were living when the novel was published. It was received in a friendly spirit and even with admiration in some quarters — more, indeed, than Hardy had expected — one experienced critic going so far as to write that it was the finest ideal comedy since the days of Shakespeare. 'Show me the lady in the flesh', he said in a letter to the author, 'and I vow on my honour as a bachelor to become a humble addition to her devoted train.' It did not, however, win the cordiality that had greeted its two forerunners, the chief objection seeming to be that it was 'impossible'. It was, in fact, thirty years too soon for a Comedy of Society of that kind — just as *The Poor Man and the Lady* had been too soon for a socialist story, and as other of his writings — in prose and verse — were too soon for their date. The most impossible situation in it was said to be that of the heroine sitting at table at a dinner-party of 'the best people', at which her father was present by the sideboard as butler. Yet a similar situation has been applauded in a play in recent years by Mr. Bernard Shaw, without any sense of improbability.

This ended Hardy's connection with Leslie Stephen as editor, though not as friend ; and in the course of a letter expressing a hope that it might be renewed, Stephen wrote (May 16, 1876) :

'My remark about modern lectures [?] was of course "wrote sarcastic", as Artemus Ward says, and intended for a passing dig in the ribs of some modern critics, who think that they can lay down laws in art like the Pope in religion ; *e.g.* the whole Rossetti-Swinburne school —— I think as a critic, that the less authors read of criticism the better. You, *e.g.*, have a perfectly fresh and original vein, and I think the less you bother yourself about critical canons the less chance there is of your becoming self-conscious and cramped. . . . Ste. Beuve, and Mat Arnold (in a smaller way), are the only modern critics who seem to me worth reading. . . . We are generally a poor lot, horribly afraid of not being in the fashion, and disposed to give ourselves airs on very small grounds.'

'*May.* In an orchard at Closeworth. Cowslips under trees. A light proceeds from them, as from Chinese lanterns or glow-worms.'

# CHAPTER VIII

# HOLLAND, THE RHINE, AND STURMINSTER NEWTON

1876–1878 : *Aet.* 36–37

FROM their lodgings in Yeovil they set out at the end of May for Holland and the Rhine — the first thing that struck them being that 'the Dutch seemed like police perpetually keeping back an unruly crowd composed of waves'. They visited Rotterdam — 'looking over-clean and new, with not enough shadow, and with houses nearly all out of the perpendicular' ; then The Hague, Scheveningen, Emmerich, and Cologne, where Hardy was disappointed by the machine-made Gothic of the Cathedral, and whence in a few days they went on 'between the banks that bear the vine', to Bonn, Coblentz, Ehrenbreitstein, and Mainz, where they were impressed by a huge confirmation in the cathedral which, by the way, was accompanied by a tune like that of Keble's Evening Hymn. Heidelberg they loved, and looking west one evening from the top of the tower on the Königsstuhl, Hardy remarks on a singular optical effect that was almost tragic. Owing to mist the wide landscape itself was not visible, but 'the Rhine glared like a riband of blood, as if it serpentined through the atmosphere above the earth's surface'. Thence they went to Carlsruhe, where they attended a fair, and searched for a German lady Hardy had known in England, but were unable to find her. Baden and the Black Forest followed, and next they proceeded to Strassburg, and then they turned back, travelling by way of Metz to Brussels. Here Hardy — maybe with his mind on *The Dynasts* — explored the field of Waterloo, and a day or two later spent some time in investigating the problem of the actual scene of the Duchess of Richmond's Ball, with no result that satisfied him, writing a letter while here to some London paper to that effect — a letter which has not been traced.

A short stay in Brussels was followed by their homeward course through Antwerp, where they halted awhile ; and Harwich, having a miserable passage on a windy night in a small steamer with cattle on board.

In London they were much astonished and amused to see in large letters on the newspaper-posters that there had been riots at Antwerp ; and they recalled that they had noticed a brass band parading the streets with about a dozen workmen walking quietly behind.

*June* (1876). Arriving at Yeovil again after another Waterloo-day visit to Chelsea by Hardy (where, in the private parlour of 'The Turk's Head' over glasses of grog, the battle was fought yet again by the dwindling number of pensioners who had taken part in it), his first consideration was the resumed question of a cottage, having ere this received hints from relatives that he and his wife 'appeared to be wandering about like two tramps' ; and also growing incommoded by an accumulation of luggage in packing-cases, mostly books, for of other furniture they had as yet not a stick ; till they went out one day to an auction and bought a door-scraper and a book-case, with which two articles they laid the foundation of household goods and effects.

'*June* 25. The irritating necessity of conforming to rules which in themselves have no virtue.'

'*June* 26. If it be possible to compress into a sentence all that a man learns between 20 and 40, it is that all things merge in one another — good into evil, generosity into justice, religion into politics, the year into the ages, the world into the universe. With this in view the evolution of species seems but a minute and obvious process in the same movement.'

A pretty cottage overlooking the Dorset Stour — called 'Riverside Villa' — offered itself at Sturminster Newton, and this they took at midsummer, hastily furnished it in part by going to Bristol and buying £100 worth of mid-Victorian furniture in two hours ; entering on July 3. It was their first house and, though small, probably that in which they spent their happiest days. Several poems commemorate their term there of nearly two years. A memorandum dated just after their entry runs as follows :

'Rowed on the Stour in the evening, the sun setting up the river. Just afterwards a faint exhalation visible on surface of water as we stirred it with the oars. A fishy smell from the numerous eels and other fish beneath. Mowers salute us. Rowed among the water-lilies to gather them. Their long ropy stems.

'Passing the island drove out a flock of swallows from the bushes and sedge, which had gone there to roost. Gathered meadow-sweet.

Rowed with difficulty through the weeds, the rushes on the border standing like palisades against the bright sky. . . . A cloud in the sky like a huge quill-pen.'

Another entry at this time :

'A story has been told me of a doctor at Maiden Newton, who attended a woman who could not pay him. He said he would take the dead baby in payment. He had it, and it was kept on his mantel-piece in a large glass jar in spirits, which stained the body brown. The doctor, who was a young man, afterwards married and used his wife badly, insisting on keeping the other woman's dead baby on his mantelpiece.'

Another :

'Mr. Warry says that a farmer who was tenant of a friend of his, used to take the heart of every calf that died, and, sticking it full of black thorns, hang it on the cotterel, or cross-bar, of his chimney : this was done to prevent the spread of the disease that had killed the calf. When the next tenant came the chimney smoked very much, and examining it, they found it choked with hearts treated in the manner described — by that time dry and parched.'

Another :

'"Toad Fair." An old man, a wizard, used to bring toads' legs in little bags to Bagber Bridge [close to where Hardy was living], where he was met by crowds of people who came in vehicles and on foot, and bought them as charms to cure scrofula by wearing them round the neck. These legs were supposed to twitch occasionally in the bag, and probably did, when it gave the wearer's blood a "turn", and changed the course of the disease.'

'There are two sorts of church people ; those who go, and those who don't go : there is only one sort of chapel-people ; those who go.'

'"All is vanity", saith the Preacher. But if all were only vanity, who would mind? Alas, it is too often worse than vanity ; agony, darkness, death also.'

'A man would never laugh were he not to forget his situation, or were he not one who never has learnt it. After risibility from comedy, how often does the thoughtful mind reproach itself for forgetting the truth? Laughter always means blindness — either from defect, choice, or accident.'

During a visit to London in December Hardy attended a Conference on the Eastern Question at St. James's Hall, and heard speak Mr. Gladstone, Lord Shaftesbury, Hon. E. Ashley, Anthony Trollope, and the Duke of Westminster. 'Trollope outran the five or seven minutes allowed for each speech, and the Duke, who was chairman, after various soundings of the bell, and other hints that he must stop, tugged at Trollope's coat-tails in desperation. Trollope turned round, exclaimed parenthetically, "Please leave my coat alone," and went on speaking.'

They spent Christmas with Hardy's father and mother; and while there his father told them that when he was a boy the hobby-horse was still a Christmas amusement. On one occasion the village band of West Stafford was at Mr. Floyer's (the landowner's) at a party, where among other entertainments was that of the said hobby-horse. One of the servants was terrified death-white at the sight of it running about, and rushed into an adjoining dark room where the band's violoncello was lying, entering with such force as to knock off the neck of the instrument.

*A Pair of Blue Eyes* was much to the taste of French readers, and was favourably criticized in the *Revue des Deux Mondes* early the next year (1877). It appears to have been also a romance that Hardy himself did not wish to let die, for we find him writing to Mr. George Smith in the following April:

'There are circumstances in connection with *A Pair of Blue Eyes* which make me anxious to favour it, even at the expense of profit, if I can possibly do so. . . . I know that you do sometimes, not to say frequently, take an interest in producing a book quite apart from commercial views as a publisher, and I should like to gain such interest for this one of mine. . . . I can get a photograph of the picturesque Cornish coast, the scene of the story, from which a drawing could be made for the frontispiece.'

Mr. Smith replied that though he had not printed the original edition he would take it up, profit or no profit; but for some unexplained reason the book was published at other hands, the re-issue receiving much commendatory notice.

'*May* 1. A man comes every evening to the cliff in front of our house to see the sun set, timing himself to arrive a few minutes before the descent. Last night he came, but there was a cloud. His disappointment.'

'*May* 30. Walking to Marnhull. The prime of bird-singing. The thrushes and blackbirds are the most prominent, — pleading earnestly rather than singing, and with such modulation that you seem to see their little tongues curl inside their bills in their emphasis. A bullfinch sings from a tree with a metallic sweetness piercing as a fife.  Further on I come to a hideous carcase of a house in a green landscape, like a skull on a table of dessert.'

Same date :

'I sometimes look upon all things in inanimate Nature as pensive mutes.'

'*June* 3.  Mr. Young says that his grandfather [about 1750–1830] was very much excited, as was everybody in Sturminster, when a mail-coach ran from Poole to Bristol.  On the morning it ran for the first time he got up early, swept *the whole street*, and sprinkled sand for the vehicle and horses to pass over.'

Same date :

'The world often feels certain works of genius to be great, without knowing why : hence it may be that particular poets and novelists may have had the wrong quality in them noticed and applauded as that which makes them great.'

We also find in this June of 1877 an entry that adumbrates *The Dynasts* yet again — showing that the idea by this time has advanced a stage — from that of a ballad, or ballad-sequence, to a 'grand drama', viz. :

'Consider a grand drama, based on the wars with Napoleon, or some one campaign (but not as Shakespeare's historical dramas).  It might be called "Napoleon", or "Josephine", or by some other person's name.'

He writes also, in another connection :

'There is enough poetry in what is left [in life], after all the false romance has been abstracted, to make a sweet pattern : *e.g.* the poem by H. Coleridge :

'"She is not fair to outward view".

'So, then, if Nature's defects must be looked in the face and transcribed, whence arises the *art* in poetry and novel-writing? which must certainly show art, or it becomes merely mechanical reporting. I think the art lies in making these defects the basis of a hitherto unperceived beauty, by irradiating them with "the light that never was" on their surface, but is seen to be latent in them by the spiritual eye.'

'*June* 28.  Being Coronation Day there are games and dancing on the green at Sturminster Newton.  The stewards with white rosettes. One is very anxious, fearing that while he is attending to the runners the leg of mutton on the pole will go wrong ; hence he walks hither and thither with a compressed countenance and eyes far ahead.

Thomas Hardy senior, 1877

Jemima Hardy, 1876

'The pretty girls, just before a dance, stand in inviting positions on the grass. As the couples in each figure pass near where their immediate friends loiter, each girl-partner gives a laughing glance at such friends, and whirls on.'

'*June* 29. Have just passed through a painful night and morning. Our servant, whom we liked very much, was given a holiday yesterday to go to Bournemouth with her young man. Came home last night at ten, seeming oppressed. At about half-past twelve, when we were supposed to be asleep, she crept downstairs, went out, and on looking from the back window of our bedroom I saw her come from the outhouse with a man. She appeared to have only her nightgown on and something round her shoulders. Beside her slight white figure in the moonlight his form looked dark and gigantic. She preceded him to the door. Before I had thought what to do E. had run downstairs, and met her, and ordered her to bed. The man disappeared. Found that the bolts of the back-door had been oiled. He had evidently often stayed in the house.

'She remained quiet till between four and five, when she got out of the dining-room window and vanished.'

'*June* 30. About one o'clock went to her father's cottage in the village, where we thought she had gone. Found them poorer than I expected (for they are said to be an old county family). Her father was in the field hay-making, and a little girl fetched him from the haymakers. He came across to me amid the windrows of hay, and seemed to read bad news in my face. She had not been home. I remembered that she had dressed up in her best clothes, and she probably has gone to Stalbridge to her lover.'

The further career of this young woman is not recorded, except as to one trifling detail.

'*July* 4. Went to Stalbridge. Mrs. —— is a charming woman. When we were looking over the church she recommended me to try a curious seat, adding, though we were only talking about the church itself, "That's where I sat when Jamie was christened, and I could see him very well". Another seat she pointed out with assumed casualness as being the one where she sat when she was churched; as if it were rather interesting that she did sit in those places, in spite of her not being a romantic person. When we arrived at her house she told us that Jamie really could not be seen — he was in a dreadful state — covered with hay; half laughing and catching our eyes while she spoke, as if we should know at once how intensely humorous he must appear under those circumstances. Jamie was evidently her life, and flesh, and raiment. . . . Her husband is what we call a "yopping, or yapping man". He strains his countenance hard in smiling, and keeps it so for a distinct length of time, so that you may on no account whatever miss his smile and the point of the words that gave rise to it. Picks up pictures and china for eighteenpence worth ever so much more. Gives cottagers a new set of tea-cups with handles for old ones without handles — an exchange which they are delighted to make.

'Country life at Sturminster. Vegetables pass from growing to boiling, fruit from the bushes to the pudding, without a moment's halt, and the gooseberries that were ripening on the twigs at noon are in the tart an hour later.'

'*July* 13. The sudden disappointment of a hope leaves a scar which the ultimate fulfilment of that hope never entirely removes.'

'*July* 27. James Bushrod of Broadmayne saw the two German soldiers [of the York Hussars] shot [for desertion] on Bincombe Down in 1801. It was in the path across the Down, or near it. James Selby of the same village thinks there is a mark.' [The tragedy was used in *The Melancholy Hussar*, the real names of the deserters being given.]

'*August* 13. We hear that Jane, our late servant, is soon to have a baby. Yet never a sign of one is there for us.'

'*September* 25. Went to Shroton Fair. In a twopenny show saw a woman beheaded. In another a man whose hair grew on one side of his face. Coming back across Hambledon Hill (where the Club-Men assembled, *temp*. Cromwell) a fog came on. I nearly got lost in the dark inside the earthworks, the old hump-backed man I had parted from on the other side of the hill, who was going somewhere else before coming across the earthworks in my direction, being at the bottom as soon as I. A man might go round and round all night in such a place.'

'*September* 28. An object or mark raised or made by man on a scene is worth ten times any such formed by unconscious Nature. Hence clouds, mists, and mountains are unimportant beside the wear on a threshold, or the print of a hand.'

'*October* 31. To Bath. Took lodgings for my father near the baths and Abbey. Met him at G.W. Station. Took him to the lodgings. To theatre in the evening. Stayed in Bath. Next day went with father to the baths, to begin the cure.'

During this year 1877 Hardy had the sadness of hearing of the death of Raphael Brandon, the literary architect whom he had been thrown with seven years earlier, at a critical stage in his own career. He also at this time entered into an interesting correspondence with Mrs. Chatteris, daughter of Admiral Sir Thomas Hardy, upon some facts in the life of the latter. But his main occupation at Riverside Villa (or 'Rivercliff' as they sometimes called it) was writing *The Return of the Native*. The only note he makes of its progress is that, on November 8, parts 3, 4, and 5 of the story were posted to Messrs. Chatto and Windus for publication in (of all places) *Belgravia* — a monthly magazine then running. Strangely enough, the rich alluvial district of Sturminster Newton in which the author was now living was not used by him at this time as a setting for the story he was constructing there, but the heath country twenty miles off. It may be mentioned here that the name 'Eustacia' which he gave to his heroine was that of the wife of the owner of the manor of Ower Moigne in the reign of Henry IV, which parish includes part of the 'Egdon' Heath of the story (*vide* Hutchins's *Dorset*); and that 'Clement', the name of the hero, was suggested by its being borne by one of his supposed ancestors, Clement le Hardy, of Jersey, whose family migrated from that isle to the west of England at the beginning of the sixteenth century.

On the same day he jots down:

'*November* 8. Mr. and Mrs. Dashwood came to tea. Mr. Dashwood [a local solicitor and landowner] says that poachers elevate a pan of brimstone on a stick under pheasants at roost, and so stupefy them that they fall.

'Sometimes the keepers make dummy pheasants and fix them in places where pheasants are known to roost: then watch by them. The poachers come; shoot and shoot again, when the keepers rush out.

'At a *battue* the other day lots of the birds ran into the keeper's *house* for protection.

'Mr. D. says that a poacher he defended at Quarter Sessions asked for time to pay the fine imposed, and they gave him till the next Justice-meeting. He said to Mr. D., "I shall be able to get it out of 'em before then", and in fact he had in a week poached enough birds from the Justices' preserves to pay the five pounds.'

'*November* 12. A flooded river after the incessant rains of yesterday. Lumps of froth float down like swans in front of our house. At the arches of the large stone bridge the froth has accumulated and lies like hillocks of salt against the bridge; then the arch chokes, and after a silence coughs out the air and froth, and gurgles on.'

'*End of November.* This evening the west is like some vast foundry where new worlds are being cast.'

'*December* 22. In the evening I went with Dr. Leach the coroner to an inquest which was to be held at Stourton Caundell on the body of a boy. Arrived at the Trooper Inn after a lonely drive through dark and muddy lanes. Met at the door by the Superintendent of Police and a policeman in plain clothes. Also by Mr. Long, who had begun the *post-mortem.* We then went to the cottage ; a woman or two, and children, were sitting by the fire, who looked at us with a cowed expression. Upstairs the body of the boy lay on a box covered with a sheet. It was uncovered, and Mr. Long went on with his autopsy, I holding a candle, and the policeman another. Found a clot in the heart, but no irritant poison in the stomach, as had been suspected. The inquest was then held at the inn.'

'*December* 26. In literature young men usually begin their careers by being judges, and as wisdom and old experience arrive they reach the dignity of standing as culprits at the bar before new young bloods who have in their turn sprung up in the judgment-seat.'

A correspondence with Baron Tauchnitz in reference to Continental editions of his books was one of the businesses of the year-end.

Despite the pleasure of this life at Sturminster Newton Hardy had decided that the practical side of his vocation of novelist demanded that he should have his headquarters in or near London. The wisdom of his decision, considering the nature of his writing, he afterwards questioned. So in the first week of February he and Mrs. Hardy went up to look for a house, and about the middle of the month he signed an agreement for a three-years' lease of one at Upper Tooting, close to Wandsworth Common.

'*March* 5. Concert at Sturminster. A Miss Marsh of Sutton [Keinton?] Mandeville sang "Should he upbraid", to Bishop's old tune. She is the sweetest of singers — thrush-like in the descending scale, and lark-like in the ascending — drawing out the soul of listeners in a gradual thread of excruciating attenuation like silk from a cocoon.'

Many years after Hardy was accustomed to say that this was the most marvellous old song in English music in its power of touching an audience. There was no surer card to play as an *encore,* even when it was executed but indifferently well. He wrote some lines thereon entitled 'The Maid of Keinton Mandeville'.

'*March* 18. End of the Sturminster Newton idyll . . .' [The following is written in later] 'Our happiest time.'

It was also a poetical time.  Several poems in *Moments of Vision* contain memories of it, such as 'Overlooking the River Stour', 'The Musical Box', and 'On Sturminster Foot-Bridge'.

That evening of March 18 a man came to arrange about packing their furniture, and the next day it was all out of the house.  They slept at Mrs. Dashwood's, after breakfasting, lunching, and dining there ; and in the morning saw their goods off, and left Sturminster for London.

# CHAPTER IX

# LIFE AND LITERATURE IN A
# LONDON SUBURB

1878–1880 : *Aet.* 37–39

Two days later they beheld their furniture descending from a pair of vans at 1 Arundel Terrace ('The Larches'), Trinity Road, just beyond Wandsworth Common. They had stayed at Bolingbroke Grove to be near.

'*March* 22. We came from Bolingbroke Grove to Arundel Terrace and slept here for the first time. Our house is the south-east corner one where Brodrick Road crosses Trinity Road down towards Wandsworth Common Station, the side door being in Brodrick Road.'

'*April* — Note. A Plot, or Tragedy, should arise from the gradual closing in of a situation that comes of ordinary human passions, prejudices, and ambitions, by reason of the characters taking no trouble to ward off the disastrous events produced by the said passions, prejudices, and ambitions.

'The advantages of the letter-system of telling a story (passing over the disadvantages) are that, hearing what one side has to say, you are led constantly to the imagination of what the other side must be feeling, and at last are anxious to know if the other side does really feel what you imagine.'

'*April* 22. The method of Boldini, the painter of "The Morning Walk" in the French Gallery two or three years ago (a young lady beside an ugly blank wall on an ugly highway) — of Hobbema, in his view of a road with formal lopped trees and flat tame scenery — is that of infusing emotion into the baldest external objects either by the presence of a human figure among them, or by mark of some human connection with them.

'This accords with my feeling about, say, Heidelberg and Baden *versus* Scheveningen — as I wrote at the beginning of *The Return of the Native* — that the beauty of association is entirely superior to the beauty of aspect, and a beloved relative's old battered tankard to the finest Greek vase. Paradoxically put, it is to see the beauty in ugliness.'

'*April* 29. Mr. George Smith (Smith Elder and Co.) informs me that how he first got to know Thackeray was through "a mutual friend" — to whom Smith said, "Tell Thackeray that I will publish everything he likes to write". This was before Thackeray was much known, and when he had only published the Titmarsh and Yellow-plush papers. However, Thackeray did not appear. When they at length met, Thackeray said he wished to publish *Vanity Fair*, and Smith undertook it. Thackeray also said he had offered it to three or four publishers who had refused it. "Why didn't you come to me?" said Smith. "Why didn't you come to me?" said Thackeray.'

'*June* 8. To Grosvenor Gallery. Seemed to have left flesh behind, and entered a world of soul. In some of the pictures, *e.g.* A. Tadema's "Sculpture" (men at work carving the Sphinx), and "Ariadne abandoned by Theseus" (an uninteresting dreary shore, little tent one corner, etc.) the principles I have mentioned have been applied to choice of subject.'

'*June* 16. Sunday evening. At Mr. Alexander Macmillan's with E. He told me a story the late Mrs. Carlyle told him. One day when she was standing alone on Craigenputtock Moor, where she and Mr. Carlyle were living, she discerned in the distance a red spot. It proved to be the red cloak of a woman who passed for a witch in those parts. Mrs. Carlyle got to know her, and ultimately learnt her history. She was the daughter of a laird owning about eighty acres, and there had come to their house in her young-womanhood a young dealer in cattle. The daughter and he fell in love, and were married, and both lived with her father, whose farm the young man took in hand to manage. But he ran the farmer into debt, and ultimately (I think) house and property had to be sold. The young man vanished. A boy was born to the wife, and after a while she went away to find her husband. She came back in a state of great misery, but would not tell where she had been. It leaked out that the husband was a married man. She was proud and would not complain ; but her father died ; the boy grew up and was intended for a schoolmaster, but he was crossing the moor one night and lost his way ; was buried in the snow, and frozen to death. She lived on in a hut there, and became the red-cloaked old woman who was Mrs. Carlyle's witch-neighbour.'

In June he was elected a member of the Savile Club, and by degrees fell into line as a London man again. Dining at Mr. Kegan

Paul's, Kensington Square, the same summer, they met Mr. Leighton (Sir F. Leighton's father), his daughter Mrs. Sutherland Orr, who had been in India during the Mutiny, and Professor Huxley, whom they had met before at Mr. Macmillan's. 'We sat down by daylight, and as we dined the moon brightened the trees in the garden, and shone under them into the room.' For Huxley Hardy had a liking which grew with knowledge of him — though that was never great — speaking of him as a man who united a fearless mind with the warmest of hearts and the most modest of manners.

'*July.* When a couple are shown to their room at an hotel, before the husband has seen that it is a room at all, the wife has found the looking-glass and is arranging her bonnet.'

'*August* 3. Minto dined with me at the club. Joined at end of dinner by W. H. Pollock, and we all three went to the Lyceum. It was Irving's last night, in which he appeared in a scene from *Richard III.* ; then as "Jingle" ; then recited "Eugene Aram's Dream" — (the only piece of literature outside plays that actors seem to know of). As "Jingle", forgetting his part, he kept up one shoulder as in *Richard III.* We went to his dressing-room, found him naked to the waist ; champagne in tumblers.'

'*August* 31. to *Sept.* 9. In Dorset. Called on William Barnes the poet. Went to Kingston Lacy to see the pictures. Dined at West-Stafford Rectory. Went with C. W. Moule [Fellow of Corpus, Cambridge] to Ford Abbey.'

'*September* 20. Returned and called on G. Smith. Agreed to his terms for publishing *The Return of the Native*.'

Shortly after he wrote to Messrs. Smith and Elder :

'I enclose a sketch-map of the supposed scene in which *The Return of the Native* is laid, copied from the one I used in writing the story ; and my suggestion is that we place an engraving of it as frontispiece to the first volume. Unity of place is so seldom preserved in novels that a map of the scene of action is as a rule quite impracticable. But since the present story affords an opportunity of doing so I am of opinion that it would be a desirable novelty.' The publishers fell in with the idea and the map was made.

A peculiarity in the local descriptions running through all Hardy's writings may be instanced here — that he never uses the word 'Dorset', never names the county at all (except possibly in an explanatory footnote), but obliterates the names of the six counties, whose area he traverses in his scenes, under the general appellation of 'Wessex' — an old word that became quite popular after the date of *Far from the Madding Crowd*, where he first introduced it. So far did he carry this idea of the unity of Wessex that he used to say he had grown to forget the crossing of county boundaries within the ancient kingdom — in this respect being quite unlike the poet Barnes, who was 'Dorset' emphatically.

Mrs. Hardy used to relate that during this summer, she could not tell exactly when, she looked out of a window at the back of the house, and saw her husband running without a hat down Brodrick Road, and disappearing round a corner into a by-street. Before she had done wondering what could have happened, he returned, and all was explained. While sitting in his writing-room he had heard a street barrel-organ of the kind that used to be called a 'harmoniflute', playing somewhere near at hand the very quadrille over which the jaunty young man who had reached the end of his time at Hicks's had spread such a bewitching halo more than twenty years earlier by describing the glories of dancing round to its beats on the Cremorne platform or at the Argyle Rooms, and which Hardy had never been able to identify. He had thrown down his pen, and, as she had beheld, flown out and approached the organ-grinder with such speed that the latter, looking frightened, began to shuffle off. Hardy called out, 'What's the name of that tune?' The grinder — a young foreigner, who could not speak English — exclaimed trembling as he stopped, 'Quad-ree-ya! quad-ree-ya!' and pointed to the index in front of the instrument. Hardy looked: 'Quadrille' was the only word there. He had till then never heard it since his smart senior had whistled it; he never heard it again, and never ascertained its name. It was possibly one of Jullien's — then gone out of vogue — set off rather by the youthful imagination of Hardy at sixteen than by any virtue in the music itself.

'*October* 27. Sunday. To Chelsea Hospital and Ranelagh Gardens: met a palsied pensioner — deaf. He is 88 — was in the Seventh (?) Hussars. He enlisted in 1807 or 1808, served under Sir John Moore in the Peninsula, through the Retreat, and was at Waterloo. It was extraordinary to talk and shake hands with a man who had shared in that terrible winter march to Coruña, and had seen Moore face to face.

'Afterwards spoke to two or three others. When an incorrigible was drummed out of barracks to the tune of the Rogue's March — (as my father had told me) — all the facings and the buttons were previously cut from his uniform, and a shilling given him. The fifes and drums accompanied him only just beyond the barrack-gates.

'In those days if you only turned your eye you were punished. My informant had known men receive 600 lashes — 300 at a time, or 900, if the doctor said it could be borne. After the punishment salt was rubbed on the victim's back, to harden it. He did not feel the pain of this, his back being numbed by the lashes. The men would hold a bullet between their teeth and chew it during the operation.'

*The Return of the Native* was published by Messrs. Smith and Elder in November, *The Times*' remark upon the book being that the reader found himself taken farther from the madding crowd than ever. Old Mrs. Procter's amusing criticism in a letter was: 'Poor Eustacia. I so fully understood her longing for the Beautiful. I love the Common; but still one may wish for something else. I rejoice that Venn [a character] is happy. A man is never cured when he loves a stupid woman [Thomasin]. Beauty fades, and intelligence and wit grow irritating; but your dear Dulness is always the same.'

'*November* 28. Woke before it was light. Felt that I had not enough staying power to hold my own in the world.'

On the last day of the year Hardy's father wrote, saying that his mother was unwell, and that he had 'drunk both their healths in gin and rhubarb wine, with hopes that they would live to see many and many a New Year's day'. He suggested that they should come ere long.

'1879. *January* 1. New Year's thought. A perception of the FAILURE of THINGS to be what they are meant to be, lends them, in place of the intended interest, a new and greater interest of an unintended kind.'

The poem 'A January Night. 1879' in *Moments of Vision* relates to an incident of this new year (1879) which occurred here at Tooting, where they seemed to begin to feel that 'there had past away a glory from the earth'. And it was in this house that their troubles began. This, however, is anticipating unduly.

'*January* 30. 1879. In Steven's book-shop, Holywell Street. A bustling, vigorous young curate comes in — red-faced and full of life — the warm breath puffing from his mouth in a jet into the frosty air, and religion sitting with an ill grace upon him.

'"Have you *Able to Save*?"

'Shopman addressed does not know, and passes on the inquiry to the master standing behind with his hat on: "*Able to Save*?"

'"I don't know — hoi! (to boy at other end). Got *Able to Save*? Why the devil can't you attend!"

'"What, Sir?"

'"*Able to Save!*"

'Boy's face a blank.  Shopman to curate: "Get it by to-morrow afternoon, Sir."

'"And please get *Words of Comfort*."

'"*Words of Comfort*.  Yes, Sir."  Exit curate.

'Master: "Why the h—— don't anybody here know what's in stock?"  Business proceeds in a subdued manner.'

'*February* 1.  To Dorchester.  Cold.  Rain on snow.  Henry seen advancing through it, with wagonette and Bob [their father's horse], to the station entrance.  Drove me to Bockhampton through the sleet and rain from the East, which shaved us like a razor.  Wind on Fordington Moor cut up my sleeves and round my wrists — even up to my elbows.  The light of the lamp at the bottom of the town shone on the reins in Henry's hands, and showed them glistening with ice.  Bob's behind-part was a mere grey arch; his foreparts invisible.'

'*February* 4.  To Weymouth and Portland.  As to the ruined walls in the low part of Chesil, a woman says the house was washed down in the November gale of 1824.  The owner never rebuilt it, but emigrated with his family.  She says that in her house one person was drowned (they were all in bed except the fishermen) and next door two people.  It was about four in the morning that the wave came.'

'*February* 7.  Father says that when there was a hanging at Dorchester in his boyhood it was carried out at one o'clock, it being the custom to wait till the mail-coach came in from London in case of a reprieve.

'He says that at Puddletown Church, at the time of the old west-gallery violin, oboe, and clarionet players, Tom Sherren (one of them) used to copy tunes during the sermon.  So did my grandfather at Stinsford Church.  Old Squibb the parish-clerk used also to stay up late at night helping my grandfather in his "prick-noting" (as he called it).

'He says that William, son of Mr. S—— the Rector of W——, became a miller at O—— Mill, and married a German woman whom he met at Puddletown Fair playing her tambourine.  When her husband was gone to market she used to call in John Porter, who could play the fiddle, and lived near, and give him some gin, when she would beat the tambourine to his playing.  She was a good-natured woman with blue eyes, brown hair, and a round face; rather slovenly.

Her husband was a hot, hasty fellow, though you could hear by his speech that he was a better educated man than ordinary millers.

'G. R.——— (who is a humorist) showed me his fowl-house, which was built of old church-materials bought at Wellspring the builder's sale. R.'s chickens roost under the gilt-lettered Lord's Prayer and Creed, and the cock crows and flaps his wings against the Ten Commandments. It reminded me that I had seen these same Ten Commandments, Lord's Prayer, and Creed, before, forming the sides of the stone-mason's shed in that same builder's yard, and that he had remarked casually that they did not prevent the workmen "cussing and damning" the same as ever. It also reminded me of seeing the old font of ——— Church, Dorchester, in a garden, used as a flower-vase, the initials of ancient godparents and Churchwardens still legible upon it. A comic business — church restoration.

'A villager says of the parson, who has been asked to pray for a sick person : "His prayers wouldn't save a mouse".'

'*February* 12. Sketched the English Channel from Mayne Down.

'I am told that when Jack Ketch had done whipping by the Town Pump [Dorchester] the prisoners' coats were thrown over their bleeding backs, and, guarded by the town constables with their long staves, they were conducted back to prison. Close at their heels came J. K., the cats held erect — there was one cat to each man — the lashes were of knotted whipcord.

'Also that in a village near Yeovil about 100 years ago, there lived a dumb woman, well known to my informant's mother. One day the woman suddenly spoke and said :

> '"A cold winter, a forward spring,
> A bloody summer, a dead King" ;

'She then dropped dead. The French Revolution followed immediately after.'

'*February* 15. Returned to London.'

'*April* 5. Mary writes to tell me that "there is a very queer quire at Steepleton Church. It consists only of a shoemaker who plays the bass-viol, and his mother who sings the air."'

'*June* 9. To the International Literary Congress at the rooms of the Society of Arts. Met M. de Lesseps. A few days afterwards to the Soirée Musicale at the Hanover Square Club, to meet members of the Literary Congress and the Comédie Française : A large gathering. The whole thing a free-and-easy mix-up. I was a total stranger, and wondered why I was there : many others were total strangers to everybody else; sometimes two or three of these total strangers would fraternize from very despair.  A little old Frenchman, however, who bustled about in a skull cap and frilled shirt, seemed to know everybody.'

'*June* 21.  With E. to Bosworth Smith's, Harrow (for the week-end).  In the aviary he has a raven and a barn owl.  One ridiculously small boy was in tails — he must have been a bright boy, but I forgot to ask about him.  One of the boys in charity-tails could have eaten him.

'Bos's brother Henry the invalid has what I fear to be a church-yard cough [he died not so very long after].  His cough pleases the baby, so he coughs artificially much more than required by his disease, to go on pleasing the baby.  Mrs. H. S. implores her husband not to do so; but he does, nevertheless, showing the extraordinary non-chalance about death that so many of his family show.

'In chapel — which we attended — the little tablets in memory of the boys who have died at school there were a moving sight.

'Sunday night we went with Bos, to the boys' dormitories.  One boy was unwell, and we talked to him as he lay in bed, his arm thrown over his head.  Another boy has his room hung with proof engravings after Landseer.  In another room were the two K————s of Clyffe.  In another a big boy and a little boy — the little boy being very earnest about birds' eggs, and the big boy silently affecting a mind above the subject, though covertly interested.'

'27.  From Tooting to Town again.  In railway carriage a *too* statuesque girl; but her features were absolutely perfect.  She sat quite still, and her smiles did not extend further than a finger-nail's breadth from the edge of her mouth.  The repose of her face was such that when the train shook her it seemed painful.  Her mouth was very small, and her face not unlike that of a nymph.  In the train coming home there was a contrasting girl of sly humour — the pupil of her eye being mostly half under the eyelid.'

It was in this year that pourparlers were opened with Leslie Stephen about another story for the *Cornhill*; and Hardy informed him that he was writing a tale of the reign of George III; on which Stephen remarks in respect of historical novels:

'I can only tell you what is my own taste, but I rather think that my taste is in this case the common one.  I think that a historical character in a novel is almost always a nuisance; but I like to have a bit of history in the background, so to speak; to feel that George III. is just round the corner, though he does not present himself in full front.'

Since coming into contact with Leslie Stephen about 1873, as has been shown, Hardy had been much influenced by his philosophy, and also by his criticism. He quotes the following sentence from Stephen in his note-book under the date of July 1, 1879 :

'The ultimate aim of the poet should be to touch our hearts by showing his own, and not to exhibit his learning, or his fine taste, or his skill in mimicking the notes of his predecessors.' That Hardy adhered pretty closely to this principle when he resumed the writing of poetry can hardly be denied.

'*July* 8 or 9. With E. to Mrs. [Alexander] Macmillan's garden-party at Knapdale, near our house. A great many present. Talked to Mr. White of Harvard University, and Mr. Henry Holt the New York publisher, who said that American spelling and idiom must prevail over the English, as it was sixty millions against thirty. I forgot for the moment to say that it did not follow, the usage set up by a few people of rank, education, and fashion being the deciding factor. Also to John Morley, whom I had not seen since he read my first manuscript. He remembered it, and said in his level uninterested voice: "Well, since we met, you have . . ." etc. etc. Also met a Mrs. H., who pretended to be an admirer of my books, and apparently had never read one. She had with her an American lady, sallow, with black dancing eyes, dangling earrings, yellow costume, and gay laugh.' It was at this garden-party at Mrs. Macmillan's that the thunderstorm came on which Hardy made use of in a similar scene in *A Laodicean*.

'*July* 12. To Chislehurst to funeral of young Louis Napoleon. Met [Sir G.] Greenhill in the crowd. We stood on the common while the procession passed. Was struck by the profile of Prince Napoleon as he walked by bareheaded, a son on each arm : complexion dark, sallow, even sinister : a round projecting chin : countenance altogether extraordinarily remindful of Boney.' Hardy said long after that this sight of Napoleon's nephew — 'Plon-Plon' — had been of enormous use to him, when writing *The Dynasts*, in imagining the Emperor's appearance. And it has been remarked somewhere in print that when the Prince had been met, without warning in Paris at night, crossing one of the bridges over the Seine, the beholder had started back aghast under the impression that he was seeing the spirit of the great Napoleon.

'*July* 29. Charles Leland — a man of higher literary rank than ever was accorded him [the American author of *Hans Breitmann's Ballads* and translator of Heine] — told some of his gipsy tales at the Savile Club, including one of how he visited at a country mansion and while there went to see a gipsy-family living in a tent on the squire's land. He talked to them in Romany, and was received by the whole family as a bosom-friend. He was told by the head gipsy that his, the gipsy's, brother would be happy to know him when he came out of gaol, but that at present he was doing six months for a horse. While Leland was sitting by the fire drinking brandy-and-water with this friend, the arrival of some gentlemen and ladies, fellow-guests at the house he was staying at, was announced. They had come to see the gipsies out of curiosity. Leland threw his brandy from his glass into the fire, not to be seen tippling there, but as they entered it blazed up in a blue flare much to their amazement, as if they thought it some unholy libation, which added to their surprise at discovering him. How he explained himself I cannot remember.'

In the latter half of August Hardy paid a visit to his parents in Dorset and a week later Mrs. Hardy joined him there. They spent a few days in going about the district, and then took lodgings at Weymouth, right over the harbour, his mother coming to see them, and driving to Portland, Upwey, etc., in their company. Their time in the port was mostly wet; 'the [excursion] steamer-bell ringing persistently, and nobody going on board except an unfortunate boys' school that had come eight miles by train that morning to spend a happy day by the sea. The rain goes into their baskets of provisions, and runs out a strange mixture of cake-juice and mustard-water, but they try to look as if they were enjoying it — all except the pale thin assistant-master who has come with them, and whose face is tragic with his responsibilities. The Quay seems quite deserted till, on going along it, groups of boatmen are discovered behind each projecting angle of wall — martyrs in countenance, talking of what their receipts would have been if the season had turned out fine; and the landladies' faces at every lodging-house window watching the drizzle and the sea it half obscures. Two adventurous visitors have emerged from their lodgings as far as the doorway, where they stand in their waterproof cloaks and goloshes, saying cheerfully, "the air will do us good, and we can change as soon as we come in". Young men rush to the bathing machines in ulsters, and the men engaged in loading a long-voyage steamer lose all patience, and say: "I'm blanked, if it goes on much longer like this we shall be rotted alive!" The tradespeople are exceptionally civil, and fancy prices have miraculously disappeared. . . .

'Am told that —— has turned upon her drunken husband at last, and knocks him down without ceremony. In the morning he holds out his trembling hand and says, "Give me a sixpence for a drop o' brandy — please do ye, my dear!"' This was a woman Hardy had known as a pretty laughing girl, who had been married for the little money she had.

# CHAPTER X

# LONDON, NORMANDY, AND CAMBRIDGE

1879–1880 : *Aet.* 39–40

AFTER their return to London they visited and dined out here and there, and as Mrs. Hardy had never seen the Lord Mayor's Show Hardy took her to view it from the upper windows of *Good Words* in Ludgate Hill. She remarked that the surface of the crowd seemed like a boiling cauldron of porridge. He jots down that 'as the crowd grows denser it loses its character of an aggregate of countless units, and becomes an organic whole, a molluscous black creature having nothing in common with humanity, that takes the shape of the streets along which it has lain itself, and throws out horrid excrescences and limbs into neighbouring alleys ; a creature whose voice exudes from its scaly coat, and who has an eye in every pore of its body. The balconies, stands, and railway-bridge are occupied by small detached shapes of the same tissue, but of gentler motion, as if they were the spawn of the monster in their midst.'

On a Sunday in the same November they met in Mr. Frith's studio, to which they had been invited, Sir Percy Shelley (the son of Percy Bysshe) and Lady Shelley. Hardy said afterwards that the meeting was as shadowy and remote as were those previous occasions when he had impinged on the penumbra of the poet he loved — that time of his sleeping at the Cross-Keys, St. John Street, and that of the visits he paid to Old St. Pancras Churchyard. He was to enter that faint penumbra twice more, once when he stood beside Shelley's dust in the English cemetery at Rome, and last when by Mary Shelley's grave at Bournemouth.

They also met in the studio a deaf old lady, introduced as 'Lady Bacon' (though she must have been Lady Charlotte Bacon), who 'talked vapidly of novels, saying she never read them — not thinking them *positively wicked*, but, well . . .'. Mr. Frith afterwards explained that she was Byron's Ianthe, to whom he dedicated the First and Second Cantos of *Childe Harold* when she was Lady Charlotte Harley. That 'Peri of the West', with an eye 'wild as the Gazelle's', and a voice that had entered Byron's ear, was now a feeble beldame muffled up in black and furs. (It may be mentioned that she died the following year.)

Hardy met there too — a distinctly modern juxtaposition — Miss Braddon, who 'had a broad, thought-creased, world-beaten face — a most amiable woman', whom he always liked.

In December Hardy attended the inaugural dinner of the Rabelais Club at the Tavistock Hotel, in a 'large, empty, dimly-lit, cheerless apartment, with a gloomy crimson screen hiding what remained of the only cheerful object there — the fire.  There was a fog in the room as in the streets, and one man only came in evening dress, who, Walter Pollock said, looked like the skull at the banquet, but who really looked like a conjuror dying of the cold among a common set of thick-jacketed men who could stand it.  When I came in Leland turned his high flat façade to me — like that of a clock-tower ; his face being the clock-face, his coat swaying like a pendulum ; features earnest and energetic, altogether those of a single-minded man.  There were also Fred Pollock, girlish-looking ; and genial Walter Besant, with his West-of-England sailor face and silent pantomimic laughter. Sir Patrick Colquhoun was as if he didn't know what he was there for, how he arrived there, or how he was going to get home again. Two others present, Palmer [afterwards murdered in the East] and Joe Knight [the dramatic critic] also seemed puzzled about it.

'When dinner was over and things had got warmer, Leland in his speech remarked with much emphasis that we were men who ought to be encouraged, which sentiment was applauded with no misgivings of self-conceit.  D——, now as always, made himself the clown of our court, privileged to say anything by virtue of his office.  Hence when we rose to drink the health of absent members, he stayed firmly sitting, saying he would not drink it because they ought to have been there, afterwards lapsing into Spanish on the strength of his being going some day to publish a translation of Don Quixote.  Altogether we were as Rabelaisian as it was possible to be in the foggy circumstances, though I succeeded but poorly.'

It should be explained that this Rabelais Club, which had a success-ful existence for many years, had been instituted by Sir Walter Besant — a great lover of clubs and societies — as a declaration for virility in literature.  Hardy was pressed to join as being the most virile writer of works of imagination then in London ; while, it may be added, Henry James after a discussion was rejected for the lack of that quality, though he was afterwards invited as a guest.

On the first of February 1880 Hardy observed a man skating by himself on the pond by the Trinity-Church Schools at Upper Tooting, near his own house, and was moved to note down :

'It is a warm evening for the date, and there has been a thaw for two or three days, so that the birds sing cheerfully. A buttercup is said to be visible somewhere, and spring has, in short, peeped in upon us. What can the sentiments of that man be, to enjoy *ice* at such a time? The mental jar must overcome physical enjoyment in any well-regulated mind. He skates round the edge, it being unsafe to go into the middle, and he seems to sigh as he puts up with a limitation resulting from blessed promise.'

> '1 ARUNDEL TERRACE, TRINITY ROAD,
> 'UPPER TOOTING, S.W.
> '*Feb.* 2, 1880.

'DEAR MR. LOCKER,

'I can hardly express to you how grateful I am to get your letter. When I consider the perfect literary taste that is shown in all your own writings, apart from their other merits, I am not sure that I do not value your expressions of pleasure more highly than all the printed criticisms put together. It is very generous of you to pass over the defects of style in the book which, whenever I look into it, seem blunders that any child ought to have avoided.

'In enjoying your poems over again, I felt — will you mind my saying it? — quite ill-used to find you had altered two of my favourite lines which I had been in the habit of muttering to myself for some years past. I mean

> '"They never do so now — because
> I'm not so handsome as I was."

'I shall stick to the old reading as much the nicest, whatever you may choose to do in new editions.

'One other remark of quite a different sort. I unhesitatingly affirm that nothing more beautiful and powerful, for its length, than "the Old Stone-Mason" has been done by any modern poet. The only poem which has affected me at all in the same way is Wordsworth's "Two April Mornings", but this being less condensed than yours does not strike through one with such sudden power as yours in the last verse.

'I will not forget to give myself the pleasure of calling some Sunday afternoon. Meanwhile I should hope that you will be so

kindly disposed as to give us a few more "old stone-masons" as well
as ballads of a lighter kind.

> 'Believe me, Yours very truly,
>
> 'THOMAS HARDY.'

The same week Hardy met Matthew Arnold — probably for the
first time — at a dinner given by Mr. G. Murray Smith, the publisher,
at the Continental Hotel, where also were present Henry James and
Richard Jefferies — the latter a modest young man then getting into
notice as a writer, through having a year or so earlier published his
first successful book, entitled *The Gamekeeper at Home.*

Arnold, according to Hardy's account of their meeting much
later, 'had a manner of having made up his mind upon everything
years ago, so that it was a pleasing futility for his interlocutor to begin
thinking new ideas, different from his own, at that time of day'. Yet
he was frank and modest enough to assure Hardy deprecatingly that
he was only a hard-worked school-inspector.

He seems to have discussed the subject of literary style with the
younger writer, but all the latter could recall of his remarks thereon
was his saying that 'the best man to read for style — narrative style
— was Swift' — an opinion that may well be questioned, like many
more of Arnold's pronouncements, despite his undoubtedly true ones.

At dinner an incident occurred in which he was charmingly
amusing. Mrs. Murray Smith having that afternoon found herself
suddenly too unwell to preside, her place had to be taken at the last
minute by her daughter, and, it being the latter's first experience of
the kind, she was timorous as to the time of withdrawal, murmuring
to Arnold, 'I — think we must retire now?' Arnold put his hand
upon her shoulder and pressed her down into her seat as if she were
a child — she was not much more, — saying, 'No, no! what's the
use of going into that room? Now I'll pour you out a glass of sherry
to keep you here.' And kept there she and the other ladies were.

> 'SAVILE CLUB,
> 'SAVILE ROW, W.
> '*February* 11, 1880.

'DEAR MR. HANDLEY MOULE,

'I have just been reading in a Dorset paper a report of your
sermon on the death of the Rev. H. Moule, and I cannot refrain from
sending you a line to tell you how deeply it has affected me, and —
what is more to the point — to express my sense of the singular

power with which you have brought Mr. Moule's life and innermost
heart before all readers of that address.

'You will, I am sure, believe me when I say that I have been
frequently with you and your brothers in spirit during the last few
days. Though not, topographically, a parishioner of your father's I
virtually stood in that relation to him, and his home generally, during
many years of my life, and I always feel precisely as if I had been one.
I had many times resolved during the year or two before his death
to try to attend a service in the old Church in the old way before he
should be gone : but to-morrow, and to-morrow, and to-morrow!
— I never did.

'A day or two ago Matthew Arnold talked a good deal about him
to me : he was greatly struck with an imperfect description I gave
him (from what I had heard my father say) of the state of Fordington
50 years ago, and its state after the vicar had brought his energies to
bear upon the village for a few years. His words "energy is genius"
express your father very happily.

'Please give my kind remembrances to Mr. Charles Moule and
your other brothers who have not forgotten me — if they are with
you — and believe me,
                    'Sincerely yours,
                              'THOMAS HARDY.'

The first week in March the Hardys called by arrangement on
Mrs. Procter — the widow of 'Barry Cornwall' — at her flat in
Queen Anne's Mansions. Hardy had been asked to her house when
he first made her acquaintance before his marriage, and when her
husband was living, though bedridden : but being then, as always,
backward in seeking new friends, Hardy had never gone — to his
regret. He was evidently impressed newly by her on this call, as one
who was a remarkable link with the literary past, though she herself
was not a literary woman ; and the visit on this Sunday afternoon
was the first one of a long series of such, extending over many years
almost to her death, for she showed a great liking for Hardy and his
wife, and she always made them particularly welcome. It was here,
on these Sunday afternoons, that they used frequently to meet
Browning.

Hardy said after her death that on such occasions she sat in a fixed
attitude, almost as if placed in her seat like an unconscious image of
Buddha. Into her eyes and face would come continually an expression from a time fifty or sixty years before, when she was a handsome

coquette, a faint tendency to which would show even in old age in
the momentary archness of her glance now and then. 'You would
talk to her', he said, 'and believe you were talking to a person of the
same date as yourself, with recent emotions and impulses : you would
see her sideways when crossing the room to show you something,
and realize her, with sudden sadness, to be a withered woman whose
interests and emotions must be nearly extinct.'

Of the poets she had met she expressed herself to have been un-
attracted by Wordsworth's personality, but to have had a great liking
for Leigh Hunt. She remembered that the latter called one day,
bringing with him 'a youth whom nobody noticed much', and who
remained in the background, Hunt casually introducing him as 'Mr.
Keats'.

She would also tell of an experience she and her husband had,
shortly after their marriage, when they were living in fashionable
lodgings in Southampton Row. They went to see Lamb at Edmonton,
and caused him much embarrassment by a hint that she would like
to wash her hands, it being a hot day. He seemed bewildered and
asked stammeringly if she would mind washing them in the kitchen,
which she did.

A little later she wrote to Hardy concerning his short story *Fellow-
Townsmen*, which had lately come out in a periodical :

'You are cruel. Why not let him come home again and marry
his first love? But I see you are right. He should not have deserted
her. I smiled about the Tombstone. Sir Francis Chantrey told me
that he had prepared fine plans — nothing could be too beautiful
and too expensive at first, and the end was generally merely a headstone.'

It was in the same month, and in the company of Mrs. Procter,
that Hardy lunched at Tennyson's at a house Tennyson had temporarily taken in Belgrave Street; Mrs. Tennyson, though an invalid,
presiding at the table, at the end of which she reclined, and his friends
F. Locker, Countess Russell (Lord John's widow), Lady Agatha
Russell, and others, being present. 'When I arrived Mrs. Tennyson
was lying as if in a coffin, but she got up to welcome me.' Hardy
often said that he was surprised to find such an expression of humour
in the Poet-Laureate's face, the corners of his mouth twitching with
that mood when he talked ; 'it was a genial human face, which all
his portraits belied' ; and it was enhanced by a beard and hair
straggling like briars, a shirt with a large loose collar, and old steel
spectacles. He was very sociable that day, asking Mrs. Procter

absurd riddles, and telling Hardy amusing stories, and about mis-
prints in his books that drove him wild, one in especial of late, where
'airy does' had appeared as 'hairy does'. He said he liked *A Pair of
Blue Eyes* the best of Hardy's novels. Tennyson also told him that
he and his family were compelled to come to London for a month or
two every year, though he hated it, because they all 'got so rusty'
down in the Isle of Wight if they did not come at all. Hardy often
regretted that he never again went to see them, though warmly invited
that day both by Tennyson and his wife to pay them a visit at
Freshwater.

'*March* 24. Lunched with Mrs. Procter. She showed me one
of her late husband's love-letters, date 1824. Also a photo of Henry
James. She says he has made her an offer of marriage. Can it be
so?' Mrs. Procter was born in 1800.

At this time he writes down, 'A Hint for Reviewers — adapted
from Carlyle :

'Observe what is true, not what is false ; what is to be loved and
held fast, and earnestly laid to heart ; not what is to be contemned,
and derided, and sportfully cast out-of-doors.'

The Hardys' house at Upper Tooting stood in a rather elevated
position, and when the air was clear they could see a long way from
the top windows. The following note on London at dawn occurs
on May 19, a night on which he could not sleep, partly on account
of an eerie feeling which sometimes haunted him, a horror at lying
down in close proximity to 'a monster whose body had four million
heads and eight million eyes' :

'In upper back bedroom at daybreak : just past three. A golden
light behind the horizon ; within it are the Four Millions. The
roofs are damp gray : the streets are still filled with night as with a
dark stagnant flood whose surface brims to the tops of the houses.
Above the air is light. A fire or two glares within the mass. Behind
are the Highgate Hills. On the Crystal Palace hills in the other
direction a lamp is still burning up in the daylight. The lamps are
also still flickering in the street, and one policeman walks down it as
if it were noon.'

Two days later they were sitting in the chairs by Rotten Row
and the Park Drive, and the chief thing he noticed against the sun
in the west was that 'a sparrow descends from the tree amid the
stream of vehicles, and drinks from the little pool left by the watering-
cart' — the same sunlight causing 'a glitter from carriage-lamp
glasses, from Coachmen's and footmen's buttons, from silver carriage

handles and harness mountings, from a matron's bracelet, from four
parasols of four young ladies in a landau, their parasol-hems touching
like four mushrooms growing close together.'

On the 26th, the Derby Day, Hardy went alone to Epsom. On
his way he noticed that 'all the people going to the races have a
twinkle in their eye, particularly the old men'. He lunched there
with a friend, and together they proceeded, by permission, through
Lord Rosebery's grounds to the Down. They saw and examined
the favourite before he emerged — neither one of the twain knowing
anything of race-horses or betting — 'the jockeys in their great-
coats; little ghastly men looking half putrid, standing silent and
apathetic while their horses were rubbed down, and saddles adjusted';
till they passed on into the paddock, and the race was run, and the
shouts arose, and they 'were greeted by a breeze of tobacco-smoke
and orange-peels'.

During the summer he dined at clubs, etc., meeting again Lord
Houghton, Du Maurier, Henry Irving, and Alma-Tadema, among
others. Toole, who was at one of these dinners, imitated a number
of other actors, Irving included; and though the mimicry was funny
and good, 'ghostliness arose, in my mind at least, when after a few
living ones had been mimicked, each succeeding representation
turned out to be that of an actor then in his grave. "What did they
go dying for, stupids!" said somebody, when Toole's face suddenly
lost its smiling.'

In July he met Lord Houghton again at dinner, and was introduced by him to James Russell Lowell, who was also present. His
opinion of Lowell was that as a man he was charming, as a writer one
of extraordinary talent, but of no instinctive and creative genius.

In the same month he arranged with Messrs. Smith and Elder for
the three-volume publication of *The Trumpet-Major*, which had been
coming out in a periodical, and on the 27th started with Mrs. Hardy
for Boulogne, Amiens — 'the misfortune of the Cathedral is that it
does not look half so lofty as it really is' — and several towns in
Normandy, including Étretat, where they put up at the Hôtel Blan-
quet, and stayed some time, bathing every day — a recreation which
cost Hardy dear, for being fond of swimming he was apt to stay too
long in the water. Anyhow he blamed these frequent immersions
for starting the long illness from which he suffered the following
autumn and winter.

From Étretat they went to Havre, and here they had half an hour
of whimsical uneasiness. The hotel they chose was on the Quay,

one that had been recommended to Hardy by a stranger on the coach, and was old and gloomy in the extreme when they got inside. Mrs. Hardy fancied that the landlord's look was sinister; also the landlady's; and the waiter's manner seemed queer. Their room was hung with heavy dark velvet, and when the chambermaid came, and they talked to her, she sighed continually and spoke in a foreboding voice; as if she knew what was going to happen to them, and was on their side, but could do nothing. The floor of the bedroom was painted a bloody red, and the wall beside the bed was a little battered, as if struggles had taken place there. When they were left to themselves Hardy suddenly remembered that he had told the friendly stranger with whom he had travelled on the coach from Étretat, and who had recommended the inn, that he carried his money with him in Bank notes to save the trouble of circular notes. He had known it was a thing one never should do; yet he had done it.

They then began to search the room, found a small door behind the curtains of one of their beds, and on opening it there was revealed inside a closet of lumber, which had at its innermost recess another door, leading they did not know whither. With their luggage they barricaded the closet door, so jamming their trunks and portmanteau between the door and the nearest bedstead that it was impossible to open the closet. They lay down and waited, keeping the light burning a long time. Nothing happened, and they slept soundly at last, and awoke to a bright sunny morning.

*August* 5. They went on to Trouville, to the then fashionable Hôtel Bellevue, and thence to Honfleur, a place more to Hardy's mind, after the fast life of Trouville. On a gloomy gusty afternoon, going up the steep incline through the trees behind the town they came upon a Calvary tottering to its fall; and as it rocked in the wind like a ship's mast Hardy thought that the crudely painted figure of Christ upon it seemed to writhe and cry in the twilight: 'Yes, Yes! I agree that this travesty of me and my doctrines should totter and overturn in this modern world!' They hastened on from the strange and ghastly scene.

Thence they went to Lisieux and Caen, where they spent some days, returning to London by the way they had come.

Going down to Dorset in September, Hardy was informed of a curious bit of family history; that his mother's grandfather was a man who worried a good deal about the disposition of his property as he grew old. It was mostly in the form of long leasehold and lifehold houses, and he would call on his lawyer about once a fortnight to make some alteration in his will.  The lawyer lived at Bere Regis, and her grandfather used to talk the matter over with the man who was accustomed to drive him there and back — a connection of his by marriage.  Gradually this man so influenced the testator on each journey, by artfully playing on his nervous perplexities as they drove along, that he got three-quarters of the property, including the houses, bequeathed to himself.

The same month he replied to a letter from J. R. Lowell, then American Minister in London :

'DEAR MR. LOWELL :

'I have read with great interest the outline of the proposed Copyright treaty that you have communicated to me in your letter of the 16th.

'For my own part I should be quite ready to accept some such treaty — with a modification in detail mentioned below — since whatever may be one's opinion on an author's abstract right to manufacture his property in any country most convenient to him, the treaty would unquestionably remove the heaviest grievances complained of under the existing law.

'The modification I mention refers to the three-months term of grace to be allowed to foreign authors who do not choose to print in both countries simultaneously.

'If I clearly understand the provisions under this head it may happen that in the event of any difficulty about terms between the author and his foreign publishers the author would be bound to give way as the end of the three months approached, or lose all by lapse of copyright.  With some provision to meet such a contingency as this the treaty would seem to me satisfactory.'

Accompanying Mrs. Hardy on a day's shopping in October Hardy makes this remark on the saleswoman at a fashionable dressmaking establishment in Regent Street, from observing her while he sat waiting :

'She is a woman of somewhat striking appearance, tall, thin, decided ; one who knows what life is, and human nature, to plenitude. Hence she acts as by clockwork ; she puts each cloak on herself, turns round, makes a remark, puts on the next cloak, and the next, and so on, like an automaton.  She knows by heart every mood in which a feminine buyer of cloaks can possibly be, and has a machine-made answer promptly ready for each.'

On the 16th of October he and his wife paid a visit of a week to

Cambridge, in spirits that would have been considerably lower if they had known what was to befall them on their return. They received much hospitality, and were shown the usual buildings and other things worth seeing, though Cambridge was not new to Hardy. After the first day or two he felt an indescribable physical weariness, which was really the beginning of the long illness he was to endure; but he kept going.

Attending the 5 o'clock service at King's Chapel, he comments upon the architect 'who planned this glorious work of fine intelligence'; also upon Milton's 'dim religious light' beheld here, and the scene presented by the growing darkness as viewed from the stalls where they sat. 'The reds and the blues of the windows became of one indistinguishable black, the candles guttered in the most fantastic shapes I ever saw — and while the wicks burnt down these weird shapes changed form; so that you were fascinated into watching them, and wondering what shape those wisps of wax would take next, till they dropped off with a click during a silence. They were stalactites, plumes, laces; or rather they were surplices, — frayed shreds from those of bygone "white-robed scholars", or from their shrouds — dropping bit by bit in a ghostly decay. Wordsworth's ghost, too, seemed to haunt the place, lingering and wandering on somewhere alone in the fan-traceried vaulting.'

# PART III
# ILLNESS, NOVELS, AND ITALY

# CHAPTER XI

# A DIFFICULT PERIOD; AND A CHANGE

1880–1881 : *Aet.* 40–41

THEY returned to London on October the 23rd — the very day *The Trumpet-Major* was published, Hardy feeling by this time very unwell, so unwell that he had to write and postpone an engagement or two, and decline an invitation to Fryston by Lord Houghton. On the Sunday after he was worse, and seeing the name of a surgeon on a brass plate opposite his house, sent for him. The surgeon came at once, and came again on that and the two or three succeeding days ; he said that Hardy was bleeding internally. Mrs. Hardy, in her distress, called on their neighbours the Macmillans, to ask their opinion, and they immediately sent their own doctor. He agreed about the bleeding, said the case was serious ; and that the patient was not to get up on any account.

Later it was supposed that a dangerous operation would be necessary, till the doctor inquired how long Hardy could lie in bed — could he lie there, if necessary, for months? — in which case there possibly need be no operation.

Now he had already written the early chapters of a story for *Harper's Magazine* — *A Laodicean*, which was to begin in the (nominally) December number, issued in November. The first part was already printed, and Du Maurier was illustrating it. The story had to go on somehow, it happening, unfortunately, that the number containing it was the first number also of the publication of *Harper's* as an English and not exclusively American magazine as hitherto, and the success of its launch in London depended largely upon the serial tale. Its writer was, during the first few weeks, in considerable pain, and compelled to lie on an inclined plane with the lower part of his body higher than his head. Yet he felt determined to finish the novel, at whatever stress to himself — so as not to ruin the new venture of the publishers, and also in the interests of his wife, for whom as yet he had made but a poor provision in the event of his own decease. Accordingly from November onwards he began dictating it to her from the awkward position he occupied; and continued to do so — with greater ease as the pain and hæmorrhage went off. She worked bravely both at writing and nursing, till at the beginning of the following May a rough draft was finished by one shift and another.

'*November* 20. Freiherr von Tauchnitz Junior called.' This was probably about a Continental edition of *The Trumpet-Major*. But Hardy was still too ill to see him. *The Trumpet-Major*, however, duly appeared in the Tauchnitz series.

It is somewhat strange that at the end of November he makes a note of an intention to resume poetry as soon as possible. Having plenty of time to think he also projected as he lay what he calls a 'Great Modern Drama' — which seems to have been a considerable advance on his first conception, in June 1875, of a Napoleonic chronicle in ballad form — a sequence of such making a lyrical whole. Yet it does not appear to have been quite the same in detail as that of *The Dynasts* later on. He also made the following irrelative note of rather vague import:

'Discover for how many years, and on how many occasions, the organism, Society, has been standing, lying, etc., in varied positions, as if it were a tree or a man hit by vicissitudes.

'There would be found these periods:
1. Upright, normal or healthy periods.
2. Oblique or cramped periods.
3. Prostrate periods (intellect counterpoised by ignorance or narrowness, producing stagnation).
4. Drooping periods.
5. Inverted periods.'

George Eliot died during the winter in which he lay ill, and this set him thinking about Positivism, on which he remarks:

'If Comte had introduced Christ among the worthies in his calendar it would have made Positivism tolerable to thousands who, from position, family connection, or early education, now decry what in their heart of hearts they hold to contain the germs of a true system. It would have enabled them to modulate gently into the new religion by deceiving themselves with the sophistry that they still continued one-quarter Christians, or one-eighth, or one-twentieth, as the case might be: This as a matter of *policy*, without which no religion succeeds in making way.'

Also on literary criticism:

'Arnold is wrong about provincialism, if he means anything more than a provincialism of style and manner in exposition. A certain provincialism of feeling is invaluable. It is of the essence of individuality, and is largely made up of that crude enthusiasm without which no great thoughts are thought, no great deeds done.'

Some days later he writes :

'Romanticism will exist in human nature as long as human nature itself exists. The point is (in imaginative literature) to adopt that form of romanticism which is the mood of the age.'

Also on adversity — no doubt suggested by the distresses he was undergoing :

'There is mercy in troubles coming in battalions — they neutralize each other. Tell a man in prosperity that he must suffer the amputation of a limb, and it is a horror to him ; but tell him this the minute after he has been reduced to beggary and his only son has died : it hurts him but feebly.'

'*January* 1881. My third month in bed. Driving snow : fine, and so fast that individual flakes cannot be seen.' In sheltered places they occasionally stop, and balance themselves in the air like hawks. . . . It creeps into the house, the window-plants being covered as if out-of-doors. Our passage (downstairs) is sole-deep, Em says, and feet leave tracks on it.'

(Same month.) 'Style — Consider the Wordsworthian dictum (the more perfectly the natural object is reproduced, the more truly poetic the picture). This reproduction is achieved by seeing into the *heart of a thing* (as rain, wind, for instance), and is realism, in fact, though through being pursued by means of the imagination it is confounded with invention, which is pursued by the same means. It is, in short, reached by what M. Arnold calls "the imaginative reason".'

'*January* 30. Sunday. Dr. S. called as usual. I can by this time see all round his knowledge of my illness. He showed a lost manner on entering, as if among his many cases he had forgotten all about my case and me, which has to be revived in his mind by looking hard at me, when it all comes back.

'He told us of having been called in to an accident which, do the best he possibly could, would only end in discredit to him. A lady had fallen down, and so badly broken her wrist that it must always be deformed even after the most careful treatment. But, seeing the result, she would give him a bad name for want of skill in setting it. These cases often occur in a surgeon's practice, he says.'

'*January* 31. Incidents of lying in bed for months. Skin gets fair : corns take their leave : feet and toes grow shapely as those of a Greek statue. Keys get rusty ; watch dim, boots mildewed ; hat and clothes old-fashioned ; umbrella eaten out with rust ; children seen through the window are grown taller.'

'*February* 7. Carlyle died last Saturday. Both he and George Eliot have vanished into nescience while I have been lying here.'

'*February* 17. Conservatism is not estimable in itself, nor is Change, or Radicalism. To conserve the existing good, to supplant the existing bad by good, is to act on a true political principle, which is neither Conservative nor Radical.'

'*February* 21. A. G. called. Explained to Em about Aerostation, and how long her wings would have to be if she flew, — how light her weight, etc., and the process generally of turning her into a flying person.'

'*March* 22. Maggie Macmillan called. Sat with Em in my room — had tea. She and Em worked, watching the sun set gorgeously. That I should also be able to see it Miss Macmillan conceived the kind idea of reflecting the sun into my face by a looking-glass.' [The incident was made use of in *Jude the Obscure* as a plan adopted by Sue when the schoolmaster was ill.]

'*March* 27. A Homeric Ballad, in which Napoleon is a sort of Achilles, to be written.' [This entry, of a kind with earlier ones, is, however, superseded a few days later by the following :] 'Mode for a historical Drama. Action mostly automatic ; reflex movement, etc. Not the result of what is called *motive*, though always ostensibly so, even to the actors' own consciousness. Apply an enlargement of these theories to, say, "The Hundred Days"!'

This note is, apparently, Hardy's first written idea of a philosophic scheme or framework as the larger feature of *The Dynasts*, enclosing the historic scenes.

On the 10th of April he went outside the door again for the first time since that October afternoon of the previous year when he returned from Cambridge, driving out with his wife and the doctor. On the 19th occurred the death of Disraeli, whom Hardy had met twice, and found unexpectedly urbane. On Sunday the 1st of May he finished *A Laodicean* in pencil, and on the 3rd went with Mrs. Hardy by appointment to call on Sir Henry Thompson for a consultation.

'*May* 9. After infinite trying to reconcile a scientific view of life with the emotional and spiritual, so that they may not be interdestructive I come to the following :

'General Principles. Law has produced in man a child who cannot but constantly reproach its parent for doing much and yet not all, and constantly say to such parent that it would have been better never to have begun doing than to have *over*done so indecisively; that is, than to have created so far beyond all apparent first intention (on the emotional side), without mending matters by a second intent and execution, to eliminate the evils of the blunder of overdoing. The emotions have no place in a world of defect, and it is a cruel injustice that they should have developed in it.

'If Law itself had consciousness, how the aspect of its creatures would terrify it, fill it with remorse!'

Though he had been out in vehicles it was not till a day early in May, more than six months after he had taken to his bed, that he went forth on foot alone; and it being a warm and sunny morning he walked on Wandsworth Common, where, as he used to tell, standing still he repeated out loud to himself:

> See the wretch that long has tost
>     On the thorny bed of pain,
> At length repair his vigour lost,
>     And breathe and walk again:
>
> The meanest flowret of the vale,
> The simplest note that swells the gale,
> The common sun, the air, the skies,
> To him are opening Paradise.

Immediately on Hardy's recovery the question arose of whereabouts he and his wife should live. The three years' lease of the house at Upper Tooting had run out on the preceding Lady Day, when Hardy was too ill to change, and he had been obliged to apply for a three months' extension, which was granted. During the latter part of May they searched in Dorset, having concluded that it would be better to make London a place of sojourn for a few months only in each year, and establish their home in the country, both for reasons of health and for mental inspiration, Hardy finding, or thinking he found, that residence in or near a city tended to force mechanical and ordinary productions from his pen, concerning ordinary society-life and habits.

They found a little house called 'Llanherne' in the Avenue, Wimborne, that would at any rate suit them temporarily, and till they could discover a better, or perhaps build one. Hardy makes a note that on June 25 they slept at Llanherne for the first time, and saw the new comet from the conservatory. 'Our garden', he says a few days later, 'has all sorts of old-fashioned flowers, in full bloom : Canterbury Bells, blue and white, and Sweet Williams of every variety, strawberries and cherries that are ripe, currants and goose-berries that are almost ripe, peaches that are green, and apples that are decidedly immature.'

In July he jots down some notes on fiction, possibly for an article that was never written :

'The real, if unavowed, purpose of fiction is to give pleasure by gratifying the love of the uncommon in human experience, mental or corporeal.

'This is done all the more perfectly in proportion as the reader is illuded to believe the personages true and real like himself.

'Solely to this latter end a work of fiction should be a precise transcript of ordinary life : but,

'The uncommon would be absent and the interest lost.  Hence,

'The writer's problem is, how to strike the balance between the uncommon and the ordinary so as on the one hand to give interest, on the other to give reality.

'In working out this problem, human nature must never be made abnormal, which is introducing incredibility.  The uncommonness must be in the events, not in the characters ; and the writer's art lies in shaping that uncommonness while disguising its unlikelihood, if it be unlikely.'

On August 23rd Hardy and his wife left Wimborne for Scotland. Arriving at Edinburgh on the 24th, they discovered to their dismay that Queen Victoria was to review the Volunteers in that city on the very next day, and that they could get no lodging anywhere.  They took train to Roslin and put up at the Royal Hotel there.  At sight of the crowds in the city Hardy had made the entry : 'There are, then, some Scotch people who stay at home '.

The next day or two, though wet, they spent in viewing Roslin Castle and Chapel, and Hawthornden, the old man who showed them the castle saying that he remembered Sir Walter Scott.  Returning to Edinburgh, now calm and normal, they stayed there a few days, and at the beginning of September went on to Stirling, where they were laid up with colds.  They started again for Callander and the Tros-sachs, where Hardy made a sketch of Ben Venue, and followed the usual route across Loch Katrine, by coach to Inversnaid, down Loch Lomond, and so on to Glasgow.  On their way back they visited Windermere and Chester, returning through London to Wimborne.

During some sunny days in September Hardy corrected *A Laodicean* for the issue in volumes, sitting under the vine on their stable-wall, 'which for want of training hangs in long arms over my head nearly to the ground. The sun tries to shine through the great leaves, making a green light on the paper, the tendrils twisting in every direction, in gymnastic endeavours to find something to lay hold of.'

Though they had expected to feel lonely in Wimborne after London, they were visited by many casual friends, were called in to Shakespeare readings, then much in vogue, and had a genial neighbour in the county-court judge, Tindal-Atkinson, one of the last of the Serjeants-at-Law, who took care they should not mope if dinners and his and his daughter's music could prevent it. They kept in touch with London, however, and were there in the following December, where they met various friends, and Hardy did some business in arranging for the publication in the *Atlantic Monthly* of a novel that he was about to begin writing, called off-hand by the title of *Two on a Tower*, a title he afterwards disliked, though it was much imitated. An amusing experience of formality occurred to him in connection with this novel. It was necessary that he should examine an observatory, the story moving in an astronomical medium, and he applied to the Astronomer Royal for permission to see Greenwich. He was requested to state before it could be granted if his application was made for astronomical and scientific reasons or not. He therefore drew up a scientific letter, the gist of which was that he wished to ascertain if it would be possible for him to adapt an old tower, built in a plantation in the West of England for other objects, to the requirements of a telescopic study of the stars by a young man very ardent in that pursuit (this being the imagined situation in the proposed novel). An order to view Greenwich Observatory was promptly sent.

The year was wound up by Hardy and his wife at a ball at Lady Wimborne's, Canford Manor, where he met Sir Henry Layard. Lord Wimborne in a conversation about the house complained that it was rendered damp by the miller below penning the water for grinding, and, on Hardy's suggesting the removal of the mill, his host amused him by saying that was out of the question, because the miller paid him £50 a year in rent. However that might have been, Hardy felt glad the old mill was to remain, having as great a repugnance to pulling down a mill where (to use his own words) they ground food for the body, as to pulling down a church where they ground food for the soul.

Thus ended 1881 — with a much brighter atmosphere for the author and his wife than the opening had shown.

# CHAPTER XII

# WIMBORNE AND 'TWO ON A TOWER'

## 1882–1883 : *Aet.* 41–43

'*January* 26. Coleridge says, aim at *illusion* in audience or readers — *i.e.*, the mental state when dreaming, intermediate between complete *delusion* (which the French mistakenly aim at) and a clear perception of falsity.'

'*February* 4 and 11. Shakespeare readings at ——'s, "The Tempest" being the play chosen. The host was omnivorous of parts — absorbing other people's besides his own, and was greedily vexed when I read a line of his part by mistake. When I praise his reading he tells me meditatively, "Oh, yes ; I've given it a deal of study — thrown myself into the life of the character, you know ; thought of what my supposed parents were, and my early life". The firelight shone out as the day diminished, the young girl N.P. crouching on a footstool, the wealthy Mrs. B. impassive and grand in her unintelligence, like a Carthaginian statue. . . . The General reads with gingerly caution, telling me privately that he blurted out one of Shakespeare's improprieties last time before he was aware, and is in fear and trembling lest he may do it again.'

In this month's entries occurs another note which appears to be related to the philosophic scheme afterwards adopted as a framework for *The Dynasts* :

'*February* 16. Write a history of human automatism, or impulsion — viz., an account of human action in spite of human knowledge, showing how very far conduct lags behind the knowledge that should really guide it.'

A dramatization of *Far from the Madding Crowd*, prepared by Mr. J. Comyns Carr some months earlier, was produced during March at the Prince of Wales's Theatre, Liverpool, and Hardy and his wife took the trouble to make a trip to Liverpool to be present. The play, with Miss Marion Terry as the heroine, was not sufficiently near the novel to be to Hardy's liking, but it was well received, and was staged in London at the Globe Theatre in April, where it ran for many nights, but brought Hardy no profit, nor the adapter, as he was informed. During his stay in London he attended, on April 26, the funeral of Darwin in Westminster Abbey. As a young man he had been among the earliest acclaimers of *The Origin of Species*.

'*May* 13. The slow meditative lives of people who live in habitual solitude. . . . Solitude renders every trivial act of a solitary full of interest, as showing thoughts that cannot be expressed for want of an interlocutor.'

'*June* 3. . . . As, in looking at a carpet, by following one colour a certain pattern is suggested, by following another colour, another; so in life the seer should watch that pattern among general things which his idiosyncrasy moves him to observe, and describe that alone. This is, quite accurately, a going to Nature; yet the result is no mere photograph, but purely the product of the writer's own mind.'

'*June* 18. M. F., son of Parson F., was well known by sight to my mother in her childhood. He had taken his degree and had been ordained. But he drank. He worked with the labourers and "yarn-barton-wenches" (as they were called in the village) in the yarn-barton. After a rollick as they worked he would suddenly stop, down his implement, and mounting a log or trestle, preach an excellent sermon to them; then go on cursing and swearing as before. He wore faded black clothes, and had an allowance of some small sum from his family, to which he liked to add a little by manual labour. He was a tall, upright, dignified man. She did not know what became of him.'

'*August.* — An ample theme : the intense interests, passions, and strategy that throb through the commonest lives.

'This month blackbirds and thrushes creep about under fruit-bushes and in other shady places in gardens rather like four-legged animals than birds. . . . I notice that a blackbird has eaten nearly a whole pear lying in the garden-path in the course of the day.'

'*September* 9. Dr. and Mrs. Brine . . . came to tea. Brine says that Jack White's gibbet (near Wincanton) was standing as late as 1835 — *i.e.* the oak-post with the iron arm sticking out, and a portion of the cage in which the body had formerly hung. It would have been standing now if some young men had not burnt it down by piling faggots round it one fifth of November.'

Later in the month he went with Mrs. Hardy on a small circular tour in the adjoining counties — taking in Salisbury, Axminster, Lyme Regis, Charmouth, Bridport, Dorchester, and back to Wimborne.

From Axminster to Lyme the journey on the coach was spoilt for them by the condition of one of the horses.

'The off-horse was weak and worn. "O yes, tender on his vore veet", said the driver with nonchalance. The coach itself weighed a ton. The horse swayed, leant against the pole, then outwards. His head hung like his tail. The straps and brass rings of the harness seemed barbarously harsh on his shrinking skin. E., with her admirable courage, would have interfered, at the cost of walking the rest of the distance: then we felt helpless against the anger of the other passengers who wanted to get on.' They were, in fact, on the tableland half-way between the two towns. But they complained when they alighted — with what effect Hardy could not remember.

At Lyme they 'met a cheerful man who had turned his trousers hind part before, because the knees had worn through'.

On The Cobb they encountered an old man who had undergone an operation for cataract:

'It was like a red-hot needle in yer eye whilst he was doing it. But he wasn't long about it. Oh no. If he had been long I couldn't ha' beared it. He wasn't a minute more than three-quarters of an hour at the outside. When he had done one eye, 'a said, "Now my man, you must make shift with that one, and be thankful you bain't left wi' narn." So he didn't do the other. And I'm glad 'a didn't. I've saved half-crowns and half-crowns out of number in only wanting one glass to my spectacles. T'other eye would never have paid the expenses of keeping en going.'

From Charmouth they came to Bridport on the box of a coach better horsed, and driven by a merry coachmen, 'who wore a lavish quantity of wool in his ears, and in smiling checked his smile in the centre of his mouth by closing his lips, letting it continue at the corners'. (A sketch of the coachman's mouth in the act of smiling was attached to illustrate this.)

Before returning to Wimborne Hardy called on the poet Barnes at Came Rectory. Mr. Barnes told him of an old woman who had asked him to explain a picture she possessed. He told her it was the family of Darius at the feet of Alexander. She shook her head, and said: 'But that's not in the Bible', looking up and down his clerical attire as if she thought him a wicked old man who disgraced his cloth by speaking of profane history.

This autumn *Two on a Tower*, which was ending its career in the *Atlantic Monthly*, came out in three volumes, and at the beginning of October its author and his wife started for Cherbourg *via* Weymouth, and onward to Paris, where they took a little *appartement* of two bedrooms and a sitting room, near the left bank of the Seine. Here they stayed for some weeks, away from English and American tourists, roving about the city and to Versailles, studying the pictures at the Louvre and the Luxembourg, practising housekeeping in the Parisian bourgeois manner, buying their own groceries and vegetables, dining at restaurants, and catching bad colds owing to the uncertain weather. He seems to have done little in the French capital besides these things, making only one memorandum beyond personal trifles, expenses, and a few picture notes :

'Since I discovered, several years ago, that I was living in a world where nothing bears out in practice what it promises incipiently, I have troubled myself very little about theories. . . . Where development according to perfect reason is limited to the narrow region of pure mathematics, I am content with tentativeness from day to day.'

At the end of the autumn Mrs. Hardy received news at Wimborne of the death of her brother-in-law, the Rev. C. Holder, at St. Juliot Rectory, Cornwall, of which he had long been the incumbent ; and they realized that the scene of the fairest romance of their lives, in the picturesque land of Lyonnesse, would have no more kinship with them. By this loss Hardy was reminded of the genial and genuine humour of his clerical relative and friend despite his fragility and ill-health ; of his qualities ; among them, of a mysterious power he had (as it seemed to his brother-in-law) of counting his congregation to a man before he had got half a dozen lines down the page in 'Dearly beloved brethren' ; and of his many strange and amusing stories of his experiences, such as that of the sick man to whose bedside he was called to read a chapter in the Bible, and who said when it was ended that it did him almost as much good as a glass of gin-and-water : or of the astonishing entry in the marriage register of Holder's parish before he was rector, by which the bridegroom and bridesmaid had made themselves husband and wife, and the bride and best man the witnesses. Hardy himself had seen the entry.

Of another cast was the following. Holder as a young man was a curate in Bristol during the terrible cholera visitation. He related that one day at a friend's house he met a charming young widow, who invited him to call on her. With pleasant anticipations he went at tea-time a day or two later, and duly inquired if she was at home. The servant said with a strange face : 'Why, Sir, you buried her this morning!' He found that amongst the many funerals of cholera victims he had conducted that day, as on every day, hers had been one.

At another of these funerals the clerk or sexton rushed to him immediately before the procession arrived to ask him to come and look at the just opened grave, which was of brick, with room for two or more, the first place being occupied by the coffin of the deceased person's husband, who had died three weeks before. The coffin was overturned into the space beside it. Holder hastily told the sexton to turn it back into its place, and say nothing, to avoid distressing the relatives by the obvious inference.

He also remembered a singular alarm to which he had once been subjected. He was roused one night by a voice calling from below, 'Holder, Holder! Can you help me?' It was the voice of a neighbouring incumbent named Woodman, and wondering what terrible thing had happened he rushed downstairs as soon as he could, seizing a heavy stick on the way. He found his neighbour in great agitation, who explained that the news had come late the previous evening that a certain noble lord the patron, who was a great critic of sermons, had arrived in the parish, and was going to attend next morning's service. 'Have you a sermon that will do? I have nothing — nothing!' The conjuncture had so preyed upon his friend's nerves during the night that he had not been able to resist getting up and coming. Holder found something he thought might suit the noble critic, and Woodman departed with it under his arm, much relieved.

Some of Holder's stories to him were, as Hardy guessed, rather well-found than well-founded, but they were always told with much solemnity. Yet he would sometimes recount one 'the truth of which he could not quite guarantee'. It was what had been related to him by some of his aged parishioners concerning an incumbent of that or an adjacent living many years before. This worthy ecclesiastic was a bachelor addicted to drinking habits, and one night when riding up Boscastle Hill fell off his horse. He lay a few minutes in the road, when he said 'Help me up, Jolly!' and a local man who was returning home behind him saw a dark figure with a cloven foot emerge from the fence, and toss him upon his horse in a jiffy. The end of him was that on one night of terrific lightning and thunder he was missed, and was found to have entirely disappeared.

Holder had kept up a friendly acquaintance with Hawker of Morwenstow, who predeceased him by seven years, though the broad and tolerant views of the rector of St. Juliot did not quite chime in with the poet-vicar's precisianism; and the twenty miles of wild Cornish coast that separated their livings was a heavy bit of road for

the rector's stout cob to traverse both ways in a day. Hardy regretted the loss of his relative, and was reminded sadly of the pleasure
he used to find in reading the lessons in the ancient church when
his brother-in-law was not in vigour. The poem 'Quid hic agis?'
in *Moments of Vision* is in part apparently a reminiscence of these
readings.

In December Hardy was told a story by a Mrs. Cross, a very old
country-woman he met, of a girl she had known who had been betrayed and deserted by a lover. She kept her child by her own exertions, and lived bravely and throve. After a time the man returned
poorer than she, and wanted to marry her; but she refused. He
ultimately went into the Union workhouse. The young woman's
conduct in not caring to be 'made respectable' won the novelist-
poet's admiration, and he wished to know her name; but the old
narrator said, 'Oh, never mind their names! they be dead and rotted
by now'.

The eminently modern idea embodied in this example — of a
woman's not becoming necessarily the chattel and slave of her seducer
— impressed Hardy as being one of the first glimmers of woman's
enfranchisement; and he made use of it in succeeding years in more
than one case in his fiction and verse.

In the same month the Hardys attended Ambulance-Society
lectures — First-Aid teaching being in fashion just then. He makes
a note concerning a particular lecture:

'A skeleton — the one used in these lectures — is hung up inside
the window. We face it as we sit. Outside the band is playing, and
the children are dancing. I can see their little figures through the
window past the skeleton dangling in front.'

Another note — this on the wintry weather:

'Heard of an open cart being driven through the freezing rain.
The people in it became literally packed in ice; the men's beards and
hair were hung with icicles. Getting one of the men into the house
was like bringing in a chandelier of lustres.'

In the same month he replied as follows to a question asked him
by letter:

'To A. A. Reade, Esq.
'DEAR SIR,

'I can say that I have never found alcohol helpful to literary production in any degree. My experience goes to prove that the effect
of wine, taken as a preliminary to imaginative work, as it is called,

is to blind the writer to the quality of what he produces rather than to raise its quality.

'When walking much out of doors, and particularly when on Continental rambles, I occasionally drink a glass or two of claret or mild ale. The German beers seem really beneficial at these times of exertion, which (as wine seems otherwise) may be owing to some alimentary qualities they possess apart from their stimulating property. With these rare exceptions I have taken no alcoholic liquor for the last two years.
'Yours truly,
'T. HARDY.'

'*February* 25, 1883. Sent a short hastily written novel to the *Graphic* for Summer Number.' [It was *The Romantic Adventures of a Milkmaid.*]

'*February* 28. Walked with Walter Fletcher (County Surveyor) to Corfe Mullen. He says that the scene of the auction of turnpike tolls used to be curious. It was held at an inn, and at one end of the room would be the auctioneer and trustees, at the other a crowd of strange beings, looking as not worth sixpence among them. Yet the biddings for the Poole Trust would sometimes reach £1400. Sometimes the bidders would say, "Beg yer pardon, gentlemen, but will you wait to let us step outside a minute or two?" Perhaps the trustees would say they could not. The men would say, "then we'll step out without your letting us". On their return only one or two would bid, and the peremptory trustees be nettled.

'Passed a lonely old house formerly an inn. The road-contractor now living there showed us into the stable, and drew our attention to the furthest stall. When the place was an inn, he said, it was the haunt of smugglers, and in a quarrel there one night a man was killed in that stall. If an old horse is put there on certain nights, at about two in the morning (when the smuggler died) the horse cries like a child, and on entering you find him in a lather of sweat.

'The huge chestnut tree which stood in front of this melancholy house is dead, but the trunk is left standing. In it are still the hooks to which horses were fastened by the reins while their owners were inside.'

'*March* 13. M. writes to me that when a farmer at Puddlehinton who did not want rain found that a neighbouring farmer had sent to the parson to pray for it, and it had come, he went and abused the other farmer, and told him 'twas a very dirty trick of his to catch God A'mighty unawares, and he ought to be ashamed of it.

'Our servant Ann brings us a report, which has been verified, that the carpenter who made a coffin for Mr. W. who died the other day, made it too short. A bystander said satirically, "Anybody would think you'd made it for yourself, John!" (the carpenter was a short man). The maker said, "Ah — they would!" and fell dead instantly.'

In reply to a letter from Miss Mary Christie :

'WIMBORNE, *April* 11, 1883.

'DEAR MADAM,

'I have read with great interest the account of your scheme for encouraging a feeling for art in National schools, and if my name be of any service in support of the general proposition, I willingly consent to your using it. As to the details of such a scheme, my views differ somewhat from your own. For instance, I think for children between 9 and 12 or 13 — the great mass of those in elementary schools — fairly good engravings, such as those in the *Graphic*, *Illustrated News*, etc., (not the coloured pictures) to be as conducive to the end desired as more finished pictures and photographs. A child's imagination is so powerful that it only requires the idea to set it to work : and hence a dozen suggestions of scenes and persons by as many prints would seem to me to be of more value to him or her than the perfect representation of one, — while the latter would cost as much as the former. This, however, is altogether a secondary point, and I daresay that if we were to talk over the subject we should soon be quite at one about it. . . .'

Hardy and his wife were in London off and on during May and June, seeing pictures, plays, and friends. At a lunch at Lord Houghton's, who with his sister Lady Galway had taken a small house off Park Lane for this season, Hardy met Robert Browning again, Rhoda Broughton for the first time, and several others, including Mrs. —— from America, 'a large-eyed lady-owner of ten serial publications, which, she told me, she called her ten children. Also Lady C. who talked to me about Rabelais — without knowledge obviously — having heard that I belonged to the Rabelais Club. She said she meant to read him through. She had read one chapter, but couldn't get on with the old French, so was looking for a literal translation. Heaven bless her reading!

'Houghton, seeing Browning about to introduce me to Rhoda Broughton, hastened forward before Browning, and emphatically introduced us with the manner of a man who means to see things properly done in his own house ; then walked round, pleased with himself as the company dropped in ; like one who, having set a machinery in motion, has now only to wait and observe how it goes.'

'*June* 24. Sunday. Went in the afternoon to see Mrs. Procter at Albert Hall Mansions. Found Browning present. He told me that Mrs. ——, whom he and I had met at Lord Houghton's, had made £200,000 by publishing pirated works of authors who had made comparatively nothing. Presently Mrs. Sutherland Orr and Mrs. Frank Hill (*Daily News*) came in. Also two Jewesses — the Misses Lazarus — from America. Browning tried the elder with Hebrew, and she appeared to understand so well that he said he perceived she knew the tongue better than he. When these had gone George Smith [the publisher] called. He and Mrs. Procter declared that there was something tender between Mrs. Orr and Browning. "Why don't they settle it!" said Mrs. P.

'In the evening went to the Irving dinner. Sir Frederick Pollock, who took the chair, and made a speech, said that the departure of Irving for America would be a loss that would eclipse the gaiety of nations (!) Irving in his reply said that in the twenty-seven years he had been on the stage he had enacted 650 different characters.'

'*June* 25. Dined at the Savile with Gosse. Met W. D. Howells of New York there. He told me a story of Emerson's loss of memory. At the funeral of Longfellow he had to make a speech. "The brightness and beauty of soul", he began, "of him we have lost, has been acknowledged wherever the English language is spoken. I've known him these forty years ; and no American, whatever may be his opinions, will deny that in — in — in — I can't remember the gentleman's name — beat the heart of a true poet."

'Howells said that Mark Twain usually makes a good speech. But once he heard him fail. In his speech he was telling a story of an occasion when he was in some western city, and found that some impostors personating Longfèllow, Emerson, and others had been there. Mark began to describe these impostors, and while doing it found that Longfellow, Emerson, etc., were present, listening, and, from a titter or two, found also that his satirical description of the impostors was becoming regarded as an oblique satirical description of the originals. He was overspread by a sudden cold chill, and struggled to a lame ending. He was so convinced that he had given offence that he wrote to Emerson and Longfellow, apologizing. Emerson could not understand the letter, his memory of the incident having failed him, and wrote to Mark asking what it meant. Then Mark had to tell him what he wished he had never uttered ; and altogether the fiasco was complete.'

CHAPTER XIII

# THE COUNTY TOWN

1883–1885 : *Aet.* 43–45

IN this month of June the Hardys removed from Wimborne to
Dorchester, which town and its neighbourhood, though they did
not foresee it, was to be their country-quarters for the remainder of
their lives. But several months of each spring and summer were to
be spent in London during the ensuing twenty years, and occasionally
spells abroad. This removal to the county town, and later to a spot
a little outside it, was a step they often regretted having taken ; but
the bracing air brought them health and renewed vigour, and in the
long run it proved not ill-advised.

'*July* 19. In future I am not going to praise things because the
accumulated remarks of ages say they are great and good, if those
accumulated remarks are not based on observation. And I am not
going to condemn things because a pile of accepted views raked
together from tradition, and acquired by instillation, say antecedently
that they are bad.'

'*July* 22. To Winterborne-Came Church with Gosse, to hear
and see the poet Barnes. Stayed for sermon. Barnes, knowing we
should be on the watch for a prepared sermon, addressed it entirely
to his own flock, almost pointedly excluding us. Afterwards walked
to the rectory and looked at his pictures.

'Poetry versus reason : *e.g.*, A band plays "God save the
Queen", and being musical the uncompromising Republican joins
in the harmony : a hymn rolls from a church-window, and the
uncompromising No-God-ist or Unconscious God-ist takes up the
refrain.'

Mr. T. W. H. Tolbort, a friend of Hardy's from youth, and a
pupil of Barnes's, who years earlier had come out at the top in the
Indian Civil Service examination, died at the beginning of the
next month, after a bright and promising career in India, and Hardy
wrote an obituary notice of him in the *Dorset Chronicle*. The only

note Hardy makes on him in addition to the printed account is as follows :

'*August* 13. Tolbort lived and studied as if everything in the world were so very much worth while. But what a bright mind has gone out at one-and-forty!'

He writes elsewhere of an anecdote told him by Barnes touching his tuition of Tolbort. Barnes had relinquished his school and retired to the country rectory in which he ended his days, when Tolbort's name, and Barnes's as his schoolmaster, appeared in *The Times* at the head of the Indian examination list, a wide proportion of marks separating it from the name following. It was in the early days when these lists excited great interest. In a few mornings Barnes was deluged with letters from all parts of the country requesting him at almost any price to take innumerable sons, and produce upon them the same successful effect. 'I told them that it took two to do it', he would say, adding sadly that a popularity which would have been invaluable during the hard-working years of his life came at almost the first moment when it was no longer of use to him.

In this month of August he made a memorandum on another matter :

'Write a list of things which everybody thinks and nobody says ; and a list of things that everybody says and nobody thinks.'

At this time too Hardy encountered an old man named P——, whose father, or grandfather, had been one of the keepers of the Rainbarrows' Beacon, 1800–1815, as described in *The Dynasts*, the remains of whose hut are still to be seen on the spot. It may be interesting to mention that the daughter of a travelling waxwork proprietor had some years before, when exhibiting at Puddletown, entirely lost her heart to P——'s brother, a handsome young labourer of the village, and he had married her. As her father grew old and infirm the son-in-law and his wife succeeded to the showman's business and carried it on successfully. They were a worthy and happy couple, and whenever in their rounds they came to P——'s native village the husband's old acquaintance were admitted gratis to the exhibition, which was of a highly moral and religious cast, including Solomon's Judgment, and Daniel in the Den of Lions, where the lions moved their heads, tails, eyes, and paws terrifically, while Daniel lifted his hands in prayer. Heads of murderers were ranged on the other side, as a wholesome lesson to evildoers. Hardy duly attended the show because the man's forefather had kept Rainbarrows' Beacon (described in *The Dynasts*) ; and the last he saw of old P—— was in the private tent attached to the exhibition, where he was sitting as a glorified figure drinking gin-and-water with his relatives.

Not having been able when he came to Dorchester to find a house to suit him, Hardy had obtained a plot of land of the Duchy of Cornwall in Fordington Field, about a mile into the country, on which to build one; and at the beginning of October marked out as a preliminary the spot where the well was to be sunk. The only drawback to the site seemed to him to be its newness. But before the well-diggers had got deeper than three feet they came upon Romano-British urns and skeletons. Hardy and his wife found the spot was steeped in antiquity, and thought the omens gloomy; but they did not prove so, the extreme age of the relics dissipating any sense of gruesomeness. More of the sort were found in digging the house-foundations, and Hardy wrote an account of the remains, which he read at the Dorchester Meeting of the Dorset Field Club, 1884. It was printed in the 'Proceedings' of the Club in 1890.

'*November* 3. *The Athenæum* says: "The glass-stainer maintains his existence at the sacrifice of everything the painter holds dear. In place of the freedom and sweet abandonment which is nature's own charm and which the painter can achieve, the glass-stainer gives us splendour as luminous as that of the rainbow . . . in patches, and stripes, and bars." The above canons are interesting in their conveyance of a half truth. All art is only approximative — not exact, as the reviewer thinks; and hence the methods of all art differ from that of the glass-stainer but in degree.'

'*November* 17. Poem. We [human beings] have reached a degree of intelligence which Nature never contemplated when framing her laws, and for which she consequently has provided no adequate satisfactions.' [This, which he had adumbrated before, was clearly the germ of the poem entitled 'The Mother Mourns' and others.]

'*December* 23. There is what we used to call "The Birds' Bedroom" in the plantation at Bockhampton. Some large hollies grow among leafless ash, oak, birch, etc. At this time of year the birds select the hollies for roosting in, and at dusk noises not unlike the creaking of withy-chairs arise, with a busy rustling as of people going to bed in a lodging-house; accompanied by sundry shakings, adjustings, and pattings, as if they were making their beds vigorously before turning in.

'Death of old Billy C—— at a great age. He used to talk enthusiastically of Lady Susan O'Brien [the daughter of Lord Ilchester, who excited London by eloping with O'Brien the actor, as so inimitably described in Walpole's *Letters*, and who afterwards settled in the Hardys' parish as before mentioned]. — "She kept a splendid house — a cellarful of home-brewed strong beer that would a'most knock you down; everybody drank as much as he liked. The head-gardener [whom Billy as a youth assisted] was drunk every morning before breakfast. There are no such houses now! On wet days we used to make a point of working opposite the drawing-room window, that she might pity us. She would send out and tell us to go indoors, and not expose ourselves to the weather so reckless."' [A kind-hearted woman, Lady Susan.]

On the eve of the New Year 1884 Hardy planted some trees on his new property at Max Gate, Dorchester, and passed part of the January following in London, where he saw Henry James, Gosse, and Thornycroft, and talked to Alma-Tadema about the Anglo-Roman remains he was finding on the site of his proposed house, over which discovery Tadema was much excited, as he was painting, or about to paint, a picture expressing the art of that date.

'*February*. "Ye shall weep and mourn, and the world shall rejoice." Such shows the natural limitation of the Christian view when the Christians were a small and despised community. The widened view of nowadays perceives that the world weeps and mourns all round. — Nevertheless, if "the world" denotes the brutal and thoughtless merely, the text is eternally true.'

'James S—— [the quaint old man already mentioned, who worked forty years for Hardy's father, and had been a smuggler], once heard a hurdlemaker bet at the "Black Dog", Broadmayne, that he would make a hurdle sooner than the other man (not a hurdler) could pull one to pieces. They put it to the test, and the hurdlemaker won the stakes.

'When trees and underwood are cut down, and the ground bared, three crops of flowers follow. First a sheet of yellow; they are primroses. Then a sheet of blue; they are wild hyacinths, or as we call them, graegles. Then a sheet of red; they are ragged robins, or as they are called here, robin-hoods. What have these plants been doing through the scores of years before the trees were felled, and how did they come there?'

'*March*. Write a novel entitled *Time against Two*, in which the antagonism of the parents of a Romeo and Juliet *does* succeed in separating the couple and stamping out their love, — alas, a more probable development than the other!' [The idea is briefly used in *The Well-Beloved*.]

*March* or *April*. 'Every error under the sun seems to arise from thinking that you are right yourself because you *are* yourself, and other people wrong because they are not you.

'It is now spring; when, according to the poets, birds pipe, and (the householder adds) day-labourers get independent after their preternatural civility through the frost and snow.'

'*April* 26. Curious scene. A fine poem in it :

'Four girls — itinerant musicians — sisters, have been playing opposite Parmiter's in the High Street. The eldest had a fixed, old, hard face, and wore white roses in her hat. Her eyes remained on one close object, such as the buttons of her sister's dress; she played the violin. The next sister, with red roses in her hat, had rather bold dark eyes, and a coquettish smirk. She too played a violin. The next, with her hair in ringlets, beat the tambourine. The youngest, a mere child, dinged the triangle. She wore a bead necklace. All wore large brass earrings like Jews'-harps, which dangled to the time of the jig.

'I saw them again in the evening, the silvery gleams from Saunders's [silver-smith's] shop shining out upon them. They were now sublimed to a wondrous charm. The hard face of the eldest was flooded with soft solicitous thought; the coquettish one was no longer bold but archly tender; her dirty white roses were pure as snow; her sister's red ones a fine crimson : the brass earrings were golden; the iron triangle silver; the tambourine Miriam's own; the third child's face that of an angel; the fourth that of a cherub. The pretty one smiled on the second, and began to play 'In the gloaming', the little voices singing it. *Now* they were what Nature made them, before the smear of "civilization" had sullied their existences.' [An impression of a somewhat similar scene is given in the poem entitled 'Music in a Snowy Street'.]

'Rural low life may reveal coarseness of considerable leaven; but that libidinousness which makes the scum of cities so noxious is not usually there.'

'*June* 2. At Bockhampton. My birthday — 44. Alone in the plantation, at 9 o'clock. A weird hour : strange faces and figures formed by dying lights. Holm leaves shine like human eyes, and the sky glimpses between the trunks are like white phantoms and cloven tongues. It is so silent and still that a footstep on the dead leaves could be heard a quarter of a mile off. Squirrels run up the trunks in fear, stamping and crying "chut-chut-chut!"' [There is not a single squirrel in that plantation now.]

The following letter was written to Hardy on his birthday :

'BURFORD BRIDGE,
'BOX HILL,
'*June* 2, 1884.

'What a good day this was for Anne Benson Procter, when Thomas Hardy was born! She little knew what stores of delightful reading she would owe to the Baby of 1840.

'If she could write an Ode — or, even worse, a Sonnet!

'He has something to be thankful for. He *must* have read the verses — and he is so good and kind that he would have praised them.

'We go home on Wednesday next, having been here for ten days — sitting by the fire, for the summer comes slowly up this way.

'Your old admirer,

'ANNE B. PROCTER.'

'*June* 3. The leaves are approaching their finished summer shape, the evergreens wear new pale suits over the old deep attire. I watered the thirsty earth at Max Gate, which drank in the liquid with a swallowing noise. In the evening I entered Tayleure's Circus in Fordington Field for a short time during the performance. There is a dim haze in the tent, and the green grass in the middle, within the circular horse-track, looks amazingly fresh in the artificial light. The damp orbits of the spectators' eyes gleam in its rays. The clowns, when "off", lounge and smoke cigarettes, and chat with serious cynicism, and as if the necessity of their occupation to society at large were not to be questioned, their true domestic expression being visible under the official expression given by the paint. This sub-expression is one of good-humoured pain.'

Hardy seems to have had something of a craze for circuses in these years, and went to all that came to Dorchester. In one performance the equestrienne who leapt through hoops on her circuit missed her footing and fell with a thud on the turf. He followed her into the dressing-tent, and became deeply interested in her recovery. The incident seems to have some bearing on the verses of many years after entitled 'Circus-Rider to Ringmaster'.

They were in London part of June and July, and among other places went to an evening party at Alma-Tadema's, meeting an artistic crowd which included Burne-Jones ; and to another at Mrs.

Murray Smith's with Mrs. Procter, where they met again Matthew
Arnold, whom Hardy liked better now than he did at their first
meeting; also Du Maurier; also Henry James 'with his nebulous
gaze'. Mrs. Procter, though so old, 'swam about through the crowd
like a swan'.

Of Madame Judic's acting in *Niniche*, Hardy says, 'This woman
has genius. The picture of the pair of them — Judic and Lassouche
— putting their faces side by side and bumping each other in making
love, was the most comic phase of real art I ever saw. . . . And
yet the world calls —— a great actress.'

'*July* 14. Assizes. Dorchester — The Lord Chief Justice,
eminent counsel, etc., reveal more of their weaknesses and vanities
here in the country than in London. Their foibles expand, being
off their guard. A shabby lad on trial for setting fire to a common,
holds an amusingly familiar conversation with the C. J. (Coleridge)
when asked if he has anything to say. Witnesses always begin their
evidence in sentences containing ornamental words, evidently prepared beforehand, but when they get into the thick of it this breaks
down to struggling grammar and lamentably jumbled narrative.'

'*August* 14. Strolling players at Dorchester in the market-field.
Went to *Othello*. A vermilion sunset fell on the west end of the booth,
where, while the audience assembled, Cassio, in supposed Venetian
costume, was lounging and smoking in the red light at the bottom of
the van-steps behind the theatre : Othello also lounging in the same
sunlight on the grass by the stage door, and touching up the black
of his face.

'The play begins as the dusk comes on, the theatre-lights within
throwing the spectators' and the actors' profiles on the canvas, so
that they are visible outside, and the immortal words spread through
it into the silence around, and to the trees, and stars.

'I enter. A woman plays Montano, and her fencing with Cassio
leaves much to the imagination. Desdemona's face still retains its
anxiety about the supper that she had been cooking a few minutes
earlier in the stove without.

'Othello is played by the proprietor, and his speeches can be
heard as far as to the town-pump. Emilia wears the earrings I saw
her wearing when buying the family vegetables this morning. The
tragedy goes on successfully, till the audience laughs at the beginning
of the murder scene. Othello stops, and turning, says sternly to
them after an awful pause : "Is this the Nineteenth Century?" The
conscience-stricken audience feel the justice of the reproof, and

preserve an abashed silence as he resumes.  When he comes to the pillow-scene they applaud with tragic vehemence, to show that their hearts are in the right place after all.'

*August* 16.  Hardy took a trip to the Channel Islands from Weymouth with his brother.  They went to Guernsey, Jersey, and Sark ; and at one of the hotels found that every man there except themselves was a commercial traveller.  As they seemed so lonely they were allowed to dine with these gentlemen, and became very friendly with them.  Manners at the dinner-table were highly ceremonious : 'Can I send you a cut of this boiled mutton, Mr. President?' 'No, thank you, Mr. Vice.  May I help you to beef?' At the end of dinner : 'Gentlemen, you can leave the table.'  Chorus of diners : 'Thank you, Mr. President.'

Conversation turned on a certain town in England, and it was defined as being a 'warm place'.  Hardy, who had lived there, was puzzled, and said he had not noticed that it was particularly warm. The speaker scarcely condescended to reply that he did not understand the meaning they attached to the word.

Off and on he was now writing *The Mayor of Casterbridge* ; but before leaving London he agreed with the Macmillans to take in hand later a story of twelve numbers for their magazine, no time being fixed.  It came out two years later under the title of *The Woodlanders*.

'*October* 20.  Query : Is not the present quasi-scientific system of writing history mere charlatanism?  Events and tendencies are traced as if they were rivers of voluntary activity, and courses reasoned out from the circumstances in which natures, religions, or what-not, have found themselves.  But are they not in the main the outcome of *passivity* — acted upon by unconscious propensity?'

'*November* 16.  My sister Mary says that women of the past generation have faces now out of fashion.  Face-expressions have their fashions like clothes.'

During the general election about this time Mr. John Morley wrote to Hardy from Newcastle :

'Your letter recalls literature, art, and sober reason — visitants as welcome as they are rare in the heats of electioneering.'  And a few days later he heard from Professor Beesly, who had been beaten at the Westminster poll : 'I suppose there is not a more hopeless seat in England.  We might have made head against its Toryism alone, or the clergy, or the Baroness's legitimate influence from her almsgiving of old date there (it being her special preserve), or the special tap of philanthropy turned on for the occasion.  But all united were much too strong for us. . . . I return to my work in much contentment.'

Leslie Stephen (like Hardy himself, quite outside politics) wrote the same week : 'I am glad to have got that book off my hands, though any vacuum in my occupations is very soon filled up (not that *my* nature abhors it!) and though in many ways I am very ill-satisfied with the result. However I meant well, and I can now begin to forget it.'

'*December* 4. A gusty wind makes the raindrops hit the windows in stars, and the sunshine flaps open and shut like a fan, flinging into the room a tin-coloured light. . . .

'Conjuror Mynterne [of whom mention has already been made], when consulted by Patt P—— (a strapping handsome woman), told her that her husband would die on a certain day, and showed her the funeral in a glass of water. She said she could see the bearers moving along. She made her mourning. She used to impress all this on her inoffensive husband, and assure him that he would go to hell if he made the conjuror a liar. He didn't, but died on the day foretold. Oddly enough she never married again.'

'*December* 31. To St. Peter's belfry to the New-Year's-Eve ringing. The night-wind whiffed in through the louvres as the men prepared the mufflers with tar-twine and pieces of horse-cloth. Climbed over the bells to fix the mufflers. I climbed with them and looked into the tenor bell : it is worn into a bright pit where the clapper has struck it so many years, and the clapper is battered with its many blows.

'The ringers now put their coats and waistcoats and hats upon the chimes and clock and stand to. Old John is fragile, as if the bell would pull him up rather than he pull the rope down, his neck being withered and white as his white neckcloth. But his manner is severe as he says "Tenor out?" One of the two tenor men gently eases the bell forward — that fine old E flat [?] (probably D in modern sharpened pitch), my father's admiration, unsurpassed in metal all the world over — and answers, "Tenor's out". Then old John tells them to "Go!" and they start. Through long practice he rings with the least possible movement of his body, though the youngest ringers — strong, dark-haired men with ruddy faces — soon perspire with their exertions. The red, green, and white sallies bolt up through the holes like rats between the huge beams overhead.

'The grey stones of the fifteenth-century masonry have many of their joints mortarless, and are carved with many initials and dates.

On the sill of one louvred window stands a great pewter pot with a hinged cover and engraved : "For the use of the ringers 16—"' [It is now in the County Museum.]

In the early part of the next year (1885) Hardy accepted a long-standing invitation to Eggesford by his friend Lady Portsmouth, whither he was to bring his work and continue it as if at home, but Mrs. Hardy was unable to accompany him.  He found her there surrounded by her daughters, and their cousin Lady Winifred Herbert, afterwards Lady Burghclere ; making altogether a lively house-party, Lady Portsmouth apologizing for its being mostly composed of 'better halves'.  Hence, though the library was placed at his disposal, and entry forbidden, that his labours should not be interrupted, very little work indeed was done while he stayed there, most of the time being spent in driving about the villages with his hosts and walking in the Park.  Lord Portsmouth he found to be 'a farmer-like man with a broad Devon accent.  He showed me a bridge over which bastards were thrown and drowned, even down to quite recent times.' Lady Dorothea, one of the daughters, told him of some of the escapades of her uncle Auberon Herbert — whom Hardy afterwards got to know very well — one of the most amusing being how he had personated a groom of his father's at a Drawing-room, and by that trick got to see a flame of his who was to be there.  Altogether they were an extraordinarily sympathetic group of women, and among other discussions was, of course, one on love, in which Lady Camilla informed him that 'a woman is never so near being in love with a man she does not love as immediately he has left her after she has refused him'.

'Lady P. tells me she never knew real anxiety till she had a family of daughters.  She wants us to come to Devonshire and live near them.  She says they would find a house for us.  Cannot think why we live in benighted Dorset.  Em would go willingly, as it is her native county ; but alas, my house at Dorchester is nearly finished.'

'*Easter Sunday*.  Evidences of art in Bible narratives.  They are written with a watchful attention (though disguised) as to their effect on their reader.  Their so-called simplicity is, in fact, the simplicity of the highest cunning.  And one is led to inquire, when even in these latter days artistic development and arrangement are the qualities least appreciated by readers, who was there likely to appreciate the art in these chronicles at that day?

'Looking round on a well-selected shelf of fiction or history, how few stories of any length does one recognize as well told from begin-

ning to end! The first half of this story, the last half of that, the middle
of another. . . . The modern art of narration is yet in its infancy.

'But in these Bible lives and adventures there is the spherical
completeness of perfect art. And our first, and second, feeling that
they must be true because they are so impressive, becomes, as a third
feeling, modified to, "Are they so very true, after all? Is not the fact
of their being so convincing an argument, not for their actuality, but
for the actuality of a consummate artist who was no more content with
what Nature offered than Sophocles and Pheidias were content?" '

'*Friday, April* 17. Wrote the last page of *The Mayor of Casterbridge*, begun at least a year ago, and frequently interrupted in the
writing of each part.'

'*April* 19. The business of the poet and novelist is to show the
sorriness underlying the grandest things, and the grandeur underlying
the sorriest things.'

He was in London at the end of April, and probably saw Leslie
Stephen there, since he makes the following remark : 'Leslie Stephen
as a critic. His approval is disapproval minimized.'

They went to the Academy this year as usual. On the Private
View Hardy remarks : 'The great difference between a Private View
and a public one is the loud chatter that prevails at the former, everybody knowing everybody else'. In the evening of the same day they
were at a party at Lady Carnarvon's, where Hardy met Lord Salisbury
for the first time, and had an interesting talk with him on the art of
making speeches — 'whether it is best to plunge *in medias res,* or to
adopt a developing method'. In the middle of May they were at
another of these parties of Lady Carnarvon's, where they met Browning again ; also Mrs. Jeune (afterwards Lady St. Helier), and the
usual friends whom they found there.

'*May* 28. Waiting at the Marble Arch while Em called a little
way further on. . . . This hum of the wheel — the roar of London!
What is it composed of? Hurry, speech, laughters, moans, cries of
little children. The people in this tragedy laugh, sing, smoke, toss
off wines, etc., make love to girls in drawing-rooms and areas ; and
yet are playing their parts in the tragedy just the same. Some wear
jewels and feathers, some wear rags. All are caged birds ; the
only difference lies in the size of the cage. This too is part of the
tragedy.'

'*Sunday May* 31. Called on Mrs. Procter. Shocked to find her
in mourning for Edith. Can't tell why I did not see announcement
of her death. Browning also present.

'Mrs. Procter was vexed with Browning and myself for sending cards to Victor Hugo's funeral to attach to wreaths.'

At one of these crushes in the early part of 1885 they found themselves on a particular evening amid a simmer of political excitement. It was supposed to be a non-political 'small-and-early', but on their arrival the house was already full to overflowing; and a well-known Conservative peeress of that date, who had lately invited Hardy to her friendship, came up to him as if she must express her feelings to somebody, and said, 'I'm ashamed of my party! They are actually all hoping that General Gordon is murdered, in order that it may ruin Gladstone!' It seems to have been this rumour of Gordon's death, which had just been circulated, that had brought so many brilliant and titled people there. Auberon Herbert, who was also there, told Hardy privately that it was true. Presently another and grimmer lady, the Dowager Viscountess Galway, said to him that she half-believed Gordon was still alive, because no relic, bloody rag, or any scrap of him had been produced, which from her experience of those countries she knew to be almost the invariable custom. So the crowd waited, and conjectured, and did not leave till a late hour, the truth as to Gordon's fate not being generally known till some days after.

It must have been his experiences at these nominally social but really political parties that gave rise to the following note at the same date:

'History is rather a stream than a tree. There is nothing organic in its shape, nothing systematic in its development. It flows on like a thunderstorm-rill by a road side; now a straw turns it this way, now a tiny barrier of sand that. The offhand decision of some commonplace mind high in office at a critical moment influences the course of events for a hundred years. Consider the evenings at Lord Carnarvon's, and the intensely average conversation on politics held there by average men who two or three weeks later were members of the Cabinet. A row of shopkeepers in Oxford Street taken just as they came would conduct the affairs of the nation as ably as these.

'Thus, judging by bulk of effect, it becomes impossible to estimate the intrinsic value of ideas, acts, material things: we are forced to appraise them by the curves of their career. There were more beautiful women in Greece than Helen; but what of them?

'What Ruskin says as to the cause of the want of imagination in works of the present age is probably true — that it is the flippant sarcasm of the time. "Men dare not open their hearts to us if we are to broil them on a thorn fire."'

At the end of the month of June Hardy was obliged to go down to Dorset to superintend the removal of his furniture from the house he had temporarily taken in Dorchester to the one he had built in the fields at Max Gate, a mile out of the town.

This house, one mile east of Dorchester, had been about eighteen months in building, commencing November 26, 1883, during which time Hardy was constantly overlooking operations. The plot of ground, which he bought from the Duchy of Cornwall, was $1\frac{1}{2}$ acres in extent, and nearly forty years later another half-acre was added to the garden.

A visitor to Max Gate in 1886 gives the following description :

'The house that is, from its position, almost the first object in the neighbourhood to catch the sun's morning rays, and the last to relinquish the evening glow, is approached . . . along the Wareham road across an open down. From this side the building appears as an unpretending red-brick structure of moderate size, somewhat quaintly built, and standing in a garden which is divided from the upland without by an enclosing wall. . . . The place is as lonely as it is elevated ; and it is evident that from the narrow windows of a turret which rises at the salient angle an extensive view of the surrounding country may be obtained.

'From the white entrance gate in the wall a short drive, planted on the windward side with beech and sycamore, leads up to the house, arrivals being notified to the inmates by the voice of a glossy black setter [Moss], who comes into view from the stable at the back as far as his chain will allow him. Within, we find ourselves in a small square hall, floored with dark polished wood, and resembling rather a cosy sitting-room with a staircase in it than a hall as commonly understood. It is lighted by a window of leaded panes, through which may be seen Conygar Hill, Came Plantation, and the elevated sea-mark of Culliford Tree.'

Some two or three thousand small trees, mostly Austrian pines, were planted around the house by Hardy himself, and in later years these grew so thickly that the house was almost entirely screened from the road, and finally appeared, in summer, as if at the bottom of a dark green well of trees.

To the right of the front door upon entering is the drawing-room, and to the left the dining-room. Above the drawing-room is the room which Hardy used as his first study at Max Gate, and in this room *The Woodlanders* was written. Later he moved his study to the back of the house with a window facing west, where *Tess of the d'Urbervilles* took shape. In after years another study was built over a new kitchen, and here *The Dynasts* and all the later poems were written, with the remaining literary work of Hardy's life. The rather large window of this, the last of all his workrooms, faced east, and the full moon rising over the tops of the dark pines was a familiar sight.

When Max Gate was built Hardy intended to have a sundial affixed to the easternmost turret, as shown in an illustration drawn by himself for *Wessex Poems*. This design, constantly in his mind, never matured during his life, though at the time of his death the sundial was actually being made in Dorchester, from a model prepared by himself, more than forty years after it was first planned.

A description of his personal appearance at this time, by a careful observer, is as follows:

'A somewhat fair-complexioned man, a trifle below the middle-height [he was actually 5 ft. 6½ ins.] of slight build, with a pleasant thoughtful face, exceptionally broad at the temples, and fringed by a beard trimmed after the Elizabethan manner [this beard was shaved off about 1890, and he never grew another, but had always a moustache]; a man readily sociable and genial, but one whose mien conveys the impression that the world in his eyes has rather more of the tragedy than the comedy about it.'

His smile was of exceptional sweetness, and his eyes were a clear blue-grey. His whole aspect was almost childlike in its sincerity and simplicity, the features being strongly marked, and his nose, as he himself once described it, more Roman than aquiline. The nobility of his brow was striking. When young he had abundant hair of a deep chestnut colour, which later became a dark brown, almost black, until it turned grey. His hands were well shaped, with long deft fingers; his shoulders particularly neat, and his gait light and easy. He walked very rapidly. He was always a spare man, though not actually thin, and he never in his life allowed himself to be weighed, as he said he considered that to be unlucky.

# CHAPTER XIV

# MAX GATE AND 'THE WOODLANDERS'

## 1885–1887 : *Aet.* 45–46

ON June 29 the Hardys slept at Max Gate for the first time — the house being one they were destined to occupy permanently thence onward, except during the four or five months in each year that were spent in London or abroad. Almost the first visitor at their new house was R. L. Stevenson, till then a stranger to Hardy, who wrote from Bournemouth to announce his coming, adding characteristically: 'I could have got an introduction, but my acquaintance with your mind is already of old date. . . . If you should be busy or unwilling, the irregularity of my approach leaves you the safer retreat.' He appeared two days afterwards, with his wife, wife's son, and cousin. They were on their way to Dartmoor, the air of which Stevenson had learnt would be good for his complaint. But, alas, he never reached Dartmoor, falling ill at Exeter and being detained there till he was well enough to go home again.

'*September* 16. Dined with [Hon. Aubrey] Spring-Rice [who lived at Dorchester]. Met there his cousin Aubrey de Vere the poet, and Father Poole. De Vere says that his father used to say a Greek drama was the fifth act of an Elizabethan one, which of course it is, when not a sixth.'

'*October* 17. Called on William Barnes. Talked of old families. He told me a story of Louis Napoleon. During his residence in England he was friendly with the Damers, and used to visit at Winterborne-Came House, near Dorchester, where they lived. (It was a current tradition that he wished to marry Miss Damer; also that he would dreamily remark that it was fated he should be the Emperor of the French to avenge the defeat of Waterloo.) It was the fashion then for the Dorchester people to parade in full dress in the South Walk on Sunday afternoons, and on one occasion the Damers with their guest came in from their house a mile off and joined in the promenade. Barnes, who kept a school in the town, had an usher from Blackmore Vale named Hann (whose people seem to have been of my mother's stock), and Barnes and his usher also promenaded. For a freak Louis Napoleon, who was walking with Colonel Damer, slipt his cane between Hann's legs when they brushed past each other in opposite directions, and nearly threw the usher down. Hann was peppery, like all of that pedigree, my maternal line included, and almost before Barnes knew what was happening had pulled off his coat, thrown it on Barnes, and was challenging Louis Napoleon to fight. The latter apologized profusely, said it was quite an accident, and laughed the affair off; so the burghers who had stood round expecting a fight resumed their walk disappointed.'

'*November* 17-19. In a fit of depression, as if enveloped in a leaden cloud. Have gone back to my original plot for *The Woodlanders* after all. Am working from half-past ten A.M. to twelve P.M., to get my mind made up on the details.'

'*November* 21-22. Sick headache.'

'Tragedy. It may be put thus in brief: a tragedy exhibits a state of things in the life of an individual which unavoidably causes some natural aim or desire of his to end in a catastrophe when carried out.'

'*November* 25. Letter from John Morley [probably about *The Woodlanders*, he being then editor of *Macmillan's Magazine* in which it was to appear]; and one from Leslie Stephen, with remarks on books he had read between whiles.'

'*December* 9. "Everything looks so little — so ghastly little!" A local exclamation heard.'

'*December* 12. Experience *un*teaches — (what one at first thinks to be the rule in events).'

'*December* 21. The Hypocrisy of things. Nature is an arch-dissembler. A child is deceived completely; the older members of society more or less according to their penetration; though even they seldom get to realize that *nothing* is as it appears.'

'*December* 31. This evening, the end of the old year 1885 finds me sadder than many previous New Year's Eves have done. Whether building this house at Max Gate was a wise expenditure of energy is one doubt, which, if resolved in the negative, is depressing enough. And there are others. But:

'"This is the chief thing: Be not perturbed; for all things are according to the nature of the universal."' [Marcus Aurelius.]

1886. — '*January* 2, *The Mayor of Casterbridge* begins to-day in the *Graphic* newspaper and *Harper's Weekly*. — I fear it will not be so good as I meant, but after all, it is not improbabilities of incident but improbabilities of character that matter. . . .

'Cold weather brings out upon the faces of people the written marks of their habits, vices, passions, and memories, as warmth brings out on paper a writing in sympathetic ink. The drunkard looks still more a drunkard when the splotches have their margins made distinct by frost, the hectic blush becomes a stain now, the cadaverous complexion reveals the bone under, the quality of handsomeness is reduced to its lowest terms.'

'*January* 3. My art is to intensify the expression of things, as is done by Crivelli, Bellini, etc., so that the heart and inner meaning is made vividly visible.'

'*January* 6. Misapprehension. The shrinking soul thinks its weak place is going to be laid bare, and shows its thought by a suddenly clipped manner. The other shrinking soul thinks the clipped manner of the first to be the result of its own weakness in some way, not of its strength, and shows its fear also by its constrained air! So they withdraw from each other and misunderstand.'

'*March* 4. Novel-writing as an art cannot go backward. Having reached the analytic stage it must transcend it by going still further in the same direction. Why not by rendering as visible essences, spectres, etc., the abstract thoughts of the analytic school?'

This notion was approximately carried out, not in a novel, but through the much more appropriate medium of poetry, in the supernatural framework of *The Dynasts* as also in smaller poems. And a further note of the same date enlarges the same idea:

'The human race to be shown as one great network or tissue which quivers in every part when one point is shaken, like a spider's web if touched. Abstract realisms to be in the form of Spirits, Spectral figures, etc.

'The Realities to be the true realities of life, hitherto called abstractions. The old material realities to be placed behind the former, as shadowy accessories.'

In the spring and summer they were again in London, staying in Bloomsbury to have the Reading Room of the Museum at hand. It was the spring during which Gladstone brought in his Home Rule Bill for Ireland. The first that Hardy says about it occurs in an entry dated *April* 8, 9, 10, 11:

'A critical time, politically. I never remember a debate of such absorbing interest as this on Gladstone's Bill for Irish Government. He spoke lucidly: Chamberlain with manly practical earnestness; Hartington fairly forcibly; Morley without much effect (for him). Morley's speech shows that in Parliament a fine intelligence is not appreciated without sword-and-buckler doggedness. Chamberlain impresses me most of all, as combining these qualities.'

And on *May* 10 : 'Saw Gladstone enter the Houses of Parliament. The crowd was very excited, not only waving their hats and shouting and running, but leaping in the air. His head was bare, and his now bald crown showed pale and distinct over the top of Mrs. Gladstone's bonnet.'

On the 13th Hardy was in the House, the debate on the Government of Ireland still continuing :

'Gladstone was suave in replying to Bradlaugh, almost unctuous. "Not accustomed to recognize Parliamentary debts after five years", etc. He would shake his head and smile contradictions to his opponents across the table and red box, on which he wrote from time to time. Heard Morley say a few words, also Sir W. Harcourt, and Lord Hartington ; a speech from Sir H. James, also from Lord G. Hamilton, Campbell-Bannerman, etc. Saw the dandy party enter in evening-dress, eye-glasses, diamond rings, etc. They were a great contrast to Joseph Arch and the Irish members in their plain, simple, ill-fitting clothes. The House is a motley assembly nowadays. Gladstone's frock-coat dangled and swung as he went in and out with a white flower in his button-hole and open waistcoat. Lord Randolph's manner in turning to Dillon, the Irish member, was almost arrogant. Sir R. Cross was sturdy, like T. B. the Dorchester butcher, when he used to stand at the chopping-block on market-days. The earnestness of the Irish members who spoke was very impressive ; Lord G. Hamilton was entirely wanting in earnestness ; Sir H. James quite the reverse ; E. Clarke direct, firm, and incisive, but inhumane.

'To realize the difficulty of the Irish question it is necessary to *see* the Irish phalanx sitting tight : it then seems as if one must go with Morley, and get rid of them at any cost.

'Morley kept trying to look used to it all, and not as if he were a consummate man of letters there by mistake. Gladstone was quite distinct from all others in the House, though he sits low in his seat from age. When he smiled one could see benevolence on his face. Large-heartedness *versus* small-heartedness is a distinct attitude which the House of Commons takes up to an observer's eye.'

Though he did not enter it here Hardy often wrote elsewhere, and said of Home Rule that it was a staring dilemma, of which good policy and good philanthropy were the huge horns. Policy for England required that it should not be granted ; humanity to Ireland that it should. Neither Liberals nor Conservatives would honestly own up to this opposition between two moralities, but speciously insisted that humanity and policy were both on one side — of course their own.

'*May.* Reading in the British Museum. Have been thinking over the dictum of Hegel — that the real is the rational and the rational the real — that real pain is compatible with a formal pleasure — that the idea is all, etc., but it doesn't help much. These venerable philosophers seem to start wrong; they cannot get away from a prepossession that the world must somehow have been made to be a comfortable place for man. If I remember, it was Comte who said that metaphysics was a mere sorry attempt to reconcile theology and physics.'

'*May* 17. At a curious soirée in Bond Street. Met a Hindu Buddhist, a remarkably well-educated man who speaks English fluently. He is the coach of the Theosophical Society. Also encountered a Mr. E. Maitland, author of a book called *The Pilgrim and the Shrine*, which I remember. He mentioned also another, written, I think he said, by himself and Dr. Anna Kingsford in collaboration. If he could not get on with the work on any particular night he would go to her next morning and she would supply him with the sentences, written down by her on waking, as sentences she had dreamt of without knowing why. Met also Dr. Anna Kingsford herself, and others; all very strange people.'

*The Mayor of Casterbridge* was issued complete about the end of May. It was a story which Hardy fancied he had damaged more recklessly as an artistic whole, in the interest of the newspaper in which it appeared serially, than perhaps any other of his novels, his aiming to get an incident into almost every week's part causing him in his own judgment to add events to the narrative somewhat too freely. However, as at this time he called his novel-writing 'mere journeywork' he cared little about it as art, though it must be said in favour of the plot, as he admitted later, that it was quite coherent and organic, in spite of its complication. And others thought better of it than he did himself, as is shown by the letter R. L. Stevenson writes thereon:

'SKERRYVORE,
'BOURNEMOUTH,
[1886]

'MY DEAR HARDY,

'I have read "The Mayor of Casterbridge" with sincere admiration: Henchard is a great fellow, and Dorchester is touched in with the hand of a master.

'Do you think you would let me 'try to dramatize it? I keep unusually well, and am

'Yours very sincerely,
'ROBERT LOUIS STEVENSON.'

What became of this dramatic project there is no evidence to show in the *Life of Stevenson*, so far as is remembered by the present writer. The story in long after years became highly popular; but it is curious to find that Hardy had some difficulty in getting it issued in volume-form, James Payn, the publishers' reader, having reported to Smith, Elder and Co. that the lack of gentry among the characters made it uninteresting — a typical estimate of what was, or was supposed to be, mid-Victorian taste.

During the remainder of this month, and through June and July, they were dining and lunching out almost every day. Hardy did not take much account of these functions, though some remarks he makes are interesting. For instance, he describes the charming daughter of a then popular hostess with whom he and his wife had been lunching:

'M—— W—— is still as childlike as when I first met her. She has an instinct to *give* something which she cannot resist. Gave me a flower. She expresses as usual contrary opinions at different moments. At one time she is going to marry; then she never is: at one moment she has been ill; at another she is always well. Pities the row of poor husbands at Marshall and Snelgrove's. Gave a poor crossing-sweeper a shilling; came back and found her drunk. An emotional delicate girl, in spite of what she calls her "largeness", *i.e.* her being bigly built.'

In these weeks Hardy met Walter Pater, 'whose manner is that of one carrying weighty ideas without spilling them'. Also a lot of politicians, on whom he notes: 'Plenty of form in their handling of politics, but no matter, or originality.' Either on this occasion or a few days later the hostess, Mrs. Jeune, drew the attention of Justin McCarthy — also a guest — to the Conservative placard in her window. 'I hope you don't mind the blue bill?' 'Not at all,' said the amiable McCarthy blandly. 'Blue is a colour I have liked from a boy.'

At Mr. and Mrs. Gosse's they met Dr. Oliver Wendell Holmes and his daughter:

'His is a little figure, that of an aged boy. He said markedly that he did not read novels; I did not say I had never read his essays, though it would have been true, I am ashamed to think. . . . But authors are not so touchy as they are supposed to be on such matters — at least I am not — and I found him a very bright, pleasant, juvenile old man.' At a Rabelais Club dinner a few days later he renewed acquaintance with Dr. Holmes, and with Henry James, 'who has a ponderously warm manner of saying nothing in infinite sentences'; and also talked to George Meredith. This may possibly have been the first time he and Meredith had met since Hardy received Meredith's advice about novel-writing; but it is not clear that it was so. At dinners elsewhere in these weeks he met Whistler and Charles Keene, Bret Harte, Sambourne, and others — most of them for the first and last time; at Sidney Colvin's he renewed acquaintance with R. L. Stevenson, then in London; and at another house sat next to a genial old lady, Lady Camperdown, and 'could not get rid of the feeling that I was close to a great naval engagement'.

On some music of Wagner's listened to at a concert at this time when it was less familiar to the public than after, Hardy remarks: 'It was *weather* and *ghost* music — whistling of wind and storm, the strumming of a gale on iron railings, the creaking of doors; low screams of entreaty and agony through key-holes, amid which trumpet-voices are heard. Such music, like any other, may be made to express emotion of various kinds; but it cannot express the subject or reason of that emotion.'

Apropos of this it may be mentioned here that, many years after, Hardy met Grieg, and in doing his best to talk about music Hardy explained that Wagner's compositions seemed to him like the wind-effects above described. 'I would rather have the wind and rain myself,' Grieg replied, shaking his head.

Mrs. Procter, who was still strong enough to go out, came to the Hardys to tea, and among her stores of anecdotes told one that was amusing about Macaulay and Sydney Smith, who had dined at her house in years gone by: when Macaulay had gone she said to Sydney Smith: 'You gave him no chance at all to talk.' 'On the contrary,' said Sydney Smith, 'I gave him several opportunities — which you took advantage of.'

It was during this summer that the Hardys either began or renewed their acquaintance with Mrs. Henry Reeve and her sister Miss Gollop, whose family was an old Dorset one; and with Reeve himself, the well-known editor of the *Edinburgh Review* and of the famous *Greville Memoirs*. Notwithstanding a slight pompousness of manner he attracted the younger man by his wide experience of Continental men of letters, musicians, and princes, and of English affairs political and journalistic.

'*June* 29.  Called on Leslie Stephen.  He is just the same or worse; as if dying to express sympathy, but suffering under some terrible curse which prevents his saying any but caustic things, and showing antipathy instead.'  [Hardy was not aware that Stephen was unwell, and growing deaf, or he would not have put in this form his impression of a man he so much liked, and who had been so much to him.]

'Afterwards had a good talk with Auberon Herbert at Lady Portsmouth's.  He said that the clue to Gladstone's faults was personal vanity.  His niece Lady Winifred Herbert, who was present, said that politics had revealed themselves to her as a horror of late.  Nevertheless she insisted that to listen to our conversation on the same horror was not an infliction.'

Mr. George Gissing, finding that Hardy was in London this summer, had asked if he might call upon him for some advice about novel-writing; which he did.  Sending one of his own novels afterwards, Gissing writes at the end of June:

'It is possible you will find *The Unclassed* detestable.  I myself should not dare to read it now, it is too saturated with bygone miseries of every kind. . . .  May I add in one word what very real pleasure it has given me to meet and speak with you?  I have not been the least careful of your readers, and in your books I have constantly found refreshment and onward help.  That aid is much needed now-a-days by anyone who wishes to pursue literature as distinct from the profession of letters.  In literature my interests begin and end; I hope to make my life and all its acquirements subservient to my ideal of artistic creation.  The end of it all may prove ineffectual, but as well spend one's strength thus as in another way.  The misery of it is that, writing for English people, one may not be thorough: reticences and superficialities have so often to fill places where one is willing to put in honest work.'

'*July* 11.  Met and talked to Browning at Mrs. Procter's again, and a day or two later at Mrs. Skirrow's, where was also Oscar Wilde, etc.

'In Rotten Row.  Every now and then each woman, however interesting, puts on her *battle face*.

'In evening to bookstalls in Holywell Street known to me so many years ago.'

Hardy by this time had quite resigned himself to novel-writing as a trade, which he had never wanted to carry on as such.  He now went about the business mechanically. He was in court a part of the time during which the Crawford-Dilke case was proceeding. He makes no comment on the case itself, but a general remark on the court :

'The personality which fills the court is that of *the witness*. The judge's personality during the cross-examination contracts to his corporeal dimensions merely. So do they all save that of the pervasive witness aforesaid. . . . The witness is also the fool of the court. . . . The witness's little peculiarities supersede those of all the other personages together. He is at once king and victim.

'As to the architecture of the courts, there are everywhere religious art-forces masquerading as law symbols! The leaf, flower, fret, suggested by spiritual emotion, are pressed into the service of social strife.'

The remainder of his spare time in London this year appears to have been spent in the British Museum Library and elsewhere, considering the question of *The Dynasts*.

At the end of July they returned to Max Gate, where he went on with *The Woodlanders* ; and in October they paid another visit to Lady Portsmouth in Devon, where they had a pleasant week, visiting local scenes and surroundings down to the kennels (Lord Portsmouth being Master of Hounds) and the dogs' cemetery. 'Lord Portsmouth made his whipper-in tell Emma the story of the hunted fox that ran up the old woman's clock-case, adding corroborative words with much gravity as the story proceeded and enjoying it more than she did, though he had heard it 100 times.'

In October the Dorset poet William Barnes died. Hardy had known him ever since his schoolmastering time in South Street, Dorchester, next door to the architect under whom Hardy had served his years of pupillage. In 1864 Barnes had retired from school-keeping, and accepted the living of Winterborne-Came-cum-Whit-combe, the rectory house being, by chance, not half a mile from the only spot Hardy could find convenient for building a dwelling on. Hardy's walk across the fields to attend the poet's funeral was marked by the singular incident to which he alludes in the poem entitled 'The Last Signal'. He also wrote an obituary notice of his friend for the *Athenæum*, which was afterwards drawn upon for details of his life in the *Dictionary of National Biography*. It was not till many years after that he made and edited a selection of Barnes's poems.

The beginning of December covers this entry :

'I often view society-gatherings, people in the street, in a room, or elsewhere, as if they were beings in a somnambulistic state, making their motions automatically — not realizing what they mean.'

And a few days later another, when going to London :

'*December* 7. Winter. The landscape has turned from a painting to an engraving : the birds that love worms fall back upon berries : the back parts of homesteads assume, in the general nakedness of the trees, a humiliating squalidness as to their details that has not been contemplated by their occupiers.

'A man I met in the train says in a tone of bitter regret that he wore out seven sets of horseshoes in riding from Sturminster Newton to Weymouth when courting a young woman at the latter place. He did not say whether he won and married her, or not ; but I fancy he did.

'At the Society of British Artists there is good technique in abundance ; but ideas for subjects are lacking. The impressionist school is strong. It is even more suggestive in the direction of literature than in that of art. As usual it is pushed to absurdity by some. But their principle is, as I understand it, that what you carry away with you from a scene is the true feature to grasp ; or in other words, *what appeals to your own individual eye and heart in particular* amid much that does not so appeal, and which you therefore omit to record.

'Talked to Bob Stevenson — Louis's cousin — at the Savile. A more solid character than Louis.

'Called on Mrs. Jeune. She was in a rich pinky-red gown, and looked handsome as we sat by the firelight *en tête-à-tête* : she was, curiously enough, an example of Whistler's study in red that I had seen in the morning at the Gallery.

'To Lady Carnarvon's "small and early". Snow falling : the cabman drove me furiously — I don't know why. The familiar man with the lantern at the door. Her drawing-room was differently arranged from its method during her summer crushes. They seemed glad to see me. Lady Winifred told me she was going to be married on the 10th of January at the Savoy Chapel, with other details of the wedding. She was serious and thoughtful — I fancied a little careworn. Said she was not going to let her honeymoon interfere with her reading, and means to carry a parcel of books. Spoke of her betrothed as 'He' — as a workman speaks of his employer — never mentioning his name. Wants me to call my heroine "Winifred", but it is too late to alter it.

'Talked to Lady Carnarvon about the trees at Highclere in relation to my work in hand [*The Woodlanders*]. Lord C. told me he had filled several bookshelves with books all written by members of his own family — from Sir Philip Sidney, who was his mother's mother's mother's, etc. brother, downwards.

'The last time, I suppose, that I shall see friendly Winifred Herbert pouring out tea from the big tea-pot in that house, as I have seen her do so many times. Lady Carnarvon went about the room weaving little webs of sympathy between her guests.'

So came the end of 1886.

January 1887 was uneventful at Max Gate, and the only remark its occupier makes during the month is the following:

'After looking at the landscape ascribed to Bonington in our drawing-room I feel that Nature is played out as a Beauty, but not as a Mystery. I don't want to see landscapes, *i.e.*, scenic paintings of them, because I don't want to see the original realities — as optical effects, that is. I want to see the deeper reality underlying the scenic, the expression of what are sometimes called abstract imaginings.

'The "simply natural" is interesting no longer. The much decried, mad, late-Turner rendering is now necessary to create my interest. The exact truth as to material fact ceases to be of importance in art — it is a student's style — the style of a period when the mind is serene and unawakened to the tragical mysteries of life; when it does not bring anything to the object that coalesces with and translates the qualities that are already there, — half hidden, it may be — and the two united are depicted as the All.'

'*February* 4, 8.20 P.M. Finished *The Woodlanders*. Thought I should feel glad, but I do not particularly, — though relieved.' In after years he often said that in some respects *The Woodlanders* was his best novel.

'*February* 6. Sunday. To see my father. It was three men whom he last saw flogged in Dorchester by the Town-pump — about 1830. He happened to go in from Stinsford about mid-day. Some soldiers coming down the street from the Barracks interfered, and swore at Davis [Jack Ketch] because he did not "flog fair"; that is to say he waited between each lash for the flesh to recover sensation, whereas, as they knew from experience, by striking quickly the flesh remained numb through several strokes.'

'*February* 13. You may regard a throng of people as containing a certain small minority who have sensitive souls; these, and the aspects of these, being what is worth observing. So you divide them into the mentally unquickened, mechanical, soulless ; and the living, throbbing, suffering, vital.   In other words, into souls and machines, ether and clay.

'I was thinking a night or two ago that people are somnambulists — that the material is not the real — only the visible, the real being invisible optically.   That it is because we are in a somnambulistic hallucination that we think the real to be what we see as real.

'Faces.   The features to beholders so commonplace are to their possessor lineaments of high estimation, striking, hopeful.'

Having now some leisure, and the spring drawing near, Hardy carried into effect an idea that he had long entertained, and on Monday, March 14, 1887, left Dorchester with Mrs. Hardy for London on their way to Italy, the day before *The Woodlanders* was published by the Messrs. Macmillan.

CHAPTER XV

# ITALIAN JOURNEY

1887: *Aet.* 46

THE month had been mild hitherto, but no sooner had they started than the weather turned to snow; and a snowstorm persistently accompanied them across the Channel and southward beyond. They broke the journey at Aix-les-Bains, at which place they arrived past midnight, and the snow being by this time deep a path was cleared with spades for them to the fly in waiting, which two horses, aided by men turning the wheels, dragged with difficulty up the hill to the Hôtel Château Durieux — an old-fashioned place with stone floors and wide fireplaces. They were the only people there — the first visitors of the season — and in spite of a huge fire in their bedroom they found the next morning a cone of snow within each casement, and a snow film on the floor sufficient to show their tracks in moving about. Hardy used to speak of a curious atmospheric effect then witnessed: he was surprised that the windows of the room they occupied — one of the best — should command the view of a commonplace paddock only, with a few broken rails and sheds. But presently 'what had seemed like the sky evolved a scene which un-curtained itself high up in the midst of the aerial expanse, as in a magic lantern, and vast mountains appeared there, tantalizingly with-drawing again as if they had been a mere illusion'.

They stayed here a day or two, 'the mountains showing again coquettish signs of uncovering themselves, and again coquettishly pulling down their veil'.

Leaving for Turin they stayed there awhile, then duly reached Genoa, concerning the first aspect of which from the train Hardy wrote a long time after the lines entitled 'Genoa and the Mediter-ranean', though that city — so pre-eminently the city of marble — 'everything marble', he writes, 'even little doorways in slums' — nobly redeemed its character when they visited its palaces during their stay.

At Pisa after visiting the Cathedral and Baptistery they stood at

the top of the leaning tower during a peal of the bells, which shook
it under their feet, and saw the sun set from one of the bridges over
the Arno, as Shelley had probably seen it from the same bridge many
a time.   Thence by 'melancholy olives and cheerful lemons' they
proceeded to Florence, where they were met by an inhabitant of that
city, Lucy Baxter, the daughter of the poet Barnes, married and
settled there since Hardy had known her in girlhood, and who wrote
under the name of 'Leader Scott'.   She had obtained lodgings for
them at the Villa Trollope, in the Piazza dell' Indipendenza ; and there
they remained all the time they were in Florence.   Their Florentine
experiences onward were much like those of other people visiting for
the first time the buildings, pictures, and historic sites of that city.
They were fortunately able to see the old Market just before its
destruction.   Having gone through the galleries and churches of
Florence, they drove out and visited another English resident in the
country near, and also went over the Certosa di Val d'Ema.   Then
they travelled on to Rome, their first glimpse of it being of the Dome
of St. Peter's across the stagnant flats of the Campagna.

They put up at the Hôtel d'Allemagne, in the Via Condotti, a
street opposite the Piazza di Spagna and the steps descending from
the church of SS. Trinità dei Monti, on the south side of which stands
the house where Keats died.   Hardy liked to watch of an evening,
when the streets below were immersed in shade, the figures ascending
and descending these steps in the sunset glow, the front of the church
orange in the same light ;  and also the house hard by, in which no
mind could conjecture what had been lost to English literature in the
early part of the same century that saw him there.

After some days spent in the Holy City Hardy began to feel, he
frequently said, its measureless layers of history to lie upon him like
a physical weight.   The time of their visit was not so long after the
peeling of the Colosseum and other ruins of their vast accumulations
of parasitic growths, which, though Hardy as an architect defended
the much-deplored process on the score of its absolute necessity if
the walls were to be preserved, he yet wished had not been taken in
hand till after his inspection of them.   This made the ruins of the
ancient city, the 'altae moenia Romae' as he called them from the
*Aeneid*, more gaunt to the vision and more depressing to the mind
than they had been to visitors when covered with greenery, and
accounts for his allusions to the city in the poems on Rome written
after his return, as exhibiting 'ochreous gauntness', 'umbered walls',
and so forth.

He mentions in a note the dustiness of the Pincio : 'Dust rising in clouds from the windy drive to the top, whitening the leaves of the evergreen oaks, and making the pale splotches on the trunks of the plane trees yet paler. The busts of illustrious Romans seem to require hats and goggles as a protection. But in the sheltered gardens beneath palms spread, and oranges still hang on the trees.'

There was a great spurt of building going on at this time, on which he remarks, 'I wonder how anybody can have any zest to erect a new building in Rome, in the overpowering presence of decay on the mangy and rotting walls of old erections, originally of fifty times the strength of the new.' This sentiment was embodied in the sonnet called 'Building a New Street in the Ancient Quarter.'

A visit to the graves of Shelley and Keats was also the inspiration of more verses — probably not written till later ; his nearly falling asleep in the Sala delle Muse of the Vatican was the source of another poem, the weariness being the effect of the deadly fatiguing size of St. Peter's ; and the musical incident, which as he once said, took him by surprise when investigating the remains of Caligula's palace, that of another.

'The quality of the faces in the streets of Rome : Satyrs : Emperors : Faustinas.'

Hardy's notes of Rome were of a very jumbled and confusing kind. But, probably from a surviving architectural instinct, he made a few measurements in the Via Appia Antica, where he was obsessed by a vision of a chained file of prisoners plodding wearily along towards Rome, one of the most haggard of whom was to be famous through the ages as the founder of Pauline Christianity. He also noticed that the pavement of the fashionable promenade, the Corso, was two feet six inches wide. Of a different kind was his note that

'The monk who showed us the hole in which stood Saint Peter's Cross in the Church of S. Pietro in Montorio, and fetched up a pinch of clean sand from it, implying it had been there ever since the apostle's crucifixion, was a man of cynical humour, and gave me an indescribably funny glance from the tail of his eye as if to say : "You see well enough what an imposture it all is!" I have noticed this sly humour in some more of these Roman monks, such as the one who sent me on alone into the vaults of the Cappuccini [among the thousands of skulls there], not knowing that I was aware of them, and therefore not startled at the ghastly scene. Perhaps there is something in my appearance which makes them think me a humorist also.'

On the Roman pictures and statuary the only remark he makes except in verse is : 'Paintings. In Roman art the kernel of truth has acquired a thick rind of affectation : *e.g.* I find that pictures by Giotto have been touched up so thoroughly that what you see is not Giotto at all, but the over-lying renovations. A disappointing sight. Alas for this "wronged great soul of an ancient master"!' (The remark, though written at Rome, seems to refer more particularly to Florence.)

By curious chance Hardy was present at a wedding at the church of S. Lorenzo-in-Lucina, and was vexed with himself that he did not recollect till afterwards that it was the church of Pompilia's marriage in *The Ring and the Book*. But he was on the whole more interested in Pagan than in Christian Rome, of the latter preferring churches in which he could detect columns from ancient temples. Christian Rome, he said, was so rambling and stratified that to comprehend it in a single visit was like trying to read Gibbon through at a sitting. So that, for instance, standing on the meagre remains of the Via Sacra then recently uncovered, he seemed to catch more echoes of the inquisitive bore's conversation there with the poet Horace than of worship from the huge basilicas hard by, which were in point of time many centuries nearer to him. But he was careful to remind one to whom he spoke about this that it was really a question of familiarity, time being nothing beside knowledge, and that he happened to remember the scene in the Satires which he, like so many school-boys, had read, while his mind was a blank on the most august cere-monial of the Middle-Age Christian services in the Basilica Julia or the Basilica of Constantine.

'*April.* Our spirits. As we get older they are less subject to steep gradients than in youth. We lower the elevations, and fill the hollows with sustained judgments.'

While here he received among other letters one from Mrs. Procter containing the following remarks :

'It is very kind of you to think of me in Rome, and stretch out a friendly hand. Perhaps, as you are living amidst the Ancient, there is a propriety in thinking of the Oldish, and, I must say, the truest, friend you have. ——

'We are still in Winter : to-day a bitter East wind, and tiles and chimney pots flying about. Never have we had so long a season of cold weather — all our Money gone in Coals and Gas.

'I have been displeased, so much as one ever is by a Man whom you care nothing about, by an Article written by a Dr. Wendell Holmes the American. He comes here, and then says, "the most wonderful thing I saw in England were the Old Ladies — they are so active, and tough like Old Macaws" — Now am I like an Old Macaw? — He might have said Parrots.

'Then Mr. Thackeray's letters [to Mrs. Brookfield] : so common, so vulgar! You will see them in *Scribner's Magazine*. — He was never in love with me, but the 200 letters he wrote me were very superior to these.'

It was with a sense of having grasped very little of its history that he left the city, though with some relief, which may have been partly physical and partly mental.

Returning to Florence on 'a soft green misty evening following rain', he found the scenery soothing after the gauntness of Rome. On a day of warm sun he sat down for a long time, he said, on the steps of the Lanzi, in the Piazza della Signoria, and thought of many things :

'It is three in the afternoon, and the faces of the buildings are steeped in afternoon stagnation. The figure of Neptune is looking an intense white against the brown-grey houses behind, and the bronze forms round the basin [of the fountain] are starred with rays on their noses, elbows, knees, bosoms and shoulders. The shade from the Loggia dei Lanzi falls half across the Piazza. Turning my head there rise the three great arches with their sculptures, then those in the middle of the Loggia, then the row of six at the back with their uplifted fingers, as if ——' [sentence unfinished].

'In the caffè near there is a patter of speech, and on the pavement outside a noise of hoofs. The reflection from that statue of Neptune throws a secondary light into the caffè.

'Everybody is thinking, even amid these art examples from various ages, that this present age is the ultimate climax and upshot of the previous ages, and not a link in a chain of them.

'In a work of art it is the accident which *charms*, not the intention ; *that* we only like and admire. Instance the amber tones that pervade the folds of drapery in ancient marbles, the deadened polish of the surfaces, and the cracks and the scratches.'

In visiting Fiesole they met with a mishap which might have ended in a serious accident. With Mrs. Baxter they had journeyed out from Florence to the foot of the hill on which the little town stands, and were about to walk up the height when on second thoughts they entered a gimcrack omnibus that plied to the top. The driver went to have a drink before starting, and left the omnibus untended, only one of the two horses being put to. The horse immediately started with the three inside at a furious pace towards Florence. The highway was dotted with heaps of large stones for repair, but he avoided them by a miracle, until the steam tram from Florence appeared a little way ahead, and a collision seemed inevitable. Two workmen, however, seeing the danger, descended from the roof of a house and stepping in front of the horse stopped it. They again attempted Fiesole, and climbed up — this time on foot despite all invitations from flymen.

In a sonnet on Fiesole called 'In the Old Theatre' Hardy makes use of an incident that occurred while he was sitting in the stone Amphitheatre on the summit of the hill.

A few more looks at Florence, including the Easter ceremony of the Scoppio del Carro, a visit to Mrs. Browning's tomb, and to the supposed scene in the Piazza dell' Annunziata of one of Browning's finest poems, 'The Statue and the Bust', ended their visit to this half-English city, and after seeing Siena they left for Bologna, Ferrara, and Venice by the railway across the Apennines, not forgetting to gaze at the Euganean Hills so inseparable from thoughts of Shelley. It is rather noticeable that two such differing poets as Browning and Shelley, in their writings, their mentality, and their lives, should have so mingled in Hardy's thoughts during this Italian tour, almost to the exclusion of other English poets equally, or nearly so, associated with Italy, with whose works he was just as well acquainted.

Hardy seems to have found more pleasure in Venice than in any Italian city previously visited, in spite of bad weather during a part of his stay there. Byron of course was introduced here among the other phantom poets marshalled through his brain in front of the sea-queen's historic succession of scenes.

A wet windy morning accompanied their first curious examination of the Ducal Palace, 'the shining *ferri* of the gondolas curtseying down and up against the wharf wall, and the gondoliers standing looking on at us. The wet draught sweeps through the colonnade by Münster's shop, not a soul being within it but Münster, whose face brightens at sight of us like that of a man on a desert island. . . . The dumb boy who showed us the way to the Rialto has haunted us silently ever since.

'The Hall of the Great Council is saturated with Doge-domry. The faces of the Doges pictured on the frieze float out into the air of the room in front of me. "We know nothing of you", say these spectres. "Who may you be, pray?" The draught brushing past seems like inquiring touches by their cold hands, feeling, feeling like blind people what you are. Yes: here to this visionary place I solidly bring in my person Dorchester and Wessex life; and they may well ask why do I do it. . . . Yet there is a connection. The bell of the Campanile of S. Marco strikes the hour, and its sound has exactly that tin-tray *timbre* given out by the bells of Longpuddle and Weatherbury, showing that they are of precisely the same-proportioned alloy.'

Hardy had been, for many reasons, keen to see St. Mark's; and he formed his own opinion on it:

'Well. There is surely some conventional ecstasy, exaggeration, — shall I say humbug? — in what Ruskin writes about this, if I remember (though I have not read him lately), when the church is looked at *as a whole*. One architectural defect nothing can get over — its squatness as seen from the natural point of view — the glassy marble pavement of the Grand Piazza. Second, its weak, flexuous, constructional lines. Then, the fantastic Oriental character of its details makes it barbaric in its general impression, in spite of their great beauty.

'Mosaics, mosaics, mosaics, gilding, gilding, everywhere inside and out. The domes like inverted china-bowls within — much gilt also.

'This being said, see what good things are left to say — of its art, of its history! That floor, of every colour and rich device, is worn into undulations by the infinite multitudes of feet that have trodden it, and *what* feet there have been among the rest!

'A commonplace man stoops in a dark corner where he strikes a common match, and shows us — what — a lost article? — a purse, pipe, or tobacco-pouch? no; shows us — drags from the depths of time as by a miracle — wonderful diaphanous alabaster pillars that were once in Solomon's temple.'

On Venice generally he makes the following desultory remarks: 'When it rains in Italy it makes one shrink and shiver; it is so far more serious a matter than in England. We have our stern gray stone and brick walls, and weathered copings, and buttress-slopes, to fend such. But here there are exposed to the decaying rain marbles, and frescoes, and tesserae, and gildings, and endless things — driving one to implore mentally that all these treasures may be put under a glass case!'

When the weather was finer:

'Venice is composed of blue and sunlight. Hence I incline, after all, to "sun-girt" rather than "sea-girt", which I once upheld.' [In Shelley's poem, 'Many a Green Isle needs must be.']

'Venice requires *heat* to complete the picture of her. Heat is an artistic part of the portrait of all southern towns.'

They were most kindly received and entertained during their brief stay by friends to whom they had introductions. Browning's friend Mrs. Bronson showed them many things; and in respect of an evening party given for them by Mrs. Daniel Curtis at the Palazzo Barbarigo, it could not be said that 'silent rows the songless gondolier', several boats lit by lanterns pausing in front of the open windows on the Grand Canal while their rowers and the singers they brought serenaded the guests within. But alas, it was true that 'Tasso's echoes were no more', the music being that of the latest popular song of the date:

'Fu-ni-cu-lì, fu-ni-cu-là,
Fu-ni-cu-lì-cu-là !'

However, the scene was picturesque, Hardy used to say — the dark shapes of the gondoliers creeping near to them silently, like cats or other nocturnal animals, the gleam of a *ferro* here and there: then the lanterns suddenly lighting up over the heads of the singers, throwing diffused light on their faces and forms; a sky as of black velvet stretching above with its star points, as the notes flapped back from the dilapidated palaces behind with a hollow and almost sepulchral echo, as if from a vault.

Quoting Byron brings to the mind a regret which Hardy some-times expressed, that though he possibly encountered some old native man or woman of fourscore or over who could remember Byron's residence at the Spinelli and Mocenigo palaces, he never questioned any likely one among them on the point, though once in especial he stood on the Riva degli Schiavoni beside such an aged personage whose appearance made him feel her to be an instance of such recollection.

He was curious to know if any descendants of the powerful Doges were left in decayed modern Venice. Mr. Curtis told him that there were some in Venetian society still — poor, but proud, though not offensively so. The majority were extinct, their palaces being ruinous. Going on to Mrs. Bronson's immediately afterwards, the Contessa M—— called. She was a great beauty, having the well-defined hues and contours of foreigners in the south; and she turned out to be one of the very descendants Hardy had inquired about. When asked afterwards how she was dressed, he said in a green velvet jacket with fluffy tags, a grey hat and feathers, a white veil with seed pearls, and a light figured skirt of a yellowish colour.  She had a charming manner, her mind flying from one subject to another like a child's as she spoke her pretty attempts at English.  'But I li—eek moch to do it!' . . . 'Si, si!' . . . 'Oh noh, noh!'

However, Hardy was not altogether listening, he afterwards recalled.  This correct, modest, modern lady, the friend of his English and American acquaintance in Venice, and now his own, was to him primarily the symbol and relic of the bygone ancient families ; and the chief effect, he said, of her good looks and pretty voice on him was to carry him at one spring back to those behind the centuries, who here took

> their pleasure when the sea was warm in May,
> Balls and masks begun at midnight, burning ever to midday,
> When they made up fresh adventures for the morrow. . . .

It is not known whether the Italian Contessa in *A Group of Noble Dames* was suggested by her ; but there are resemblances.

Then they left Venice.  'The Riva degli Schiavoni is interested along its whole length in our departure, just as nautical people at ports always are, and as we left the station we could see the tops of the Alps floating in the sky above the fog.'  They had been unable to follow Ruskin's excellent advice to approach Venice by water, but they had seen it from the water a good deal while there.

'The Cathedral, Milan.  Yes, perhaps it is architectural filigree : and yet I admire it.  The vaulting of the interior is infinite quadrilles in carved-work.  A momentary vexation comes when I am reminded that it is not real — even a disgust.  And yet I admire.  The sense of space alone demands admiration, being beyond that expressed anywhere except at St. Peter's.'

The cheerful scenes of life and gaiety here after the poetical decay of Venice came as the greatest possible contrast, and a not unwelcome change.  Here Hardy's mind reverted to Napoleon, particularly when he was sitting in the sun with his wife on the roof of the Cathedral, and regarding the city in vistas between the flying buttresses.  It was while here on the roof, he thought in after years, though he was not quite sure, that he conceived the Milan Cathedral scene in *The Dynasts*.

Hardy had lately been obsessed by an old French tune of his father's, 'The Bridge of Lodi', owing to his having drawn near the spot of that famous Napoleonic struggle ; and at a large music-shop in the Gallery of Victor Emmanuel he inquired about it ; as may be expected, his whimsical questioning met with no success. He felt it could meet with none, and yet went on with his search. At dinner at the Grand Hôtel de Milan that evening, where the Hardys had put up, they became friendly with a young Scotch officer of Foot returning from India, and Hardy told him about Lodi, and how he could not get the old tune.

'The Bridge of Lodi?' said the Scotchman (apparently a sort of Farfrae). 'Ay, but I've never heard of it!'

'But you've heard of the battle, anyhow?' says the astonished Hardy.

'Nay, and I never have whatever!' says the young soldier.

Hardy then proceeded to describe the conflict, and by degrees his companion rose to an enthusiasm for Lodi as great as Hardy's own. When the latter said he would like to go and see the spot, his friend cried 'And I'll go too!'

The next morning they started and passing through levels of fat meads and blooming fruit-trees, reached the little town of their quest, and more especially the historic bridge itself — much changed, but at any rate sufficiently well denoting the scene of Napoleon's exploit in the earlier and better days of his career. Over the quiet flowing of the Adda the two re-enacted the fight, and the 'Little Corporal's' dramatic victory over the Austrians.

The pleasant jingle in *Poems of the Past and the Present* named after the bridge, and written some time after the excursion to the scene, fully enough describes the visit, but the young Scotch lieutenant from India is not mentioned, though his zest by this time had grown more than equal to Hardy's — the latter's becoming somewhat damped at finding that the most persevering inquiries at Lodi failed to elicit any tradition of the event, and the furthest search to furnish any photograph of the town and river.

They returned to England by way of Como and the St. Gothard, one of the remarks Hardy makes on the former place being on the vying of 'the young greens with the old greens, the greens of yesterday and the greens of yesteryear'. It was too early in the year for Lucerne, and they stayed there only a day. Passing through Paris, they went to see the Crown jewels that chanced just then to be on exhibition, previous to their sale.

# PART IV

# BETWEEN TOWN AND COUNTRY

# CHAPTER XVI

# LONDON FRIENDS, PARIS, AND SHORT STORIES

1887–1888 : *Aet.* 47–48

REACHING London in April 1887, Hardy attended the annual dinner of the Royal Academy. He remarks thereon :

'The watching presence of so many portraits gives a distinct character to this dinner. . . . In speaking, the Duke of Cambridge could not decide whether he had ended his speech or not, and so tagged and tagged on a bit more, and a bit more, till the sentences were like acrobats hanging down from a trapeze. Lord Salisbury's satire was rather too serious for after-dinner. Huxley began well but ended disastrously ; the Archbishop was dreary ; Morley tried to look a regular dining-out man-of-the-world, but really looked what he is by nature, the student. Everybody afterwards walked about, the Prince of Wales included, remaining till 12. I spoke to a good many ; was apparently unknown to a good many more I knew. At these times men do not want to talk to their equals, but to their superiors.'

On the Sunday after, the Hardys again met Browning at Mrs. Procter's, and being full of Italy, Hardy alluded to 'The Statue and the Bust' (which he often thought one of the finest of Browning's poems) ; and observed that, looking at 'the empty shrine' opposite the figure of Ferdinand in the Piazza dell' Annunziata, he had wondered where the bust had gone to, and had been informed by an officious waiter standing at a neighbouring door that he remembered seeing it in its place ; after which he gave further interesting details about it, for which information he was gratefully rewarded. Browning smiled and said, 'I invented it.'

Shortly afterwards they settled till the end of July at a house in Campden-Hill Road.

Speaking of this date Hardy said that in looking for rooms to stay at for the season he called at a house-agent's as usual, where, not seeing the man at the desk who had been there a day or two before, and who knew his wants in flats and apartments, he inquired for the man and was told he was out. Saying he would call again in an hour, Hardy left. On coming back he was told he was still out. He called a day or two afterwards, and the answer then was that the clerk he wanted was away.

'But you said yesterday he was only out,' exclaimed Hardy. His informant looked round him as if not wishing to be overheard, and replied :

'Well, *strictly* he is not *out*, but *in*.'

'Why didn't you say so?'

'Because you can't speak to him. He's dead and buried.'

'*May* 16. Met Lowell at Lady Carnarvon's.'

'*May* 29. Instance of a *wrong* (*i.e.* selfish) philosophy in poetry :

> 'Thrice happy he who on the sunless side
> Of a romantic mountain. . . .
> Sits coolly calm ; while all the world without,
> Unsatisfied and sick, tosses at noon.
>
> THOMSON.'

'*June* 2. The forty-seventh birthday of Thomas the Unworthy.'

'*June* 8. Met at a dinner at the Savile Club : Goschen, Chancellor of the Exchequer ; Lord Lytton, A. J. Balfour, and others.'

'*June* 9. At dinner at (Juliet) Lady Pollock's. Sir F. told Emma that he had danced in the same quadrille with a gentleman who had danced with Marie Antoinette.

'Sir Patrick Colquhoun said that Lord Strath—— (illegible) told him he was once dining with Rogers when Sir Philip Francis was present. The conversation turned on "Junius". Rogers said he would ask Sir Philip point-blank if he really were the man, so going to him he said "Sir Philip, I want to ask you a question". Sir P. "At your peril, Sir!" Rogers retreated saying "He's not only Junius, but Junius *Brutus*!"

'He also told us that Lord S—— once related to him how George III. met him on Richmond Hill, and said to him : "Eton boy, what are you doing here?" —— "Taking a walk, Sir." —— "What form are you in?" —— "The sixth." —— "Then you have that which I couldn't give you." —— (Characteristic.)'

'*Sunday*. To Mrs. Procter's. Browning there. He was sleepy. In telling a story would break off, forgetting what he was going to say.'

On the 21st was Queen Victoria's Jubilee, and Hardy took his

wife to see the procession from the Savile Club in Piccadilly. 'The
Queen was very jolly-looking. The general opinion is that there
will certainly never be another jubilee in England ; anyhow, probably
never such a gathering of royal personages again.'

'25. At a concert at Prince's Hall I saw Souls outside Bodies.'

'26. We were at Mrs. Procter's when Browning came in as usual.
He seemed galled at not having been invited to the Abbey (Jubilee)
ceremony. He says that so far from receiving (as stated in the *Pall
Mall*) an invitation even so late as twenty-four hours before, he
received absolutely no invitation from the Lord Chamberlain (Lord
Lathom) at all. The Dean offered him one of his own family tickets,
but B. did not care to go on such terms, so went off to Oxford to
stay with Jowett. People who were present say there were crowds
of Court-servants and other nobodies there. An eminent actor had
25 tickets sent him . . . Millais, Huxley, Arnold, Spencer, etc., had
none. Altogether Literature, Art, and Science had been unmistake-
ably snubbed, and they should turn republican forthwith.' An
interesting comment on the reign of Queen Victoria!

The remainder of the London season in the brilliant Jubilee-year
was passed by the Hardys gaily enough. At some houses the scene
was made very radiant by the presence of so many Indian princes in
their jewelled robes. At a certain reception Hardy was rather struck
by one of the Indian dignitaries (who seems to have been the Raja
of Kapurthala) ; remarking of him :

'In his mass of jewels and white turban and tunic he stood and
sat apart amid the babble and gaiety, evidently feeling himself *alone*,
and having too much character to pretend to belong to and throw
himself into a thoughtless world of chit-chat and pleasure which he
understood nothing of.'

'*June* 30. Talked to Matthew Arnold at the Royal Academy
*Soirée*. Also to Lang, du Maurier, Thornycrofts, Mrs. Jeune, etc.

'With E. to lunch at Lady Stanley's (of Alderley). Met there
Lord Halifax, Lady Airlie, Hon. Maude Stanley, her brother Monsignor Stanley, and others. An exciting family dispute supervened,
in which they took no notice of us guests at all.'

But Hardy does not comment much on these society-gatherings,
his thoughts running upon other subjects, as is shown by the following memorandum made on the same day as the above. (It must
always be borne in mind that these memoranda on people and things
were made by him only as personal opinions for private consideration,
which he meant to destroy, and not for publication ; an issue which

has come about by his having been asked when old if he would object to their being printed, as there was no harm in them, and his saying passively that he did not mind.)

'*July* 14. It is the on-going — *i.e.* the "becoming" — of the world that produces its sadness. If the world stood still at a felicitous moment there would be no sadness in it. The sun and the moon standing still on Ajalon was not a catastrophe for Israel, but a type of Paradise.'

In August he was back again at Max Gate, and there remarks on the difference between children who grow up in solitary country places and those who grow up in towns — the former being imaginative, dreamy, and credulous of vague mysteries; giving as the reason that 'The Unknown comes within so short a radius from themselves by comparison with the city-bred'.

At the end of the month Mr. Edmund Gosse wrote to inform Hardy among other things that R. L. Stevenson was off to Colorado as a last chance, adding in the course of a humorous letter: 'I hope your spirits have been pretty good this summer. I have been scarcely fit for human society, I have been so deep in the dumps. I wonder whether climate has anything to do with it? It is the proper thing nowadays to attribute to physical causes all the phenomena which people used to call spiritual. But I am not sure. One may be dyspeptic and yet perfectly cheerful, and one may be quite well and yet no fit company for a churchyard worm. For the last week I should not have ventured to say unto a flea, "Thou art my sister".'

'*September* 3. Mother tells me of a woman she knew named Nanny Priddle, who when she married would never be called by her husband's name "because she was too proud", she said; and to the end of their lives the couple were spoken of as "Nanny Priddle and John Cogan".'

'*September* 25. My grandmother used to say that when sitting at home at Bockhampton she had heard the tranter "beat out the tune" on the floor with his feet when dancing at a party in his own house, which was a hundred yards or more away from hers.'

'*October* 2. Looked at the thorn-bushes by Rushy Pond [on an exposed spot of the heath]. In their wrath with the gales their forms resemble men's in like mood.

'A variant of the superstitions attached to pigeon's hearts is that, when the counteracting process is going on, the person who has bewitched the other *enters*. In the case of a woman in a village near here, who was working the spell at midnight, a neighbour knocked at the door and said; "Do ye come in and see my little maid.  She is so ill that I don't like to bide with her alone!"'

'*October* 7.  During the funeral of Henry Smith, the rector's son at West Stafford, the cows looked mournfully over the churchyard wall from the adjoining barton at the grave, resting their clammy chins on the coping; and at the end clattered their horns in a farewell volley.'

Another outline scheme for *The Dynasts* was shaped in November, in which Napoleon was represented as haunted by an Evil Genius or Familiar, whose existence he has to confess to his wives.  This was abandoned, and another tried in which Napoleon by means of necromancy becomes possessed of an insight, enabling him to see the thoughts of opposing generals.  This does not seem to have come to anything either.

But in December he quotes from Addison :

'In the description of Paradise the poet [Milton] has observed Aristotle's rule of lavishing all the ornaments of diction on the weak, inactive parts of the fable.'  And although Hardy did not slavishly adopt this rule in *The Dynasts*, it is apparent that he had it in mind in concentrating the 'ornaments of diction' in particular places, thus following Coleridge in holding that a long poem should not attempt to be poetical all through.

'*December* 11.  Those who invent vices indulge in them with more judgment and restraint than those who imitate vices invented by others.'

'*December* 31.  A silent New Year's Eve — no bell, or band, or voice.

'The year has been a fairly friendly one to me.  It showed me the south of France — Italy, above all Rome — and it brought me back unharmed and much illuminated.  It has given me some new acquaintances, too, and enabled me to hold my own in fiction, whatever that may be worth, by the completion of *The Woodlanders*.

'Books read or pieces looked at this year :

'Milton, Dante, Calderon, Goethe.

'Homer, Virgil, Molière, Scott.

'The Cid, Nibelungen, Crusoe, Don Quixote.

'Aristophanes, Theocritus, Boccaccio.

'Canterbury Tales, Shakespeare's Sonnets, Lycidas.

'Malory, Vicar of Wakefield, Ode to West Wind, Ode to Grecian Urn.

'Christabel, Wye above Tintern.

'Chapman's Iliad, Lord Derby's ditto, Worsley's Odyssey.'

'*January* 2.  1888.  Different purposes, different men.  Those in the city for money-making are not the same men as they were when at home the previous evening.  Nor are these the same as they were when lying awake in the small hours.'

'*January* 5.  Be rather curious than anxious about your own career ;  for whatever result may accrue to its intellectual and social value, it will make little difference to your personal well-being.  A naturalist's interest in the hatching of a queer egg or germ is the utmost introspective consideration you should allow yourself.'

'*January* 7.  On New Year's Eve and day I sent off five copies of the magazine containing a story of mine, and three letters — all eight to friends by way of New Year's greeting and good wishes.  *Not a single reply.*  Mem. :  Never send New Year's letters, etc., again.'

[Two were dying :  one ultimately replied.  The story was either 'The Withered Arm', in *Blackwood*, or 'The Waiting Supper' in *Murray's Magazine*, both of which appeared about this time.]

'Apprehension is a great element in imagination.  It is a semi-madness, which sees enemies, etc., in inanimate objects.'

'*January* 14.  A "sensation-novel" is possible in which the sensationalism is not casualty, but evolution ;  not physical but psychical. . . .  The difference between the latter kind of novel and the novel of physical sensationalism — *i.e.* personal adventure, etc., — is this :  that whereas in the physical the adventure itself is the subject of interest, the psychical results being passed over as commonplace, in the psychical the casualty or adventure is held to be of no intrinsic interest, but the effect upon the faculties is the important matter to be depicted.'

'*January* 24.  I find that my politics really are neither Tory nor Radical.  I may be called an Intrinsicalist.  I am against privilege derived from accident of any kind, and am therefore equally opposed to aristocratic privilege and democratic privilege.  (By the latter I mean the arrogant assumption that the only labour is hand-labour — a worse arrogance than that of the aristocrat, — the taxing of the worthy to help those masses of the population who will not help themselves when they might, etc.)  Opportunity should be equal for all, but those who will not avail themselves of it should be cared for merely — not be a burden to, nor the rulers over, those who do avail themselves thereof.'

'*February* 5.  Heard a story of a farmer who was "over-looked" [malignly affected] by *himself*.  He used to go and examine his stock

every morning before breakfast with anxious scrutiny.  The animals
pined away.  He went to a conjuror or white witch, who told him
he had no enemy ;  that the evil was of his own causing, the eye of a
fasting man being very blasting :  that he should eat a "dew-bit"
before going to survey any possession about which he had hopes.'

In the latter part of this month there arrived the following :

'The Rev. Dr. A. B. Grosart ventures to address Mr. Hardy on a
problem that is of life and death ;  personally, and in relation to young
eager intellects for whom he is responsible. . . . Dr. Grosart finds
abundant evidence that the facts and mysteries of nature and human
nature have come urgently before Mr. Hardy's penetrative brain.'

He enumerated some of the horrors of human and animal life,
particularly parasitic, and added :

'The problem is how to reconcile these with the absolute goodness and non-limitation of God.'

Hardy replied :  'Mr. Hardy regrets that he is unable to suggest
any hypothesis which would reconcile the existence of such evils as
Dr. Grosart describes with the idea of omnipotent goodness.  Perhaps
Dr. Grosart might be helped to a provisional view of the universe
by the recently published Life of Darwin, and the works of Herbert
Spencer and other agnostics.'

He met Leslie Stephen shortly after, and Stephen told him that he
too had received a similar letter from Grosart ;  to which he had replied that as the reverend doctor was a professor of theology, and he
himself only a layman, he should have thought it was the doctor's
business to explain the difficulty to his correspondent, and not his to
explain it to the doctor.

Two or three days later the Bishop (Wordsworth) of Salisbury
wrote to Hardy for his views on the migration of the peasantry,
'which is of considerable social importance and has a very distinct
bearing on the work of the Church', adding that Hardy with his very
accurate knowledge of the custom was well-qualified to be the historian of its causes and its results.  'Are they good or bad morally
and in respect of religion, respectability, etc., to men, women, and
children.'  Hardy's answer cannot be discovered, but he is known to
have held that these modern migrations are fatal to local traditions,
and to cottage horticulture.  Labourers formerly, knowing they were
permanent residents, would plant apple-trees and fruit-bushes with
zealous care, to profit from them : but now they scarce ever plant
one, knowing they will be finding a home elsewhere in a year or two ;
or if they do happen to plant any, digging them up and selling them

before leaving! Hence the lack of picturesqueness in modern labourers' dwellings.

'*March* 1. Youthful recollections of four village beauties :

'1. Elizabeth B——, and her red hair. [She seems to appear in the poem called "Lizbie Browne", and was a gamekeeper's daughter, a year or two older than Hardy himself.]

'2. Emily D——, and her mere prettiness.

'3. Rachel H——, and her rich colour, and vanity, and frailty, and clever artificial dimple-making. [She is probably in some respects the original of Arabella in *Jude the Obscure*.]

'4. Alice P—— and her mass of flaxen curls.'

'*March*. At the Temperance Hotel. The people who stay here appear to include religious enthusiasts of all sorts. They talk the old faiths with such new fervours and original aspects that such faiths seem again arresting. They open fresh views of Christianity by turning it in reverse positions, as Gérôme the painter did by painting the *shadow* of the Crucifixion instead of the Crucifixion itself as former painters had done.

'In the street outside I heard a man coaxing money from a prostitute in slang language, his arm round her waist. The outside was a commentary on the inside.'

'*March* 9. British Museum Reading Room. Souls are gliding about here in a sort of dream — screened somewhat by their bodies, but imaginable behind them. Dissolution is gnawing at them all, slightly hampered by renovations. In the great circle of the library Time is looking into Space. Coughs are floating in the same great vault, mixing with the rustle of book-leaves risen from the dead, and the touches of footsteps on the floor.'

'*March* 28. On returning to London after an absence I find the people of my acquaintance abraded, their hair disappearing, also their flesh, by degrees.

'People who to one's-self are transient singularities are to themselves the permanent condition, the inevitable, the normal, the rest of mankind being to them the singularity. Think, that those (to us) strange transitory phenomena, *their* personalities, are with them always, at their going to bed, at their uprising!

'Footsteps, cabs, etc., are continually passing our lodgings. And every echo, pit-pat, and rumble that makes up the general noise has behind it a motive, a prepossession, a hope, a fear, a fixed thought forward ; perhaps more — a joy, a sorrow, a love, a revenge.

'London appears not to *see itself*. Each individual is conscious of *himself*, but nobody conscious of themselves collectively, except perhaps some poor gaper who stares round with a half-idiotic aspect.

'There is no consciousness here of where anything comes from or goes to — only that it is present.

'In the City. The fiendish precision or mechanism of town-life is what makes it so intolerable to the sick and infirm. Like an acrobat performing on a succession of swinging trapezes, as long as you are at particular points at precise instants, everything glides as if afloat; but if you are not up to time ——'

'*April* 16. News of Matthew Arnold's death, which occurred yesterday. . . . The *Times* speaks quite truly of his "enthusiasm for the nobler and detestation of the meaner elements in humanity".'

'*April* 19. Scenes in ordinary life that are insipid at 20 become interesting at 30, and tragic at 40.'

'*April* 21. Dr. Quain told me some curious medical stories when we were dining at Mrs. Jeune's. He said it was a mistake for anyone to have so many doctors as the German Emperor has, because neither feels responsible. Gave an account of Queen Adelaide, who died through her physicians' ignorance of her malady, one of them, Dr. Chambers, remarking, when asked why he did not investigate her disorder, "Damn it, I wasn't going to pull about the Queen" — she being such a prude that she would never have forgiven him for making an examination that, as it proved, would have saved her life.

'Mary Jeune says that when she tries to convey some sort of moral or religious teaching to the East-end poor, so as to change their views from wrong to right, it ends by their convincing her that their view is the right one — not by her convincing them.'

'*April* 23. To Alma-Tadema's musical afternoon. Heckmann Quartett. The architecture of his house is incomplete without sunlight and warmth. Hence the dripping wintry afternoon without mocked his marble basin and brass steps and quilted blinds and silver apse.'

'*April* 26. Thought in bed last night that Byron's *Childe Harold* will live in the history of English poetry not so much because of the beauty of parts of it, which is great, but because of its good fortune in being an accretion of descriptive poems by the most fascinating personality in the world — for the English — not a common plebeian, but a romantically wicked noble lord. It affects even Arnold's judgment.'

'*April* 28. A short story of a young man — "who could not go to Oxford"—His struggles and ultimate failure. Suicide. [Probably the germ of *Jude the Obscure*.] There is something [in this] the world ought to be shown, and I am the one to show it to them—though I was not altogether hindered going, at least to Cambridge, and could have gone up easily at five-and-twenty.

'In Regent Street, which commemorates the Prince Regent. It is in the fitness of things that The Promenade of Prostitutes should be here. One can imagine *his shade* stalking up and down every night, smiling approvingly.'

'*May* 13. Lord Houghton tells me to-day at lunch at Lady Catherine Gaskell's of a young lady who gave a full description of a ball to her neighbour during the Chapel Royal service by calling out at each response in the Litany as many details as she could get in. Also of Lord —— who saves all his old tooth-brushes affectionately.

'The Gaskells said that Lord and Lady Lymington and themselves went to the city in an omnibus, and one of them nearly sat on an Irishwoman's baby. G. apologized, when she exclaimed, "Och, 'twas not you : 'twas the ugly one!" (pointing to Lord L.).

'Lady C. says that the central position of St. James's Square (where their house is) enables her to see so many more people. When she first comes to Town she feels a perfect lump the first fortnight—she knows nothing of the new phrases, and does not understand the social telegraphy and allusions.'

*May* 28. They went to Paris *via* London and Calais : and stayed in the Rue du Commandant Rivière several weeks, noticing on their arrival as they always did 'the sour smell of a foreign city'.

*June* 4 and 7. At the Salon. 'Was arrested by the sensational picture called "The Death of Jezebel" by Gabriel Guays, a horrible tragedy, and justly so, telling its story in a flash.'

'*June* 10. To Longchamps and the Grand Prix de Paris. Roar from the course as I got near. It was Pandemonium : not a blade of grass : half overshoe in dust : the ground covered with halves of white, yellow, and blue tickets : bookmakers with staring brass-lettered names and addresses, in the very exuberance of honesty. The starter spoke to the jockeys entirely in English, and most of the cursing and swearing was done in English likewise, and done well. The horses passed in a volley, so close together that it seemed they must be striking each other. Excitement. Cries of "Vive la France!" (a French horse having won).'

'*June* 11. To the Embassy. Bon Marché with Em. Walked to l'Etoile in twilight. The enormous arch stood up to its knees in lamplight, dark above against the deep blue of the upper sky. Went under and read some names of victories which were never won.'

'*June* 12. To see the tombs of St. Denis with E. A lantern at the slit on one side of the vault shows the coffins to us at the opposite slit.'

'*June* 13. Exhibition of Victor Hugo's manuscripts and drawings. Thence to one of the Correctional Courts : heard two or three trivial cases. Afterwards to the Salle des Conférences.'

'*June* 14. Sunny morning. View from l'Etoile. Fresh, after rain ; air clear. Could see distinctly far away along the Avenue de la Grande Armée — down into the hollow and on to rising ground beyond, where the road tapers to an obelisk standing there. Also could see far along the Avenue Wagram. In the afternoon I went to the Archives Nationales. Found them much more interesting than I had expected. As it was not a public day the attendant showed me round alone, which, with the gloomy wet afternoon, made the relics more solemn ; so that, mentally, I seemed close to those keys from the Bastille, those letters of the Kings of France, those Edicts, and those corridors of white boxes, each containing one year's shady documents of a past monarchy.'

Next day, coming out of the Bourse, he learnt of the death of the Emperor of Germany.

On returning to London Hardy had a rheumatic attack which kept him in bed two or three days, after which they entered lodgings at Upper Phillimore Place, Kensington, where they remained till the third week in July. Walter Pater sometimes called on them from over the way, and told them a story of George III anent the row of houses they were living in. These, as is well known, have their fronts ornamented with the stone festooning of their date, and the King would exclaim when returning from Weymouth : 'Ah, there are the dish-clouts. Now I shall soon be home!' Acquaintance was renewed with various friends, among them, after a dozen years of silence, Mrs. Ritchie (Miss Thackeray), later Lady Ritchie. 'Talked of the value of life, and its interest. She admits that her interest in the future lies largely in the fact that she has children, and says that when she calls on L. Stephen and his wife she feels like a ghost, who arouses sad feelings in the person visited.'

As to the above remark on the value of life, Hardy writes whimsically a day or two later :

'I have attempted many modes [of finding it]. For my part, if there is any way of getting a melancholy satisfaction out of life it lies in dying, so to speak, before one is out of the flesh ; by which I mean putting on the manners of ghosts, wandering in their haunts, and taking their views of surrounding things. To think of life as passing away is a sadness ; to think of it as past is at least tolerable. Hence even when I enter into a room to pay a simple morning call I have unconsciously the habit of regarding the scene as if I were a spectre not solid enough to influence my environment ; only fit to behold and say, as another spectre said : "Peace be unto you!"'

'*July* 3. Called on [Eveline] Lady Portsmouth. Found her alone and stayed to tea. Looked more like a model countess than ever I have seen her do before, her black brocaded silk fitting her well and suiting her eminently. She is not one of those marble people who can be depended upon for their appearance at a particular moment, but like all mobile characters uncertain as to aspect. She is one of the few, very few, women of her own rank for whom I would make a sacrifice : a woman too of talent, part of whose talent consists in concealing that she has any.'

'*July* 5. A letter lies on the red velvet cover of the table ; staring up, by reason of the contrast. I cover it over, that it may not hit my eyes so hard.'

'*July* 7. One o'clock A.M. I got out of bed, attracted by the never-ending procession [of market-carts to Covent Garden] as seen from our bedroom windows, Phillimore Place. Chains rattle, and each cart cracks under its weighty pyramid of vegetables.'

'*July* 8. A service at St. Mary Abbots, Kensington. The red plumes and ribbon in two stylish girls' hats in the foreground match the red robes of the persons round Christ on the Cross in the east window. The pale crucified figure rises up from a parterre of London bonnets and artificial hair-coils, as viewed from the back where I am. The sky over Jerusalem seems to have some connection with the corn-flowers in a fashionable hat that bobs about in front of the city of David. . . . When the congregation rises there is a rustling of silks like that of the Devils' wings in Paradise Lost. Every woman then, even if she had forgotten it before, has a single thought to the folds of her clothes. They pray in the litany as if under enchantment. Their real life is spinning on beneath this apparent one of calm, like the District Railway-trains underground just by — throbbing, rushing, hot, concerned with next week, last week. . . . Could these true scenes in which this congregation is living be brought into church bodily with the personages, there would be a churchful of jostling phantasmagorias crowded like a heap of soap bubbles, infinitely intersecting, but each seeing only his own. That bald-headed man is surrounded by the interior of the Stock Exchange ; that girl by the jeweller's shop in which she purchased yesterday. Through this bizarre world of thought circulates the recitative of the parson — a thin solitary note without cadence or change of intensity — and getting lost like a bee in the clerestory.'

'*July* 9. To "The Taming of the Shrew". A spirited unconventional performance, revitalizing an old subject. The brutal mediaeval view of the sex which animates the comedy does not bore us by its obsoleteness, the Shrew of Miss Ada Rehan being such a real shrew. Her attitude of sad, impotent resignation, when her husband wears out her endurance, in which she stands motionless and almost unconscious of what is going on around her, was well done. At first she hears the cracks of the whip with indifference ; at length she begins to shrink at the sound of them, and when he literally whips the domestics out of the room she hides away. At first not looking at him in his tantrums, she gets to steal glances at him, with an awestruck arrested attention. ' The scene in which the sun-and-moon argument comes in contained the best of acting. Drew's aspect of inner humorous opinion, lively eye, and made-up mind, is eminently suited to the husband's character.

'Reading H. James's *Reverberator*. After this kind of work one feels inclined to be purposely careless in detail. The great novels of the future will certainly not concern themselves with the minutiae of manners. . . . James's subjects are those one could be interested in at moments when there is nothing larger to think of.'

'*July* 11. At the Savile. [Sir] Herbert Stephen declares that he met S——r [another member of the Club] in Piccadilly, a few minutes ago, going away from the direction of the club house door, and that S——r nodded to him ; then arriving quickly at the Club he saw S——r seated in the back room. S——r, who is present during the telling, listens to this story of his wraith, and as H. S. repeats it to the other members, becomes quite uncomfortable at the weirdness of it. H. S. adds that he believes S——r is in the back room still, and S——r says he is afraid to go in to himself.'

'*July* 13. After being in the street : What was it on the faces of those horses? — Resignation. Their eyes looked at me, haunted me. The absoluteness of their resignation was terrible. When afterwards I heard their tramp as I lay in bed, the ghosts of their eyes came in to me, saying, "Where is your justice, O man and ruler?"'

'Lady Portsmouth told me at a dinner party last night that once she sat between Macaulay and Henry Layard in dining at Lord

Lansdowne's, and whenever one of them had got the ear of the table the other turned to her and talked, to show that the absolute vacuity of his rival's discourse had to be filled in somehow with any rubbish at hand.'

'*July* 14.   Was much struck with Gladstone's appearance at Flinders Petrie's Egyptian Exhibition.   The full curves of his Roman face ;   and his cochin-china-egg complexion was not at all like his pallor when I last saw him, and there was an utter absence of any expression of senility or mental weakness. — We dined at Walter Pater's.   Met Miss ——, an Amazon, more, an Atalanta, most, a Faustine.   Smokes : handsome girl : cruel small mouth : she's of the class of interesting women one would be afraid to marry.'

Here follow long lists of books read, or looked into, or intended to be read, during the year.

# CHAPTER XVII

# MORE TOWN FRIENDS AND A NOVEL'S DISMEMBERMENT

### 1888–1889 : *Aet.* 48–49

RETURNING to Dorchester two days later, he notes down : 'Thought of the determination to enjoy. We see it in all nature, from the leaf on the tree to the titled lady at the ball. . . . It is achieved, of a sort, under superhuman difficulties. Like pent-up water it will find a chink of possibility somewhere. Even the most oppressed of men and animals find it, so that out of a thousand there is hardly one who has not a sun of some sort for his soul.'

'*August* 5, 1888. To find beauty in ugliness is the province of the poet.'

'8. The air is close, the sunshine suddenly disappears, and a bad kind of sea-fog comes up, smelling like a laundry or wash-house.'

'19. Sent a story to H. Quilter, by request, for his Magazine, entitled *A Tragedy of Two Ambitions.*'

'21. The literary productions of men of rigidly good family and rigidly correct education, mostly treat social conventions and contrivances — the artificial forms of living — as if they were cardinal facts of life.

'Society consists of Characters and No-characters — nine at least of the latter to one of the former.'

'*September* 9. My Father says that Dick Facey used to rivet on the fetters of criminals when they were going off by coach (Facey was journeyman for Clare the smith). He was always sent for secretly, that people might not know and congregate at the gaol entrance. They were carried away at night, a stage-coach being specially ordered. One K. of Troytown, on the London Road, a poacher, who was in the great fray at Westwood Barn near Lulworth Castle about 1825, was brought past his own door thus, on his way to transportation : he called to his wife and family ; they heard his shout and ran out to bid him good-bye as he sat in chains. He was never heard of again by them.

'T. Voss used to take casts of heads of executed convicts. He took those of Preedy and Stone. Dan Pouncy held the heads while it was being done. Voss oiled the faces, and took them in halves, afterwards making casts from the masks. There was a groove where the rope went, and Voss saw a little blood in the case of Stone, where the skin had been broken, — not in Preedy's.'

'*September* 10. Destitution sometimes reaches the point of grandeur in its pathetic grimness : *e.g.*, as shown in the statement of the lodging-house keeper in the Whitechapel murder :

'"He had seen her in the lodging-house as late as half-past one o'clock or two that morning. He knew her as an unfortunate, and that she generally frequented Stratford for a living. He asked her for her lodging-money, when she said, 'I have not got it. I am weak and ill, and have been in the infirmary.' He told her that she knew the rules, whereupon she went out to get some money." (*Times* report.)

'O richest City in the world! "She knew the rules."'

'*September* 15. Visited the old White Horse Inn, Maiden Newton. Mullioned windows, queer old bedrooms. Fireplace in the late Perpendicular style. The landlady tells me that the attic was closed up for many years, and that on opening it they found a suit of clothes, supposed to be those of a man who was murdered.' [This fine old Tudor inn is now pulled down.]

'*September* 30. "The Valley of the Great Dairies" — Froom.
'"The Valley of the Little Dairies" — Blackmoor.
'In the afternoon by train to Evershot. Walked to Woolcombe, a property once owned by a — I think the senior — branch of the Hardys. Woolcombe House was to the left of where the dairy now is. On by the lane and path to Bubb-Down. Looking east you see High Stoy and the escarpment below it. The Vale of Blackmoor is almost entirely green, every hedge being studded with trees. On the left you see to an immense distance, including Shaftesbury.

'The decline and fall of the Hardys much in evidence hereabout. An instance : Becky S.'s mother's sister married one of the Hardys of this branch, who was considered to have bemeaned himself by the marriage. "All Woolcombe and Froom Quintin belonged to them at one time," Becky used to say proudly. She might have added Up-Sydling and Toller Welme. This particular couple had an enormous lot of children. I remember when young seeing the man — tall and thin — walking beside a horse and common spring trap, and my mother pointing him out to me and saying he represented what was once the leading branch of the family. So we go down, down, down.'

'*October* 7. The besetting sin of modern literature is its insincerity. Half its utterances are qualified, even contradicted, by an aside, and this particularly in morals and religion. When dogma has to be balanced on its feet by such hair-splitting as the late Mr. M. Arnold's it must be in a very bad way.'

'*October* 15–21. Has the tradition that Cerne-Abbas men have no whiskers any foundation in the fact of their being descendants of a family or tribe or clan who have not intermarried with neighbours on account of their isolation? They are said to be hot-tempered people.

'Stephen B. says that he has "never had the nerve" to be a bearer at a funeral. Now his brother George, who has plenty of nerve, has borne many neighbours to their graves.

'If you look beneath the surface of any farce you see a tragedy; and, on the contrary, if you blind yourself to the deeper issues of a tragedy you see a farce.

'My mother says that my [paternal] grandmother told her she was ironing her best muslin gown (then worn by young women at any season) when news came that the Queen of France was beheaded. She put down her iron, and stood still, the event so greatly affecting her mind. She remembered the pattern of the gown so well that she would recognize it in a moment.' Hardy himself said that one hot and thundery summer in his childhood she remarked to him : 'It was like this in the French Revolution, I remember.'

'*December* 10. . . . He, she, had blundered; but not as the Prime Cause had blundered. He, she, had sinned; but not as the Prime Cause had sinned. He, she, was ashamed and sorry; but not as the Prime Cause would be ashamed and sorry if it knew.' (The reference is unexplained.)

Among the letters received by Hardy for the New Year (1889) was one from Mr. Gosse, who wrote thanking him for *A Tragedy of Two Ambitions*, which he thought one of the most thrilling and most complete stories Hardy had written — 'I walked under the moral burden of it for the remainder of the day. . . . I am truly happy — being an old faded leaf and disembowelled bloater and wet rag myself — to find your genius ever so fresh and springing.'

They were in London the first week of the year, concerning which Hardy remarks :

'On arriving in London I notice more and more that it (viz. London proper — the central parts) is becoming a vast hotel or caravan, having no connection with Middlesex — whole streets which were not so very long ago mostly of private residences consisting entirely of lodging-houses, and having a slatternly look about them.

'Called on Lady ——. She is a slim girl still, and continually tells her age, and speaks practically of "before I was married". Tells humorously of how she and Lord —— her father, who is a nervous man, got to the church too soon, and drove drearily up and down the Thames Embankment till the right time. She has just now the fad of adoring art. When she can no longer endure the ugliness of London she goes down to the National Gallery and sits in front of the great Titian.'

'*January* 8. To the City. Omnibus horses, Ludgate Hill. The greasy state of the streets caused constant slipping. The poor creatures struggled and struggled but could not start the omnibus. A man next me said: "It must take all heart and hope out of them! I shall get out." He did; but the whole remaining selfish twenty-five of us sat on. The horses despairingly got us up the hill at last. I *ought* to have taken off my hat to him and said: "Sir, though I was not stirred by your humane impulse I will profit by your good example"; and have followed him. I should like to know that man; but we shall never meet again!'

'*January* 9. At the Old Masters, Royal Academy. Turner's water-colours: each is a landscape *plus* a man's soul. . . . What he paints chiefly is *light as modified by objects*. He first recognizes the impossibility of really reproducing on canvas all that is in a landscape; then gives for that which cannot be reproduced a something else which shall have upon the spectator an approximative effect to that of the real. He said, in his maddest and greatest days: "What pictorial drug can I dose man with, which shall affect his eyes somewhat in the manner of this reality which I cannot carry to him?" — and set to make such strange mixtures as he was tending towards in "Rain, Steam and Speed", "The Burial of Wilkie", "Agrippina landing with the ashes of Germanicus", "Approach to Venice", "Snowstorm and a Steamboat", etc. Hence, one may say, Art is the secret of how to produce by a false thing the effect of a true. . . .

'I am struck by the red glow of Romney's backgrounds, and his red flesh shades. . . . Watteau paints claws for hands. They are unnatural — hideous sometimes. . . . Then the pictures of Sir Joshua, in which middle-aged people sit out of doors without hats,

on damp stone seats under porticoes, and expose themselves imprudently to draughts and chills, as if they had lost their senses. . . .
Besides the above there were also the Holls, and the works of other
recent English painters, such as Maclise. . . .

'How Time begins to lift the veil and show us by degrees the truly
great men among these, as distinct from the vaunted and the fashionable. The false glow thrown on them by their generation dies down,
and we see them as they are.'

'*January* 28. Alfred Parsons, the landscape painter, here. He
gave as a reason for living in London and mixing a good deal with
people (intellectual I presume) that you can let them do your thinking
for you. A practice that will be disastrous to A. P.'s brush, I fear.'

'*February* 6. (After reading Plato's dialogue "Cratylus"): A
very good way of looking at things would be to regard everything
as having an actual or false name, and an intrinsic or true name, to
ascertain which all endeavour should be made. . . . The fact is that
nearly all things are falsely, or rather inadequately, named.'

'*February* 19. The story of a face which goes through three
generations or more, would make a fine novel or poem of the passage
of Time. The differences in personality to be ignored.' [This idea
was to some extent carried out in the novel *The Well-Beloved*, the
poem entitled 'Heredity', etc.]

'*February* 26. In time one might get to regard every object, and
every action, as composed, not of this or that material, this or that
movement, but of the qualities pleasure and pain in varying proportions.'

'*March* 1. In a Botticelli the soul is outside the body, permeating
its spectator with its emotions. In a Rubens the flesh is without, and
the soul (possibly) within. The very odour of the flesh is distinguishable in the latter.'

'*March* 4. A Village story recalled to me yesterday:

'Mary L., a handsome wench, had come to Bockhampton, leaving
a lover at Askerswell, her native parish. William K. fell in love with
her at the new place. The old lover, who was a shoemaker, smelling
a rat, came anxiously to see her, with a present of a dainty pair of
shoes he had made. He met her by chance at the pathway stile, but
alas, on the arm of the other lover. In the rage of love the two men
fought for her till they were out of breath, she looking on and holding
both their hats the while; till William, wiping his face, said: "Now,
Polly, which of we two do you love best? Say it out straight!" She
would not state then, but said she would consider (the hussy!). The

young man to whom she had been fickle left her indignantly — throwing the shoes at her and her new lover as he went. She never saw or heard of him again, and accepted the other. *But she kept the shoes, and was married in them.* I knew her well as an old woman.'

'*March* 15. What has been written cannot be blotted. Each new style of novel must be the old with added ideas, not an ignoring and avoidance of the old. And so of religion, and a good many other things!'

'*April* 5. London. Four million forlorn hopes!'

'*April* 7. A woeful fact — that the human race is too extremely developed for its corporeal conditions, the nerves being evolved to an activity abnormal in such an environment. Even the higher animals are in excess in this respect. It may be questioned if Nature, or what we call Nature, so far back as when she crossed the line from invertebrates to vertebrates, did not exceed her mission. This planet does not supply the materials for happiness to higher existences. Other planets may, though one can hardly see how.'

A day or two later brought him a long and interesting letter from J. Addington Symonds at Davos Platz concerning *The Return of the Native*, which he had just met with and read, and dwelling enthusiastically on 'its vigour and its freshness and its charm'. The last week in April they went off to London again for a few months, staying at the West Central Hotel till they could find something more permanent, which this year chanced to be two furnished floors in Monmouth Road, Bayswater.

'*May* 5. Morning. Sunday. To Bow Church, Cheapside, with Em. The classic architecture, especially now that it has been regilt and painted, makes one feel in Rome. About twenty or thirty people present. When you enter, the curate from the reading-desk and the rector from the chancel alm ost smile a greeting as they look up in their surplices, so glad are they that you have condescended to visit them in their loneliness.

'That which, socially, is a great tragedy, may be in Nature no alarming circumstance.'

'*May* 12. Evening. Sunday. To St. James's, Westmoreland Street, with Em. Heard Haweis — a small lame figure who could with difficulty climb into the pulpit. His black hair, black beard, hollow cheeks and black gown, made him look like one of the skeletons in the Church of the Capuchins, Rome. The subject of his discourse was Cain and Abel, his first proposition being that Cain had excellent qualities, and was the larger character of the twain, though Abel might have been the better man in some things. Yet, he reminded us, good people are very irritating sometimes, and the occasion was probably one of agricultural depression like the present, so that Cain said to himself: "'Tis this year as it was last year, and all my labour wasted!" (titter from the congregation). Altogether the effect was comical. But one sympathized with the preacher, he was so weak, and quite in a perspiration when he had finished.'

'*May* 20. Called on the Alma-Tademas. Tadema is like a school-boy, with untidy hair, a sturdy inquiring look, and bustling manner. I like this phase of him better than his man-of-the-world phase. He introduced me to M. Taine, a kindly, nicely trimmed old man with a slightly bent head.'

Earlier in the year Hardy had asked one of the Miss Sheridans, a daughter of Mr. and Mrs. A. Brinsley Sheridan, Hardy's neighbours at Frampton Court, Dorset, if she could sing to him 'How oft, Louisa!' the once celebrated song in her ancestor's comic opera 'The Duenna'. (It was not a woman's song, by the way.) His literary sense was shocked by her telling him that she had never heard of it, since he himself had sung it as a youth, having in fact been in love with a Louisa himself. Now he was in London he remembered that he had promised it to her, and looked for a copy, but, much to his surprise, to find one seemed beyond his power. At last he called at a second-hand music-shop that used to stand where the Oxford Circus Tube-Station now is, and repeated hopelessly, 'How oft, Louisa?' The shop was kept by an old man, who was sitting on an office stool in a rusty dress-suit and very tall hat, and at the sound of the words he threw himself back in his seat, spread his arms like an opera-singer, and sang in a withered voice by way of answer:

> How oft, Louisa, hast thou told,
> (Nor wilt thou the fond boast disown)
> Thou would'st not lose Antonio's love
> To reign the partner of a throne!

'Ah, that carries me back to times that will never return!' he added. 'Yes; when I was a young man it was my favourite song. As to my having it, why, certainly, it is here *somewhere*. But I could not find it in a week.' Hardy left him singing it, promising to return again.

When his shop was pulled down the delightful old man disappeared, and though Hardy searched for him afterwards he never saw him any more.

'*May* 29. That girl in the omnibus had one of those faces of marvellous beauty which are seen casually in the streets but never among one's friends. It was perfect in its softened classicality — a Greek face translated into English. Moreover she was fair, and her hair pale chestnut. Where do these women come from? Who marries them? Who knows them?'

They went to picture-galleries, concerts, French plays, and the usual lunches and dinners during the season; and in June Hardy ran down to Dorchester for a day or two, on which occasion, taking a walk in the meadows, he remarks: 'The birds are so passionately happy that they introduce variations into their songs to an outrageous degree — which are not always improvements.'

In London anew: 'One difference between the manners of the intellectual middle class and of the nobility is that the latter have more flexibility, almost a dependence on their encompassment, as if they were waiting upon future events; while the former are direct, and energetic, and crude, as if they were manufacturing a future to please them.'

'*July* 9. Love lives on propinquity, but dies of contact.'

'*July* 14. Sunday. Centenary of the fall of the Bastille. Went to Newton Hall to hear Frederic Harrison lecture on the French Revolution. The audience sang "The Marseillaise". Very impressive.'

'*July* 23. Of the people I have met this summer, the lady whose mouth recalls more fully than any other beauty's the Elizabethan metaphor "Her lips are roses full of snow" (or is it Lodge's?) is Mrs. Hamo Thornycroft — whom I talked to at Gosse's dinner.'

'*July* 24. B. Museum:

'Εἰ δέ τι πρεσβύτερον, etc. Soph. *Oed. Tyr.* 1365 ("and if there be a woe surpassing woes, it hath become the portion of Oedipus" — Jebb. Cf. Tennyson: "a deeper deep").'

About this time Hardy was asked by a writer of some experience in adapting novels for the theatre — Mr. J. T. Grein — if he would grant permission for *The Woodlanders* to be so adapted. In his reply he says:

'You have probably observed that the ending of the story — hinted rather than stated — is that the heroine is doomed to an unhappy life with an inconstant husband. I could not accentuate this strongly in the book, by reason of the conventions of the libraries, etc. Since the story was written, however, truth to character is not considered quite such a crime in literature as it was formerly; and it is therefore a question for you whether you will accent this ending, or prefer to obscure it.'

It appears that nothing arose out of the dramatization, it becoming obvious that no English manager at this date would venture to defy the formalities to such an extent as was required by the novel, in which some of the situations were approximately of the kind afterwards introduced to English playgoers by translations from Ibsen.

At the end of the month they gave up their rooms in Bayswater and returned to Dorchester; where during August Hardy settled down daily to writing the new story he had conceived, which was *Tess of the d'Urbervilles*, though it had not as yet been christened. During the month he jots down as a casual thought:

'When a married woman who has a lover kills her husband, she does not really wish to kill the husband; she wishes to kill the situation. Of course in Clytaemnestra's case it was not exactly so, since there was the added grievance of Iphigenia, which half-justified her.'

'*September* 21. For carrying out that idea of Napoleon, the Empress, Pitt, Fox, etc., I feel continually that I require a larger canvas. . . . A spectral tone must be adopted. . . . Royal ghosts. . . . Title: "A Drama of Kings". [He did not use it, however; preferring *The Dynasts*.]

'*October* 13. Three wooden-legged men used to dance a three-handed reel at Broadmayne, so my father says.'

In November Leslie Stephen wrote concerning a Dorset character for the *Dictionary of National Biography*, then in full progress under his hands:

'I only beg that you will not get into the Dictionary yourself. You can avoid it by living a couple of years — hardly a great price to pay for the exemption. But I will not answer for my grandson, who will probably edit a supplement.'

About the same time Hardy answered some questions by Mr. Gosse:

'"Oak-apple day" is exotic; "sic-sac day" or "shic-sac day", being what the peasantry call it.

'"Ich." This and kindred words, *e.g.* — "Ich woll", "er woll", etc., are still used by old people in N.W. Dorset and Somerset (*vide* Gammer Oliver's conversation in *The Woodlanders*, which is an attempted reproduction). I heard "Ich" only last Sunday; but it is dying rapidly.'

However, the business immediately in hand was the new story *Tess of the d'Urbervilles*, for the serial use of which Hardy had three requests, if not more, on his list; and in October as much of it as was written was offered to the first who had asked for it, the editor of *Murray's Magazine*. It was declined and returned to him in the middle of November virtually on the score of its improper explicitness. It was at once sent on to the second, the editor of *Macmillan's Magazine*, and on the 25th was declined by him for practically the same reason. Hardy would now have much preferred to finish the story and bring it out in volume form only, but there were reasons why he could not afford to do this; and he adopted a plan till then, it is believed, unprecedented in the annals of fiction. This was not to offer the novel intact to the third editor on his list (his experience with the first two editors having taught him that it would be useless to send it to the third as it stood), but to send it up with some chapters or parts of chapters cut out, and instead of destroying these to publish them, or much of them, elsewhere, if practicable, as episodic adventures of anonymous personages (which in fact was done, with the omission of a few paragraphs); till they could be put back in their places at the printing of the whole in volume form. In addition several passages were modified. Hardy carried out this unceremonious concession to conventionality with cynical amusement, knowing the novel was moral enough and to spare. But the work was sheer drudgery, the modified passages having to be written in coloured ink, that the originals might be easily restored, and he frequently asserted that it would have been almost easier for him to write a new story altogether. Hence the labour brought no profit. He resolved to get away from the supply of family fiction to magazines as soon as he conveniently could do so.

However, the treatment was a complete success, and the mutilated novel was accepted by the editor of the *Graphic*, the third editor on Hardy's list, and an arrangement come to for beginning it in the pages of that paper in July 1891. It may be mentioned that no complaint of impropriety in its cut-down form was made by readers, except by one gentleman with a family of daughters, who thought the blood-stain on the ceiling indecent — Hardy could never understand why.

'*December* 1. It was the custom at Stinsford down to 1820 or so to take a corpse to church on the Sunday of the funeral, and let it remain in the nave through the service, after which the burial took place. The people liked the custom, and always tried to keep a corpse till Sunday. The funeral psalms were used for the psalms of the day, and the funeral chapter for the second lesson.'

'*December* 13. Read in the papers that Browning died at Venice yesterday.' He was buried in Westminster Abbey on December 31.

'"Incidents in the development of a soul! little else is worth study," — Browning.

'What the *Athenæum* says is true, though not all the truth, that intellectual subtlety is the disturbing element in his art.'

Among other poems written about this time was the one called 'At Middle-Field Gate in February', describing the field-women of the author's childhood. On the present writer's once asking Hardy the names of those he calls the 'bevy now underground', he said they were Unity Sargent, Susan Chamberlain, Esther Oliver, Emma Shipton, Anna Barrett, Ann West, Elizabeth Hurden, Eliza Trevis, and others, who had been young women about twenty when he was a child.

# CHAPTER XVIII

# OBSERVATIONS ON PEOPLE AND THINGS

1890 : *Aet.* 49–50

'*January* 5. Looking over old *Punches.* Am struck with the frequent wrong direction of satire, and of commendation, when seen by the light of later days.'

'*January* 29. I have been looking for God 50 years, and I think that if he had existed I should have discovered him. As an external personality, of course — the only true meaning of the word.'

'*March* 5. A staid, worn, weak man at the railway station. His back, his legs, his hands, his face, were longing to be out of the world. His brain was not longing to be, because, like the brain of most people, it was the last part of his body to realize a situation.

'In the train on the way to London. Wrote the first four or six lines of "Not a line of her writing have I". It was a curious instance of sympathetic telepathy. The woman whom I was thinking of — a cousin — was dying at the time, and I quite in ignorance of it. She died six days later. The remainder of the piece was not written till after her death.'

'*March* 15. With E. to a crush at the Jeunes'. Met Mrs. T. and her great eyes in a corner of the rooms, as if washed up by the surging crowd. The most beautiful woman present. . . . But these women! If put into rough wrappers in a turnip-field, where would their beauty be?'

He observes later in respect of such scenes as these: 'Society, *collectively*, has neither seen what any ordinary person can see, read what every ordinary person has read, nor thought what every ordinary person has thought.'

'*March–April* :

'Altruism, or The Golden Rule, or whatever "Love your Neighbour as Yourself" may be called, will ultimately be brought about I think by the pain we see in others reacting on ourselves, as if we and they were a part of one body. Mankind, in fact, may be and possibly will be viewed as members of one corporeal frame.

'Tories will often do by way of exception to their principles more extreme acts of democratism or broad-mindedness than Radicals do by rule — such as help on promising plebeians, tolerate wild beliefs, etc.

'Art consists in so depicting the common events of life as to bring out the features which illustrate the author's idiosyncratic mode of regard ; making old incidents and things seem as new.'

'*Easter.* Sir George Douglas came. Went to Barnes's grave with him ; next day to Portland. Lunched at the Mermaid.

'In an article on Ibsen in the *Fortnightly* the writer says that his manner is wrong. That the drama, like the novel, should not be for edification. In this I think the writer errs. It should be so, but the edified should not perceive the edification. Ibsen's edifying is too obvious.'

'*April* 26. View the Prime Cause or Invariable Antecedent as "It" and recount its doings.' [This was done in *The Dynasts.*]

In May the Hardys were again resident in London, and went their customary round of picture-viewing, luncheons, calls, dinners, and receptions. At the Academy he reminds himself of old Academy exhibitions, *e.g.* the years in which there was a rail round Frith's pictures, and of the curious effect upon an observer of the fashionable crowd — seeming like people moving about under enchantment, or as somnambulists. At an evening service at St. George's, Hanover Square, 'everything looks the Modern World : the electric light and old theology seem strange companions ; and the sermon was as if addressed to native tribes of primitive simplicity, and not to the Nineteenth-Century English.' Coming out of church he went into the Criterion for supper, where, first going to the second floor, he stumbled into a room whence proceeded 'low laughter and murmurs, the light of lamps with pink shades ; where the men were all in evening clothes, ringed and studded, and the women much uncovered in the neck and heavily jewelled, their glazed and lamp-blacked eyes wandering'. He descended and had his supper in the grill-room.

'*May* 9. MS. of *A Group of Noble Dames* sent to the *Graphic* as promised.

'In the streets I see patient hundreds, labouring on, and boxes on wheels packed with men and women. There are charcoal trees in the squares. A man says : "When one is half-drunk London seems a wonderfully enjoyable place, with its lamps, and cabs moving like fire-flies." Yes, man has done more with his materials than God has done with his.

'A physician cannot cure a disease, but he can change its mode of expression.'

'*May* 15. Coming home from seeing Irving in *The Bells*. Between 11 and 12. The 4,000,000 suggest their existence now, when one sees the brilliancy about Piccadilly Circus at this hour, and notices the kiln-dried features around.'

At Mr. Gosse's this month they met Miss Balestier — an attractive and thoughtful young woman on her first visit to England from America, who remarked to him that it was so reposeful over here; 'In America you feel at night, "I must be quick and sleep; there is not much time to give to it".' She afterwards became Mrs. Rudyard Kipling. About the same date Hardy also met — it is probable for the first time — Mr. Kipling himself. 'He talked about the East, and he well said that the East is the world, both in numbers and in experiences. It has passed through our present bustling stages, and has become quiescent. He told curious details of Indian life.'

Hardy remarks that June 2 is his fiftieth birthday: and during the month went frequently to the Savile Club, sometimes dining there with acquaintances, among others J. H. Middleton, Slade Professor of Fine Art at Cambridge. Hardy used to find fault with Middleton as having no sense of life as such; as one who would talk, for instance, about bishops' copes and mitres with an earnest, serious, anxious manner, as if there were no cakes and ale in the world, or laughter and tears, or human misery beyond tears. His sense of art had caused him to lose all sense of relativity, and of art's subsidiary relation to existence.

This season also Hardy seems to have had a humour for going the round of the music-halls, and pronounces upon the beauties 'whose lustrous eyes and pearly countenances show that they owe their attractions to art', that they are seldom well-formed physically; notes the 'round-hatted young men gaping at the stage, with receding chins and rudimentary mouths'; and comments upon the odd fact that though there were so many obvious drunkards around him, the character on the stage which always gave the most delight was that of a drunkard imitated. At Bizet's opera of *Carmen* he was struck, as he had been struck before, with the manner in which people conducted themselves on the operatic stage; that of being 'possessed, maudlin, distraught, as if they lived on a planet whose atmosphere was intoxicating'. At a ballet at the Alhambra he noticed 'the air of docile obedience on the faces of some of the dancing women, a passive resignation like that of a plodding horse, as if long accustomed to correction.  Also marks of fatigue.  The morality of actresses, dancers, etc., cannot be judged by the same standard as that of people who lead slower lives.  Living in a throbbing atmosphere they are perforce throbbed by it in spite of themselves.  We should either put down these places altogether because of their effect upon the performers, or forgive the performers as irresponsibles. . . . The Première Danseuse strokes each calf with the sole of her other foot like a fly — on her mouth hanging a perpetual smile.'

'*June* 23.  Called on Arthur Locker [editor] at the *Graphic* office in answer to his letter.  He says he does not object to the stories [*A Group of Noble Dames*] but the Directors do.  Here's a pretty job!  Must smooth down these Directors somehow I suppose.'

In the same month he met Mr. (afterwards Sir) H. M. Stanley, the explorer, at a dinner given by the publishers of his travels.  Hardy does not seem to have been much attracted by his personality.  He observed that Stanley was shorter than himself, 'with a disdainful curve on his mouth and look in his eye which would soon become resentment'.  He made a speech in the worst taste, in Hardy's opinion, being to the effect that everybody who had had to do with producing his book was, rightly, delighted with the honour.  At the same dinner Hardy talked to Du Chaillu, who had also spoken a few words.  Hardy asked him : 'Why didn't you claim more credit for finding those dwarfs?'  The good-natured Du Chaillu said with a twinkle : 'Noh, noh!  It is *his* dinner.'  Hardy also made the acquaintance of the Bishop of Ripon at that dinner, from what he says : 'He [the Bishop] has a nice face — a sort of ingenuous archness in it — as if he would be quite willing to let supernaturalism down easy, if he could.'

At the police courts, where just at this time he occasionally spent half an hour, being still compelled to get novel padding, he noticed that 'the public' appeared to be mostly represented by grimy gentlemen who had had previous experience of the courts from a position in the dock : that there were people sitting round an anteroom of the courts as if waiting for the doctor ; that the character of the witness usually deteriorated under cross-examination ; and that the magistrate's spectacles as a rule endeavoured to flash out a strictly just manner combined with as much generosity as justice would allow.

On the last day of the month he wound up his series of visits to London entertainments and law-offices with the remark, 'Am getting tired of investigating life at music-halls and police-courts'.  About the same time he lost his friend Lord Carnarvon, who had written with prophetic insight when proposing him for the Athenæum that it would have been better if his proposer had been a younger man. Before leaving London he met Miss Ada Rehan, for whom he had a great liking, and, in some of her parts, admiration, that of the Shrew being of course one of them. He says of her: 'A kindly natured, winning woman with really a heart. I fear she is wearing herself out with too hard work.' Two days later they were present at the Lyceum to see her as Rosalind in *As You Like It*. She was not so real — indeed could not be — in the character as in *The Shrew*. Before starting Hardy wrote: 'Am going with E. to see Rosalind, after not seeing her for more than twenty years. This time she is composed of Ada Rehan.' After going he added: 'At the end of the second act I went round, and found her alone, in a highly strung throbbing state — and rather despondent. "O yes — it goes smoothly," she said. "But I am in a whirlwind. . . . Well, it is an old thing, and Mr. Daly liked to produce it!" I endeavoured to assure her that it was going to be satisfactory, and perhaps succeeded, for in the remaining acts she played full of spirit.' It is possible that the dramatic poem entitled 'The Two Rosalinds' was suggested by this performance combined with some other; but there is no certainty about this, and dates and other characteristics do not quite accord.

Mrs. Hardy had to leave London shortly after, on account of the illness and death of her father; but her husband had promised to write an Epilogue to be spoken by Miss Rehan at a performance on behalf of Mrs. Jeune's Holiday Fund for Children. So he remained in London till he had written it, and it had been duly delivered. He did not go himself to the performance, but in the evening of the same day was present at a debate at the St. James's Hall between Messrs. Hyndman and Bradlaugh, in which he was much struck by the extraordinary force in the features of the latter.

'*July* 24. Mary Jeune delighted with the verses: says Miss Rehan's hand shook so much when she read them that she seemed scarcely able to follow the lines.'

'*August* 5. Reflections on Art. Art is a changing of the actual proportions and order of things, so as to bring out more forcibly than might otherwise be done that feature in them which appeals most strongly to the idiosyncrasy of the artist. The changing, or distortion, may be of two kinds: (1) The kind which increases the sense of vraisemblance: (2) That which diminishes it. (1) is high art: (2) is low art.

'High art may choose to depict evil as well as good, without losing its quality. Its choice of evil, however, must be limited by the sense of worthiness.' A continuation of the same note was made a little later, and can be given here :

'Art is a disproportioning — (*i.e.* distorting, throwing out of proportion) — of realities, to show more clearly the features that matter in those realities, which, if merely copied or reported inventorially, might possibly be observed, but would more probably be overlooked. Hence "realism" is not Art.'

'*August* 8–17. With E. to Weymouth and back. Alfred Parsons [R.A.] came. Went to see some Sir Joshuas and Pinturicchios belonging to Pearce-Edgcumbe. Then drove to Weymouth over Ridgeway Hill with Parsons. Lunch at the Royal.' This was the Old Royal Hotel, now pulled down, where George III and his daughters used to dance at the town assemblies, a red cord dividing the royal dancers from the townspeople. The sockets for the standards bearing the cord were still visible in the floor while the building was standing.

Later in this month of August Hardy started with his brother for Paris by way of Southampton and Havre, leaving the former port at night, when 'the Jersey boat and ours were almost overwhelmed by the enormous bulk of the "Magdalena" (Brazil and River Plate) — the white figure of her at the ship's head stretching into the blue-black sky above us'. The journey was undertaken by Hardy solely on his brother's account, and they merely went the usual round of sight-seeing. As was the case with Hardy almost always, a strange bizarre effect was noticed by him at the Moulin Rouge — in those days a very popular place of entertainment. As everybody knows, or knew, it was close to the cemetery of Montmartre, being, it seems, only divided therefrom by a wall and erection or two, and as he stood somewhere in the building looking down at the young women dancing the *cancan*, and grimacing at the men, it appears that he could see through some back windows over their heads to the last resting-place of so many similar gay Parisians silent under the moonlight, and, as he notes, to near the grave of Heinrich Heine.

Coming back towards Havre he sees 'A Cleopatra in the railway carriage. Her French husband sits opposite, and seems to study her ; to keep wondering why he married her ; and why she married him. She is a good-natured amative creature by her voice, and her heavy moist lips.'

The autumn was passed in the country, visiting and entertaining neighbours, and attending garden-parties. In September, to their great grief, their watch-dog 'Moss' died — an affectionate retriever whose grave can still be seen at Max Gate.

In the latter part of this year, having finished adapting *Tess of the d'Urbervilles* for the serial issue, he seems to have dipped into a good many books — mostly the satirists : including Horace, Martial, Lucian, 'the Voltaire of Paganism', Voltaire himself, Cervantes, Le Sage, Molière, Dryden, Fielding, Smollett, Swift, Byron, Heine, Carlyle, Thackeray, *Satires and Profanities* by James Thomson, and Weismann's *Essays on Heredity*.

In December, staying in London, Hardy chanced to find himself in political circles for a time, though he never sought them. At one house he was a fellow-guest with Mr. (afterwards Lord) Goschen, then Chancellor of the Exchequer, and the 'I forgot Goschen' story was still going about. At another house just afterwards he chanced to converse with the then Dowager Duchess of Marlborough, Lord Randolph Churchill's mother : 'She is a nice warm-feeling woman, and expressed her grief at what had happened to her son, though her hostess had told her flatly it was his own doing. She deplores that young men like ——— should stand in the fore-front of the Tory party, and her son should be nowhere. She says he has learnt by bitter experience, and would take any subordinate position the Government might offer him. Poor woman — I was sorry for her, as she really suffers about it. Parnell, however, was the main thing talked about, and not Randolph.'

'*December* 4. I am more than ever convinced that persons are successively various persons, according as each special strand in their characters is brought uppermost by circumstances.'

'*December* 8 onwards. Lodging at the Jeunes. Lord Rowton, who is great on lodging-houses, says I am her "dosser".'

'*December* 18. Mr. E. Clodd this morning gives an excellently neat answer to my question why the superstitions of a remote Asiatic and a Dorset labourer are the same : "The attitude of man", he says, "at corresponding levels of culture, before like phenomena, is pretty much the same, your Dorset peasants representing the persistence of the barbaric idea which confuses persons and things, and founds wide generalizations on the slenderest analogies."

'(This "barbaric idea which confuses persons and things" is, by the way, also common to the highest imaginative genius — that of the poet.)'

'*Christmas Day*. While thinking of resuming "the viewless wings of poesy" before dawn this morning, new horizons seemed to open, and worrying pettinesses to disappear.

'Heard to-day an old country tradition; that if a woman goes off her own premises before being churched, *e.g.* crosses a road that forms the boundary of her residence — she may be made to do penance, or be excommunicated. I cannot explain this, but it reminds me of what old Mr. Hibbs of Bere Regis told me lately; that a native of that place, now ninety, says he remembers a young woman doing penance in Bere Church for singing scandalous songs about "a great lady". The girl stood in a white sheet while she went through "the service of penance", whatever that was.

'Also heard another curious story. Mil [Amelia] C—— had an illegitimate child by the parish doctor. She christened him all the doctor's names, which happened to be a mouthful — Frederick Washington Ingen — and always called him by the three names complete. Moreover the doctor had a squint, and to identify him still more fully as the father she hung a bobbin from the baby's cap between his eyes, and so trained him to squint likewise.'

Next day they lunched with a remote cousin of Hardy's on the maternal side — Dr. Christopher Childs of Weymouth — to meet his brother and sister-in-law Mr. and Mrs. Borlase Childs on a visit from Cornwall, and heard from Borlase Childs (whose grandfather had married into the Borlase family) some traditions of his and Hardy's common ancestors, on which Hardy remarks: 'The Christopher Childs, brother of my great-grandmother, who left Dorset, was a Jacobite, which accounted for the fall in their fortunes. There is also a tradition — that I had heard before from my mother — that one of the family added the "s" to the name, and that it was connected with the Josiah Child who founded Child's Bank, and with the family of Lord Jersey. I doubt the first statement, and have no real evidence of the latter.'

'*New Year's Eve.* Looked out of doors just before twelve, and was confronted by the toneless white of the snow spread in front, against which stood the row of pines breathing out: "'Tis no better with us than with the rest of creation, you see!" I could not hear the church bells.'

# CHAPTER XIX

# THE NOVEL 'TESS' RESTORED AND PUBLISHED

## 1891 : *Aet.* 50–51

AT the beginning of January 1891, he was at home arranging *A Group of Noble Dames* for publication in a volume. He was also in London a part of the month, where he saw 'what is called sunshine up here — a red-hot bullet hanging in a livid atmosphere — reflected from window-panes in the form of bleared copper eyes, and inflaming the sheets of plate-glass with smears of gory light. A drab snow mingled itself with liquid horsedung, and in the river puddings of ice moved slowly on. The steamers were moored, with snow on their gangways. A captain, in sad solitude, smoked his pipe against the bulk-head of the cabin stairs. The lack of traffic made the water like a stream through a deserted metropolis. In the City George Peabody sat comfortably in his easy chair, with snow on the folds of his ample waistcoat, the top of his bare head, and shoulders, and knees.'

After seeing Irving at the Lyceum, and admiring the staging : 'But, after all, scenic perfection such as this only banishes one plane further back the jarring point between illusion and disillusion. You must have it *somewhere*, and begin calling in "make believe" forthwith, and it may as well be soon as late — immediate as postponed — and no elaborate scenery be attempted.

'I don't care about the fashionable first night at a play : it is so insincere, meretricious ; the staginess behind the footlights seem to flow over upon the audience.'

On the Sunday following a number of people dined at the house where Hardy was staying. 'Presently Ellen Terry arrived — diaphanous — a sort of balsam or sea-anemone, without shadow. Also Irving, Sir Henry Thompson, Evelyn Ashley, Lady Dorothy [Nevill], Justin McCarthy, and many others. Ellen Terry was like a machine in which, if you press a spring, all the works fly open. E. Ashley's laugh is like a clap, or report ; it was so loud that it woke the children asleep on the third floor. Lady Dorothy said she collected death's-heads — (what did she mean?). Ashley told me about his electioneering experiences. The spectacle of another guest — a Judge of the Supreme Court — telling broad stories with a broad laugh in a broad accent, after the ladies had gone, reminded one of Baron Nicholson of "Judge-and-Jury" fame. "Tom" Hughes and Miss Hughes came in after dinner. Miss Hilda Gorst said that at dinner we made such a noise at our end of the table that at her end they wondered what we had to amuse us so much. (That's how it always seems.) . . . A great crush of people afterwards, till at one o'clock they dwindled away, leaving nothing but us, blank, on the wide polished floor.'

At the end of the month he and his wife were at a ball at Mrs. Sheridan's at Frampton Court, Dorset, where he saw a friend of his 'waltzing round with a face of ambition, not of slightest pleasure, as if he were saying to himself "this has to be done". We are all inveterate joy-makers: some do it more successfully than others; and the actual fabrication is hardly pleasure.'

'*February* 10. Newman and Carlyle. The former's was a feminine nature, which first decides and then finds reasons for having decided. He was an enthusiast with the absurd reputation of a logician and reasoner. Carlyle was a poet with the reputation of a philosopher. Neither was truly a *thinker*.'

On the 21st Hardy notes that Mrs. Hardy rode on horse-back for what turned out to be the last time in her life. It was to Mrs. Sheridan's at Frampton, and a train crossed a bridge overhead, causing the mare to rear; but happily not throwing the rider. Very few horses could.

In March they were again in London. A deep snow came on shortly after, but they had got home. It was in drifts:

'Sculptured, scooped, gouged, pared, trowelled, moulded, by the wind. Em says it is architectural. . . . A person aged 50 is an old man in winter and a young man in summer. . . . Was told by J. A. of a poor young fellow who is dying of consumption, so that he has to sit up in the night, and to get up because he cannot sleep. Yet he described to my informant that one night he had such a funny dream of pigs knocking down a thatcher's ladder that he lay awake laughing uncontrollably.'

In the same month Hardy erected what he called 'The Druid Stone' on the lawn **at** Max Gate. This was a large block they discovered about three feet underground in the garden, and the labour of getting it from the hole where it had lain for perhaps two thousand years was a heavy one even for seven men with levers and other appliances. — 'It was a primitive problem in mechanics, and the scene was such a one as may have occurred in building the Tower of Babel.' Round the stone, which had been lying flat, they had found a quantity of ashes and half charred bones.

Though Hardy was at this time putting the finishing touches to *Tess* he was thinking of 'A Bird's-Eye View of Europe at the beginning of the Nineteenth Century. . . . It may be called "A Drama of the Times of the First Napoleon".' He does not appear to have done more than think of it at this date.

In April he was at a morning performance at the old Olympic Theatre of that once popular play *The Stranger*, by Kotzebue; and he 'thought of the eyes and ears that had followed the acting first and last, including Thackeray's'. Miss Winifred Emery was Mrs. Haller on this occasion. During his time in London he notes the difference between English and French stage-dancing; 'The English girls dance as if they had learned dancing; the French as if dancing had produced them.' He also while in Town dined at the Lushingtons' 'and looked at the portrait of Lushington's father, who had known Lady Byron's secret'. He went to hear Spurgeon preach, for the first and last time. As Spurgeon died soon after, he was glad he had gone, the preacher having been a great force in his day, though it had been spent for many years. He witnessed the performance of *Hedda Gabler* at the Vaudeville, on which he remarks that it seems to him that the rule for staging nowadays should be to have no scene which would not be physically possible in the time of acting. [An idea carried out years after in *The Queen of Cornwall*.]

The Hardys were now as usual looking for a place in which to spend three or four months in London. Much as they disliked handling other people's furniture, taking on their breakages, cracks, and stains, and paying for them at the end of the season as if they had made them themselves, there was no help for it in their inability to afford a London house or flat all the year round. 'The dirty house-fronts, leaning gate-piers, rusty gates, broken bells, Doré monstrosities of womankind who showed us the rooms, left Em nearly fainting, and at one place she could not stay for the drawing-room floor to be exhibited.' They found a flat at last in Mandeville Place, just about the time that Hardy learnt of his being elected to the Athenæum Club by the Committee under Rule 2.

'*April* 28. Talking to Kipling to-day at the Savile, he said that he once as an experiment took the ideas of some mature writer or speaker (on Indian politics, I think) and translating them into his own language used them as his. They were pronounced to be the crude ideas of an immature boy.'

The Royal Academy this year struck Hardy as containing some good colouring but no creative power, and that as visitors went by names only the new geniuses, even if there were any, were likely to be overlooked. He recalled in respect of the fair spring and summer landscapes that 'They were not pictures of *this* spring and summer, although they seem to be so. All this green grass and fresh leafage perished yesterday; after withering and falling, it is gone like a dream.'

In the Gallery of the English Art Club: 'If I were a painter, I would paint a picture of a room as viewed by a mouse from a chink under the skirting.'

Hardy's friend Dr. (afterwards Sir) Joshua Fitch took him over Whitelands Training College for schoolmistresses, where it was the custom in those days, and may be now, to choose a May Queen every year, a custom originated by Ruskin. Hardy did not, however, make any observation on this, but merely: 'A community of women, especially young women, inspires not reverence but protective tenderness in the breast of one who views them. Their belief in circumstances, in convention, in the rightness of things, which you know to be not only wrong but damnably wrong, makes the heart ache, even when they are waspish and hard. . . . You feel how entirely the difference of their ideas from yours is of the nature of misunderstanding. . . . There is much that is pathetic about these girls, and I wouldn't have missed the visit for anything. How far nobler in its aspirations is the life here than the life of those I met at the crush two nights back!'

Piccadilly at night. 'A girl held a long-stemmed narcissus to my nose as we went by each other. At the Circus, among all the wily crew, there was a little innocent family standing waiting, I suppose for an omnibus. How pure they looked! A man on a stretcher, with a bloody bandage round his head, was wheeled past by two policemen, stragglers following. Such is Piccadilly.'

He used to see Piccadilly under other aspects, however, for the next day, Sunday, he attended the service at St. James's — as he did off and on for many years — because it was the church his mother had been accustomed to go to when as a young woman she was living for some months in London. 'The preacher said that only five per cent of the inhabitants entered a church, according to the

Bishop of London. On coming out there was a drizzle across the
electric lights, and the paper-boys were shouting, not, "Go to church!"
but, "Wee-naw of the French Oaks!"'

Next day — wet — at the British Museum : 'Crowds parading
and gaily traipsing round the mummies, thinking to-day is for ever,
and the girls casting sly glances at young men across the swathed
dust of Mycerinus [?]. They pass with flippant comments the illuminated MSS. — the labours of years — and stand under Rameses the
Great, joking. Democratic government may be justice to man, but
it will probably merge in proletarian, and when these people are our
masters it will lead to more of this contempt, and possibly be the
utter ruin of art and literature! . . . Looking, when I came out, at
the Oxford Music Hall, an hour before the time of opening, there
was already a queue.'

'*May* 3. Sunday. Em and I lunch at the Jeunes' to see the house
they have just moved into — 79 Harley St. Sun came in hot upon
us through back windows, the blinds not being yet up. Frederic
Harrison called afterwards. He is leaving London to live in the
country.'

During the month of May he was much impressed by a visit paid
with his friend Dr. (later Sir) T. Clifford Allbutt, then a Commissioner
in Lunacy, to a large private lunatic asylum, where he had intended
to stay only a quarter of an hour, but became so interested in the
pathos of the cases that he remained the greater part of the day. He
talked to 'the gentleman who was staying there of his own will, to
expose the devices of the Commissioners ; to the old man who offers
snuff to everybody ; to the scholar of high literary aims, as sane in
his conversation as any of us ; to the artist whose great trouble was
that he could not hear the birds sing ; "which as you will see, Mr.
Hardy, is hard on a man of my temperament" ; and, on the women's
side, listened to their stories of their seduction ; to the Jewess who
sang to us ; to the young woman who, with eyes brimming with
reproach, said to the doctor, "When are you going to let me out of
this?" [Hardy appealed for a re-examination of her, which was
done afterwards.] Then came the ladies who thought themselves
queens — less touching cases, as they were quite happy — one of
them, who was really a Plantagenet by descent, perversely insisted
on being considered a Stuart. All the women seemed prematurely
dried, faded, *flétries*.'

In June he visited Stockwell Training College. 'A pretty custom
among the girls here is that of each senior student choosing *a daughter*

from the list of junior girls who are coming. The senior is *mother* to the daughter for the whole year, and looks after her. Sometimes the pair get fond of each other; at other times not. I gather that they are chosen blindly before arrival, from the names only. There must be singular expectancies, confrontings, and excitements resulting therefrom.'

In July he took Mrs. Hardy to the balcony of the Athenæum Club to see the German Emperor William II pass to the City; the next day he met W. E. Henley at the Savile. 'He is paler, and his once brown locks are getting iron-grey.' On the 13th, lunching at Lady Wynford's, Grosvenor Square, Hardy discovered, or thought he did, that the ceiling of the drawing-room contained oval paintings by Angelica Kauffmann, and that the house was built by the Adams; 'I was amused by Ld. Wynford, who told me he would not live in Dorset for £50,000 a year, and wanted me to smoke cigarettes made of tobacco from Lebanon — "same as smoked by Laurence Oliphant". Wynford's nose is two sides of a spherical triangle in profile.' In the same week, on a visit with his wife to G. F. Watts, the painter, he was much struck with his host; 'that old small man with a grey coat and black velvet skull-cap, who, when he saw one of his picture-frames pressing against a figure on canvas, moved it away gently, as if the figure could feel.'

'Dining at the Milnes-Gaskells', Lady Catherine told me that the Webbs of Newstead have buried the skulls that Byron used to drink from, but that the place seems to throw "a sort of doom on the family". I then told her of the tragic Damers of the last century, who owned Abbey property, and thought she rather shrank from what I said; I afterwards remembered to my dismay that her own place was an Abbey.' Hardy, however, found later that this was only a moment's mood, she being as free from superstitions as any woman.

'*July* 19. Note the weight of a landau and pair, the coachman in his grey great-coat, footmen ditto. All this mass of matter is moved along with brute force and clatter through a street congested and obstructed, to bear the *petite* figure of the owner's young wife in violet velvet and silver trimming, slim, small; who could be easily carried under a man's arm, and who, if held up by the hair and slipped out of her clothes, carriage, etc. etc., aforesaid, would not be much larger than a skinned rabbit, and of less use.

'At Mary Jeune's lunch to-day sat between a pair of beauties. Mrs. A. G—— with her violet eyes, was the more seductive; Mrs. R. C—— the more vivacious. The latter in yellow: the former in pale brown, and more venust and warm-blooded than Mrs. C——, who is large-eyed, somewhat slight, with quick impulsive motions, and who neglects the dishes and the coffee because possessed by some idea.' At another luncheon or dinner at this time 'the talk was entirely political — of when the next election would be — of the probable Prime Minister — of ins and outs — of Lord This and the Duke of That — everything except the people for whose existence alone these politicians exist. Their welfare is never once thought of.'

The same week: 'After a day of headache, went to I——'s Hotel to supper. This is one of the few old taverns remaining in London, whose frequenters after theatre-closing know each other, and talk across from table to table. The head waiter is called William. There is always something homely when the waiter is called William. He talks of his affairs to the guests, as the guests talk of theirs to him. He has whiskers of the rare old mutton-chop pattern, and a manner of confidence. He has shaved so many years that his face is of a bluish soap-colour, and if wetted and rubbed would raise a lather of itself. . . . Shakespeare is largely quoted at the tables; especially "How long will a man lie i' the earth ere he rot?" Theatrical affairs are discussed neither from the point of view of the audience, nor of the actors, but from a third point — that of the recaller of past appearances.

'Old-fashioned country couples also come in, their fathers having recommended the tavern from recollections of the early part of the century. They talk on innocently-friendly terms with the theatrical young men, and handsome ladies who enter with them as their "husbands", after the play.'

They annexed to their London campaign this year a visit to Sir Brampton and Lady Camilla Gurdon at Grundesburgh Hall, Suffolk — a house standing amid green slopes timbered with old oaks. The attraction was its possession of the most old-fashioned and delightful — probably Elizabethan — garden with high buttressed walls that Hardy had ever seen, which happily had been left unimproved and unchanged, owing to the Hall having been used merely as a farm-house for a century or two, and hence neglected. The vegetables were planted in the middle of square plots surrounded by broad green alleys, and screened by thickets and palisades of tall flowers, 'so that one does not know any vegetables are there'.

Hardy spent a good deal of time in August and the autumn correcting *Tess of the d'Urbervilles* for its volume form, which process consisted in restoring to their places the passages and chapters of the original MS. that had been omitted from the serial publication. The name 'Talbothays', given to the dairy, was based on that of a farm belonging to his father, which, however, had no house on it at that time.

In September he and his wife paid a visit to his friend Sir George Douglas at Springwood Park, in fulfilment of a long promise, passing on their way north by the coastline near Holy Isle or Lindisfarne, at that moment glowing reddish on a deep blue sea under the evening sun, with all the romance of *Marmion* about its aspect. It was the place which he afterwards urged Swinburne to make his headquarters, as being specially suited for him — a Northumbrian — an idea which Swinburne was much attracted by, though he owned that 'to his great shame' he had never been on the isle. They had a very charming time in Scotland, visiting many Scott scenes, including Edie Ochiltree's grave, and one that Hardy had always been anxious to see — Smaylho'me Tower — the setting of the 'Eve of St. John' — a ballad which was among the verse he liked better than any of Scott's prose. At Springwood they met at dinner one evening old Mr. Usher, aged eighty-one, who had known Scott and Lady Scott well, and whose father had sold Scott the land called Huntley Burn. He said that when he was a boy Scott asked him to sing, which he did; and Scott was so pleased that he gave him a pony. When Hardy wondered why Lady Scott should have taken the poet's fancy, Mr. Usher replied grimly, 'She wadna' ha' taken mine!'

They finished this autumn visit by a little tour to Durham, Whitby, Scarborough, York, and Peterborough. At the last-mentioned place the verger 'told us of a lady's body found in excavating, of which the neck and bosoms glistened, being coated with a species of enamel. She had been maid of honour to Catherine of Arragon who lies near. . . . In the train there was a woman of various ages — hands old, frame middle-aged, and face young. What her mean age was I had no conception of.'

'*October* 28. It is the incompleteness that is loved, when love is sterling and true. This is what differentiates the real one from the imaginary, the practicable from the impossible, the Love who returns the kiss from the Vision that melts away. A man sees the Diana or the Venus in his Beloved, but what he loves is the difference.'

'*October* 30. Howells and those of his school forget that a story *must* be striking enough to be worth telling. Therein lies the problem — to reconcile the average with that uncommonness which alone makes it natural that a tale or experience would dwell in the memory and induce repetition.'

Sir Charles Cave was the judge at the Dorset assizes this autumn, and Hardy dined with him and Mr. Frith his marshal while they were in the town. Cave told him, among other things, that when he and Sir J. F. Stephen, also on the bench, were struggling young men the latter came to him and said a man was going to be hanged at the Old Bailey, jocularly remarking as an excuse for proposing to go and see it: 'Who knows; we may be judges some day; and it will be well to have learnt how the last sentence of the law is carried out.'

During the first week in November the Rev. Dr. Robertson Nicoll, editor of the *Bookman*, forwarded particulars of a discussion in the papers on whether national recognition should be given to eminent men of letters. Hardy's reply was:

'I daresay it would be very interesting that literature should be honoured by the state. But I don't see how it could be satisfactorily done. The highest flights of the pen are mostly the excursions and revelations of souls unreconciled to life, while the natural tendency of a government would be to encourage acquiescence in life as it is. However, I have not thought much about the matter.'

As the year drew to a close an incident that took place during the publication of *Tess of the d'Urbervilles* as a serial in the *Graphic* might have prepared him for certain events that were to follow. The editor objected to the description of Angel Clare carrying in his arms, across a flooded lane, Tess and her three dairymaid companions. He suggested that it would be more decorous and suitable for the pages of a periodical intended for family reading if the damsels were wheeled across the lane in a wheel-barrow. This was accordingly done.

Also the *Graphic* refused to print the chapter describing the christening of the infant child of Tess. This appeared in Henley's *Scots Observer*, and was afterwards restored to the novel, where it was considered one of the finest passages.

*Tess of the d'Urbervilles ; a Pure Woman faithfully Presented* was published complete about the last day of November, with what results Hardy could scarcely have foreseen, since the book, notwithstanding its exceptional popularity, was the beginning of the end of his career as a novelist.

PART V

'TESS', 'JUDE', AND THE END OF PROSE

# THE RECEPTION OF THE BOOK

1892 : *Aet.* 51–52

As *Tess of the d'Urbervilles* got into general circulation it attracted an attention that Hardy had apparently not foreseen, for at the time of its publication he was planning something of quite a different kind, according to an entry he made :

'Title : — "Songs of Five-and-Twenty Years". Arrangement of the songs : Lyric Ecstasy inspired by music to have precedence.'

However, reviews, letters, and other intelligence speedily called him from these casual thoughts back to the novel, which the tedious-ness of the alterations and restorations had made him weary of. From the prefaces to later editions can be gathered more or less clearly what happened to the book as, passing into great popularity, an endeavour was made by some critics to change it to scandalous notoriety — the latter kind of clamour, raised by a certain small section of the public and the press, being quite inexplicable to the writer himself.

Among other curious results from the publication of the book was that it started a rumour of Hardy's theological beliefs, which lived, and spread, and grew, so that it was never completely extin-guished. Near the end of the story he had used the sentence, 'The President of the Immortals had finished his sport with Tess', and the first five words were, as Hardy often explained to his reviewers, but a literal translation of Aesch. *Prom.* 169 : Μακάρων πρύτανις. The classical sense in which he had used them is best shown by quoting a reply he wrote thirty years later to some unknown critic who had said in an article :

'Hardy postulates an all-powerful being endowed with the baser human passions, who turns everything to evil and rejoices in the mischief he has wrought' ; another critic taking up the tale by adding : 'To him evil is not so much a mystery, a problem, as the wilful malice of his god.'

Hardy's reply was written down but (it is believed), as in so many

cases with him, never posted ; though I am able to give it from the
rough draft :

'As I need hardly inform any thinking reader, I do not hold, and
never have held, the ludicrous opinions here assumed to be mine —
which are really, or approximately, those of the primitive believer in
his man-shaped tribal god. And in seeking to ascertain how any
exponent of English literature could have supposed that I held them
I find that the writer of the estimate has harked back to a passage in
a novel of mine, printed many years ago, in which the forces opposed
to the heroine were allegorized as a personality (a method not unusual
in imaginative prose or poetry) by the use of a well-known trope,
explained in that venerable work, Campbell's *Philosophy of Rhetoric*,
as "one in which life, perception, activity, design, passion, or any
property of sentient beings, is attributed to things inanimate".

'Under this species of criticism if an author were to say "Aeolus
maliciously tugged at her garments, and tore her hair in his wrath",
the sapient critic would no doubt announce that author's evil creed
to be that the wind is "a powerful being endowed with the baser
human passions", etc., etc.

'However, I must put up with it, and say as Parrhasius of Ephesus
said about his pictures : There is nothing that men will not find fault
with.'

The deep impression produced on the general and uncritical
public by the story was the occasion of Hardy's receiving strange
letters — some from husbands whose experiences had borne a resemblance to that of Angel Clare, though more, many more, from
wives with a past like that of Tess, but who had *not* told their husbands,
and asking for his counsel under the burden of their concealment.
Some of these were educated women of good position, and Hardy
used to say the singular thing was that they should have put themselves in the power of a stranger by these revelations (their names
having often been given, though sometimes initials at a post-office
only), when they would not trust persons nearest to them with their
secret. However, they did themselves no harm, he would add, for
though he was unable to advise them, he carefully destroyed their
letters, and never mentioned their names, or suspected names, to a
living soul. He owed them that much, he said, for their trust in his
good faith. A few, too, begged that he would meet them privately,
or call on them, and hear their story instead of their writing it. He
talked the matter over with his friend Sir Francis Jeune, who had had

abundant experience of the like things in the Divorce Court, where he presided, and who recommended him not to meet the writers alone, in case they should not be genuine. He himself, he said, also got such letters, but made it a rule never to notice them. Nor did Hardy, though he sometimes sadly thought that they came from sincere women in trouble.

*Tess of the d'Urbervilles* was also the cause of Hardy's meeting a good many people of every rank during that spring, summer, and onwards, and of opportunity for meeting a good many more if he had chosen to avail himself of it. Many of the details that follow concerning his adventures in the world of fashion at dinner-parties, crushes, and other social functions, which Hardy himself did not think worth recording, have been obtained from diaries kept by the late Mrs. Hardy.

It must be repeated that his own notes on these meetings were set down by him as private memoranda only ; and that they, or some of them, are reproduced here to illustrate what contrasting planes of existence he moved in — vibrating at a swing between the artificial gaieties of a London season and the quaintnesses of a primitive rustic life.

Society remarks on *Tess* were curious and humorous. Strangely enough, Lord Salisbury, with whom Hardy had a slight acquaintance, was a supporter of the story. Also : 'The Duchess of Abercorn tells me that the novel has saved her all future trouble in the assortment of her friends. They have been almost fighting across her dinner-table over Tess's character. What she now says to them is "Do you support her or not?" If they say "No indeed. She deserved hanging. A little harlot!" she puts them in one group. If they say "Poor wronged innocent!" and pity her, she puts them in the other group where she is herself.' He was discussing the question thus with another noble dame who sat next him at a large dinner-party, when they waxed so contentious that they were startled to find the whole table of two-and-twenty silent, listening to their theories on this vexed question. And a well-known beauty and statesman's wife, also present, snapped out at him : 'Hanged? They ought all to have been hanged!'

'Took Arthur Balfour's sister in to dinner at the Jeunes'. Liked her frank, sensible, womanly way of talking. The reviews have made me shy of presenting copies of *Tess*, and I told her plainly that if I gave her one it might be the means of getting me into hot water with her. She said : "Now don't I really look old enough to read any

novel with safety by this time!" Some of the best women don't
marry — perhaps wisely.'

'*April* 10. Leslie Ward, in illustration of the calamities of artists,
tells me of a lady's portrait, life-size, he has on his hands, that he was
requested by her husband to paint. When he had just completed
the picture she eloped with a noble earl, whereupon her husband
wrote to say he did not want the painting, and Ward's labour was
wasted, there being no contract. The end of the story was that the
husband divorced her, and, like Edith in Browning's "Too Late",
she "married the other", and brought him a son and heir. At a
dinner the very same evening the lady who was my neighbour at the
table told me that her husband was counsel in the case, which was
hurried through, that the decree might be made absolute and the
remarriage take place before the baby was born.'

'11. In the evening with Sir F. and Lady J. to the Gaiety Theatre
to hear Lottie Collins in her song "Ta-ra-ra". A rather striking tune
and performance, to foolish words.'

'15. *Good Friday*. Read review of *Tess* in *The Quarterly*. A
smart and amusing article; but it is easy to be smart and amusing if
a man will forgo veracity and sincerity. . . . How strange that one
may write a book without knowing what one puts into it — or
rather, the reader reads into it. Well, if this sort of thing continues
no more novel-writing for me. A man must be a fool to deliberately
stand up to be shot at.'

Moreover, the repute of the book was spreading not only through
England, and America, and the Colonies, but through the European
Continent and Asia; and during this year translations appeared in
various languages, its publication in Russia exciting great interest.
On the other hand, some local libraries in English-speaking countries
'suppressed' the novel — with what effect was not ascertained.
Hardy's good-natured friends Henry James and R. L. Stevenson
(whom he afterwards called the Polonius and the Osric of novelists)
corresponded about it in this vein: 'Oh, yes, dear Louis: "Tess of
the d'Urbervilles" is vile. The pretence of sexuality is only equalled
by the absence of it [?], and the abomination of the language by the
author's reputation for style.' (*Letters of Henry James.*)

'16. Dr. Walter Lock, Warden of Keble, Oxford, called. "*Tess*",
he said, "is the Agamemnon without the remainder of the Oresteian
trilogy." This is inexact, but suggestive as to how people think.

'Am glad I have got back from London and all those dinners:
— London, that *hot-plate* of humanity, on which we first sing, then

simmer, then boil, then dry away to dust and ashes!'

'*Easter Sunday.* Was told a story of a handsome country-girl. Her lover, though on the point of matrimony with her, would not perform it because of the temper shown by her when they went to buy the corner-cupboard and tea-things, her insistence on a different pattern, and so on. Their child was born illegitimate. Leaving the child at home she went to Jersey, for this reason, that a fellow village girl had gone there, married, and died; and the other thought that by going and introducing herself to the widower as his late wife's playmate and friend from childhood he would be interested in her and marry her too. She carried this out, and he did marry her. But her temper was so bad that he would not live with her; and she went on the streets. On her voyage home she died of disease she had contracted, and was thrown into the sea — some say before she was quite dead. Query: What became of the baby?'

He notes that on the 27th of the month his father, away in the country, 'went upstairs for the last time'. On the 31st he received a letter from his sister Mary on their father's illness, saying that it being of a mild lingering kind there was no immediate hurry for his return, and hence he dined with Lady Malmesbury on his birthday, June 2nd, in fulfilment of a three weeks' engagement, before returning to Dorchester. This, however, he did the next day, arriving at his house just when his brother had come to fetch him.

He found his father much changed; and yet he rallied for some weeks onward.

In the town one day Hardy passed by chance the tent just erected for Sanger's Circus, when the procession was about to start. 'Saw the Queen climb up on her lofty gilt-and-crimson throne by a step-ladder. Then the various nations personified climbed up on theirs. They, being men, mounted anyhow, "No swearin'!" being said to them as a caution. The Queen, seated in her chair on the terrestrial globe, adjusts her crimson and white robes over her soiled satin shoes for the start, and looks around on Hayne's trees, the church-tower, and Egdon Heath in the distance. As she passes along the South-walk Road she is obliged to duck her head to avoid the chestnut boughs tearing off her crown.'

'*June* 26. Considered methods for the Napoleon drama. Forces; emotions, tendencies. The characters do not act under the influence of reason.'

'*July* 1. We don't always remember as we should that in getting at the truth, we get only at the true nature of the impression that an object, etc., produces on us, the true thing in itself being still, as Kant shows, beyond our knowledge.

'The art of observation (during travel, etc.) consists in this: the seeing of great things in little things, the whole in the part — even the infinitesimal part. For instance, you are abroad: you see an English flag on a ship-mast from the window of your hotel: you realize the English navy. Or, at home, in a soldier you see the British Army; in a bishop at your club, the Church of England; and in a steam hooter you see Industry.'

He was paying almost daily visits to his father at this time. On the 19th his brother told him the patient was no worse, so he did not go that day. But on the 20th Crocker, one of his brother's men, came to say that their father had died quietly that afternoon — in the house in which he was born. Thus, in spite of his endeavours, Hardy had not been present.

Almost the last thing his father had asked for was water fresh drawn from the well — which was brought and given him; he tasted it and said, 'Yes — that's our well-water. Now I know I am at home.'

Hardy frequently stated in after years that the character of Horatio in *Hamlet* was his father's to a nicety, and in Hardy's copy of that play his father's name and the date of his death are written opposite the following lines:

> 'Thou hast been
> As one, in suffering all, that suffers nothing,
> A man that fortune's buffets and rewards
> Hast ta'en with equal thanks.'

He was buried close to his father and mother, and near the knights of various dates in the seventeenth and eighteenth centuries, with whom the Hardys had been connected.

'*August* 14. Mother described to-day the three Hardys as they used to appear passing over the brow of the hill to Stinsford Church on a Sunday morning, three or four years before my birth. They were always hurrying, being rather late, their fiddles and violoncello in green-baize bags under their left arms. They wore top hats, stick-up shirt collars, dark blue coats with great collars and gilt buttons, deep cuffs and black silk "stocks" or neckerchiefs. Had curly hair, and carried their heads to one side as they walked. My grandfather wore drab cloth breeches and buckled shoes, but his sons wore trousers and Wellington boots.'

In August they received at Max Gate a long-promised visit from Sir Arthur Blomfield, who had taken a house a few miles off for a month or two. Contrary to Hardy's expectations Blomfield liked the design of the Max Gate house. The visit was a very pleasant one, abounding in reminiscences of 8 Adelphi Terrace, and included a drive to 'Weatherbury' (Puddletown) Church and an examination of its architecture.

'*August* 31. My mother says she looks at the furniture and feels she is nothing to it. All those belonging to it, and the place, are gone, and it is left in her hands, a stranger. (She has, however, lived there these fifty-three years!)'

'*August.* I hear of a girl of Maiden Newton who was shod by contract like a horse, at so much a year.'

'*September* 4. There is a curious Dorset expression — "tankard-legged". This style of leg seems to have its biggest end downwards, and I have certainly seen legs of that sort. My mother says that my Irish ancestress had them, the accomplished lady who is reputed to have read the Bible through seven times; though how my mother should know what the legs of her husband's great-great-grandmother were like I cannot tell.

'Among the many stories of spell-working that I have been told, the following is one of how it was done by two girls about 1830. They killed a pigeon, stuck its heart full of pins, made a tripod of three knitting needles, and suspended the heart on them over a lamp, murmuring an incantation while it roasted, and using the name of the young man in whom one or both were interested. The said young man felt racking pains about the region of the heart, and suspecting something went to the constables. The girls were sent to prison.'

This month they attended a Field-Club meeting at Swanage, and were introduced to 'old Mr. B——, "the King of Swanage". He had a good profile, but was rougher in speech than I should have expected after his years of London — being the ordinary type of Dorset man, self-made by trade, whenever one of the county does self-make himself, which is not often. . . . Met Dr. Yeatman, the Bishop of Southwark [afterwards of Worcester]. He says the Endicotts [Mrs. J. Chamberlain's ancestors] are a Dorset family.'

'*September* 17. Stinsford House burnt. Discovered it to be on fire when driving home from Dorchester with E. I left the carriage and ran across the meads. She drove on, having promised to dine at Canon R. Smith's. I could soon see that the old mansion was

doomed, though there was not a breath of wind.  Coppery flames
were visible in the sun through the trees of the park, and a few figures
in shirt-sleeves on the roof.  Furniture on the lawn : several servants
perspiring and crying.  Men battering out windows to get out the
things — a bruising of tender memories for me.  I worked in carrying
books and other articles to the vicarage.  When it grew dark the
flames entered the drawing and dining rooms, lighting up the chambers
of so much romance.  The delicate tones of the wall-painting seemed
pleased at the illumination at first, till the inside of the rooms became
one roaring oven ; and then the ceiling fell, and then the roof, sending
a fountain of sparks from the old oak into the sky.

'Met Mary in the churchyard, who had been laying flowers on
Father's grave, on which the firelight now flickered.

'Walked to Canon Smith's dinner-party just as I was, it being
too late to change.  E. had preceded me there, since I did not arrive
until nine.  Dinner disorganized and pushed back between one and
two hours, they having been to the fire.  Met Bosworth Smith
[Harrow master], who had taken E. to the fire, though I saw neither
of them.  Late home.

'I am sorry for the house.  It was where Lady Susan Strangways,
afterwards Lady Susan O'Brien, lived so many years with her actor-
husband, after the famous elopement in 1764, so excellently described
in Walpole's Letters, Mary Frampton's Journal, etc.

'As stated, she knew my grandfather well, and he carefully heeded
her tearful instructions to build the vault for her husband and later
herself, "just large enough for us two".  Walpole's satire on her
romantic choice — that "a footman were preferable" — would have
missed fire somewhat if tested by time.

'My father when a boy-chorister in the gallery of the church
used to see her, an old and lonely widow, walking in the garden in
a red cloak.'

'*End of September*.  In London.  This is the time to realize
London as an old city, all the pulsing excitements of May being
absent.

'Drove home from dining with McIlvaine at the Café Royal,
behind a horse who had no interest in me, was going a way he had
no interest in going, and was whipped on by a man who had no
interest in me, or the horse, or the way.  Amid this string of com-
pulsions reached home.'

'*October*.  At Great Fawley, Berks.  Entered a ploughed vale
which might be called the Valley of Brown Melancholy.  The silence

is remarkable. . . . Though I am alive with the living I can only see the dead here, and am scarcely conscious of the happy children at play.'

'*October* 7.  Tennyson died yesterday morning.'

'*October* 12.  At Tennyson's funeral in Westminster Abbey. The music was sweet and impressive, but as a funeral the scene was less penetrating than a plain country interment would have been. Lunched afterwards at the National Club with E. Gosse, Austin Dobson, Theodore Watts, and William Watson.'

'18.  Hurt my tooth at breakfast-time. I look in the glass. Am conscious of the humiliating sorriness of my earthly tabernacle, and of the sad fact that the best of parents could do no better for me. . . . Why should a man's mind have been thrown into such close, sad, sensational, inexplicable relations with such a precarious object as his own body!'

'*October* 24.  The best tragedy — highest tragedy in short — is that of the WORTHY encompassed by the INEVITABLE. The tragedies of immoral and worthless people are not of the best.'

'*December*.  At the "Empire" [Music-Hall]. The dancing-girls are nearly all skeletons. One can see drawn lines and puckers in their young flesh. They should be penned and fattened for a month to round out their beauty.'

'*December* 17.  At an interesting legal dinner at Sir Francis Jeune's. They were all men of law but myself — mostly judges. Their stories, so old and boring to one another, were all new to me, and I was delighted. Hawkins told me his experiences in the Tichborne case, and that it was by a mere chance that he was not on the other side. Lord Coleridge (the cross-examiner in the same case, with his famous, "Would you be surprised to hear?") was also anecdotic. Afterwards, when Lady J. had a large reception, the electric-lights all went out, just when the rooms were most crowded, but fortunately there being a shine from the fire we all stood still till candles were brought in old rummaged-up candlesticks.'

# CHAPTER XXI

# VISITS AND INTERMITTENT WRITING

1893 : *Aet.* 52–53

'*January* 13. *The Fiddler of the Reels* (short story) posted to Messrs. Scribner, New York.'

'*February* 16. Heard a curious account of a grave that was ordered (by telegraph?) at West Stafford, and dug. But no funeral ever came, the person who had ordered it being unknown ; and the grave had to be filled up.' This entry had probably arisen from Hardy's occupation during some days of this winter in designing his father's tombstone, of which he made complete drawings for the stonemason ; and it was possibly his contact with the stonemason that made him think of that trade for his next hero, though in designing church stonework as an architect's pupil he had of course met with many.

'*February* 22. There cannot be equity in one kind. Assuming, *e.g.*, the possession of £1,000,000 sterling or 10,000 acres of land to be the coveted ideal, all cannot possess £1,000,000 or 10,000 acres. But there is a practicable equity possible : that the happiness which one man derives from one thing shall be equalled by what another man derives from another thing. Freedom from worry, for instance, is a counterpoise to the lack of great possessions, though he who enjoys that freedom may not think so.'

'*February* 23. A story must be exceptional enough to justify its telling. We tale-tellers are all Ancient Mariners, and none of us is warranted in stopping Wedding Guests (in other words, the hurrying public) unless he has something more unusual to relate than the ordinary experience of every average man and woman.

'The whole secret of fiction and the drama — in the constructional part — lies in the adjustment of things unusual to things eternal and universal. The writer who knows exactly how exceptional, and how non-exceptional, his events should be made, possesses the key to the art.'

'*April.* I note that a clever thrush, and a stupid nightingale, sing very much alike.

'Am told that Nat C——'s good-for-nothing grandson has "turned ranter " — *i.e.* street-preacher — and, meeting a girl he used to carry on with, the following dialogue ensued :

HE : "Do you read your Bible for your spiritual good?"

SHE : "Ho-ho!  Git along wi' thee!"

HE : "But do you, my dear young woman?"

SHE : "Haw-haw!  Not this morning!"

HE : "Do you read your Bible, I implore?"

SHE : (*tongue out*) "No, nor you neither.  Come, you can't act in that show, Natty!  You haven't the guts to carry it off!"  The discussion was ended by their going off to Came Plantation.'

In London this spring they again met many people, the popularity of Hardy as an author now making him welcome anywhere.  For the first time they took a whole house, 70 Hamilton Terrace, and brought up their own servants, and found themselves much more comfortable under this arrangement than they had been before.

At such crushes, luncheons, and dinners the Hardys made or renewed acquaintance also with Mrs. Richard Chamberlain, Mr. Charles Wyndham, Mr. Goschen, and the Duke, Duchess, and Princess May of Teck, afterwards Queen Mary.  'Lady Winifred Gardner whispered to me that meeting the Royal Family always reminded her of family prayers.  The Duke confused the lady who introduced me to him by saying it was unnecessary, as he had known me for years, adding privately to me when she was gone, "That's good enough for her : of course I meant I had known you spiritually".'

'13.  Whibley dined with me at the Savile, and I afterwards went with him to the Trocadero Music-Hall.  Saw the great men — famous performers at the Halls — drinking at the bar in long coats before going on : on their faces an expression of not wishing in the least to emphasize their importance to the world.'

'*April* 19.  Thought while dressing, and seeing people go by to their offices, how strange it is that we should talk so glibly of "this cold world which shows no sympathy", when this is the feeling of so many components of the same world — probably a majority — and nearly everyone's neighbour is waiting to give and receive sympathy.'

'25.  Courage has been idealized ; why not Fear? — which is a higher consciousness, and based on a deeper insight.'

'27.  A great lack of tact in A. J. B., who was in the chair at the Royal Literary Fund dinner which I attended last night.  The purpose of the dinner was, of course, to raise funds for poor authors, largely from the pockets of the more successful ones who were present with the other guests. Yet he dwelt with much emphasis on the decline of the literary art, and on his opinion that there were no writers of high rank living in these days. We hid our diminished heads, and buttoned our pockets. What he said may have been true enough, but alas for saying it then!'

'28. At Academy Private View. Find that there is a very good painting here of Woolbridge Manor-House under the (erroneous) title of "Tess of the d'Urbervilles' ancestral home". Also one entitled "In Hardy's Country, Egdon Heath".

'The worst of taking a furnished house is that the articles in the rooms are saturated with the thoughts and glances of others.'

'*May* 10. Spent a scientific evening at the conversazione of the Royal Society, where I talked on the exhibits to Sir R. Quain, Dr. Clifford Allbutt, Humphry Ward, Bosworth Smith, Sir J. Crichton-Browne, F. and G. Macmillan, Ray Lankester, and others, without (I flatter myself) betraying excessive ignorance in respect of the points in the show.'

'*May* 18. Left Euston by 9 o'clock morning train with E. for Llandudno, *en route* for Dublin. After arrival at Llandudno drove round Great Orme's Head. Magnificent deep purple-grey mountains, the fine colour being on account of an approaching storm.'

'19. Went on to Holyhead and Kingstown. Met on board John Morley, the Chief Secretary, and Sir John Pender. Were awaited at Dublin by conveyance from the Viceregal Lodge as promised, this invitation being one renewed from last year, when I was obliged to postpone my visit on account of my father's death. We were received by Mrs. Arthur Henniker, the Lord-Lieutenant's sister. A charming, *intuitive* woman apparently. Lord Houghton (the Lord-Lieutenant) came in shortly after.

'Our bedroom windows face the Phœnix Park and the Wicklow Mountains. The Lodge appears to have been built some time in the last century. A roomy building with many corridors.'

'20. To Dublin Castle, Christ Church, etc., conducted by Mr. Trevelyan, Em having gone with Mrs. Henniker, Mrs. Greer, and Miss Beresford to a Bazaar. Next day (Sunday) she went to Christ Church with them, and Trevelyan and I, after depositing them at the church door, went on to Bray, where we found the Chief Secretary and the Lord Chancellor at the grey hotel by the shore, "making magistrates by the dozen", as Morley said.'

'22. *Whit Monday*. Several went to the races. Mr. Lucy (who is also here) and I, however, went into Dublin, and viewed the public buildings and some comical drunken women dancing, I suppose because it was Whitsuntide.

'A larger party at dinner. Mr. Dundas, an A.D.C., played banjo and sang : Mrs. Henniker the zithern.'

'23. Morley came to lunch. In the afternoon I went with H. Lucy to the scene of the Phœnix Park murders.'

'24. Queen's birthday review. Troops and carriages at door at ½ past 11. The Aides — of whom there are about a dozen — are transformed by superb accoutrements into warriors — Mr. St. John Meyrick into a Gordon Highlander [he was killed in the South African War], Mr. Dundas into a dashing hussar. Went in one of the carriages of the procession with E. and the rest. A romantic scene, pathetically gay, especially as to the horses in the gallop past. "Yes : very pretty!" Mr. Dundas said, as one who knew the real thing.

'At lunch Lord Wolseley told me interesting things about war. On the other side of me was a young lieutenant, grandson of Lady de Ros, who recalled the Napoleonic wars. By Wolseley's invitation I visited him at the Military Hospital. Thence drove to Mrs. Lyttelton's to tea at the Chief Secretary's Lodge (which she rented). She showed me the rooms in which the bodies of Lord F. Cavendish and Mr. Burke were placed, and told some gruesome details of the discovery of a roll of bloody clothes under the sofa after the entry of the succeeding Secretary. The room had not been cleaned out since the murders.

'We dined this evening at the Private Secretary's Lodge with Mrs. Jekyll. Met Mahaffy there, a rattling, amusing talker, and others. Went back to the Viceregal Lodge soon enough to join the state diners in the drawing-room. Talked to several, and the Viceroy. Very funny altogether, this little Court.'

'25. Went over Guinness's Brewery, with Mrs. Henniker and several of the Viceregal guests, in the morning. Mr. Guinness conducted us. On the miniature railway we all got splashed with porter, or possibly dirty water, spoiling Em's and Mrs. Henniker's clothes. E. and I left the Lodge after lunch and proceeded by 3 o'clock train to Killarney, Lord Houghton having given me a copy of his poems. Put up at the Great Southern Railway Hotel.'

'26. Drove in car round Middle Lake, first driving to Ross Castle. Walked in afternoon about Killarney town, where the cows stand about the streets like people.'

'27. Started in wagonette for the Gap of Dunloe. Just below

Kate Kearney's house Em mounted a pony and I proceeded more leisurely on foot by the path. The scenery of the Black Valley is deeply impressive. Here are beauties of Nature to delight man, and to degrade him by attracting all the vagabonds in the country. Boats met us at the head of the Upper Lake, and we were rowed through the three to Ross Castle, whence we drove back to Killarney town.'

On the following Sunday they left and passed through Dublin, sleeping at the Marine Hotel at Kingstown, and early the next morning took the boat to Holyhead. Reached London the same evening.

Early in June Hardy attended a rehearsal at Terry's Theatre of his one-act play called *The Three Wayfarers* — a dramatization of his story *The Three Strangers*, made at the suggestion of J. M. Barrie. On the 3rd June the play was produced with one equally short by his friend, and another or two. The Hardys went with Lady Jeune and some more friends, and found that the little piece was well received.

During the week he saw Ibsen's *Hedda Gabler* and *Rosmersholm*, in which Miss Elizabeth Robins played. The former he had already seen, but was again impressed by it, as well as by the latter. Hardy could not at all understand the attitude of the English press towards these tragic productions — the culminating evidence of our blinkered insular taste being afforded by the nickname of the 'Ibscene drama' which they received.

On the eighth he met for the first time (it is believed) that brilliant woman Mrs. Craigie; and about this date various other people, including Mr. Hamilton Aidé, an old friend of Sir Arthur Blomfield's. In the week he still followed up Ibsen, going to *The Master Builder* with Sir Gerald and Lady Fitzgerald and her sister, Mrs. Henniker, who said afterwards that she was so excited by the play as not to be able to sleep all night; and on Friday lunched with General Milman at the Tower, inspecting 'Little-ease', and other rooms not generally shown at that time. In the evening he went with Mrs. Hardy and Miss Milman to Barrie's play, *Walker, London*, going behind the scenes with Barrie, and making the acquaintance of J. L. Toole, who said he could not go on even now on a first night without almost breaking down with nervousness. In a letter to Mrs. Henniker Hardy describes this experience:

'The evening of yesterday I spent in what I fear you will call a frivolous manner — indeed, during the time, my mind reverted to our Ibsen experience; and I could not help being regretfully struck

by the contrast — although I honestly was amused.   Barrie had
arranged to take us and Maarten Maartens to see B.'s play of *Walker,
London*, and lunching yesterday with the Milmans at the Tower we
asked Miss Milman to be of the party.   Mr. Toole heard we had come
and invited us behind the scenes.   We accordingly went and sat with
him in his dressing-room, where he entertained us with hock and
champagne, he meanwhile in his paint, wig, and blazer, as he had
come off the stage, amusing us with the drollest of stories about a
visit he and a friend paid to the Tower some years ago : how he
amazed the custodian by entreating the loan of the crown jewels for
an amateur dramatic performance for a charitable purpose, offering
to deposit 30s. as a guarantee that he would return them, etc., etc.,
etc.   We were rather late home as you may suppose.'

Some ten days later Hardy was at Oxford.   It was during the
Encaenia, with the Christ Church and other college balls, garden-
parties, and suchlike bright functions, but Hardy did not make himself known, his object being to view the proceedings entirely as a
stranger.   It may be mentioned that the recipients of Honorary
Degrees this year included Lord Rosebery, the Bishop of Oxford,
Dr. Liddell, and Sir Charles Euan Smith, a friend of his own.   He
viewed the Commemoration proceedings from the undergraduates'
gallery of the Sheldonian, his quarters while at Oxford being at the
Wilberforce Temperance Hotel.

The remainder of their season in London this year was of the
usual sort.   A memorial service to Admiral Tryon, a view of the
marriage procession of the Duke of York and Princess May from the
Club window, performances by Eleanora Duse and Ada Rehan in
their respective theatres, with various dinners and luncheons, brought
on the end of their term in Hamilton Terrace, and they returned to
Dorchester.   A note he made this month runs as follows :

'I often think that women, even those who consider themselves
experienced in sexual strategy, do not know how to manage an *honest*
man.'

In the latter part of July Hardy had to go up to town again for a
few days, when he took occasion to attend a lecture by Stepniak on
Tolstoi, to visit City churches, and to go with Lady Jeune and her
daughters to a farewell performance by Irving.   His last call this
summer was on Lady Londonderry, who remained his friend through
the ensuing years.   'A beautiful woman still', he says of her ; 'and
very glad to see me, which beautiful women are not always.   The

Duchess of Manchester [Consuelo] called while I was there, and Lady Jeune. All four of us talked of the marriage-laws, a conversation which they started, not I; also of the difficulties of separation, of terminable marriages where there are children, and of the nervous strain of living with a man when you know he can throw you over at any moment.'

It may be mentioned here that after the Duchess of Manchester's death a good many years later Hardy described her as having been when he first knew her 'a warm-natured woman, laughing-eyed, and bubbling with impulses, in temperament very much like "Julie-Jane" in one of my poems'.

'*At Dorchester. July* 31st. Mrs. R. Eliot lunched. Her story of the twins, "May" and "June". May was born between 11 and 12 on the 31st May, and June between 12 and 1 on June the 1st.'

The following month, in reply to an inquiry by the editors of the Parisian paper *L'Ermitage*, he wrote:

'I consider a social system based on individual spontaneity to promise better for happiness than a curbed and uniform one under which all temperaments are bound to shape themselves to a single pattern of living. To this end I would have society divided into *groups of temperaments*, with a different code of observances for each group.'

It is doubtful if this Utopian scheme possessed Hardy's fancy for any long time.

In the middle of August Hardy and his wife accepted an invitation to visit the Milnes-Gaskells at Wenlock Abbey, on their way thither calling at Hereford to see the Cathedral, Hardy always making a point of not missing such achievements in architecture, even if familiar. Lady Catherine and her daughter met them at the station. 'Lady C. is as sweet as ever, and almost as pretty, and occasionally shows a quizzical wit. The pet name "Catty" which her dearest friends give her has, I fear, a suspicious tremor of malice.' They were interested to find their bedroom in the Norman part of the building, Hardy saying he felt quite mouldy at sleeping within walls of such high antiquity.

Their time at the Abbey appears to have been very pleasant. They idled about in the shade of the ruins, and Milnes-Gaskell told an amusing story of a congratulatory dinner by fellow-townsmen to a burgher who had obtained a divorce from his wife, where the mayor made a speech beginning 'On this auspicious occasion'. During their stay they went with him to Stokesay Castle and Shrewsbury.

Lady Wenlock came one day ; and on Sunday Hardy and Lady C.
walked till they were tired, when they 'sat down on the edge of a
lonely sandpit and talked of suicide, pessimism, whether life was
worth living, and kindred dismal subjects, till we were quite miserable.  After dinner all sat round a lantern in the court under the stars
— where Lady C. told stories in the Devonshire dialect, moths flying
about the lantern as in *In Memoriam*.  She also defined the difference
between coquetting and flirting, considering the latter a grosser form
of the first, and alluded to Zola's phrase, "a woman whose presence
was like a caress", saying that some women could not help it being
so, even if they wished it otherwise.  I doubted it, considering it but
their excuse for carrying on.'

On their way back the Hardys went to Ludlow Castle, and deplored the wanton treatment which had led to the rooflessness of the
historic pile where *Comus* was first performed and *Hudibras* partly
written.  Hardy thought that even now a millionaire might be able
to re-roof it and make it his residence.

On a flying visit to London at the end of this month, dining at
the Conservative Club with Sir George Douglas, he had 'an interesting scientific conversation' with Sir James Crichton-Browne.  'A
woman's brain, according to him, is as large in proportion to her
body as a man's.  The most passionate women are not those selected
in civilized society to breed from, as in a state of nature, but the
colder ; the former going on the streets (I am sceptical about this).
The doctrines of Darwin require readjusting largely ; for instance,
the survival of the fittest in the struggle for life.  There is an altruism
and coalescence between cells as well as an antagonism.  Certain cells
destroy certain cells; but others assist and combine.  Well, I can't say.'

'*September* 13.  At Max Gate.  A striated crimson sunset ;
opposite it I sit in the study writing by the light of a shaded lamp,
which looks primrose against the red.'  This was Hardy's old study
facing west (now altered) in which he wrote *Tess of the d'Urbervilles*,
before he removed into his subsequent one looking east, where he
wrote *The Dynasts* and all his later poetry, and which is still unchanged.

'*September* 14.  Drove with Em. to the Sheridans', Frampton.
Tea on lawn.  Mrs. Mildmay, young Harcourt, Lord Dufferin, etc.
On our return all walked with us as far as the first park-gate.  May
[afterwards Lady Stracey] looked remarkably well.'

'*September* 17.  At Bockhampton heard a story about eels that
was almost gruesome — how they jumped out of a bucket at night,
crawled all over the house and half-way up the stairs, their tails being

heard swishing in the dark, and were ultimately found in the garden ; and when water was put to them to wash off the gravel and earth they became lively and leapt about.'

At the end of the month Hardy and his wife went on a visit to Sir Francis and Lady Jeune at Arlington Manor, finding the house when they arrived as cheerful as the Jeunes' house always was in those days, Hardy saying that there was never another house like it for cheerfulness. Among the other house-guests were Mrs. Craigie ('John Oliver Hobbes'), Lewis Morris, Mr. Stephen (a director of the North-Western Railway), and Hubert Howard, son of Lord Carlisle. On Sunday morning Hardy took a two hours' walk with Mrs. Craigie on the moor, when she explained to him her reasons for joining the Roman Catholic Church, a step which had vexed him somewhat. Apparently he did not consider her reasons satisfactory, but their friendship remained unbroken. While staying there they went to Shaw House, an intact Elizabethan mansion, and to a picnic in Savernake Forest, 'where Lady Jeune cooked luncheon in a great saucepan, with her sleeves rolled up and an apron on'.

'*October* 7-10. Wrote a song.' (Which of his songs is not mentioned.)

'*November* 11. Met Lady Cynthia Graham. In appearance she is something like my idea of Tess, though I did not know her when the novel was written.'

'*November* 23. Poem. "The Glass-stainer" (published later on).'

'*November* 28. Poem. "He views himself as an automaton" (published).'

'*December*. Found and touched up a short story called "An Imaginative Woman".

'In London with a slight cold in the head. Dined at the Dss. of Manchester's. Most of the guests had bad colds, and our hostess herself a hacking cough. A lively dinner all the same. As some people had not been able to come I dined with her again a few days later, as did also George [afterwards Lord] Curzon. Lady London-derry told me that her mother's grandmother was Spanish, whence the name of Theresa. There were also present the Duke of Devon-shire, Arthur Balfour, and Mr. and Mrs. Lyttelton. When I saw the Duchess again two or three days later, she asked me how I liked her relation, the Duke. I said not much ; he was too heavy for one thing. "That's because he's so shy!" she urged. "I assure you he is quite different when it wears off." I looked as if I did not believe much in the shyness. However, I'll assume it was so.'

After looking at a picture of Grindelwald and the Wetterhorn at somebody's house he writes: 'I could argue thus: "There is no real interest or beauty in this mountain, which appeals only to the childish taste for colour or size. The little houses at the foot are the real interest of the scene".' Hardy never did argue so, nor intend to, nor quite believe the argument; but one understands what he means.

Finishing his London engagements, which included the final revision with Mrs. Henniker of a weird story in which they had collaborated, entitled 'The Spectre of the Real', he spent Christmas at Max Gate as usual, receiving the carol-singers there on Christmas Eve, where, 'though quite modern, with a harmonium, they made a charming picture with their lanterns under the trees, the rays diminishing away in the winter mist'. On New Year's Eve it was calm, and they stood outside the door listening to the muffled peal from the tower of Fordington St. George.

# CHAPTER XXII

# ANOTHER NOVEL FINISHED, MUTILATED, AND RESTORED

1894–1895 : *Aet.* 53–55

'*February* 4, 1894. Curious scene encountered this (Sunday) evening as I was walking back to Dorchester from Bockhampton very late — nearly 12 o'clock. A girl almost in white on the top of Stinsford Hill, beating a tambourine and dancing. She looked like one of the "angelic quire", who had tumbled down out of the sky, and I could hardly believe my eyes. Not a soul there or near but her and myself. Was told she belonged to the Salvation Army, who beat tambourines devotionally.' The scene was afterwards put into verse.

One day this month he spent in Stinsford Churchyard with his brother, superintending the erection of their father's tombstone.

At Londonderry House the subject arose of social blunders. The hostess related some amusing ones of hers ; but Sir Redvers Buller capped everybody by describing what he called a 'double-barrelled' one of his own. He inquired of a lady next him at dinner who a certain gentleman was, 'like a hippopotamus', sitting opposite them. He was the lady's husband ; and Sir Redvers was so depressed by the disaster that had befallen him that he could not get it off his mind ; hence at a dinner the next evening he sought the condolences of an elderly lady, to whom he related his misfortune ; and remembered when he had told the story that his listener was the gentleman's mother.

At a very interesting luncheon at the Bachelors' Club given by his friend George Curzon he made the acquaintance of Mr. F. C. Selous, the mighty hunter, with the nature of whose fame he was not, however, quite in sympathy, wondering how such a seemingly humane man could live for killing ; and also of Lord Roberts and Lord Lansdowne.

After these cheerful doings he returned to Max Gate for a while, but when in London again, to look for a house for the spring and summer, he occasionally visited a friend he had earlier known by correspondence, Lord Pembroke, author of *South Sea Bubbles*, a fellow Wessex man, as he called himself, for whom Hardy acquired a very warm feeling. He was now ill at a nursing home in London, and an amusing incident occurred while his visitor was sitting by his bedside one afternoon, thinking what havoc of good material it was that such a fine and handsome man should be prostrated. He whispered to Hardy that there was a 'Tess' in the establishment, who always came if he rang at that time of the day, and that he would do so then that Hardy might see her. He accordingly rang, whereupon Tess's chronicler was much disappointed at the result; but endeavoured to discern beauty in the very indifferent figure who responded, and at last persuaded himself that he could do so. When she had gone the patient apologized, saying that for the first time since he had lain there a stranger had attended to his summons.

On Hardy's next visit to his friend Pembroke said with the faintest reproach: 'You go to the fashionable house in front, and you might come round to the back to see me.' The nursing home was at the back of Lady Londonderry's. They never met again, and when he heard of Pembroke's unexpected death Hardy remembered the words and grieved.

'*April* 7. Wrote to Harper's asking to be allowed to cancel the agreement to supply a serial story to *Harper's Magazine*.' This agreement was the cause of a good deal of difficulty afterwards (the story being *Jude the Obscure*), as will be seen.

This year they found a house at South Kensington, and moved into it with servants brought from the country, to be surprised a little later by the great attention their house received from butchers' and bakers' young men, postmen, and other passers-by; when they found their innocent country servants to have set up flirtations with all these in a bold style which the London servant was far too cautious to adopt.

At the end of April he paid a visit to George Meredith at his house near Box Hill, and had an interesting and friendly evening there, his son and daughter-in-law being present. 'Meredith', he said, 'is a shade artificial in manner at first, but not unpleasantly so, and he soon forgets to maintain it, so that it goes off quite.'

At a dinner at the Grand Hotel given by Mr. Astor to his contributors in May, Hardy had a talk with Lord Roberts, who spoke most modestly of his achievements. It was 'an artistic and luxuriant banquet, with beds of roses on the tables, electric lights shining up like glow-worms through their leaves and petals [an arrangement somewhat of a novelty then], and a band playing behind the palms'.

This month he spared two or three days from London to go to Aldeburgh in Suffolk, where at the house of Mr. Edward Clodd, his host, he met Grant Allen and Whymper, the mountaineer, who told of the tragedy on the Matterhorn in 1865 in which he was the only survivor of the four Englishmen present — a reminiscence which specially impressed Hardy from the fact that he remembered the particular day, thirty years before, of the arrival of the news in this country. He had walked from his lodgings in Westbourne Park Villas to Harrow that afternoon, and on entering the place was surprised to notice people standing at the doors discussing something with a serious look. It turned out to be the catastrophe, two of the victims being residents of Harrow. The event lost nothing by Whymper's relation of it. He afterwards marked for Hardy on a sketch of the Matterhorn a red line showing the track of the adventurers to the top and the spot of the accident — a sketch which is still at Max Gate with his signature.

On a day in the week following he was at the Women Writers' Club — probably its first anniversary meeting — and, knowing what women writers mostly had to put up with, was surprised to find himself in a group of fashionably dressed youngish ladies, the Princess Christian being present with other women of rank. 'Dear me — are women-writers like this!' he said with changed views.

During the same week they fulfilled likewise day or night invitations to Lady Carnarvon's, Mrs. Pitt-Rivers's, and other houses. At Lady Malmesbury's one of her green linnets escaped from its cage, and he caught it — reluctantly, but feeling that a green linnet at large in London would be in a worse predicament than as a prisoner. At the Countess of ——'s 'a woman very rich and very pretty' [Marcia, Lady Yarborough] informed him mournfully in *tête-à-tête* that people snubbed her, which so surprised him that he could hardly believe it, and frankly told her it was her own imagination. She was the lady of the 'Pretty pink frock' poem, though it should be stated that the deceased was not her husband but an uncle. And at an evening party at her house later he found her in a state of nerves, lest a sudden downpour of rain which had occurred should prevent people coming, and spoil her grand gathering. However, when the worst of the thunderstorm was over they duly streamed in, and she touched him joyfully on the shoulder and said, 'You've conjured them!' 'My entertainer's sister, Lady P——, was the most beautiful woman there.

On coming away there were no cabs to be got [on account of a strike it seems], and I returned to S.K. on the top of a 'bus. No sooner was I up there than the rain began again. A girl who had scrambled up after me asked for the shelter of my umbrella and I gave it — when she startled me by holding on tight to my arm and bestowing on me many kisses for the trivial kindness. She told me she had been to "The Pav", and was tired, and was going home. She had not been drinking. I descended at the South Kensington Station and watched the 'bus bearing her away. An affectionate nature wasted on the streets! It was a strange contrast to the scene I had just left.'

Early in June they were at the first performance of a play by Mrs. Craigie at Daly's Theatre, and did some entertaining at their own house, after which Mrs. Hardy was unwell, and went to Hastings for a change of air, Hardy going to Dorchester to look at some alterations he was making in his Max Gate house. At the end of a week he fetched his wife from Hastings, and after more dinners and luncheons he went to a melodrama at the Adelphi, which was said to be based without acknowledgement on *Tess of the d'Urbervilles*. He had received many requests for a dramatic version of the novel, but he found that nothing could be done with it among London actor-managers, all of them in their notorious timidity being afraid of the censure from conventional critics that had resisted Ibsen ; and he abandoned all idea of producing it, one prominent actor telling him frankly that he could not play such a dubious character as Angel Clare (which would have suited him precisely) 'because I have my name to make, and it would risk my reputation with the public if I played anything but a heroic character without spot'. Hardy thought of the limited artistic sense of even a leading English actor. Yet before and after this time Hardy received letters or oral messages from almost every actress of note in Europe asking for an opportunity of appearing in the part of 'Tess' — among them being Mrs. Patrick Campbell, Ellen Terry, Sarah Bernhardt, and Eleanora Duse.

During July Hardy met Mrs. Asquith for the first time ; and at another house he had an interesting conversation with Dr. W. H. Russell on the battles in the Franco-Prussian war, where Russell had been correspondent for *The Times*, and was blamed by some readers for putting too much realism into his accounts. Russell told Hardy a distressing story of a horse with no under jaw, laying its head upon his thigh in a dumb appeal for sympathy, two or three days after the battle of Gravelotte, when he was riding over the field ; and other such sickening experiences.

Whether because he was assumed to have written a notorious novel or not Hardy could not say, but he found himself continually invited hither and thither to see famous beauties of the time — some of whom disappointed him ; but some he owned to be very beautiful, such as Lady Powis, Lady Yarborough, Lady de Grey — 'handsome, tall, glance-giving, arch, friendly' — the Duchess of Montrose, Mrs. John Hanbury, Lady Cynthia Graham, Amélie Rives, and many others. A crush at Lady Spencer's at the Admiralty was one of the last of the parties they attended this season. But he mostly was compelled to slip away as soon as he could from these gatherings, finding that they exhausted him both of strength and ideas, few of the latter being given him in return for his own, because the fashionable throng either would not part from those it possessed, or did not possess any.

On the day of their giving up their house at South Kensington a curious mishap befell him. He had dispatched the servants and luggage in the morning ; Mrs. Hardy also had driven off to the station, leaving him, as they had arranged, to look over the house, see all was right, and await the caretaker, when he and his portmanteau would follow the rest to Dorchester. He was coming down the stairs of the silent house dragging the portmanteau behind him when his back gave way, and there he had to sit till the woman arrived to help him. In the course of the afternoon he was better and managed to get off, the acute pain turning out to be rheumatism aggravated by lifting the portmanteau.

'*August* 1–7. Dorchester : Seedy : back got better by degrees.'

'*October* 16. To London to meet Henry Harper on business.'

'*October* 20. Dined at the Guards' Mess, St. James's, with Major Henniker. After dinner went round with him to the sentries with a lantern.'

'*October* 23. Dining at the Savile last Sunday with Ray Lankester we talked of hypnotism, will, etc. He did not believe in silent influence, such as making a person turn round by force of will without communication. But of willing, for example, certain types of women by speech to do as you desire — such as "You *shall*, or you *are to*, marry me", he seemed to have not much doubt. If true, it seems to open up unpleasant possibilities.'

'*November*. Painful story. Old P——, who narrowly escaped hanging for arson about 1830, returned after his imprisonment, died at West Stafford, his native village, and was buried there. His widow long after died in Fordington, having saved £5 to be buried with her husband. The rector of the village made no objection, and the grave was dug. Meanwhile the daughter had come home, and said the money was not enough to pay for carrying the body of her mother out there in the country; so the grave was filled in, and the woman buried where she died.'

'*November* 11. Old song heard:

> "And then she arose,
> And put on her best clothes,
> And went off to the north with the Blues."

'Another:

> "Come ashore, Jolly Tar, with your trousers on."

'Another (sung at J. D.'s wedding):

> "Somebody here has been . . .
> Or else some charming shepherdess
> That wears the gown of green."'

In December he ran up to London alone on publishing business, and stayed at a temporary room off Piccadilly, to be near his club. It was then that there seems to have occurred, according to what he said later, some incident of the kind possibly adumbrated in the verses called 'At Mayfair Lodgings', in *Moments of Vision*. He watched during a sleepless night a lighted window close by, wondering who might be lying there ill. Afterwards he discovered that a woman had lain there dying, and that she was one whom he had cared for in his youth, when she was a girl in a neighbouring village.

In March of the next year (1895) Hardy was going about the neighbourhood of Dorchester and other places in Wessex with Mr. Macbeth Raeburn, the well-known etcher, who had been commissioned by the publishers to make sketches on the spot for frontispieces to the Wessex Novels. To those scenes which Hardy could not visit himself he sent the artist alone, one of which places, Charborough Park, the scene of *Two on a Tower*, was extremely difficult of access, the owner jealously guarding ingress upon her estate, and particularly to her park and house. Raeburn came back in the evening full of his adventures. Reaching the outer park-gate he found it locked, but the lodge-keeper opened it on his saying he had important business at the house. He then reached the second park-gate, which was unfastened to him on the same representation of urgency, but more dubiously. He then got to the front door of the mansion, rang, and asked permission to sketch the house. 'Good God!' said the butler, 'you don't know what you are asking. You had better be off before the mis'ess sees you, or the bailiff comes across you!' He started away discomfited, but thought he would make an attempt at a sketch behind the shadow of a tree. Whilst doing this he heard a voice shouting, and beheld a man running up to him — the redoubtable bailiff — who promptly ordered him out of the park. Raeburn as he moved off thought he detected something familiar in the accent of the bailiff, and turning, said, 'Surely you come from my country?' 'An' faith, man, it may be so!' the bailiff suddenly replied, whereon they compared notes, and found they had grown up in the same Scottish village. Then matters changed. 'Draw where you like and what you like, only don't let her see you from the windows at a'. She's a queer auld body, not bad at bottom, though it's rather far down. Draw as ye will, an' if I see her coming I'll haud up my hand.' Mr. Raeburn finished his sketch in peace and comfort, and it stands to this day at the beginning of the novel as evidence of the same.

During the spring they paid a visit of a few days to the Jeunes at Arlington Manor, where they also found Sir H. Drummond Wolff, home from Madrid, Lady Dorothy Nevill, Sir Henry Thompson, and other friends; and in May entered a flat at Ashley Gardens, West-minster, for the season. While here a portrait of Hardy was painted by Miss Winifred Thomson. A somewhat new feature in their doings this summer was going to teas on the terrace of the House of Com-mons — in those days a newly fashionable form of entertainment. Hardy was not a bit of a politician, but he attended several of these, and of course met many Members there.

On June 29 Hardy attended the laying of the foundation stone of the Westminster Cathedral, possibly because the site was close to the flat he occupied, for he had no leanings to Roman Catholicism. However, there he was, and deeply impressed by the scene. In July he visited St. Saviour's, Southwark, by arrangement with Sir Arthur Blomfield, to see how he was getting on with the restoration. Dinners and theatres carried them through the month, in which he also paid a visit to Burford Bridge, to dine at the hotel with the Omar Khayyám Club and meet George Meredith, where the latter made a speech, and Hardy likewise, said to be the first and last ever made by either of them; at any rate it was the first, and last but one or two, by Hardy.

Hardy's entries of his doings were always of a fitful and irregular kind, and now there occurs a hiatus which cannot be filled. But it is clear that at the end of the summer at Max Gate he was 'restoring the MS. of *Jude the Obscure* to its original state' — on which process he sets down an undated remark, probably about the end of August, when he sent off the restored copy to the publishers :

'On account of the labour of altering *Jude the Obscure* to suit the magazine, and then having to alter it back, I have lost energy for revising and improving the original as I meant to do.'

In September they paid a week's visit to General and Mrs. Pitt-Rivers at Rushmore, and much enjoyed the time. It was on the occasion of the annual sports at the Larmer Tree, and a full moon and clear sky favouring, the dancing on the green was a great success. The local paper gives more than a readable description of the festivity for this particular year :

'After nightfall the scene was one of extraordinary picturesqueness and poetry, its great features being the illumination of the grounds by thousands of Vauxhall lamps, and the dancing of hundreds of couples under these lights and the mellow radiance of the full moon. For the dancing a space was especially enclosed, the figures chosen being mostly the polka-mazurka and schottische, though some country dances were started by the house-party, and led off by the beautiful Mrs. Grove, the daughter of General Pitt-Rivers, and her charming sister-in-law, Mrs. Pitt. Probably at no other spot in England could such a spectacle have been witnessed at any time. One could hardly believe that one was not in a suburb of Paris, instead of a corner in old-fashioned Wiltshire, nearly ten miles from a railway-station in any direction.'

It may be worth mentioning that, passionately fond of dancing as Hardy had been from earliest childhood, this was the last occasion on which he ever trod a measure, according to his own recollection ; at any rate on the greensward, which is by no means so springy to the foot as it looks, and left him stiff in the knees for some succeeding days. It was he who started the country dances, his partner being the above-mentioned Mrs. (afterwards Lady) Grove.

A garden-party of their own at Max Gate finished the summer doings of the Hardys this year ; and a very different atmosphere from that of dancing on the green soon succeeded for him, of the coming of which, by a strange divination, he must have had a suspicion, else why should he have made the following note beforehand?

'"Never retract. Never explain. Get it done and let them howl." Words said to Jowett by a very practical friend.'

On the 1st November *Jude the Obscure* was published.

A week after, on the 8th, he sets down :

'England seventy years ago. — I have heard of a girl, now a very old woman, who in her youth was seen following a goose about the common all the afternoon to get a quill from the bird, with which the parish-clerk could write for her a letter to her lover. Such a first-hand method of getting a quill-pen for important letters was not infrequent at that date.' It may be added that Hardy himself had written such love-letters, and read the answers to them: but this was after the use of the quill had been largely abandoned for that of the steel pen, though old people still stuck to quills, and Hardy himself had to practise his earliest lessons in writing with a quill.

The onslaught upon *Jude* started by the vituperative section of the press — unequalled in violence since the publication of Swinburne's *Poems and Ballads* thirty years before — was taken up by the anonymous writers of libellous letters and post-cards, and other such gentry. It spread to America and Australia, whence among other appreciations he received a letter containing a packet of ashes, which the virtuous writer stated to be those of his iniquitous novel.

Thus, though Hardy with his quick sense of humour could not help seeing a ludicrous side to it all, and was well enough aware that the evil complained of was what these 'nice minds with nasty ideas' had read into his book, and not what he had put there, he underwent the strange experience of beholding a sinister lay figure of himself constructed by them, which had no sort of resemblance to him as he was, and which he, and those who knew him well, would not have recognized as being meant for himself if it had not been called by his name. Macaulay's remark in his essay on Byron was well illustrated by Thomas Hardy's experience at this time: 'We know of no spectacle so ridiculous as the British public in one of its periodical fits of morality.'

In contrast to all this it is worth while to quote what Swinburne wrote to Hardy after reading *Jude the Obscure*:

'The tragedy — if I may venture an opinion — is equally beautiful and terrible in its pathos. The beauty, the terror, and the truth, are all yours and yours alone. But (if I may say so) how cruel you are! Only the great and awful father of "Pierrette" and "L'Enfant Maudit" was ever so merciless to his children. I think it would hardly be seemly to enlarge on all that I admire in your work — or on half of it. — The man who can do such work can hardly care about criticism or praise, but I will risk saying how thankful we should be (I know that I may speak for other admirers as cordial as myself) for another admission into an English paradise "under the greenwood tree".

But if you prefer to be — or to remain — ποιητῶν τραγικώτατος [1] no doubt you may; for Balzac is dead, and there has been no such tragedy in fiction — on anything like the same lines — since he died.

'Yours most sincerely,

'A. C. SWINBURNE.'

Three letters upon this same subject, written by Hardy himself to a close friend, may appropriately be given here.

### LETTER I

'MAX GATE,
'DORCHESTER,
'*November* 10*th*, 1895.

'. . . Your review (of *Jude the Obscure*) is the most discriminating that has yet appeared. It required an artist to see that the plot is almost geometrically constructed — I ought not to say *constructed*, for, beyond a certain point, the characters necessitated it, and I simply let it come. As for the story itself, it is really sent out to those into whose souls the iron has entered, and has entered deeply at some time of their lives. But one cannot choose one's readers.

'It is curious that some of the papers should look upon the novel as a manifesto on 'the marriage question' (although, of course, it involves it), seeing that it is concerned first with the labours of a poor student to get a University degree, and secondly with the tragic issues of two bad marriages, owing in the main to a doom or curse of hereditary temperament peculiar to the family of the parties. The only remarks which can be said to bear on the *general* marriage question occur in dialogue, and comprise no more than half a dozen pages in a book of five hundred. And of these remarks I state (p. 362) that my own views are not expressed therein. I suppose the attitude of these critics is to be accounted for by the accident that, during the serial publication of my story, a sheaf of "purpose" novels on the matter appeared.

'You have hardly an idea how poor and feeble the book seems to me, as executed, beside the idea of it that I had formed in prospect.

'I have received some interesting letters about it already — yours not the least so. Swinburne writes, too enthusiastically for me to quote with modesty.

'Believe me, with sincere thanks for your review,

'Ever yours,

'THOMAS HARDY.

[1] The most tragic of authors.

'*P.S.* One thing I did not answer. The "grimy" features of the story go to show the contrast between the ideal life a man wished to lead, and the squalid real life he was fated to lead. The throwing of the pizzle, at the supreme moment of his young dream, is to sharply initiate this contrast. But I must have lamentably failed, as I feel I have, if this requires explanation and is not self-evident. The idea was meant to run all through the novel. It is, in fact, to be discovered in *everybody's* life, though it lies less on the surface perhaps than it does in my poor puppet's. 'T. H.'

LETTER II

'MAX GATE,
'DORCHESTER,
'*November 20th*, 1895.

'I am keen about the new magazine. How interesting that you should be writing this review for it! I wish the book were more worthy of such notice and place.

'You are quite right; there is nothing perverted or depraved in Sue's nature. The abnormalism consists in disproportion, not in inversion, her sexual instinct being healthy as far as it goes, but unusually weak and fastidious. Her sensibilities remain painfully alert notwithstanding, as they do in nature with such women. One point illustrating this I could not dwell upon: that, though she has children, her intimacies with Jude have never been more than occasional, even when they were living together (I mention that they occupy separate rooms, except towards the end), and one of her reasons for fearing the marriage ceremony is that she fears it would be breaking faith with Jude to withhold herself at pleasure, or altogether, after it; though while uncontracted she feels at liberty to yield herself as seldom as she chooses. This has tended to keep his passion as hot at the end as at the beginning, and helps to break his heart. He has never really possessed her as freely as he desired.

'Sue is a type of woman which has always had an attraction for me, but the difficulty of drawing the type has kept me from attempting it till now.

'Of course the book is all contrasts — or was meant to be in its original conception. Alas, what a miserable accomplishment it is, when I compare it with what I meant to make it! — *e.g.* Sue and her heathen gods set against Jude's reading the Greek testament; Christminster academical, Christminster in the slums; Jude the saint, Jude the sinner; Sue the Pagan, Sue the saint; marriage, no marriage; &c., &c.

'As to the "coarse" scenes with Arabella, the battle in the schoolroom, etc., the newspaper critics might, I thought, have sneered at them for their Fieldingism rather than for their Zolaism. But your everyday critic knows nothing of Fielding. I am read in Zola very little, but have felt akin locally to Fielding, so many of his scenes having been laid down this way, and his home near.

'Did I tell you I feared I should seem too High-Churchy at the end of the book where Sue recants? You can imagine my surprise at some of the reviews.

'What a self-occupied letter!

'Ever sincerely,

'T. H.'

LETTER III

'MAX GATE,
'DORCHESTER,
'*January* 4, 1896.

'For the last three days I have been tantalized by a difficulty in getting *Cosmopolis*, and had only just read your review when I received your note. My sincere thanks for the generous view you take of the book, which to me is a mass of imperfections. We have both been amused — or rather delighted — by the sub-humour (is there such a word?) of your writing. I think it a rare quality in living essayists, and that you ought to make more of it — I mean write more in that vein than you do.

'But this is apart from the review itself, of which I will talk to you when we meet. The rectangular lines of the story were not premeditated, but came by chance: except, of course, that the involutions of four lives must necessarily be a sort of quadrille. The only point in the novel on which I feel sure is that it makes for morality; and that delicacy or indelicacy in a writer is according to his object. If I say to a lady "I met a naked woman", it is indelicate. But if I go on to say "I found she was mad with sorrow", it ceases to be indelicate. And in writing Jude my mind was fixed on the ending.

'Sincerely yours,

'T. H.'

In London in December they went to see Forbes-Robertson and Mrs. Patrick Campbell as Romeo and Juliet, supping with them afterwards at Willis's Rooms, a building Hardy had known many years earlier, when it was still a ballroom unaltered in appearance from that of its famous days as 'Almack's' — indeed, he had himself danced on the old floor shortly after his first arrival in London in 1862, as has been mentioned.

When they got back to Dorchester during December Hardy had plenty of time to read the reviews of *Jude* that continued to pour out. Some paragraphists knowingly assured the public that the book was an honest autobiography, and Hardy did not take the trouble to deny it till more than twenty years later, when he wrote to an inquirer with whom the superstition still lingered that no book he had ever written contained less of his own life, which of course had been known to his friends from the beginning. Some of the incidents were real in so far as that he had heard of them, or come in contact with them when they were occurring to people he knew; but no more. It is interesting to mention that on his way to school he did once meet with a youth like Jude who drove the bread-cart of a widow, a baker, like Mrs. Fawley, and carried on his studies at the same time, to the serious risk of other drivers in the lanes; which youth asked him to lend him his Latin grammar. But Hardy lost sight of this featful student, and never knew if he profited by his plan.

Hardy makes a remark on one or two of the reviews:

'Tragedy may be created by an opposing environment either of things inherent in the universe, or of human institutions. If the former be the means exhibited and deplored, the writer is regarded as impious; if the latter, as subversive and dangerous; when all the while he may never have questioned the necessity or urged the non-necessity of either....'

During this year 1895, and before and after, *Tess of the d'Urbervilles* went through Europe in translations, German, French, Russian, Dutch, Italian, and other tongues, Hardy as a rule stipulating that the translation should be complete and unabridged, on a guarantee of which he would make no charge. Some of the renderings, however, were much hacked about in spite of him. The Russian translation appears to have been read and approved by Tolstoi during its twelve months' career in a Moscow monthly periodical.

In December he replied to Mr. W. T. Stead, editor of *The Review of Reviews*:

'I am unable to answer your inquiry as to "Hymns that have helped me".

'But the undermentioned have always been familiar and favourite hymns of mine as poetry :

'1. "Thou turnest man, O Lord, to dust". Ps. xc. *vv.* 3, 4, 5, 6. (Tate and Brady.)

'2. "Awake, my soul, and with the sun." (Morning Hymn, Ken.).

'3. "Lead, kindly Light." (Newman.)'

So ended the year 1895.

# CHAPTER XXIII

# MORE ON 'JUDE', AND ISSUE OF 'THE WELL-BELOVED'

1896–1897 : *Aet.* 55–57

HARDY found that the newspaper comments on *Jude the Obscure* were producing phenomena among his country friends which were extensive and peculiar, they having a pathetic reverence for press opinions. However, on returning to London in the spring he discovered somewhat to his surprise that people there seemed not to be at all concerned at his having been excommunicated by the press, or by at least a noisy section of it, and received him just the same as ever ; so that he and his wife passed this season much as usual, going to Lady Malmesbury's wedding and also a little later to the wedding of Sir George Lewis's son at the Jewish Synagogue ; renewing acquaintance with the beautiful Duchess of Montrose and Lady Londonderry, also attending a most amusing masked ball at his friends Mr. and Mrs. Montagu Crackanthorpe's, where he and Henry James were the only two not in dominoes, and were recklessly flirted with by the women in consequence.

This year they took again the house in South Kensington they had occupied two years earlier, and gave some little parties there. But it being a cold damp spring Hardy caught a chill by some means, and was laid up with a rheumatic attack for several days, in May suffering from a relapse. He was advised to go to the seaside for a change of air, and leaving the London house in the charge of the servants went with Mrs. Hardy to lodgings at Brighton.

While there he received a request from the members of the Glasgow University Liberal Club to stand as their candidate in the election of a Lord Rector for the University : the objection to Mr. Joseph Chamberlain, who had been nominated, being that he was not a man of letters. Hardy's reply to the Honorary Secretary was written from Brighton on May 16, 1896.

'DEAR SIR,

'Your letter has just reached me here, where I am staying for a few days for change of air after an illness.

'In reply let me assure you that I am deeply sensible of the honour of having been asked by the members of the Glasgow University Liberal Club to stand as their candidate for the Lord Rectorship.

'In other circumstances I might have rejoiced at the opportunity. But personal reasons which it would be tedious to detail prevent my entertaining the idea of coming forward for the office, and I can only therefore request you to convey to the Club my regrets that such should be the case ; and my sincere thanks for their generous opinion of my worthiness.

> 'I am, dear Sir,
> 'Yours faithfully,
> 'THOMAS HARDY.'

There they stayed about a week and, finding little improvement effected, returned to South Kensington. By degrees he recovered, and they resumed going out as usual, and doing as much themselves to entertain people as they could accomplish in a house not their own. This mostly took a form then in vogue, one very convenient for literary persons, of having afternoon parties, to the invitations to which their friends of every rank as readily responded as they had done in former years, notwithstanding the fact that at the very height of the season the Bishop of Wakefield announced in a letter to the papers that he had thrown Hardy's novel into the fire. Knowing the difficulty of burning a thick book even in a good fire, and the infrequency of fires of any sort in summer, Hardy was mildly sceptical of the literal truth of the bishop's story ; but remembering that Shelley, Milton, and many others of the illustrious, reaching all the way back to the days of Protagoras, had undergone the same sort of indignity at the hands of bigotry and intolerance he thought it a pity in the interests of his own reputation to disturb the episcopal narrative of adventures with *Jude*. However, it appeared that, further, — to quote the testimony in the Bishop's *Life* — the scandalized prelate was not ashamed to deal a blow below the belt, but 'took an envelope out of his paperstand and addressed it to W. F. D. Smith, Esq., M.P. The result was the quiet withdrawal of the book from the library, and an assurance that any other books by the same author would be carefully examined before they were allowed to be circulated.' Of this precious conspiracy Hardy knew nothing, or it might have moved a mind which the burning could not stir to say a word on literary garrotting. In his ignorance of it he remained silent, being fully aware of one thing, that the ethical teaching of the novel, even if somewhat crudely put, was as high as that of any of the bishop's sermons — (indeed, Hardy was afterwards reproached for its being 'too much of a sermon'). And thus feeling quite calm on the ultimate verdict of Time he merely reflected on the shallowness of the episcopal view of the case and of morals generally, which brought to his memory a witty remark he had once read in a *Times* leading article, to the effect that the qualities which enabled a man to become a bishop were often the very reverse of those which made a good bishop when he became one.

The only sad feature in the matter to Hardy was that if the bishop could have known him as he was, he would have found a man whose personal conduct, views of morality, and of the vital facts of religion, hardly differed from his own.[1]

Possibly soured by all this he wrote a little while after his birthday :

'Every man's birthday is a first of April for him ; and he who lives to be fifty and won't own it is a rogue or a fool, hypocrite or simpleton.'

At a party at Sir Charles Tennant's, to which Hardy and his wife were invited to meet the Eighty Club, Lord Rosebery took occasion in a conversation to inquire 'why Hardy had called Oxford "Christminster".' Hardy assured him that he had not done anything of the sort, 'Christminster' being a city of learning that was certainly suggested by Oxford, but in its entirety existed nowhere else in the world but between the covers of the novel under discussion. The answer was not so flippant as it seemed, for Hardy's idea had been, as he often explained, to use the difficulty of a poor man's acquiring learning at that date merely as the 'tragic mischief' (among others) of a dramatic story, for which purpose an old-fashioned university at the very door of the poor man was the most striking method ; and though the architecture and scenery of Oxford were the best in England adapted for this, he did not slavishly copy them ; indeed in some details he departed considerably from whatever of the city he took as a general model. It is hardly necessary to add that he had no feeling

---

[1] That the opinions thus expressed by Bishop How in 1895 are not now shared by all the clergy may be gathered from the following extract from an article in *Theology*, August 1928 :

'If I were asked to advise a priest preparing to become a *village* rector I would suggest first that he should make a good retreat . . . and then that he should make a careful study of Thomas Hardy's novels. . . . From Thomas Hardy he would learn the essential dignity of country people and what deep and often passionate interest belongs to every individual life. You cannot treat them in the mass : each single soul is to be the object of your special and peculiar prayer.'

The author of this article is an eminent clergyman of the Church of England.

in the matter, and used Jude's difficulties of study as he would have used war, fire, or shipwreck for bringing about a catastrophe.

It has been remarked above that Hardy with his quick sense of humour could not help seeing a ludicrous side to his troubles over *Jude*, and an instance to that effect now occurred. The *New York World* had been among those papers that fell foul of the book in the strongest terms, the critic being a maiden lady who expressed herself thus :

'What has happened to Thomas Hardy? . . . I am shocked, appalled by this story! . . . It is almost the worst book I ever read. . . . I thought that *Tess of the d'Urbervilles* was bad enough, but that is milk for babes compared to this. . . . It is the handling of it that is the horror of it. . . . I do not believe that there is a newspaper in England or America that would print this story of Thomas Hardy's as it stands in the book. Aside from its immorality there is coarseness which is beyond belief. . . . When I finished the story I opened the windows and let in the fresh air, and I turned to my bookshelves and I said : "Thank God for Kipling and Stevenson, Barrie and Mrs. Humphry Ward. Here are four great writers who have never trailed their talents in the dirt".'

It was therefore with some amazement that in the summer, after reading the above and other exclamations grossly maligning the book and the character of its author, to show that she would not touch him with a pair of tongs, he received a letter from the writer herself. She was in London, and requested him to let her interview him 'to get your side of the argument'. He answered :

'SAVILE CLUB,
'*July* 16, 1896.

'MY DEAR MADAM :

'I have to inform you in answer to your letter that ever since the publication of *Jude the Obscure* I have declined to be interviewed on the subject of that book ; and you must make allowance for human nature when I tell you that I do not feel disposed to depart from this rule in favour of the author of the review of the novel in the *New York World*.

'I am aware that the outcry against it in America was only an echo of its misrepresentation here by one or two scurrilous papers which got the start of the more sober press, and that dumb public opinion was never with these writers. But the fact remains that such a meeting would be painful to me and, I think, a disappointment to you.

'Moreover, my respect for my own writings and reputation is so very slight that I care little about what happens to either, so that the rectification of judgements, etc., and the way in which my books are interpreted, do not much interest me.  Those readers who, like yourself, could not see that *Jude* (though a book quite without a "purpose" as it is called) makes for morality more than any other book I have written, are not likely to be made to do so by a newspaper article, even from your attractive pen.

'At the same time I cannot but be touched by your kindly wish to set right any misapprehension you may have caused about the story.  Such a wish will always be cherished in my recollection, and it removes from my vision of you some obviously unjust characteristics I had given it in my mind.  This is, at any rate on my part, a pleasant gain from your letter, whilst I am "never the worse for a touch or two on my speckled hide" as the consequence of your review.

> 'Believe me, dear Madam,
> > 'Yours sincerely,
> > > 'THOMAS HARDY.

'To Miss JEANNETTE GILDER.'


It may be interesting to give Miss Gilder's reply to this:

> > > > 'HOTEL CECIL,
> > > > > '*July* 17, '96.

'DEAR MR. HARDY,

'I knew that you were a great man, but I did not appreciate your goodness until I received your letter this morning.

> > > 'Sincerely yours,
> > > > 'JEANNETTE L. GILDER.'

Hardy must indeed have shown some magnanimity in condescending to answer the writer of a review containing such contumelious misrepresentations as hers had contained.  But, as he said, she was a woman, after all — one of the sex that makes up for lack of justice by excess of generosity — and she had screamed so grotesquely loud in her article that Hardy's sense of the comicality of it had saved his feelings from being much hurt by the outrageous slurs.

Here, he thought, the matter had ended.  But make the doors upon a woman's wit, and it will out at the casement.  The amusing sequel to the episode was that the unsuspecting Hardy was invited to an evening party a few days later by an American lady resident in

London, and though he knew her but slightly he went, having nothing better to do. While he was talking to his hostess on the sofa a strange lady drew up her chair rather near them, and listened to the conversation, but did not join in it. It was not till afterwards that he discovered that this silent person had been his reviewer, who was an acquaintance of his entertainer, and that the whole thing had been carefully schemed.

Various social events took them into and through July ; Hardy's chief pleasure, however, being none of these, but a pretty regular attendance with his wife in this, as in other summers, at the Imperial Institute, not far from their house, where they would sit and listen to the famous bands of Europe that were engaged year after year by the management, but were not, to Hardy's regret, sufficiently appreciated by the London public. Here one evening they met, with other of their friends, the beautiful Mrs., afterwards Lady, Grove ; and the 'Blue Danube' Waltz being started, Hardy and the latter lady danced two or three turns to it among the promenaders, who eyed them with a mild surmise as to whether they had been drinking or not. In such wise the London season drew to a close and was wound up, as far as they were concerned, with the wedding of one of Lady Jeune's daughters, Miss Dorothy Stanley, at St. George's, Hanover Square, to Mr. Henry Allhusen.

When he reached Dorchester he paid a visit to his mother, on whom he remarks that she was well, but that 'her face looked smaller'.

On the 12th August they left Dorchester for Malvern, where they put up at the Foley Arms, climbed the Beacon, Hardy on foot, Mrs. Hardy on a mule ; drove round the hills, visited the Priory Church, and thence went on to Worcester to see the Cathedral and porcelain works ; after which they proceeded to Warwick and Kenilworth, stopping to correct proofs at the former place, and to go over the castle and church. A strange reminder of the transitoriness of life was given to Hardy in the church, where, looking through a slit by chance, he saw the coffin of the then recent Lord Warwick, who, a most kindly man, some while before, on meeting him in London, had invited him to Warwick Castle, an invitation which he had been unable to accept at the time, though he had promised to do so later. 'Here I am at last', he said to the coffin as he looked ; 'and here are you to receive me!' It made an impression on Hardy which he never forgot.

They took lodgings for a week at Stratford-on-Avon, and visited the usual spots associated with Shakespeare's name ; going on to

Coventry and to Reading, a town which had come into the life of Hardy's paternal grandmother, who had lived here awhile ; after which they went to Dover, where Hardy read *King Lear*, which was begun at Stratford. He makes the following observation on the play :

'*September* 6. Finished reading *King Lear*. The grand scale of the tragedy, scenically, strikes one, and also the large scheme of the plot. The play rises from and after the beginning of the third act, and Lear's dignity with it. Shakespeare did not quite reach his intention in the King's character, and the splitting of the tragic interest between him and Gloucester does not, to my mind, enhance its intensity, although commentators assert that it does.'

'*September* 8. Why true conclusions are not reached, notwithstanding everlasting palaver : Men endeavour to hold to a mathematical consistency in things, instead of recognizing that certain things may both be good and mutually antagonistic : *e.g.*, patriotism and universal humanity ; unbelief and happiness.

'There are certain questions which are made unimportant by their very magnitude. For example, the question whether we are moving in Space this way or that ; the existence of a God, etc.'

Having remained at Dover about a fortnight they crossed to Ostend in the middle of September, and went on to Bruges. He always thought the railway station of this town the only satisfactory one in architectural design that he knew. It was the custom at this date to admire the brick buildings of Flanders, and Hardy himself had written a prize essay as a young man on Brick and Terra-Cotta architecture ; but he held then, as always, that nothing can really compensate in architecture for the lack of stone, and would say on this point — with perhaps some intentional exaggeration — that the ashlar back-yards of Bath had more dignity than any brick front in Europe. From Bruges they went on to Brussels, Namur, and Dinant, through scenes to become synonymous with desolation in the war of after years.

'*September* 23. At dinner at the public table [of the hotel] met a man possessed of the veritable gambling fever. He has been playing many days at the Casino (roulette and trente-et-quarante). He believes thoroughly in his "system", and yet, inconsistently, believes in luck : *e.g.*, 36 came into his head as he was walking down the street towards the Casino to-day ; and it made him back it, and he won. He plays all the afternoon and all the evening.

'His system appears to be that of watching for numbers which have not turned up for a long time ; but I am not sure.

'He is a little man ; military looking ; large iron-grey moustache standing out detached ; iron-grey hair ; fresh crimson skin. Produces the book, ruled in vertical columns, in which he records results. Discusses his system incessantly with the big grey-bearded man near. Can talk of nothing else. . . . Has lost to-day 4500 francs. Has won back some — is going to play to-night till he has won it all back, and if he can profit enough to pay the expenses of his trip on the Continent he will be satisfied. His friend with the beard, who seems to live in the hotel permanently, commends him by a nod and a word now and then, but not emphatically.'

'*September* 24. After breakfast unexpectedly saw the gambler standing outside the hotel-entrance without a hat, looking wild, and by comparison with the previous night like a tree that has suddenly lost its leaves. He came up to me ; said he had had no luck on the previous night ; had plunged, and lost heavily. He had not enough money left to take him home third-class. Is going to Monte Carlo in November with £2000 to retrieve his losses. . . .

'We left between 12 and 1. The gambler left at the same time by a train going in the opposite direction, and was carefully put into a third-class carriage by his friend of the hotel, who bought his ticket. He wore a green-grey suit and felt hat, looking bleak-faced and absent, and seemed passive in the other's hands. His friend is apparently a decoy from the Casino.'

Mrs. Hardy, not being a good walker, had brought her bicycle as many people did just then, bicycling being wildly popular at the time, and Flanders being level. After they had paid twenty-four francs duty at Ostend for importing it, it had several adventures in its transit from place to place, was always getting lost, and miraculously turned up again when they were just enjoying the relief of finding themselves free of it. At Liège it really did seem gone, Hardy having watched the transfer of all the luggage at a previous junction, and the bicycle not being among it. Having given up thinking of it they were hailed by an official, who took them with a mysterious manner to a store-room some way off, unlocked it, and with a leer said, to Hardy's dismay : '*Le véloçe!*' How it had got there they did not know.

At Spa they drove to the various fountains, examined the old gaming-house in the Rue Vauxhall where those that were now cold skeletons had burnt hot with the excitement of play, thought of the town's associations in fact and fiction, of the crowned heads of all the countries of Europe who had found their pleasure and cure at this

Mother of Watering-places — now shrunk small like any other ancient matron.

Getting back to Brussels they put up for association's sake at the same hotel they had patronized twenty years before, but found it had altered for the worse since those bright days. Hardy again went out to Waterloo, which had been his chief reason for stopping at the Belgian capital, and no doubt made some more observations with a view to *The Dynasts*, to which he at this time had given the provisional name of 'Europe in Throes'. All he writes thereon in his pocket-book while in Brussels is :

'Europe in Throes.
'Three Parts.   Five Acts each.
'*Characters :* Burke, Pitt, Napoleon, George III., Wellington. . . .
and many others.'

But he set down more copious notes for the drama elsewhere. It is believed he gave time to further conjectures as to the scene of the Duchess's Ball, which he had considered when here before, and on which it may be remembered there is a note in *The Dynasts*, ending, 'The event happened less than a century ago, but the spot is almost as phantasmal in its elusive mystery as towered Camelot, the Palace of Priam, or the Hill of Calvary'.

Concerning the scene of the battle itself he writes :

'*October* 2.   To Field of Waterloo.   Walked alone from the English line along the Charleroi Road to "La Belle Alliance".   Struck with the *nearness* of the French and English lines to each other. Shepherds with their flocks and dogs, men ploughing, two cats, and myself, the only living creatures on the field.'

Returning homeward through Ostend a little later they found the hotels and shops closed and boarded up, and the Digue empty, Mrs. Hardy being the single woman bicyclist where there had been so many.

'MAX GATE.   *October* 17.   A novel, good, microscopic touch in Crabbe [which would strike one trained in architecture].   He gives surface without outline, describing his church by telling *the colour of the lichens.*

'Poetry.   Perhaps I can express more fully in verse ideas and emotions which run counter to the inert crystallized opinion — hard as a rock — which the vast body of men have vested interests in supporting.   To cry out in a passionate poem that (for instance) the

Supreme Mover or Movers, the Prime Force or Forces, must be either limited in power, unknowing, or cruel — which is obvious enough, and has been for centuries — will cause them merely a shake of the head ; but to put it in argumentative prose will make them sneer, or foam, and set all the literary contortionists jumping upon me, a harmless agnostic, as if I were a clamorous atheist, which in their crass illiteracy they seem to think is the same thing. . . . If Galileo had said in verse that the world moved, the Inquisition might have let him alone.'

'1897. *January* 27. To-day has length, breadth, thickness, colour, smell, voice. As soon as it becomes *yesterday* it is a thin layer among many layers, without substance, colour, or articulate sound.'

'*January* 30. Somebody says that the final dictum of the *Ion* of Plato is "inspiration, not art". The passage is θεῖον καὶ μὴ τεχνικόν. And what is really meant by it is, I think, more nearly expressed by the words "inspiration, not technicality" — "art" being too comprehensive in English to use here.'

'*February* 4. Title : "Wessex Poems : with Sketches of their Scenes by the Author".'

'*February* 10. In spite of myself I cannot help noticing countenances and tempers in objects of scenery, *e.g.* trees, hills, houses.'

'*February* 21. My mother's grandfather, Swetman — a descendant of the Christopher Swetman of 1631 mentioned in the History of the County as a small landed proprietor in the parish — used to have an old black bedstead, with the twelve apostles on it in carved figures, each about one foot six inches high. Some of them got loose, and the children played with them as dolls. What became of that bedstead?'

'*March* 1. Make a lyric of the speech of Hyllus at the close of the *Trachiniae*.' (It does not appear that this was ever carried out.)

At the beginning of March a dramatization of *Tess of the d'Urbervilles* was produced in America with much success by Mr. Fiske. About the same date Hardy went with Sir Francis Jeune to a banquet at the Mansion House in honour of Mr. Bayard, the American Ambassador, on his leaving England, which Hardy described as a 'brilliant gathering', though the night was so drenching and tempestuous as to blow off house-roofs and flood cellars. In the middle of the month a revised form of a novel of his which had been published serially in 1892 as *The Pursuit of the Well-Beloved: A Sketch of a Temperament*, was issued in volume form as *The Well-Beloved*. The theory on which this fantastic tale of a subjective idea was constructed is explained in the preface to the novel, and again exemplified in a poem bearing the same name, written about this time and published with *Poems of the Past and the Present* in 1901 — the theory of the trans-migration of the ideal beloved one, who only exists in the lover, from material woman to material woman — as exemplified also by Proust many years later. Certain critics affected to find unmentionable moral atrocities in its pages, but Hardy did not answer any of the charges further than by defining in a letter to a literary periodical the scheme of the story somewhat more fully than he had done in the preface :

'Not only was it published serially five years ago but it was sketched many years before that date, when I was comparatively a young man, and interested in the Platonic Idea, which, considering its charm and its poetry, one could well wish to be interested in always. . . . There is, of course, underlying the fantasy followed by the visionary artist the truth that all men are pursuing a shadow, the Unattainable, and I venture to hope that this may redeem the tragi-comedy from the charge of frivolity. . . . "Avice" is an old name common in the county, and "Caro" (like all the other surnames) is an imitation of a local name . . . this particular modification having been adopted because of its resemblance to the Italian for "dear".'

In reply to an inquiry from an editor he wrote :

'No : I do not intend to answer the article on *The Well-Beloved*. Personal abuse best answers itself. What struck me, next to its mendacious malice, was its maladroitness, as if the writer were blinded by malignity. . . . Upon those who have read the book the review must have produced the amazed risibility I remember feeling at Wilding's assertions when as a youth I saw Foote's comedy of *The Liar.* . . . There is more fleshliness in *The Loves of the Triangles* than in this story — at least to me. To be sure, there is one explana-tion which should not be overlooked : a reviewer *himself* afflicted with "sex mania" might review so — a thing terrible to think of.'

Such were the odd effects of Hardy's introduction of the sub-jective theory of love into modern fiction, and so ended his prose contributions to literature (beyond two or three short sketches to fulfil engagements), his experiences of the few preceding years having killed all his interest in this form of imaginative work, which had ever been secondary to his interest in verse.

A letter from him to Swinburne was written about this time, in which he says :

'I must thank you for your kind note about my fantastic little tale [*The Well-Beloved*], which, if it can make, in its better parts, any faint claim to imaginative feeling, will owe something of such feeling to you, for I often thought of lines of yours during the writing ; and indeed, was not able to resist the quotation of your words now and then.

'And this reminds me that one day, when examining several English imitations of a well-known fragment of Sappho, I interested myself in trying to strike out a better equivalent for it than the commonplace "Thou, too, shalt die", etc., which all the translators had used during the last hundred years. I then stumbled upon your "Thee, too, the years shall cover", and all my spirit for poetic pains died out of me. Those few words present, I think, the finest *drama* of Death and Oblivion, so to speak, in our tongue.

.        .        .        .        .        .

'Believe me to be
'Yours very sincerely,
'THOMAS HARDY.

1

'*P.S.* — I should have added that *The Well-Beloved* is a fancifu exhibition of the artistic nature, and has, I think, some little foundation in fact. I have been much surprised, and even grieved, by a ferocious review attributing an immoral quality to the tale. The writer's meaning is beyond me. T. H.'

# PART VI

## VERSE, TO THE END OF 'THE DYNASTS'

# CHAPTER XXIV

# COLLECTING OLD POEMS AND
# MAKING NEW

1897–1898 : *Aet.* 57–58

THE misrepresentations of the last two or three years affected but little, if at all, the informed appreciation of Hardy's writings, being heeded almost entirely by those who had not read him ; and turned out ultimately to be the best thing that could have happened ; for they wellnigh compelled him, in his own judgment at any rate, if he wished to retain any shadow of self-respect, to abandon at once a form of literary art he had long intended to abandon at some indefinite time, and resume openly that form of it which had always been more instinctive with him, and which he had just been able to keep alive from his early years, half in secrecy, under the pressure of magazine writing. He abandoned it with all the less reluctance in that the novel was, in his own words, 'gradually losing artistic form, with a beginning, middle, and end, and becoming a spasmodic inventory of items, which has nothing to do with art'.

The change, after all, was not so great as it seemed. It was not as if he had been a writer of novels proper, and as more specifically understood, that is, stories of modern artificial life and manners showing a certain smartness of treatment. He had mostly aimed at keeping his narratives close to natural life and as near to poetry in their subject as the conditions would allow, and had often regretted that those conditions would not let him keep them nearer still.

Nevertheless he had not known, whilst a writer of prose, whether he might not be driven to society novels, and hence, as has been seen, he had kept, at casual times, a record of his experiences in social life, though doing it had always been a drudgery to him. It was now with a sense of great comfort that he felt he might leave off further chronicles of that sort. But his thoughts on literature and life were often written down still, and from his notes much of which follows has been abridged.

He had already for some time been getting together the poems which made up the first volume of verse that he was about to publish. In date they ranged from 1865 intermittently onwards, the middle period of his novel-writing producing very few or none, but of late years they had been added to with great rapidity, though at first with some consternation he had found an awkwardness in getting back to an easy expression in numbers after abandoning it for so many years ; but that soon wore off.

He and his wife went to London as usual this year (1897), but did not take a house there. After two or three weeks' stay they adopted the plan of living some way out, and going up and down every few days, the place they made their temporary centre being Basingstoke. In this way they saw London friends, went to concerts at the Imperial Institute (the orchestra this season being the famous Vienna band under Edouard Strauss), saw one or two Ibsen plays, and the year's pictures. Being near they also went over the mournful relics of that city of the past, Silchester ; till in the middle of June they started for Switzerland, thus entirely escaping the racket of the coming Diamond Jubilee, and the discomfort it would bring upon people like them who had no residence of their own in London.

All the world, including the people of fashion habitually abroad, was in London or arriving there, and the charm of a lonely Continent impressed the twain much. The almost empty Channel steamer, the ease with which they crossed France from Havre by Paris, Dijon, and Pontarlier to Neuchâtel, the excellent rooms accorded them by obsequious hosts at the hotels in Switzerland, usually frequented by English and American tourists, made them glad they had come. On the actual day, the 20th, they were at Berne, where they celebrated it by attending a Jubilee Concert in the Cathedral, with the few others of their fellow-countryfolk who remained in the town. At Interlaken the comparative solitude was just as refreshing, the rosy glow from the Jungfrau, visible at three in the morning from Hardy's bedroom, seeming an exhibition got up for themselves alone ; and a pathetic procession of empty omnibuses went daily to and from each railway train between shops that looked like a banquet spread for people who delayed to come. They drove up the valley to Grindelwald, and having been conveyed to Scheidegg, walked thence to the Wengern Alp — overlooking the scene of *Manfred* — where a baby had just been born, and where Hardy was more impressed by the thundering rumble of unseen avalanches on the immense Jungfrau immediately facing than by the sight of the visible ones.

The next day, or the next following, *The Times'* account of the celebration in London of Queen Victoria's Diamond Jubilee reached Hardy's hands, and he took it out and read it in the snowy presence of the maiden-monarch that dominated the whole place.

It was either in the train as it approached Interlaken, or while he was there looking at the peak, that there passed through his mind the sentiments afterwards expressed in the lines called 'The Schreckhorn : with thoughts of Leslie Stephen'.

After a look at Lauterbrunnen, the Staubbach, the Lake and Castle of Thun, they stopped at the Hôtel Gibbon, Lausanne, Hardy not having that aversion from the historian of the *Decline and Fall* which Ruskin recommended. He found that, though not much might remain of the original condition of the building or the site, the remoter and sloping part of the garden, with its acacias and irregular contours, could not have been much changed from what it was when Gibbon haunted it, and finished his history. Accordingly his recaller sat out there till midnight on June 27, and imagined the historian closing his last page on the spot, as described in his *Autobiography* :

'It was on the day, or rather the night, of the 27th of June 1787, between the hours of eleven and twelve, that I wrote the last lines of the last page, in a summer house in my garden. After laying down my pen I took several turns in a *berceau*, or covered walk of acacias, which commands a prospect of the country, the lake, and the mountains.'

It is uncertain whether Hardy chose that particular evening for sitting out in the garden because he knew that June 27th was Gibbon's date of conclusion, or whether the coincidence of dates was accidental. The later author's imaginings took the form of the lines subjoined, which were printed in *Poems of the Past and the Present*.

## LAUSANNE

*In Gibbon's old garden:* 11-12 *p.m.*

*June* 27, 1897

A spirit seems to pass,
Formal in pose, but grave withal and grand :
He contemplates a volume in his hand,
And far lamps fleck him through the thin acacias.

Anon the book is closed,
With 'It is finished!' And at the alley's end
He turns, and when on me his glances bend
As from the Past comes speech — small, muted, yet composed.

'How fares the Truth now? — Ill?
— Do pens but slily further her advance?
May one not speed her but in phrase askance?
Do scribes aver the Comic to be Reverend still?

'Still rule those minds on earth
At whom sage Milton's wormwood words were hurled :
"*Truth like a bastard comes into the world
Never without ill-fame to him who gives her birth*"?' [1]

From Lausanne, making excursions to Ouchy, and by steamer to
Territet, Chillon, Vevey, and other places on the lake, they afterwards
left for Zermatt, going along the valley of the Rhone amid intense
heat till they gradually rose out of it beside the roaring torrent of the
Visp. That night Hardy looked out of their bedroom window in
the Hôtel Mt. Cervin, and 'Could see where the Matterhorn was by the
absence of stars within its outline', it being too dark to see the surface
of the mountain itself although it stood facing him.  He meant to
make a poem of the strange feeling implanted by this black silhouette
of the mountain on the pattern of the constellation ; but never did,
so far as is known.  However, the mountain inspired him to begin
one sonnet, finished some time after — that entitled 'To the Matterhorn' — the terrible accident on whose summit, thirty-two years
before this date, had so impressed him at the time of its occurrence.

While walking from Zermatt with a Russian gentleman to the
Riffel-Alp Hotel, whither Mrs. Hardy had preceded him on a pony,
he met some English ladies, who informed him of the mysterious
disappearance of an Englishman somewhere along the very path he
had been following.  Having lunched at the hotel and set his wife
upon the pony again he sent her on with the guide, and slowly searched
all the way down the track for some clue to the missing man, afterwards writing a brief letter to *The Times* to say there was no sign
visible of foul play anywhere on the road.  The exertion of the
search, after walking up the mountain-path in the hot morning sun,
so exhausted his strength that on arriving at Geneva, whither they
went after leaving Zermatt, he was taken so ill at the Hôtel de la Paix
that he had to stay in bed.  Here as he lay he listened to the plashing
of a fountain night and day just outside his bedroom window, the

---

[1] The quotation is from *The Doctrine and Discipline of Divorce*, the passage running
as follows : 'Truth is as impossible to be soiled by any outward touch, as the sunbeam ;
though this ill hap wait on her nativity, that she never comes into the world, but like a
bastard, to the ignominy of him that brought her forth ; till Time, the midwife rather
than the mother of truth, have washed and salted the infant and declared her legitimate.

casements of which were kept widely open on account of the heat. It was the fountain beside which the Austrian Empress was murdered shortly after by an Italian anarchist.  His accidental nearness in time and place to the spot of her doom moved him much when he heard of it, since thereby hung a tale.  She was a woman whose beauty, as shown in her portraits, had attracted him greatly in his youthful years, and had inspired some of his early verses, the same romantic passion having also produced the outline of a novel upon her, which he never developed.

While he was recovering at Geneva Mrs. Hardy found by chance the tomb of an ancestor who had died there.  But of Geneva, its lake, Diodati, Montalègre, Ferney, and the neighbourhood, he merely remarks : 'These haunts of the illustrious!  Ah, but *they* are gone now, and care for their chosen nooks no more!'

Again in London in July he expressed views on scenery in the following letter :

### To the Editor of the 'Saturday Review'

'Sir, — I am unable to reply to your inquiry on "The Best Scenery I know".  A week or two ago I was looking at the inexorable faces of the Jungfrau and the Matterhorn : a few days later at the Lake of Geneva with all its soft associations.  But, which is "best" of things that do not compare at all, and hence cannot be reduced to a common denominator?  At any given moment we like best what meets the mood of that moment.

'Not to be entirely negative, however, I may say that, in my own neighbourhood, the following scenes rarely or never fail to delight beholders :

'1. View from Castle Hill, Shaftesbury.
'2. View from Pilsdon Pen.
'3. New Forest vistas near Brockenhurst.
'4. The River Dart.
'5. The coast from Trebarwith Strand to Beeny Cliff, Cornwall.'

From London he returned to Max Gate, and with Mrs. Hardy wandered off to Wells Cathedral, and onwards to Frome and Longleat, whence after examining the library and the architecture he proceeded to Salisbury, a place in which he was never tired of sojourning, partly from personal associations and partly because its graceful cathedral pile was the most marked instance in England of an architectural intention carried out to the full.

'*August* 10, *Salisbury.* Went into the Close late at night. The moon was visible through both the north and south clerestory windows to me standing on the turf on the north side. . . . Walked to the west front, and watched the moonlight creep round upon the statuary of the façade — stroking tentatively and then more and more firmly the prophets, the martyrs, the bishops, the kings, and the queens. . . . Upon the whole the Close of Salisbury, under the full summer moon on a windless midnight, is as beautiful a scene as any I know in England — or for the matter of that elsewhere.

'Colonel T. W. Higginson of the United States, who is staying at the same hotel as ourselves, introduced himself to us. An amiable well-read man, whom I was glad to meet. He fought in the Civil War. Went with him to hunt up the spot of the execution of the Duke of Buckingham, whose spirit is said to haunt King's House still.'

After revisiting Stonehenge he remarks :

'The misfortune of ruins — to be beheld nearly always at noonday by visitors, and not at twilight.

'*August* 10, *continued.* "The day goeth away . . . the shadows of the evening are stretched out . . . I set watchmen over you, saying, Hearken to the sound of the trumpet. But they said, We will not hearken. Therefore hear, ye nations. . . . To what purpose cometh there to me incense from Sheba, and the sweet cane from a far country? Your burnt offerings are not acceptable, nor your sacrifices sweet unto me." Passages from the first lesson (Jer. vi.) at the Cathedral this afternoon. E. and I present. A beautiful chapter, beautifully read by the old Canon.'

'*August* 13. All tragedy is grotesque — if you allow yourself to see it as such. A risky indulgence for any who have an aspiration towards a little goodness or greatness of heart! Yet there are those who do.'

'*August* 15. It is so easy nowadays to call any force above or under the sky by the name of "God" — and so pass as orthodox cheaply, and fill the pocket!'

In September he passed a few pleasant days in bicycling about the neighbourhood with Mr. Rudyard Kipling, who had an idea just at that time that he would like to buy a house near Weymouth. They found a suitable house for sale at Rodwell, commanding a full view of Portland Roads ; but difficulties arose when inquiries were made, and Mr. Kipling abandoned the idea.

Bicycling was now in full spirit with the Hardys — and, indeed, with everybody — and many were the places they visited by that means.

'*October* 10. Am told a singularly creepy story — absolutely true, I am assured — of a village girl near here who was about to be married. A watch had been given her by a former lover, his own watch, just before their marriage was prevented by his unexpected death of consumption. She heard it *going* in her box at waking on the morning of the wedding with the second lover, though it had not been touched for years.

'Lizzy D—— [the monthly nurse who had attended at Hardy's birth] told my mother that she walked eighteen (?) miles the day after her own baby was born. . . . She was an excellent nurse, much in demand ; of infinite kindheartedness, humour, and quaintness, and as she lived in a cottage quite near our house at Bockhampton, she as it were kept an eye upon the Hardy family always, and being her neighbour gave my mother the preference in clashing cases. She used to tell a story of a woman who came to her to consult her about the ghost of another woman she declared she had seen, and who "troubled her" — the deceased wife of the man who was courting her.

'"How long hev' the woman been dead?" I said.

'"Many years!"

'"Oh, that were no ghost. Now if she'd only been dead a month or two, and you were making her husband your fancy-man, there might have been something in your story. But Lord, much can she care about him after years and years in better company!"'

To return to 1897. Nothing more of much account occurred to Hardy during its lapse, though it may be mentioned that *Jude*, of which only a mutilated version could be printed as a serial in England and America, appeared in a literal translation in Germany, running through several months of a well-known periodical in Berlin and Stuttgart without a single abridgement.

'1898. *February* 5. Write a prayer, or hymn, to One not Omnipotent, but hampered ; striving for our good, but unable to achieve it except occasionally.' [This idea of a limited God of goodness, often dwelt on by Hardy, was expounded ably and at length in MacTaggart's *Some Dogmas of Religion* several years later, and led to a friendship which ended only with the latter's death.]

As the spring drew on they entered upon their yearly residence of a few months in London — this time taking a flat in Wynnstay

Gardens, Kensington. Hardy did some reading at the British Museum with a view to *The Dynasts*, and incidentally stumbled upon some details that suggested to him the Waterloo episode embodied in a poem called 'The Peasant's Confession'. He also followed up the concerts at the Imperial Institute, mostly neglected by Londoners. One visit gave him occasion for the following note, the orchestra this year being from the Scala, Milan :

'Scene at the Imperial Institute this afternoon. Rain floating down in wayward drops. Not a soul except myself having tea in the gardens. The west sky begins to brighten. The red, blue, and white fairy lamps are like rubies, sapphires, turquoises, and pearls in the wet. The leaves of the trees, not yet of full size, are dripping, and the waiting-maids stand in a group with nothing to do. Band playing a "Contemplazione" by Luzzi.'

On June 24th, declining to write an Introduction to a proposed Library Edition of Fielding's novels, he remarks :

'Fielding as a local novelist has never been clearly regarded, to my mind : and his aristocratic, even feudal, attitude towards the peasantry (*e.g.* his view of Molly as a "slut" to be ridiculed, not as a simple girl, as worthy a creation of Nature as the lovely Sophia) should be exhibited strongly. But the writer could not well be a working novelist without his bringing upon himself a charge of invidiousness.'

Back in Dorset in July he resumed cycling more vigorously than ever, and during the summer went to Bristol, Gloucester, Cheltenham, Sherborne, Poole, Weymouth, and many other places — sometimes with Mrs. Hardy, sometimes with his brother.

In the middle of December *Wessex Poems* was published ; and verse being a new mode of expression with him in print he sent copies to friends, among them one to Leslie Stephen, who said :

'It gave me a real pleasure. I am glad to think that you remember me as a friend. . . . I am always pleased to remember that *Far from the Madding Crowd* came out under my command. I then admired the poetry which was diffused through the prose ; and can recognize the same note in the versified form. . . . I will not try to criticize or distinguish, but will simply say that they have pleased me and re-minded me vividly of the old time. I have, as you probably know, gone through much since then. . . .'

# CHAPTER XXV

# 'WESSEX POEMS' AND OTHERS

1899–1900 : *Aet.* 58–60

IN the early weeks of this year the poems were reviewed in the customary periodicals — mostly in a friendly tone, even in a tone of respect, and with praise for many pieces in the volume ; though by some critics not without umbrage at Hardy's having taken the liberty to adopt another vehicle of expression than prose-fiction without consulting them.  It was probably these reviews that suggested to Hardy several reflections on poetry and criticism about this time, and the following gleanings of his opinions are from the rough entries he made thereon.  Some no doubt were jotted down hastily, and might have been afterwards revised.

He observes that he had been under no delusion about the coldness and even opposition he would have to encounter — at any rate from some voices — in openly issuing verse after printing nothing (with trifling exceptions) but prose for so many years.

Almost all the fault-finding was, in fact, based on the one great antecedent conclusion that an author who has published prose first, and that largely, must necessarily express himself badly in verse, no reservation being added to except cases in which he may have published prose for temporary or compulsory reasons, or prose of a poetical kind, or have written verse first of all, or for a long time intermediately.

In criticism generally, the fact that the date of publication is but an accident in the life of a literary creation, that the printing of a book is the least individual occurrence in the history of its contents, is often overlooked.  In its visible history the publication is what counts, and that alone.  It is then that the contents start into being for the outside public.  In the present case, although it was shown that many of the verses had been written before their author dreamt of novels, the critics' view was little affected that he had 'at the eleventh hour', as they untruly put it, taken up a hitherto uncared-for art.

It may be observed that in the art-history of the century there was an example staring them in the face of a similar modulation from one style into another by a great artist. Verdi was the instance, 'that amazing old man' as he was called. Someone of insight wrote concerning him : 'From the ashes of his early popularity, from *Il Trovatore* and its kind, there arose on a sudden a sort of phœnix Verdi. Had he died at Mozart's death-age he would now be practically unknown.' And another : 'With long life enough Verdi might have done almost anything ; but the trouble with him was that he had only just arrived at maturity at the age of threescore and ten or thereabouts, so that to complete his life he ought to have lived a hundred and fifty years.'

But probably few literary critics discern the solidarity of all the arts. Curiously enough Hardy himself dwelt upon it in a poem that seems to have been little understood, though the subject is of such interest. It is called 'Rome : The Vatican : Sala delle Muse' ; in which a sort of composite Muse addresses him :

> 'Be not perturbed', said she. 'Though apart in fame,
> I and my sisters are one.'

In short, this was a particular instance of the general and rather appalling conclusion to which he came — had indeed known before — that a volume of poetry, by clever manipulation, can be made to support any *a priori* theory about its quality. Presuppose its outstanding feature to be the defects aforesaid ; instances can be found. Presuppose, as here was done, that it is overloaded with derivations from the Latin or Greek when really below the average in such words ; they can be found. Presuppose that Wordsworth is unorthodox : instances can be found ; that Byron is devout ; instances can also be found. [The foregoing paragraphs are abridged from memoranda which Hardy set down, apparently for publication ; though he never published them.]

He wrote somewhere : 'There is no new poetry ; but the new poet — if he carry the flame on further (and if not he is no new poet) — comes with a new note. And that new note it is that troubles the critical waters.

'Poetry is emotion put into measure. The emotion must come by nature, but the measure can be acquired by art.'

In the reception of this and later volumes of Hardy's poems there was, he said, as regards form, the inevitable ascription to ignorance of what was really choice after full knowledge. That the author loved the art of concealing art was undiscerned.  For instance, as to rhythm.  Years earlier he had decided that too regular a beat was bad art.  He had fortified himself in his opinion by thinking of the analogy of architecture, between which art and that of poetry he had discovered, to use his own words, that there existed a close and curious parallel, both arts, unlike some others, having to carry a rational content inside their artistic form.  He knew that in architecture cunning irregularity is of enormous worth, and it is obvious that he carried on into his verse, perhaps in part unconsciously, the Gothic art-principle in which he had been trained — the principle of spontaneity, found in mouldings, tracery, and such like — resulting in the 'unforeseen' (as it has been called) character of his metres and stanzas, that of stress rather than of syllable, poetic texture rather than poetic veneer;  the latter kind of thing, under the name of 'constructed ornament', being what he, in common with every Gothic student, had been taught to avoid as the plague.  He shaped his poetry accordingly, introducing metrical pauses, and reversed beats ; and found for his trouble that some particular line of a poem exemplifying this principle was greeted with a would-be jocular remark that such a line 'did not make for immortality'.  The same critic might have gone to one of our cathedrals (to follow up the analogy of architecture), and on discovering that the carved leafage of some capital or spandrel in the best period of Gothic art strayed freakishly out of its bounds over the moulding, where by rule it had no business to be, or that the enrichments of a string-course were not accurately spaced ;  or that there was a sudden blank in a wall where a window was to be expected from formal measurement, have declared with equally merry conviction, 'This does not make for immortality'.

One case of the kind, in which the poem 'On Sturminster Foot-Bridge' was quoted with the remark that one could make as good music as that out of a milk-cart, betrayed the reviewer's ignorance of any perception that the metre was intended to be onomatopoeic, plainly as it was shown ;  and another in the same tone disclosed that the reviewer had tried to scan the author's sapphics as heroics.

If any proof were wanted that Hardy was not at this time and later the apprentice at verse that he was supposed to be, it could be found in an examination of his studies over many years.  Among his papers were quantities of notes on rhythm and metre : with outlines and experiments in innumerable original measures, some of which he adopted from time to time.  These verse skeletons were mostly blank, and only designated by the usual marks for long and short syllables, accentuations, etc., but they were occasionally made up of 'nonsense verses' — such as, he said, were written when he was a boy by students of Latin prosody with the aid of a 'Gradus'.

Lastly, Hardy had a born sense of humour, even a too keen sense occasionally: but his poetry was sometimes placed by editors in the hands of reviewers deficient in that quality. Even if they were accustomed to Dickensian humour they were not to Swiftian. Hence it unfortunately happened that verses of a satirical, dry, caustic, or farcical cast were regarded by them with the deepest seriousness. In one case the tragic nature of his verse was instanced by the ballad called 'The Bride-night Fire', or 'The Fire at Tranter Sweatley's', the criticism being by an accomplished old friend of his own, Frederic Harrison, who deplored the painful nature of the bridegroom's end in leaving only a bone behind him. This piece of work Hardy had written and published when quite a young man, and had hesitated to reprint because of its too pronounced obviousness as a jest.

But he had looked the before-mentioned obstacles in the face, and their consideration did not move him much. He had written his poems entirely because he liked doing them, without any ulterior thought; because he wanted to say the things they contained and would contain. He offered his publishers to take on his own shoulders the risk of producing the volume, so that if nobody bought it they should not be out of pocket. They were kind enough to refuse this offer, and took the risk on themselves; and fortunately they did not suffer.

A more serious meditation of Hardy's at this time than that on critics was the following:

'*January* (1899). No man's poetry can be truly judged till its last line is written. What is the last line? The death of the poet. And hence there is this quaint consolation to any writer of verse — that it may be imperishable for all that anybody can tell him to the contrary; and that if worthless he can never know it, unless he be a greater adept at self-criticism than poets usually are.'

Writing to Hardy in March about her late husband's tastes in literature Mrs. Coventry Patmore observes:

'. . . It shows how constant he was to his *loves*. From 1875 [when he first met with the book — *vide ante*] to 1896 he continually had *A Pair of Blue Eyes* read aloud to him. Each time he felt the same shock of surprise and pleasure at its consummate art and pathos. In illness, when he asked for *A Pair of Blue Eyes* one knew he was able to *enjoy* again.'

A correspondence on another matter than literature may be alluded to here. Mr. W. T. Stead had asked Hardy to express his opinion on 'A Crusade of Peace' in a periodical he was about to publish under the name of *War against War*. In the course of his reply Hardy wrote :

'As a preliminary, all civilized nations might at least show their humanity by covenanting that no horses should be employed in battle except for transport. Soldiers, at worst, know what they are doing, but these animals are denied even the poor possibilities of glory and reward as a compensation for their sufferings.'

His reply brought upon Hardy, naturally, scoffs at his unpractical tender-heartedness, and on the other hand, strong expressions of agreement.

In the following April (1899) the Hardys were again in London where as in the previous year they took a flat in Wynnstay Gardens, though not the same one. They saw their friends as usual, on one of whom Hardy makes this observation after a call from him :

'When a person has gone, though his or her presence was not much desired, we regret the withdrawal of the grain of value in him, and overlook the mass of chaff that spoilt it. We realize that the essence of his personality was a human heart, though the form was uninviting.'

'It would be an amusing fact, if it were not one that leads to such bitter strife, that the conception of a First Cause which the theist calls "God", and the conception of the same that the so-styled atheist calls "no-God", are nowadays almost exactly identical. So that only a minor literary question of terminology prevents their shaking hands in agreement, and dwelling together in unity ever after.'

At the beginning of June Hardy was staying at a country-house not many miles from London, and among the guests was the young Duchess of M——, a lady of great beauty, who asked him if he would conduct her to the grave of the poet Gray, which was within a walk. Hardy did so and, standing half-balanced on one foot by the grave (as is well known, it was also that of Gray's mother) his friend recited in a soft voice the 'Elegy' from the first word to the last in leisurely and lengthy clearness without an error (which Hardy himself could not have done without some hitch in the order of the verses). With startling suddenness, while duly commending her performance, he seemed to have lived through the experience before.

Then he realized what it was that had happened : in love of recitation, attitude, and poise, tone of voice, and readiness of memory, the fair lady had been the duplicate of the handsome dairymaid who had insisted on his listening to her rehearsal of the long and tedious gospels, when he taught in the Sunday school as a youth of fifteen. What a thin veneer is that of rank and education over the natural woman, he would remark.

On the 18th he met A. E. Housman (the Shropshire Lad) for the first time probably, and on the 20th he visited Swinburne at Putney, of which visit he too briefly speaks ; observing, 'Again much inclined to his engaging, fresh, frank, almost childlike manner. Showed me his interesting editions, and talked of the play he was writing. Promised to go again.' He also went a day or two later, possibly owing to his conversation with Swinburne (though he had been there before), to St. Mildred's, Bread Street, with Sir George Douglas, where Shelley and Mary Godwin were married, and saw the register, with the signatures of Godwin and his wife as witnesses. The church was almost unaltered since the poet and Mary had knelt there, and the vestry absolutely so, not having even received a coat of paint as it seemed. Being probably in the calling mood he visited George Meredith just afterwards, and found him 'looking ruddy and well in the upper part ; quite cheerful, enthusiastic and warm. Would gladly see him oftener, and must try to do so.' At the end of the month he rambled in Westminster Abbey at midnight by the light of a lantern, having with some friends been admitted by Miss Bradley through the Deanery.

Hardy had suffered from rather bad influenza this summer in Town, and it left an affection of the eye behind it which he had never known before ; and though he hoped it might leave him on his return to Dorchester it followed him there. He was, indeed, seldom absolutely free from it afterwards.

In July he replied to a communication from the Rationalist Press Association, of which his friend Leslie Stephen was an honorary associate :

'Though I am interested in the Society I feel it to be one which would naturally compose itself rather of writers on philosophy, science, and history, than of writers of imaginative works, whose effect depends largely on detachment. By belonging to a philosophic association imaginative writers place themselves in this difficulty, that they are misread as propagandist when they mean to be simply artistic and delineative.'

The pleasures of bicycling were now at their highest appreciation, and many miles did Hardy and his wife, and other companions, cover during the latter part of this summer.  He was not a long-distance cyclist, as was natural at fifty-nine, never exceeding forty to fifty miles a day, but he kept vigorously going within the limit, this year and for several years after.  His wife, though an indifferent walker, could almost equal him in cycle distances.

In October his sonnet on the departure of the troops for the Boer War, which he witnessed at Southampton, appeared in the *Daily Chronicle*, and in November the very popular verses called 'The Going of the Battery' were printed in the *Graphic*, the scene having been witnessed at Dorchester.  In December 'The Dead Drummer' (afterwards called 'Drummer Hodge') appeared in *Literature*, and 'A Christmas Ghost-Story' in the *Westminster Gazette*.

The latter months of this same year (1899) were saddened for him by the sudden death of Sir Arthur Blomfield, shortly before the date which had been fixed for a visit to him at Broadway by Hardy and his wife.  Thus was snapped a friendship which had extended over thirty-six years.

Hardy's memoranda on his thoughts and movements — particularly the latter — which never reached the regularity of a diary — had of late grown more and more fitful, and now (1900) that novels were past and done with, nearly ceased altogether, such notes on scenes and functions having been dictated by what he had thought practical necessity ; so that it becomes difficult to ascertain what mainly occupied his mind, or what his social doings were.  His personal ambition in a worldly sense, which had always been weak, dwindled to nothing, and for some years after 1895 or 1896 he requested that no record of his life should be made.  His verses he kept on writing from pleasure in them.  The poetic fantasy entitled 'The Souls of the Slain' was published in the *Cornhill* in the April of this year, and he and his wife went to London this month according to custom, though instead of taking a flat or house as in former years they stayed on at the West Central Hotel in Southampton Row.  He possibly thought it advisable to economize, seeing that he had sacrificed the chance of making a much larger income by not producing more novels.  When one considers that he might have made himself a man of affluence in a few years by taking the current of popularity as it served, writing 'best sellers', and ringing changes upon the novels he had already written, his bias towards poetry must have been instinctive and disinterested.

In a pocket-book of this date appears a diagram illustrating 'the language of verse' :

Verse

| Fanciful | Meditative | Sentimental | Passionate |

Language of Common Speech.

Poetic Diction

and the following note thereon :

'The confusion of thought to be observed in Wordsworth's teaching in his essay in the Appendix to *Lyrical Ballads* seems to arise chiefly out of his use of the word "imagination". He should have put the matter somewhat like this : In works of *passion and sentiment* (not "imagination and sentiment") the language of verse is the language of prose. In works of *fancy* (or *imagination*), "poetic diction" (of the real kind) is proper, and even necessary. The diagram illustrates my meaning.'

For some reason he spent time while here in hunting up Latin hymns at the British Museum, and copies that he made of several have been found, of dates ranging from the thirteenth to the seventeenth century, by Thomas of Celano, Adam of S. Victor, John Mombaer, Jacob Balde, etc. That English prosody might be enriched by adapting some of the verse-forms of these is not unlikely to have been his view.

When they left London this year is uncertain, but we find Hardy at the latter part of July bicycling about Dorset with his friend Mr. (later Sir) Hamo Thornycroft, and in August entertaining Mr. A. E. Housman, Mr. Clodd, and Sir Frederick Pollock, bicycling from Max Gate to Portland Bill and back in one day with the last named, a performance whose chief onerousness lay in roughness of road surface and steepness of gradient. Cycling went merrily along through August, September, and into October, mostly with Mrs. Hardy and other companions, reaching to the outskirts of the county and into Somerset, Devon, and Hants. In October, declining to be interviewed by the representative of the American National Red Cross Society, he wrote as a substitute :

'A society for the relief of suffering is entitled to every man's gratitude ; and though, in the past century, material growth has been out of all proportion to moral growth, the existence of your Society

Thomas Hardy's study about 1900

leaves one not altogether without hope that during the next hundred years the relations between our inward and our outward progress may become less of a reproach to civilization.'

In the same month he replied to the Rev. J. Alexander Smith:

'On referring to the incident in *Tess of the d'Urbervilles* to which you draw my attention, I do not find there anything more than an opinion, or feeling, on lay baptism by a person who was nettled at having his clerical ministration of the rite repulsed. The truth or error of his opinion is therefore immaterial. Nevertheless if it were worth while it might be plausibly argued that to refuse clerical performance and substitute lay performance not from necessity but from pure obstinacy (as he held), might deprive that particular instance of lay baptism of its validity.'

At the very close of the year Hardy's much admired poem on the Century's End, entitled 'The Darkling Thrush', was published in a periodical.

[END OF THE NINETEENTH CENTURY]

# CHAPTER XXVI

# 'POEMS OF THE PAST AND THE PRESENT', AND OTHERS

### 1901–1903 : *Aet.* 60–63

M AY found them in London, and hearing music. At an Ysaye Concert at Queen's Hall a passage in the descriptive programme evidently struck him — whether with amusement at the personifica-tions in the rhetoric, or admiration for it, is not mentioned — for he takes the trouble to copy it :

'" The solo enters at the twelfth bar. . . . Later in the movement a new theme is heard — a brief episode, the thematic material of the opening sufficing the composer's needs. In the Adagio the basses announce and develop a figure. Over this the soloists and first violins enter", etc. (Bach's Concerto in E.) I see them : black-headed, lark-spurred fellows, marching in on five wires.'

'*May* 11. Leslie Stephen says : "The old ideals have become obsolete, and the new are not yet constructed. . . . We cannot write living poetry on the ancient model. The gods and heroes are too dead, and we cannot seriously sympathize with . . . the idealized prize-fighter."'

A few days later Hardy chronicles a feat of execution by Kubelik at a concert he attended at St. James's Hall — that of playing 'pizzi-cato' on his violin the air of 'The Last Rose of Summer' with Ernst's variations, and fingering and bowing a rapid accompaniment at the same time. At Mr. Maurice Hewlett's Madame Sarah Bernhardt talked to him pensively on her consciousness that she was getting old, but on his taking his wife a day or two later to see her as the Duc in M. Rostand's *L'Aiglon* she appeared youthful enough, he said, 'though unfortunately too melodramatically lime-lighted for natural-ness'.

At the end of the month the well-known literary and journalistic fraternity called the Whitefriars Club paid Hardy a visit at Max Gate, where they were entertained in a tent on the lawn. To diversify their journey from London they had travelled the last ten miles by road in open carriages, and the beautiful new summer dresses of the ladies were encrusted with dust. But nobody minded — except perhaps some of the ladies themselves — and the visit was a most lively one, though the part of the country they had driven through was not the most picturesque part.

Thomas Hardy's mother, now in her eighty-eighth year, was greatly interested to hear of this visit of the Club to the home of her son. Her devoted daughters, Mary and Katherine, promised to take her in her wheeled chair, for she was no longer able to walk abroad as formerly, to see the carriages drive past the end of a lane leading from Higher Bockhampton to the foot of Yellowham Hill, some three miles from Max Gate.

On the day appointed, the chair, its two attendants, and its occupant, a little bright-eyed lady in a shady hat, waited under some trees bordering the roadside for the members of the Whitefriars Club to pass.

Mrs. Hardy had announced gaily that she intended to wave her handkerchief to the travellers, but her more sedate daughters urged that this was not to be done. However, as soon as the dusty vehicles had whirled past the old lady pulled out a handkerchief which she had concealed under the rug covering her knees, and waved it triumphantly at the disappearing party. So unquenchable was her gay and youthful spirit even when approaching her ninetieth year.

Long afterwards one member of the visiting party said to the present writer : 'If we had known who that was, what cheers there would have been, what waving of handkerchiefs, what a greeting for Thomas Hardy's mother!'

In a letter on Rationalism written about this time, but apparently not sent, he remarks :

'My own interest lies largely in non-rationalistic subjects, since non-rationality seems, so far as one can perceive, to be the principle of the Universe. By which I do not mean foolishness, but rather a principle for which there is no exact name, lying at the indifference point between rationality and irrationality.'

In reply to the letter of an inquirer as to the preservation of the prospect from Richmond Hill, he wrote, 10th June 1901 :

'I have always been in love with Richmond Hill — the Lass included — and though I think I could produce a few specimens from this part of the country that would be fairly even with it, or her, in point of beauty, I am grieved to hear that the world-famed view is in danger of disfigurement. I cannot believe that any such foolish local policy will be persevered in.'

### To Dr. Arnaldo Cervesato of Rome

'*June* 20, 1901.

'I do not think that there will be any permanent revival of the old transcendental ideals ; but I think there may gradually be developed an Idealism of Fancy ; that is, an idealism in which fancy is no longer tricked out and made to masquerade as belief, but is frankly and honestly accepted as an imaginative solace in the lack of any substantial solace to be found in life.'

'*July* 8. Pictures. My weakness has always been to prefer the large intention of an unskilful artist to the trivial intention of an accomplished one : in other words, I am more interested in the high ideas of a feeble executant than in the high execution of a feeble thinker.'

During the seven weeks ensuing he was preparing for the press a number of lyrics and other verses which had accumulated since *Wessex Poems* appeared, and sent off the manuscript to the publishers at the end of August. It was published in the middle of November under the title of *Poems of the Past and the Present*. He seems to have taken no notice of the reception accorded to the book by the press, though it might have flattered him to find that some characteristic ideas in this volume — which he never tried to make consistent — such as in the pieces entitled 'The Sleep-worker', 'The Lacking Sense', 'Doom and She', and others — ideas that were further elaborated in *The Dynasts*, found their way into many prose writings after this date.

On the last day of the year he makes the following reflection : 'After reading various philosophic systems, and being struck with their contradictions and futilities, I have come to this : *Let every man make a philosophy for himself out of his own experience.* He will not be able to escape using terms and phraseology from earlier philosophers, but let him avoid adopting their theories if he values his own mental life. Let him remember the fate of Coleridge, and save years of labour by working out his own views as given him by his surroundings.'

'*January* 1 (1902).   A Pessimist's apology.   Pessimism (or rather what is called such) is, in brief, playing the sure game.   You cannot lose at it; you may gain.   It is the only view of life in which you can never be disappointed.   Having reckoned what to do in the worst possible circumstances, when better arise, as they may, life becomes child's play.'

In reply this month to a writer in the Parisian *Revue Bleue* he gave it as his opinion that the effect of the South African War on English literature had been:

'A vast multiplication of books on the war itself, and the issue of large quantities of warlike and patriotic poetry.   These works naturally throw into the shade works that breathe a more quiet and philosophic spirit; a curious minor feature in the case among a certain class of writers being the disguise under Christian terminology of principles not necessarily wrong from the point of view of international politics, but obviously anti-Christian, because inexorable and masterful.'

In view of the approaching centenary of Victor Hugo's birth, Hardy, amongst other European men of letters, was asked at this time by a Continental paper for a brief tribute to the genius of the poet; and he sent the following:

'His memory must endure.   His works are the cathedrals of literary architecture, his imagination adding greatness to the colossal and charm to the small.'

'*March*.   Poetry.   There is a latent music in the sincere utterance of deep emotion, however expressed, which fills the place of the actual word-music in rhythmic phraseology on thinner emotive subjects, or on subjects with next to none at all.   And supposing a total poetic effect to be represented by a unit, its component fractions may be either, say:

'Emotion three-quarters, plus Expression one quarter, or

'Emotion one quarter, plus Expression three-quarters.

'This suggested conception seems to me to be the only one which explains all cases, including those instances of verse that apparently infringe all rules, and yet bring unreasoned convictions that they are poetry.'

In April of this year he was writing 'A Trampwoman's Tragedy' — a ballad based on some local story of an event more or less resembling the incidents embodied, which took place between 1820 and 1830. Hardy considered this, upon the whole, his most successful poem.

To Mr. (afterwards Sir) Rider Haggard, who was investigating the conditions of agriculture and agricultural labourers, he gave the following information:

'*March*, 1902.

'My dear Haggard,

'As to your first question, my opinion on the past of the agricultural labourers in this county: I think, indeed know, that down to 1850 or 1855 their condition was in general one of great hardship. I say in general, for there have always been fancy-farms, resembling St. Clair's in *Uncle Tom's Cabin*, whereon they lived as smiling exceptions to those of their class all around them. I recall one such, the estate-owner being his own farmer, and ultimately ruining himself by his hobby. To go to the other extreme: as a child I knew a sheep-keeping boy who to my horror shortly afterwards died of want — the contents of his stomach at the autopsy being raw turnip only. His father's wages were six shillings a week, with about two pounds at harvest, a cottage rent free, and an allowance of thorn faggots from the hedges as fuel. Between these examples came the great bulk of farms — wages whereon ranged from seven to nine shillings a week, and perquisites being better in proportion.

'Secondly: as to the present. Things are of course widely different now. I am told that at the annual hiring-fair just past, the old positions were absolutely reversed, the farmers walking about and importuning the labourers to come and be hired, instead of, as formerly, the labourers anxiously entreating the stolid farmers to take them on at any pittance. Their present life is almost without exception one of comfort, if the most ordinary thrift be observed. I could take you to the cottage of a shepherd not many miles from here that has a carpet and brass-rods to the staircase, and from the open door of which you hear a piano strumming within. Of course bicycles stand by the doorway, while at night a large paraffin lamp throws out a perfect blaze of light upon the passer-by.

'The son of another labourer I know takes dancing lessons at a quadrille-class in the neighbouring town. Well, why not?

'But changes at which we must all rejoice have brought other changes which are not so attractive. The labourers have become more and more migratory — the younger families in especial, who enjoy nothing so much as fresh scenery and new acquaintance. The consequences are curious and unexpected. For one thing, village tradition — a vast mass of unwritten folk-lore, local chronicle, local topography, and nomenclature — is absolutely sinking, has nearly sunk, into eternal oblivion. I cannot recall a single instance of a labourer who still lives on the farm where he was born, and I can only recall a few who have been five years on their present farms. Thus you see, there being no continuity of environment in their lives, there is no continuity of information, the names, stories, and relics of one place being speedily forgotten under the incoming facts of the next. For example, if you ask one of the workfolk (they always used to be called "workfolk" hereabout — "labourers" is an imported word) the names of surrounding hills, streams; the character and circumstances of people buried in particular graves; at what spots parish personages lie interred; questions on local fairies, ghosts, herbs, etc., they can give no answer: yet I can recollect the time when the places of burial even of the poor and tombless were all remembered, and the history of the parish and squire's family for 150 years back known. Such and such ballads appertained to such and such a locality, ghost tales were attached to particular sites, and nooks wherein wild herbs grew for the cure of divers maladies were pointed out readily.

'On the subject of the migration to the towns I think I have printed my opinions from time to time: so that I will only say a word or two about it here. In this consideration the case of the farm labourers merges itself in that of rural cottagers generally, including jobbing labourers, artizans, and nondescripts of all sorts who go to make up the body of English villagery. That these people have removed to the towns of sheer choice during the last forty years it would be absurd to argue, except as to that percentage of young, adventurous and ambitious spirits among them which is found in all societies. The prime cause of the removal is, unquestionably, insecurity of tenure. If they do not escape this in the towns it is not fraught with such trying consequences there as in a village, whence they may have to travel ten or twenty miles to find another house and other work. Moreover, if in a town lodgings an honest man's daughter should have an illegitimate child, or his wife should take to drinking, he is not compelled by any squire to pack up his furniture and get his living elsewhere, as is, or was lately, too often the case in the country. (I am neither attacking nor defending this order of things; I merely relate it: the landlord sometimes had reason on his side; sometimes not.)

'Now why such migrations to cities did not largely take place till within the last forty years or so is, I think (in respect of farm labourers), that they had neither the means nor the knowledge in old times that they have now. And owing to the then stability of villagers of the other class — such as mechanics and small traders, the backbone of village life — they had not the inclination. The tenure of these latter was, down to about fifty years ago, a fairly secure one, even if they were not in the possession of small freeholds. The custom of granting leaseholds for three lives, or other life-holding privileges, obtained largely in our villages, and though tenures by lifehold may not be ideally good or fair, they did at least serve the purpose of keeping the native population at home. Villages in which there is now not a single cottager other than a weekly tenant were formerly occupied almost entirely on the life-hold principle, the term extending over seventy or a hundred years; and the young man who knows that he is secure of his father's and grandfather's cottage for his own lifetime thinks twice and three times before he embarks on the uncertainties of a wandering career. Now though, as I have said, these cottagers were not often farm labourers, their permanency reacted on the farm labourers, and made their lives with such comfortable associates better worth living.

'Thirdly: as to the future, the evils of instability, and the ultimate results from such a state of things, it hardly becomes me to attempt to prophesy here. That remedies exist for them and are easily applicable you will easily gather from what I have stated above.'

'*April* 20. Vagg Hollow, on the way to Load Bridge (Somerset) is a place where "things" used to be seen — usually taking the form of a wool-pack in the middle of the road. Teams and other horses always stopped on the brow of the hollow, and could only be made to go on by whipping. A waggoner once cut at the pack with his whip: it opened in two, and smoke and a hoofed figure rose out of it.'

'*May* 1. Life is what we make it as Whist is what we make it; but not as Chess is what we make it; which ranks higher as a purely intellectual game than either Whist or Life.'

Letter sent to and printed in *The Academy and Literature*, May 17, 1902, concerning a review of Maeterlinck's *Apology for Nature*:

'SIR,

'In your review of M. Maeterlinck's book you quote with seeming approval his vindication of Nature's ways, which is (as I understand it) to the effect that, though she does not appear to be just from our point of view, she may practise a scheme of morality unknown to us, in which she is just. Now, admit but the bare possibility of such a hidden morality, and she would go out of court without the slightest stain on her character, so certain should we feel that indifference to morality was beneath her greatness.

'Far be it from my wish to distrust any comforting fantasy, if it can be barely tenable. But alas, no profound reflection can be needed to detect the sophistry in M. Maeterlinck's argument, and to see that the original difficulty recognized by thinkers like Schopenhauer, Hartmann, Haeckel, etc., and by most of the persons called pessimists, remains unsurmounted.

'Pain has been, and pain is : no new sort of morals in Nature can remove pain from the past and make it pleasure for those who are its infallible estimators, the bearers therof. And no injustice, however slight, can be atoned for by her future generosity, however ample, so long as we consider Nature to be, or to stánd for, unlimited power. The exoneration of an omnipotent Mother by her retrospective justice becomes an absurdity when we ask, what made the foregone injustice necessary to her Omnipotence?

'So you cannot, I fear, save her good name except by assuming one of two things : that she is blind and not a judge of her actions' or that she is an automaton, and unable to control them : in either of which assumptions, though you have the chivalrous satisfaction of screening one of her sex, you only throw responsibility a stage further back.

'But the story is not new. It is true, nevertheless, that, as M. Maeterlinck contends, to dwell too long amid such reflections does no good, and that to model our conduct on Nature's apparent conduct, as Nietzsche would have taught, can only bring disaster to humanity.

'Yours truly,
'THOMAS HARDY.
'MAX GATE, DORCHESTER.'

In June Hardy was engaged in a correspondence in the pages of the *Dorset County Chronicle* on Edmund Kean's connection with Dorchester, which town he visited as a player before he became famous, putting up with his wife and child at an inn called 'The Little Jockey' on Glyde-Path Hill (standing in Hardy's time). His child died whilst here, and was buried in Trinity Churchyard near at hand. The entry in the register runs as follows :

'Burials in the Parish of Holy Trinity in Dorchester in the County of Dorset in the year 1813 :

'Name, Howard, son of Edmund and Mary Kean. Abode, Residing at Glyde Path Hill in this Parish. When buried, Nov. 24. Age 4. By whom the Ceremony was performed, Henry John Richman.'

Readers of the life of Kean will remember the heaviness of heart with which he noted his experience at Dorchester on this occasion — that it was a very wet night, that there was a small audience, that, unless we are mistaken, the play was *Coriolanus* (fancy playing *Coriolanus* at Dorchester *now*!), that he performed his part badly. Yet he was standing on the very brink of fame, for it was on this very occasion that the emissary from Old Drury — Arnold, the stage manager — witnessed his performance, and decided that he was the man for the London boards.

In his letters to the paper under the pseudonym of 'History' Hardy observed :

'Your correspondent "Dorset" who proposes to "turn the hose" upon the natural interest of Dorchester people in Edmund Kean, should, I think, first turn the hose upon his own uncharitableness. His contention amounts to this, that because one of the greatest, if not the very greatest, of English tragedians was not without blemish in his morals, no admiration is to be felt for his histrionic achievements, or regard for the details of his life. So, then, Lord Nelson should have no place in our sentiment, nor Burns, nor Byron — not even Shakespeare himself - - nor unhappily many another great man whose flesh has been weak. With amusing maladroitness your correspondent calls himself by the name of the county which has lately commemorated King Charles the Second — a worthy who seduced scores of men's wives, to Kean's one.

'Kean was, in truth, a sorely tried man, and it is no wonder that he may have succumbed. The illegitimate child of a struggling actress, the vicissitudes and hardships of his youth and young manhood left him without moral ballast when the fire of his genius brought him success and adulation. The usual result followed, and owing to the publicity of his life it has been his misfortune ever since to have, like Cassius in *Julius Cæsar*,

All his faults observed,<br>
Set in a note-book, learn'd and conn'd by rote,

by people who show the Christian feeling of your correspondent.'

The following week Hardy sent a supplementary note :

'One word as to the building [in Dorchester] in which Kean performed in 1813. There is little doubt that it was in the old theatre yet existing [though not as such], stage and all, at the back of Messrs. Godwin's china shop ; and for these among other reasons. A new theatre in North Square [Qy. Back West Street?], built by Curme, was opened in February 1828, while there are still dwellers in Dorchester who have heard persons speak of seeing plays in the older theatre about 1821 or 1822, Kean's visit having been only a few years earlier.'

During the latter half of this year 1902 Hardy was working more or less on the first part of *The Dynasts*, which was interrupted in August and September by bicycle trips, and in October by a short stay in Bath, where the cycling was continued. On one of these occasions, having reached Bristol by road, and suddenly entered on the watered streets, he came off into the mud with a side-slip, and was rubbed down by a kindly coal-heaver with one of his sacks. In this condition he caught sight of some rare old volume in a lumber-shop ; and looking him up and down when he asked the price, the woman who kept the shop said : 'Well, sixpence won't hurt ye, I suppose?' He used to state that if he had proposed threepence he would doubtless have got the volume.

To a correspondent who was preparing a Report on Capital Punishment for the Department of Economics, Stanford University, California, and who asked for the expression of his opinion on the advisability of abolishing it in highly civilized communities, he replied about this time :

'As an acting magistrate I think that Capital Punishment operates as a deterrent from deliberate crimes against life to an extent that no other form of punishment can rival. But the question of the moral right of a community to inflict that punishment is one I cannot enter into in this necessarily brief communication.'

It may be observed that the writer describes himself as an 'acting magistrate', yet he acted but little at sessions. He was not infrequently, however, on Grand Juries at the Assizes, where he would meet with capital offences.

Returning to the country in July he sat down to finish the first part of *The Dynasts*, the MS. of which was sent to the Messrs. Macmillan at the end of September. He then corrected the proofs of 'A Trampwoman's Tragedy' for the *North American Review*, in which pages it was published in November. When the ballad was read in England by the few good judges who met with it, they reproached Hardy with sending it out of the country for publication, not knowing that it was first offered to the *Cornhill Magazine*, and declined by the editor on the ground of it not being a poem he could possibly print in a family periodical. That there was any impropriety in the verses had never struck the author at all, nor did it strike any readers, so far as he was aware.

In December he answered an inquiry addressed to him by the editor of *L'Européen*, an international journal published in Paris:

'I would say that I am not of opinion that France is in a decadent state. Her history seems to take the form of a serrated line, thus:

and a true judgement of her general tendency cannot be based on a momentary observation, but must extend over whole periods of variation.

'What will sustain France as a nation is, I think, her unique accessibility to new ideas, and her ready power of emancipation from those which reveal themselves to be *effete*.'

In the same month of December the first part of *The Dynasts* was published.

It was some time in this year that Hardy, in concurrence with his brother and sisters, erected in Stinsford Church a brass tablet to commemorate the connection of his father, grandfather, and uncle with the musical services there in the early part of the previous century — the west gallery, wherein their ministrations had covered altogether about forty years, having been removed some sixty years before this date. The inscription on the brass runs as follows:

Memoriae · Sacrum · Thomae · Hardy · patris · Jacobi · et · Thomae filiorum · qui · olim · in · hac · Ecclesia · per · annos · quadraginta (MDCCCII — MDCCCXLI) · fidicinis · munere · sunt · perfuncti. Ponendum · curaverunt · Thomae · junioris · filii · et · filiae: Thomas: Henricus: Maria: Catherina. MDCCCCIII.

In drawing up this inscription Hardy was guided by his belief that the English language was liable to undergo great alterations in the future, whereas Latin would remain unchanged.

# CHAPTER XXVII

# PART FIRST OF 'THE DYNASTS'

1904–1905 : *Aet.* 63–65

As *The Dynasts* contained ideas of some freshness, and was not a copy of something else, a large number of critics were too puzzled by it to be unprejudiced. The appraisement of the work was in truth, while nominally literary, at the core narrowly Philistine, and even theosophic. Its author had erroneously supposed that by writing a frank preface on his method — that the scheme of the drama was based on a tentative theory of things which seemed to accord with the mind of the age; but that whether such theory did or not so accord, and whether it were true or false, little affected his object, which was a poetical one wherein nothing more was necessary than that the theory should be plausible — a polemic handling of his book would be avoided. Briefly, that the drama being advanced not as a reasoned system of philosophy, nor as a new philosophy, but as a poem, with the discrepancies that are to be expected in an imaginative work, as such it would be read.

However, the latitude claimed was allowed but in few instances, and an unfavourable reception was pretty general, the substance of which was 'On what ground do you arrogate to yourself a right to express in poetry a philosophy which has never been expressed in poetry before?'

Notwithstanding his hopes, he had a suspicion that such might be the case, as we may gather from a note he had written:

'The old theologies may or may not have worked for good in their time. But they will not bear stretching further in epic or dramatic art. The Greeks used up theirs: the Jews used up theirs: the Christians have used up theirs. So that one must make an independent plunge, embodying the real, if only temporary, thought of the age. But I expect that I shall catch it hot and strong for attempting it!'

Hardy replied to one of these criticisms written by the dramatic critic of *The Times* in the *Literary Supplement* (*Times Literary*

*Supplement*, Feb. 5 and Feb. 19, 1904), but did not make many private memoranda on the reviews. One memorandum is as follows :

'I suppose I have handicapped myself by expressing, both in this drama and previous verse, philosophies and feelings as yet not well established or formally adopted into the general teaching ; and by thus over-stepping the standard boundary set up for the thought of the age by the proctors of opinion, I have thrown back my chance of acceptance in poetry by many years. The very fact of my having tried to spread over art the latest illumination of the time has darkened counsel in respect of me.

'What the reviewers really assert is, not "This is an untrue and inartistic view of life", but "This is not the view of life that we people who thrive on conventions can permit to be painted". If, instead of the machinery I adopted, I had constructed a theory of a world directed by fairies, nobody would have objected, and the critics would probably have said, "What a charming fancy of Mr. Hardy's!" But having chosen a scheme which may or may not be a valid one, but is presumably much nearer reality than the fancy of a world ordered by fairies would be, they straightway lift their brows.'

Writing to his friend Edward Clodd on March 22, he says :

'I did not quite think that the *Dynasts* would suit your scientific mind, or shall I say the scientific side of your mind, so that I am much pleased to hear that you have got pleasure out of it.

'As to my having said nothing or little (I think I did just allude to it a long while ago) about having it in hand, the explanation is simple enough — I did not mean to publish Part I. by itself until after a quite few days before I sent it up to the publishers : and to be engaged in a desultory way on a MS. which may be finished in five years (the date at which I thought I might print it, complete) does not lead one to say much about it. On my return here from London I had a sudden feeling that I should never carry the thing any further, so off it went. But now I am better inclined to go on with it. Though I rather wish I had kept back the parts till the whole could be launched, as I at first intended.

'What you say about the "Will" is true enough, if you take the word in its ordinary sense. But in the lack of another word to express precisely what is meant, a secondary sense has gradually arisen, that of effort exercised in a reflex or unconscious manner. Another word would have been better if one could have had it, though "Power" would not do, as power can be suspended or withheld, and the forces of Nature cannot: However, there are inconsistencies in the Phantoms, no doubt. But that was a point to which I was somewhat indifferent, since they are not supposed to be more than the best human intelligences of their time in a sort of quint-essential form. I speak of the "Years". The "Pities" are, of course, merely Humanity, with all its weaknesses.

'You speak of Meredith. I am sorry to learn that he has been so seriously ill. Leslie Stephen gone too. They are thinning out ahead of us. I have just lost an old friend down here, of forty-seven years' standing. A man whose opinions differed almost entirely from my own on most subjects, and yet he was a good and sincere friend — the brother of the present Bishop of Durham, and like him in old-fashioned views of the Evangelical school.'

His mind was, however, drawn away from the perils of attempting to express his age in poetry by a noticeable change in his mother's state of health. She was now in her ninety-first year, and though she had long suffered from deafness was mentally as clear and alert as ever. She sank gradually, but it was not till two days before her death that she failed to comprehend his words to her. She died on Easter Sunday, April 3, and was buried at Stinsford in the grave of her husband. She had been a woman with an extraordinary store of local memories, reaching back to the days when the ancient ballads were everywhere heard at country feasts, in weaving shops, and at spinning-wheels ; and her good taste in literature was expressed by the books she selected for her children in circumstances in which opportunities for selection were not numerous. The portraits of her which appeared in the *Sphere*, the *Gentlewoman*, the *Book Monthly*, and other papers — the best being from a painting by her daughter Mary — show a face of dignity and judgment.

A month earlier he had sent a reply to the Rev. S. Whittell Key, who had inquired of him concerning 'sport' :

'I am not sufficiently acquainted with the many varieties of sport to pronounce which is, quantitatively, the most cruel. I can only say generally that the prevalence of those sports which consist in the pleasure of watching a fellow-creature, weaker or less favoured than ourselves, in its struggles, by Nature's poor resources only, to escape the death-agony we mean to inflict by the treacherous contrivances of science, seems one of the many convincing proofs that we have not yet emerged from barbarism.

'In the present state of affairs there would appear to be no logical reason why the smaller children, say, of overcrowded families, should not be used for sporting purposes. Darwin has revealed that there

would be no difference in principle ; moreover, these children would
often escape lives intrinsically less happy than those of wild birds and
other animals.'

During May he was in London reading at the British Museum on
various days — probably historic details that bore upon *The Dynasts*
— and went to Sunday concerts at the Queen's Hall, and to afternoon
services at St. Paul's whenever he happened to be near the Cathedral,
a custom of his covering many years before and after.

On June 28 *The Times* published the following letter :

'SIR,

'I should like to be allowed space to express in the fewest words
a view of Count Tolstoy's philosophic sermon on war, of which you
print a translation in your impression of to-day and a comment in
your leading article.

'The sermon may show many of the extravagances of detail to
which the world has grown accustomed in Count Tolstoy's alter
writings. It may exhibit, here and there, incoherence as a moral
system. Many people may object to the second half of the dissertation — its special application to Russia in the present war (on which
I can say nothing). Others may be unable to see advantage in the
writer's use of theological terms for describing and illustrating the
moral evolutions of past ages. But surely all these objectors should
be hushed by his great argument, and every defect in his particular
reasonings hidden by the blaze of glory that shines from his masterly
general indictment of war as a modern principle, with all its senseless
and illogical crimes.

'Your obedient servant,

'THOMAS HARDY.'

Again in the country in August, Hardy resumed his cycling tours,
meeting by accident Mr. William Watson, Mr. Francis Coutts (Lord
Latymer), and Mr. John Lane at Glastonbury, and spending a romantic
day or two there among the ruins.

In October Hardy learnt by letter from Madras of the death ot
Mrs. Malcolm Nicolson — the gifted and impassioned poetess known
as 'Laurence Hope', whom he had met in London ; and he wrote a
brief obituary notice of her in the *Athenæum* at the end of the month.
But beyond this, and the aforesaid newspaper letters, he appears to
have printed very little during this year 1904. A German translation
of *Life's Little Ironies* was published in *Aus fremden Zungen*, in
Berlin, and a French translation of *The Well-Beloved* undertaken.

His memoranda get more and more meagre as the years go on, until we are almost entirely dependent on letter-references, reviews, and casual remarks of his taken down by the present writer. It is a curious reversal of what is usually found in lives, where notes and diaries grow more elaborate with maturity of years. But it accords with Hardy's frequent saying that he took little interest in himself as a person, and his absolute refusal at all times to write his reminiscences.

In January (1905) he served as Grand Juror at the winter Assizes, and in the latter part of the month met Dr. Shipley, Mr. Asquith, Lord Monteagle, Sir Edgar Vincent, and others at a dinner at the National Club given by Mr. Gosse. At this time he was much interested in the paintings of Zurbarán, which he preferred to all others of the old Spanish school, venturing to think that they might some day be held in higher estimation than those of Velazquez.

About this time the romantic poem entitled 'The Noble Lady's Tale' was printed in the *Cornhill Magazine.*

The first week in April Hardy left Dorchester for London *en route* for Aberdeen, the ancient University of which city had offered him the honorary degree of LL.D. In accepting it he remarked :

'I am impressed by its coming from Aberdeen, for though a stranger to that part of Scotland to a culpable extent I have always observed with admiration the exceptional characteristics of the northern University, which in its fostering encouragement of mental effort seems to cast an eye over these islands that is unprejudiced, unbiased, and unsleeping.'

It was a distance of near 700 miles by the route he would have to take — almost as far as to the Pyrenees — and over the northern stage of it winter still lingered ; but his journey there and back was an easy one. The section from Euston Square to the north was performed in a train of sleeping-cars which crunched through the snow as if it were January, the occasion coinciding with the opening of the new sculpture gallery, a function that brought many visitors from London. Hardy was hospitably entertained at the Chanonry Lodge, Old Aberdeen, by Principal and Mrs. Marshall Lang, which was the beginning of a friendship that lasted till the death of the Principal. Among others who received the like honour at the same time were Professor Bury and Lord Reay.

In the evening there was a reception in the Mitchell Hall, Marischal College, made lively by Scotch reels and bagpipers ; and the next day, after attending at the formal opening of the sculpture gallery, he was a guest at the Corporation Dinner at the Town Hall, where friends were warm, but draughts were keen to one from a southern county, and speeches, though good, so long that he and the Principal did not get back to Chanonry Lodge till one o'clock.

On Sunday morning Hardy visited spots in and about Aberdeen associated with Byron and others, and lunched at the Grand Hotel by the invitation of Mr. (afterwards Sir) James Murray, dining at the same place with the same host, crossing hands in 'Auld Lang Syne' with delightful people whom he had never seen before and, alas, never saw again. This was the 'hearty way' (as it would be called in Wessex) in which they did things in the snowy north. To Hardy the whole episode of Aberdeen, he said, was of a most pleasant and unexpected kind, and it remained with him like a romantic dream.

Passing through London on his way south he breakfasted at the Athenæum, where he was shocked to learn of the death of his friend Lord St. Helier (Sir Francis Jeune), who had been ailing more or less since the loss of his only son in the previous August. Hardy on his way down to Dorset was led to think of the humorous stories connected with the Divorce Court that the genial judge sometimes had told him when they were walking in the woods of Arlington Manor in the summer holidays ; among them the tale of that worthy couple who wished to be divorced but disliked the idea of such an unpleasant person as a co-respondent being concerned in it, and so hit upon the plan of doing without him. The husband, saying he was going to Liverpool for a day or two, got a private detective to watch his house ; but instead of leaving stayed in London, and at the dead of night went to his own house in disguise, and gave a signal. His wife came down in her dressing-gown and let him in softly, letting him out again before it was light. When the husband inquired of the detective he was informed that there was ample evidence ; and the divorce was duly obtained.

Hardy could not remember whether it was a story of the same couple or of another, in which Sir Francis had related that being divorced they grew very fond of each other, the former wife becoming the husband's mistress, and living happily with him ever after.

As they had taken a flat at Hyde Park Mansions for this spring and summer Hardy did not stay long in Dorset, and they entered the flat the week before Easter. During April he followed up Tchaikowsky at the Queen's Hall concerts, saying of the impetuous march-piece in the third movement of the Pathetic Symphony that it was the only music he knew that was able to make him feel exactly as if he were in a battle.

'*May* 5. To the Lord Mayor's farewell banquet to Mr. Choate at the Mansion House. Thought of the continuity of the institution, and the teeming history of the spot. A graceful speech by Arthur Balfour : a less graceful but more humorous one by Mr. Choate. Spoke to many whom I knew. Sat between Dr. Butler, Master of Trinity, and Sir J. Ramsay, Came home with Sir F. Pollock.'

This month he was seeing Ben Jonson's play, *The Silent Woman*, and Shaw's *John Bull's Other Island* and *Man and Superman*, and went to the Royal Society's Conversazione ; though for some days confined to the house by a sore throat and cough. At a lunch given by Sidney Lee at the Garrick Club in June he talked about Shakespeare with Sir Henry Irving, and was reconfirmed in his opinion that actors never see a play as a whole and in true perspective, but in a false perspective from the shifting point of their own part in it, Sir Henry having shied at Hardy's suggestion that he should take the part of Jaques.

In this June, too, he paid a promised visit to Swinburne, and had a long talk with him ; also with Mr. Watts-Dunton. 'Swinburne's grey eyes are extraordinarily bright still — the brightness of stars that do not twinkle — planets namely. In spite of the nervous twitching of his feet he looked remarkably boyish and well, and rather impish. He told me he could walk twenty miles a day, and was only an old man in his hearing, his sight being as good as ever. He spoke with amusement of a paragraph he had seen in a Scottish paper : "Swinburne planteth, Hardy watereth, and Satan giveth the increase." He has had no honours offered him. Said that when he was nearly drowned his thought was, "My *Bothwell* will never be finished!" That the secret reason for Lady Byron's dismissal of Lord Byron was undoubtedly his *liaison* with Augusta. His (Swinburne's) mother [Lady Jane, *née* Ashburnham] used to say that it was the talk of London at the time. That the last time he visited his friend Landor the latter said plaintively that as he wrote only in a dead language (Latin), and a dying language (English), he would soon be forgotten. Talking of poets, he said that once Mrs. Procter told him that Leigh Hunt on a visit to her father one day brought an unknown youth in his train and introduced him casually as Mr. John Keats. (I think, by the way, that she also told me of the incident.[1]) We laughed and condoled with each other on having been the two most abused of living writers ; he for *Poems and Ballads*, I for *Jude the Obscure*.'

[1] See p. 136.

Later on in June he went to Mr. Walter Tyndale's exhibition of
Wessex pictures, some of which Hardy had suggested, and during the
remainder of their stay in London they did little more than entertain
a few friends at Hyde Park Mansions, and dine and lunch with others.

'*June* 26, 1905. To the Hon. Sec. of the Shakespeare Memorial
Committee :

'I fear that I shall have to leave town before the meeting of the
Committee takes place.

'All I would say on the form of the Memorial is that one which
embodies the calling of an important *street* or *square* after Shakespeare
would seem to be as effectual a means as any of keeping his name on
the tongues of citizens, and his personality in their minds.'

In July they went back to Dorset. Here, in the same month, a
Nelson-and-Hardy exhibition was opened in Dorchester, the relics
shown being mainly those of the Captain of the *Victory*, who had
been born and lived near, and belonged to a branch of the Dorset
Hardys, the subject of this memoir belonging to another.

On September 1 Hardy received a visit from 200 members of the
Institute of Journalists at their own suggestion, as they had arranged
a driving tour through his part of the country. There was an understanding that no interviews should be printed, and to this they honourably adhered. Their idea had been a call on him only, but they were
entertained at tea, for which purpose a tent 150 feet long had to be
erected on Max Gate lawn. 'The interior with the sun shining through
formed a pretty scene when they were sitting down at the little tables',
Mrs. Hardy remarks in a diary. 'They all drove off in four-in-hand
brakes and other vehicles to Bockhampton, Puddletown, Bere Regis,
and Wool.' After they had gone it came on to rain, and Hardy,
returning from Dorchester at ten o'clock, met the vehicles coming
back in a procession, empty ; 'the horses tired and steaming after
their journey of thirty miles, and their coats and harness shining with
rain and perspiration in the light of the lamps'.

In pursuance of the above allusion to interviewing, it may be
stated that there are interviewers and interviewers. It once happened
that an interviewer came specially from London to Hardy to get his
opinions for a popular morning paper. Hardy said positively that he
would not be interviewed on any subject. 'Very well', said the interviewer, 'then back I go, my day and my expenses all wasted.' Hardy
felt sorry, his visitor seeming to be a gentlemanly and educated man,
and said he did not see why he should hurry off, if he would give his
word not to write anything. This was promised, and the interviewer

stayed, and had lunch, and a pleasant couple of hours' conversation on all sorts of subjects that would have suited him admirably. Yet he honourably kept his promise, and not a word of his visit appeared anywhere in the pages of the paper.

In the middle of this month the 150th anniversary of the birth of the poet Crabbe at Aldeburgh in Suffolk was celebrated in that town, and Hardy accepted the invitation of Mr. Edward Clodd to be present. There were some very good *tableaux vivants* of scenes from the poems exhibited in the Jubilee Hall, some good lectures on the poet, and a sermon also in the parish church on his life and work, all of which Hardy attended, honouring Crabbe as an apostle of realism who practised it in English literature three-quarters of a century before the French realistic school had been heard of.

Returning to Max Gate he finished the second part of *The Dynasts* — that second part which the New York *Tribune* and other papers had been positive would never be heard of, so ridiculous was the first — and sent off the MS. to the Messrs. Macmillan in the middle of October.

'*First week in November*. The order in which the leaves fall this year is: Chestnuts; Sycamores; Limes; Hornbeams; Elm; Birch; Beech.'

A letter written November 5 of this year :

'All I know about my family history is that it is indubitably one of the several branches of the Dorset Hardys — having been here-abouts for centuries. But when or how it was connected with the branch to which Nelson's Hardy's people belonged — who have also been hereabouts for centuries — I cannot positively say.[1] The branches are always asserted locally to be connected, and no doubt are, and there is a strong family likeness. I have never investigated the matter, though my great-uncle knew the ramifications. The Admiral left no descendant in the male line, as you may know.

'As to your interesting remarks on honours for men of letters, I have always thought that any writer who has expressed unpalatable or possibly subversive views on society, religious dogma, current morals, and any other features of the existing order of things, and who wishes to be free and to express more if they occur to him, must feel hampered by accepting honours from any government — which are different from academic honours offered for past attainments merely.'

[1] Since writing the above I have received from a correspondent what seems to me indubitable proof of the connection of these two branches of the Hardy family. — F. E. H.

To Mr. Israel Zangwill on November 10 :

'It would be altogether presumptuous in me — so entirely outside Jewish life — to express any positive opinion on the scheme
embodied in the pamphlet you send to me.  I can only say a word
or two of the nature of a fancy.  To found an autonomous Jewish
state or colony, under British suzerainty or not, wears the look of a
good practical idea, and it is possibly all the better for having no
retrospective sentiment about it.  But I cannot help saying that this
retrospective sentiment among Jews is precisely the one I can best
enter into.

'So that if I were a Jew I should be a rabid Zionist no doubt.
I feel that the idea of ultimately getting to Palestine is the particular
idea to make the imaginative among your people enthusiastic —
"like unto thèm that dream" — as one of you said in a lyric which
is among the finest in any tongue, to judge from its power in a translation.  You, I suppose, read it in the original ; I wish I could.  (This
is a digression.)

'The only plan that seems to me to reconcile the traditional feeling
with the practical is that of regarding the proposed Jewish state on
virgin soil as a stepping-stone to Palestine.  A Jewish colony united
and strong and grown wealthy in, say, East Africa, could make a bid
for Palestine (as a sort of annexe) — say 100 years hence — with far
greater effect than the race as scattered all over the globe can ever do ;
and who knows if by that time altruism may not have made such
progress that the then ruler or rulers of Palestine, whoever they may
be, may even hand it over to the expectant race, and gladly assist
them, or part of them, to establish themselves there.

'This expectation, nursed throughout the formation and development of the new territory, would at any rate be serviceable as an
ultimate ideal to stimulate action.  With such an idea lying behind
the immediate one, perhaps the Zionists would reunite and co-operate
with the New Territorialists.

'I have written, as I said, only a fancy.  But, as I think you know,
nobody outside Jewry can take a deeper interest than I do in a people
of such extraordinary character and history ; who brought forth,
moreover, a young reformer who, though only in the humblest walk
of life, became the most famous personage the world has ever known.'

At the end of 1905 a letter reached him from a correspondent in
the Philippine Islands telling him that to its writer he was 'like some
terrible old prophet crying in the wilderness'.

# CHAPTER XXVIII

# THE REMAINDER OF 'THE DYNASTS'

1906–1908 : *Aet.* 65–67

*The Dynasts*, Part II, was not published till the first week in February 1906, and its reception by the reviews was much more congratulatory than their reception of the first part, an American critical paper going so far as to say, 'Who knows that this work may not turn out to be a masterpiece ?'

This year they reoccupied the flat in Hyde Park Mansions that had been let to them by Lady Thompson the year before, and paid the customary visits to private views, concerts, and plays that are usually paid to such by people full of vigour from the country. Of the Wagner concerts he says :

'I prefer late Wagner, as I prefer late Turner, to early (which I suppose is all wrong in taste), the idiosyncrasies of each master being more strongly shown in these strains. When a man not contented with the grounds of his success goes on and on, and tries to achieve the impossible, then he gets profoundly interesting to me. To-day it was early Wagner for the most part : fine music, but not so particularly his — no spectacle of the inside of a brain at work like the inside of a hive.'

An attack of influenza, which he usually got while sojourning in London, passed off, and they entertained many friends at the flat as usual, and went out to various meetings and dinners, though he does not write them down in detail as when he thought he must. They included one at Vernon Lushington's, where Hardy was interested in the portrait of his host's father, the Lushington of the Lady Byron mystery, who kept his secret honourably ; also a luncheon in a historic room weighted with its antiquity, the vaulted dining-room of the house in Dean's Yard then occupied by Dr. Wilberforce as Arch-deacon of Westminster. It was this year that Hardy met Dr. Grieg, the composer, and his wife, and when, discussing Wagner music, he said to Grieg that the wind and rain through trees, iron railings, and

keyholes fairly suggested Wagner music; to which the rival composer responded severely that he himself would sooner have the wind
and rain.

On the 21st May the following letter, in which Hardy gives a
glimpse of himself as a young man in London, appeared in *The Times*:

'SIR,

'This being the 100th anniversary of J. Stuart Mill's birth, and
as writers like Carlyle, Leslie Stephen, and others have held that
anything, however imperfect, which affords an idea of a human
personage in his actual form and flesh, is of value in respect of him,
the few following words on how one of the profoundest thinkers of
the last century appeared forty years ago to the man in the street
may be worth recording as a footnote to Mr. Morley's admirable
estimate of Mill's life and philosophy in your impression of Friday.

'It was a day in 1865, about three in the afternoon, during Mill's
candidature for Westminster. The hustings had been erected in
Covent Garden, near the front of St. Paul's Church; and when I —
a young man living in London — drew near to the spot, Mill was
speaking. The appearance of the author of the treatise *On Liberty*
(which we students of that date knew almost by heart) was so different
from the look of persons who usually address crowds in the open air
that it held the attention of people for whom such a gathering in
itself had little interest. Yet it was, primarily, that of a man out of
place. The religious sincerity of his speech was jarred on by his
environment — a group on the hustings who, with few exceptions,
did not care to understand him fully, and a crowd below who could
not. He stood bareheaded, and his vast pale brow, so thin-skinned
as to show the blue veins, sloped back like a stretching upland, and
conveyed to the observer a curious sense of perilous exposure. The
picture of him as personified earnestness surrounded for the most
part by careless curiosity derived an added piquancy — if it can be
called such — from the fact that the cameo clearness of his face
chanced to be in relief against the blue shadow of a church which,
on its transcendental side, his doctrines antagonized. But it would
not be right to say that the throng was absolutely unimpressed by
his words; it felt that they were weighty, though it did not quite
know why.

'Your obedient servant,

'THOMAS HARDY.

'HYDE PARK MANSIONS,
    '*May* 20.'

The same month Mrs. Hardy makes the following note : 'May 30. Returned to Max Gate for a day or two. I gardened a little, and had the first strange fainting-fit [I had known]. My heart seemed to stop ; I fell, and after a while a servant came to me.' (Mrs. Hardy died of heart-failure six years after.)

During the summer in London M. Jacques Blanche, the well-known French painter, who had a studio in Knightsbridge, painted Hardy's portrait in oils. And a paper called 'Memories of Church Restoration', which he had written, was read in his enforced absence by Colonel Eustace Balfour at the annual meeting of the Society for the Protection of Ancient Buildings.

At the end of the lecture great satisfaction was expressed by speakers that Hardy had laid special emphasis on the value of the human associations of ancient buildings, for instance, the pews of churches, since they were generally slighted in paying regard to artistic and architectural points only.

As the June month drew on Hardy seems to have been at the British Museum Library verifying some remaining details for *The Dynasts*, Part Third ; also incidentally going to see the *Daily Telegraph* printed, and to meet a group of German editors on a visit to England. He returned with his wife to Dorset towards the latter part of July.

At the end of July he wrote to Pittsburgh, U.S.A. :

'The handsome invitation of the Trustees of the Pittsburgh Institute that I should attend the dedication with wife or daughter, free of expense to us from the time we leave home till we return again, is a highly honouring and tempting one. But I am compelled to think of many contingent matters that would stand in the way of my paying such a visit, and have concluded that I cannot undertake it.

'Please convey my thanks to Mr. Carnegie and the trustees.'

'*August* 15. Have just read of the death of Mrs. Craigie in the papers. . . . Her description of the artistic temperament is clever ; as being that which "thinks more than there is to think, feels more than there is to feel, sees more than there is to see". . . . It reveals a bitterness of heart that was not shown on the surface by that brilliant woman.'

On August 17 he started with his brother on a tour to some English cathedrals, which included Lincoln, Ely, the Cambridge

Colleges, and Canterbury; and finished out the summer with bicycling in Dorset and Somerset. He must have been working at the
third part of *The Dynasts* at intervals this year, though there is
apparently no record of his doing so.

## 1907

The poem entitled 'New Year's Eve', written in 1906, was issued
in the January number of the *Fortnightly Review*, 1907 (afterwards
reprinted in the volume called *Time's Laughingstocks*). Some time
in the same month he made the following notes on kindred subjects:

'An ephemeral article which might be written: "The Hard Case
of the Would-be-Religious. By Sinceritas."

'Synopsis. Many millions of the most thoughtful people in
England are prevented entering any church or chapel from year's
end to year's end.

'The days of creeds are as dead and done with as days of
Pterodactyls.

'Required: services at which there are no affirmations and no
supplications.

'Rationalists err as far in one direction as Revelationists or Mystics
in the other; as far in the direction of logicality as their opponents
away from it.

'*Religious, religion*, is to be used in the article in its modern sense
entirely, as being expressive of nobler feelings towards humanity and
emotional goodness and greatness, the old meaning of the word —
ceremony, or ritual — having perished, or nearly.

'We enter church, and we have to say, "We have erred and
strayed from Thy ways like lost sheep", when what we want to say
is, "Why are we made to err and stray like lost sheep?" Then we
have to sing, "My soul doth magnify the Lord", when what we
want to sing is, "O that my soul could find some Lord that it could
magnify! Till it can, let us magnify good works, and develop all
means of easing mortals' progress through a world not worthy of
them."

'Still, being present, we say the established words full of the
historic sentiment only, mentally adding, "How happy our ancestors
were in repeating in all sincerity these articles of faith!" But we
perceive that none of the congregation recognizes that we repeat the
words from an antiquarian interest in them, and in a historic sense,
and solely in order to keep a church of some sort afoot — a thing

indispensable ; so that we are pretending what is not true : that we are believers. This must not be ; we must leave. And if we do, we reluctantly go to the door, and creep out as it creaks complainingly behind us.'

Hardy, however, was not a controversialist in religion or anything else, and it should be added here that he sometimes took a more nebulous view, that may be called transmutative, as in a passage that he wrote some time later :

'Christianity nowadays as expounded by Christian apologists has an entirely different meaning from that which it bore when I was a boy. If I understand, it now limits itself to the religion of emotional morality and altruism that was taught by Jesus Christ, or nearly so limits itself. But this teaching does not appertain especially to Christianity : other moral religions within whose sphere the name of Christ has never been heard, teach the same thing! Perhaps this is a mere question of terminology, and does not much matter. That the dogmatic superstitions read every Sunday are merely a commemorative recitation of old articles of faith held by our grandfathers, may not much matter either, as long as this is well understood. Still, it would be more honest to make these points clearer, by recasting the liturgy, for their real meaning is often misapprehended. But there seems to be no sign of such a clearing up, and I fear that, since the "Apology" [in *Late Lyrics*], in which I expressed as much some years ago, no advance whatever has been shown ; rather, indeed, a childish back-current towards a belief in magic rites.'

'*February* 8. E. goes to London to walk in the suffragist procession to-morrow.'

In March occurred the death of a friend — the Rev. T. Perkins, rector of Turnworth, Dorset — with whom Hardy was in sympathy for his humane and disinterested views, and staunch support of the principle of justice for animals, in whose cause he made noble sacrifices, and spent time and money that he could ill afford. On the 29th of the month Hardy enters a memorandum :

'Eve of Good Friday. 11.30 P.M. Finished draft of Part III. of *The Dynasts*.' He had probably been so far influenced by the reception of the first two parts as not to expect the change of view which was about to give to the third part, and the whole production, a warm verdict of success, or he would not have followed the entry by the addendum :

'Critics can never be made to understand that the failure may be greater than the success. It is their particular duty to point this out; but the public points it out to them. To have strength to roll a stone weighing a hundredweight to the top of the mount is a success, and to have the strength to roll a stone of ten hundredweight only half-way up that mount is a failure. But the latter is two or three times as strong a deed.'

They again took the flat in Hyde Park Mansions for the spring and summer, and moved thither the third week in April, whence they made their usual descent on friends and acquaintances, picture-galleries, and concert-rooms. It was this year that they met Mr. and Mrs. Bernard Shaw — it is believed for the first time. They also received at the flat their customary old friends, including Mr. and Mrs. J. M. Barrie, M. and Madame Jacques Blanche, and many others.

In May he was present at an informal but most interesting dinner at the house of his friend Dr. Hagberg Wright, where he met M. and Mme. Maxim Gorky, Mr. H. G. Wells, Mr. Bernard Shaw, Mr. Conrad, Mr. Richard Whiteing, and others. A disconcerting but amusing accident was the difficulty of finding Dr. Wright's flat, on account of which the guests arrived at intervals and had their dinners in succession, the Gorkys coming last after driving two hours about London, including the purlieus of Whitechapel, which he had mis-taken for 'Westminster'. Naturally it was a late hour when the party broke up.

*June* 2. Hardy's birthday, which he kept by dining at Lady St. Helier's.

On the same day he wrote to Mr. Edward Wright:

'Your interesting letter on the philosophy of *The Dynasts* has reached me here. I will try to answer some of your inquiries.

'I quite agree with you in holding that the word "Will" does not perfectly fit the idea to be conveyed — a vague thrusting or urging internal force in no predetermined direction. But it has become accepted in philosophy for want of a better, and is hardly likely to be supplanted by another, unless a highly appropriate one could be found, which I doubt. The word that you suggest — Impulse — seems to me to imply a driving power behind it; also a spasmodic movement unlike that of, say, the tendency of an ape to become a man and other such processes.

'In a dramatic epic — which I may perhaps assume *The Dynasts* to be — some philosophy of life was necessary, and I went on using that which I had denoted in my previous volumes of verse (and to some extent prose) as being a generalized form of what the thinking world had gradually come to adopt, myself included.  That the Unconscious Will of the Universe is growing aware of Itself I believe I may claim as my own idea solely — at which I arrived by reflecting that what has already taken place in a fraction of the whole (*i.e.* so much of the world as has become conscious) is likely to take place in the mass ; and there being no Will outside the mass — that is, the Universe — the whole Will becomes conscious thereby : and ultimately, it is to be hoped, sympathetic.

'I believe, too, that the Prime Cause, this Will, has never before been called "It" in any poetical literature, English or foreign.

'This theory, too, seems to me to settle the question of Free-will v. Necessity.  The will of a man is, according to it, neither wholly free nor wholly unfree.  When swayed by the Universal Will (which he mostly must be as a subservient part of it) he is not individually free ;  but whenever it happens that all the rest of the Great Will is in equilibrium the minute portion called one person's will is free, just as a performer's fingers are free to go on playing the pianoforte of themselves when he talks or thinks of something else and the head does not rule them.

'In the first edition of a drama of the extent of *The Dynasts* there may be, of course, accidental discrepancies and oversights which seem not quite to harmonize with these principles ;  but I hope they are not many.

'The third part will probably not be ready till the end of this or the beginning of next year ;  so that I have no proofs as yet.  I do not think, however, that they would help you much in your proposed article.  The first and second parts already published, and some of the poems in *Poems of the Past and the Present*, exhibit fairly enough the whole philosophy.'

Concerning Hardy's remark in this letter on the Unconscious Will being an idea already current, though that its growing aware of Itself might be newer, and that there might be discrepancies in the Spirits' philosophy, it may be stated that he had felt such questions of priority and discrepancy to be immaterial where the work was offered as a poem and not as a system of thought.

On the 22nd of June they were guests at King Edward's Garden Party at Windsor Castle, and a few days later at Mr. Reginald Smith's

met Sir Theodore Martin, then nearly ninety-one. Hardy remembering when as a young man he had frequented the pit of Drury Lane
to see Lady Martin — then Miss Helen Faucit — in Shakespeare
characters. His term at Hyde Park Mansions came to an end in the
latter part of July, and they returned to Max Gate, though Hardy
attended a dinner a week later given by the Medico-Psychological
Society, where he had scientific discussions with Sir James Crichton-
Browne and Sir Clifford Allbutt, and where one of the speakers
interested Hardy by saying that all great things were done by men
'who were not at ease'.

That autumn Sir Frederick and Lady Treves took a house near
Max Gate, and Hardy frequently discussed with the Serjeant-surgeon
a question which had drawn their attention for a long time, both
being Dorset men; that of the 'poor whites' in Barbados, a degenerate, decadent race, descendants of the Dorset and Somerset 'rebels'
who were banished there by Judge Jeffreys, and one of whom had
been a collateral ancestor of Hardy's on the maternal side.

He was now reaching a time of life when shadows were continually
falling. His friend Pretor, Fellow of St. Catherine's College, Cambridge, wrote to tell him he was dying, and asked him for an epitaph.
Hardy thought of an old one:

> If a madness 'tis to weepe
> For a man that's fall'n asleepe,
> How much more for that we call
> Death — the sweetest sleepe of all!

They still kept up a little bicycling this autumn, but he did some
writing, finishing the third part of *The Dynasts* in September, and
posting the MS. to the publishers shortly after.

In November he complied with a request from the Dorsetshire
Regiment in India, which had asked him for a marching tune with
the required local affinity for the use of the fifes and drums, and sent
out an old tune of his grandfather's called 'The Dorchester Hornpipe',
which he himself had fiddled at dances as a boy. He wound up the
year by sending to the Wessex Society of Manchester, also at their
request, a motto for the Society:

> While new tongues call, and novel scenes unfold,
> Meet may it be to bear in mind the old. . . .
> Vain dreams, indeed, are thoughts of heretofore;
> What then? Your instant lives are nothing more.

About the same time he forwarded 'A Sunday Morning Tragedy' to the *English Review* as wished, where it appeared shortly after; and also in fulfilment of a promise, sent the following old-fashioned psalm tunes associated with Dorsetshire to the Society of Dorset Men in London of which he was President-elect for the ensuing year:

Frome; Wareham; Blandford; New Poole; Bridport; Lulworth; Rockborne; Mercy; Bridehead; Charmouth.

The concluding part of *The Dynasts* was published about six weeks later and was the cause of his receiving many enthusiastic letters from friends and strangers, among which the following from the far west of Australia may be given as a specimen:

'My thanks for your tremendous new statement in *The Dynasts* of the world-old problem of Freewill versus Necessity. You have carried me on to the mountain with Jesus of Nazareth, and, viewing with Him the great conflict below, one chooses with Him to side with the Spirit of the Pities, in the belief that they will ultimately triumph; and even if they do not we at least will do our little to add to the joy rather than to the woe of the world. . . . The Spirit of the Pities is indeed young in comparison with The Years, and so we must be patient. . . . Your conception of the Immanent Will — irresponsible, blind, but possibly growing into self-consciousness, was of great significance to me, from my knowledge of Dr. Bucke's theory of the Cosmic Consciousness.'

In connection with this subject it may be here recalled, in answer to writers who now and later were fond of charging Hardy with postulating a malignant and fiendish God, that he never held any views of the sort, merely surmising an indifferent and unconscious force at the back of things 'that neither good nor evil knows'. His view is shown, in fact, to approximate to Spinoza's — and later Einstein's — that neither Chance nor Purpose governs the universe, but Necessity.

END OF PART VI

## PART VII

'TIME'S LAUGHINGSTOCKS',
'SATIRES OF CIRCUMSTANCE', AND
'MOMENTS OF VISION'

# CHAPTER XXIX

# DEATHS OF SWINBURNE AND MEREDITH

1908–1909 : *Aet. 67–69*

In March he finished preparing a book of selections from the poems of William Barnes, for the Clarendon Press, Oxford, with a critical preface and glossary.

In April Lady St. Helier and a party motored from beyond Newbury to Max Gate and back, arriving within five minutes of the time specified, although the distance each way was seventy-five miles. It was considered a good performance in those days. At the end of the month he dined at the Royal Academy, but was in Dorchester at a performance by the local Dramatic Society of some scenes from *The Dynasts* — the first attempt to put on the stage a dramatic epic that was not intended for staging at all. In May he sent his Presidential Address to the Society of Dorset Men in London, to be read by the Secretary, as he was always a victim to influenza and throat-trouble if he read or spoke in London himself; afterwards on request he sent the original manuscript. (By the way, the address never was read, so he might have saved himself the trouble of writing it. What became of the manuscript is unknown.)

The following letter to Mr. Robert Donald in May explains itself :

'If I felt at all strongly, or indeed weakly, on the desirability of a memorial to Shakespeare in the shape of a theatre, I would join the Committee. But I do not think that Shakespeare appertains particularly to the theatrical world nowadays, if ever he did. His distinction as a minister to the theatre is infinitesimal beside his distinction as a poet, man of letters, and seer of life, and that his expression of himself was cast in the form of words for actors and not in the form of books to be read was an accident of his social circumstances that he himself despised. I would, besides, hazard the guess that he, of all poets of high rank whose works have taken a stage direction, will some day cease altogether to be acted, and be simply studied.

'I therefore do not see the good of a memorial theatre, or for that matter any other material monument to him, and prefer not to join the Committee.

'Nevertheless I sincerely thank you for letting me know how the movement is progressing, and for your appreciative thought that my joining the promoters would be an advantage.'

Hardy afterwards modified the latter part of the above opinion in favour of a colossal statue in some public place.

It appears that the Hardys did not take any house or flat in London this year, contenting themselves with short visits and hotel quarters, so that there is not much to mention. From letters it can be gathered that at a dinner his historic sense was appealed to by the Duchess of St. Albans taking a diamond pin from her neck and telling him it had been worn by Nell Gwynne; and in May or June he paid a few days' visit to Lord Curzon at Hackwood Park, where many of the house-party went into the wood by moonlight to listen to the nightingale, but made such a babble of conversation that no nightingale ventured to open his bill.

In July Hardy was again in London with Mrs. Hardy, and was present at the unveiling by Lord Curzon of the memorial to 'John Oliver Hobbes' (Mrs. Craigie), at University College, where he had the pleasure of hearing his writings cried down by a speaker, nobody knowing him to be present. During some of these days he sat to Sir Hubert Herkomer for his portrait, kindly presented to him by the painter. He went on to Cambridge to the Milton Celebration, where at the house of his friend Sir Clifford Allbutt he met Mr. Robert Bridges, the Poet-Laureate, for the first time, and made the acquaintance of Dr. Peile, the Master of Christ's College, Sir James ('Dictionary') Murray, and others. *Comus* was played at the theatre, in which performance young Rupert Brooke appeared as the attendant Spirit, but Hardy did not speak to him, to his after regret.

The remainder of the month was spent in Dorset, where he met for the last time his friend Bosworth Smith, long a house-master at Harrow, who told him he was soon to undergo a severe surgical operation — under which indeed he sank and died three months after. This was the fourth of his friends and relations that had sunk under the surgeon's knife in four years — leaving a blank that nothing could fill.

'*August* 18. The Poet takes note of nothing that he cannot feel emotively.

'If all hearts were open and all desires known — as they would be if people showed their souls — how many gapings, sighings, clenched fists, knotted brows, broad grins, and red eyes should we see in the market-place!'

The autumn was filled by little journeys to cathedrals and a visit to his sister at Swanage, whither she had gone for change of air ; and in December he attended a dinner at the Mansion House to commemorate Milton, from which he returned in company with his friend Mr. S. H. Butcher, walking up and down with him late that night in Russell Square, conversing on many matters as if they knew they would never meet again.   Hardy had a great liking for him, and was drawn to him for the added reason that he and his family had been warm friends of Hardy's dead friend Horace Moule.

In the following January (1909) the University of Virginia invited him to attend the celebration of the 100th anniversary of the birth of Edgar Allan Poe, and in writing his thanks for the invitation Hardy adds :

'The University of Virginia does well to commemorate the birthday of this poet.   Now that lapse of time has reduced the insignificant and petty details of his life to their true proportion beside the measure of his poetry, and softened the horror of the correct classes at his lack of respectability, that fantastic and romantic genius shows himself in all his rarity.   His qualities, which would have been extraordinary anywhere, are much more extraordinary for the America of his date.

'Why one who was in many ways disadvantageously circumstanced for the development of the art of poetry should have been the first to realize to the full the possibilities of the English language in rhyme and alliteration is not easily explicable.

'It is a matter for curious conjecture whether his achievements in verse would have been the same if the five years of childhood spent in England had been extended to adult life.   That "unmerciful disaster" hindered those achievements from being carried further must be an endless regret to lovers of poetry.'

At the beginning of this year Hardy was appointed by the Dorset Court of Quarter Sessions a Representative Governor of the Dorchester Grammar School, a position he filled till the end of 1925.   He said he was not practical enough to make a good governor, but was influenced to accept the office by the fact that his namesake, Thomas Hardy of Melcombe Regis, who died in 1599, was the founder of the school.   The latter has a monument in St. Peter's Church, Dorchester,[1]

[1] See p. 5.

and is believed to have been of the same stock as the Thomas Hardy of this memoir.

In March came the last letter he was ever to receive from George Meredith, in which the elder writes :

'The French review herewith comes to my address and is, as you see by the superscription, intended for you.

'I am reminded that you are among the kind souls who thought of me on my 80th [birthday] and have not been thanked for their testimony of it. . . . The book [*The Dynasts*] was welcome all the more as being a sign that this big work was off your mind. How it may have been received I cannot say, but any book on so large a scale has to suffer the fate of a Panorama, and must be visited again and again for a just impression of it to be taken. I saw that somewhere in your neighbourhood it was represented in action. That is the way to bring it more rapidly home to the mind. But the speaker of Josephine's last words would have to be a choice one.'

The representation had been in Dorchester, and was limited to a few of the country scenes.

On the 10th April he heard of the death of Swinburne, which was the occasion of his writing the following letter :

'MAX GATE, *April* 12, 1909.

'For several reasons I could not bring myself to write on Swinburne immediately I heard that, to use his own words, "Fate had undone the bondage of the gods" for him. . . .

'No doubt the press will say some good words about him now he is dead and does not care whether it says them or no. Well, I remember what it said in 1866, when he did care, though you do not remember it, and how it made the blood of some of us young men boil.

'Was there ever such a country — looking back at the life, work, and death of Swinburne — is there any other country in Europe whose attitude towards a deceased poet of his rank would have been so ignoring and almost contemptuous? I except *The Times*, which has the fairest estimate I have yet seen. But read the *Academy* and the *Nation*.

'The kindly cowardice of many papers is overwhelming him with such toleration, such theological judgements, hypocritical sympathy, and misdirected eulogy that, to use his own words again, "it makes one sick in a corner" — or as we say down here in Wessex, "it is enough to make every little dog run to mixen".

'However, we are getting on in our appreciativeness of poets. One thinks of those other two lyricists, Burns and Shelley, at this time, for obvious reasons, and of how much harder it was with them. We know how Burns was treated at Dumfries, but by the time that Swinburne was a young man Burns had advanced so far as to be regarded as no worse than "the glory and the shame of literature" (in the words of a critic of that date). As for Shelley, he was not tolerated at all in his lifetime. But Swinburne has been tolerated — at any rate since he has not written anything to speak of. And a few months ago, when old and enfeebled, he was honoured by a rumour that he had been offered a complimentary degree at Oxford. And Shelley too, in these latter days of our memory, has been favoured so far as to be considered no lower than an ineffectual angel beating his luminous wings in vain. . . .

'I was so late in getting my poetical barge under way, and he was so early with his flotilla — besides my being between three and four years younger, and being nominally an architect (an awful impostor at that, really) — that though I read him as he came out I did not personally know him till many years after the *Poems and Ballads* year. . . .

.        .        .        .                      .

'T. H.'

'*April* 13. A genius for repartee is a gift for saying what a wise man thinks only.'

'*April* 15. Day of Swinburne's funeral. Find I cannot go with this rheumatism, though it is but slight, the journey being so roundabout.

'Thought of some of Swinburne's lines : *e.g.*,

'On Shelley : "O sole thing sweeter than thine own songs were".

'On Newman and Carlyle : "With all our hearts we praise you whom ye hate".

'On Time : "For time is as wind and as waves are we".

'On Man : "Save his own soul he hath no star".' [1]

In May Hardy was in London, and walking along Dover Street on his way to the Academy saw on a poster the announcement of the death of Meredith. He went on to the Athenæum and wrote some memorial lines on his friend, which were published a day or two later in *The Times*, and reprinted in *Time's Laughingstocks*.

[1] But Isaiah had said before him : 'Mine own arm brought salvation unto me'.

On the 22nd he attended a memorial service to Meredith in West-
minster Abbey — meeting there Maurice Hewlett, Henry James, Max
Beerbohm, Alfred Austin, and other acquaintance — and returned to
Dorchester the same afternoon.

In June he was asked to succeed Meredith as President of the
Society of Authors; and wrote to Mr. Maurice Hewlett, who had
brought the proposal before him:

'I am moved more than I can say by learning that in the view of
the Council I should be offered the succession to the Presidentship.
But I must nevertheless perform the disagreeable duty of acting upon
my own conviction of what is for the Society's good, and tell you that
I feel compelled to decline the honour. I have long had an opinion
that although in the early years of the Society it may perhaps have
been not unwise to have at its head men who took no part in its
management — indeed the mere names of Tennyson and Meredith
were in themselves of use to the institution — the time has now come
when the President should be one who takes an active part in the
Council's deliberations, and if possible one who lives in or near
London — briefly, that he should preside over its affairs. Now this
I could never do. I will not go into the reasons why, as they are
personal and unavoidable. . . .

'I may perhaps add that if there should still be a preponderat-
ing opinion in the Council that an inactive President of the old
kind is still desirable, the eminent name of Lord Morley suggests
itself.'

However, the matter ended by the acceptance of the Presidency
by Hardy on further representations by the Council. His first diffi-
dence had, in fact, arisen, as he stated, out of consideration for the
Society's interests, for he remembered that the Society included
people of all sorts of views, and that since Swinburne's death there
was no living English writer who had been so abused by sections of
the press as he himself had been in previous years; 'and who knows',
he would drily add, 'that I may not be again?'

But, as said above, his objections were overruled.

As usual his stay in London had given him influenza, and he could
not go to Aldeburgh as he had intended. About this time he wrote
to a lady of New York in answer to an inquiry she made:

'The discovery of the law of evolution, which revealed that all
organic creatures are of one family, shifted the centre of altruism
from humanity to the whole conscious world collectively. Therefore
the practice of vivisection, which might have been defended while

the belief ruled that men and animals are essentially different, has been left by that discovery without any logical argument in its favour. And if the practice, to the extent merely of inflicting slight discomfort now and then, be defended [as I sometimes hold it may] on grounds of it being good policy for animals as well as men, it is nevertheless in strictness a wrong, and stands precisely in the same category as would stand its practice on men themselves.'

In July the influenza had nearly passed off, and he fulfilled his engagement to go to Aldeburgh — the air of which he always sought if possible after that malady, having found it a quicker restorative than that of any other place he knew.

In the second week of this month he was at rehearsals of Baron F. d'Erlanger's opera *Tess* at Covent Garden, and on the 14th was present with Mrs. Hardy at the first performance. Though Italianized to such an extent that Hardy scarcely recognized it as his novel, it was a great success in a crowded house, Queen Alexandra being among the distinguished audience. Destinn's voice suited the title-character admirably ; her appearance less so.

In response to an invitation by Dr. Max Dessoir, a professor at the University of Berlin, who wished to have an epitome of the culture and thought of the time — the 'Weltanschauung' of a few representa-tive men in England and Germany — Hardy wrote the following during August this year :

'We call our age an age of Freedom. Yet Freedom, under her incubus of armaments, territorial ambitions smugly disguised as patriotism, superstitions, conventions of every sort, is of such stunted proportions in this her so-called time, that the human race is likely to be extinct before Freedom arrives at maturity.'

In the meantime he had been putting together poems written between-whiles, some of them already printed in periodicals — and in addition hunting up quite old ones dating from 1865, and over-looked in his earlier volumes, out of which he made a volume called *Time's Laughingstocks*, and sent off the MS. to his publishers the first week in September.

In continuance of the visits to cathedrals he went this autumn to Chichester, York, Edinburgh, and Durham ; and on returning to Dorchester was at a rehearsal of a play by Mr. A. H. Evans, the dramatist of the local Debating and Dramatic Society, based on *Far from the Madding Crowd*, which was performed there in the Corn Exchange, and a few days later before the Society of Dorset Men in London. Hardy had nothing to do with the adaptation, but thought

it a neater achievement than the London version of 1882 by Mr.
Comyns Carr.

In December *Time's Laughingstocks* was published, and Hardy
was in London, coming back as usual with a choking sore throat
which confined him to his bed till the New Year, on the eve of which
at twelve o'clock he crouched by the fire and heard in the silence of
the night the ringing of the muffled peal down the chimney of his
bedroom from the neighbouring church of St. George.

# CHAPTER XXX

# THE FREEDOM OF THE BOROUGH

1910 : *Aet.* 69–70

In March, being at Ventnor, Hardy visited Swinburne's grave at Bonchurch, and composed the poem entitled 'A Singer Asleep'. It is remembered by a friend who accompanied him on this expedition how that windy March day had a poetry of its own, how primroses clustered in the hedges, and noisy rooks wheeled in the air over the little churchyard. Hardy gathered a spray of ivy and laid it on the grave of that brother-poet of whom he never spoke save in words of admiration and affection.

'*To the Secretary of the Humanitarian League*

'THE ATHENÆUM, PALL MALL, S.W.'
'10*th April* 1910.'

'SIR :

'I am glad to think that the Humanitarian League has attained the handsome age of twenty years — the Animals Defence Department particularly.

'Few people seem to perceive fully as yet that the most far-reaching consequence of the establishment of the common origin of all species is ethical; that it logically involved a readjustment of altruistic morals by enlarging as a *necessity of rightness* the application of what has been called "The Golden Rule" beyond the area of mere mankind to that of the whole animal kingdom. Possibly Darwin himself did not wholly perceive it, though he alluded to it. While man was deemed to be a creation apart from all other creations, a secondary or tertiary morality was considered good enough towards the "inferior" races; but no person who reasons nowadays can escape the trying conclusion that this is not maintainable. And though I myself do not at present see how the principle of equal justice all round is to be carried out in its entirety, I recognize that the League is grappling with the question.'

It will be seen that in substance this agrees with a letter written earlier, and no doubt the subject was much in his mind just now.

About this time Hardy was asked by the editor of *Harper's Magazine* to publish his reminiscences in the pages of that periodical month by month. He replied :

'I could not appear in a better place. But it is absolutely unlikely that I shall ever change my present intention not to produce my reminiscences to the world.'

In the same month of April he was looking for a flat again in London, and found one at Blomfield Court, Maida Vale, which he and his wife and servants entered in May. Looking out of the window while at breakfast on the morning after their arrival, they beheld placarded in the street an announcement of the death of King Edward.

Hardy saw from the Athenæum the procession of the removal of the King's body to Westminster, and the procession of the funeral from Westminster three days later. On account of the suggestiveness of such events it must have been in these days that he wrote 'A King's Soliloquy on the Night of his Funeral'. His own seventieth birthday a fortnight later reminded him that he was a year older than the monarch who had just died.

There was general satisfaction when Hardy's name appeared as a recipient of the Order of Merit in the Birthday List of Honours in June 1910. He received numerous and gratifying telegrams and letters of congratulation from both friends and strangers, and, though he accepted the award with characteristic quietude, it was evident that this sign of official approval of his work brought him pleasure.

At the flat — the last one they were to take, as it happened — they received their usual friends as in previous years, and there were more performances of the *Tess* opera; but in the middle of June they were compelled to cancel all engagements suddenly owing to Hardy's illness, which was happily but brief. In July he was able to go out again, and on the 19th went to Marlborough House to be invested with the Order of Merit. The King received him pleasantly : 'but afterwards I felt that I had failed in the accustomed formalities'.

Back in the country at the end of the month they entertained some visitors at Max Gate. A brief visit to Aldeburgh, where he met Professor Bury and Dr. (afterwards Sir James) Frazer, and a few cycle rides, diversified the close of this summer.

In September he sat to Mr. William Strang for a sketch-portrait, which was required for hanging at Windsor Castle among those of

other recipients of the Order of Merit; and on November 16 came
the interesting occasion of the presentation of the freedom of Dorchester to Hardy, which appealed to his sentiment more perhaps than
did many of those recognitions of his literary achievements that had
come from the uttermost parts of the earth at a much earlier time.
Among the very few speeches or lectures that he ever delivered, the
one he made on this occasion was perhaps the most felicitous and
personal :

'Mr. Mayor and Gentlemen of the Corporation — This is an
occasion that speaks for itself, and so, happily, does not demand
many remarks from me.  In simply expressing my sincere thanks for
the high compliment paid me by having my name enrolled with those
of the Honorary Freemen of this historic town, I may be allowed to
confess that the freedom of the Borough of Dorchester did seem to
me at first something that I had possessed a long while, had helped
myself to (to speak plainly), for when I consider the liberties I have
taken with its ancient walls, streets, and precincts through the medium
of the printing-press, I feel that I have treated its external features
with the hand of freedom indeed.  True, it might be urged that my
Casterbridge (if I may mention seriously a name coined off-hand in
a moment with no thought of its becoming established and localized)
is not Dorchester — not even the Dorchester as it existed sixty years
ago, but a dream-place that never was outside an irresponsible book.
Nevertheless, when somebody said to me that "Casterbridge" is a
sort of essence of the town as it used to be, "a place more Dorchester
than Dorchester itself", I could not absolutely contradict him, though
I could not quite perceive it.  At any rate, it is not a photograph in
words, that inartistic species of literary produce, particularly in respect
of personages.  But let me say no more about my own doings.  The
chronicle of the town has vivid marks on it.  Not to go back to events
of national importance, lurid scenes have been enacted here within
living memory, or not so many years beyond it, whippings in front
of the town-pump, hangings on the gaol-roof.  I myself saw a woman
hanged not 100 yards from where we now stand, and I saw, too, a
man in the stocks in the back part of this very building.  Then, if one
were to recount the election excitements, Free Trade riots, scenes of
soldiers marching down the town to war, the proclamation of Sove-
reigns now crumbled to dust, it would be an interesting local story.

'Miss Burney, in her diary, speaks of its aspect when she drove
through with the rest of King George's Court on her way to Weymouth.  She says : "The houses have the most ancient appearance

of any that are inhabited that I have happened to see." This is not
quite the case now, and though we may regret the disappearance of
these old buildings, I cannot be blind to the difficulty of keeping a
town in what may be called working order while retaining all its
ancient features. Yet it must not be forgotten that these are its chief
attractions for visitors, particularly American visitors. Old houses,
in short, have a far larger commercial value than their owners always
remember, and it is only when they have been destroyed, and tourists
who have come to see them vow in their disappointment that they
will never visit the spot again, that this is realized. An American
gentleman came to me the other day in quite a bad temper, saying
that he had diverged from his direct route from London to Liverpool
to see ancient Dorchester, only to discover that he knew a hundred
towns in the United States more ancient-looking than this (*laughter*).
Well, we may be older than we look, like some ladies ; but if, for
instance, the original All-Saints and Trinity Churches, with their
square towers, the castle, the fine mansion of the Trenchards at the
corner of Shirehall Lane, the old Three Mariners Inn, the old Grey-
hound, the old Antelope, Lady Abingdon's house at the corner of
Durngate Street, and other mediaeval buildings were still in their
places, more visitors of antiquarian tastes would probably haunt the
town than haunt it now. Old All-Saints was, I believe, demolished
because its buttresses projected too far into the pavement. What a
reason for destroying a record of 500 years in stone! I knew the
architect who did it ; a milder-mannered man never scuttled a sacred
edifice. Milton's well-known observation in his *Areopagitica* —
"Almost as well kill a man as kill a good book" — applies not a
little to a good old building ; which is not only a book but a unique
manuscript that has no fellow. But corporations as such cannot help
these removals ; they can only be prevented by the education of
their owners or temporary trustees, or, in the case of churches, by
Government guardianship.

'And when all has been said on the desirability of preserving as
much as can be preserved, our power to preserve is largely an illusion.
Where is the Dorchester of my early recollection — I mean the
human Dorchester — the kernel — of which the houses were but
the shell? Of the shops as I first recall them not a single owner
remains ; only in two or three instances does even the name remain.
As a German author has said, "Nothing is permanent but change".
Here in Dorchester, as elsewhere, I see the streets and the turnings
not far different from those of my schoolboy time ; but the faces

that used to be seen at the doors, the inhabitants, where are they?
I turn up the Weymouth Road, cross the railway-bridge, enter an
iron gate to "a slope of green access", and there they are! There is
the Dorchester that I knew best; there are names on white stones
one after the other, names that recall the voices, cheerful and sad,
anxious and indifferent, that are missing from the dwellings and
pavements. Those who are old enough to have had that experience
may feel that after all the permanence or otherwise of inanimate
Dorchester concerns but the permanence of what is minor and
accessory.

'As to the future of the town, my impression is that its tendency
is to become more and more a residential spot, and that the nature
of its business will be mainly that of administering to the wants of
"private residents" as they are called. There are several reasons for
supposing this. The dryness of its atmosphere and subsoil is unex-
celled. It has the great advantage of standing near the coast without
being on it, thus escaping the objections some people make to a
winter residence close to the sea; while the marine tincture in its
breezes tempers the keenness which is felt in those of high and dry
chalk slopes further inland. Dorchester's future will not be like its
past; we may be sure of that. Like all other provincial towns, it
will lose its individuality — has lost much of it already. We have
become almost a London suburb owing to the quickened locomotion,
and, though some of us may regret this, it has to be.

'I will detain you no longer from Mr. Evans's comedy that is
about to be played downstairs. Ruskin somewhere says that comedy
is tragedy if you only look deep enough. Well, that is a thought to
remember; but to-night, at any rate, we will all be young and not
look too deeply.'

After the presentation — which was witnessed by Mrs. Hardy, by
Mr. (afterwards Sir Henry) Newbolt, by the writer of this memoir,
and by other friends, the Dorchester Dramatic Society gave for the
first time, at the hands of their own dramatist, an adaptation of *Under
the Greenwood Tree* entitled *The Mellstock Quire* — the second title
of the novel — Hardy himself doing no more than supply the original
carols formerly sung by the Quire of the parish outshadowed by the
name 'Mellstock' — the village of Stinsford, a mile from the town.

In December the American fleet paid a visit to Portland Roads,
and though the weather was bad while they were lying there Hardy
went on board the battleship *Connecticut*, where he met the captain,
commander, and others; who, with several more officers, afterwards

visited him and Mrs. Hardy at Max Gate.   On the 29th they went
on board the English *Dreadnought*, which was also lying there, and
thence to a dance on board the United States flagship *Louisiana*, to
which they were welcomed by Admiral Vreeland.

It was at the end of this year that Hardy published in the *Fortnightly
Review* some verses entitled 'God's Funeral'.   The alternative title he
had submitted for the poem was 'The Funeral of Jahveh' — the subject being the gradual decline and extinction in the human race of a
belief in an anthropomorphic god of the King of Dahomey type —
a fact recognized by all bodies of theologians for many years.   But the
editor, thinking the longer title clumsy and obscure, chose the other,
to which Hardy made no objection, supposing the meaning of his
poem would be clear enough to readers.

# CHAPTER XXXI

# BEREAVEMENT

1911–1912 : *Aet.* 70–72

IN March (1911) Hardy received a letter from M. Emile Bergerat of Paris asking him to let his name appear as one of the Committee for honouring Théophile Gautier on his approaching centenary, to which Hardy readily agreed. In the same month he visited Bristol Cathedral and Bath Abbey, and in April attended the funeral of the Mayor of Dorchester, who had presented him with the freedom of the borough but a few months earlier. A sequence of verses by Hardy, entitled 'Satires of Circumstance', which were published in the *Fortnightly Review* at this juncture, met with much attention both here and in America.

In April he and his brother, in pursuance of a plan of seeing or re-seeing all the English cathedrals, visited Lichfield, Worcester, and Hereford.

He makes only one note this spring : 'View the matrices rather than the moulds'.

Hardy had been compelled to decline in February an invitation from the Earl-Marshal to the Coronation in Westminster Abbey in the coming June. That month found him on a tour with his brother in the Lake Country, including Carlisle Cathedral and Castle, where the dungeons were another reminder to him of how 'evil men out of the evil treasure of their hearts have brought forth evil things'. However, the tour was agreeable enough despite the wet weather, and probably Hardy got more pleasure out of Coronation Day by spending it on Windermere than he would have done by spending it in a seat at the Abbey.

Of Grasmere Churchyard he says : 'Wordsworth's headstone and grave are looking very trim and new. A group of tourists who have never read a line of him sit near, addressing and sending off picture postcards. . . . Wrote some verses.' He visited Chester Cathedral coming homeward, called at Rugby, and went over the school and chapel ; and returned to Dorchester through London.

After his return he signed, with many other well-known people, a protest against the use of aerial vessels in war; appealing to all governments 'to foster by any means in their power an international understanding which shall preserve the world from warfare in the air'. A futile protest indeed!

In July Hardy took his sister Katherine on an excursion to North Somerset, stopping at Minehead, and going on by coach to Porlock and Lynmouth. Thence they went by steamer to Ilfracombe, intending to proceed through Exeter to South Devon. But the heat was so great that further travelling was abandoned, and after going over the cathedral they returned home.

In the preceding month, it may be remarked, had died Mr. W. J. Last, A.M.Inst.C.E., Director of the Science Museum, South Kensington, who was a son of Hardy's old Dorchester schoolmaster, Isaac Glandfield Last. The obituary notices that appeared in *The Times* and other papers gave details of a life more successful than his father's, though not of higher intellectual ability than that by which it had been Hardy's good fortune to profit.

At the end of the month Mr. Sydney Cockerell, director of the Fitzwilliam Museum, Cambridge, called, mainly to inquire about Hardy's old manuscripts, which was the occasion of his looking up those that he could find and handing them over to Mr. Cockerell to distribute as he thought fit among any museums that would care to possess one, Hardy himself preferring to have no voice in the matter. In the course of October this was done by Mr. Cockerell, the MSS. of *The Dynasts* and *Tess of the d'Urbervilles* being accepted by the British Museum, of *Time's Laughingstocks* and *Jude the Obscure* by the Fitzwilliam, and of *Wessex Poems*, with illustrations by the author himself (the only volume he ever largely illustrated), by Birmingham. Others were distributed from time to time by Mr. Cockerell, to whom Hardy had sent all the MSS. for him to do what he liked with, having insisted that 'it would not be becoming for a writer to send his own MSS. to a museum on his own judgement'.

It may be mentioned in passing that in these months Mr. F. Saxelby of Birmingham, having been attracted to Hardy's works by finding in them a name which resembled his own, published 'A Hardy Dictionary', containing the names of persons and places in the author's novels and poems. Hardy had offered no objection to its being issued but accepted no responsibility for its accuracy.

In November the Dorchester Debating and Dramatic Society

gave another performance of plays from the Wessex novels. This time the selection was the short one-act piece that Hardy had drama-tized himself many years before, from the story called *The Three Strangers*, entitled *The Three Wayfarers*; and a rendering by Mr. A. H. Evans of the tale of *The Distracted Preacher*. The Hardys' friend, Mrs. Arthur Henniker, came all the way from London to see it, and went with his wife and himself.

The curator of the Dorset County Museum having expressed a wish for a MS. of Hardy's, he sent this month the holograph of *The Mayor of Casterbridge*.

Being interested at this time in the only Gothic style of archi-tecture that can be called especially and exclusively English — the perpendicular style of the fifteenth century — Hardy made a journey to Gloucester to investigate its origin in that cathedral, which he ascertained to be in the screen between the south aisle and the transept — a fact long known probably to other investigators, but only recently to him. He was so much impressed by the thought that the inventor's name, like the names of the authors of so many noble songs and ballads, was unknown, that on his return he composed a poem there-on, called 'The Abbey Mason', which was published a little later in *Harper's Magazine*, and later still was included in a volume with other poems.

The illness of his elder sister Mary saddened the close of 1911; and it was during this year that his wife wrote the Reminiscences printed in the earlier pages of this book, as if she had premonitions that her end was not far off; though nobody else suspected it.

The year 1912, which was to advance and end in such gloom for Hardy, began serenely. In January he went to London for a day or two and witnessed the performance of *Oedipus* at Covent Garden. But in February he learnt of the death of his friend General Henniker, and in April occurred the disaster to the *Titanic* steamship, upon which he wrote the poem called 'The Convergence of the Twain' in aid of the fund for the sufferers.

On the 22nd April Hardy was correcting proofs for a new edition of his works, the Wessex Edition, concerning which he wrote to a friend:

'. . . I am now on to p. 140 of *The Woodlanders* (in *copy* I mean, not in proofs, of course). That is vol. vi. Some of the later ones will be shorter. I read ten hours yesterday — finishing the *proofs* of the *Native* (wh. I have thus got rid of). I got to like the character of

Clym before I had done with him. I think he is the nicest of all my heroes, and *not a bit* like me. On taking up *The Woodlanders* and reading it after many years I think I like it, *as a story*, the best of all. Perhaps that is owing to the locality and scenery of the action, a part I am very fond of. It seems a more quaint and fresh story than the *Native*, and the characters are very distinctly drawn. . . . Seven o'clock P.M. It has come on to rain a little : a blackbird is singing outside. I have read on to p. 185 of *The Woodlanders* since the early part of my letter.'

The Hardys dined with a few friends in London this season, but did not take a house, putting up at a hotel with which Hardy had long been familiar, the West Central in Southampton Row.

On June 1 at Max Gate they had a pleasant week-end visit from Henry Newbolt and W. B. Yeats, who had been deputed by the Royal Society of Literature to present Hardy with the Society's gold medal on his seventy-second birthday. The two eminent men of letters were the only people entertained at Max Gate for the occasion ; but everything was done as methodically as if there had been a large audience. Hardy says : 'Newbolt wasted on the nearly empty room the best speech he ever made in his life, and Yeats wasted a very good one : mine in returning thanks was as usual a bad one, and the audience was quite properly limited'.

In the middle of June he was in London at Lady St. Helier's, and went to the play of *Bunty pulls the Strings* with her. An amusing anticlimax to a story of the three-crow type occurred in connection with this or some other popular play of the date. It was currently reported and credited that Mr. Asquith had gone to see it eight times, and Mr. Balfour sixteen. Taking Miss Balfour in to dinner and discussing the play, Hardy told her of the report, and she informed him that her brother had been only once. How few the visits of Mr. Asquith were could not be ascertained. Possibly he had not gone at all.

Later on in the autumn a letter was addressed to him on a gross abuse which was said to have occurred — that of publishing details of a lately deceased man's life under the guise of a novel, with assurances of truth scattered in the newspapers. In the course of his reply he said :

'What should certainly be protested against, in cases where there is no authorization, is the mixing of fact and fiction in unknown proportions. Infinite mischief would lie in that. If any statements in the dress of fiction are covertly hinted to be fact, all must be fact, and nothing else but fact, for obvious reasons. The power of getting lies believed about people through that channel after they are dead, by stirring in a few truths, is a horror to contemplate.'

'*June.* Here is a sentence from the *Edinburgh Review* of a short time back which I might have written myself: "The division [of poems] into separate groups [ballad, lyrical, narrative, &c.] is frequently a question of the preponderance, not of the exclusive possession, of certain aesthetic elements."'

Meanwhile in July he had returned to Max Gate just in time to be at a garden-party on July 16 — the last his wife ever gave — which it would have much grieved him afterwards to have missed. The afternoon was sunny and the guests numerous on this final one of many occasions of such a gathering on the lawn there, and nobody foresaw the shadow that was so soon to fall on the house, Mrs. Hardy being then, apparently, in her customary health and vigour. In the following month, August, she was at Weymouth for the last time; and Hardy took her and her niece to see the performance of *Bunty* at the Pavilion Theatre. It was her last play.

However, she was noticed to be weaker later on in the autumn, though not ill, and complained of her heart at times. Strangely enough, she one day suddenly sat down to the piano and played a long series of her favourite old tunes, saying at the end she would never play any more. The poem called 'The Last Performance' approximately describes this incident.

She went out up to the 22nd November, when, though it was a damp, dark afternoon, she motored to pay a visit six miles off. The next day she was distinctly unwell, and the day after that was her birthday, when she seemed depressed. On the 25th two ladies called; and though she consulted with her husband whether or not to go downstairs to see them, and he suggested that she should not in her weak state, she did go down. The strain obliged her to retire immediately they had left. She never went downstairs again.

The next day she agreed to see a doctor, who did not think her seriously ill, but weak from want of nourishment through indigestion. In the evening she assented quite willingly to Hardy's suggestion that he should go to a rehearsal in Dorchester of a play made by the local company, that he had promised to attend. When he got back at eleven o'clock all the house was in bed and he did not disturb her.

The next morning the maid told him in answer to his inquiry that when she had as usual entered Mrs. Hardy's room a little earlier she had said she was better, and would probably get up later on;

but that she now seemed worse. Hastening to her he was shocked to find her much worse, lying with her eyes closed and unconscious. The doctor came quite quickly, but before he arrived her breathing softened and ceased.

It was the day fixed for the performance of *The Trumpet-Major* in Dorchester, and it being found impossible to put off the play at such short notice, so many people having come from a distance for it, it was produced, an announcement of Mrs. Hardy's unexpected death being made from the stage.

Many years earlier she had fancied that she would like to be buried at Plymouth, her native place ; but on going there to the funeral of her father she found that during a 'restoration' the family vault in Charles Churchyard, though it was not full, had been broken into, if not removed altogether, either to alter the entrance to the church, or to erect steps ; and on coming back she told her husband that this had quite destroyed her wish to be taken there, since she could not lie near her parents.

There was one nook, indeed, which in some respects was pre-eminently the place where she might have lain — the graveyard of St. Juliot, Cornwall — whose dilapidated old church had been the cause of their meeting, and in whose precincts the early scenes of their romance had a brief being. But circumstances ordered other-wise. Hardy did not favour the thought of her being carried to that lonely coast unless he could be carried thither likewise in due time ; and on this point all was uncertain. The funeral was accordingly at Stinsford, a mile from Dorchester and Max Gate, where the Hardys had buried for many years.

She had not mentioned to her husband, or to anybody else so far as he could discover, that she had any anticipations of death before it occurred so suddenly. Yet on his discovery of the manuscript of her 'Recollections', written only a year earlier, it seemed as if some kind of presentiment must have crossed her mind that she was not to be much longer in the world, and that if her brief memories were to be written it were best to write them quickly. This is, however, but conjecture.

# CHAPTER XXXII

# REVISITINGS, SECOND MARRIAGE, AND WAR WRITINGS

1913–1914 : *Aet.* 72–74

MANY poems were written by Hardy at the end of the previous year and the early part of this — more than he had ever written before in the same space of time — as can be seen by referring to their subjects, as well as to the dates attached to them. To adopt Walpole's words concerning Gray, Hardy was 'in flower' in these days, and, like Gray's, his flower was sad-coloured.

On March 6 — almost to a day, forty-three years after his first journey to Cornwall — he started for St. Juliot, putting up at Boscastle, and visiting Pentargan Bay and Beeny Cliff, on which he had not once set foot in the long interval.

He found the Rectory and other scenes with which he had been so familiar changed a little, but not greatly, and returning by way of Plymouth arranged for a memorial tablet to Mrs. Hardy in the church with which she had been so closely associated as organist before her marriage, and in other ways. The tablet was afterwards erected to his own design, as was also the tomb in Stinsford Churchyard — in the preparation of which memorials he had to revive a species of work that he had been unaccustomed to since the years of his architectural pupillage.

In June he left for Cambridge to receive the honorary degree of Litt.D., and lunched with the Master of Magdalene (also Vice-Chancellor), Dr. Donaldson, and Lady Albinia Donaldson, meeting — some for the first and last time — the Master of Trinity and Mrs. Butler, John Sargent, Arthur Benson, Henry Jackson, Vice-Master of Trinity and the Regius Professor of Greek, Sir James Murray, and many others. The visit was full of interest for Hardy as the sequel to his long indirect connection with the University in several ways, partly through the many graduates who were his friends, his frequent visits to the place, and his intention in the eighteen-sixties to go up himself for a pass-degree, which was abandoned mainly owing to his discovery that he could not conscientiously carry out his idea of taking Orders. A few weeks later he was elected an Honorary Fellow of Magdalene, as will be seen.

In July he was in London once or twice, meeting Dr. Page, the American Ambassador, Mr. and Mrs. Asquith, and others here and there. A German translation of *The Mayor of Casterbridge* under the title of *Der Bürgermeister* was begun as a serial in Germany at this time, and in the same month the gift of the MS. of his poem on Swinburne's death was acknowledged by the Newnes Librarian at Putney, an offer which had originated with Mr. Sydney Cockerell. In response to a request from the Secretary of the General Blind Association, he gave his permission to put some of his books in prose and verse into Braille type for the use of the blind, adding:

'I cannot very well suggest which, as I do not know the length you require. . . . If a full-length novel, I would suggest *The Trumpet-Major*. If verse, the Battle of Trafalgar scenes or the Battle of Waterloo scenes from *The Dynasts*, or a selection from the Poems. . . . I am assuming that you require scenes of action rather than those of reflection or analysis.'

In August he was at Blandford with Mr. John Lane searching about for facts and scenes that might illustrate the life of Alfred Stevens, the sculptor, whose best-known work is the Wellington monument in St. Paul's, and who was born and grew up in this town. Hardy had suggested that it ought to be written before it was too late, and Mr. Lane had taken up the idea. The house of his birth was discovered, but not much material seems to have been gained. It was not till a year or two later that Hardy discovered that Stevens's father painted the Ten Commandments in the church of Blandford St. Mary, his name being in the corner: 'G. Stevens, Blandford, 1825'.

'*September* 15. Thoughts on the recent school of novel-writers. They forget in their insistence on life, and nothing but life, in a plain slice, that a story *must be worth the telling*, that a good deal of life is not worth any such thing, and that they must not occupy a reader's time with what he can get at first hand anywhere around him.'

The autumn glided on with its trifling incidents. In the muddle of Hardy's unmistressed housekeeping animal pets of his late wife died, strayed, or were killed, much to Hardy's regret; short visits were paid by friends, including Mr. Frederic Harrison; and in November, while staying with the Master of his College, Hardy was admitted in chapel as Honorary Fellow. 'The ceremony, which

Thomas Hardy, 1913

consists of a Latin formula of admission before the Altar, and the handing-in of the new Fellow into his stall, was not unimpressive', said the *Cambridge Review*. Hardy had read the lessons in church in his young manhood, besides having had much to do with churches in other ways, and the experience may have recalled the old ecclesiastical times. In the evening he dined in Hall, where 'the Master proposed the health of him who was no longer a guest, but one of the Society, and the day's proceedings terminated happily', continued the *Cambridge Review*. It was an agreeable evening for Hardy, Mr. A. E. Housman and Sir Clifford Allbutt being present as guests among others of his friends.

A good sketch-painting of him was made this autumn by Mr. Fuller Maitland for his friend Arthur Benson, to be hung with the other portraits in the hall of Magdalene College; and in the middle of November the Dorchester amateurs' version of *The Woodlanders*, adapted by themselves, was performed on the Dorchester stage, but Hardy was not present on the occasion.

In the December of this year M. Anatole France was entertained at a dinner in London by a committee of men of letters and of affairs. Hardy was much disappointed at being unable to attend; and he wrote to express his regret, adding:

'In these days when the literature of narrative and verse seems to be losing its qualities as an art, and to be assuming a structureless and conglomerate character, it is a privilege that we should have come into our midst a writer who is faithful to the principles that make for permanence, who never forgets the value of organic form and symmetry, the force of reserve, and the emphasis of understatement, even in his lighter works.'

In February of the year following (1914) the subject of this memoir married the present writer.

In the spring of the same year Hardy was at the dinner of the Royal Academy, and he and his wife saw several friends in London, afterwards proceeding to Cambridge, where they spent a pleasant week in visiting and meeting Mr. Arthur Benson, Professor and Mrs. Bury, Mr. and Mrs. Cockerell, Professor Quiller-Couch, the Master of Jesus, Dr. James, Provost of King's, Dr. and Mrs. MacTaggart, and the oldest friend of Hardy's in Cambridge, or for that matter anywhere, Mr. Charles Moule, President and formerly Tutor of Corpus, who had known him as a boy. A dinner at St. John's — the 'Porte-Latin Feast' — with the mellow radiance of the dark mahogany tables, curling tobacco smoke, and old red wine, charmed Hardy, in spite of his drinking very little, and not smoking at all. A visit to Girton and tea with Miss Jones and members of her staff ended the Cambridge week for them.

Although Hardy had no sort of anticipation of the restrictions that the war was so soon to bring on motoring, he went about in a car this early summer almost as if he foresaw what was coming, taking his wife to Exeter, Plymouth, and back across Dartmoor.

After serving as a Grand Juror at the Assizes he dined during June with the Royal Institute of British Architects, a body of which he had never lost sight on account of his early associations with the profession, though nearly all the members he had known — except his old acquaintance, the Vice-President, John Slater, and the Blomfields — had passed away.

A communication from men of letters and art in Germany who thought of honouring the memory of Friedrich Nietzsche on the seventieth anniversary of his birth, was the occasion of Hardy's writing at this date :

'It is a question whether Nietzsche's philosophy is sufficiently coherent to be of great ultimate value, and whether those views of his which seem so novel and striking appear thus only because they have been rejected for so many centuries as inadmissible under humane rule.

'A continuity of consciousness through the human race would be the only justification of his proposed measures.

'He assumes throughout the great worth intrinsically of human masterfulness. The universe is to him a perfect machine which only requires thorough handling to work wonders. He forgets that the universe is an imperfect machine, and that to do good with an ill-working instrument requires endless adjustments and compromises.'

There was nothing to tell of the convulsion of nations that was now imminent, and in Dorset they visited various friends and stayed a week-end with Sir Henry and Lady Hoare at Stourhead (where they met as their fellow-guests Mr. and Mrs. Charles Whibley, the former of whom Hardy had long known, though they had not met for years). To Hardy as to ordinary civilians the murder at Serajevo was a lurid and striking tragedy, but carried no indication that it would much affect English life. On July 28th they were at a quiet little garden-party near Dorchester, and still there was no sign of the coming storm : the next day they lunched about five miles off with friends at Islington, and paid a call or two — this being the day on

which war was declared by Austria on Serbia.  Hardy made a few
entries just after this date :

'*August* 4, 11 P.M.  War declared with Germany.'

On this day they were lunching at Athelhampton Hall, six miles
off, where a telegram came announcing the rumour to be fact.  A
discussion arose about food, and there was almost a panic at the table,
nobody having any stock.  But the full dimensions of what the
English declaration meant were not quite realized at once.  Their
host disappeared to inquire into his stock of flour.  The whole news
and what it involved burst upon Hardy's mind next morning, for
though most people were saying the war would be over by Christmas
he felt it might be a matter of years and untold disaster.

'*August* 9-15.  English Expeditionary Force crosses the Channel
to assist France and Belgium.'

'*August* onwards.  War excitement.  "Quicquid delirant reges,
plectuntur Achivi!"'  It was the quotation Hardy had made at the
outbreak of the Franco-Prussian war forty-four years earlier, when
he was quite a young man.

He had been completely at fault, as he often owned, on the coming
so soon of such a convulsion as the war, though only three or four
months before it broke out he had printed a prophetic poem in the
*Fortnightly* entitled 'Channel Firing', whereof the theme,

> All nations striving strong to make
> Red war yet redder,

was, to say the least, a perception singularly coincident.  However,
as stated, that it would really burst, he doubted.  When the noisy
crew of music-hall Jingoes said exultingly, years earlier, that Germany
was as anxious for war as they were themselves, he had felt convinced
that they were wrong.  He had thought that the play, *An Englishman's Home*, which he witnessed by chance when it was produced,
ought to have been suppressed as provocative, since it gave Germany,
even if pacific in intention beforehand, a reason, or excuse, for directing her mind on a war with England.  A long study of the European
wars of a century earlier had made it appear to him that common
sense had taken the place of bluster in men's minds ;  and he felt this
so strongly that in the very year before war burst on Europe he wrote
some verse called 'His Country', bearing on the decline of antagonism
between peoples ;  and as long before as 1901 he composed a poem
called 'The Sick Battle-God', which assumed that zest for slaughter
was dying out.  It was seldom he had felt so heavy at heart as in

seeing his old view of the gradual bettering of human nature, as expressed in these verses of 1901, completely shattered by the events of 1914 and onwards. War, he had supposed, had grown too coldly scientific to kindle again for long all the ardent romance which had characterized it down to Napoleonic times, when the most intense battles were over in a day, and the most exciting tactics and strategy led to the death of comparatively few combatants. Hence nobody was more amazed than he at the German incursion into Belgium, and the contemplation of it led him to despair of the world's history thenceforward. He had not reckoned on the power still retained there by the governing castes whose interests were not the people's. It was, however, no use to despair, and since Germany had not shown the rationality he had expected of her, he presently began to consider if there was anything he — an old man of seventy-four — could do in the critical circumstances. A slight opening seemed to offer when he received a letter from the Government asking his attendance at a private Conference in which eminent literary men and women who commanded confidence abroad 'should take steps to place the strength of the British case and the principles for which the British troops and their allies are fighting before the populations of neutral countries'. He went to London expressly to attend, as explained in the following memorandum :

'*September* 2. To London in obedience to a summons by Mr. Masterman, Chancellor of the Duchy of Lancaster, at the instance of the Cabinet, for the organization of public statements of the strength of the British case and principles in the war by well-known men of letters.'

This meeting was at Wellington House, Buckingham Gate, and in view of what the country was entering on has a historic significance. There was a medley of writers present, including, in addition to the Chairman, Mr. Masterman, among Hardy's friends and acquaintance, Sir James Barrie, Sir Henry Newbolt, J. W. Mackail, Arthur and Monsignor Benson, John Galsworthy, Sir Owen Seaman, G. M. Trevelyan, H. G. Wells, Arnold Bennett, John Masefield, Robert Bridges, Anthony Hope Hawkins, Gilbert Murray, and many others. Whatever the effect of the discussion, the scene was impressive to more than one of them there. In recalling it Hardy said that the yellow September sun shone in from the dusty street with a tragic cast upon them as they sat round the large blue table, full of misgivings, yet unforeseeing in all their completeness the tremendous events that were to follow. The same evening Hardy left London

— 'the streets hot and sad, and bustling with soldiers and recruits' — to set about some contribution to the various forms of manifesto that had been discussed.

In Dorset the Hardys kept up between-whiles their motoring through September, visiting Broadwindsor, Axminster, the summit called 'Cross-in-hand', from which both the Bristol and English Channels are visible, and on which many years earlier Hardy had written a traditional poem, 'The Lost Pyx'; also Bridport, Abbotsbury, Portisham, including the old residence of Admiral Hardy's father, still intact with its dial in the garden, dated 1767.

In the same month he published in *The Times* the soldiers' war-song called 'Men who March Away', which won an enormous popularity; and in October wrote 'England to Germany', a sonnet 'On the Belgian Expatriation' for *King Albert's Book*, and in the papers a letter on the destruction of Reims Cathedral. This month, too, he brought out another volume of verses entitled *Satires of Circumstance, Lyrics and Reveries* — the book being made up of the 'Satires in Fifteen Glimpses', published in a periodical in 1911, and other poems of a very different kind with which the satires ill harmonized — the latter filling but fifteen pages in a volume of 230 pages. These were caustically humorous productions which had been issued with a light heart before the war. So much shadow, domestic and public, had passed over his head since he had written the satires that he was in no mood now to publish humour or irony, and hence he would readily have suppressed them if they had not already gained such currency from magazine publication that he could not do it. The 'Lyrics and Reveries', which filled the far greater part of the volume, contained some of the tenderest and least satirical verse that ever came from his pen.

In November he and his wife went to London to a rehearsal of a portion of *The Dynasts*, which Mr. Granville-Barker was then preparing for the stage at the Kingsway Theatre, and which was produced there on the 25th November, though the author had never dreamt of a single scene of it being staged. Owing to a cold Hardy was unable to be present on the first representation, but he went up two or three weeks later.

Hardy's idea had been that the performance should be called what it really was, namely, 'Scenes from *The Dynasts*' — as being less liable to misconception than the book-title unmodified, since people might suppose the whole epic-drama was to be presented, which was quite an impossibility. However, as the scheme of the production was Mr. Granville-Barker's own, as he had himself selected all the scenes, Hardy did not interfere, either with this or any other detail. The one feature he could particularly have wished altered was that of retaining indoor architecture for outdoor scenes, it being difficult for the spectator to realize — say in the Battle of Waterloo — that an open field was represented when pillars and architraves hemmed it in. He thought that for the open scenes a perfectly plain green floorcloth and blue backcloth would have suited better. But the theatre's resources of space were very limited. However, the production was artistically successful.

More verses on the war were written by Hardy in December, including 'An Appeal to America'. A sad vigil, during which no bells were heard at Max Gate, brought in the first New Year of this unprecedented 'breaking of nations'.

It may be added here that the war destroyed all Hardy's belief in the gradual ennoblement of man, a belief he had held for many years, as is shown by poems like 'The Sick Battle-God', and others. He said he would probably not have ended *The Dynasts* as he did end it if he could have foreseen what was going to happen within a few years.

Moreover, the war gave the *coup de grâce* to any conception he may have nourished of a fundamental ultimate Wisdom at the back of things. With his views on necessitation, or at most a very limited free will, events seemed to show him that a fancy he had often held and expressed, that the never-ending push of the Universe was an unpurposive and irresponsible groping in the direction of the least resistance, might possibly be the real truth. 'Whether or no', he would say,

'Desine fata Deûm flecti sperare precando.'

# CHAPTER XXXIII

# WAR EFFORTS, DEATHS OF RELATIVES, AND 'MOMENTS OF VISION'

## 1915–1917 : *Aet.* 74–77

HE seems to have been studying the *Principia Ethica* of Dr. G. E. Moore early this year ; and also the philosophy of Bergson. Writing on the latter in answer to a letter from Dr. C. W. Saleeby on the subject, he states :

'I suppose I may think that you are more or less a disciple of his, or fellow-philosopher with him. Therefore you may be rather shocked at some views I hold about his teaching — or did hold, anyhow. His theories are much pleasanter ones than those they contest, and I for one would gladly believe them ; but I cannot help feeling all the time that his is rather an imaginative and poetical mind than a reasoner's, and that for his charming and attractive assertions he does not adduce any proofs whatever. His use of the word "creation" seems to me loose and vague. Then as to conduct : I fail to see how, if it is not mechanism, it can be other than caprice, though he denies it. Yet I quite agree with him in regarding finalism as an erroneous doctrine. He says, however, that mechanism and finalism are only external views of our conduct — "Our conduct extends between them, and slips much further". Well, it may, but he nowhere shows that it does.

'Then again : "A mechanistic conception . . . treats the living as the inert. . . . Let us, on the contrary, trace a line of demarcation between the inert and the living." Well, let us, to our great pleasure, if we can see why we should introduce an inconsistent rupture of Order into a uniform and consistent Law of the same.

'You will see how much I want to have the pleasure of being a Bergsonian. But I fear his theory is, in the bulk, only our old friend Dualism in a new suit of clothes —an ingenious fancy without real foundation, and more complicated than the fancies he endeavours to overthrow.

'You must not think me a hard-headed rationalist for all this.

Half my time — particularly when writing verse — I "believe" (in the modern sense of the word) not only in the things Bergson believes in, but in spectres, mysterious voices, intuitions, omens, dreams, haunted places, etc., etc.  But I do not believe in them in the old sense of the word any more for that. . . .

'By the way, how do you explain the following from the *Cambridge Magazine,* by a writer whom I imagine to be of a school of thinkers akin to your own, concerning Herbert Spencer's doctrine of the Unknowable?

'"We doubt if there is a single philosopher alive to-day who would subscribe to it.  Even men of science are gradually discarding it in favour of Realism and Pragmatism."

'I am utterly bewildered to understand how the doctrine that, beyond the knowable, there must always be an unknown, can be displaced.'

In April a distant cousin of promising ability — a lieutenant in the 5th Batt. Dorset Regiment — came to see him before going abroad, never to be seen by him again; and in the following month he sat to Mr. [Sir Hamo] Thornycroft for a model of a head which the sculptor wished to make.  At home he heard that two single-page songs in manuscript which he had sent to the Red Cross Sale at Christie's had fetched £48 — 'Men who March Away' and 'The Night of Trafalgar'.

'*May* 14.  Have been reading a review of Henry James.  It is remarkable that a writer who has no grain of poetry, or humour, or spontaneity in his productions, can yet be a good novelist.  Meredith has some poetry, and yet I can read James when I cannot look at Meredith.'

'*May* 27.  "Georgian Poets".  It is a pity that these promising young writers adopted such a title.  The use of it lacks the modesty of true genius, as it confuses the poetic chronology, and implies that the hitherto recognized original Georgians — Shelley, Keats, Wordsworth, Byron, etc., are negligible; or at any rate says that they do not care whether it implies such or no.'

'*June* 10.  Motored with F. to Bridport, Lyme, Exeter, and Torquay.  Called on Mr. and Mrs. Eden Phillpotts.  Saw their garden and beautiful flowers.  Then back to Teignmouth, Dawlish, and Exeter, putting up at the "Clarence" opposite the Cathedral.'

'*June* 11.  To Cathedral — then home via Honiton, Chard, Crewkerne.'

Thomas and Florence Emily Hardy at Max Gate, 1914

In July they were in London on a visit to Lady St. Helier, and paid a long-promised call on Sir Frederick and Lady Treves in Richmond Park. Later on in the month he was at the funeral at Stinsford of a suddenly lost friend, Mr. Douglas Thornton the banker, and received visits from Sir Henry Hoare, who motored over from Stourhead, and Professor Flinders Petrie, whom he had known but not seen for many years.

In August he learnt of the loss of his second cousin's son, Lieutenant George, who had been killed that month in Gallipoli during a brave advance. Hardy makes this note of him:

'Frank George, though so remotely related, is the first one of my family to be killed in battle for the last hundred years, so far as I know. He might say Militavi non sine gloria — short as his career has been.'

In the autumn Hardy sometimes, and his wife continually, assisted in the evenings at the soldiers' tea-room established in the Dorchester Corn Exchange; they visited the Australian Camp near Weymouth, and spent two or three days at Melbury House. On returning he learnt that his elder sister was again seriously ill. She died the same week, at his brother's house at Talbothays. The two poems, 'Logs on the Hearth' and 'In the Garden', in *Moments of Vision*, evidently refer to her, as also the Fourth person in 'Looking Across', in the same volume.

The hobby of her life had been portrait-painting, and she had shown her aptitude in catching a likeness, particularly of her relations, her picture of her mother in oils bearing a striking resemblance to the striking original. But she had been doomed to school-teaching, and organ-playing in this or that village church during all her active years, and hence was unable to devote sufficient time to pictorial art till leisure was too late to be effective. Her character was a somewhat unusual one, being remarkably unassertive, even when she was in the right, and could easily have proved it; so that the point of the following remark about her is manifest:

'*November* 29. Buried her under the yew-tree where the rest of us lie. As Mr. Cowley read the words of the psalm "Dixi Custodiam" they reminded me strongly of her nature, particularly when she was young: "I held my tongue and spake nothing: I kept silence, yea, even from good words." That was my poor Mary exactly. She never defended herself; and that not from timidity, but indifference to opinion.'

The funeral day had been cold and wet, and Hardy was laid up till the end of the year with a violent bronchitis and racking cough. Nevertheless, during December, in response to a request from Winchester House for a contribution to a 'Pro-Ally Film' of paragraphs in facsimile from authors' writings, which was 'to be exhibited throughout the world and make its appeal particularly to the neutral nations', he was able to send the following passages from Pitt's actual speech in the House of Commons a hundred years earlier, as closely paraphrased in *The Dynasts* :

### ENGLAND AT BAY

The strange fatality that haunts the times
Wherein our lot is cast, has no example ;
Times are they fraught with peril, trouble, gloom ;
We have to mark their lourings and to face them.

### ENGLAND RESOLUTE

Unprecedented and magnificent
As were our strivings in the previous wars,
Our efforts in the present shall transcend them,
As men will learn.

In January of the next year (1916) a war ballad of some weirdness, called 'The Dead and the Living One', which had been written several months before, was published in the *Sphere* and the *New York World*, and later reprinted in *Moments of Vision*.

In February he was again confined to his room with a cold, the previous one never having quite gone off. But he managed to send to the Red Cross Sale for this year, not any work of his own, but 'A Sheaf of Victorian Letters', written to T. H. by many other writers, nearly all deceased, and of a very interesting kind. Mrs. Hardy also sent to the same sale three short MSS. of his: 'The Oxen', 'The Breaking of Nations', and a fragment of a story — the whole fetching £72 : 10s.

A *Book of Homage* to Shakespeare was printed in April, for which Hardy had written a piece entitled 'To Shakespeare after three hundred years', afterwards included in the volume called *Moments of Vision*.

In June he served again as Grand Juror at the Assizes, and was at a rehearsal in Dorchester of *Wessex Scenes from The Dynasts*. This, made by 'The Hardy Players', was quite a different selection from that of Mr. Granville-Barker, embracing scenes of a local character only, from which could be gathered in echoes of drum and

trumpet and alarming rumours, the great events going on elsewhere
Though more limited in scope than the former, it was picturesque and.
effective as performed by the local actors at the Weymouth Pavilion
a fortnight later, and was well appreciated by the London press.

In the same month of June he paid a visit with his wife and remaining sister to a house he had never entered for forty years. This
was Riverside Villa, Sturminster Newton — the first he had furnished
after his first marriage, and in which he had written *The Return of
the Native*. He found it much as it had been in the former years ;
and it was possibly this visit which suggested the poems about
Sturminster that were published in *Moments of Vision*. Motorings
to Melbury again, to Swanage, and again to Bridport, passed the
midsummer days.

'*July* 27. *Times Literary Supplement* on "What is Militarism?"
The article suggests a term to express the cause of the present war,
"hypochondria" (in the Prussians). I should rather have said
"*apprehensiveness*". The term would fit some of the facts like a
glove.'

In September they set out by train for Cornwall, breaking the
journey at Launceston. Thence they went on to Camelford, Boscastle, and St. Juliot, to see if Hardy's design and inscription for the
tablet in the church had been properly carried out and erected. At
Tintagel they met quite by accident Hardy's friends the Stuart-
Wortleys, which made their sojourn at that romantic spot a very
pleasant one.

'*September* 10. Sunday. To Tintagel Church. We sat down
in a seat bordering the passage to the transept, but the vicar appalled
us by coming to us in his surplice and saying we were in the way of
the choir, who would have to pass there. He banished us to the back
of the transept. However, when he began his sermon we walked out.
He thought it was done to be even with him, and looked his indigna-
tion ; but it was really because we could not see the nave lengthwise,
which my wife, Emma, had sketched in watercolours when she was
a young woman before it was "restored", so that I was interested in
noting the changes, as also was F., who was familiar with the sketch.
It was saddening enough, though doubtless only a chance, that we
were inhospitably received in a church so much visited and appreciated by one we both had known so well. The matter was somewhat
mended, however, by their singing the beautiful 34th Psalm to Smart's
fine tune, "Wiltshire". By the by, that the most poetical verse of
that psalm is omitted from it in *Hymns Ancient and Modern* shows

the usual ineptness of hymn selectors. We always sang it at Stinsford. But then, we sang there in the good old High-and-Dry Church way — straight from the New Version.'

Multifarious matters filled up the autumn — among others a visit to the large camp of some 5000 German prisoners in Dorchester ; also visits to the English wounded in hospital, which conjunction led him to say :

'At the German prisoners' camp, including the hospital, operating-room, etc., were many sufferers. One Prussian, in much pain, died whilst I was with him — to my great relief, and his own. Men lie helpless here from wounds : in the hospital a hundred yards off other men, English, lie helpless from wounds — each scene of suffering caused by the other!

'These German prisoners seem to think that we are fighting to exterminate Germany, and though it has been said that, so far from it, we are fighting to save what is best in Germany, Cabinet ministers do not in my opinion speak this out clearly enough.'

In October the *Selected Poems of Thomas Hardy* were published in Macmillan's Golden Treasury Series, a little book that received some very good reviews ; and in December the *Wessex Scenes from The Dynasts*, which had been produced earlier at Weymouth, were performed at Dorchester. Some of Hardy's friends, including Sir James Barrie and Mr. Sydney Cockerell, came to see the piece, but Hardy could not accompany them, being kept in bed by another cold. The performances were for Red Cross Societies.

'*January* 1, 1917. Am scarcely conscious of New Year's Day.'

'*January* 6. I find I wrote in 1888 that "Art is concerned with seemings only", which is true.'

*To the Secretary of the Royal Society of Literature*

'*February* 8, 1917.

'DEAR SIR,

'I regret that as I live in a remote part of the country I cannot attend the meeting of the Entente Committee.

'In respect of the Memorandum proposing certain basic principles of international education for promoting ethical ideals that shall conduce to a League of Peace, I am in hearty agreement with the proposition.

'I would say in considering a *modus operandi* :

'That nothing effectual will be accomplished in the cause of *Peace* till the sentiment of *Patriotism* be freed from the narrow meaning attaching to it in the past (still upheld by Junkers and Jingoists) and be extended to the whole globe.

'On the other hand, that the sentiment of *Foreignness* — if the sense of a contrast be really rhetorically necessary — attach only to other planets and their inhabitants, if any.

'I may add that I have been writing in advocacy of those views for the last twenty years.'

### To Dr. L. Litwinski

'*March* 7, 1917.

'DEAR SIR,

'I feel much honoured by your request that I should be a member of the Committee for commemorating two such writers of distinction as Verhaeren and Sienkiewicz. But for reasons of increasing years and my living so far from London I have latterly been compelled to give up membership with several associations ; and I am therefore sorry to say that I must refrain from joining any new committee in which I should be unable actively to support the cause, even when so worthy as the present one.'

In this March also a sonnet by him named 'A Call to National Service' was printed in the newspapers. An article in the April *Fortnightly* by Mr. Courtney, the editor, on Hardy's writings, especially *The Dynasts*, interested him not only by its appreciativeness, but also by the aspect some features of the drama assumed in the reviewer's mind :

'Like so many critics, Mr. Courtney treats my works of art as if they were a scientific system of philosophy, although I have repeatedly stated in prefaces and elsewhere that the views in them are *seemings*, provisional impressions only, used for artistic purposes because they represent approximately the impressions of the age, and are plausible, till somebody produces better theories of the universe.

'As to his winding up about a God of Mercy, etc. — if I wished to make a smart retort, which I really should hate doing, I might say that the Good-God theory having, after some thousands of years of trial, produced the present infamous and disgraceful state of Europe — that most Christian Continent ! — a theory of a Goodless-and-Badless

God (as in *The Dynasts*) might perhaps be given a trial with advantage.

'Much confusion has arisen and much nonsense has been talked latterly in connection with the word "atheist". I have never understood how anybody can be one except in the sense of disbelieving in a tribal god, man-shaped, fiery-faced and tyrannous, who flies into a rage on the slightest provocation ; or as (according to Horace Walpole) Sir Francis Dashwood defined the Providence believed in by the Lord Shrewsbury of that date to be — a figure like an old angry man in a blue cloak. . . . Fifty meanings attach to the word "God" nowadays, the only reasonable meaning being the *Cause of Things*, whatever that cause may be.[1] Thus no modern thinker can be an atheist in the modern sense, while all modern thinkers are atheists in the ancient and exploded sense.'

In this connection he said once — perhaps oftener — that although invidious critics had cast slurs upon him as Nonconformist, Agnostic, Atheist, Infidel, Immoralist, Heretic, Pessimist, or something else equally opprobrious in their eyes, they had never thought of calling him what they might have called him much more plausibly — churchy ; not in an intellectual sense, but in so far as instincts and emotions ruled. As a child, to be a parson had been his dream ; moreover, he had had several clerical relatives who held livings ; while his grandfather, father, uncle, brother, wife, cousin, and two sisters had been musicians in various churches over a period covering altogether more than a hundred years. He himself had frequently read the church lessons, and had at one time as a young man begun reading for Cambridge with a view to taking Orders.

His vision had often been that of so many people brought up under Church of England influences, a giving of liturgical form to modern ideas, and expressing them in the same old buildings that had already seen previous reforms successfully carried out. He would say to his friends, the Warden of Keble, Arthur Benson, and others, that if the bishops only had a little courage, and would modify the liturgy by dropping preternatural assumptions out of it, few churchgoers would object to the change for long, and congregations would be trebled in a brief time. The idea was clearly expressed in the 'Apology' prefixed to *Late Lyrics and Earlier*.

'*June* 9. It is now the time of long days, when the sun seems reluctant to take leave of the trees at evening — the shine climbing

[1] In another place he says 'Cause' means really but the 'invariable antecedent'.

up the trunks, reappearing higher, and still fondly grasping the tree-tops till long after.'

Later in the month his friend J. M. Barrie suggested that Hardy should go with him to France, to which proposal Hardy replied :

'MAX GATE, DORCHESTER,
'23 *June* 1917.

'MY DEAR BARRIE,

'It was so kind of you to concoct that scheme for my accompanying you to the Front — or Back — in France. I thought it over carefully, as it was an attractive idea. But I have had to come to the conclusion that old men cannot be young men, and that I must content myself with the past battles of our country if I want to feel military. If I had been ten years younger I would have gone.

'I hope you will have a pleasant, or rather, impressive, time, and the good company you will be in will be helpful all round. I am living in hope of seeing you on the date my wife has fixed and of renewing acquaintance with my old friend Adelphi Terrace.

'Always sincerely yours,
'THOMAS HARDY.'

In July his poem 'Then and Now' was printed in *The Times*, and in the latter half of the month he and his wife paid a visit of two days to J. M. Barrie at Adelphi Terrace — a spot with which Hardy had had years of familiarity when their entertainer was still a child, and which was attractive to him on that account. Here they had some interesting meetings with other writers. Upon one memorable evening they sat in a large empty room, which was afterwards to be Sir James's study but was then being altered and decorated. From the windows they had a fine view over the Thames, and searchlights wheeled across the sky. The only illumination within the room was from candles placed on the floor to avoid breaking war regulations, which forbade too bright lighting.

He came back to pack up in August his MS. of *Moments of Vision* and send to the Messrs. Macmillan.

In October he went with Mrs. Hardy to Plymouth, calling for a day or two upon Mr. and Mrs. Eden Phillpotts at Torquay on their way. But the weather being wet at Plymouth they abandoned their stay there and came home.

'I hold that the mission of poetry is to record impressions, not convictions. Wordsworth in his later writings fell into the error of recording the latter. So also did Tennyson, and so do many poets when they grow old. *Absit omen!*

'I fear I have always been considered the Dark Horse of contemporary English literature.

'I was quick to bloom; late to ripen.

'I believe it would be said by people who knew me well that I have a faculty (possibly not uncommon) for burying an emotion in my heart or brain for forty years, and exhuming it at the end of that time as fresh as when interred. For instance, the poem entitled "The Breaking of Nations" contains a feeling that moved me in 1870, during the Franco-Prussian war, when I chanced to be looking at such an agricultural incident in Cornwall. But I did not write the verses till during the war with Germany of 1914, and onwards. Query: where was that sentiment hiding itself during more than forty years?'

Hardy's mind seems to have been running on himself at this time to a degree quite unusual with him, who often said — and his actions showed it — that he took no interest in himself as a personage.

'*November* 13. I was a child till I was 16; a youth till I was 25; a young man till I was 40 or 50.'

The above note on his being considered a Dark Horse was apt enough, when it is known that none of the society men who met him suspected from his simple manner the potentialities of observation that were in him. This unassertive air, unconsciously worn, served him as an invisible coat almost to uncanniness. At houses and clubs where he encountered other writers and critics and world-practised readers of character, whose bearing towards him was often as towards one who did not reach their altitudes, he was seeing through them as though they were glass. He set down some cutting and satirical notes on their qualities and compass, but destroyed all of them, not wishing to leave behind him anything which could be deemed a gratuitous belittling of others.

This month *Moments of Vision and Miscellaneous Verses* was published, and it may have been his occupation with the proofs that had set him thinking of himself; and also caused him to make the following entry: 'I do not expect much notice will be taken of these poems: they mortify the human sense of self-importance by showing, or suggesting, that human beings are of no matter or appreciable value in this nonchalant universe.' He subjoined the Dedication of *Sordello*, where the author remarks: 'My own faults of expression are many ; but with care for a man or book such would be sur-mounted, and without it what avails the faultlessness of either?'

It was in this mood that he read such reviews of the book as were sent him.

'*December* 31. *New Year's Eve.* Went to bed at eleven. East wind. No bells heard. Slept in the New Year, as did also those "out there".'

This refers to the poem called 'Looking Across' published in the new volume, Stinsford Churchyard lying across the mead from Max Gate.

PART VIII

LIFE'S DECLINE

# CHAPTER XXXIV

# REFLECTIONS ON POETRY

1918 : *Aet.* 77–78

On January 2 Hardy attended a performance of the women land-workers in the Corn Exchange. 'Met there Mrs. Alfred Lyttelton, Lady Shaftesbury, and other supporters of the movement. The girls looked most picturesque in their raiment of emancipation, which they evidently enjoyed wearing.'

Meanwhile the shadows lengthened. In the second week of the month he lost his warm-hearted neighbour, Mrs. A. Brinsley Sheridan, *née* Motley, of Frampton Court. 'An old friend of thirty-two years' standing. She was, I believe, the first to call when we entered this house at Max Gate, and she remained staunch to the end of her days.'

'*January* 16. As to reviewing. Apart from a few brilliant exceptions, poetry is not at bottom criticized as such, that is, as a particular man's artistic interpretation of life, but with a secret eye on its theological and political propriety. Swinburne used to say to me that so it would be two thousand years hence ; but I doubt it.

'As to pessimism. My motto is, first correctly diagnose the complaint — in this case human ills — and ascertain the cause : then set about finding a remedy if one exists. The motto or practice of the optimists is : Blind the eyes to the real malady, and use empirical panaceas to suppress the symptoms.

'Browning said (in a line cited against me so often) :

Never dreamed though right were worsted wrong would triumph.

'Well, that was a lucky dreamlessness for Browning. It kept him comfortably unaware of those millions who cry with the Chorus in *Hellas*: "Victorious Wrong, with vulture scream, Salutes the rising sun!"[1] — or with Hyllus in the *Trachiniae* : "Mark the vast injustice of the gods!"'[2]

'*January* 24. It is *the unwilling mind* that stultifies the contemporary criticism of poetry.'

[1] Shelley's *Hellas*, line 940.      [2] Sophocles' *Trachiniae*, 1266.

'*January* 25. The reviewer so often supposes that where Art is not visible it is unknown to the poet under criticism. Why does he not think of the art of concealing art? There is a good reason why.'

'*January* 30. English writers who endeavour to appraise poets, and discriminate the sheep from the goats, are apt to consider that all true poets must be of one pattern in their lives and developments. But the glory of poetry lies in its largeness, admitting among its creators men of infinite variety. They must all be impractical in the conduct of their affairs ; nay, they must almost, like Shelley or Marlowe, be drowned or done to death, or like Keats, die of consumption. They forgot that in the ancient world no such necessity was recognized ; that Homer sang as a blind old man, that Aeschylus wrote his best up to his death at nearly seventy, that the best of Sophocles appeared between his fifty-fifth and ninetieth years, that Euripides wrote up to seventy.

'Among those who accomplished late, the poetic spark must always have been latent ; but its outspringing may have been frozen and delayed for half a lifetime.'

'*January* 31. Performance of *The Mellstock Quire* at the Corn Exchange, Dorchester, by the local Company for Hospital purposes. Arranged for the admission of the present "Mellstock" Quire to see the resuscitated ghosts of their predecessors.'

The romantic name of 'Little Hintock' in *The Woodlanders* was advanced to a practical application in the February of this year by a request from Mr. Dampier Whetham, once Fellow and Tutor of Trinity College, Cambridge, whose hobby when in his Dorset home was dairy farming, to be allowed to define as the 'Hintock' herd, the fine breed of pedigree cattle he was establishing in the district which Hardy had described under that fictitious name.

In a United States periodical for March it was stated that 'Thomas Hardy is a realistic novelist who . . . has a grim determination to go down to posterity wearing the laurels of a poet'. This writer was a glaring illustration of the danger of reading motives into actions. Of course there was no 'grim determination', no thought of 'laurels'. Thomas Hardy was always a person with an unconscious, or rather unreasoning, *tendency*, and the poetic tendency had been his from the earliest. He would tell that it used to be said to him at Sir Arthur Blomfield's : 'Hardy, there can hardly have been anybody in the world with less ambition than you.' At this time the real state of his mind was, in his own words, that 'A sense of the truth of poetry, of its supreme place in literature, had awakened itself in me. At the risk of ruining all my worldly prospects I dabbled in it . . . was forced out of it. . . . It came back upon me. . . . All was of the nature of being led by a mood, without foresight, or regard to whither it led.'

*To Professor D. A. Robertson, University of Chicago*

'*February 7th*, 1918.

'In reply to your inquiry if I am likely to visit the United States after the war, I am sorry to say that such an event is highly improbable. . . .

'The opinion you quote from Lord Bryce to the effect that Americans do not think internationally, leads one to ask, Does any country think internationally? I should say, none. But there can be no doubt that some countries think thus more nearly than others ; and in my opinion the people of America far more than the people of England.'

In April there was sold at Christie's Red Cross Sale the manuscript of *Far from the Madding Crowd*. The interest of the latter — at least to Hardy himself — lay in the fact of it being a *revenant* — that for forty years he had had no other idea but that the manuscript had been 'pulped' after its use in the *Cornhill Magazine* in 1874, since it had completely disappeared, not having been sent back with the proofs. Hardy's rather whimsical regret was that he had not written it on better paper, unforeseeing the preservation. It afterwards came to his knowledge that after the sale it went to America, and ultimately was bought off a New York dealer for the collection of Mr. A. E. Newton of Pennsylvania.

'*April* 30. By the will of God some men are born poetical. Of these some make themselves practical poets, others are made poets by lapse of time who were hardly recognized as such. Particularly has this been the case with the translators of the Bible. They translated into the language of their age ; then the years began to corrupt that language as spoken, and to add grey lichen to the translation ; until the moderns who use the corrupted tongue marvel at the poetry of the old words. When new they were not more than half so poetical. So that Coverdale, Tyndale, and the rest of them are as ghosts what they never were in the flesh.'

'*May* 8.  A letter from Sir George Douglas carries me back to
Wimborne and the time when his brother Frank lived opposite us
there in the Avenue :

> They are great trees, no doubt, by now,
>     That were so thin in bough —
>         That row of limes —
> When we housed there ; I'm loth to reckon when ;
>     The world has turned so many times,
>         So many, since then !'

Whether any more of this poem was written is not known.

Two days later Hardy was seized with a violent cough and cold
which confined him for a week.  However, he was well enough by
the 23rd to adjudicate at the Police Court on several food-profiteering
cases, undertaken as being 'the only war-work I was capable of', and
to receive some old friends, including Sydney Cockerell, John Powys,
Lady Ilchester, and her mother, Lady Londonderry, of whom he
says : 'Never saw her again : I had known her for more than twenty-
five years'.  A little later came Mrs. Henry Allhusen, whom he had
known from her childhood, Sir Frederick Treves, and Mr. H. M.
and Mrs. Rosalind Hyndman (a charming woman), who were staying
at Dorchester for the benefit of the air.

Some sense of the neglect of poetry by the modern English may
have led him to write at this time :

'The poet is like one who enters and mounts a platform to give
an address as announced.  He opens his page, looks around, and
finds the hall — *empty*.'

A little later he says :

'It bridges over the years to think that Gray might have seen
Wordsworth in his cradle, and Wordsworth might have seen me in
mine.'

Some days later :

'The people in Shakespeare act as if they were not quite closely
thinking of what they are doing, but were great philosophers giving
the main of their mind to the general human situation.

'I agree with Tennyson, who said he could form no idea how
Shakespeare came to write his plays.

'My opinion is that a poet should express the emotion of all the
ages and the thought of his own.'

# CHAPTER XXXV

# POETICAL QUESTIONS: AND MELLSTOCK CLUB-ROOM

1918–1919 : *Aet.* 78–79

'*Sunday, June* 2. Seventy-eighth birthday. Several letters.' Among others was an interesting one from a lady who informed him that some years earlier she had been made the happiest woman in the world by accidentally meeting for the first time, by the 'Druid Stone' on his lawn, at the late Mrs. Hardy's last garden-party, the man who was now her husband. And a little later came one he much valued, from a man he long had known — Mr. Charles Moule, Senior Fellow and President of Corpus, Cambridge, enclosing a charming poem to Hardy as his 'almost lifelong friend . . . Too seldom seen since far-off times' — times when the two had visited mediæval buildings together, and dived from a boat on summer mornings into the green water of Weymouth Bay.

In September 1918 he received a circular letter asking him to assist in bringing home to people certain facts relating to the future with a view to finding a remedy, and stating that, 'It is agreed by all students of modern military methods that this war, horrible as it seems to us, is merciful in comparison with what future wars must be. Scientific munition-making is only in its infancy. The next world-war, if there is another, will find the nations provided not with thousands, but with hundreds of thousands of submarines, and all these as far surpassing the present types in power and destructiveness as they surpass the feeble beginnings of ten years ago. . . .'

In his reply he remarked :

'If it be all true that the letter prophesies, I do not think a world in which such fiendishness is possible to be worth the saving. Better let Western "civilization" perish, and the black and yellow races have a chance.

'However, as a meliorist (not a pessimist as they say) I think better of the world.'

'*December* 31. New Year's Eve. Did not sit up.'

At the beginning of the year 1919 Hardy received a letter and volume of verses from Miss Amy Lowell, the American poetess, who reminded him of her call at the beginning of the war — 'two bedraggled ladies', herself and her friend. Hardy did remember, and their consternation lest they should not be able to get back to their own country.

In February he signed a declaration of sympathy with the Jews in support of a movement for 'the reconstitution of Palestine as a National Home for the Jewish People', and during the spring he received letters from Quiller-Couch, Crichton-Browne, and other friends on near and dear relatives they had lost in the war ; about the same time there appeared a relevant poem by Hardy in the *Athenæum* which was much liked, entitled in words from the Burial Service, 'According to the Mighty Working'.

In May Edmund Gosse wrote that he was very curious to know who drew the rather unusual illustration on the cover of the first edition of *The Trumpet-Major*. Hardy was blank on the matter for a time, until, finding a copy, he remembered that he drew it himself.

Being in London for a few days the same month he went to the dinner of the Royal Academy — the first held since the war — with his friend J. M. Barrie, with whom he was then staying, and was saddened to find how many of the guests and Academicians that he had been formerly accustomed to meet there had disappeared from the scene. He felt that he did not wish to go again, and, indeed, he never did. Among the incidents of this visit was a meeting at Lady St. Helier's with Dr. Bernard, Archbishop of Dublin, and a discussion with him on Coverdale's translation of the Psalms, and the inferiority of the Latin Vulgate in certain passages of them, with which Dr. Bernard agreed, sending him afterwards the two versions in parallel readings.

On his birthday in June he did what he had long intended to do — took his wife and sister to Salisbury by the old road which had been travelled by his and their forefathers in their journeys to London — via Blandford, Woodyates Inn, and Harnham Hill, whence Constable had painted his famous view of the cathedral, and where the track was still accessible to wheels. Woodyates Inn — now no longer such, to the surprise of everybody since the revival of road traffic — still retained its genial hostelry appearance, and reminded Hardy of the entry in the diary of one of the daughters of George the Third after she and the rest of the family had halted there : 'At Woodyates Inn . . . had a beastly breakfast'. It is said that Browning's great-grandfather was once the landlord of this famous inn.

In a reply to a letter of this date concerning a new literary periodical started in Canada, he adds, after some commendatory remarks :

'But why does the paper stultify its earlier articles by advertising "The Best Sellers"? Of all marks of the *un*-literary journal this is the clearest. If the *Canadian Bookman* were to take a new line and advertise eulogistically the *worst* sellers, it might do something towards its object.'

Replying to a birthday letter from Mrs. Arthur Henniker, Hardy writes :

'MAX GATE, 5 *June* 1919.

'Sincere thanks for your good wishes, my dear friend, which I echo back towards you. I should care more for my birthdays if at each succeeding one I could see any sign of real improvement in the world — as at one time I fondly hoped there was ; but I fear that what appears much more evident is that it is getting worse and worse. All development is of a material and scientific kind — and scarcely any addition to our knowledge is applied to objects philanthropic and ameliorative. I almost think that people were less pitiless towards their fellow-creatures — human and animal — under the Roman Empire than they are now ; so why does not Christianity throw up the sponge and say, I am beaten, and let another religion take its place?

'I suddenly remember that we had a call from our Bishop and his wife two or three days ago, so that perhaps it is rather shabby of me to write as above. By a curious coincidence we had motored to Salisbury that very day, and were in his cathedral when he was at our house.

'Do you mean to go to London for any length of time this summer? We are not going again till I don't know when. We squeezed a good deal into the four days we were there, and I got a bad throat as usual, but it has gone off. At Lady St. Helier's we met the Archbishop of Dublin (English Church), and found him a pleasant man. We also met several young poets at Barrie's, where we were staying.

'We do hope you are well — in "rude health" as they call it. Florence sends her love, and I am,

'Ever affectionately,

'TH. H.'

Shortly after his birthday he received a charming volume of holograph poems, beautifully bound, from some forty or fifty living

poets. The mark of recognition so appealed to him that he determined to answer every one of the contributors by letter, and ultimately did so, though it took him a long while; saying that if they
could take the trouble to write the poems he could certainly take the
trouble to write the letters. It was almost his first awakening to the
consciousness that an opinion had silently grown up as it were in the
night, that he was no mean power in the contemporary world of poetry.

This 'Poets' Tribute' had been arranged by his friend Siegfried
Sassoon, who brought the gift and placed it in Hardy's hand.

It had impressed him all the more as coming just after his reading
quite by chance in an Australian paper a quotation from a recent
English review of his verse — belittling one of the poems — that
called 'On Sturminster Foot-Bridge' — in a manner that showed the
critic to be quite unaware of what was called 'onomatopoeia' in
poetry, the principle on which the lines had been composed. They
were intended to convey by their rhythm the impression of a clucking
of ripples into riverside holes when blown upon by an up-stream
wind; so that when his reviewer jested on the syllables of the verse
sounding like milk in a cart he was simply stating that the author had
succeeded in doing what he had tried to do — the sounds being
similar. As the jest by the English review had come back to England
from Australia, where it had been quoted to Hardy's damage without
the context, he took the trouble to explain the matter to the writer
of the article, which he would probably have left undone if it had not
so frequently happened that his intentions were shown up as blunders.
But he did not get a more satisfactory reply than that the critics, like
the writer, were sheep in wolves' clothing, and meant no harm.

Hardy's loyalty to his friends was shown by his devotion to the
Moule family, members of which he had known intimately when he
was a young man. The following is probably the last letter he wrote
to one whom he could remember as a small boy:

'29 *June* 1919.

'MY DEAR BISHOP OF DURHAM,

'You may agree with me in thinking it a curious coincidence that
the evening before your letter arrived, and when it probably was just
posted, we were reading a chapter in Job, and on coming to the verse,
"All the days of my appointed time will I wait, till my change come",
I interrupted and said: "That was the text of the Vicar of Fordington
one Sunday evening about 1860". And I can hear his voice repeating

the text as the sermon went on — in the way they used to repeat it in those days — just as if it were yesterday. I wonder if you have ever preached from that text; I daresay you have. I should add that he delivered his discourse without note of any kind.

'My warm thanks for your good feeling about my birthday. The thoughts of friends about one at these times take off some of the sadness they bring as one gets old.

'The study of your father's life (too short, really) has interested me much. I well remember the cholera years in Fordington; you might have added many details. For instance, every morning a man used to wheel the clothing and bed-linen of those who had died in the night out into the mead, where the Vicar had a large copper set. Some was boiled there, and some burnt. He also had large fires kindled in Mill Street to carry off infection. An excellent plan I should think.

'Many thanks, too, for the volume of poems which duly came. 'Apollo at Pherae' seems to me remarkably well constructed in "plot", and the verse facile: I don't quite know how you could have acquired such readiness at such an early date, and the influence of Milton is not excessive — at least I think not.

'I hope you will let us know when you come this way again.'

*August.* The Collected edition of Hardy's poems was published about this time in two volumes, the first containing the shorter poems, and the second *The Dynasts.*

*October.* A curious question arose in Hardy's mind at this date on whether a romancer was morally justified in going to extreme lengths of assurance — after the manner of Defoe — in respect of a tale he knew to be absolutely false. Thirty-seven years earlier, when much pressed to produce something of the nature of a fireside yarn, he had invented a picturesque account of a stealthy nocturnal visit to England by Napoleon in 1804, during the war, to spy out a good spot for invasion. Being struck with the extreme improbability of such a story, he added a circumstantial framework describing it as an old local tradition to blind the reader to the hoax. When it was published he was much surprised at people remarking to him: 'I see you have made use of that well-known tradition of Napoleon's landing'. He then supposed that, strange as it seemed, such a story must have been in existence without his knowledge, and that perhaps the event had happened. So the matter rested till the time at which we have arrived, when a friend who was interested made inquiries, and was assured by historians and annalists whom he consulted that such a visit would have been fatuous, and wellnigh impossible. Moreover, that there had never existed any such improbable tradition. Hence arose Hardy's aforesaid case of conscience as to being too natural in the art he could practise so well. Had he not long discontinued the writing of romances he would, he said, have put at the beginning of each new one: 'Understand that however true this book may be in essence, in fact it is utterly untrue'.

Being interested in a dramatic case of piracy on the high seas, which might have happened a hundred or two hundred years before, Hardy and his wife went to the October assizes, on the invitation of Mr. Justice Darling, and sat through the case. Such sensational trials came to quiet Dorset whenever the port of landing was in the county, even if they happened a thousand miles off.

On October 30 the following was written at his request:

'In reply to your letter I write for Mr. Hardy, who is in bed with a chill, to say that he cannot furnish you with any biographical details. . . . To your inquiry if *Jude the Obscure* is autobiographical, I have to answer that there is not a scrap of personal detail in it, it having the least to do with his own life of all his books. The rumour, if it still persists, was started some years ago. Speaking generally, there is more autobiography in a hundred lines of Mr. Hardy's poetry than in all the novels.'

It is a tribute to Hardy's powers of presentation that readers would not for many years believe that such incidents as Jude's being smacked when bird-keeping, his driving a baker's cart, his working as a journeyman mason, as also many situations described in verse, were not actual transcripts from the writer's personal experience, although the briefest reference to biographical date-books would have shown the impossibility of anything of the sort.

Hardy had been asked this autumn if he would object to a representation of some of the scenes in *The Dynasts* by the Oxford University Dramatic Society in the following year, and on his making no objection some correspondence ensued with the President and Manager on certain details.

*To Mr. Maurice Colbourne*

'*November* 11, 1919.

'Your plan for showing the out-of-doors scenes is very ingenious and attractive — and more elaborate than I imagined, my idea having been just a backcloth coloured greyish-blue, and a floorcloth coloured greenish-grey — a purely conventional representation for all open-air scenes. . . . My feeling was the same as yours about the Strophe and Antistrophe — that they should be unseen, and, as it were, speaking from the sky. But it is, as you hint, doubtful if the two ladies will like to have their charms hidden. Would boys do instead, or ugly ladies with good voices? But I do not wish to influence largely your methods of presentation. It will be of the greatest interest to me, whether I can get to Oxford for the performance or not, to see how the questions that arise in doing the thing have been grappled with by younger brains than mine.'

'*November* 18. To my father's grave (he was born Nov. 18, 1811) with F. [Mrs. Hardy]. The funeral psalm formerly sung at the graveside to the tune of "St. Stephen" was the xc. in Tate and Brady's version. Whether Dr. Watts's version, beginning "O God, our help in ages past" — said to be a favourite with Gladstone — was written before or after T. and B.'s (from Coverdale's prose of the same psalm) I don't know, but I think it inferior to the other, which contains some good and concise verse, *e.g.*,
    'T. and B. :

> For in Thy sight a thousand years
>     Are like a day that's past,
> Or like a watch at dead of night
>     Whose hours unnumbered waste.
> Thou sweep'st us off as with a flood,
>     We vanish hence like dreams. . . .

'Watts (more diffusely) :

> A thousand ages in Thy sight
>     Are like an evening gone ;
> Short as the watch that ends the night
>     Before the rising sun.
> Time, like an ever-rolling stream,
>     Bears all its sons away ;
> They fly forgotten, as a dream
>     Dies at the opening day.'

In December Sir George Douglas writes concerning a lecture he is going to give in Edinburgh on Hardy's poems, and incidentally remarks : 'Those Aeschylean poems in *The Past and the Present* . . .

how would Wordsworth have regarded them, I wonder, differing so markedly as they do from his view of Nature?' His friend Sir Frederick Pollock also sent a letter containing an impromptu scene of a humorous kind : 'Overheard at the sign of the Mermaid in Elysium', purporting to be a conversation between the shades of Shakespeare, Campion, and Heine, 'on a book newly received' — (*i.e.* Hardy's Collected Poems) — in which Shakespeare says :

> 'Twas pretty wit, friend Thomas, that you spoke ;
> You take the measure of my Stratford folk,

the lines referring to Hardy's poem 'To Shakespeare after three hundred years'.

In December he opened a village war memorial in the form of a club-room in Bockhampton. It was close to his first school, erected, as has been told, by the manor lady of his early affections, and here he danced, for the last time in his life, with the then lady of the manor. The room was erected almost on the very spot where had stood Robert Reason's shoe-making shop when Hardy was a boy, described in *Under the Greenwood Tree* as 'Mr. Robert Penny's'.

A speech made by Hardy at the opening of the Bockhampton Reading-room and Club on the 2nd December 1919 was not reported in any newspaper, but the following extracts from it may be of interest :

'I feel it an honour — and an honour of a very interesting kind — to have been asked by your President to open this Club as a memorial to the gallant men of this parish who fought in the last great war — a parish I know so well, and which is only about a mile from my own door.

'This room is, it seems, to be called "The Mellstock Club". I fancy I have heard the name of "Mellstock" before. But we will let that pass. . . .

'The village of Bockhampton has had various owners. In the time of the Conqueror it belonged to a Norman countess ; later to a French Priory ; and in the time of Queen Elizabeth to the Dean and Chapter of Exeter, who at the beginning of the last century sold it to Mr. Morton Pitt, a cousin of Pitt the Premier. What a series of scenes does this bare list of owners bring back!

'At one time Bockhampton had a water-mill. Where was that mill, I wonder? It had a wood. Where was that wood?

'To come to my own recollections. From times immemorial the

village contained several old Elizabethan houses, with mullioned windows and doors, of Ham Hill stone. They stood by the withy bed. I remember seeing some of them in process of being pulled down, but some were pulled down before I was born. To this attaches a story. Mr. Pitt, by whose orders it was done, came to look on, and asked one of the men several questions as to why he was doing it in such and such a way. Mr. Pitt was notorious for his shabby clothes, and the labourer, who did not know him, said at last, 'Look here, old chap, don't you ask so many questions, and just go on. Anybody would think the house was yours!" Mr. Pitt obeyed orders, and meekly went on, murmuring, "Well, 'tis mine, after all!"

'Then there were the Poor-houses, I remember — just at the corner turning down to the dairy. These were the homes of the parish paupers before workhouses were built. In one of them lived an old man who was found one day rolling on the floor, with a lot of pence and halfpence scattered round him. They asked him what was the matter, and he said he had heard of people rolling in money, and he thought that for once in his life he would do it, to see what it was like.

'Then there used to be dancing parties at Christmas, and some weeks after. This kind of party was called a Jacob's Join, in which every guest contributed a certain sum to pay the expenses of the entertainment — it was mostly half-a-crown in this village. They were very lively parties I believe. The curious thing is that the man who used to give the house-room for the dances lived in a cottage which stood exactly where this Club-house stands now — so that when you dance here you will be simply carrying on the tradition of the spot.

'In conclusion, I have now merely to say I declare the Mellstock Club and reading-room to be open.'

To a correspondent, on December 30, Hardy writes :

'I am sorry to say that your appeal for a poem that should be worthy of the event of the 8th August 1918 reaches me at too late a time of life to attempt it. . . . The outline of such a poem, which you very cleverly sketch, is striking, and ought to result at the hands of somebody or other who may undertake it, in a literary parallel to the "Battle of Prague" — a piece of music which ceased to be known long before your time, but was extraordinarily popular in its day — reproducing the crashing of guns nearer and nearer, the groans of the wounded, and the final fulfilment, with great fidelity.

'The length of the late war exhausted me of all my impromptu poems dealing with that tragedy. . . . I quite think that one of our young poets would rise to the occasion if you were to give him the opportunity.'

This year went out quietly with Hardy, as is shown by the brief entry : 'New Year's Eve.  Did not sit up.'

CHAPTER XXXVI

# 'THE DYNASTS' AT OXFORD; HON. DEGREE; A DEPUTATION; A CONTROVERSY

1920; *Aet.* 79–80

'*January* 19. Coming back from Talbothays by West Stafford Cross I saw Orion upside-down in a pool of water under an oak.'

On February 2 Hardy was invited to receive an honorary degree of Doctor of Letters during the time he was to be in Oxford at the performance of *The Dynasts* at the theatre, which he had promised to attend; and on the 9th he set out by train for Oxford with Mrs. Hardy, though the members of the O.U.D.S. had offered to send a car for him all the way. The day was unusually fine for February, and they were met at the station by enthusiastic representatives of the society, driven round Oxford, and conducted to the house of Sir Walter and Lady Raleigh, who were their hosts.

The next day, after lunching with friends, they went to the Sheldonian and the degree was received.

In presenting Hardy, the Public Orator, Mr. A. D. Godley, made one of the most felicitous of his many excellent speeches. He said:

'Scilicet ut Virgilio nostro sic huic quoque "molle atque facetum adnuerunt gaudentes rure Camenae". Hic est, qui divini gloriam ruris sicut nemo alius nostrorum idylliis suis intertexuit: hic est, qui agricolarum sensus et colloquia ita vivide verbis effinxit ut videre rusticos consessus, ut ipsos inter se sermocinantes, cum legimus, audire videamur. Obruit multos cita oblivio qui in rebus transitoriis versantur: qui insitos animorum sensus et naturae humanae immutabilitatem exprimit, cuius scripta aeternam silvarum et camporum amoenitatem spirant, hunc diu vivum per ora virum volitaturum esse praedicimus. Quid quod idem in poesi quoque eo evasit ut hoc solo scribendi genere, nisi fabularum narratio vel magis suum aliquid et proprium habeat, immortalem famam assequi possit?'[1]

[1] 'Surely as with Virgil, so with him, have the Muses that rejoice in the countryside approved his smoothness and elegance. This is he who has interwoven in his (pastoral) poems, as no other has done, the (heavenly) glory of the (heavenly) countryside: this

397

And then, after a reference to the production that evening by the O.U.D.S. of *The Dynasts* — 'opus eius tam scriptoris facundia quam rerum quae tractantur magnitudine insignitum'[1] — he concluded :

'Nunc ut homini si quis alius Musis et dis agrestibus amico titulum debitum dando, non tantum illi quantum nobis ipsis decus addatis, duco ad vos senem illustrem Thomam Hardy. . . .'[2]

His wife, Evelyn Gifford, and her sister were present among others. Evelyn, daughter of the late Archdeacon Gifford, was his bright and affectionate cousin by marriage, whom Hardy was never to see again. Had he known it when he was parting from her outside the Sheldonian in the rain that afternoon, his heart would have been heavier than it was.

In the afternoon he met the Poet-Laureate (Robert Bridges), Mr. Masefield, and many friends at the Raleighs', and also at the theatre in the evening, from which they did not return till one o'clock — the whole day having been of a most romantic kind.

AN ACCOUNT OF THOMAS HARDY'S COMING TO OXFORD in 1920 to
    witness a performance of *The Dynasts* by the Oxford University
    Dramatic Society, and of a later meeting with him in Dorchester
    when *A Desperate Remedy* was produced there : written in
    1929, at Mrs. Hardy's request, by Charles Morgan, who in 1920
    was Manager for the O.U.D.S., in 1921 its President, and after-
    wards dramatic critic of *The Times*.

When the University reassembled after the war, the Oxford University Dramatic Society was in low water. The tradition was broken, the surviving membership was not more than half a dozen, and the treasury was empty. During 1919 new members joined and life began to flicker in the Society, but its future largely depended

---

is he who has portrayed in words the feelings and conversations of rustics so clearly that when we read of them we seem to picture their meetings and hear them discoursing one with another. Speedy forgetfulness overwhelms many who treat of life's fleeting things, but of him who unfolds the inborn feelings of man's soul and the unchangeable-ness of his nature, whose writings breathe the eternal charm of (the) woods and fields, we foretell that his living fame shall long hover on the lips of men.

'Why now, is not the excellence of his poems such that, by this type of writing alone, he can achieve immortal fame, even if the narration of his stories has not something about them more peculiarly his own ?'

[1] 'His work marked not only by the eloquence of the author, but by the magnitude of the events which he describes.'

[2] 'Now that you may confer distinction, not so much on him as on our own selves, by granting a deserved title to one who is a friend of the Muses and pastoral gods, I present to you the revered and renowned Thomas Hardy.'

upon the success or failure of the first annual play in the new series.

An undergraduate was instructed to consider, during the long vacation of 1919, what play should be performed and to report to the Committee. His choice was *The Dynasts*, and he had to defend it against those who objected that it was not Shakespearian and that Shakespeare was a tradition of the Society : and against those more dangerous critics who said that *The Dynasts* would be costly, and, pointing to the balance-sheet, asked whence the money would come. The financial objection was at last overcome by personal guarantees.

The Committee endorsed the choice, and the Vice-Chancellor, whose special consent was needed for the performance of so modern a work, allowed it. The arguments in its favour were, indeed, unanswerable.

*The Dynasts* was unique in literature, an epic-drama without predecessor in its own kind. Its writer was a living Englishman : its subject was closely linked with the tragedy in which nearly all the players had lately participated : and, except for those who had seen Granville-Barker's production, it would be a new theatrical experience.

One difficulty remained : the play was copyright, and it seemed to us very probable that Hardy would refuse permission to perform it. He is an old man, we said, and set fast in Dorset ; he will not give a fig for what he will call amateur theatricals, nor will he be troubled with our affairs. It was the impression of us all that he would be forbidding and formidable, and he was approached with misgiving. He gave his play to us, not grudgingly nor with any air of patronage, but with so gracious a courtesy that we were made to feel that he was genuinely pleased to find young men eager to perform his work. I do not remember the text of his reply to the original request, but I remember well the impression made by it — an impression increased by his later correspondence. Long before he came to Oxford his individuality had become established among us. Without whittling away his legend by any of the affectations of modesty, he had, by his gentle plainness, banished our fear of it.

Even so, when we invited him and Mrs. Hardy to come to Oxford to see the play, we had little hope that he would accept, for our ideas had overestimated his age — or, rather, underestimated the vigour of it — and his withdrawal into Wessex was believed to be permanent. But he said he would come, and Sir Walter Raleigh invited him to be his guest. So soon as it was known that he would visit Oxford, everyone perceived what hitherto few had been able to perceive — that, in withholding her highest honour from the author of *The*

*Dynasts* and *The Return of the Native* (perhaps, whispered Cambridge and the world, because he was also the author of *Jude the Obscure*), Christminster was making herself ridiculous. A D.C.L. was offered him. Authority must have sighed with relief when he did not refuse.

It fell to me to meet him at the station. I give my impression of him then and afterwards, not because it is of value as being mine, but for two reasons — first, that Mrs. Hardy has asked it ; secondly, that I should dearly love to see some great writer of the past as a contemporary undergraduate saw him. In days to come, even so slight a record as this may have an interest that it cannot now possess.

Hardy made it easy for a young man to be his host — made it easy, not by any loose affability of manner or by a parade of that heartiness which, in too many celebrated men, is a form of patronage, but simply by making no attempt whatever to impress or to startle me. I had not expected cleverness or volubility in him ; and his speech was, at first, slight and pleasantly conventional. He introduced me to Mrs. Hardy, asked how long the drive would be to Sir Walter's, used, in brief, the small talk of encounter, giving me time to become accustomed to his presence and to break free of the thought : I must remember this ; I shall remember and tell of it when I am an old man. He himself seemed to me prodigiously old, not because there was any failure in his powers — he was, on the contrary, sprightly, alert, bird-like — but because his head had an appearance of being much older than his body, his neck having the thinness and his brow the tightness of great age, and his eyes — so old that age itself seemed to have swung full circle within them — being the eyes of some still young man who had been keeping watch at sea since the beginning of time. I remember that, sitting opposite him in the cab, I began to think of the sea and to imagine his head appearing above the bridge-ladder of a warship. Then I thought of a bird again, a small bird with a great head. And I made another discovery that pleased me : in external things he was deeply old-fashioned, and, fearing perhaps some assertive, new-fangled conduct in an undergraduate, timid and a little suspicious. I knew at once that I had nothing to fear from an old gentleman who by no means wished to pretend that he was young, and would never embarrass me by forsaking those little formalities of ordinary behaviour to which I myself had been trained.

Thus, because he made no attempt to break it, the ice melted easily and naturally. He asked of the play, saying that it had not been intended for the stage and that he wondered at our having chosen it.

Then, breaking off from this and reminded, I think, by Mrs. Hardy, he said : 'We thought we should like to make a little tour of Oxford before going out to the Raleighs'. I don't know it well as it is to-day, and Mrs. Hardy knows it less.' He knew it, however, well enough to have planned a route with precision. We drove slowly, stopping now and then when he commanded it, and of each place he spoke in a different tone as if some mood were connected with it. *Jude* was, of course, the inevitable thought of one who had read that book in a midshipman's hammock when to him also Oxford was a beckoning dream. It seemed very strange to be driving solemnly down the High and up the Broad with the author of *Jude*. It seemed strange because, after all, it was so natural. Here was an old man taking a normal and reasonable interest in the place where he was — quietly 'seeing the sights' in the fashion of his own time and without the self-consciousness of ours.

But when we are undergraduates we expect writers to be literary men in all things ; we cannot easily dissociate them from their works ; and it seemed to me very odd that Thomas Hardy should bother about the Martyrs' Memorial.

When the tour was over, we went forward towards our destination. Hardy began to ask me about the age of undergraduates, and what effect the war has had upon us. I told him that my own war service delivered me from one examination and from compulsory chapels. 'Compulsory chapels . . .' said Hardy, and no more ; then, opening a little case on the seat beside him and producing from it a handful of small volumes, he asked me if I knew what they were. 'Poems', he said, 'written by young men. They very kindly send them to me.' Very kindly — was there irony in that? But Hardy, reading my thought, dismissed it. He left no doubt that he was glad to have these volumes sent to him, seeing in them a tribute to himself as a poet, not a novelist — and he cared deeply for that. And from this there came to me an opportunity to ask a question that I had been afraid to ask : whether he would ever write another tale? 'No,' he answered, 'I gave it up long ago. I wanted to write poetry in the beginning ; now I can. Besides, it is so long since I wrote a novel that novel readers must have forgotten me.' And, when I had said something, he added : 'No. Much depends on the public expectation. If I wrote a story now, they would want it to be what the old ones were. Besides, my stories are written.'

I have no recollection of any conversation after that, nor any picture of Hardy in my mind until, going to Dorchester in 1922 to see the Hardy Players perform a dramatization of *Desperate Remedies*, I was invited by him to Max Gate, where we sat round the fire after tea and he told me of his early days in London, and how he would go to Shakespearian plays with the text in his hands and, seated in the front rows, follow the dialogue by the stage light. He told me, too, that he had written a stage version of *Tess*, and something of its early history; how, after the success of the novel, the great ones of the earth had pressed him to dramatize it; how he had done so, and the play had been prepared for the stage; by what mischance the performance of it had been prevented. Where was it now?

In a drawer. Would he allow it to be performed? He smiled, gave no answer, and began at once to talk of criticism — first of dramatic criticism which, he said, in the few newspapers that took it seriously was better than literary criticism, the dramatic critics having less time 'to rehearse their prejudices'; then of literary criticism itself — a subject on which he spoke with a bitterness that surprised me. The origin of this bitterness was in the past where, I believe, there was indeed good reason for it, but it was directed now against contemporary critics of his own work, and I could not understand what general reason he had to complain of them. He used no names; he spoke with studied reserve, sadly rather than querulously; but he was persuaded — and there is evidence of this persuasion in the preface to the posthumous volume of his verse — that critics approached his work with an ignorant prejudice against his 'pessimism' which they allowed to stand in the way of fair reading and fair judgment.

This was a distortion of facts as I knew them. It was hard to believe that Hardy honestly thought that his genius was not recognized; harder to believe that he thought his work was not read. Such a belief indicated the only failure of balance, the only refusal to seek the truth, which I perceived in Hardy, and I was glad when the coming of a visitor, who was, I think, secretary of the Society of Dorset Men, led him away from criticism to plainer subjects. When the time came for me to go, seeing that he proposed to come out with me, I tried to restrain him, for the night was cold; but he was determined, and Mrs. Hardy followed her own wise course of matching her judgment with his vitality. So he came down among the trees to the dark road, and I saw the last of him standing outside his gate with a lantern swaying in his hand. I shall not know a greater man, nor have I ever known one who had, in the same degree, Hardy's power of drawing reverence towards affection.

He was not simple ; he had the formal subtlety peculiar to his own generation ; there was something deliberately 'ordinary' in his demeanour which was a concealment of extraordinary fires — a method of self-protection common enough in my grandfather's generation, though rare now.

There are many who might have thought him unimpressive because he was content to be serious and determined to be unspectacular. But his was the kind of character to which I lay open. He was an artist, proud of his art, who yet made no parade of it ; he was a traditionalist and, therefore, suspicious of fashion ; he had that sort of melancholy, the absence of which in any man has always seemed to me to be a proclamation of blindness.

There was in him something timid as well as something fierce, as if the world had hurt him and he expected it to hurt him again. But what fascinated me above all was the contrast between the plainness, the quiet rigidity of his behaviour, and the, passionate boldness of his mind, for this I had always believed to be the tradition of English genius, too often and too extravagantly denied.

*To Mr. Joseph McCabe, who wrote proposing to include Hardy in a Biographical Dictionary of Modern Rationalists*

'*February* 18, 1920.

'DEAR SIR,

'As Mr. Hardy has a cold which makes writing trying to his eyes, I answer your letter for him. He says he thinks he is rather an irrationalist than a rationalist, on account of his inconsistencies. He has, in fact, declared as much in prefaces to some of his poems, where he explains his views as being mere impressions that frequently change. Moreover, he thinks he could show that no man is a rationalist, and that human actions are not ruled by reason at all in the last resort. But this, of course, is outside the question. So that he cannot honestly claim to belong to the honourable body you are including in your dictionary, whom he admires for their straightforward sincerity and permanent convictions, though he does not quite · think they can claim their title.

'Yours very truly,

'F. E. HARDY.'

On March 7, 1920, Hardy writes to an old friend of nearly fifty years' standing, Mr. John Slater, F.R.I.B.A. :

L.T.H.—2 D

'. . . As to your question whether I should like to be nominated as an Hon. Fellow of the R.I.B.A., I really don't know what to say. Age has naturally made me, like Gallio, care for none of these things, at any rate very much, especially as I am hardly ever in London. But at the same time I am very conscious of the honour of such a proposition, and like to be reminded in such a way that I once knew what a T-square was. So, shall I leave the decision to your judgment?'

Hardy was duly nominated and elected, and it was a matter of regret to him that he could not attend the meetings of the Institute, held still in the same old room in Conduit Street in which he had received the prize medal for his essay in 1863 from the hands of Sir Gilbert Scott. Mr. John Slater was almost the only surviving friend of Hardy's architectural years in London since the death of Arthur Blomfield.

'*March* 25. Joined National Committee for acquiring Wentworth Place — the house once occupied by John Keats.'

'*April* 7. A would-be author, not without humour, writing from South Africa for a "foreword" from me, adds : "Mr. Balfour when writing asked me not to use his remarks mentioning the number of books sent him from all parts of the world (for forewords). But mental dexterity greatly inferior to yours, Sir, could contrive to do somewhat, and yet avoid the consequences contemplated" — *i.e.* multitudes of other would-be novelists asking the same favour.'

'*April* 21. Went with F. to St. Margaret's, Westminster, to the wedding of Harold Macmillan and Lady Dorothy Cavendish. Sat with Lord Morley, and signed as one of the witnesses. Morley, seeing Bryce close by us, and the Duke of Devonshire near, whispered to F., "Which weigh most, three O.M.'s or one Duke?"'

This was Hardy's last visit to London. He, with his wife, stayed for two nights only at J. M. Barrie's flat, so near the house in Adelphi Terrace where he had worked as an architect's assistant nearly sixty years before.

'*May* 14. Motored with F. and K. to Exeter. Called on the Granville-Barkers at Sidmouth. Cathedral service : the beautiful anthem "God is gone up" (Croft). Well sung. Psalms to Walker in E flat. Felt I should prefer to be a cathedral organist to anything in the world. "Bidding my organ obey, calling its keys to their work, claiming each slave of the sound." A fine May day.'

At the end of May a letter came from C. W. Moule in reply to Hardy's note of sympathy on his loss of his only remaining brother,

Handley, the Bishop of Durham, with whom Hardy had had occasion to correspond the year before. As it was the last letter Hardy received from his correspondent, who himself passed away within the next year, the following passages are quoted:

'In condolence "the half is more than the whole", as the wise Greek paradox saith (πλέον ἥμισυ παντός). . . . Your friendly acceptance of those stanzas was answered by me, but that in which you told me that dear Horace was one of "The Five Students" in *Moments of Vision* I fear was never answered. . . . I did not know of Handley's nearness in age to your sister Mary (they were only two days apart), nor did I know that your mother and mine knew each other well enough to compare notes on the point. . . . I am glad you saw him at Max Gate. We wish that we could see you here. I may try to send you some book in memoriam H. C. G. M. . . . "Not one is there among us that understandeth any more", as a snapshot of the current generation, is worthy of you.' [Hardy had quoted the words from the 74th Psalm in the letter to which this was an answer, alluding probably to the memories familiar to all three.]

On June 2nd of this year came Hardy's eightieth birthday, and he received a deputation from the Society of Authors, consisting of Mr. Augustine Birrell, Sir Anthony Hope Hawkins, and Mr. John Galsworthy. The occasion was a pleasant one, and the lunch lively. Many messages were received during the day, including one from the King, the Lord Mayor of London, the Cambridge Vice-Chancellor, and the Prime Minister.

Hardy pencilled down the following as 'Birthday notes':

'When, like the Psalmist, "I call mine own ways to remembrance", I find nothing in them that quite justifies this celebration.

'The value of old age depends upon the person who reaches it. To some men of early performance it is useless. To others, who are late to develop, it just enables them to complete their job.

'We have visited two cathedrals during the last month, and I could not help feeling that if men could get a little more of the reposefulness and peace of those buildings into their lives how much better it would be for them.

'Nature's indifference to the advance of her species along what we are accustomed to call civilized lines makes the late war of no importance to her, except as a sort of geological fault in her continuity.

'Though my life, like the lives of my contemporaries, covers a period of more material advance in the world than any of the same length can have done in other centuries, I do not find that real

civilization has advanced equally. People are not more humane, so far
as I can see, than they were in the year of my birth. Disinterested
kindness is less. The spontaneous goodwill that used to characterize
manual workers seems to have departed. One day of late a railway
porter said to a feeble old lady, a friend of ours, "See to your luggage
yourself". Human nature had not sunk so low as that in 1840.

'If, as has been lately asserted, only the young and feeble League
of Nations stands between us and the *utter destruction of Civilization*,
it makes one feel he would rather be old than young. For a person
whose chief interest in life has been the literary art — poetry in
particular — the thought is depressing that, should such an overturn
arrive, poetry will be the first thing to go, probably not to revive
again for many centuries. Anyhow, it behoves young poets and
other writers to endeavour to stave off such a catastrophe.'

Among others who remembered his birthday, Mr. John Lane sent
a glass goblet which had come into his possession many years before,
remarking, . . . 'no doubt it was intended as a gift for you from
some fair but probably shy admirer'; to which Hardy replied :

'Also, for the mysterious goblet inscribed to the mysterious namesake of mine. He must, or may, have been a jockey from the dia-
grams. . . . Anyhow, no woman ever took the trouble to inscribe
her love for me on a cup of crystal — of that you may be sure ; and
it is best on the whole to leave the history of the glass in vague
obscurity.'

The next week J. M. Barrie came to Max Gate on a visit, and in
July Hardy and his wife were motoring about Dorset, showing some
features of the county to their friend Mrs. Arthur Henniker, who
was staying at Weymouth, and at that time had ideas of buying a
house in the neighbourhood. He was also engaged in further correspondence on the scheme of establishing a South-western University
at Exeter.

*To Mr. G. Herbert Thring*

'*August* 23, 1920.

'The address from the Members of the Council, representing the
Society of Authors all, has reached me safely, and though I knew its
contents — its spiritual part — on my actual birthday when the
deputation came here, I did not realize its bodily beauty till now.

'As to the address itself, I can only confirm by this letter what I
told the deputation by word of mouth — how much I have been

moved by such a mark of good feeling — affection as I may truly call it — in the body of writers whose President I have had the distinction of being for many years — a do-nothing President, a *roi-fainéant*, I very greatly fear, in spite of their assurances! However, the Society has been good enough to take me as worth this tribute, and I thank them heartily for it and what it expresses. It will be a cheering reminder of bright things whenever I see it or think o íit, which will be often and often.'

'*September* 6. Death of Evelyn Gifford, at Arlington House, Oxford. Dear Evelyn! whom I last parted from in apparently perfect health.' She was the daughter of Dr. Gifford, who married Margaret Jeune, and the poem 'Evelyn G. of Christminster' was written on this occasion.

'*November* 11. Hardy's poem 'And there was a great calm' appeared in *The Times* Armistice Supplement.

The request to write this poem had been brought to him from London by one of the editorial staff. At first Hardy was disinclined, and all but refused, being generally unable to write to order. In the middle of the night, however, an idea seized him, and he was heard moving about the house looking things up. The poem was duly written and proved worthy of the occasion.

On the 13th the Dorchester Amateurs performed *The Return of the Native* in Dorchester, as dramatized by Mr. Tilley.

'More interested than I expected to be. The dancing was just as it used to be at Higher Bockhampton in my childhood.'

In declining to become a Vice-President of a well-known Society, Hardy writes :

'I may be allowed to congratulate its members upon their wise insistence on the word "English" as the name of this country's people, and in not giving way to a few short-sighted clamourers for the vague, unhistoric and pinchbeck title of "British" by which they would fain see it supplanted.'

Towards the end of the year Hardy was occupied with the following interesting correspondence :

### To Mr. Alfred Noyes

'DORCHESTER, 13*th December* 1920.

'DEAR MR. NOYES,

'Somebody has sent me an article from the *Morning Post* of December 9 entitled "Poetry and Religion", which reports you as saying, in a lecture, that mine is "a philosophy which told them (readers) that the Power behind the Universe was an imbecile jester".

'As I hold no such "philosophy", and, to the best of my recollection, never could have done so, I should be glad if you would inform me whereabouts I have seriously asserted such to be my opinion.

'Yours truly,

'TH. HARDY.'

It should be stated that Mr. Noyes had always been a friendly critic of Hardy's writings, and one with whom he was on good terms, which was probably Hardy's reason for antagonism in his letter.

Mr. Noyes replied that he was sorry the abbreviated report of his address did not contain the tribute he had paid Hardy as a writer with artistic mastery and at the head of living authors, although he did disagree with his pessimistic philosophy ; a philosophy which, in his opinion, led logically to the conclusion that the Power behind the Universe was malign ; and he referred to various passages in Hardy's poems that seemed to bear out his belief that their writer held the views attributed to him in the lecture ; offering, however, to revise it when reprinted, if he had misinterpreted the aforesaid passages.

### To Mr. Alfred Noyes

'December 19t h, 1920.

'I am much obliged for your reply, which I really ought not to have troubled you to write. I may say for myself that I very seldom do give critics such trouble, usually letting things drift, though there have been many occasions when a writer who has been so much abused for his opinions as I have been would perhaps have done well not to hold his peace.

'I do not know that there can be much use in my saying more than I did say. It seems strange that I should have to remind a man of letters of what, I should have supposed, he would have known as well as I — of the very elementary rule of criticism that a writer's works should be judged as a whole, and not from picked passages that contradict them as a whole — and this especially when they are scattered over a period of fifty years.

'Also that I should have to remind him of the vast difference between the expression of fancy and the expression of belief. My imagination may have often run away with me ; but all the same, my sober opinion — so far as I have any definite one — of the Cause of Things, has been defined in scores of places, and is that of a great many ordinary thinkers :  that the said Cause is neither moral nor immoral, but *un*moral :  "loveless and hateless" I have called it, "which neither good nor evil knows" — etc., etc. — (you will find plenty of these definitions in *The Dynasts* as well as in short poems, and I am surprised that you have not taken them in).  This view is quite in keeping with what you call a Pessimistic philosophy (a mere nickname with no sense in it), which I am quite unable to see as "leading logically to the conclusion that the Power behind the universe is malign".

'In my fancies, or poems of the imagination, I have of course called this Power all sorts of names — never supposing they would be taken for more than fancies.  I have even in prefaces warned readers to take them as such — as mere impressions of the moment, exclamations in fact.  But it has always been my misfortune to presuppose a too intelligent reading public, and no doubt people will go on thinking that I really believe the Prime Mover to be a malignant old gentleman, a sort of King of Dahomey — an idea which, so far from my holding it, is to me irresistibly comic.  "What a fool one must have been to write for such a public!" is the inevitable reflection at the end of one's life.

'The lines you allude to, "A Young Man's Epigram", dated 1866, I remember finding in a drawer, and printed them merely as an amusing instance of early cynicism.  The words "Time's Laughingstocks" are legitimate imagery all of a piece with such expressions as "Life, Time's fool", and thousands in poetry and I am amazed that you should see any *belief* in them.  The other verses you mention, "New Year's Eve", "His Education", are the same fanciful impressions of the moment.  The poem called "He abjures Love", ending with "And then the curtain", is a love-poem, and lovers are chartered irresponsibles.  A poem often quoted against me, and apparently in your mind in the lecture, is the one called "Nature's Questioning", containing the words, "some Vast Imbecility", etc. — as if these definitions were my creed.  But they are merely enumerated in the poem as fanciful alternatives to several others, having nothing to do with my own opinion.  As for "The Unborn", to which you allude, though the form of it is imaginary, the sentiment is one which I should think, especially since the war, is not uncommon or unreasonable.

'This week I have had sent me a review which quotes a poem

entitled "To my Father's Violin", containing a Virgilian reminiscence of mine of Acheron and the Shades. The writer comments: "Truly this pessimism is insupportable. . . . One marvels that Hardy is not in a madhouse". Such is English criticism, and I repeat, why did I ever write a line! And perhaps if the young ladies to whom you lectured really knew that, so far from being the wicked personage they doubtless think me at present to be, I am a harmless old character much like their own grandfathers, they would consider me far less romantic and attractive.'

Mr. Noyes in a further interesting letter, after reassuring Hardy that he would correct any errors, gave his own views, one of which was that he had 'never been able to conceive a Cause of Things that could be less in any respect than the things caused'. To which Hardy replied:

'Many thanks for your letter. The Scheme of Things is, indeed, incomprehensible; and there I suppose we must leave it — perhaps for the best. Knowledge might be terrible.'


### To the 'New York World'

'*December* 23, 1920.

'Yes I approve of international disarmament, on the lines indicated by the *New York World*.'


The following letter, written to someone about December 1920, obviously refers to his correspondence with Mr. Noyes:

'A friend of mine writes objecting to what he calls my "philosophy" (though I have no philosophy — merely what I have often explained to be only a confused heap of impressions, like those of a bewildered child at a conjuring show). He says he has never been able to conceive a Cause of Things that could be less in any respect than the things caused. This apparent impossibility to him, and to so many, is very likely owing to his running his head against a *Single* Cause, and perceiving no possible other. But if he would discern that what we call the first Cause should be called First Causes, his difficulty would be lessened. Assume a thousand unconscious causes — lumped together in poetry as one Cause, or God — and bear in mind that a coloured liquid can be produced by the mixture of colourless ones, a noise by the juxtaposition of silences, etc., etc., and you see that the assumption that intelligent beings arise from the combined action of unintelligent forces is sufficiently probable for imaginative writing, and I have never attempted scientific. It is my misfortune that people *will* treat all my mood-dictated writing as a single scientific theory.'

About Christmas the song entitled 'When I set out for Lyonnesse' was published as set to music by Mr. Charles A. Speyer. It was one of his own poems that Hardy happened to like, and he was agreeably surprised that it should be liked by anybody else, his experience being that an author's preference for particular verses of his own was usually based on the circumstances that gave rise to them, and not on their success as art.

On Christmas night the carol singers and mummers came to Max Gate as they had promised, the latter performing the *Play of Saint George*, just as he had seen it performed in his childhood. On the last day of the old year a poem by Hardy called 'At the Entering of the New Year' appeared in the *Athenæum*.

CHAPTER XXXVII

# SOME FAREWELLS

1921–1925 : *Aet.* 80–85

THE New Year found Hardy sitting up to hear the bells, which he had not done for some time.

Early in January he was searching through registers of Stinsford for records of a family named Knight, connected with his own. Many generations of this family are buried in nameless graves in Stinsford Churchyard.

J. M. Barrie paid him a brief visit on May 11, staying at Max Gate for one night, and visiting Hardy's birthplace at Bockhampton on the morning of May 12. The same day Hardy learned of the death of a friend, an elder brother of the confidant and guide of his youth and early manhood. In his note-book he writes :

'*May* 11. Charles Moule died. He is the last of "the seven brethren".'

On June 2 he notes that his birthday was remembered by the newspapers, and that he received an address from younger writers. Accompanying this was a fine copy of the first edition of 'Lamia', 'Isabella', 'The Eve of St. Agnes', and other poems by John Keats, in the original boards with the half-title and eight pages of advertisements.

The idea had originated with Mr. St. John Ervine, who summoned a committee to consider the nature of the tribute. The address was signed by a hundred and six younger writers, and ran as follows :

'DEAR MR. HARDY,

'We, who are your younger comrades in the craft of letters, wish on this your eighty-first birthday to do honour to ourselves by praising your work, and to thank you for the example of high endeavour and achievement which you have set before us. In your novels and poems you have given us a tragic vision of life which is informed by your knowledge of character and relieved by the charity of your humour, and sweetened by your sympathy with human suffering and endurance. We have learned from you that the proud heart can subdue the hardest fate, even in submitting to it. . . . In all that you have written you have shown the spirit of man, nourished by tradition and sustained by pride, persisting through defeat.

'You have inspired us both by your work and by the manner in which it was done. The craftsman in you calls for our admiration as surely as the artist, and few writers have observed so closely as you have the Host's instruction in the *Canterbury Tales* :

> 'Your termes, your colours, and your figures,
> Keep them in store, till so be ye indite
> High style, as when that men to kinges write.

'From your first book to your last, you have written in the "high style, as when that men to kinges write", and you have crowned a great prose with a noble poetry.

'We thank you, Sir, for all that you have written . . . but most of all, perhaps, for *The Dynasts*.

'We beg that you will accept the copy of the first edition of *Lamia* by John Keats which accompanies this letter, and with it, accept also our grateful homage.'

A few days later, on June 9, he motored to Sturminster Newton with his wife and Mr. Cecil Hanbury to see a performance of *The Mellstock Quire* by the Hardy Players in the Castle ruins. Afterwards he went to Riverside, the house where he had written *The Return of the Native*, and where the Players were then having tea.

On June 16 Mr. de la Mare arrived for a visit of two nights. The following day he walked to Stinsford with Hardy and was much interested in hearing about the various graves, and in reading a poem that Hardy had just lately written, 'Voices from Things growing in a Country Churchyard'. The first verse of the poem runs thus :

> These flowers are I, poor Fanny Hurd,
>     Sir or Madam,
> A little girl here sepultured.
> Once I flit-fluttered like a bird
> Above the grass, as now I wave
> In daisy shapes above my grave,
>     All day cheerily,
>     All night eerily!

Fanny Hurd's real name was Fanny Hurden, and Hardy remembered her as a delicate child who went to school with him. She died when she was about eighteen, and her grave and a head-stone with her name are to be seen in Stinsford Churchyard.  The others mentioned in this poem were known to him by name and repute.

Early in July a company of film actors arrived in Dorchester for the purpose of preparing a film of *The Mayor of Casterbridge*.  Hardy met them outside The King's Arms, the hotel associated with the novel.  Although the actors had their faces coloured yellow and were dressed in the fashion of some eighty years earlier, Hardy observed, to his surprise, that the townsfolk passed by on their ordinary affairs and seemed not to notice the strange spectacle, nor did any interest seem aroused when Hardy drove through the town with the actors to Maiden Castle, that ancient earthwork which formed the background to one part of the film.

About this time he went to St. Peter's Church, to a morning service, for the purpose of hearing sung by the choir the morning hymn, 'Awake, my Soul', to Barthélémon's setting.  This had been arranged for him by Dr. Niven, the Rector of St. Peter's.  Church music, as has been shown, had appealed strongly to Hardy from his earliest years.  On July 23 a sonnet, 'Barthélémon at Vauxhall', appeared in *The Times*.  He had often imagined the weary musician, returning from his nightly occupation of making music for a riotous throng, lingering on Westminster Bridge to see the rising sun and being thence inspired to the composition of music to be heard hereafter in places very different from Vauxhall.

In the same month he opened a bazaar in aid of the Dorset County Hospital, and in the evening of that day he was driven into Dorchester again to see some dancing in the Borough Gardens.  Of this he writes :

'Saw "The Lancers" danced (for probably the last time) at my request.   Home at 10 :  outside our gate full moon over cottage : band still heard playing.'

At the beginning of September Hardy stood sponsor at the christening of the infant daughter of Mr. and Mrs. Cecil Hanbury of Kingston Maurward.  His gift to his little godchild was the manuscript of a short poem contained in a silver box.  This appeared afterwards in *Human Shows* under the title 'To C. F. H.'.

Three days later he was again at Stinsford Church, attending the evening service.  In his notebook he records :  'A beautiful evening. Evening Hymn Tallis.'

During the latter half of September Hardy was sitting to his friend Mr. Ouless for his portrait, which now hangs in the National

Portrait Gallery.   On October 14 he received a visit from Mr. and
Mrs. John Masefield, who brought with them a gift: a full-rigged
ship made by John Masefield himself.   This ship had been named by
its maker *The Triumph*, and was much valued by Hardy, who showed
it with pride to callers at Max Gate, with the story of how it arrived.
Four days later Hardy writes:

'*October* 18.   In afternoon to Stinsford with F.   A matchless
October: sunshine, mist and turning leaves.'

The first month of 1922 found him writing an energetic preface
to a volume of poems entitled *Late Lyrics and Earlier*, the MS. of
which he forwarded to the publishers on January 23.   Some of his
friends regretted this preface, thinking that it betrayed an oversensi-
tiveness to criticism which it were better the world should not know.
But sensitiveness was one of Hardy's chief characteristics, and without it his poems would never have been written, nor, indeed, the
greatest of his novels.   He used to say that it was not so much the
force of the blow that counted, as the nature of the material that
received the blow.

An interesting point in this preface was his attitude towards
religion.   Through the years 1920 to 1925 Hardy was interested in
conjectures on rationalizing the English Church.   There had been
rumours for some years of a revised Liturgy, and his hopes were
accordingly raised by the thought of making the Established Church
comprehensive enough to include the majority of thinkers of the
previous hundred years who had lost all belief in the supernatural.

When the new Prayer Book appeared, however, his hopes were
doomed to disappointment, and he found that the revision had not
been in a rationalistic direction, and from that time he lost all expectation of seeing the Church representative of modern thinking minds.

In April J. M. Barrie stayed at Max Gate for one night.   The 23rd
May saw the publication of *Late Lyrics and Earlier*, and on the following day Hardy motored to Sturminster Newton to call at the house
where he had spent some of the early years of his first marriage, and
where he wrote *The Return of the Native*.   Two days later he notes:
'Visited Stinsford and Higher Bockhampton.   House at the latter
shabby, and garden.   Just went through into heath, and up plantation
to top of garden.'   It was becoming increasingly painful to Hardy to
visit this old home of his, and often when he left he said that he
would go there no more.

On May 29 he copied some old notes made before he had contemplated writing *The Dynasts*.

'We — the people — Humanity, a collective personality — (Thus "we" could be engaged in the battle of Hohenlinden, say, and in the battle of Waterloo) — dwell with genial humour on "our" getting into a rage for we knew not what.

'The intelligence of this collective personality Humanity is pervasive, ubiquitous, like that of God. Hence *e.g.* on the one hand we could hear the roar of the cannon, discern the rush of the battalions, on the other hear the voice of a man protesting, etc.

'Title "self-slaughter"; "divided against ourselves".

'Now these 3 (or 3000) whirling through space at the rate of 40 miles a second — (God's view). "Some of our family who" (the we of one nation speaking of the "we" of another).

'A battle. Army as somnambulists — not knowing what it is for.

'We were called "Artillery" etc. "We were so under the spell of habit that" (drill).

'It is now necessary to call the reader's attention to those of us who were harnessed and collared in blue and brass. . . .

'*Poem* — the difference between what things are and what they ought to be. (Stated as by a god to the gods — *i.e.* as God's story.)

'*Poem* — I — First Cause, omniscient, not omnipotent — limitations, difficulties, etc., from being only able to work by Law (His only failing is lack of foresight).

'We will now ask the reader to look eastward with us . . . at what the contingent of us out that way were doing.

'*Poem*. A spectral force seen acting in a man (*e.g.* Napoleon) and he acting under it — a pathetic sight — this compulsion.

'Patriotism, if aggressive and at the expense of other countries, is a vice; if in sympathy with them, a virtue.'

From these notes it will be seen how *The Dynasts* had been slowly developing in his mind. Unfortunately they are not dated, but there is in existence a notebook filled with details of the Napoleonic wars, and reflection upon them, having been written at the time he was gathering material for *The Trumpet-Major*, which was first published in 1880.

During July Hardy had visits from many friends. Florence Henniker came early in the month, and went for a delightful drive with him and his wife in Blackmore Vale, and to Sherborne, the scene of *The Woodlanders*. Later Siegfried Sassoon arrived with

Edmund Blunden, and then E. M. Forster, who accompanied him to
an amateur performance of *A Midsummer Night's Dream* on the lawn
of Trinity Rectory.

In August he was well enough to cycle (no small feat for a man
of eighty-two) with his wife to Talbothays to visit his brother and
his sister.

On August 11 he writes in his notebook :

'Motored to Sturminster Newton, and back by Dogbury Gate.
Walked to top of High Stoy with Flower (probably for the last time),
thence back home. A beautiful drive.'

'*October* 12. Walked across Boucher's Close to Ewelease Stile.'
[Boucher's Close is a green-wooded meadow next to Stinsford
Vicarage, and the Ewelease Stile is the one whereon, more than fifty
years before this date, he had sat and read the review of *Desperate
Remedies* in the *Spectator*.]

On the same day Hardy wrote to J. H. Morgan as follows :

'DEAR GENERAL MORGAN,

'I had already begun to reply to your interesting letter from Berlin,
which opened up so many points that had engaged me 20 years ago,
but had rather faded in my memory. Now that you are at home I
will write it in a more succinct form, for it is not likely that amid
the many details you have to attend to after your absence you will
want to think much about Napoleonic times.

'I cannot for my life recall where I obtained the idea of N's entry
into Berlin by the Potsdamer-strasse, though I don't think I should
have written it without authority. However, you have to remember
that the events generally in *The Dynasts* had to be pulled together
into dramatic scenes, to show themselves to the mental eye of the
reader as a picture viewed from one point ; and hence it was sometimes necessary to see round corners, down crooked streets, and to
shift buildings nearer each other than in reality (as Turner did in his
landscapes) ; and it may possibly happen that I gave "A Public
Place" in Berlin these convenient facilities without much ceremony.

'You allude to Leipzig. That battle bothered me much more
than Jena or Ulm (to which you also allude) — in fact more than
any other battle I had to handle. I defy any human being to synchro-
nize with any certainty its episodes from descriptions by historians.
My time-table was, I believe, as probable a one as can be drawn up
at this date. But I will go no further with these stale conjectures,
now you are in London.

'I have quite recently been reading a yellow old letter written from Berlin in June, 1815, by a Dorset man whose daughter is a friend of ours, and who lately sent it to me. The writer says what is oddly in keeping with your remarks on the arrogance of Prussian officers. "Buonaparte has rendered Germany completely military ; at the inns and post-houses a private Gentleman exacts not half the respect exacted by a soldier. This contempt for those who wear no swords displays itself in no very pleasant shape to travellers. About 3 weeks ago I might have died of damp sheets if my German servant had not taken upon him to assure a brute of a Post-master that I was an English General travelling for my health. . . . I have since girded on a sabre, got a military cap, and let my moustache grow : soldiers now present arms as we pass."

'It would be strange to find that Napoleon was really the prime cause of German militarism! What a Nemesis for the French nation!

'Well, I have gone back to Boney again after all : but no more of him. I hope you find the change to London agreeable, and keep well in your vicissitudes.

'Sincerely yours,

'THOMAS HARDY.'

Early in November he was visited by Mrs. Henry Allhusen, his friend from her girlhood, when she was Miss Dorothy Stanley, daughter of Lady Jeune, afterwards Lady St. Helier. With Mrs. Allhusen and her daughter Elizabeth he motored to Dogbury Gate and other beautiful parts of Dorset. Elizabeth Allhusen, a charming girl, died soon after, to Hardy's grief.

A few days later came a letter from the Pro-Provost of Queen's College, Oxford, to say that it had been decided to elect him to an Honorary Fellowship, which he accepted, an announcement to that effect being made in *The Times* on the 20th of the month.

Another entry in his notebook :

'*November* 27. E's death-day, ten years ago. Went with F. and tidied her tomb and carried flowers for her and the other two tombs.'

'*New Year's Eve.* Henry and Kate came to 1 o'clock dinner, stayed to tea, left 5.30. Did not sit up.'

Early in January 1923 Hardy was appointed Governor of the Dorchester Grammar School for three years.

'*February* 26. A story (rather than a poem) might be written in the first person, in which "I" am supposed to live through the centuries in my ancestors, in one person, the particular line of descent chosen being that in which *qualities* are most continuous.' (From an old note.)

A few days after this entry is the following :

'*April* 5. In to-day's *Times* :

"Henniker. — on the 4th April 1923, of heart failure, the Honourable Mrs. Arthur Henniker. R.I.P."

'After a friendship of 30 years!'

'*April* 10. F. Henniker buried to-day at 1 o'clock at Thornham Magna, Eye, Suffolk.'

During the month of April Hardy finished the rough draft of his poetical play *The Queen of Cornwall*, and in May he made, with infinite care, his last drawing, an imaginary view of Tintagel Castle. This is delicately drawn, an amazing feat for a man in his eighty-third year, and it indicates his architectural tastes and early training. It was used as an illustration when *The Queen of Cornwall* was published.

In April, replying to a letter from Mr. John Galsworthy, he writes :

'. . . The exchange of international thought is the only possible salvation for the world : and though I was decidedly premature when I wrote at the beginning of the South African War that I hoped to see patriotism not confined to realms, but circling the earth, I still maintain that such sentiments ought to prevail.

'Whether they will do so before the year 10,000 is of course what sceptics may doubt.'

Towards the end of May Mr. and Mrs. Walter de la Mare stayed at Max Gate for two nights, and early in June, the day after Hardy's birthday, Mr. and Mrs. Granville-Barker came to see him, bringing with them friends he had not seen for many years, Mr. and Mrs. Max Beerbohm.

'*June* 10. Relativity. That things and events always were, are, and will be (*e.g.* Emma, Mother and Father are living still in the past).'

'*June* 21. Went with F. on board the *Queen Elizabeth* on a visit to Sir John de Robeck, Lady de Robeck, and Admiral W. W. Fisher.' More than once, upon the invitation of Admiral Fisher, he had had a pleasant time on board a battleship off Portland.

On June 25 Hardy and his wife went to Oxford by road to stay at Queen's College for two nights. This was the last long journey that Hardy was to make, and the last time that he was to sleep away from Max Gate. It was a delightful drive, by way of Salisbury,

Hungerford, and Wantage.  At Salisbury they stopped for a little
while to look at the Cathedral, as Hardy always loved doing, and at
various old buildings, including the Training College which he had
visited more than fifty years before when his two sisters were students
there, and which is faithfully described in *Jude the Obscure.*

They paused also at Fawley, that pleasant Berkshire village described in the same novel under the name of Marygreen.  Here some
of Hardy's ancestors were buried, and he searched fruitlessly for their
graves in the little churchyard.  His father's mother, the gentle,
kindly grandmother who lived with the family at Bockhampton
during Hardy's childhood, had spent the first thirteen years of her
life here as an orphan child, named Mary Head, and her memories
of Fawley were so poignant that she never cared to return to the
place after she had left it as a young girl.  The surname of Jude was
taken from this place.

So well had their journey been timed that on their arrival at
Oxford they found awaiting them under the entrance gateway of
Queen's, Mr. Godfrey Elton, who was to be their cicerone, and whose
impressions of their visit are given herewith.

'Having been elected an Honorary Fellow Hardy paid Queen's
College a visit on June 25th and 26th, just after the end of the summer
term of 1923.  With a colleague, Dr. Chattaway, I was delighted to
meet him at the College gate — he was to come by road with Mrs.
Hardy from Dorchester.  Neither Chattaway nor I had met Hardy
before, but I felt confident that we should recognise the now legendary
figure from his portraits.  It was almost like awaiting a visit from
Thackeray or Dickens. . . .

'The car arrived punctually, and a smallish, fragile, bright-eyed
man, elderly certainly but as certainly not old, climbed out of it.  An
elderly gentleman, one would have said, who had always lived in the
country and knew much of the ways of wild creatures and crops. . . .

'We left Mr. and Mrs. Hardy at tea in the Provost's lodgings.
The Provost was only one year Mr. Hardy's senior, but with his
patriarchal white beard appeared a great deal older, and as we left
the party — Hardy sitting bright-eyed and upright on the edge of
his chair — it seemed almost like leaving a new boy in charge of his
headmaster. . . . Next day there was a lunch in Common-room, at
which the Fellows and their wives met Mr. and Mrs. Hardy, and a
photograph in the Fellows' garden in which Hardy appeared in his
Doctor's gown with his new colleagues.  In the morning he was
shown the sights of the College.  He was obviously happy to be in

Oxford, and happy, I think, too, to be of it, and I wished that it had been term-time and that he could have seen the younger life of the place, which one felt in some ways he would have preferred to Tutors and Professors. We took him round College a trifle too fast. He would pause reflectively before Garrick's copy of the First Folio or the contemporary portrait of Henry V., and seem about to make some comment when his conductors would be passing on again and some new historical information would be being offered him. It was characteristic of him that in some pause in this perambulation he found occasion to say some kind words to me of some youthful verse of mine he had chanced to see. . . . Afterwards he asked me to take him into the High Street to see the famous curve, and we spent some minutes searching for the precise spot from which it can best be viewed, while in my mind memories of *Jude the Obscure* and an earlier Oxford conflicted with anxieties as to the traffic of the existing town — to which he seemed quite indifferent. Then, apparently unwearied, he asked for the Shelley Memorial. . . .

'After this came the Common-room lunch, and afterwards Mrs. Hardy invited me to accompany them on a visit to the Masefields. We drove to Boar's Hill, paying a visit in Christ Church on the way. Had it not been for my constant consciousness that I was sitting before a Classic, I should not have guessed that I was with a man who wrote; rather an elderly country gentleman with a bird-like alertness and a rare and charming youthfulness — interested in everything he saw, and cultured, but surely not much occupied with books : indeed almost all of us, his new colleagues, would have struck an impartial observer as far more *bookish* than the author of the Wessex novels. . . .

'At the Masefields' Hardy was asked a question or two about Jude's village, which it was thought he might have passed on the road from Dorchester, and he spoke briefly and depreciatingly of "that fictitious person. If there ever was such a person. . . ." When we left, Hardy holding a rose which Mr. Masefield had cut from his garden, there was still time to see more. I had expected that he would wish to rest but no ; he wanted to see the Martyrs' Memorial and New College, Cloisters. Obviously there were certain of the Oxford sights which he had resolved to see again. I am ashamed to remember that, by some error which I cannot now explain, I conducted our guests to the Chapel, instead of the Cloisters, at New College. But perhaps it was a fortunate error, for the choir were about to sing the evening service, and at Hardy's wish we sat about twenty minutes in the ante-chapel listening in silence to the soaring boys' voices. . . .

'Next morning Mr. and Mrs. Hardy left. He spoke often afterwards of his pleasure at having seen his College, and he contemplated another visit. This too brief membership and his one visit remain a very happy memory to his colleagues.'

The Hardys motored back to Max Gate by way of Newbury, Winchester, and Ringwood, having lunch in a grassy glade in the New Forest in the simple way that Hardy so much preferred.

This occasion was an outstanding one during the last years of his life.

On July 20 the Prince of Wales paid a visit to Dorchester, to open the new Drill Hall for the Dorset Territorials, and Hardy was invited to meet him there, and to drive back to Max Gate where the Prince and the party accompanying him were to lunch. It was a hot day, and the whole episode might well have proved fatiguing and irksome to a man of Hardy's years and retiring nature, but owing to the thoughtfulness of the Prince and his simple and friendly manner, all passed off pleasantly.

At lunch, besides the Prince and the Hardys, there were present Lord Shaftesbury, Admiral Sir Lionel Halsey, Sir Godfrey Thomas, Mr. (afterwards Sir) Walter Peacock, and Messrs. Proudfoot and Wilson, the Duchy Stewards.

The Prince had a friendly talk with Hardy in the garden, before leaving to visit certain Duchy farms in Dorchester : the main characteristic of the visit was its easy informality.

The next few months saw a certain activity on Hardy's part. He visited several friends either for lunch or tea, as he did not go out in the evening except for a short walk, nor did he again sleep away from Max Gate. Many from a distance also called upon him, including his ever faithful friend Lady St. Helier, who travelled from Newbury to Max Gate on October 3rd, this being their last meeting.

On November 15th the poetic drama *The Famous Tragedy of the Queen of Cornwall* was published. Hardy's plan in writing this is clearly given in a letter to Mr. Harold Child :

'The unities are strictly preserved, whatever virtue there may be in that. (I, myself, am old-fashioned enough to think there *is* a virtue in it, if it can be done without artificiality. The only other case I remember attempting it in was *The Return of the Native*.) The original events could have been enacted in the time taken up by the performance, and they continue unbroken throughout. The change of persons on the stage is called a change of scene, there being no change of background.

'My temerity in pulling together into the space of an hour events that in the traditional stories covered a long time will doubtless be criticized, if it is noticed. But there are so many versions of the famous romance that I felt free to adapt it to my purpose in any way — as, in fact, the Greek dramatists did in their plays — notably Euripides.

'Wishing it to be thoroughly English I have dropped the name of Chorus for the conventional onlookers, and called them Chanters, though they play the part of a Greek Chorus to some extent. I have also called them Ghosts (I don't for the moment recall an instance of this in a Greek play). . . . Whether the lady ghosts in our performance will submit to have their faces whitened I don't know! . . .

'I have tried to avoid turning the rude personages of, say, the fifth century into respectable Victorians, as was done by Tennyson, Swinburne, Arnold, etc. On the other hand it would have been impossible to present them as they really were, with their barbaric manners and surroundings.'

On the 28th of the same month the play was produced by the Hardy Players at the Corn Exchange at Dorchester. The great difficulties which the play presented to amateur actors, unaccustomed to reciting blank verse, who were at their best in rustic comedy, were more or less overcome, but naturally a poetic drama did not make a wide appeal. However, the performance, and particularly the rehearsals, gave Hardy considerable pleasure.

On December 10 the death was announced of Sir Frederick Treves, Hardy's fellow-townsman, the eminent surgeon. Frederick Treves as a child had attended the same school as Hardy's elder sister Mary, and it was from the shop of Treves's father that Hardy as a boy purchased his first writing-desk. The care which he took of all his possessions during his whole life is shown by the fact that this desk was in his study without a mark or scratch upon it at the time of his death. Because of the early association and the love which they both bore to the county, there was a strong link between these two Dorset men.

On the last day but one of the year Mr. and Mrs. G. Bernard

Shaw and Colonel T. E. Lawrence lunched with the Hardys and spent several hours with them. The following entry in his notebook ends his brief chronicle of the year's doings :

'31. *New Year's Eve.* Did not sit up. Heard the bells in the evening.'

## 1924

'*January* 2. Attended Frederick Treves's funeral at St. Peter's. Very wet day. Sad procession to the cemetery. Casket in a little white grave.

'Lord Dawson of Penn and Mr. Newman Flower came out to tea afterwards.'

On January 5 a poem by Hardy, 'In Memoriam, F. T.', appeared in *The Times,* a last tribute to an old friend.

During February *The Queen of Cornwall* was performed in London by the Hardy Players of Dorchester, but it was not altogether a success, partly owing to the only building available having no stage suitable for the performance, a rather small concert platform having to be used.

On March 7 Hardy notes :

'To Stinsford with F. (E. first met 54 years ago).'

And later, on April 3 :

'Mother died 20 years ago to-day.'

Among the many letters which arrived on June 2, the 84th anniversary of his birth, was one from a son of the Baptist minister, Mr. Perkins, whom, in his youth, Hardy had so respected. This correspondent was one of the young men who had met him at the Baptist Chapel at the eastern end of the town for a prayer-meeting which was hindered by the arrival of a circus.

More than sixty years had elapsed since Hardy had had any contact with this friend of his youth, and for a little while he was strongly tempted to get into touch with him again. However, too wide a gulf lay between and, as might have been told in one of his poems, the gesture was never made and the days slipped on into oblivion.

On June 11 Mr. Rutland Boughton arrived at Max Gate for a visit of two days, the purpose of which was to consult Hardy about a plan he had for setting *The Queen of Cornwall* to music. Hardy was greatly interested, though he had heard no modern compositions, not even the immensely popular 'Faerie Song' from *The Immortal Hour.* 'The Blue Danube', 'The Morgenblätter Waltz', and the 'Overture to *William Tell*' interested him more strongly, and also church music, mainly on account of the association with his early days.

But he found Mr. Boughton a stimulating companion, and was interested in his political views, though he could not share them. After Mr. Boughton's departure he said with conviction, 'If I had talked to him for a few hours I would soon have converted him'.

One feature of this visit was a drive the Hardys took with their guests across parts of Egdon Heath, which were then one blaze of purple with rhododendrons in full bloom.

On June 16 a poem by Hardy entitled 'Compassion' appeared in *The Times*. It was written in answer to a request, and was intended to celebrate the Centenary of the Royal Society for the Prevention of Cruelty to Animals.

Although not one of his most successful efforts, as he was never happy when writing to order, it served to demonstrate the poet's passionate hatred of injustice and barbarity.

> Much has been won — more, maybe, than we know —
>   And on we labour hopeful. 'Ailinon!'
> A mighty voice calls : 'But may the good prevail!'
>   And 'Blessed are the merciful!'
>     Calls a yet mightier one.

On July 1 the Balliol Players, a party of undergraduates from Oxford, visited Max Gate, during the course of a tour in the west of England, to perform on the lawn *The Oresteia* as *The Curse of the House of Atreus*. This was a pleasant and informal occasion which gave delight to Hardy. Always sympathetic to youth, and a lifelong admirer of Greek tragedy, he fully appreciated this mark of affection and respect. The performance was not without an amusing side. The day was a windy one, and cold for July, hence the players with their bare arms and legs and scanty costumes must have been none too comfortable. However, they ran about the lawn and pranced into the flower-beds with apparent enjoyment. Finding that the carrying of lighted torches in the sunlight was ineffective, they carried instead tall spikes of a giant flowering spiræa which they plucked from a border. While having tea after the play they gathered round Hardy, who talked to them with a sincerity and simplicity that few but he could have shown. Among the names of the players that he jotted down in his notebook were those of Mr. A. L. Cliffe — Clytemnestra : Mr. Anthony Asquith — Cassandra ; Mr. Walter Oakshott — Orestes ; Mr. H. T. Wade-Gery — Agamemnon ; Mr. A. A. Farrer

— Electra; and he also notes, 'The Balliol Players had come on bicycles, sending on their theatrical properties in a lorry that sometimes broke down'. Mr. and Mrs. Granville-Barker were present as spectators on this occasion.

A day or two later, with reference to what is not clear, Hardy copies a quotation from Emerson:

'The foolish man wonders at the unusual, but the wise man at the usual.'

On August 4, noted by Hardy as being the day on which war was declared ten years before, he and Mrs. Hardy motored to Netherton Hall in Devon to lunch with Mr. and Mrs. Granville-Barker. Two days later he received a visit from Siegfried Sassoon and Colonel T. E. Lawrence.

About this time Rutland Boughton's music version of *The Queen of Cornwall* was produced at Glastonbury, and on August 28 Hardy with his wife went to see and hear it, making the journey to Glastonbury by car.

From the 25th to the 30th Hardy was sitting to the Russian sculptor Serge Youriévitch for his bust. This was made in Hardy's study at Max Gate, and though he enjoyed conversation with the sculptor he was tired by the sittings, probably on account of his age, and definitely announced that he would not sit again for anything of the kind.

For several years some of the members of the Dorchester Debating and Dramatic Society had wished to perform a dramatization of *Tess of the d'Urbervilles*. After much hesitation Hardy handed over his own dramatization, although, as he notes in his diary, he had come to the conclusion that to dramatize a novel was a mistake in art; moreover, that the play ruined the novel and the novel the play. However, the result was that the company, self-styled 'The Hardy Players', produced *Tess* with such unexpected success at Dorchester and Weymouth that it was asked for in London, and the following year produced there by professional actors for over a hundred nights, Miss Gwen Ffrangçon-Davies taking the part of 'Tess'.

On the 22nd of October Hardy with his wife visited for the first time since childhood the old barn at the back of Kingston Maurward. Here, as a small boy, he had listened to village girls singing old ballads. He pointed out to his wife the corner where they had sat. He looked around at the dusty rafters and the debris, considering possibly the difference that seventy years had made, and his manner as he left the barn was that of one who wished he had not endeavoured to revive a scene from a distant past. Almost certainly he was the only human being left of that once gay party.

A characteristic note ends Hardy's diary for 1924:

'*December* 31. *New Year's Eve.* Sat up and heard Big Ben and the London church bells by wireless ring in the New Year.'

On this day also he copied a quotation from an essay by L. Pearsall Smith:

'In every representation of Nature which is a work of art there is to be found, as Professor Courthope said, something which is not to be found in the aspect of Nature which it represents; and what that something is has been a matter of dispute from the earliest days of criticism.'

'The same writer adds', notes Hardy, '"Better use the word 'inspiration' than 'genius' for inborn daemonic genius as distinct from conscious artistry".

'(It seems to me it might be called "temperamental impulse", which, of course, must be inborn.)'

Early in January 1925 Hardy sent to the *Nineteenth Century Magazine* a poem entitled 'The Absolute Explains'.

In the spring of this year, in connection with Hardy's dog 'Wessex', an incident occurred which was impossible to explain. This dog, a wire-haired terrier, was of great intelligence and very friendly to many who visited Max Gate, though he had defects of temper, due perhaps to a want of thorough training. Among those to whom he showed a partiality was Mr. William Watkins, the honorary secretary to the Society of Dorset Men in London.

About nine o'clock on the evening of April 18, Mr. Watkins called at Max Gate to discuss with Hardy certain matters connected with his society. The dog, as was his wont, rushed into the hall and greeted his friend with vociferous barks. Suddenly these gave way to a piteous whine, and the change was so startling that Wessex's mistress went to see what had happened.

Nothing, however, seemed amiss, and the dog returned into the room where Hardy was sitting and where he was joined by Mr. Watkins. But even here Wessex seemed ill at ease, and from time to time went to the visitor and touched his coat solicitously with his paw, which he always withdrew giving a sharp cry of distress.

Mr. Watkins left a little after ten o'clock, apparently in very good spirits. Early the next morning there came a telephone message from his son to say that the father, Hardy's guest of the night before, had died quite suddenly about an hour after his return to the hotel from Max Gate. As a rule the dog barked furiously when he heard the telephone ring, but on this occasion he remained silent, his nose between his paws.

On May 26 a letter and a leading article appeared in *The Times* on the subject of a Thomas Hardy Chair of Literature and a Wessex University. The letter was signed by many eminent writers and educationalists. At the date of writing, however, the Chair has not been endowed.

Later in the summer, on July 15, a deputation from Bristol University arrived at Max Gate to confer on Hardy the honorary degree of Doctor of Literature. This was the fifth degree he had received from English and Scottish Universities, the others being, in the order in which the degrees were bestowed — Aberdeen, Cambridge, Oxford, and St. Andrews.

At the end of July Hardy sent off the manuscript of his volume of poems, *Human Shows*, to the publishers, and a month later he made arrangements for the performance of his dramatization of *Tess* at the Barnes Theatre. About this time he enters in his notebook:

'"Truth is what will work", said William James (Harpers). A worse corruption of language was never perpetrated.'

Few other events were of interest to him during the year. *Tess of the d'Urbervilles* was produced in London, but he felt he had not sufficient strength to go up to see it. After nearly two months at Barnes Theatre the play was removed on November 2 to the Garrick Theatre, where the hundredth performance took place.

The many pilgrimages Hardy made with his wife to Stinsford Church took place usually in the evening during the summer, and in the afternoon during the winter. On October 9, however, contrary to his usual custom, he walked to Stinsford in the morning. The bright sunlight shone across the face of a worn tomb whose lettering Hardy had often endeavoured to decipher, so that he might recarve the letters with his penknife. This day, owing to the sunlight, they were able to read:

SACRED
to the memory of
ROBERT REASON
who departed this life
December 26th 1819
Aged 56 years

Dear friend should you mourn for me
I am where you soon must be.

Although Robert Reason had died twenty-one years before the birth of the author of *Under the Greenwood Tree*, he was faithfully described in that novel as Mr. Penny, the shoemaker, Hardy having heard so much of him from old inhabitants of Bockhampton. He used to regret that he had not used the real name, that being much better for his purpose than the one he had invented.

On December 6 the company of players from the Garrick Theatre arrived at Max Gate in the evening for the purpose of giving a performance of *Tess* in the drawing-room. The following description of this incident is taken from a letter written by one of the company to a correspondent in America who had particularly desired her impression of the visit :

'Mr. and Mrs. Hardy behaved as if it were a most usual occurrence for a party of West-End actors to arrive laden with huge theatrical baskets of clothes and props.

'They met us in the hall and entertained us with tea, cakes and sandwiches, and Mr. Hardy made a point of chatting with everyone.

'The drawing-room was rather a fortunate shape — the door facing an alcove at one end of the room, and we used these to make our exits and entrances, either exiting into the hall or sitting quietly in the alcove.

'Mr. and Mrs. Hardy, a friend of the Hardys, and two maids who, in cap and apron, sat on the floor — made up our audience. I think I am correct in saying there was no one else. The room was shaded — lamps and firelight throwing the necessary light on our faces.

'We played the scenes of Tess's home with chairs and a tiny drawing-room table to represent farm furniture — tea-cups for drinking mugs — when the chairs and tables were removed the corner of the drawing-room became Stonehenge, and yet in some strange way those present said the play gained from the simplicity.

'It had seemed as if it would be a paralysingly difficult thing to do, to get the atmosphere at all within a few feet of the author himself and without any of the usual theatrical illusion, but speaking for myself, after the first few seconds it was perfectly easy, and Miss Ffrangçon-Davies's beautiful voice and exquisite playing of the Stonehenge scene in the shadows thrown by the firelight was a thing that I shall never forget. It was beautiful.

'Mr. Hardy insisted on talking to us until the last minute. He talked of Tess as if she was someone real whom he had known and liked tremendously. I think he enjoyed the evening. I may be quite wrong, but I got the impression that to him it seemed quite a proper and usual way to give a play — and he seemed to have very little conception of the unusualness and difficulties it might present to us.

'The gossip of the country has it that his house was designed and the garden laid out with the idea of being entirely excluded from the gaze of the curious. Of course it was dark when we arrived, but personally I should say he had succeeded.'

On December 20 he heard with regret of the death of his friend Sir Hamo Thornycroft, the sculptor, whose bronze head of Hardy was presented later to the National Portrait Gallery by Lady Thornycroft.

Siegfried Sassoon, a nephew of Sir Hamo's, happened to be paying Hardy a visit at the time. He left to go to the funeral of his uncle at Oxford, carrying with him a laurel wreath which Hardy had sent to be placed on the grave. Hardy had a warm regard for the sculptor, whose fine upstanding mien spoke truly of his nobility of character. The hours Hardy had spent in Sir Hamo's London studio and at his home were pleasant ones, and they had cycled together in Dorset while Sir Hamo was staying at Max Gate.

'*December* 23. Mary's birthday. She came into the world . . . and went out . . . and the world is just the same . . . not a ripple on the surface left.'

'*December* 31. *New Year's Eve.* F. and I sat up. Heard on the wireless various features of New Year's Eve in London: dancing at the Albert Hall, Big Ben striking twelve, singing Auld Lang Syne, God Save the King, Marseillaise, hurrahing.'

# CHAPTER XXXVIII

# THE LAST SCENE

1926–*January* 1928 : *Aet.* 86–87

EARLY in January 1926, feeling that his age compelled him to such a step, Hardy resigned the Governorship of the Dorchester Grammar School. He had always been reluctant to hold any public offices, knowing that he was by temperament unfitted to sit on committees that controlled or ordained the activities of others. He preferred to be 'the man with the watching eye'.

On April 27, replying to a letter from an Oxford correspondent, who was one of four who had signed a letter to the *Manchester Guardian* upon the necessity of the reformation of the Prayer Book Services, Hardy writes from Max Gate :

'I have read your letter with interest: also the enclosure that you and your friends sent to the *Manchester Guardian*, particularly because, when I was young, I had a wish to enter the Church.

'I am now too old to take up the questions you lay open, but I may say that it has seemed to me that a simpler plan than that of mental reservation in passages no longer literally accepted (which is puzzling to ordinary congregations) would be just to abridge the creeds and other primitive parts of the Liturgy, leaving only the essentials. Unfortunately there appears to be a narrowing instead of a broadening tendency among the clergy of late, which if persisted in will exclude still more people from Church. But if a strong body of young reformers were to make a bold stand, in a sort of New Oxford Movement, they would have a tremendous backing from the thoughtful laity, and might overcome the retrogressive section of the clergy.

'Please don't attach much importance to these casual thoughts, and believe me,

'Very truly yours,
'T. H.'

In May he received from Mr. Arthur M. Hind a water-colour sketch of an attractive corner in the village of Minterne, which the artist thought might be the original of 'Little Hintock' in the *Wood-landers*. In thanking Mr. Hind, Hardy writes:

'The drawing of the barn that you have been so kind as to send me has arrived uninjured, and I thank you much for the gift. I think it a charming picture, and a characteristic reproduction of that part of Dorset.

'As to the spot being the "Little Hintock" of *The Woodlanders* — that is another question. You will be surprised and shocked at my saying that I myself do not know where "Little Hintock" is! Several tourists have told me that they have found it, in every detail, and have offered to take me to it, but I have never gone.

'However, to be more definite, it has features which were to be found fifty years ago in the hamlets of Hermitage, Middlemarsh, Lyons-Gate, Revels Inn, Holnest, Melbury Bubb, etc. — all lying more or less under the eminence called High Stoy, just beyond Minterne and Dogbury Gate, where the country descends into the Vale of Blackmore.

'The topographers you mention as identifying the scene are merely guessers and are wrong. . . .'

On June 29 he again welcomed the Balliol Players, whose chosen play this summer, the *Hippolytus* of Euripides, was performed on the lawn of Max Gate. About the same time he sent by request a message of congratulation and friendship to Weymouth, Massachusetts, by a deputation which was then leaving England to visit that town.

'*July* 1926. Note — It appears that the theory exhibited in *The Well-Beloved* in 1892 has been since developed by Proust still further:

'Peu de personnes comprennent le caractère purement subjectif du phénomène qu'est l'amour, et la sorte de création que c'est d'une personne supplémentaire, distincte de celle qui porte le même nom dans le monde, et dont la plupart des éléments sont tirés de nous-mêmes.' (*Ombre*, i. 40.)

'Le désir s'élève, se satisfait, disparaît — et c'est tout. Ainsi, la jeune fille qu'on épouse n'est pas celle dont on est tombé amoureux.' (*Ombre*, ii. 158, 159.)

On September 8 a dramatization of *The Mayor of Casterbridge* by Mr. John Drinkwater was produced at the Barnes Theatre, and on the 20th the play was brought to Weymouth, where Hardy went to see it. He received a great ovation in the theatre, and also, on his return to Max Gate, from an enthusiastic crowd that collected round the Pavilion Theatre on the pier. From balconies and windows people were seen waving handkerchiefs as he drove past. In his diary he notes :

'20 *September*. Performance of *Mayor of Casterbridge* at Weymouth by London Company, a "flying matinée". Beautiful afternoon, scene outside the theatre finer than within.'

Writing to a friend about a proposed dramatization of *Jude the Obscure*, he observes :

'I may say that I am not keen on the new mode (as I suppose it is regarded, though really Elizabethan) of giving a series of episodes in the film manner instead of set scenes.

'Of the outlines I sent you which suggested themselves to me many years ago, I thought the one I called (I think) "4th Scheme" most feasible.

'Would not Arabella be the villain of the piece? — or Jude's personal constitution? — so far as there is any villain more than blind Chance. Christminster is of course the tragic influence of Jude's drama in one sense, but innocently so, and merely as crass obstruction. By the way it is not meant to be exclusively Oxford, but any old-fashioned University about the date of the story, 1860–1870, before there were such chances for poor men as there are now. I have somewhere printed that I had no feeling against Oxford in particular.'

A few days later he visited Mrs. Bankes at Kingston Lacy in Dorset, and was greatly interested in the priceless collection of pictures shown him. Of this occasion he writes :

'*End of September*. With F. on a visit to Mrs. Bankes at Kingston Lacy. She told me an amusing story when showing me a letter to Sir John Bankes from Charles the First, acknowledging that he had borrowed £500 from Sir John. Many years ago when she was showing the same letter to King Edward, who was much interested in it, she said, "Perhaps, Sir, that's a little matter which could now be set right". He replied quickly, "Statute of Limitations, Statute of Limitations".'

Another note :

'1 *November*. Went with Mr. Hanbury to Bockhampton and looked at fencing, trees, etc., with a view to tidying and secluding the Hardy house.'

That was his last visit to the place of his birth. It was always a matter of regret to him if he saw this abode in a state of neglect, or the garden uncherished.

During this month, November, his friend Colonel T. E. Lawrence called to say good-bye, before starting for India. Hardy was much affected by this parting, as T. E. Lawrence was one of his most valued friends. He went into the little porch and stood at the front door to see the departure of Lawrence on his motor-bicycle. This machine was difficult to start, and, thinking he might have to wait some time Hardy turned into the house to fetch a shawl to wrap round him. In the meantime, fearing that Hardy might take a chill, Lawrence started the motor-bicycle and hurried away. Returning a few moments after, Hardy was grieved that he had not seen the actual departure, and said that he had particularly wished to see Lawrence go.

The sight of animals being taken to market or driven to slaughter always aroused in Hardy feelings of intense pity, as he well knew, as must anyone living in or near a market-town, how much needless suffering is inflicted. In his notebook at this time he writes :

'*December* (1st Week). Walking with F. by railway saw bullocks and cows going to Islington (?) for slaughter.' Under this he drew a little pencil sketch of the rows of trucks as they were seen by him, with animals' heads at every opening, looking out at the green countryside they were leaving for scenes of horror in a far-off city. Hardy thought of this sight for long after. It was found in his will that he had left a sum of money to each of two societies 'to be applied so far as practicable to the investigation of the means by which animals are conveyed from their houses to the slaughter-houses with a view to the lessening of their sufferings in such transit'.

The year drew quietly to an end. On the 23rd of December a band of carol-singers from St. Peter's, Dorchester, came to Max Gate and sang to Hardy 'While Shepherds Watched' to the tune which used to be played by his father and grandfather, a copy of which he had given to the Rector.

A sadness fell upon the household, for Hardy's dog, Wessex, now thirteen years old, was ill and obviously near his end.

Two days after Christmas Day Hardy makes this entry :

'27 *December*. Our famous dog "Wessex" died at ½ past 6 in the evening, thirteen years of age.'

'28. Wessex buried.'

'28. *Night*. Wessex sleeps outside the house the first time for thirteen years.'

The dog lies in a small turfed grave in the shrubbery on the west side of Max Gate, where also were buried several pet cats and one other dog, Moss. On the headstone is this inscription drawn up by Hardy, and carved from his design :

THE
FAMOUS DOG
WESSEX
August 1913–27 Dec. 1926
Faithful. Unflinching.

There were those among Hardy's friends who thought that his life was definitely saddened by the loss of Wessex, the dog having been the companion of himself and his wife during twelve years of married life. Upon summer evenings or winter afternoons Wessex would walk with them up the grassy slope in the field in front of their house, to the stile that led into Came Plantation, and while Hardy rested on the stile the dog would sit on the ground and survey the view as his master was doing. On Frome Hill when his companions sat on the green bank by the roadside, or on the barrow that crowns the hill, he would lie in the grass at their feet and gaze at the landscape, 'as if', to quote Hardy's oft-repeated comment on this, 'it were the right thing to do'.

Those were happy innocent hours. A poem written after the dog's death, 'Dead " Wessex ", the dog to the household', well illustrates Hardy's sense of loss. Two of its verses are :

Do you look for me at times,
Wistful ones?
Do you look for me at times
Strained and still?
Do you look for me at times,
When the hour for walking chimes,
On that grassy path that climbs
Up the hill?

You may hear a jump or trot,
Wistful ones,
You may hear a jump or trot —
Mine, as 'twere —
You may hear a jump or trot
On the stair or path or plot;
But I shall cause it not,
Be not there.

On December 29 Hardy wrote to his friends Mr. and Mrs. Granville-Barker from Max Gate :

'. . . This is intended to be a New Year's letter, but I don't know if I have made a good shot at it. How kind of you to think of sending me Raymond Guyot's *Napoleon*. I have only glanced at it, at the text that is, as yet, but what an interesting collection of records bearing on the life of the man who finished the Revolution with "a whiff of grapeshot", and so crushed not only its final horrors but all the worthy aspirations of its earlier time, made them as if they had never been, and threw back human altruism scores, perhaps hundreds of years.'

'31 *December*. *New Year's Eve*. Did not sit up.'

In January 1927 'A Philosophical Fantasy' appeared in the *Fortnightly Review*. Hardy liked the year to open with a poem of this type from him in some leading review or newspaper. The quotation at the heading, 'Milton . . . made God argue', gives the keynote, and the philosophy is much as he had set forth before, but still a ray of hope is shown for the future of mankind.

> Aye, to human tribes nor kindlessness
> Nor love I've given, but mindlessness,
> Which state, though far from ending,
> May nevertheless be mending.

Weeks passed through a cold spring and Hardy's eighty-seventh birthday was reached. This year, instead of remaining at Max Gate, he motored with his wife to Netherton Hall in Devonshire, to spend a part of the day with friends, Helen and Harley Granville-Barker. In a letter written some months later, Mrs. Granville-Barker describes this visit.

'. . . There were no guests, just the peaceful routine of everyday life, for that last birthday here. Mr. Hardy said to you afterwards, you told me, that he thought it might be the last, but at the time he was not in any way sad or unlike himself. He noticed, as always, and unlike most old people, the smallest things. At luncheon, I remember, one of the lace doilies at his place got awry in an ugly way, showing the mat underneath, and I saw him, quietly and with the most delicate accuracy, setting it straight again — all the time taking his part in the talk.

'Wasn't it that day he said, speaking of Augustus John's portrait of him :

'"I don't know whether that is how I look or not — but that is how I *feel*"?

'In the afternoon we left him alone in the library because we thought he wanted to rest a little. It was cold, for June, and a wood fire was lighted.

'Once we peeped in at him through the garden window. He was not asleep but sitting, walled in with books, staring into the fire with that deep look of his. The cat had established itself on his knees and he was stroking it gently, but half-unconsciously.

'It was a wonderful picture of him. I shall not forget it. Nor shall I forget the gay and startlingly youthful gesture with which he flourished his hat towards us as, once in the motor-car, later that afternoon, he drove away from us.'

At the end of the day he seemed in a sad mood, and his wife sought to amuse him by a forecast of small festivities she had planned for his ninetieth birthday, which she assured him would be a great occasion. With a flash of gaiety he replied that he intended to spend that day in bed.

Once again the Balliol Players appeared at Max Gate, this year on July 6. As before, their visit gave Hardy considerable pleasure, and after their performance on the lawn of *Iphigenia in Aulis* he talked with them freely, appreciating their boyish ardour and their modesty.

A few days later he received visits from his friends Siegfried Sassoon and Mr. and Mrs. John Masefield, and on July 21 he laid the foundation-stone of the new building of the Dorchester Grammar School, which was to be seen clearly from the front gate of his house, looking towards the Hardy Monument, a noticeable object on the sky-line, to the south-west. It was Hardy's custom nearly every fine morning after breakfast in the summer to walk down to the gate to see what the weather was likely to be by observing this tower in the distance.

The day chosen for the stone-laying was cold and windy, by no means a suitable day for a man of Hardy's advanced years to stand in the open air bareheaded. Nevertheless he performed his task with great vigour, and gave the following address in a clear resonant voice that could be heard on the outskirts of the crowd that collected to hear him :

'I have been asked to execute the formal part of to-day's function, which has now been done, and it is not really necessary that I should add anything to the few words that are accustomed to be used at the laying of foundation or dedication stones. But as the circumstances of the present case are somewhat peculiar, I will just enlarge upon them for a minute or two.   What I have to say is mainly concerning the Elizabethan philanthropist, Thomas Hardy, who, with some en- couragement from the burgesses, endowed and rebuilt this ancient school after its first humble shape — him whose namesake I have the honour to be, and whose monument stands in the church of St. Peter, visible from this spot.   The well-known epitaph inscribed upon his tablet, unlike many epitaphs, does not, I am inclined to think, exag- gerate his virtues, since it was written, not by his relatives or depen- dents, but by the free burgesses of Dorchester in gratitude for his good action towards the town.   This good deed was accomplished in the latter part of the sixteenth century, and the substantial stone building in which it merged eventually still stands to dignify South Street, as we all know, and hope it may remain there.

'But what we know very little about is the personality of this first recorded Thomas Hardy of the Froome Valley here at our back, though his work abides.   He was without doubt of the family of the Hardys who landed in this county from Jersey in the fifteenth century, acquired small estates along the river upwards towards its source, and whose descendants have mostly remained hereabouts ever since, the Christian name of Thomas having been especially affected by them.   He died in 1599, and it is curious to think that though he must have had a modern love of learning not common in a remote county in those days, Shakespeare's name could hardly have been known to him, or at the most vaguely as that of a certain ingenious Mr. Shake- speare who amused the London playgoers ;  and that he died before Milton was born.

'In Carlylean phraseology, what manner of man he was when he walked this earth, we can but guess, or what he looked like, what he said and did in his lighter moments, and at what age he died.   But we may shrewdly conceive that he was a far-sighted man, and would not be much surprised, if he were to revisit the daylight, to find that his building had been outgrown, and no longer supplied the needs of the present inhabitants for the due education of their sons.   His next feeling might be to rejoice in the development of what was possibly an original design of his own, and to wish the reconstruction every success.

'We living ones all do that, and nobody more than I, my retire- ment from the Governing body having been necessitated by old age only.   Certainly everything promises well.   The site can hardly be surpassed in England for health, with its open surroundings, elevated and bracing situation, and dry subsoil, while it is near enough to the

sea to get very distinct whiffs of marine air.  Moreover, it is not so
far from the centre of the borough as to be beyond the walking powers
of the smallest boy.  It has a capable headmaster, holding every
modern idea on education within the limits of good judgement, and
assistant masters well equipped for their labours, which are not sine-
cures in these days.

'I will conclude by thanking the Governors and other friends for
their kind thought in asking me to undertake this formal initiation of
the new building, which marks such an interesting stage in the history
of the Dorchester Grammar School.'

After the ceremony, having spoken to a few friends, Hardy went
away without waiting for the social gathering that followed.  He was
very tired, and when he reached home he said that he had made his
last public appearance.

There seemed no ill after-effects, however, and on August 9
Hardy drove with Gustav Holst to 'Egdon Heath', just then purple
with heather.  They then went on to Puddletown and entered the
fine old church, and both climbed up into the gallery, where probably
some of Hardy's ancestors had sat in the choir, more than a century
earlier.

On August 8 he wrote to Mr. J. B. Priestley :

'. . . I send my sincere thanks for your kind gift of the "George
Meredith" book, and should have done so before if I had not fallen
into the sere, and weak eyesight did not trouble me.  I have read
your essay, or rather have had it read to me, and have been much
interested in the bright writing of one in whom I had already fancied
I discerned a coming force in letters.

'I am not at all a critic, especially *of* a critic, and when the author
he reviews is a man who was, off and on, a friend of mine for forty
years ; but it seems to me that you hold the scales very fairly.  Meredith was, as you recognize, and might have insisted on even more
strongly, and I always felt, in the direct succession of Congreve and
the artificial comedians of the Restoration, and in getting his brilliancy
we must put up with the fact that he would not, or could not — at
any rate did not — when aiming to represent the "Comic Spirit",
let himself discover the tragedy that always underlies Comedy if you
only scratch it deeply enough.'

During the same month Hardy and his wife motored to Bath and
back.  On the way they had lunch sitting on a grassy bank, as they
had done in former years, to Hardy's pleasure.  But now a curious

sadness brooded over them; lunching in the open air had lost its charm, and they did not attempt another picnic of this kind.

In Bath Hardy walked about and looked long and silently at various places that seemed to have an interest for him. He seemed like a ghost revisiting scenes of a long-dead past. After a considerable rest in the Pump Room they returned home. Hardy did not seem tired by this drive.

Some weeks later they motored to Ilminster, a little country town that Hardy had long desired to visit. He was interested in the church, and also in the tomb of the founder of Wadham College therein. By his wish, on their return, they drove past the quarries where Ham Hill stone was cut.

Stopping at Yeovil they had tea in a restaurant, where a band of some three musicians were playing. One of Hardy's most attractive characteristics was his ability to be interested in simple things, and before leaving he stood and listened appreciatively to the music, saying afterwards what a delightful episode that had been.

On September 6, an exceedingly wet day, Mr. and Mrs. John Galsworthy called on their way to London. During the visit Hardy told them the story of a murder that had happened eighty years before. Mr. Galsworthy seemed struck by these memories of Hardy's early childhood, and asked whether he had always remembered those days so vividly, or only lately. Hardy replied that he had always remembered clearly. He could recall what his mother had said about the Rush murder when he was about the age of six: 'The governess hanged him'. He was puzzled, and wondered how a governess could hang a man. Mr. and Mrs. Galsworthy thought that Hardy seemed better than when they saw him last, better, in fact, than they had ever seen him.

September 7 being a gloriously fine day, Hardy with his wife walked across the fields opposite Max Gate to see the building of the new Grammar School, then in progress.

During September Hardy was revising and rearranging the *Selected Poems* in the Golden Treasury Series in readiness for a new edition. The last entry but one in his notebook refers to the sending of the copy to the publishers, and finally, on the 19th of September, he notes that Mr. Weld of Lulworth Castle called with some friends. After this no more is written, but a few notes were made by his wife for the remaining weeks of 1927.

About the 21st of September they drove to Lulworth Castle to lunch with Mr. and Mrs. Weld and a house-party, and Hardy was much interested in all that he was shown in the Castle and in the adjoining church. A few weeks later he and his wife lunched at Charborough Park, the scene of *Two on a Tower*, the first time he had entered this house.

## NOTES BY F. E. H.

'*October* 24. A glorious day. T. and I walked across the field in front of Max Gate towards Came. We both stood on a little flat stone sunk in the path that we call our wishing stone, and I wished. T. may have done so, but he did not say.

'On the way he gathered up some waste paper that was blowing about the lane at the side of our house and buried it in the hedge with his stick, and going up the path to Came he stopped for quite a long time to pull off the branches of a tree a heap of dead weeds that had been thrown there by some untidy labourer who had been cleaning the field. He says that a man has no public spirit who passes by any untidiness out of doors, litter of paper or similar rubbish.'

'*October* 27. During the evening he spoke of an experience he had a few years ago. There were four or five people to tea at Max Gate, and he noticed a stranger standing by me most of the time. Afterwards he asked who that dark man was who stood by me. I told him that there was no stranger present, and I gave him the names of the three men who were there, all personal friends. He said that it was not one of these, and seemed to think that another person had actually been there. This afternoon he said : "I can see his face now".

'Later in the evening, during a terrific gale, I said that I did not wonder that some people disliked going along the dark road outside our house at night.

'T. replied that for twelve years he walked backwards and forwards from Bockhampton to Dorchester often in the dark, and he was only frightened twice. Once was when he was going up Stinsford Hill, no habitation of any sort being in sight, and he came upon two men sitting on chairs, one on either side of the road. By the moonlight he saw that they were strangers to him ; terrified, he took to his heels ; he never heard who they were or anything to explain the incident.

'The other time was when, as a small boy walking home from school, reading *Pilgrim's Progress*, he was so alarmed by the description of Apollyon that he hastily closed his book and went on his way trembling, thinking that Apollyon was going to spring out of a tree whose dark branches overhung the road. He remembered his terror, he said, that evening, seventy-five years afterwards.'

'*October* 30. At lunch T. H. talked about Severn, speaking with admiration of his friendship towards Keats. He said that it must have been quite disinterested, as Keats was then comparatively obscure.'

'*October* 31. Henry Williamson, the author of *Tarka the Otter*, called.'

'*November* 3. While he was having tea to-day, T. H. said that whenever he heard any music from *Il Trovatore*, it carried him back to the first year when he was in London and when he was strong and vigorous and enjoyed his life immensely. He thought that *Il Trovatore* was good music.'

'*November* 4. We drove in the afternoon to Stinsford, to put flowers on the family graves. The tombs are very green, being covered with moss because they are under a yew-tree. T. H. scraped off most of the moss with a little wooden implement like a toy spade, six inches in length, which he made with his own hands and which he carries in his pocket when he goes to Stinsford. He remarked that Walter de la Mare had told him that he preferred to see the gravestones green.

'Then we drove to Talbothays (his brother's house). As we turned up Dark Hill, T. H. pointed out the place where, as a small boy, he had left an umbrella in the hedge, having put it down while he cut a stick. He did not remember it until he reached home and his mother asked him where was his umbrella. As he went to school next morning he looked in the hedge and found it where he had left it.

'After having been with H. H. and K. H. (the brother and sister) for half an hour we returned home.'

Thus ended a series of visits paid regularly to his family extending over forty years. While his parents were alive, Hardy went to see them at Bockhampton nearly every Sunday afternoon when he was in Dorchester, walking at first, then cycling. After his mother's death he visited his two sisters and his brother at Bockhampton, and later at Talbothays, to which house they moved in 1912. These visits continued until the last year or two of his life, when he was unable to go very often. He cycled there in fine weather until he was over eighty, and then he walked, until the distance seemed beyond his powers. Stinsford was a favourite haunt until the last few months of his life, the walk there from Max Gate, across the water-meadows, being a particularly beautiful one; and the churchyard, to him, the most hallowed spot on earth.

'*November* 4, *continued.* At tea T. H. said that he had been pleased to read that day an article by the composer Miss Ethel Smyth, saying that *Il Trovatore* was good music. He reminded me of what he said yesterday.'

'*November* 11. *Armistice Day.* T. came downstairs from his study and listened to the broadcasting of a service at Canterbury Cathedral. We stood there for the two minutes' silence. He said afterwards that he had been thinking of Frank George, his cousin, who was killed at Gallipoli.

'In the afternoon we took one of our usual little walks, around "the triangle" as we call it, that is down the lane by the side of our house, and along the cinder-path beside the railway line. We stood and watched a goods train carrying away huge blocks of Portland stone as we have done so many times. He seems never tired of watching these stone-laden trucks. He said he thought that the shape of Portland would be changed in the course of years by the continual cutting away of its surface.

'Sitting by the fire after tea he told me about various families of poachers he had known as a boy, and how, when a thatched house at Bockhampton was pulled down, a pair of swingels was found under the thatch. This was an instrument of defence used by poachers, and capable of killing a man.[1]

'He said that if he had his life over again he would prefer to be a small architect in a country town, like Mr. Hicks at Dorchester, to whom he was articled.'

'*November* 17. To-day T. H. was speaking, and evidently thinking a great deal, about a friend, a year or two older than himself, who was a fellow-pupil at Mr. Hicks's office. I felt, as he talked, that he would like to meet this man again more than anyone in the world. He is in Australia now, if alive, and must be nearly ninety. His name is Henry Robert Bastow; he was a Baptist and evidently a very religious youth, and T. H. was devoted to him. I suggested that we might find out something about him by sending an advertisement to Australian newspapers, but T. H. thought that would not be wise.'

'*Sunday, November* 27. The fifteenth anniversary of the death of Emma Lavinia Hardy; Thursday was the anniversary of the death

[1] Poachers' iron swingels. A strip of iron ran down three or four sides of the flail part, and the two flails were united by three or four links of chain, the keepers carrying cutlasses which would cut off the ordinary eel-skin hinge of a flail. — *From T. H.'s notebook, Dec. 1884.*

of Mary, his elder sister. For two or three days he has been wearing
a black hat as a token of mourning, and carries a black walking-stick
that belonged to his first wife, all strangely moving.

'T. H. has been writing almost all the day, revising poems.
When he came down to tea he brought one to show me, about a
desolate spring morning, and a shepherd counting his sheep and not
noticing the weather.' This is the poem in *Winter Words* called 'An
Unkindly May'.

'*November* 28. Speaking about ambition T. said to-day that he
had done all that he meant to do, but he did not know whether it
had been worth doing.

'His only ambition, so far as he could remember, was to have
some poem or poems in a good anthology like the Golden Treasury.

'The model he had set before him was "Drink to me only", by
Ben Jonson.'

The earliest recollection of his childhood (as he had told me before) was that when he was four years old his father gave him a small
toy concertina and wrote on it, 'Thomas Hardy, 1844'. By this
inscription he knew, in after years, his age when that happened.

Also he remembered, perhaps a little later than this, being in the
garden at Bockhampton with his father on a bitterly cold winter day.
They noticed a fieldfare, half-frozen, and the father took up a stone
idly and threw it at the bird, possibly not meaning to hit it. The
fieldfare fell dead, and the child Thomas picked it up and it was as
light as a feather, all skin and bone, practically starved. He said he
had never forgotten how the body of the fieldfare felt in his hand:
the memory had always haunted him.

He recalled how, crossing the eweleaze when a child, he went on
hands and knees and pretended to eat grass in order to see what the
sheep would do. Presently he looked up and found them gathered
around in a close ring, gazing at him with astonished faces.

An illness, which at the commencement did not seem to be serious,
began on December 11. On the morning of that day he sat at the
writing-table in his study, and felt totally unable to work. This, he
said, was the first time that such a thing had happened to him.

From then his strength waned daily. He was anxious that a poem
he had written, 'Christmas in the Elgin Room', should be copied and
sent to *The Times*. This was done, and he asked his wife anxiously
whether she had posted it with her own hands. When she assured
him that she had done so he seemed content, and said he was glad

that he had cleared everything up. Two days later he received a personal letter of thanks, with a warm appreciation of his work, from the editor of *The Times*. This gave him pleasure, and he asked that a reply should be sent.

He continued to come downstairs to sit for a few hours daily, until Christmas Day. After that he came downstairs no more.

On December 26 he said that he had been thinking of the Nativity and of the Massacre of the Innocents, and his wife read to him the gospel accounts, and also articles in the *Encyclopædia Biblica*. He remarked that there was not a grain of evidence that the gospel story was true in any detail.

As the year ended a window in the dressing-room adjoining his bedroom was opened that he might hear the bells, as that had always pleased him. But now he said that he could not hear them, and did not seem interested.

His strength still failed. The weather was bitterly cold, and snow had fallen heavily, being twelve inches deep in parts of the garden. In the road outside there were snow-drifts that in places would reach a man's waist.

By desire of the local practitioner additional advice was called in, and Hardy's friend Sir Henry Head, who was living in the neighbourhood, made invaluable suggestions and kept a watchful eye upon the case. But the weakness increased daily.

He could no longer listen to the reading of prose, though a short poem now and again interested him. In the middle of one night he asked his wife to read aloud to him 'The Listeners', by Walter de la Mare.

On January 10 he made a strong rally, and although he was implored not to do so he insisted upon writing a cheque for his subscription to the Pension Fund of the Society of Authors. For the first time in his life he made a slightly feeble signature, unlike his usual beautiful firm handwriting, and then he laid down his pen.

Later he was interested to learn that J. M. Barrie, his friend of many years, had arrived from London to assist in any way that might be possible. He was amused when told that this visitor had gone to the kitchen door to avoid any disturbance by ringing the front-door bell.

In the evening he asked that Robert Browning's poem 'Rabbi Ben Ezra' should be read aloud to him. While reading it his wife glanced at his face to see whether he were tired, the poem being a long one of thirty-two stanzas, and she was struck by the look of wistful intentness with which Hardy was listening. He indicated that he wished to hear the poem to the end.

He had a better night, and in the morning of January 11 seemed so much stronger that one at least of those who watched beside him had confident hopes of his recovery, and an atmosphere of joy prevailed in the sick-room. An immense bunch of grapes arrived from London, sent by a friend, and this aroused in Hardy great interest. As a rule he disliked receiving gifts, but on this occasion he showed an almost childlike pleasure, and insisted upon the grapes being held up for the inspection of the doctor, and whoever came into the room. He ate some, and said quite gaily, 'I'm going on with these'. Everything he had that day in the way of food or drink he seemed to appreciate keenly, though naturally he took but little. As it grew dusk, after a long musing silence, he asked his wife to repeat to him a verse from the *Rubáiyát of Omar Khayyám*, beginning

Oh, Thou, who Man of baser Earth—

She took his copy of this work from his bedside and read to him :

Oh, Thou, who Man of baser Earth didst make,
And ev'n with Paradise devise the Snake :
For all the Sin wherewith the Face of Man
Is blacken'd — Man's forgiveness give — and take!

He indicated that he wished no more to be read.

In the evening he had a sharp heart attack of a kind he had never had before. The doctor was summoned and came quickly, joining Mrs. Hardy at the bedside. Hardy remained conscious until a few minutes before the end. Shortly after nine he died.

An hour later one, going to his bedside yet again, saw on the death-face an expression such as she had never seen before on any being, or indeed on any presentment of the human countenance. It was a look of radiant triumph such as imagination could never have conceived. Later the first radiance passed away, but dignity and peace remained as long as eyes could see the mortal features of Thomas Hardy.

The dawn of the following day rose in almost unparalleled splendour. Flaming and magnificent the sky stretched its banners over the dark pines that stood sentinel around.

# APPENDIX I

On the morning of Thursday, January 12, the Dean of Westminster readily gave his consent to a proposal that Hardy should be buried in Westminster Abbey; and news of this proposal and its acceptance was sent to Max Gate. There it was well known that Hardy's own wish was to be buried at Stinsford, amid the graves of his ancestors and of his first wife. After much consideration a compromise was found between this definite personal wish and the nation's claim to the ashes of the great poet. On Friday, January 13, his heart was taken out of his body and placed by itself in a casket. On Saturday, January 14, the body was sent to Woking for cremation, and thence the ashes were taken the same day to Westminster Abbey and placed in the Chapel of St. Faith to await interment. On Sunday, January 15, the casket containing the heart was taken to the church at Stinsford, where it was laid on the altar steps.

At two o'clock on Monday, January 16, there were three services in three different churches. In Westminster Abbey the poet's wife and sister were the chief mourners, while in the presence of a great crowd, which included representatives of the King and other members of the Royal Family, and of many learned and other societies, the ashes of Thomas Hardy were buried with stately ceremonial in Poets' Corner. The pall-bearers were the Prime Minister (Mr. Stanley Baldwin) and Mr. Ramsay MacDonald, representing the Government and Parliament; Sir James Barrie, Mr. John Galsworthy, Sir Edmund Gosse, Professor A. E. Housman, Mr. Rudyard Kipling, and Mr. Bernard Shaw, representing literature; and the Master of Magdalene College, Cambridge (Mr. A. S. Ramsey), and the Pro-Provost of Queen's College, Oxford (Dr. E. M. Walker), representing the Colleges of which Hardy was an honorary Fellow. A spadeful of Dorset earth, sent by a Dorset farm labourer, Mr. Christopher Corbin, was sprinkled on the casket. In spite of the cold and wet the streets about the Abbey were full of people who had been unable to obtain admission to the service, but came as near as they might to taking part in it. At the same hour at Stinsford, where Hardy was baptized, and where as boy and man he had often worshipped, his brother,

447

Mr. Henry Hardy, was the chief mourner, while, in the presence of a rural population, the heart of this lover of rural Wessex was buried in the grave of his first wife among the Hardy tombs under the great yew-tree in the corner of the churchyard.    And in Dorchester all business was suspended for an hour, while at St. Peter's Church the Mayor and Corporation and many other dignitaries and societies attended a memorial service in which the whole neighbourhood joined.                                                                    H. C.

# APPENDIX II

I

Max Gate, Dorchester,
*Dec.* 21, 1914.

Dear Sir,

I have read with much interest the lecture on *The Longest Price of War* that you kindly send : and its perusal does not diminish the gloom with which this ghastly business on the Continent fills me, as it fills so many. The argument would seem to favour Conscription, since the inert, if not the unhealthy, would be taken, I imagine.

Your visits to *The Dynasts* show that, as Granville-Barker foretold, thoughtful people would care about it. My own opinion when I saw it was that it was the only sort of thing likely to take persons of musing turn into a theatre at this time.

I have not read M. Bergson's book, and if you should not find it troublesome to send your copy as you suggest, please do.

The theory of the Prime Force that I used in *The Dynasts* was published in Jan. 1904. The nature of the determination embraced in the theory is that of a collective will ; so that there is a proportion of the total will in each part of the whole, and each part has therefore, in strictness, *some* freedom, which would, in fact, be operative as such whenever the remaining great mass of will in the universe should happen to be in equilibrium.

However, as the work is intended to be a poetic drama and not a philosophic treatise I did not feel bound to develop this.

The assumption of unconsciousness in the driving force is, of course, not new. But I think the view of the unconscious force as gradually *becoming* conscious : *i.e.* that consciousness is creeping further and further back towards the origin of force, had never (so far as I know) been advanced before *The Dynasts* appeared. But being only a mere impressionist I must not pretend to be a philosopher in a letter, and ask you to believe me,

Sincerely yours,

Thomas Hardy.

Dr. Saleeby.

449

2

Dear Dr. Saleeby,

Your activities are unlimited. I should like to hear your address on 'Our War for International Law'. Personally I feel rather disheartened when I think it probable that the war will end by sheer exhaustion of the combatants, and that things will be left much as they were before. But I hope not.

I have been now and then dipping into your Bergson, and shall be returning the volume soon. I suppose I may assume that you are more or less disciple, or fellow-philosopher, of his. Therefore you may be rather shocked by some views I hold about his teachings — if I may say I hold any views about anything whatever, which I hardly do.

His theories are certainly much more delightful than those they contest, and I for one would gladly believe them, but I cannot help feeling all the time that he is rather an imaginative and poetical writer than a reasoner, and that for his attractive assertions he does not adduce any proofs whatever. His use of the word 'creation' seems loose to me. Then, as to 'conduct'. I fail to see how, if it is not mechanism, it can be other than Caprice, though he denies it (p. 50). And he says that Mechanism and Finalism (I agree with him as to Finalism) are only external views of our conduct.

'Our conduct extends between them, and slips much further.' Well, I hope it may, but he nowhere shows that it does. And again : 'a mechanistic conception . . . treats the living as the inert. . . . Let us, on the contrary, trace a line of demarcation between the inert and the living (208).' Well, let us, to our great pleasure, if we can see why we should introduce an inconsistent rupture of order into uniform and consistent laws of the same.

You will see how much I want to be a Bergsonian (indeed I have for many years). But I fear that his philosophy is, in the bulk, only our old friend Dualism in a new suit of clothes — an ingenious fancy without real foundation, and more complicated, and therefore less likely than the determinist fancy and others that he endeavours to overthrow.

You must not think me a hard-hearted rationalist for all this. Half my time (particularly when I write verse) I believe — in the modern use of the word — not only in things that Bergson does, but in spectres, mysterious voices, intuitions, omens, dreams, haunted places, etc., etc.

But then, I do not believe in these in the old sense of belief any more for that; and in arguing against Bergsonism I have, of course, meant belief in its old sense when I aver myself incredulous.

Sincerely yours,

THOMAS HARDY.[1]

3

MAX GATE, DORCHESTER,<br>16.3.1915.

DEAR DR. SALEEBY,

My thanks for the revised form of *The Longest Price of War*, which I am reading.

.        .        .        .        .        .

I am returning, or shall be in a day or two, your volume of Bergson. It is most interesting reading, and one likes to give way to its views and assurances without criticizing them.

If, however, we ask for reasons and proof (which I don't care to do) I am afraid we do not get them.

An *élan vital* — by which I understand him to mean a sort of additional and spiritual force, beyond the merely unconscious push of life — the 'will' of other philosophers that propels growth and development — seems much less probable than single and simple determinism, or what he calls mechanism, because it is more complex : and where proof is impossible probability must be our guide. His partly mechanistic and partly creative theory seems to me clumsy and confused.

He speaks of 'the enormous gap that separates even the lowest form of life from the inorganic world'. Here again it is more probable that organic and inorganic modulate into each other, one nature and law operating throughout. But the most fatal objection to his view of creation *plus* propulsion seems to me to lie in the existence of pain. If nature were creative she would have created painlessness, or be

[1] A great part of this letter will be found in a slightly different form on pp. 369-70 of this volume. Both versions are printed in order to illustrate Hardy's artistic inability to rest content with anything that he wrote until he had brought the expression as near to his thought as language would allow. He would, for instance, often go on revising his poems for his own satisfaction after their publication in book form.—F. E. H.

in process of creating it — pain being the first thing we instinctively fly from. If on the other hand we cannot introduce into life what is not already there, and are bound to mere recombination of old materials, the persistence of pain is intelligible.

Sincerely yours,

THOMAS HARDY.

# APPENDIX III

MAX GATE, DORCHESTER,
*New Year's Eve*, 1907.

MY DEAR CLODD,

I write a line to thank you for that nice little copy of Munro's Lucretius, and to wish you a happy New Year. I am familiar with two translations of the poet, but not with this one, so the book is not wasted.

I have been thinking what a happy man you must be at this time of the year, in having to write your name 8000 times. Nobody wants me to write mine once!

In two or three days I shall have done with the proofs of *Dynasts* III. It is well that the business should be over, for I have been living in Wellington's campaigns so much lately that, like George IV, I am almost positive that I took part in the battle of Waterloo, and have written of it from memory.

What new side of science are you writing about at present?

Yours sincerely,

THOMAS HARDY.

MAX GATE,
20:2:1908.

MY DEAR CLODD,

I must send a line or two in answer to your letter. What you remind me of — the lyrical account of the fauna of Waterloo field on the eve of the battle is, curiously enough, the page (p. 282) that struck me, in looking back over the book, as being the most original in it. Though, of course, a thing may be original without being good. However, it does happen that (so far as I know) in the many treatments of Waterloo in literature, those particular personages who were present have never been alluded to before.

Yes: I left off on a note of hope. It was just as well that the Pities should have the last word, since, like *Paradise Lost*, *The Dynasts* proves nothing.

Always yours sincerely,

THOMAS HARDY.

*P.S.*—The idea of the Unconscious Will becoming conscious with flux of time, is also new, I think, whatever it may be worth. At any rate I have never met with it anywhere.—T. H.

MAX GATE, DORCHESTER,<br>28:8:1914.

MY DEAR CLODD,

I fear we cannot take advantage of your kind invitation, and pay you a visit just now — much as in some respects we should like to. With the Germans (apparently) only a week from Paris, the native hue of resolution is sicklied o'er with the pale cast of thought. We shall hope to come when things look brighter.

Trifling incidents here bring home to us the condition of affairs not far off — as I daresay they do to you still more — sentries with gleaming bayonets at unexpected places as we motor along, the steady flow of soldiers through here to Weymouth, and their disappearance across the Channel in the silence of night, and the 1000 prisoners whom we get glimpses of through chinks, mark these fine days. The prisoners, they say, have already mustered enough broken English to say 'Shoot Kaiser!' and oblige us by playing 'God Save the King' on their concertinas and fiddles. Whether this is 'meant sarcastic', as Artemus Ward used to say, I cannot tell.

I was pleased to know that you were so comfortable, when I was picturing you in your shirt sleeves with a lot of other robust Aldeburghers digging a huge trench from Aldeburgh church to the top of those steps we go down to your house, streaming with sweat, and drinking pots of beer between the shovellings (English beer of course).

Sincerely yours,

THOMAS HARDY.

*P.S.*—Yes: everybody seems to be reading *The Dynasts* just now — at least, so a writer in the *Daily News* who called here this morning tells me.—T. H.

# INDEX

St. Margaret's, Westminster, 404
St. Mark's, Venice, 193
St. Martin's Place (No. 8), 36, 38, 45
St. Mary Abbots, Kensington, 210
St. Mary's, Kilburn, 38
St. Matthias's, Richmond, 45
St. Pancras (Old) Churchyard, 44-5, 131
St. Paul's Cathedral, 42, 322
St. Peter's, Bournemouth, 45
St. Peter's, Dorchester, 5, 169-70, 343
St. Peter's, Paddington, 101
St. Saviour's, Southwark, 268
Saleeby, Dr. C. W., letters to, 369-70, 449-52
Salisbury, 38, 153, 388, 389, 419 ; Cathedral, 295-6, 420
Salisbury, Lord, 171, 199, 245
Sambourne, Linley, 181
Sargent, John, 361
Sassoon, Siegfried, 390, 416, 426, 430, 437
'Satires in Fifteen Glimpses', see *Satires of Circumstance*
*Satires of Circumstance, Lyrics and Reveries*, 79, 355, 367
*Saturday Review*, 39, 60, 75, 88, 91, 95, 295
Savile Club, 121, 129, 160, 200, 201, 211, 226, 234, 237, 253, 266
Saxelby, F., 356
Scarborough, 239
Scheveningen, 110, 120
'Schreckhorn, The' (poem), 293
Scotland, visits to, 150, 239
*Scots Observer*, 240
Scott, Sir Gilbert, 404
Scott, Sir Walter, 49, 150, 203, 239
Scott, Lady, 239
Scribner, Messrs., 252
*Scribner's Magazine*, 191
Seaman, Sir Owen, 366
Sedgemoor, battle of, 6
Selby, James, 116
*Selected Poems of Thomas Hardy* (Golden Treasury), 374, 440
Selous, F. C., 262
Sergeant, Captain and Mrs., 91
Seven Dials, 42
Shaftesbury, 107, 214
Shaftesbury, Lady, 383
Shaftesbury, Lord, 112, 422
Shakespeare, 24, 53, 59, 77, 98, 108, 152, 203, 238, 281, 282, 325, 326, 386
'Shakespeare after three hundred years, To' (poem), 372, 394
Shakespeare Memorial Committee, the, 326, 341-2

Shaw, G. B., 108, 325, 334, 423-4, 447 ; Mrs., 334, 423-4
'She, to Him' (poem), 54
Shelley, 17, 42, 131, 188, 189, 193, 277, 304, 345, 370, 383 n., 384
Shelley, Mary, 45
Shelley, Sir Percy and Lady, 45, 131
Sheridan, Miss, 219, 259
Sheridan, Mr. and Mrs. A. Brinsley, 219, 233, 259, 383
Sherren, Tom, 125
Shipley, Dr., 323
Shorthand, Hardy's progress in, 41
Shrewsbury, 258
Shroton Fair, 116
'Sick Battle-God, The' (poem), 365, 368
Sidney, Sir Philip, 185
Silchester, 292
'Singer Asleep, A' (poem), 349
Skinner Street, 42
Skirrow, Mrs., 182
Slater, John, 364, 403-4
'Sleep-worker, The' (poem), 310
Smaylh'ome Tower, 239
Smith, Bosworth, 77, 127, 250, 254, 342
Smith, Sir Charles Euan, 257
Smith, G. M., 100, 101, 113, 134
Smith, Miss (daughter of G. M. Smith), 100
Smith, Mrs. G. M., 100, 134, 167
Smith, Henry, 127
Smith, Henry (of West Stafford), 203
Smith, Rev. J. Alexander, letter to, 307
Smith, L. Pearsall, 427
Smith, Canon R., 249-50
Smith, Reginald, 335
'Smith, Stephen' and his father, originals of, 73
Smith, Sydney, 181
Smith, Professor T. Roger, 87, 89, 90, 91
Smith, W. F. D., 277
Smith, Elder and Co., Messrs., 101, 121, 122, 124, 138, 160, 180
Smithfield, 17
Smugglers, 107-8
Smyth, Dame Ethel, 443
Society for the Protection of Ancient Buildings, 331
Society of Authors, the, 346, 404, 406-7, 445
Society of British Artists, 184
Society of Dorset Men, the, 337, 341, 347, 402
'Songs of Five-and-Twenty Years' (projected volume, 1892), 243

Thornton, Douglas, 371
Thornycroft, Sir Hamo, 164, 201, 306, 370, 430
Thornycroft, Lady, 430
*Three Wayfarers, The* (dramatic version of *The Three Strangers*), 256, 357
Thring, G. Herbert, letter to, 406-7
Tichborne Case, the, 251
Tietjens, 43
Tilley, Mr., 407
*Time against Two* (tentative title of *The Well-Beloved*), 164
*Time's Laughingstocks*, 332, 345, 347, 348, 356, 409
*Times, The*, 162, 207, 214, 265, 278, 292-3, 294, 319-20, 322, 330, 344, 345, 356, 367, 373, 398, 407, 414, 418, 419, 424, 425, 428, 444-5; reviews in, 99, 124
Tindal-Atkinson, Mr. (Serjeant-at-Law), 151
Tinsley, W., 83, 88-90
Tinsley Brothers, Messrs., 76-7, 83-4, 88-9, 101
*Tinsley's Magazine*, 89
Tintagel, 71, 75, 78, 91, 92, 373; Hardy's drawing of, 419
Tintern Abbey, 93
*Titanic* disaster, the, 357
'To C. F. H.' (poem), 414
'To My Father's Violin' (poem), 410
'To Shakespeare' (poem), 372, 394
'To the Matterhorn' (poem), 294
'Toad Fair', 112
Tolbort, T. W. Hooper, 32, 161-2
Toller-Welme, 5, 214
Tolstoy, 257, 274, 322
Toole, J. L., 138, 256-7
Tooting, Upper (1 Arundel Terrace), 118, 120, 124, 127, 133, 137, 149
Torquay, 370, 377
'Townsend' (home of the Swetmans *q.v.*), 6
'Tragedy of Two Ambitions, A' (short story), 213, 215
'Trampwoman's Tragedy, A' (poem), 311-12, 317
Trebarwith Strand, 71
Trevelyan, G. M., 366
Trevelyan, Mr., 254
Treves, Sir Frederick, 336, 371, 386, 423, 424
Treves, Lady, 336, 371
Trocadero Music Hall, 253
Trollope, Anthony, 51, 112-13
Trossachs, visit to, 150

Trouville, 139
*Trumpet-Major, The*, 17, 19, 138, 145, 146, 362, 416; dramatized, 360; Hardy's drawings for first edition, 388
Tryon, Admiral, 257
Turner, J. M. W., 185, 216, 329
Turnpike tolls, auction of, 158
Twain, Mark, 160
*Two on a Tower*, 151, 154, 267, 441
'Two Rosalinds, The' (poem), 228
Tyndale, Walter, 326

'Unborn, The' (poem), 409
*Under the Greenwood Tree*, 12, 86, 88-9, 91, 92, 97, 101, 353, 384, 394, 413, 429
dramatized, 353
'Under the Waterfall' (poem), 71 n.
'Unkindly May, An' (poem), 444
Upper Tooting, *see* Tooting
Up-Sydling, 5, 214
Upwey, 129
Usher, Mr., 239

Vaudeville Theatre, 234
Venice, 192-5, 222; St. Mark's, 193
Ventnor, visit to, 349
Verdi, 300
Versailles, 155
Victoria, Queen, 150, 200-1
Vincent, Sir Edgar, 323
Virginia, University of, 343
'Voices from Things growing in a Country Churchyard' (poem), 413
Voss, T., 92, 214
Vreeland, Admiral (of the U.S. Navy), 354

Wade-Gery, H. T., 425
Wagner, Hardy on, 181, 329-30
'Waiting Supper, The' (short story), 204
Wakefield, Bishop of, and *Jude*, 277-8
Wales, the Prince of, 37, 39, 52, 199; at Max Gate, 422
Walker, Dr. E. M. (Pro-Provost of Queen's College, Oxford), 447
Walpole, Horace, 9, 59, 164
Wandsworth Common, 118, 120, 149
War, Hardy on, 303, 387
War propaganda, conference of literary men on (Sept. 1914), 366
Ward, Humphry, 254; Mrs., 279
Ward, Leslie, 246
Wareham, 5; tune, 337
Warwick, Lord, 281

# THE ORIGINS OF THE COLD WAR
# AND CONTEMPORARY EUROPE

Modern Scholarship on European History

Henry A. Turner, Jr.
General Editor

# THE
# ORIGINS
## OF THE
# COLD WAR
## AND
# CONTEMPORARY
# EUROPE

EDITED WITH AN INTRODUCTION BY
## CHARLES S. MAIER
Modern Scholarship on European History

New Viewpoints
A Division of Franklin Watts
New York | London | 1978

New Viewpoints
A Division of Franklin Watts
730 Fifth Avenue
New York, New York 10019

92562

Library of Congress Cataloging in Publication Data
Main entry under title:

The Origins of the cold war and contemporary
Europe.

  (Modern scholarship on European history)
  Includes bibliographical references and index.
  1. World politics—1945—    —Addresses, essays,
lectures.  2.  Europe—Politics and government—
1945—    —Addresses, essays, lectures.  3.  Economic assistance, American—Europe—Addresses, essays, lectures.  I.  Maier, Charles S.
D843.|O|65         327′.09′044              78-17915
ISBN 0–531–05397–0
ISBN 0–531–05607–4 pbk.

# Acknowledgments

The author gratefully acknowledges the following authors and publishers: the Charles Warren Center for Studies in American History at Harvard University and the editors of *Perspectives in American History* for permission to reprint his own article "Revisionism and the Interpretation of Cold War Origins" from *Perspectives in American History*, IV (1970), pp. 313–347; Franz Schurmann and Pantheon Books division of Random House, Inc., for permission to reprint selections from pages 8–17, 46–53, 56–62, 64–68, 91–100, 105–107 of *The Logic of World Power: An Inquiry into the Origins, Currents and Contradictions of World Politics* (New York, 1974); Radomír Luža and Princeton University Press for permission to reprint "Czechoslovakia Between Democracy and Communism," from Luža and Victor S. Mamatey, eds., *A History of the Czechoslovak Republic, 1914– 1948* (copyright [c] 1973 by Princeton University Press), pp. 387– 415; Daniel Yergin and Houghton Mifflin Company, for permission to reprint chapter 12, "The Margin of Safety," from *Shattered Peace: The Origins of the Cold War and the National Security State* (Boston, 1977), pp. 303–335 with end notes, pp. 472–477; John Gimbel and Stanford University Press and the Board of Trustees of the Leland Stanford Junior University for permission to reproduce chapter 19 (pages 247–266) and pages 267–270, 274–279 of chapter 20 along with the end notes (pp. 325–331) from *The Origins of the Marshall Plan*, copyright (c), 1976; Hadley Arkes and Princeton University Press for permission to reprint chapter 14, "Theory and Coercion in the ECA," from *Bureaucracy, the Marshall Plan, and the National Interest* (copyright [c] 1972 by Princeton University Press), pp. 301– 321; and to Lutz Niethammer and the Bund Verlag of Cologne, Germany for permission to reprint the major portion (pp. 313–354) of the essay "Strukturreform und Wachstumspakt," from Heinz Oskar Vetter, ed., *Vom Sozialistengesetz zur Mitbestimmung. Zum 100. Geburtstag von Hans Böckler* (Cologne, 1975), pp. 303–358.

# Contents

# Introduction

The selection of essays in this volume has a purpose different from most other Cold War anthologies. I have focused less on the question of responsibility for the Cold War than upon the relationship of the Soviet-American antagonism to national political and social developments after World War II. Thus this collection intentionally omits some articles that were central to historical debate five to ten years ago. At that time scholarship centered on the question of "revisionism," or the reassessment of the respective contributions of the United States and the Soviet Union to the bitter post-World War II military and ideological confrontation. That debate, in my view, has not been neatly resolved, although issues have been narrowed and language has become less stridently polemical. Non-revisionists recognize that imperial as well as idealistic impulses motivated the American conduct of world politics, while recent critics are less accusatory than their predecessors a decade back. But just as important, the question of guilt or innocence has become less preoccupying as scholars have turned toward exploring the effect of the Cold War upon individual societies.

This volume seeks to illuminate the interaction of the Cold War with domestic politics and social structures. The emphasis is suggested by the fact that the anthology forms part of a series on "Modern Scholarship on European History." It also derives from my own scholarly interests, since I am in the midst of research on the reorganization of the European political economy after the Second World War. One aspect of that investigation must be the influence of the Cold War: the impact of the United States and the Soviet Union on countries that had toppled from an earlier preeminence into disarray and exhaustion.

On the other hand, the Cold War was only one of several factors in the formation of contemporary Europe: the reaction to the mass unemployment of the 1930s, the rejection of fascist authoritarianism, the response to decolonization, growing wealth—all have helped create the political society we have today. This collection cannot illuminate all these aspects; it can only begin to reveal the interaction of the superpowers' rivalry and the shaping of contemporary European institutions. Nevertheless, these articles summon the historian of Europe to consider the bipolar conflict that overshadowed his countries of concern. And they call upon the American historian to move outside the usual studies of Washington's diplomacy to reflect on the effects it produced within other societies.

Unfortunately, the few essays chosen here can represent only the beginning of this dual enterprise. The size of the volume alone compels a narrow selection. But there are further difficulties as well. The archival sources that most historians of Europe can utilize are less available for the period after 1945, although they can draw upon the United States diplomatic records now open for research through 1950 and the British cabinet papers, which are sequentially released with a thirty-year delay, such that 1947's records thus opened on January 1, 1978. Many of the essays published on this period are thus based upon private holdings, on the press, official statements, congressional or parliamentary debates, and the like. In some cases, too, potentially valuable chapters from larger books lack a sufficient impact when extracted: they cannot be used alone effectively. Some of the European literature, moreover, goes into a level of detail on episodes whose intensive coverage cannot easily be justified in this collection. Thus many factors have constrained selection, and scholars in the field may miss articles here that they would have preferred to see.

The first two pieces are intended to provide overviews of Cold War issues and the sources of American policy; for without the background of United States choices, European results cannot properly be appreciated. I have led off with a historiographical résumé I wrote in 1970 designed to clarify the status of debate as it then existed. Some of the outstanding works since that date will be cited in the following pages. My own work criticized revisionist scholarship, and while I sought to be fair, readers may naturally dissent. Even as a critic, moreover, one must recognize that in historical writing the question of "fruitfulness" is a different one from that of being right or wrong. For example, the Beard thesis on the origins of the Constitution and the Turner thesis on the closing of the frontier set new questions and opened up new research hypotheses even if they were later modified. So, too, the major critical histories of American policy have forced debate and compelled an inquiry into aspects of our goals and strategies that were previously unquestioned.

The second selection, a patchwork extract from Franz Schurmann's book, *The Logic of World Power*, is more an essay than a monograph. In my judgment Schurmann has written a very suggestive discussion of American objectives, though it is one that is hard to confirm with documentation. But of all the works that try to plumb the relationship between American capitalism and United States foreign policy, his is one of the most subtle and interesting. It makes full allowance for the fact that business interests in the United States have generally fallen into at least two major groups that tend to encourage different foreign-policy orientations. It further stresses the natural connection between high-technology weaponry and the centralization of executive power.

The following selections concern the formation of American policies and their impact upon European societies. The harshest impact of the Cold War fell, of course, on Eastern Europe, and I have chosen for inclusion here an essay on the history of Czechoslovakia from 1945 until the communist take-over in 1948. The author is an experienced historian of international affairs, has a command of East European languages, and offers one of the few treatments in English that concentrates on the internal developments of an East European society from its own point of view. Luža's essay reveals how difficult the maintenance of a compromise course was for the Czech democracy. On the other hand, Daniel Yergin has suggested that, for all the ruthlessness of the Czech communists and the Soviet leadership, grave deficiencies in American diplomacy facilitated the communist take-over. In a chapter of his book—not the one included here—he argues that American policymakers by and large wrote off Czechoslovakia by the fall of 1947. If Yergin's interpretation is correct, then Washington's failure takes on tragic proportions and must be seen as reminiscent of the Anglo-French write-off of Czechoslovakia that had taken place at Munich a decade earlier. For more detail on the countries of Eastern Europe and their fate, the student can turn later to Hugh Seton-Watson's account or to François Fejtö's.[1] And for a radically different perspective, Gabriel Kolko's work remains problematic but an important component of the historical debate. According to Kolko, no real grounds for democratic reconstruction had existed in most countries of Eastern Europe. Prewar elites had generally been compromised by collaboration with the Germans or presented such an artificial and narrow social base in Bulgaria, Rumania, and even Poland, that only communist-sponsored ruling groups could effectively replace them.[2] Such an assessment, in my opinion, overlooks the fact that broad-based peasant parties with social-democratic preferences did get launched after World War II, and their leadership was purposefully decimated—exiled, imprisoned, executed—by Soviet-backed communists.

Surveying Eastern Europe, most Cold War historians have felt dismayed enough by the results that they have continually asked whether American policy contributed to the outcome, either by not contesting the area more forcefully, or by not ceding influence more gracefully and thereby allowing the Soviets to feel secure without repressive measures. On this issue the recent argumentation of Lynn Etheridge Davis's *The Cold War Begins: Soviet-American Conflict Over Eastern Europe,* is challenging. Davis, currently serving as a deputy assistant secretary of defense, has suggested that Washington followed an unfruitfully ambivalent policy toward Eastern Europe. By constant verbal refusal to accept the region's incorporation into a Soviet sphere of interest, Washington envenomed relations with Moscow. American policymakers, in her critical view, indulged in a rhetorical demand for free elections and liberal procedures in the area without serious reflection as to how to press these aims. The United States did not use economic bargaining concretely nor did Washington effectively encourage institutional bulwarks for liberal government, and hardly thought out what democratic elections might have guaranteed.[3] This view tends to agree with the arguments of anti-Soviet "realist" foreign policy advisers at the time, preeminently George Kennan, who argued that a frank acceptance of spheres of influence would have kept the Soviet-American confrontation from heating up and certainly would have lost us no more influence in Eastern Europe and sacrificed no more liberty for its inhabitants than the "Wilsonian" insistence on self-determination. Before the student accepts this powerful argumentation, however, he or she should review the memoir of the then ambassador to the Soviet Union, W. Averell Harriman. In his book, Harriman illuminates the persisting and compelling hold that ideas of self-determination and democracy exerted; his account suggests that for Americans to have sanctioned a division of Europe after a war to liberate the continent was hardly possible. Harriman's chapters on the Polish issue, as seen from his Moscow vantage in 1944–45, are central narratives of the issue that lay at the beginning of Cold War hostility.[4]

The evolution of American policy from the 1944–45 disputes over Poland to the Czech coup and the Berlin Blockade of 1948–49 has been presented and interpreted many times. While it is always partially misleading to select one moment or two in a chain of events as the decisive turning point, nonetheless the period from early 1947 to early 1948 did witness accelerated crises and responses. The Truman Doctrine announced in March 1947, the communization of Hungary, the exclusion of the Western communists from the Belgian, French, and

Italian governing coalitions, announcement of the Marshall Plan, decisive steps toward the permanent division of Germany, and the Czech
coup—all contributed to a qualitative escalation of the Cold War. To
convey the progress and flavor of events in that urgent year, I have
chosen Daniel Yergin's chapter on the origins of the Marshall Plan. As
is clear from Yergin, the Marshall Plan and the division of Germany
were inextricably linked. Indeed that is the argument of John Gimbel's
work, which follows Yergin's: namely, that the Marshall Plan represented a strategy for reviving the crippled German economy—as demanded by the American War Department and our Occupation authorities—without antagonizing would-be French allies. By fusing
German recovery funds into a European-wide scheme, Gimbel argues,
the incompatible objectives could be resolved on a higher level. Gimbel's work deserves attention, and it follows his revealing book on the
effects of the American occupation in Marburg and his more inclusive
*Politics and the Military: The American Occupation of Germany,
1945-1949*.[6] This thesis may be overstressed, however. A European-
wide concept of European aid arose from broader considerations than
just those of finessing French objections to aiding German recovery. It
accompanied a new global outlook toward the contest with the Soviet
Union. What in 1945 and 1946 could still appear as local trouble spots
in Eastern Europe or the Middle East now loomed as mere probes on
the part of a persistently expansionist and ideologically hostile power.
Even when George Kennan, writing as Mr. X, counseled that Soviet
aggressiveness was probably limited to contiguous regions, Americans read not what he said about the limits of Russian aims, but
about their continuity and pervasiveness.[7] Consequently, by 1947
Washington policymakers and the community of those concerned about
America's role, such as the leadership that periodically assembled at the
Council on Foreign Relations in New York, sought a unified coordination of foreign assistance. The Truman Doctrine of March 1947 already
signaled the United States determination to judge guerrilla movements
in peripheral noncommunist regimes as part of a unitary threat of subversion. By June, the Marshall Plan's stress on recovery as a problem
of the European core region responded to the forebodings of a vast
confrontation of blocs. Whether the United States had to enter a bitter
ideological conflict with the Soviets over Europe may remain debatable;
but given the premises of the conflict, the Marshall Plan represented a
creative policy vision. First of all, it finally specified a consistent
American need to help the reconstruction of European capital and
mixed economies if liberal democracy were to prove viable; second, it
charted a continental strategy that recognized the Atlantic political
economy as a coherent arena of struggle.

Unfortunately, scholarship on the workings of the Marshall Plan remains sparse. Except for explanatory material generated at the time of the European Recovery Program itself, there is little on how the program was run. Hadley Arkes's book, *Bureaucracy, the Marshall Plan, and the National Interest,* is an exception. Although it is aimed at the concerns of political scientists, I have included in this collection a useful chapter from his book on the impact of the Marshall Plan in Europe.

The announcement of the Truman Doctrine and the carrying through of the Marshall Plan from early 1947 to mid 1948 marked a year and a half of decisive political realignment in the West European nations. During the key months from the winter crisis of 1947 through the Berlin Blockade, European political leaders interpreted the American initiative as a clear signal to establish noncommunist coalitions. On the other side, communist leaders also made the Marshall Plan the touchstone of their political decisions. Once the Czechoslovak government reversed its plans under Soviet pressure to participate in the initial conference of European countries working out a response to the American aid offer, Western communists embarked upon a bitter opposition to the Marshall Plan as an instrument of United States hegemony. Their reaction proved almost self-fulfilling in that it confirmed the end of the united postwar labor movements and accelerated the unification of the Western zones of Germany. Doubtless a whole set of issues separated communists from social democrats: memories of old post-World War I schisms, fear on the part of social democrats that communist domination of the union federations would mean loss of any autonomy, and apprehension on the part of the communists that realization of the Marshall Plan would subordinate Western societies to an American political vision. Thus the American initiative provided a year-long theme for ideological conflict, punctuated by great strikes in Italy and France from the autumn of 1947 through the summer of 1948 that consummated the division of the labor movement. For a discussion of this schism I have included here a translation of a synthetic essay by the German scholar Lutz Niethammer that examines the international breakdown of the post-1944 effort at united trade unions.

The political developments during the same years are as crucial as those in the union movement, but suitable scholarly essays are difficult to find. Increasingly the Italians are publishing significant material about the transition from the Resistance coalition comprising Communists, Socialists, Liberals, and Christian Democrats to a noncommunist Christian Democratic-dominated phalanx. Likewise, they have contributed close studies of labor-union development, but the detail involved makes selection difficult.[8] Scholarship on postwar French history is sparse and is composed predominantly of quasi-journalistic accounts, such as those by Alexander Werth, Jacques Fauvet, and Georgette Elgey, although scholarly treatments of special subjects exist.[9] I have not attempted to survey the material that might illuminate the trends in the smaller countries of Europe.

In summary, two tasks confront the historical investigator of this period. The first is simply to establish what happened, to reconstruct a narrative on the basis of documentation that, while huge, is still very incomplete. Second, the historian must try to discern in the welter of recent events relationships that future historians will see more easily—although always, of course, according to their own generation's preoccupations.

The more recent the period, the more difficult is this second task. I do not think it unfair to judge that by and large Cold War history has so far been disappointing in this regard. Too often it has become ensnared in polemics and fixed upon blame. In a search for the liveliness and excitement of journalism, some authors have tended to muster picturesque quotations—e.g., Truman's telling off Molotov—but have sometimes neglected to recreate the context of documents or the social and institutional milieu in which national policy emerged by fits and starts. The researchers who have ferreted out new documentation have often failed to achieve that sense of sovereign synthesis that good history attains, while those writers who like to convey the impression of impartially mastering the era often decline to confront uncomfortable evidence.

Yet only insofar as historians both plunge into the documents and derive underlying configurations can they go beyond just a more inclusive reportage. Only in the search for at least partial coherence can they test the given patterns that they will otherwise impose willy-nilly merely because they have grown up on the ideological concepts suggested by Cold War conflict. The historian's task involves not merely fighting the controversies of the day or even of the decade. It demands making contemporary history an object of perspective and reflection to at least the same order of relative dispassion that would be sought in judging earlier epochs. For the era of the Cold War, this scientific task remains to be accomplished. The essays here are meant as an invitation to students to participate in that intellectual enterprise.

## Notes

1. Hugh Seton-Watson, *The East European Revolution,* 3rd ed. (New York: Praeger, 1956); François Fejtö, *Histoire des démocraties populaires,* 2 vols. (Paris: Editions du Seuil, 1952, 1969).
2. Gabriel Kolko, *The Politics of War: The World and United States*

*Foreign Policy, 1943–1945* (New York: Random House, 1968). See also Gabriel and Joyce Kolko, *The Limits of Power: The World and United States Foreign Policy, 1945–54* (New York: Harper & Row, 1972).

3. Lynn Etheridge Davis, *The Cold War Begins: Soviet-American Conflict over Eastern Europe* (Princeton, N.J.: Princeton University Press, 1974).

4. W. Averell Harriman and Elie Abel, *Special Envoy to Churchill and Stalin, 1941–1946* (New York: Random House, 1975), especially chapters 14–15. See also Ito Takayuki, "The Genesis of the Cold War: Confrontation over Poland, 1941–44," which draws upon Polish and Russian sources, in Yonusuke Nagai and Akira Iriye, eds., *The Origins of the Cold War in Asia* (New York: Columbia University Press and University of Tokyo Press, 1977), pp. 147–202.

5. Daniel Yergin, *Shattered Peace: The Origins of the Cold War and the National Security State* (Boston: Houghton Mifflin, 1977), pp. 346–350.

6. John N. Gimbel, *The Origins of the Marshall Plan* (Stanford: Stanford University Press, 1976); also *The American Occupation of Germany: Politics and the Military, 1945–1949* (Stanford: Stanford University Press, 1968); also, *A German Community under American Occupation: Marburg, 1945–52* (Stanford: Stanford University Press, 1961).

7. George F. Kennan, "The Sources of Soviet Conduct," *Foreign Affairs* (July 1947). The student should also read Kennan's *Memoirs 1925–50* and *Memoirs 1950–63* (Boston: Little, Brown & Co., 1969, 1972) to get an insight into Kennan's mode of analysis: subtle, minor-key, premised on long-term national psychological characteristics, profoundly repelled by Russia even when fascinated, constantly disillusioned about the possibilities for conducting diplomacy in a democracy with a strong legislative scrutiny over foreign affairs.

8. For English-language surveys, see H. Stuart Hughes, *The United States and Italy* (Cambridge, Mass.: Harvard University Press, 1965); Norman Kogan, *Italy and the Allies* (Cambridge, Mass.: Harvard University Press, 1962); and Giuseppe Mammarella, *Italy After Fascism: A Political History 1943–1965,* Elizabeth and Victor Velen, eds. (Notre Dame, Ind.: University of Notre Dame Press, 1966). In Italian, see on the political scene, Enzo Piscitelli, *Da Parri a De Gasperi, Storia del dopoguerra 1945/1948* (Milan: Feltrinelli, 1975); A. Gambino, *Storia del dopoguerra della Liberazione al potere DC* (Bari: Laterza, 1975); and for the social struggles, Fabio Levi, Paride Rugafiori, Salvatore Vento, *Il triangolo industriale tra ricostruzione e lotta di classe 1945/48* (Milan: Feltrinelli, 1974).

9. See Alexander Werth, *France, 1940–1955* (London: R. Hale, 1956); Georgette Elgey, *La république des illusions* (Paris: A. Fayard, 1965); also Jacques Fauvet, *Histoire de la IVᵉ République* (Paris: A. Fayard, 1960). For an English-language survey, consult Phillip Williams, *Politics in Post-War France* (London: Longmans Green, 1954). For excellent bibliographical suggestions and a closely argued account of events in 1947, see Wilfried Loth, "Das Ausscheiden der französischen Kommunisten aus der Regierung 1947," *Vierteljahrshefte für die Zeitgeschichte,* vol. 26, nr. 1 (January 1978), pp. 9–65.

# THE ORIGINS OF THE COLD WAR
# AND CONTEMPORARY EUROPE

# 1

## Charles S. Maier

# Revisionism and the Interpretation of Cold War Origins

*This essay should serve to orient the reader in the "revisionist"
controversy concerning the origins of the Cold War. It surveys most
of the major literature up to 1970. Dissertations and books have
continued in full spate during the present decade. In addition to those
cited in the notes to the Introduction, the reader might also turn to
the following: John Lewis Gaddis,* The United States and the Origins
of the Cold War *(New York: Columbia University Press, 1972)—a
counter-revisionist statement that illuminates the domestic pressures
in the making of United States foreign policy; Diane Shaver Clemens,*
Yalta *(New York: Oxford University Press, 1970); Adam B. Ulam,*
The Rivals *(New York: Viking, 1971); and the revised version of
Walter LaFeber,* America, Russia and the Cold War, *3rd ed. (New
York: John Wiley and Sons, 1976). The essays in the Nagai–Iriye
volume,* The Origins of the Cold War in Asia *(full citation in Note 4
of the editor's introduction) are also very useful. For biographical
treatments see Alonzo L. Hamby,* Beyond The New Deal: Harry S.
Truman and American Liberalism *(New York: Columbia University
Press, 1973)—a somewhat defensive defense; and two biographies of
a major "cold warrior":* Gaddis Smith, Dean Acheson. The American
Secretaries of State and their Diplomacy, *vol. 16. Robert H. Ferrell,
ed. (New York: Cooper Square Publishers, 1972), and David S.
McLellan,* Dean Acheson: The State Department Years *(New York:
Dodd, Mead & Company, 1976). For a revisionist collective biography
see Lloyd C. Gardner,* Architects of Illusion *(Chicago: Quadrangle,
1972). Townsend Hoopes'* The Devil and John Foster Dulles *(Boston: Atlantic-Little, Brown, 1973) concentrates on the 1950s, but is*

*an exciting portrait of an ardent Cold War stalwart. Needless to say, these titles represent just a fragment of the continuing literature.*

*In including my own essay in this collection, I have asked myself would I have written it differently today? I do not really think so. On the other hand, I might emphasize the transition from Roosevelt to Truman more strongly. While Soviet-American antagonism was emerging in any case, the tone of diplomacy matters almost as much as the substance; and through inexperience and distrust that tone on our side became suddenly harsher and cruder. It may seem curious to assert that Truman's bluntness should really influence the reaction of a dictator capable of murdering entire cohorts of his colleagues. Yet precisely because Stalin was so sensitive to the real and imagined fluctuations in his political environment, the Truman–Byrnes diplomacy may have contributed to defensiveness, insecurity and churlishness. Whether it basically affected the outcome in those states where Soviet power was decisive, however, still seems to me an open question. Second, the issue of German reparations appears more important to me now—not because ultimately the Soviets were morally entitled to a given quota of German industrial equipment beyond what they uprooted immediately as war booty or extracted thereafter, but because the reparation issue lay at the root of all the German problems and elevated what was originally an area of cooperation into the most refractory conflict of all. Finally, I would now stress the importance of the events from early 1947 through spring of 1948, not for the "origins" of the Cold War, which lay in the East European disputes of 1944–46, but for the decisive stages in the outcome of the Cold War and the division of Europe.*

Few historical reappraisals have achieved such sudden popularity as the current revisionist critique of American foreign policy and the origins of the Cold War. Much of this impact is clearly due to Vietnam. Although the work of revision began before the United States became deeply involved in that country, the war has eroded so many national self-conceptions that many assumptions behind traditional Cold War history have been cast into doubt. For twenty years the Soviet-American conflict was attributed to Stalin's effort to expand Soviet control through revolutionary subversion,[1] or, as in a more recent formulation, to "the logic of his position as the ruler of a totalitarian society and as the supreme head of a movement that seeks security through constant expansion."[2] Revisionist assailants of this view have now found readers receptive to the contrary idea that the United States must bear the blame for the Cold War. The preoccupation with America's historical guilt distinguishes the new authors not only from anti-communist historians but from earlier writers who felt the question of blame was inappropriate. William McNeill, for example, in an out-standing account written at the height of the Cold War, stressed a nearly inevitable falling-out among allies who had never been united save to fight a common enemy.[3] This viewpoint has been preserved in some recent accounts; but since Denna Fleming's massive Cold War history of 1961, the revisionists have gone on to indict the United States for long-term antipathy to communism, insensitivity to legitimate Soviet security needs, and generally belligerent behavior after World War II.[4]

The revisionist version of Cold War history includes three major ele-ments: an interpretation of Eastern European developments; an allega-tion of anti-Soviet motives in the Americans' use of the atomic bomb; and a general Marxian critique of the alleged American search for a world capitalist hegemony. Since these three elements comprise a de-tailed reassessment of the role of the United States in world politics they deserve to be discussed and evaluated in turn; but in the end one must consider the more fundamental question of the conceptual bases of revisionist history.

The revisionists are divided among themselves about the turning points and the causes of American aggressiveness, but all agree that the traditional description of the crucial events in Eastern Europe must be radically altered. The old version of the roots of the Cold War charged Soviet Russia with progressively tightening totalitarian control from mid-1944. In effect the earlier historians only confirmed the diagnosis of Ambassador Averell Harriman in Moscow, whose cables between late 1943 and early 1945 changed from emphasizing the needs of a functioning wartime alliance to stressing the difficulties of prolonging cooperation in the face of Soviet ambitions.[5] In this evolution of views, the Russian refusal to facilitate Anglo-American supply flights to the Warsaw uprising of August 1944 and Moscow's backing for its own Polish government later in that year provoked major western disillu-sionment. It was agreed after 1945 that the germs of the Cold War lay in Stalin's intransigence on the Polish issue.

In contrast to this interpretation, the revisionists charge that the United States forced Stalin into his stubborn Polish policy by backing the excessive aspirations of the exile Polish government in London. Revisionist accounts emphasize how antagonistic the State Depart-ment's refusal to sanction any territorial changes during the war must have appeared in Moscow. They point out that the territory that the Soviets had annexed in 1939, and which the Poles were contesting, had restored the 1919 Curzon line of mediation and merely reversed Poland's own acquisitions by war in 1920–1921. At the Teheran Conference in December 1943, Churchill and Roosevelt had loosely consented to Poland's borders being shifted westward. Even Harriman backed the British in counseling the London Poles to accept the terms the Soviets were offering in October 1944.[6] Only when the Russians produced their own so-called Lublin Committee and thereafter Polish government—allegedly out of frustration and bitterness at the unyielding stance of the London Poles—did the focus switch from the question of territory to that of regimes.[7] At the Yalta conference, Stalin agreed to add some Western Poles to the communist-based government and to move toward free elections; and if the United States had continued to accept the Yalta provisions in a generous spirit, the revisionists maintain, the earlier disputes might have been overcome. Gar Alperovitz argues in detail that after Yalta Roosevelt sought to persuade Churchill to move toward the Soviet position on the key question of who would determine which Western Polish leaders might be invited to join the expanded Warsaw government. But Roosevelt's successors, notably President Truman and Secretary of State James Byrnes, put up a harsh fight to reverse this supposed acquiescence in the creation of a basically communist-dominated government.[8]

This American attitude toward Polish issues, the revisionists claim, was typical of a wide range of Eastern European questions where the United States appeared to be set upon frustrating Russia's international security. From the summer of 1945 Truman and Byrnes, it is charged, sought to reverse the pro-Soviet governments in Rumania and Bulgaria by blustering with atomic weapons.[9] The American opposition to Soviet demands for territorial security and friendly neighboring states allegedly forced the Russians away from their minimal aims of 1943–1945, which envisaged United Front coalition regimes, to the ruthless communization they imposed by 1947–1948. Had the United States not demanded total openness to Western influence, the revisionists imply, Poland, Bulgaria, and Rumania might have survived as Hungary and Czechoslovakia did until 1947–1948 and Finland thereafter. But in fact, they argue, the parties and social groups that Washington desired to entrench could only intensify Stalin's mistrust. In revisionist eyes these groups were either unworthy or unviable: unworthy because they regrouped pre-war reactionary elements who had often been pro-German, unviable because even when democratic they were doomed to fall between the more intransigent right and the Russian-backed left.[10]

Even more fundamental from the revisionist point of view, there was no legitimacy for any American concern with affairs in that distant region. However ugly the results in Eastern Europe, they should not really have worried Washington. Russia should have been willingly accorded unchallenged primacy because of her massive wartime sacrifices, her need for territorial security, and the long history of the area's reactionary politics and bitter anti-bolshevism. Only when Moscow's deserved primacy was contested did Stalin embark upon a search for exclusive control.[11]

These revisionist assessments of the United States's political choices in Eastern Europe are valid in some respects, simplistic in others. It is true that American policymakers sought to establish agrarian democracies and based their hopes upon peasant proprietors and populist-like parties whose adherents had oscillated between left and right before the war. As revisionist accounts suggest, these occupied a precarious middle ground in Polish politics and an even narrower one in the former Axis satellites, Rumania and Bulgaria, where the Russians may have felt entitled to complete hegemony. Churchill for one felt that his "percentages" agreement of October 1944 had sanctioned Soviet control over these countries as a *quid pro quo* for the Russians' acceptance of British dominance in Greece. And whatever the effective status of that arrangement, Stalin might well have considered his domination of Rumania no more than the counterpart of Allied exclusion of the Soviets from any effective voice in Italy.[12]

But despite revisionist implications to the contrary, the major offense of the middle- and pro-Western groups in Soviet eyes was not really their collusion with rightists. The Russians themselves, after all, supported the far more fascist-tainted Marshall Badoglio as Italian premier. The major crime of the pro-Western elements seems really to have been the desire to stay independent of Soviet influence in a situation of Soviet-American polarization that made independence seem enmity. Perhaps the pro-Westerners acted imprudently by looking to Washington: Benes won three years of Czech democracy by collaboration with Moscow—but one might argue from his example that either the collaboration prolonged the Czech respite or that it helped contribute to the final undermining of Prague's independence. In any case the outcome throughout the area was communist dictatorship. Between 1945 and 1947 the peasant party and social democratic leaders were harassed in their assemblies and organizations, tried for treason by communist interior ministries, driven abroad or into silence, and finally, as with the case of Nikola Petkov, the Bulgarian agrarian party leader, executed.[13]

This bleak result naturally undercut those who advocated voluntarily relinquishing United States influence in the area. Opposing the official American rejection of spheres of influence, Henry Wallace on one side, and Henry Stimson and George Kennan on the other, counseled restraint and acceptance of the new status quo; [14] but few contemporary advocates could wholeheartedly celebrate a policy of spheres of influence. It was justified from expedience and as a second-best alternative. As a former advocate recalls, it had always to be advanced as a melancholy necessity, especially as the men for whom Western liberals felt most sympathy were liquidated.[15] To follow a policy of abnegation might indeed have allowed more openness in Eastern Europe; on the other hand, the Stalinist tendencies toward repression might well have followed their own Moscow-determined momentum.

If as a group the revisionists condemn the American role in Eastern Europe, they diverge beyond that point of criticism. One major area of debate among them concerns the use of the atomic bomb, which, while it must be weighed as an important issue in its own right, also signals a basic methodological division. Although the revisionist writing that often seems most hostile to received opinion is that of Gar Alperovitz, he is not the most radical of the dissenting historians. His writings involve a less thoroughgoing critique of United States institutions than the contributions of either William Appleman Williams or Gabriel Kolko. What has elevated Alperovitz to the role of the revisionist *enfant terrible* is his thesis that the United States used nuclear weapons against the Japanese largely to overawe the Soviets. Still, his version of events hinges less on structural elements in American life than on the contingent roles of personality and technological opportunity.

There are two aspects of Alperovitz's thesis: first, that before Hiroshima, expectation of the bomb's availability caused decisive tactical changes in American diplomacy; second, that the weapon was used wantonly when it became available, in part to limit Soviet penetration into the Far East, and more generally because only a combat demonstration would create a sufficient impression to prevent absolute Soviet control over Eastern Europe. Only the desire to have the atomic bomb in hand, Alperovitz argues, led Truman to reverse his harsh diplomatic approach of late April 1945, to dispatch Harry Hopkins to Moscow, and to delay the Potsdam conference despite Churchill's misgivings.[16]

More disturbing than this charge is Alperovitz's subsequent argument that Americans did not merely wish to possess the bomb but actually used it to enhance the country's position vis-à-vis the Soviets. Alperovitz repeats the charge that by the spring of 1945 most Washington officials believed neither the bomb nor an invasion was necessary to end the war. Either continued blockade or a Russian declaration of war could achieve victory. The bomb, however, would obviate the need for Soviet participation in the Pacific war, and, allegedly, the United States wanted desperately to keep Russia out. Along with hastening the technical preparations for Hiroshima, the United States supposedly had the Chinese Nationalists prolong their negotiations with Moscow so that the Sino-Soviet treaty would remain a stumbling block to Stalin's entry.[17]

Interestingly enough, the historiographical factions in this debate have crossed the usual lines. Kolko offers the most cogent response to Alperovitz and the most plausible reconstruction of Potsdam. On the other hand, Herbert Feis—the major traditionalist historian of wartime diplomacy—has so tempered his conclusions that despite himself he grudgingly gives the Alperovitz view considerable credence.[18] Alperovitz has indeed documented a reversal in May 1945 of some initial efforts at confrontation and then a renewed American toughness after Potsdam. But whether calculations about the bomb were decisive remains unproven. The evidence adduced must remain circumstantial: the increased hostility to Russia that was thrust upon the new President; Stimson's and Byrnes' awareness that possession of nuclear weapons might bestow significant diplomatic leverage; and the pushing back of a Big Three parley. In light of this conjunction of events a calculated strategy of delay, such as Alperovitz develops, does remain a possible component of Truman's motivation. But the initial months of the new administration formed a period of contradictory needs and approaches. For a while Truman may have been thinking in terms of disengaging from the disquieting Soviet repression in Bulgaria and Rumania by withdrawing from the Allied Control Commission rather than attempting to reverse the course of events by exerting pressure within it.[19] The Hopkins mission was well suited to many purposes: perhaps an effort to appease Stalin until nuclear weapons were at hand, but more immediately an attempt to secure agreements in their own right and to halt further deterioration of relations as a worthy goal in itself. For Truman, as even Alperovitz realizes, the Hopkins trip was probably viewed not as a reversal of his earlier harsh language to Molotov on April 23, but as a complementary démarche, another approach to a dramatic unjamming of issues.[20]

What also makes the Alperovitz view so difficult to evaluate is the fact, as the author himself admits, that the debate has been largely a retrospective one. Actors at the time hardly saw the significance of the alternatives as later historians have. The place that the idea of using the bomb might have been thrashed out was in the so-called Interim Committee dominated by Stimson and Byrnes, both of whom were committed to dropping the weapon. In this forum it was easy to dismiss any alternative to the incineration of a real city as beset with one fatal obstacle or another. And beyond the Interim Committee, except for a group of scientific dissenters at Chicago who felt they had been turned into sorcerers' apprentices, there was no fundamental challenge to using the weapon. Moreover, if the bomb represented a threshold in terms of weapons technology, it no longer represented one in terms of casualties: the Tokyo incendiary raids in March of 1945 produced about 84,000 deaths; Dresden, between 60,000 and 130,000; Hiroshima, about 70,000. The significant ethical question was that of area versus precision bombing, and the allies had long since steeled their conscience on that issue. If the Navy and Air Force, moreover, were confident that they could starve the Japanese into submission, the Joint Chiefs never gave their collective imprimatur to such a view because the Army would not endorse it. Many thought the collapse of Japan was likely; official plans were drawn up to deal with a sudden surrender; but no one in authority felt he could assume official responsibility for advocating restraint so long as some prolonged Japanese resistance was remotely possible. If Byrnes, Harriman, and Admiral Leahy would have preferred to complete the Pacific war without obligations to Moscow, Truman still felt it his duty to cling to the contingency plans of the Joint Chiefs of Staff and seek Soviet help at Potsdam. Even at Potsdam when Japanese capitulation seemed near, a host of factors militated against reappraisal: the ambivalence of the Tokyo response to the Potsdam ultimatum (itself only the vaguest of warnings); concern that die-hard Japanese militarists would seek to "protect" their monarch against those who counseled surrender; the debate in Washington over retention of the Emperor, which delayed a surrender formula both sides might accept; the belief that the nation responsible for the Pearl Harbor attack could be requited from the air hundreds of times over without any injustice; and no doubt the vested interests in making the bomb contribute to the war effort.[21] If in addition to these pressures Byrnes also entertained an ulterior anti-Soviet motive, it probably represented a marginal, additional payoff of a policy long established on other grounds.

Alperovitz seems to feel it wrong that the atomic bomb became a major factor in American policy calculations. Certainly, however, it was natural to give deep consideration to the new weapon's diplomatic implications. And despite Alperovitz's linkage, there is insufficient evidence that possession of nuclear weapons was decisive in motivating a hard line on Bulgaria and Rumania in the latter half of 1945. This approach followed naturally from the administration's view of Eastern European developments since Yalta and would have been pursued without an atomic monopoly. It is questionable, too, whether the United States could have utilized a veiled atomic threat except in regard to the distant future, for Washington was not prepared to threaten the use of nuclear weapons over Russian targets in 1945.[22] Despite the revisionist view that the United States enjoyed a preponderance of power and therefore must be charged with the greater responsibility in the generation of the Cold War, the Soviet Union still exerted effective control over the area that was central to the dispute. This is not to deny that outside its borders the United States seemed to be flaunting its nuclear capacity. Harriman reported from Moscow in November that the Soviets felt America was trying to intimidate them with the atomic bomb, while to observers in Washington Truman and Byrnes often seemed bolstered by an inner assurance of American invincibility.[23]

Indeed it may have appeared by late 1945 and early 1946 as if the United States were wrapping iron fist in iron glove; but even had there been a far more sophisticated and reserved approach, the simple fact of one-sided possession of the bomb was bound to evoke mistrust. There was no way for its influence to be exorcized from international relations.

Alperovitz's charges are, of course, profoundly disquieting. But at least he suggests that things might have been different. Had Roosevelt lived he might have smoothed out differences with Moscow. Had Stimson been heeded, the United States might have bargained by offering to share atomic secrets and not by seeking, as it is alleged to have done, to intimidate with the weapon itself. Gabriel Kolko, in contrast, can dismiss Alperovitz's arguments about atomic diplomacy because they are unnecessary for what he considers the more important indictment, namely, that the United States, in order to serve its economic needs and ambitions, opposed any threat to its world-wide military and political power.

This view produces a more radical interpretation of both American foreign relations and the country's internal history. William Appleman Williams, for instance, argues that the long-term American quest for universal market and investment arenas, even into Eastern Europe, naturally collided with quite moderate Soviet wartime aspirations and thereby helped the Kremlin's own hardliners and ideologues to prevail.[24] For both Williams and Kolko, moreover, a critique of United States foreign policy forms only part of a wider reassessment of American liberal institutions. The anti-communist effort is depicted as the natural product of an industrial society in which even major reform efforts have been intended only to rationalize corporate capitalism.[25]

The more the revisionists stress the continuity of American capitalist goals and de-emphasize the importance of the Roosevelt-Truman transition, the more they tend to condemn all of America's earlier policies as contributing to the Cold War. The revisionists in general have stressed the direct pre-1945 clashes with the Soviets. They emphasize the significance of the Allies' delay in opening a Second Front in

Europe; [26] and while anti-Soviet historians duly cite Russia's non-aggression pact with Germany, the revisionists usually argue that the Soviets were forced into this arrangement by the Western powers' appeasement policies and their exclusion of Moscow from any common defense plans.[27] Finally, revisionists like Fleming recall the United States' original hostility to bolshevism and the interventions of 1918–1920.[28] In short, all revisionists are mindful of the Western treatment of the Soviets as a pariah regime.

The more radical revisionists, however, go on to depict all of twentieth-century foreign policy as woven into a large counter-revolutionary fabric of which the Cold War itself is only one portion. Their logic links a hesitant and ineffective anti-Nazi foreign policy with a zealous anti-communism and thus finds that the issues of the 1930's adumbrate Cold War attitudes. Similarly, revisionists who discuss pre-war diplomacy have attacked the usual image of American isolationism by stressing the country's persistent economic stakes abroad. All this vaguely serves to hint that the lateness of United States enlistment against Nazism is no longer explainable in terms of deep internal divisions about involvement in European quarrels: the United States responded only as it perceived threats to foreign economic interests.[29] Receding even further, the revisionists view Woodrow Wilson as a major architect of liberal but counter-revolutionary interventionism.[30] And even before Wilson the roots of the Cold War can be discerned, they feel, in the economic lobbying that backed the Open Door policy and the capitalist expansion of the late nineteenth century.[31] Finally, under the stresses of a market economy, even the otherwise virtuous farmers felt it necessary to seek world markets and back imperialist expansionism. The private economy, for Williams and others, taints with acquisitiveness the Jeffersonian Eden that America might have been.[32]

There is a further aspect of this radical revisionism. Since it concentrates on American expansionism in general, its focus shifts from the Soviet-American conflict to the alleged American imperialist drive against all forces of radicalism, or what Kolko loosely calls the New Order. Not an insouciant blundering, and not the arrogance of power, but only capitalist megalomania suffices to explain American efforts to prop up an international Old Order of discredited and outworn parties and elites. Within this perspective, Kolko's explanation of the events of 1943–1945 becomes most clear. He offers three major areas of evidence: United States policy in respect to its future enemy, that is, the effort to reduce Russia to dependency; United States policy against its own ally, that is, the insistence on an economic multilateralism designed to reduce Great Britain to dependency; and United States policy in respect to the "Third World" and the Resistance, the effort to smash all truly independent challenges to American hegemony. Under Kolko's scrutiny the policies once adjudged to be among the most enlightened emerge as the most imperialistic. Where, for example, previous critics attacked the abandonment of Morgenthau's intended ten-billion-dollar loan to Russia, Kolko sees the proposal itself as devious. Coupled with the destruction of German industry, the contemplated loan was allegedly designed to prevent Russia from refurbishing her industrial base from German factories and thus to force her into a dependency on United States capital for which she could return raw materials. Ironically enough, the plans of Harry Dexter White— abused as a communist in the 1950's—represented a massive effort to place the USSR in a state of semi-colonial subservience.[33]

American aid to England emanates from analogous motives, according to Kolko and Lloyd Gardner who have concentrated most closely on this issue. Kolko asserts that American policy aimed at keeping Britain in a viable second-rank position: rescuing her from utter collapse for reasons of world economic stability yet profiting from her distress. State Department officials, congressmen, and businessmen supporting assistance to Britain intended to penetrate the sterling bloc and the Commonwealth markets protected by tariffs since the 1930's. The celebrated Article Seven of the Mutual Aid Agreement of February 1942, the revisionists emphasize, demanded that Britain consider reduction of Commonwealth trade barriers in return for Lend-Lease, a stipulation repeated with each renewal of Lend-Lease. Finally, all the projects for post-war financial credits and arrangements, as they took form at Bretton Woods and in the 3.75-billion dollar loan negotiated in December 1945, envisaged a sterling-dollar convertibility that would also open the Commonwealth to American goods and severely test the pound.[34]

As the revisionists see it, the interest in convertibility and multilateralism represented the answer of post-Depression America to the chronic domestic under-consumption of a capitalist economy. In the final analysis American efforts amounted to a subtle neo-colonialism. While classical economic theorists helped to justify the international division of labor by comparative-advantage doctrine no matter how unequal the partners, the revisionists evidently feel that the costs to the less powerful or industrial nation outweigh the benefits. They emphasize that specialization can act to perpetuate relations of dependency and they view American policy as dedicated throughout the twentieth century to fostering the bonds of economic subordination.[35]

In this interpretative framework the Cold War, in its European aspects, arose because Soviet Russia refused to allow herself or Eastern Europe to be integrated into the American neo-colonial network.

This analysis is often illuminating but sometimes exaggerated and tendentious. One can certainly differentiate between the values of the arguments about the Soviet Union and Britain. To see de-bolshevizing Russia as Morgenthau's underlying concern in 1944–1945 is simply to ignore the central quest of his public life, which was to deny Germany any future as a world industrial power. In the policy alternatives shaping up in Washington, a bitterly anti-German policy could, moreover, only mean a desire to collaborate with the Soviet Union and not to dominate it. And by late 1944 Morgenthau viewed those opposing his projects as themselves motivated primarily by anti-communism. The major purpose of the loan to Russia was, in fact, to make it easier for the Soviets to accede to the dismantling of German industry. The economic destruction of the Reich was not designed to make the Russians dependent upon America: if the Soviets would receive no reparation from future German exports they would get many factories that would have produced the exports.[36]

Revisionist analysis of American economic relations with Great Britain is more convincing. Kolko's discussion of Anglo-American financial relations in the framework of overall United States goals probably forms the most innovative and substantive contribution of his study. Americans did push against British trade barriers and mentally relegated the country to a secondary role in a Western economic system. The pressure upon the beleaguered Ally could be harsh: "What do you want me to do," Churchill asked about Lend-Lease renewal at Quebec in the fall of 1944, "stand up and beg like Fala?"[37] Nevertheless, revisionist judgments tend to neglect the powerful ties of sentiment that motivated Roosevelt's policy, and they minimize the critical fact that British financial commitments were over-extended in terms of her own resources. Moreover, the focus by the revisionists on the free-trade rapacity of an Eastern banking establishment is inappropriate. Insofar as banking representatives formed a coherent interest it was often the friendliest to London's needs. Pressures came as much from a conservative Congress as from Wall Street.[38]

Still, as the revisionists stress, economic self-interest was woven into American policy even when it was most generous. The hard fact is that until they both felt mortally threatened by Soviet power London and Washington had conflicting economic interests. There was a desire for currency convertibility on the part of the United States Treasury which Britain naturally felt was potentially disastrous. For Britain to meet the American wishes for sterling convertibility at a moment when she had liquidated four billion pounds of overseas assets in order to fight the war meant subjecting her economy to great deflationary pressure. During the war Keynes had already asked priority for full employment and strong domestic demands over considerations of exports and stable exchanges. After the war the Labour government even more fervently stressed easy money to banish the specter of unemployment. They did not want planning, investment, and new social-service transfers to be impeded by worries about sterling outflow. The American enthusiasm for currency convertibility threatened havoc to all the delicate equilibriums in London; and it was only dire necessity that led the English to pledge an effort at convertibility as a condition for the massive credits the United States extended in late 1945. When finally the dissenting historians reach the story of 1947–1950, they will no doubt be able to depict in their terms a further effort at world economic supremacy. For similar Treasury pressures for convertibility were to continue into the America-sponsored negotiations for intra-European payments agreements in 1949 and the European Payments Union of 1950. Once again, Britain feared a flanking attack on the sterling area, and once again many of her Labour leaders worried about a deflationary thrust against schemes of economic planning.[39]

One can agree that American objectives clashed with British economic policy without accepting the larger revisionist accusation of a pervasive neo-colonialism. As of 1945, American thinking on foreign trade and investment (as well as more general questions of colonialism) was often marked by reformist ideas. American spokesmen such as Eric Johnston of the Chamber of Commerce or Donald Nelson of the War Production Board certainly emphasized the need for sustained American exports as a safeguard against renewed depression,[40] but a sense of the need for exports assumed that countries rich and industrialized enough to offer extensive markets were more helpful to the United States than economies kept in perpetual underdevelopment or one-sided dependency.[41]

Underlying much revisionist criticism of United States foreign economic relations is a desire for socialist self-sufficiency: a virtuous autarchy inflicts the least damage on the rest of the world. Indeed, in theory, there might have been one alternative for the American economy that did not require either unemployment or international trade: a great program of domestic investment to remedy urban blight, improve transportation, build new TVA's—in short an expansion of the New Deal into a semi-socialized economy. But after the domestic emphasis upon small business and competition in the "Second New Deal," and after the massive infusion of business leaders into the government to run the war economy, such a public-sector commitment

was not likely.[42] In the absence of such a program the stress on
international trade was probably the most reasonable United States
response. Finally, one must note that a United States public-sector
solution for full employment would not necessarily have benefited
foreign countries. Their problems were not entirely owing to outsiders'
exploitation; they needed investments, and socialist governments,
whether British or Soviet, were no less likely to draw profits from
abroad where they could.

The revisionists' reasoning on this point fits in analytically with one
of their major current preoccupations: the role of the United States in
the third world of peasant movements. The same revisionist argument
that sees foreign trade as a means to subordination and control also
suggests that the United States had to be hostile to movements seeking
genuine self-determination and local independence. Thus American
hostility to popular resistance movements, including those of World
War II, forms one more logical extension of the country's counter-
revolutionary and imperialist drive in the wake of World War II.
Kolko makes much of the British suppression of the Greek resistance
movement in December 1944, of the American preference for continued dealings with Vichy, of the dislike of Tito's partisans, and of
the joint Anglo-American efforts to restrain the left-wing forces in the
Italian resistance. When it is remembered that the United States is
still fighting the heirs of the Vietnamese resistance to the Japanese and
later the French, or that the Haiphong incidents between French and
Vietminh occurred within two years after the British put down the
Greek resistance cadres in Athens, the emotional thrust of the revisionist argument becomes more understandable.[43]

This concern with the continuities of counter-revolution arises in
part from the natural fact that revisionists want to explain the origins
of cold war against the background of Vietnam. Ironically enough,
the result is to downgrade the importance of the Soviet-American antagonism that originally preoccupied revisionist authors. What in fact
increasingly distinguishes the more radical historians is their emphasis
upon a Soviet "conservatism" that sought to discourage revolutionary action for the sake of acquiring territorial buffers. Stalin's
treaty with Chiang at the expense of Mao, his distrust of Tito, and
his abandonment of the Greek Communists, complement American objectives. In view of this supposed convergence of Moscow and Washington, the Cold War becomes little more than a mistaken enmity
deriving from the United States' panicky idenification of Soviet policies
with indigenous Marxist or merely democratic movements. This finding confirms a "third world" viewpoint which can indict both major
world powers and supply a "usable past" for those morally over-

whelmed by an updated Holy Alliance between Moscow and Washington.[44] Through the mid 1960's, in short, the revisionists could still be fixed upon explaining the origins of conflict with Moscow; by the end of the decade they were concerned with the antagonism with Havana, Hanoi, and Peking.

Attractive though it may be in light of current events, this third-world perspective has serious analytical deficiencies. First of all, its Marxian basis imposes an overly schematic view of motivation; it precludes any possibility that American policy makers might have acted from genuine emancipatory impulses or even in uncertainty. The war had united the country around democratic ideas that were genuinely held, even if too abstract for implementation in the areas they were aimed at. It can be argued that the economic aspirations that State Department draftsmen grafted onto the policy statements the revisionists cite were just as ritualistic as the political formulas,[45] and that there was still cause for a genuine dismay at the developments in Eastern Europe. The revisionist presentation conveys no sense of America's anti-totalitarian commitment and thus little understanding of the seeds of the post-1945 disillusionment.

Furthermore, the new revisionist writings composed under the impact of Vietnam attribute too consistently ideological an opposition to the resistance movements in Western Europe. For anyone with sympathy for the "vision" of the Resistance, vague as it was, American policy often does appear as misguided or willful. At times tactical considerations were influential; at times the wartime authority that devolved upon conservative proconsuls such as Robert Murphy was critical; at times United States policy acquiesced in a joint allied position more rightist than Washington alone would have preferred, as when the exigencies of coalition warfare led Roosevelt to accede to Churchill's reactionary policies in Italy and Greece.[46] Yet most basically what militated against the Resistance was a big-power paternalism and the wartime habit of viewing military success as an end in itself. United States spokesmen accused Resistance leaders of seeking their own political advantage above the destruction of the Germans, though what Americans saw as narrow partisanship was to Resistance leaders a battle against collaborators and a fascist or semi-fascist right—a struggle for regeneration within to match the fight against the occupying power. The British and Americans preferred to think of the Resistance as a vanguard of saboteurs who might soften up the Germans and pin down their troops but not as an army or regime in embryo. Centralization and control, the distrust of independent authority and pretensions, characterized all three great powers. But unless decentralization itself is made synonymous with radicalism while centralization is defined as reactionary *per se,* it is misleading to condemn American behavior toward the Resistance movements as consistently conservative.[47]

Finally, what is perhaps most misleading about the neo-Marxian point of view is its suggestion that Europe in 1945 was as socially malleable as underdeveloped societies today. By projecting a third-world image upon the West the revisionists overestimate the power of the radical forces and the structural possibilities for change. The United States did help to brake fundamental change especially after V-E Day, but the major limits on reconstruction were set by the internal divisions within the Resistance and the conservative attitude of the Communist parties and the other two allies.[48]

No more in institutional than in political terms did America alone abort a New Order. Kolko's New Order represents a normative image of revolution borrowed from predominantly peasant countries or Yugoslavia and applied to industrial Europe. But not even 1945 Europe was so shaky: the Germans, not the Russians, had occupied the area and left most elites intact. Even where nominally socialist remedies such as nationalization were to be tried, they rarely incorporated any revolutionary tendencies.[49] Pre-war economies had already evolved toward pluralist balances among labor, heavy industry, and small producers and merchandisers. The communists were concerned primarily with retaining their share of the trade-union component in this equilibrium of forces. They sought a social and economic buffer as Stalin sought territorial buffers. A renovation of society on new principles would have required smashing the corporate pluralism in which left-wing as well as conservative leaders found comfort. America did not really have to rescue Europe from radical change because no significant mass-based elements advocated a radical transformation. The so-called New Order—an amalgam in the revisionist mind of Yugoslavian factory councils and Algerian, Vietnamese, or Greek national resistance movements—had no solid peacetime constituency in the West.

What in fact was new in the West was precisely the conglomeration of business, labor, and government that the revisionists lament. In America the New Deal and the wartime economic effort worked to dissolve many of the old lines between public and private spheres.[50] In Fascist Italy, Vichy France, and Nazi Germany a similar interweaving occurred, as it did in a democratic Britain that submitted to extensive planning and welfare measures.[51] Revisionists such as Kolko would accept this description of trends—in fact, Kolko examined the precursor of this private-public interpenetration in his critique of Progressivism—but the revisionists regard these developments as clearly elitist and conservative. Ultimately their general interpretation conceives of the issues behind the Cold War in terms of inequality and class: the Cold War represents to them a continuation of an international civil war in which Russian and later peasant revolutionary forces have successively championed the cause of the oppressed in all countries, while the United States has become the leader of the world's elites.

But no matter what importance this conceptualization may have for today's world, it obscures the historical development. If there has been a growth in international class conflict over the past generation, so too in Western societies there has been an increase of bureaucratic and administrative solutions for social conflict—solutions to which labor contributed, solutions that were conservative in leaving intact private control and ownership, yet still social compromises that commanded wide assent. The forces for compromise sprang from the bureaucratic trends of modern industrial society as they existed in Europe as well as in the United States. The revisionist view splits the world into an industrial half that America supposedly stabilized on behalf of a bureaucratic capitalism and a peasant world where the United States has since met its match. But if peasant society has proved hard to manipulate, Western industrial society has also proved refractory; the neo-Marxians overestimate the fragility of its capitalist order, and overvalue the American contribution to counter-revolution as well as the will to impose it. There is still no well-modulated portrayal of what the United States sought in the world, even less of the real possibilities of institutional change.

No full evaluation of revisionist history, however, can be content with weighing particular interpretations against available evidence. For beneath the details of specific revisionist arguments are more fundamental historiographical problems—implicit conceptual models and underlying assumptions about the decisive factors in American foreign relations.

The revisionists' approach to international conflict and foreign policy formation is a narrow one. They are interested in certain specific modes of explanation and no others. Rejecting any model of international society that sees crucial impulses to conflict as inherent in the international system itself, they seek explanations in American domestic conditions. But for them all domestic conditions are not equally valid. They are unwilling to accept any description that tends to stress the decentralized nature of decision-making or that envisages the possibility of expansionist policy taking shape by imperceptible commitments and bureaucratic momentum. Above all, they approach history with a value system and a vocabulary that appear to make meaningful historical dialogue with those who do not share their framework impossible. The revisionists presuppose international harmony as a normal state and have a deep sense of grievance against whatever factors disturb it. This common assumption shapes their work from the outset in terms of both analysis and tone. But is international harmony a normal state? The division of sovereignty among nation-states makes it difficult to eliminate friction and tension, as theorists from the time of Machiavelli and Hobbes have pointed out.[52] The disputes of 1944–1945 especially were not easy to avoid. With a power vacuum in Central Europe created by the defeat of Germany and with the expansion of American and Soviet influence into new, overlapping regions, some underlying level of dispute was likely. Angered by the scope that the Cold War finally assumed, the revisionists do not really ask whether conflict might have been totally avoided or what level of residual disagreement was likely to emerge even with the best intentions on both sides.

Once mutual mistrust was unchained—and much already existed—all disputes were burdened by it. The initiatives that would have been required to assuage incipient conflict appeared too risky to venture in terms either of domestic public opinion or international security. By late 1945 the United States and Russia each felt itself to be at a competitive disadvantage in key disputes. Each felt that the other, being ahead, could best afford to make initial concessions, while gestures on its part would entail disproportionate or unilateral sacrifice. Perhaps more far-sighted leaders could have sought different outcomes, but there were pressures on all policy makers to take decisions that would harden conflict rather than alleviate it. Some details on this point are particularly worth considering.

In retrospect there appear to have been several areas of negotiation where compromise might at least have been possible, where accommodation demanded relatively little cost, and where the continued absence of greater concession probably deepened suspicion. Some additional flexibility on the issues of both atomic control and financial assistance might have helped to alleviate the growing estrangement. Innovative and generous as our plans for atomic energy control appeared to Americans at the time, the provisions for holding all United States weapons until controls were complete, as well as the demand that the Russians renounce their United Nations veto on all atomic-energy matters, probably doomed the proposal. With such an imbalance of obligations the Soviet advocates of their own country's atomic arsenal were likely to prevail over those willing to acquiesce in nuclear inferiority for a decade or so. As so often after 1946, the reluctance to give up an advantage that at best could only be transitory led to a further spiral in the arms race.[53]

With far less objective risk than was presented by the nuclear issue, liberality with aid might also have offered United States policy makers a chance to dissipate quarrels. Unfortunately, Lend-Lease was brusquely cut off in a way that could not help but offend the Russians, although it was slated to end with the close of the war in any case.[54] Had transitional aid or a significant post-war loan been available, the termination of Lend-Lease might not have proved so abrasive. But the loan proposal was always keyed to the extraction of political concessions, and the Russians had no need to become a suppliant.[55] As it turned out a post-war credit was less crucial to the Soviets than to the British, who faced a mammoth balance of payments crisis that Russia did not have to cope with. Washington could not really use the loan to wrest concessions; instead her failure to provide funds precluded any chance for postwar credits to help improve the general international atmosphere and re-establish some minimal trust.

Disagreement at the start over Eastern Europe had undermined the chances of those peripheral initiatives that might in turn have helped to alleviate overall tension. By becoming trapped in a position where apparently unilateral démarches were needed to break a growing deadlock, policy was far more likely to be vetoed by State Department, Congress, or the President's immediate advisers. It was far harder to justify financial assistance or atomic renunciation when Russia was already felt to be uncooperative. Domestic constraints and the suspicions fed by international rivalry interacted to intensify a serious deadlock.

Although the revisionists do not readily soften their judgments about American policy makers in light of these pressures, they do use them to make Soviet responses appear more acceptable. They explain that the Russians had to reckon with the death of an exceptionally friendly President and the replacement of his key policy makers by tougher spokesmen; with a tooth-and-nail resistance to the German reparations that Russia felt she clearly deserved; and with the curt United States dismissal of a Soviet voice in the occupation of Japan, an influence over the Dardanelles, and a base in the Mediterranean. Neither side was likely to see in the opposing moves anything but a calculated effort to expand power, or, with a little more subtlety, the upshot of a contest between the other power's doves and hawks with the doves increasingly impotent. Such interpretations tended to produce a response in kind. In the absence of any overriding commitment to conciliation, the Cold War thus contained its own momentum toward polarization and deadlock.

It would, however, also be inappropriate to fix too much blame for the origins of the Cold War upon the Hobbesian nature of the international system, though it is a major element the revisionists ignore. As revisionists insist, domestic factors are clearly required to explain the timing and trajectory of the Soviet-American antagonism. But significantly absent from revisionist writing is any sense of the bureaucratic determinants of policy—an element of increasing interest to historians and social scientists seeking to respond to the revisionist indictment. In the view of these writers, decisions are seen as the outcome of organizational disputes within an overall government structure. Policy emerges not so much as a way of maximizing a well-defined national "interest" as the outcome of struggles among bureaucratic forces each seeking to perpetuate its own *raison d'être* and to expand its corporate influence. Recent studies have shown for instance that much of the impulse toward a cold-war defense posture after 1945 came from the fact that both the Air Force and the Navy sought out new strategic conceptions and justifications to preserve their wartime size and status.[56]

Study of the German and reparations issues also reveals how American foreign policy emerged from inter-departmental contention, in this case between Henry Morgenthau and the Treasury on the one hand, and on the other a more conservative State Department desirous of recreating economic stability in Central Europe. After V-E day the Army military government agencies also demanded that their American occupation zone be as economically self-sufficient as possible. The result of these pressures, and of Morgenthau's loss of influence under Truman, was that the United States quarreled bitterly with the Soviets to limit reparations. The American insistence at Potsdam that each power largely confine its reparations to its own zone helped lead to the very division of Germany that the United States officially deplored. The intent was not to build Germany up at the expense of Russia: Byrnes after all offered the Soviets a 25- or 40-year treaty against German aggression in late 1945 and the spring of 1946. But each agency's struggle for the priorities it set in terms of its own organizational interest helped shape a narrow policy that was not subordinated to a clear sense of our more general relations with the Soviet Union.[57]

This approach to policy analysis, which opens up a new range of motivation and offers an alternative to an undue emphasis on personal factors, contrasts with the explanatory model suggested by the neo-

Marxist revisionists.[58] For the latter group what ultimately explains policy is a "system" arising out of the property and power relations within a society, a system causative in its own right and within which institutions and organizations do not lead independent lives but relate to each other dialectically. For these revisionists the explanation of events in terms of intra-governmental structure and struggles is simply formalistic, oriented to the procedural aspects of policy formation and begging the substantive questions. For them, the processes of government might as well be a black box: if one understands the distribution of wealth and influence then policy follows by an almost deductive logic. To attribute decisive influence to bureaucratic pressures seems additionally frivolous to the revisionists since allegedly only certain elites ever rise to the top of those bureaucracies.[59] For those, on the other hand, who stress the political infighting among bureaucracies what is important about history tends to be the successive modifications of action—in short, political process not social structure.

Both of these approaches are deceptive and limiting if taken to extremes. For those who stress history as bureaucratic process, all questions of historical responsibility can appear ambiguous and even irrelevant. Foreign policy emerges as the result of a competition for fiefs within governmental empires. Bureaucratic emphases can produce a neo-Rankean acquiescence in the use of power that is no less deterministic than the revisionist tendency to make all policies exploitative in a liberal capitalist order. But what is perhaps most significant about these alternative causal models is that they are addressed to different questions. The non-revisionists are asking how policies are formed and assume that this also covers the question why. The revisionists see the two questions as different and are interested in the why. And by "why?" revisionists are asking what the meaning of policies is in terms of values imposed from outside the historical narrative. The revisionists charge that the historian must pose this question of meaning consciously or he will pose it unconsciously and accept the values that help to uphold a given social system. History, they suggest, must serve the oppressors or the oppressed, if not by intent then by default. The historian who wishes to avoid this iron polarity can reply that social systems rarely divide their members into clear-cut oppressors and oppressed. He can also insist that even when one despairs of absolute objectivity there are criteria for minimizing subjectivity. On the other hand, he must also take care that the history of policy making not become so focused on organizational processes that the idea of social choice and responsibility is precluded.

In the end it is this attempt by the revisionists to analyze specific historical issues on the basis of *a priori* values about the political system that most strongly affects the controversies their writings have touched off. For their values cannot be derived from the mere amassment of historical data nor do they follow from strictly historical judgments, but rather underlie such judgments. This is true in some sense, no doubt, of history in general, but the whole of Cold War historiography seems particularly dependent upon defined value systems.

For the revisionists, on the one hand, the key issues hinge not upon facts or evidence but upon assessments as to how repressive or non-repressive contemporary liberal institutions are. These judgments in turn must be made within ground rules that allow only polar alternatives for evaluating political action. What is non-revolutionary must be condemned as counter-revolutionary, and reformist political aspirations are dismissed in advance. Similarly, the foreign policies of Western powers cannot escape the stigma of imperialism, for imperialism and exploitation are defined by the revisionists as virtually inherent in any economic intercourse between industrialized and less developed states, or just between unequals. But how can one decide whether the economic reconstruction that America financed was beneficial or "exploitative" for countries brought into a cooperative if not subordinate relationship to the United States? How does one judge the value of multilateral or bilateral trading relations that benefit each side differentially? Judgments must rest upon definitions of exploitation or fairness that logically precede the historical narrative and cannot be derived from it.

The non-revisionist, on the other hand, can refuse to accept the ground rules that presuppose exploitation, dependency, or automatic neo-colonialism; he can refuse to accept the definitions that allow no choice between revolution and reaction. But traditional Cold War historians no less than the revisionists have been involved in tautologies. Historical explanations are normally tested by efforts to find and weigh contradictory evidence, but Cold War analyses on both sides have relied upon propositions that cannot be disproven. Sometimes disproof is precluded by prior assumptions, and while revisionists may believe America's capitalist economy necessitates a voracious expansionism, Cold War theorists have similarly argued that any commitment to communism is *ipso facto* destructive of a "moderate" or "legitimate" international order.[60] Often disproof is impossible because the explanations are totalistic enough to accommodate all contradictory phenomena into one all-embracing explanatory structure. So writers who condemned the Soviets cited Marxist ideology as evidence of real intention when it preached revolution and as evidence of deviousness when it envisaged United-Front coalitions. Conversely, according to the revisionists, when the United States withdrew foreign assistance it was seeking to bring nations to heel; when it was generous, it sought to suborn. When the United States bowed to British desires to delay the Second Front it justified Soviet suspicions; when it opposed Churchill's imperial designs it did so in order to erect a new economic hegemony over what England (and likewise France or the Netherlands) controlled by direct dominion. Spokesmen for each side present the reader with a total explanatory system that accounts for all phenomena, eliminates the possibility of disproof, and thus transcends the usual processes of historical reasoning. More than in most historical controversies, the questions about what happened are transformed into concealed debate about the nature of freedom and duress, exploitation and hegemony. As a result much Cold War historiography has become a confrontation *manqué*–debatable philosophy taught by dismaying example.

## Notes

1. Herbert Feis, *Roosevelt-Churchill-Stalin. The War They Waged and the Peace They Sought* (Princeton, 1957), p. 655.
2. Adam Ulam, *Expansion and Coexistence: The History of Soviet Foreign Policy, 1917–1967* (New York, 1968), p. 377.
3. William H. McNeill, *America, Britain, and Russia, Their Cooperation and Conflict, 1941–1946* (London, 1953). For recent explorations in the same spirit: Walter LaFeber, *America, Russia, and the Cold War, 1945–1966* (New York, 1967), which stresses growing ideological militancy; Louis J. Halle, *The Cold War as History* (London, 1967), a treatment that verges on fatalism; Martin F. Herz, *Beginnings of the Cold War* (Bloomington, Ind., 1966); William L. Neumann, *After Victory: Churchill, Roosevelt, Stalin, and the Making of the Peace* (New York, 1967); André Fontaine, *History of the Cold War*, trans. D. D. Paige (2 vols.: New York, 1968); cf. also Arthur Schlesinger, Jr., "Origins of the Cold War," *Foreign Affairs,* 46 (1967), 22–52.
4. Denna F. Fleming, *The Cold War and its Origins, 1917–1960* (2 vols.: Garden City, N.Y., 1961). Unfortunately the book relies almost exclusively on newspaper accounts and commentary. Relying heavily on Fleming for its historical analysis is David Horowitz, *The Free World Colossus* (New York, 1965).
5. Harriman's assessments in Department of State, *Foreign Relations of the United States* (henceforth: *FRUS*), especially November 5, 1943 foreseeing disagreements on reparations and Poland but generally pleased with Russian cooperation (*FRUS,* 1943, III, 589–593), August 15, and August

21, 1944 (*FRUS*, 1944, III, 1376, 1382 n. 1.), March 17, 1945 (*FRUS*, 1945, III, 732), and April 4, 1945—"the Soviet program is the establishment of totalitarianism"—(*FRUS*, 1945, V, 819).

6. For the Teheran discussions of the Polish frontier, Feis, *Churchill-Roosevelt-Stalin* pp. 284–285. Harriman advice in *FRUS*, 1944, III, 1322ff.

7. For the revisionist view of the Polish dispute, Gabriel Kolko, *The Politics of War, The World and United States Foreign Policy, 1943–1945* (New York, 1968), pp. 99–122, 147–152; Gar Alperovitz, *Atomic Diplomacy: Hiroshima and Potsdam* (New York, 1965), esp. pp. 243–256; Fleming, *The Cold War and its Origins*, I, 222–248. Cf. Feis, *Churchill-Roosevelt-Stalin*, pp. 283–301, 453–460, 518–529; official summary in *FRUS, The Conferences at Malta and Yalta (1945)*, p. 202ff.; and for strong anti-communist presentations, Arthur Bliss Lane, *I Saw Poland Betrayed* (Indianapolis, 1948), and Edward J. Rozek, *Allied Wartime Diplomacy: A Pattern in Poland* (London, 1958).

8. Alperovitz, *Atomic Diplomacy*, pp. 250–253, 261–267, on Roosevelt after Yalta, and 188–225 on post-Hiroshima aggressiveness. In judging Roosevelt's correspondence it is important to remember that by March 1945 the Polish issue was just part of a larger concern about keeping the alliance together in view of the upcoming United Nations conference and preventing broad public disillusion about the Crimean agreements. Roosevelt was acting more as a mediator than as a defender of a particular Polish position. For the President's misgivings about the agreement even at Yalta see William D. Leahy, *I Was There* (New York, 1950), pp. 315–316; the mingled exultation and disillusion in the post-Yalta atmosphere is conveyed in Robert Sherwood, *Roosevelt and Hopkins* (New York, 1948), pp. 869–876. For the quarrel about the composition of the Polish government, Winston S. Churchill, *The Second World War*, vol. VI, *Triumph and Tragedy* (Boston, 1953), pp. 418–439; cf. also the reports from the Commission on Poland sitting in Moscow: *FRUS*, 1945, V, 134ff.

9. But see the American point of view in James F. Byrnes, *Speaking Frankly* (New York, 1947), pp. 72ff., 89–101, 115ff.; also the critical reports of Byrnes's observer in Rumania, Mark Ethridge, who urged firm resistance to growing aggression: *FRUS*, 1945, V, 627–630, 633–641.

10. See Kolko, *The Politics of War*, pp. 168–171 (an analysis marred by the remarkable judgment that absence of civil war in Eastern Europe showed the "flexibility and subtlety of the various Communist parties and the Russians"); also Alperovitz, *Atomic Diplomacy*, pp. 217ff.; Fleming, *The Cold War and its Origins*, I, 203, 208–210, 242–243, 250–258.

11. For a spectrum of opinions on Stalinist objectives see Ulam, *Expansion and Coexistence*, pp. 377, 381, 388–408, an anti-revisionist but rich and subtle account; J. M. Mackintosh, *Strategy and Tactics of Soviet Foreign Policy* (London, 1962), pp. 1–17, for a traditional view; also Philip E. Mosely, "Soviet Policy in a two-world System," *The Kremlin and World Politics* (New York, 1960), who sees the Russians reverting to revolutionary goals from November 1944; Kolko, *The Politics of War*, pp. 164–165, stressing Soviet conservatism; McNeill, *America, Britain, and Russia*, pp.

564–565, 609–610; LaFeber, *America, Russia, and the Cold War*, pp. 14–18, 23, 28–32, which couples Stalin's electoral address and Churchill's speech at Fulton, Missouri; Isaac Deutscher, *Stalin, A Political Biography* (New York, 1960), pp. 518–521, 529ff.

12. Cf. Kolko, *The Politics of War*, pp. 37–39, 128–131 for the Italian-Rumanian parallel; Churchill, *Triumph and Tragedy*, pp. 227–235, for the percentages agreement; cf. Alperovitz, *Atomic Diplomacy*, pp. 133–134.

13. For a pro-Western account of Balkan party politics: Hugh Seton-Watson, *The East European Revolution* (New York, 3rd ed., 1956), pp. 31–36, 174–175, 184, 197–198, 202–219.

14. For official American disavowal of spheres of influence, Cordell Hull, *The Memoirs of Cordell Hull* (London, 1948), II, 1168, 1298; *FRUS, The Conference of Berlin (The Potsdam Conference) 1945*, I, 262–264. For Stimson's dissent, Alperovitz, *Atomic Diplomacy*, p. 54; for Kennan's, George F. Kennan, *Memoirs, 1925–1950* (Boston, 1967), pp. 211–213, 222, 250; for Henry Wallace's coupling of political spheres of influence with economic universalism, LaFeber, *America, Russia and the Cold War*, pp. 37–39.

15. H. Stuart Hughes, "The Second Year of the Cold War: A Memoir & an Anticipation," *Commentary*, 48 (1969), 27–32, esp. 31.

16. Alperovitz, *Atomic Diplomacy*, pp. 19–33, 55–90, 270–275.

17. *Ibid.*, pp. 117–120 on military estimates, 176–187 and 226–242 on nuclear calculations, 120–126 and 183–186 on the Sino-Soviet treaty. The delays in the final arrangements of the treaty, however, did not all stem from the American or Chinese side; the Russians themselves were raising the price of a treaty with Chiang's government. Cf. Kolko, *The Politics of War*, pp. 556–560.

18. Kolko, *The Politics of War*, pp. 560–565: "Mechanism prevailed"; Herbert Feis, *The Atomic Bomb and the End of World War II* (Princeton, N.J., 1966), p. 194, who now feels that "to monitor" Russian behavior may have been a motive for using the weapon. Cf. Alperovitz's critique of Feis's vacillation now included as "The Use of the Atomic Bomb," in his collection of *New York Review of Books* pieces: Gar Alperovitz, *Cold War Essays* (Garden City, N.Y., 1970), pp. 51–74. A variant of the Alperovitz thesis was first advanced by P. M. S. Blackett, *Fear, War, and the Bomb* (New York, 1949). Important in the earlier debate was Henry L. Stimson's justification, "The Decision to Use the Atomic Bomb," *Harper's Magazine*, February 1947, reprinted in H. L. Stimson and McGeorge Bundy, *On Active Service in Peace and War* (New York, 1948); also Louis Morton, "The Decision to Use the Atomic Bomb," *Foreign Affairs*, 35 (1957), 334–353.

19. See Memorandum of Conversation, May 2, 1945 with President Truman, Generals Schuyler and Crane, in Joseph Grew MSS., Conversations, vol. 7, Houghton Library, Harvard University.

20. Alperovitz, *Atomic Diplomacy*, p. 80. As grounds for pushing back a summit conference, Truman himself claimed newness to office and the need to complete the preparation of a budget before the end of the fiscal

year (Grew-Eden-Truman conversation, March 14, 1945, Joseph Grew
MSS, Conversations, vol. 7). Alperovitz dismisses the budget considerations
as implausible (p. 67). Much of Alperovitz's case hinges upon the timing
and intent of the Hopkins mission. Truman's decision to dispatch Hopkins
was made earlier than Sherwood said, although the suggestion was still
Harriman's; hence Alperovitz argues it should be read as a response to
Stimson's atomic briefings and not the disputes usually cited. Cf. Harry
Truman, *Year of Decisions* (Garden City, N.Y., 1955), pp. 108–110 for
April 30 date; Sherwood, *Roosevelt and Hopkins*, p. 885, for mid-May, and
cf. Alperovitz, *Atomic Diplomacy*, p. 71n, and pp. 270–275. In fact by the
end of April there were many indications of urgent troubles warranting an
envoy's talk with Stalin: see Churchill's major letter of April 29 to Stalin,
which foresaw a divided Europe and a quarrel "that would tear the world
to pieces." *Triumph and Tragedy*, pp. 494–497.

21. For the recommendations of the Joint Chiefs of Staff see *FRUS,
The Conference of Berlin (Potsdam)*, I, 903–910, which records the White
House meeting of June 18, 1945, where Marshall outlined a November 1
landing on Kyushu, and the President said he would seek Russian help at
Potsdam and wanted to prevent an "Okinawa from one end of Japan to
another." See also the text of the JCS report, pp. 910–911, and the Combined Chiefs of Staff report as approved by Truman and the Prime Minister
on July 24, in Vol. II, 1462–1463. Cf. Alperovitz, *Atomic Diplomacy*, pp.
117–120, for discussion of this point. For divisions on the surrender debates
within the respective combatants: Waldo H. Heinrichs, Jr., *American Ambassador: Joseph C. Grew and the Development of the United States Diplomatic Tradition* (Boston, 1966), pp. 372–380; Robert J. C. Butow, *Japan's
Decision to Surrender* (Stanford, 1954), pp. 158ff. for the post-Hiroshima
situation.

22. Cf. Kolko, *The Politics of War*, p. 560; Halle, *The Cold War as
History*, p. 173.

23. Harriman's assessment is in *FRUS, 1945*, V, 922–924. On Truman
and the bomb, see Alperovitz, *Atomic Diplomacy*, p. 227; cf. Nuel Pharr
Davis, *Lawrence and Oppenheimer* (Greenwich, Conn., Fawcett ed., 1969),
pp. 257–260.

24. William Appleman Williams, *The Tragedy of American Diplomacy*
(New York, rev. ed., 1962); for similar analysis as applied to the whole
Roosevelt period cf. the work of Williams' student, Lloyd C. Gardner,
*Economic Aspects of New Deal Diplomacy* (Madison, 1964).

25. For this theme, Gabriel Kolko, *The Triumph of Conservatism* (Chi-
cago, 1963); William A. Williams, *The Contours of American History*
(Chicago, 1966), pp. 390ff.; James Weinstein, *The Corporate Ideal in the
Liberal State, 1900–1918* (Boston, 1968); Barton J. Bernstein, "The New
Deal: The Conservative Achievements of Liberal Reform," in Barton J.
Bernstein, ed., *Towards a New Past: Dissenting Essays in American History*
(New York, 1969), pp. 262–288.

26. See John Bagulley, "The World War and the Cold War," David
Horowitz, ed., *Containment and Revolution* (Boston, 1968), pp. 77–97;

Kolko, *The Politics of War,* pp. 12–30. For non-revisionist discussions of this thorny issue cf. Feis, *Churchill-Roosevelt-Stalin,* pp. 47–80, 93–102, 114–119, 134–136; Maurice Matloff and Edwin M. Snell, *Strategic Planning for Coalition Warfare, 1941–1942* (Washington, 1953), pp. 229–244, 328–349; also Maurice Matloff, *Strategic Planning for Coalition Warfare, 1943–1944* (Washington, 1959). Valuable insight into the "technical" restraints on Allied policy is provided by Robert W. Coakley and Richard M. Leighton, *Global Logistics and Strategy, 1943–1945* (Washington, 1968), pp. 3–6, 173–245.

27. See Fleming, *The Cold War and its Origins,* I, 106–134; also A. J. P. Taylor, *The Origins of the Second World War* (New York, 1962), pp. 240–241, for defenses of Stalinist diplomacy, and George F. Kennan, *Russia and the West under Lenin and Stalin* (Boston, 1960), pp. 312–336, 347–348, for a harsh critique. The recent accounts on both sides—Kolko, *The Politics of War,* pp. 13–14, and Ulam, *Expansion and Coexistence,* pp. 250–279—stress the prevailing Machiavellism and cynicism of the late 1930's and sensibly tend to divorce the period from an integral role in cold war origins.

28. Fleming, *The Cold War and its Origins,* I, 20–35.

29. One can usefully separate those accounts that stress the ineffectiveness and hesitations of Roosevelt's foreign policy—Arnold Offner, *American Appeasement: United States Foreign Policy and Germany, 1933–1938* (Cambridge, Mass., 1969); Robert A. Divine, *The Illusion of Neutrality* (Chicago, 1962)—from those questioning the old view of isolationism from economic or ideological criteria: Gardner, *Economic Aspects of New Deal Diplomacy,* pp. 86–98; Williams, "The Legend of Isolationism," in *The Tragedy of American Diplomacy,* pp. 104–159; Robert Freeman Smith, "American Foreign Relations, 1920–1942," in Bernstein, *Towards a New Past,* pp. 232–256.

30. For a presentation of Wilsonian aspirations parallel in some respects to Kolko, Arno J. Mayer, *Politics and Diplomacy of Peacemaking: Containment and Counterrevolution at Versailles, 1918–1919* (New York, 1967). Cf. also N. Gordon Levin, Jr., *Woodrow Wilson and World Politics* (New York, 1968). Common to both Mayer and Kolko, is the subordination of the German problem to the Russian one; on the other hand, Wilson exerted a more genuinely reformist impulse in Europe according to Mayer than Roosevelt did according to Kolko.

31. See Marilyn B. Young, "American Expansion, 1870–1900: The Far East," in Bernstein, *Towards a New Past,* esp. pp. 186–198, for a tempered interpretation; also Williams, *The Tragedy of American Diplomacy,* pp. 37–50; Walter LaFeber, *The New Empire: An Interpretation of American Expansion, 1860–1898* (Ithaca, N.Y., 1963).

32. See William A. Williams, *The Roots of the Modern American Empire* (New York, 1969), based upon an extensive reading of agrarian opinion, and a learned and moving, if problematic, book.

33. Kolko, *The Politics of War,* pp. 323–340.

34. For detailed treatment of these issues, see Richard N. Gardner,

*Sterling-Dollar Diplomacy* (Oxford, 1956), which covers the entire wartime period; cf. also E. F. Penrose, *Economic Planning for Peace* (Princeton, 1953). Revisionist critiques are in Lloyd Gardner, *Economic Aspects of New Deal Diplomacy,* pp. 275–291, and Kolko, *The Politics of War,* pp. 280–294, 488–492, 623–624.

35. For critiques of "exploitative" international economic relations from a Marxist viewpoint, see Harry Magdoff, *The Age of Imperialism: The Economics of United States Foreign Policy* (New York, 1969); and Paul A. Baran, *The Political Economy of Growth* (New York and London, 1957), pp. 177ff.

36. John Morton Blum, *From the Morgenthau Diaries: Years of War, 1941–1945* (Cambridge, Mass., 1967), pp. 323–347; Paul Y. Hammond, "Directives for the Occupation of Germany: The Washington Controversy," in Harold Stein, ed., *American Civil-Military Decisions* (Birmingham, Ala., 1963), pp. 348–388.

37. Cited in Blum, *From the Morgenthau Diaries,* III, 273.

38. For impulses to cooperation, Richard Gardner, *Sterling-Dollar Diplomacy,* pp. 54–58; for the spectrum of domestic opinion on aid to Britain, *ibid.,* pp. 192–199, 226–253, 208–210; cf. also Thomas Lamont's call for restoration of British prosperity, cited in Lloyd Gardner, *Economic Aspects of New Deal Diplomacy,* pp. 275–276; also Blum, *From the Morgenthau Diaries,* III, 324–326 for opposed views (Morgenthau's and Baruch's) on what to demand of Britain.

39. Richard Gardner, *Sterling-Dollar Diplomacy,* pp. 306–347; J. Keith Horsefield, *History of the International Monetary Fund* (Washington, D.C., 1970), I, 3–118. For the difficulties that convertibility presented to English policies: Sidney Pollard, *The Development of the British Economy, 1914–1950* (London, 1962), pp. 365–407; Hugh Dalton, *High Tide and After: Memoirs, 1945–1960* (London, 1962), pp. 68–89, 178–184, 254ff. For American policies of 1949–1950, William Diebold, Jr., *Trade and Payments in Western Europe: A Study in Economic Cooperation, 1947–1951* (New York, 1952), pp. 34–110.

40. See Thomas G. Paterson, "The Abortive American Loan to Russia and the Origins of the Cold War, 1943–1946," *The Journal of American History,* 56 (1969), pp. 71–72, 75–77.

41. Cf. Sumner Wells, *The Time for Decision* (New York, 1944), p. 409.

42. See Under-Secretary of State Dean Acheson's condemnation of any such tendency as bordering on Soviet autarchy cited in Williams, *The Tragedy of American Diplomacy,* p. 236; for a spectrum of economists' thinking about post-war possibilities, see Seymour Harris, ed., *Postwar Economic Problems* (New York, 1943).

43. Cf. Kolko, *The Politics of War,* pp. 55–71, 154–155, 172–193. For a pointed Greek EAM-NLF comparison, see Todd Gitlin, "Counter-Insurgency: Myth and Reality in Greece," in Horowitz, *Containment and Revolution,* pp. 140–181. The major pro-EAM Greek account is now André Kédros, *La résistance grècque (1940–1944)* (Paris, 1966).

44. Cf. Isaac Deutscher, "Myths of the Cold War," in Horowitz, *Con-*

*tainment and Revolution,* pp. 17–19; Gabriel Kolko, *The Roots of American Foreign Policy* (Boston, 1969), esp. pp. xi–xii and 85–87 on the United States relation to the third world; also Kolko, *The Politics of War,* pp. 449–451, 594–595ff. For an extensive critical discussion of the American attitudes toward the third world and Greece since the 1940's see Richard J. Barnet, *Intervention and Revolution: The United States in the Third World* (New York and Cleveland, 1968).

45. For a view of economically determined aims for Eastern Europe, see Kolko, *The Politics of War,* pp. 167–171. But is it really so true, as Kolko claims, that trade and investment were "so central to objectives in that area"? The aims stated by Stetinnius (*FRUS,* 1944, IV, 1025–1026) that Kolko cites were more inconsistent than imperialist: their cardinal point was self-determination of political and social systems. Briefing papers prepared for Yalta also said that the United States should insist on access for trade and investment, but still recognized that the Soviets would exert predominant political influence in the area. They expressed a willingness to accept the fact so long as American influence was not completely nullified, and ventured, furthermore, to say that precisely the safe assurance of a pro-Russian political orientation would let the Soviets admit United States loans. (See *FRUS, The Conferences at Malta and Yalta,* pp. 234–235.) For definition of aspirations in a concrete situation see Harriman's report on the Polish agreement, June 28, 1945, in *FRUS, The Conference of Berlin (Potsdam),* I, 728, where the matter of concern cited is administration of the Ministry of Internal Security: "the crux of whether Poland will have her independence, whether reasonable personal freedoms will be permitted and whether reasonably free elections can be held."

46. On Vichy policy: William L. Langer, *Our Vichy Gamble* (New York, 1947); Robert Murphy, *Diplomat Among Warriors* (Garden City, N.Y., 1964), pp. 49–64, 124–185; Cordell Hull, *The Memoirs of Cordell Hull,* II, 1127–1138, 1222–1226, 1241–1246. For allied differences in Italy: Norman Kogan, *Italy and the Allies* (Cambridge, Mass., 1956); for British policy in Greece, Kédros, *La résistance grècque (1940–1944),* pp. 479–513; William H. McNeill, *The Greek Dilemma* (London, 1947); and Churchill's defense in *Triumph and Tragedy,* pp. 283–325.

47. Cf. Norman Kogan, "American Policies toward European Resistance Movements," *European Resistance Movements, 1939–1945. Proceedings of the Second International Conference on the History of the Resistance Movements Held at Milan, 26–29 March 1961* (London, 1964), pp. 74–93; cf. F. W. Deakin, "Great Britain and European Resistance," and the veiled criticisms of Allied policy by Ferruccio Parri and Franco Venturi, "The Italian Resistance and the Allies," in the same collection xxvii–xxxvii.

For a critique from the Left of Allied pressure against the Northern Resistance movement in Italy (the CLNAI) see Franco Catalano, *Storia del C.L.N.A.I.* (Bari, 1956), pp. 283–315, 326–350; Kogan, *Italy and the Allies,* pp. 90–110; Kolko, *The Politics of War,* pp. 53–63.

48. It is often overlooked that the political decisions of late 1944, which led to the British suppression of the Greek resistance and the Allied pres-

sure for a compromise between the reformist Northern Italian resistance groups (the CLNAI) and the more conservative Rome government, grew out of Anglo-American differences as much as out of any quarrel with the Soviets. At the second Quebec Conference in September 1944 Roosevelt had pressed the Morgenthau plan upon the reluctant British and had threatened Lend-Lease curtailment. At the same time the President, in view of the upcoming elections, was advocating an Italian policy more favorable to the Rome government or the Resistance parties than Churchill desired and was more obdurate on the Polish issue. It was immediately after Quebec that Churchill flew to Moscow to make his "percentages" agreement with Stalin on the demarcation of Balkan spheres of influence. In the months to come Stalin increased his own domination over the Eastern European countries, but in contrast reaffirmed his policy of having Western communist leaders support the established forces in Rome and Paris. Churchill and Eden could act with a freer hand in the Mediterranean and also explore a West European bloc. In short, both Allies adopted policies that envisaged a possible falling-out with America, although the Soviet push into Central Europe was to bring Churchill quickly back into an anti-Russian posture. In the interim it was the independent forces of the local Resistance movements that bore the cost. But for the divisions within the Resistance forces themselves, which was also an important factor, see Kolko, *The Politics of War,* pp. 428–456, esp. 450–456; Franco Catalano, "Presentazione," and "Italia," in *Aspetti sociali ed economici della Resistenza in Europa: Atti del convegno . . . (Milano 26–27 marzo 1966),* pp. xviii, 114ff., 121ff.; Georgio Bocca, *Storia dell'Italia partigiana* (Bari, 1966), pp. 466–484; cf. also Leo Valiani, "Sulla storia sociale della resistanza," *Il movimento di Liberazione in Italia,* 88 (1967), 87–92 on the limits of the Resistance Left. For France, Henri Michel sees American and inherent limits on the resistance: "France," *Aspetti sociali ed economici,* pp. 17, 32–33; cf. also his *Les courants de pensée de la résistance* (Paris, 1962), pp. 387–410, 518–529, 685–706, 711–721.

49. A brief exception may have been the Communist efforts at syndical control in France, but even these appear to have been only a means to entrench the Party in a new labor fief. See Maurice Bye, Ernest Rossi, Mario Einaudi, *Nationalization in France and Italy* (Ithaca, N.Y., 1955), pp. 96–109.

50. Ellis Hawley, *The New Deal and the Problem of Monopoly* (Princeton, 1966), pp. 449ff., 489; Sherwood, *Roosevelt and Hopkins,* pp. 157–164; Barton J. Bernstein, "America in War and Peace: The Test of Liberalism," in Bernstein, *Towards a New Past,* pp. 292–295; also his "Industrial Reconversion: The Protection of Oligopoly and Military Control of the War Machine," *American Journal of Economics and Sociology,* 26 (1967), 159–172. For a good case study of military-industrial collaboration, Robert H. Connery, *The Navy and the Industrial Mobilization in World War II* (Princeton, N.J., 1951).

51. Derek H. Aldcroft, "The Development of the Managed Economy before 1939," *Journal of Contemporary History,* 4 (October 1969), 117–

137; W. K. Hancock and M. M. Gowing, *British War Economy* (London, 1949). For French initiatives, Stanley Hoffmann, "Paradoxes of the French Political Community," in Stanley H. Hoffmann, et al., *In Search of France* (New York, Harper Torchbooks, 1965), pp. 38–39. For descriptions of the German situation, Arthur Schweitzer, *Big Business in the Third Reich* (Bloomington, Ind., 1954); Franz Neumann, *Behemoth, The Structure and Practice of National Socialism* (New York, Harper Torchbook ed., 1966), pp. 221–361; David S. Landes, *The Unbound Prometheus* (Cambridge, Eng., 1969), pp. 402–417. For the origins of the IRI, Rossi, Bye, Einaudi, *Nationalization in France and Italy*, pp. 191–200.

52. For an introduction to the large body of theory that stresses the inherent logic of the international system in shaping bipolar or balance-of-power competition, see Morton Kaplan, *System and Process in International Politics* (New York, 1957), also his "Variants on Six Models of the International System," in James N. Rosenau, ed., *International Politics and Foreign Policy* (New York, 1969 ed.), pp. 291–303; cf. Karl W. Deutsch, *The Analysis of International Relations* (Englewood Cliffs, N.J., 1969), pp. 112–140. In its most abstract form in terms of an international system, the Cold War to 1948 can be reconstructed as a transition in which each side raised its criteria of tolerable political conditions in third countries from acceptance of regimes so long as they allowed some influence for its own respective supporters to an insistence on regimes that excluded its opponents' clients from any voice in policy. For elaboration of a similar logic in mathematical terms as applied to arms races, see Anatol Rapoport, "Lewis M. Richardson's Mathematical Theory of War," now included as "The Mathematics of Arms Races," in James N. Rosenau, ed., *International Politics and Foreign Policy* (New York, 1961 ed.). For a useful discrimination between causal models of war according to their focus on international, domestic, or psychological factors see Kenneth Waltz, *Man, the State, and War* (New York, 1959).

53. Richard G. Hewlett and Oscar E. Anderson, *The New World, 1939–1946* (University Park, Pa., 1962), pp. 455–481, 531–619; David Lilienthal, *The Journals of David E. Lilienthal: The Atomic Energy Years, 1945–1950* (New York, 1964), pp. 27ff.; Dean Acheson, *Present at the Creation: My Years in the State Department* (New York, 1969), pp. 151–156; critical views in Fleming, *The Cold War and its Origins*, I, 363–379; cf. also Robert Gilpin, *American Scientists and Nuclear Weapons Policy* (Princeton, 1962), pp. 52–63.

54. The best recent summary is in George Herring, Jr., "Lend-Lease to Russia and the Origins of the Cold War, 1944–1945," *The Journal of American History*, 56 (1969), 93–114. Herring emphasizes that Lend-Lease to Russia always depended upon Roosevelt's constant intervention to smooth requirements that might have disqualified the Soviets. The 3 (c) clause of the Lend-Lease agreement provided for transitional aid after the war, but the negotiations were dropped in March 1945 on the recommendation of Joseph Grew and Leo Crowley—who also engineered the cut-off in May. Grew and Crowley pleaded Congressional difficulty, but this seems

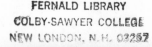

exaggerated. Cf. Morgenthau's objections to 3 (c) delays in *FRUS, The Conferences at Malta and Yalta,* p. 320.

55. See Paterson, "The Abortive American Loan to Russia and the Origins of the Cold War, 1943–1946," pp. 70–92.

56. Vincent Davis, *Postwar Defense Policy and the U.S. Navy, 1943–1946* (Chapel Hill, 1966), pp. 164ff., 186ff., 219ff.; Perry M. Smith; *The Air Force Plans for Peace, 1943–1945* (Baltimore, Md., 1970). The Army, on the other hand, was interested in maintaining Soviet participation in the war because they were unwilling to concede that air and naval power would defeat Japan; moreover Eisenhower needed Russian cooperation in administering Germany, and was personally impressed by Marshall Zhukov. See Dwight D. Eisenhower, *Crusade in Europe* (New York, 1948), pp. 458–475; Feis, *Between War and Peace,* pp. 74–76, 141–144.

57. For inter-agency contention on Germany see Hammond, "Directives for the Occupation of Germany," pp. 408–443. State Department conservatism and backwardness are well evoked in Acheson, *Present at the Creation,* pp. 17, 22–36, 38–47, 64ff; Kolko, *The Politics of War,* pp. 511–521, 569–575, and for criticism of reparations policy, 578; John M. Gimbel, *The American Occupation of Germany: Politics and the Military, 1945–1949* (Stanford, 1968), pp. xii, 9–30, 52–61, 85–87, stresses the economic needs of the American zonal administrators and the resistance of the French. For the hard-fought reparations negotiations, see also Feis, *Between War and Peace,* pp. 234, 246–258, and *FRUS, Conference of Berlin (Potsdam),* I, 510–511, 519–554; II, 274–275, 277–287, 295–298 and passim to 512–518, 830–949. Cf. Alperovitz, "How did the Cold War Begin?" *Cold War Essays,* p. 48, for recognition of the complexities of the German questions.

58. For some examples of this approach see Hammond's and other studies in Stein, *American Civil-Military Decisions;* also the studies in Werner Schilling, P. Y. Hammond, and G. H. Snyder, eds., *Strategy, Politics and Defense Budgets* (New York, 1962); Werner Schilling, "The H Bomb Decision: How to Decide Without Actually Choosing," *Political Science Quarterly,* 76 (1961), 24–46. For a methodological statement, see Graham T. Allison, "Conceptual Models and the Cuban Missile Crisis," *The American Political Science Review,* 63 (1969), 689–718.

59. See most recently Gabriel Kolko's emphasis on the permeation of business influence in the United States foreign-policy elite and his attack on bureaucratic formalism in *The Roots of American Foreign Policy,* esp. pp. xii–xiii, 3–26.

60. See Henry Kissinger's influential distinction between legitimate and revolutionary orders in *Nuclear Weapons and Foreign Policy* (Garden City, N.Y., 1958), pp. 43–49; also Henry Kissinger, "Conditions of World Order," *Daedalus,* 45 (1966), pp. 503–529.

# 2

## Franz Schurmann

# Selections from The Logic of World Power

*Franz Schurmann is a scholar of Communist China who teaches at the University of California at Berkeley. He has contributed a major study in his area of specialty:* Ideology and Organization in Communist China *(Berkeley and Los Angeles: University of California Press, 1968). The book, from which the following selections are taken (pp. 8–17, 46–53, 56–62, 64–68, 91–100, 105–109) with the permission of the publisher, Pantheon, and the author, represents an effort to place the Vietnam war in the longer perspective of three-power conflict among the United States, the Soviet Union, and China. Frankly theoretical, Schurmann's work seeks to link the foreign policies of the major states with economic structures, political and bureaucratic institutions, and ideology. The close attention paid to American "capitalism" indicates the author's debt to various strands of Marxism. But the differential analysis of United States economic interests, the critique of revisionism, and the emphasis given to the autonomous imperialist drives generated by ideas represented in the Democratic Party and the logic of nuclear weapons, all make for an unorthodox and independent critical stance. It is, of course, always problematic to link up the broad outlines of theory with day-to-day outcomes; any grand scheme will be vulnerable to charges of glossing over particular historical events that fit less well. Moreover, Schurmann's summary that American imperialism provoked the cold war regardless of Soviet aspirations will seem too clever for many readers. Still, Schurmann's theory, I think, satisfies a major criterion that should be set for any explanation in the social sciences, namely, the uncovering of testable relationships between areas of activity not otherwise plausibly linked together.*

### Vision and Executive Power:
### Toward a Theory of Ideology and Interests

If Roosevelt's vision of "one world" was an emerging doctrine of American imperialism, then one obvious and central fact about it has to be noted: it was conceived, formulated, and implemented at the highest levels of governmental power, by the President himself. Moreover, if one takes seriously the conflict between isolationists and interventionists, that vision was put forth against the opposition of a major part of the American business class, who constitute the great bulk of America's particular interests and were traditionally the most expansionist segment of American society. This points to something that people raised in or influenced by the Marxist tradition are prone to reject: the autonomous, innovative, and powerful role of the state. But one must go even further and see what was obvious at the time: that it was not from the state as a whole, the aggregate of executive, bureaucratic, and legislative agencies, but from the very pinnacle of the state that the vision originated.

Although I have begun with some historical observations, my real intent is theoretical, to sketch out a theory of relations between states in the last quarter-century. A theory is an explanatory device, neither true nor false in itself, which demonstrates its worth by generating a continuous chain of derivative explanations of phenomena that are not in conflict with conventional wisdom or certain testable hypotheses. In other words, a good theory is a satisfyingly productive one. People feel the need to construct theories when they are persistently faced with anomalies in important problems which existing theories cannot explain away. When such anomalies exist in the realm of human affairs, it is usually the historians who take command. They gather the salient facts, sort out the patterns, and construct generalizations. The process of generalization works from the bottom up, that is, from generally accepted facts. Theory construction, on the other hand, works from the top down, from the logical mind. Both, however, demonstrate their productivity by generating hypotheses that can be tested against generally accepted canons of evidence. The most exciting situation for learning occurs when theory, hypotheses, and generalization constitute a thriving, interacting trinity in which all grow.

The important problem that has produced anomalies during the quarter-century of the nuclear age is the nature of state-to-state relations. If one accepts the notion that America has been the prime mover in this new network of relations, then the important problem becomes the nature of American foreign policy since 1945, when the nuclear age began. Mounds of popular and scholarly material have been written on this subject. All the points of view, which implicitly are kinds of theories, agree that the world since 1945 has become a political whole: even minor events in a distant part of the world affect the global skein of relations. But, since the points of view are usually ideologically inspired, they naturally differ in their basic assumptions. The most popular point of view in America has been the notion that communism has been the prime aggressive force in the world, seeking to undermine and destroy the free world. The opposite point of view, initially held in the socialist countries and by the international left wing but increasingly prevalent among "revisionist" scholars, is that America has been the prime aggressive force in the world, seeking to undermine the socialist camp and destroy revolutionary movements. A third point of view, much more esoteric, is held largely by trained experts in the field of international systems. It sees global politics as a game in which the key actors are the great powers (primarily America and Russia), the key pieces are elements of power (notably nuclear), and the other pieces are a changing variety of political actors. While the first two points of view have produced the bulk of the literature, they have not been particularly theoretical. There has been little theoretical thinking in American popular anticommunist approaches. There appears to be a great deal in the Russian and Chinese approaches, particularly as expressed in their polemics during the early 1960s, but theory, dogma, and politics were too intertwined there to allow the theory to appear in simple and elegant form. "Revisionist" writers on the left in the West have only begun the process of theory construction, much of which tends to follow Marxist lines. . . .

When people do a lot of writing about a particular subject, it always means that they are bothered by it. One hardly has to press the argument that state-to-state relations since 1945, particularly with the ever-present threat of nuclear destruction, deeply bother people throughout the world. The phenomenon of nuclear power has produced the major anomaly demanding satisfying explanation in the contemporary world—not only is this power, which can virtually burn up the planet, the product of stupefyingly sophisticated technology, but the power to use it is so centralized that, at least in the United States, one person alone can make the final decision. This is symbolized by the little black box always in the presence of the President of the United States, which contains the signals to activate, deploy, and fire the nuclear weapons. This concentration of political power of enormous scope in the hands of the chief executive, only barely modified by fail-safe devices, seems to contradict all notions of politics. Politics is the realm of power, and power can be simply defined as the command over men and resources for the achievement of goals. The notion of goals is basic to politics. Men achieve power in political structures to advance or protect their own interests or those of constituencies with whom they identify. The President of the United States is presumed to wield power in the interests of all Americans, his constituency, although it is generally believed that he does so primarily for some and less so for others. In any case, politics presumes that he acts to achieve someone's interests, even if his overriding interest is entirely personal, such as assuring his re-election. Radical and liberal views of politics in America may differ on whose interests are being advocated by the President, but they agree that his power serves interests. Whether the President is the instrument of certain constituencies or their leader does not affect that argument.

The notion of politics as serving interests runs into a dilemma when one enters the nuclear field. That the President of the United States (and presumably also the chief executives of Russia and China) exercises nuclear power is obvious—he wields command over men and resources (nuclear strike forces) to achieve goals (the destruction of an enemy). But what and whose interests are served by nuclear war? Conventional (non-nuclear) wars serve real interests: that one side capture from or deny to the other side territory, populations, resources, prestige, or time. Even a war so murky as the Vietnam war can be explained in terms of interests. Nuclear war, however, does not envisage the capture or denial of anything to an adversary. It is theoretically designed to assure maximum destruction of an adversary with maximum survival for one's own side. Since it is in the "interest" of all living beings to survive, the concept of interest loses any theoretical force, for it has meaning only where interests can be differentiated into various kinds. At first, nuclear weapons were seen as just another kind of weapon with which to punish or threaten an aggressor. Then it was realized that no nation would pursue a deliberately suicidal course in order to get something it wanted, such as a chunk of another nation's territory. Notions of deterrence then became popular, implying that massive nuclear power could in effect deter a nation from trying for illegitimate gains. As the two superpowers, America and Russia, achieved overwhelming arsenals of nuclear weapons, deterrence lost its credibility, because each side simultaneously paralyzed the other with its power, thus presumably allowing the more normal politics of gain to go on. If power cannot be used, it can serve no interests. Under such circumstances, common sense and utilitarian assumptions indicate that the power should wither away to be replaced by more useful forms. Obviously nuclear power is not only not withering away, but achieving greater dimensions than ever before. If nuclear power only deters an adversary from using his own nuclear power, then we are forced to the conclusion that it exists in and for itself. Even this notion, however, can be explained in some sort of interest terms: there are productive facilities that make the weapons and thereby gain profit, research is stimulated which benefits other sectors of the economy, bureaucratic and corporate bodies get a share of the power deriving from involvement in nuclear programs. But this is true of all weapons procured by a government. The argument about a "military-industrial complex" implies that the real purpose for the vast accumulation of arms of all kinds is to service private corporate and public bureaucratic interests. It explains the baffling problem of why the government acquires weaponry far beyond the dictates of utility in terms of conventional political wisdom, which assumes that politics always serves interests. While there is some truth to this argument, closer examination quickly shows that too much is left unexplained and too much just is not so. It does not explain the quality, nature, and purpose of the strategic weapons the government decides it needs, and overlooks the fact that much military production is not particularly profitable for the corporations concerned. To say that the government acquires immense stockpiles of nuclear weapons just to fatten the profits of corporations and expand the power of certain bureaucracies strains the public imagination, which rightly senses something anomalous about the realm of nuclear weaponry. . . .

Nuclear power is obviously a realm of politics, for if politics is the game of power, and power involves command over men and resources to achieve goals, then the immense organizational and technical systems that nuclear power has generated are political. But it is a realm of politics in which interests do not play the decisive role. Governments create nuclear systems not to benefit this or that particular interest but to give security to all the people or to the free world or even to the world as a whole. Security is intangible and unquantifiable, a mood which skilled politicians sense and can take advantage of. But public moods are clearly a reality, and for centuries organizations have existed to create and service them. The Catholic Church, for example, is a gigantic organization whose basic purpose is to cultivate the faith of its adherents. It also does many more practical things, such as teaching Christian ethics, ministering to the poor and the sick, solving problems in its communities. But faith remains the living core of its entire corporate existence. It is no coincidence that the largest organized religious body in the world is headed by one man, the Pope. A sense of security is somewhat like religious faith in its belief that there is a higher being with the power, knowledge, and presence to protect people in a threatening world constantly in turmoil. Similarly, the essence of the faith from which a sense of security derives is that there is a supreme being at the apex of the political system who is the fountainhead of that faith. Nuclear power therefore has created the need for a god. This notion should not be surprising. Most civilized societies have gone through periods when kings and emperors assumed some kind of divine form. Europe had its "divine right of kings" and China had its "celestial emperors." Much of the modern political process has resulted in the erosion of supreme and autonomous executive power—absolute monarchies have turned into constitutional monarchies and democracies have turned rulers into chief executives, periodically chosen leaders who are supposed to be little more than chairmen of the board. It is obvious that supreme executive power has made its reappearance in socialist societies (Stalin and Mao Tse-tung, for example), and now the nuclear phenomenon has also generated it in America. Never in American history has executive power been so centralized, far-reaching, and autonomous as at the present time. America is making a transition comparable to that of ancient Rome from republic to empire.

The anomaly people feel when trying to explain nuclear politics in terms of an interest theory begins to dissipate if we accept the notion that there is not just one but two realms of politics: the realm of interests and the realm of ideology. Nuclear systems belong in the realm of ideology; conventional weapons in the realm of interests. There is a qualitative gap of great importance between these two kinds of weapons systems and the power and politics they represent. This, however, reflects a much more basic gap between presidential power (the White House) and all other bureaucracies of government, including the Cabinet. The theme of qualitatively different presidential and bureaucratic politics is one of the main arguments in this book.

Understanding the realm of ideology requires an analysis of the Presidency. The analysis need not just flow outward from the personality and position of the President, but can flow inward from the context of power, issues, and conflicts in which he operates. The office makes the man as much as the man makes the office. Thus, one can learn as much about presidential power from understanding nuclear politics as from analyzing a specific decision or his decision-making powers. The President is the leader of a big political world which influences him as he influences it. He also is the only one who deals with the chief executives of other countries in an international game which has generated certain rules. Understanding that game, particularly the relations among the great powers, tells us much about presidential power. But to analyze it in terms of interest quickly leads to a dead end. It has to do with intents and intentions, actual and projected capabilities, all of which must be conceived of in a systematic sense, which I call ideological. More theoretical exposition is necessary, however, before the notion of a presidential realm of ideology can become productively useful.

## Roosevelt's Vision

Roosevelt's vision involved a new world order based on the principles laid out in the Bretton Woods and Dumbarton Oaks conferences. In retrospect, one can also say that nuclear power, which today has the most powerful global force of all, had its roots in another of Roosevelt's visions. Roosevelt probably never anticipated that this new weapon, which had not even been successfully tested at the time of his death, would be one of the great determining factors of world politics for the latter half of the twentieth century. Nevertheless, the immensely costly program to develop an atomic bomb never would have been undertaken in the United States were it not for his inspiration. It can be argued that had Truman, a man steeped in interest politics, become President a few years earlier (had he been Vice President then), the atomic bomb would not have been developd. Similarly, as most historians concede, it is doubtful that the United Nations would have been formed without Roosevelt's driving force. It is also questionable whether a new monetary system and something like the World Bank would have come into being even before the war had ended without the combination of Franklin Roosevelt and Henry Morgenthau.

Roosevelt is remembered outside the United States as a visionary, a man who would have brought world peace had he lived. Within the United States, those old enough remember him either as a man devoted to peace and justice or a dictator willing to destroy the free enterprise system to feed his dreams of world grandeur. Roosevelt started out as a master politician whom even conservatives supported as a smart and forceful leader. But as he moved to resolve the crisis of depression, he evolved dreams of a new America, and as he entered the crisis of war, he began to evolve his visions of a new world. Roosevelt's long-standing interest in the Navy, in faraway places, his early global travels, gave him a world consciousness, but whatever visions he had in his earlier years went little beyond those of most stamp collectors. The conclusion that Roosevelt's global visions grew as America became involved in World War II is inescapable. War and vision were closely interrelated in Roosevelt's mind. . . .

Roosevelt's vision of atomic power, a United Nations, and a postwar monetary system was not just passive prediction that all this would come about anyway. As with scientific prediction, the President of the United States could, by virtue of his vast political power, create the conditions that would bring these new military, political, and economic systems into being. Also like scientific prediction, Roosevelt's vision was based on elements of hard realities: on a considerable array of scientific, technical, and human resource facts which convinced him—and many others—that it could be done. Many of the bricks used to build the United Nations had been available since the pre–World War I period, before the League of Nations had been formed. The most active period for the formation of international agencies dated from the turn of the century. The bricks for the new monetary system were contained in the world-wide sterling system, which survived the abandonment of the gold standard in the early 1930s and only weakened because Britain was so badly hurt during World War II. Like so many Arab mosques in Spain, which were built with older Christian masonry, Roosevelt's vision was made up of elements already in existence. What was new was the whole structure, the product of a series of flashes of insight.

Roosevelt's vision of the postwar world was, thus, a prediction of what would be, made by the only man in the world at that time who had the power to bring it about or to set up the conditions that would show that the predictions were wrong. If atomic power had fizzled, if the United Nations had quickly collapsed, and if the dollar had not been able to sustain the international monetary system, Roosevelt's visionary experiment would have been reckoned a total failure. Only America and, in America, only Roosevelt had the power to generate a global vision. Indeed, the great international structures and systems of the postwar world were American creations: nuclear power, the United Nations, and the international monetary system. Russia, which symbolically abdicated from its own internationalism during the war by dissolving the Comintern and ordering the dissolution of the American Communist party, eventually reverted to it, but only *after* the cold war had begun.

## Some Propositions and Observations

Nations (or even cities and tribes) have turned into empires in the past, and, in spite of the vast historical differences, all these transformations have something in common. I shall make some general propositions on the subject, though they relate particularly to America of the postwar period.

A nation turns into an empire not simply by direct or indirect conquest, but by creating, developing, and maintaining a larger political system to govern its new dominions, clients, and dependents.

When a nation becomes an empire, a new political realm comes into being which I call the realm of ideology. This realm centers on the chief executive, and the military and political agencies he creates or assumes power over to carry out his global policies. In empires, the dominant ideology is imperial.

A nation is primarily concerned with national interests. Empires, in addition to pursuing their own interests as nations, also pursue goals deriving from the imperial ideology, which are frequently incomprehensible in terms of national interest.

The sources of imperial ideology are popular, but it is the great leader or executive projecting a vision who succeeds in transforming ideological beliefs into structures of organizational power.

Powerful realms of ideology turn outward to impose their will abroad, that being a mark of empire, except in the case of revolutionary countries, which project their power inward to revolutionize society.

I shall also make some practical observations on the basis of the theory developed so far. America became an empire in the closing days of World War II. For reasons that have yet to be explored, America made a qualitative leap from its traditional expansionism to a new global role whereby it tried to create and implement a world order. In this it succeeded, not in the form of Roosevelt's "one world," which would have included Russia, but in the form of the later "free world," which excluded Russia. America's assumption of an imperial role was obviously in part a response to the political vacuum brought about by World War II. But the theory also points to the enormous expansion of governmental power, particularly of the executive branch, as an element in this process. This expansion began in the crisis environment of the Depression but was greatly accelerated by the war. America's transition from nation to empire cannot be understood except in terms of the political visions of Franklin D. Roosevelt, which he had already gone far to implement before his death.

What I propose, in effect, is that when any nation has a political realm of ideology concretely visible in the form of a powerful chief executive, military and political structures with global concerns, and deep ideological currents purporting to bring about peace, progress, and justice in the world, it is on the way to becoming an empire. . . .

## Interests Against Ideology

By giving Roosevelt his fourth term in 1944, the American electorate did more than signify acceptance of the United Nations. It reaffirmed a progressive New Deal philosophy widely regarded as crypto-revolutionary by many conservatives. In 1944 it was already clear that the war would soon end and that New Dealism would be the dominant ideology of the postwar period. The New Deal probably saved American capitalism by preventing the labor-business struggles of the Depression from turning into class war. But it did so with an ideology which, in the eyes of people of the time, was more leftist than centrist. In retrospect, one can say that in 1944 the American electorate voted for imperialism. In subsequent years they would do this again and again, not because they were hoodwinked by labor fakers or reactionaries in liberal clothing, but because they perceived American imperialism as a progressive force, which would bring benefit to themselves and to the world as a whole. Both during the Depression and during the war, the American people had an overriding desire for security—security of employment and income and security from external attack. They wanted security to overcome the miasma of fear that had come over the country after the euphoria of the 1920s. They looked to government guided by the progressive values of social welfare to provide this security, and they looked equally to government to provide such military power that never again would a Hitler or a Tojo threaten world peace. Because of the Depression and the war, the American electorate swung to the left. Thus, when Roosevelt went to them to secure a mandate for his postwar plans, his vision had a populist and progressive aura to it. Like Wilson, the progressive quality of his vision assured him world-wide support and acclaim, regardless of what the interests thought of it.

Whatever the end result of American imperialism, its origins were democratic. But what was to become the real imperialism in the postwar years was not a simple expansion of Roosevelt's vision, but the product of a struggle with two other major ideological currents springing from the realm of interests. These two currents, which I call internationalism and nationalism, have roots deep in American history and persist to the present time. They are also rooted in basic American interests, particularly economic. Prior to 1945, as universalism and isolationism, they sought to restrain Roosevelt's flights of

vision and channel presidential policy into more conventional directions. But once the war was over, they fought to replace Roosevelt's
vision with policies of their own.

[Early in this study], I noted three great events at the end of World
War II which shaped the postwar world: the founding of the United
Nations, the re-establishment of an international monetary system and
world bank, and the development of atomic weapons. While not so
intended, each of these events addressed itself to the key concern of
one of the three currents. For the current that was to flow out of
Roosevelt's vision, the establishment of the United Nations promised a
new world of peace, security, and progress, a New Deal on a world-
wide scale. The structures emerging from Bretton Woods addressed
themselves to the key concern of the universalist current: free trade
fueled by sound money. And the atomic bomb eventually became a
symbol of the nationalist and isolationist obsession with military power.
Actually, Roosevelt himself expressed all three currents. He was not a
starry-eyed internationalist willing to disarm America, but a hard-
headed military thinker devoted to the notion of American military
power serving American interests—he was always interested in military bases. Although not adept at handling intricate economic problems, his Eastern patrician heritage made him sympathetic to the world
trade concerns of Wall Street. And his growing stature as the leader
of the free and the friend of the poor did as much as anything to
make the United Nations into something above and beyond the League
of Nations. Roosevelt was full of contradictions, which made him a
superb politician. They sprang not so much from his pliant personality
as from the facts of American political life.

### Universalism or Internationalism

The universalist current ran strong in the State Department, the
agency of American government traditionally close to international
business. It was the obvious agency to concern itself with postwar
planning, and, as a bureaucracy with a long history, it did so from the
perspective of its own interests. The main business of the State Department was, in fact, business. The main duties of its vast diplomatic
network, particularly its consular corps, were to aid American businessmen in their dealings with foreign governments. Since the time of
John Hay, the predominant ideological current governing the State
Department was an "open door" policy, a commitment to free trade
and protection of American property and businessmen in foreign countries. The State Department feared that postwar economic chaos could
lead to a repetition of what happened after World War I: revolution

followed by fascism and war. Cordell Hull, as Secretary of State, regarded the United Nations as a political instrument which, by universality of membership, could compel members to adopt the principles of free trade and respect for property. Free trade, fueled by loans from the prosperous United States, could revive the devastated economies and thereby provide the firmest guarantee against new troubles. Peace would be the product of universally accepted free trade. The hope was entertained that even Bolshevik Russia might depart from its rigid hostility to free trade practices and thereby gradually rejoin the world community.

Free trade versus protectionism was an old issue in American politics, and the State Department traditionally stood on the side of free trade. The State Department has always been the most elitist governmental agency (its foreign service officers were recruited largely from graduates of Ivy League schools), and it is not surprising that it took its cues from the most elitist segment of American business, the Eastern Establishment. It was also the most internationally minded bureaucracy in the government. Only the State Department felt that it really understood how much America was intertwined with larger world systems, and within America only the Eastern Establishment with its far-flung business interests abroad was directly involved in the world scene.

The primary concern of the Eastern business establishment was making and keeping money on a grand scale through investments and trade that covered the world. Built into this basic commitment to money were a series of attitudes arising out of two centuries of practical experience. The Eastern Establishment loathed war and revolution. War destroyed property and increased the power of governments. Revolution was a mortal threat to property. The State Department traditionally reflected both of these attitudes. In its postwar planning, the assurance of peace was, next to free trade, its major concern. On the other hand, the State Department also held some of the most ferocious anticommunist views in government, reflected by many of its ambassadors. The coincidence of these two attitudes was manifested in State Department policies toward the Vichy government and in the person of the United States Ambassador to Vichy, William Leahy. The State Department maintained friendly ties with Vichy partly to prevent the war from spreading over the rest of France and the French Empire and partly out of instinctive support for a conservative, anticommunist regime determined to prevent Bolshevism from arising in France. It opposed de Gaulle because he wanted to drag the French Empire back into the war and create the kind of chaos that would permit the Communists to resurrect themselves.

The State Department was intellectually the heir of the Hamiltonian tradition that regarded government, particularly foreign policy, as too intricate a matter to be entrusted to the ignorant masses. How could the people be relied on to make judicious judgments about something so complex as international monetary policy? The State Department's elitism did not arise from a reactionary fear of the masses but from the comfortable conviction of men who, like bankers and financiers, held a monopoly of knowledge about the ethereal world of international relations. Its universalism was the reflection of a basic reality, that of the world market system. For two centuries, capitalism, spearheaded by Great Britain, had woven a nexus of economic and political interests spanning the entire world, on which all nations were dependent to one degree or another. The energizing force of this world market system was world trade, which, of course, was monopolized by the advanced and civilized nations. Trade brought profits to national enterprises and the raw materials which an expanding capitalism needed. While America did not approve wholeheartedly of the British Empire as the political expression of the world market system, it was regarded as irreplaceable for the preservation of that system. The pound sterling was the symbol both of the world market system as the leading reserve currency and of the British Empire by virtue of its Englishness. The British Empire was the closest thing to a world order since the Roman Empire. If World War II weakened Great Britain's ability to maintain that empire, this did not mean and should not mean that the world order too should disappear. Universalism was a further elaboration of the world order which the British Empire did most to bring about in the modern world and for the maintenance and further development of which America was to assume the guiding role in the post-1945 world.

Cordell Hull's universalism was an expression of the realm of interests. The interests were the international economy which for two centuries had been under the control of Englishmen and Americans. The internationalists saw both world wars as attempts by ferocious nationalisms to destroy the international economy. Conversely, they regarded the destruction of the international economy as the main cause for the rise of fascism, Bolshevism, and other barbaric political forms. The Bolsheviks took people's property away and the Nazis threatened to undo the world market system. While the Anglo-American elites exhibited natural tendencies to seek accommodations with both in order to avoid war, the Bolshevik and the Fascist/Nazi dangers had to be resisted when they came too close to the core of the international economic system. Hullian universalism was quite different from the American imperialism of the postwar period. It was politically and economically conservative. It wanted to restore what was and do as little new as possible. What had to be restored above all else was the world market system. If this was done, the Anglo-American business elite would have its power reaffirmed and, as the best custodian of a peaceful world order, could then do what was necessary to improve mankind's lot and prevent new barbarisms from arising. The State Department believed that if the world could be brought back to where it was before the turn of the century, before an ambitious Kaiser Wilhelm threatened its peace and security, the greatest good for the greatest number would be vouchsafed.

The insulated atmosphere of the State Department, like that of the great international banking offices, made it easy for them to think in terms of the logic of international relations and difficult for them to understand the popular furor which produced wars and revolutions. But visionary ideologies and innovative policies do not arise out of the realm of interests. Conservatism in the modern world means nothing more than a commitment to certain existing interests. Attempts to portray it as a moral or visionary force have failed for the simple reason that it can never conjure up hope and anticipation in people's minds. Hullian universalism would have liked to see a postwar world where governments came back into the hands of responsible conservatives (as eventually happened in the former enemy nations with Adenauer, Yoshida, and De Gasperi), where outlaw nations like Russia assumed international responsibilities by recognizing the obligations of participation in the world market system, and where the small and poor nations took the sensible path of slow, deliberate efforts toward improving their lot.

Universalism was, in essence, a benign, conservative internationalism. It flourished during World War II through close Anglo-American cooperation for the preservation of the existing world order. It was not nationalistic, and was willing to make major sacrifices in the area of national sovereignty. That this was possible without sacrificing national identity was due to the overriding fact that in the eyes of the universalists the English-speaking world was the world itself. No language was more widely spoken than English. Through the British Empire and America's far-flung private activities (businessmen, missionaries, educators), Anglo-American culture had become the predominant world culture, just as Roman culture had covered the known Western world two thousand years before. Above all, nowhere in the world could one find cultivated men with as deep a sense of moral responsibility as in London and the eastern seaboard of the United States. Moreover, these men had access to the greatest power in the world, the command over wealth. It seemed natural that the American and British worlds should eventually coalesce in an English-speaking union in which both would surrender archaic notions of sovereignty to the interests of a peaceful new world order.

The universalists, like all conservatives, were hostile to huge governmental power and above all to militarism. Like the Marxists, they believed that capitalism knew no boundaries. They thought that power was best invested in a class of wealthy, educated, and propertied men who had been taught responsibility in the finest schools. Government was to be their instrument, in which they served often at cost to themselves. Huge bureaucracies and huge armies would only produce the barbaric monstrosities of Nazi Germany and Bolshevik Russia. The universalist conservatives mistrusted the state as an irrational force. From it sprang lust for power and, above all, the drive toward war, which of all policies in government the conservatives most opposed. They tried to stem the drive toward war until it was inevitable, and during the war they tried to plan for postwar structures that would make a new war impossible. The universalist conservatives instinctively sympathized with Chamberlain's efforts to avoid war by appeasing Hitler. Roosevelt, as a sometime universalist, actively supported his efforts to settle the Czech crisis in 1938. The basic concern of the universalist conservatives was stability, and nothing was more conducive to stability than peace. The conservatives abhorred revolution, but they also abhorred war. Therefore, *both* Nazi Germany and Bolshevik Russia were abominations in their eyes. Yet if Germany ceased making war against other nations and Russia refrained from exporting revolution, there was no reason one could not coexist with them. It was regrettable that the German and Russian peoples allowed themselves to be governed by barbarians, but if they would just leave other people alone, there was no reason to make war against them.

This theoretical proposition suggests that conservative universalism, inclined toward a world order dominated by Anglo-American capital, was also committed to peace and to peaceful coexistence. Free, unfettered trade fueled by a stable international monetary system was the indispensable basis for any kind of rational world order. War as much as revolution was the deadly enemy of trade. Peace assured stability and stability was the necessary prerequisite for the accumulation and preservation of wealth. Peace was to be preserved at all costs except where the threat became mortal.

The universalist current, as the world view of international business, retained its power during the postwar years. It fueled postwar economic reconstruction of Europe, foreign aid to poor nations, and participation in United Nations activities, and argued for peaceful coexistence with Russia. It was not accidental that the breakthrough to peaceful coexistence with Russia came under the conservative Eisenhower and that the breakthrough to China came under Nixon. Once Russia and China opened their iron and bamboo curtains respectively, the conservatives were more ready than others to espouse peaceful coexistence. While the right-wing military opposed it and the ideological liberals (like organized labor) shrank back, the conservatives made the move. In both Eisenhower's approach to Russia and Nixon's approach to China and Russia, trade played a major role. Peaceful coexistence could be meaningful only if Russia and China agreed to join the world market system. If they did, the conservatives foresaw that conservatizing forces would set in in both countries. The more these militantly revolutionary countries were involved in world trade, the more their barbaric regimes would be civilized under the weight of international responsibility. It would be too much to hope that they would once again accept the principle of private property, but accepting foreign investment was a step in the right direction.

Universalism was a World War II expression of capitalist conservatism. As the cold war made "one world" meaningless, universalism took on more modest postures. It advocated greater unity within the "free world," fought against trade barriers, supported internationalist programs. The conservatives eagerly joined the anticommunist crusade and needed little convincing that the Russians were intent on expanding Russian national power, as well as revolutionary communism, throughout the world. But they never lost their conviction that peace was best for profits, and it mattered little from which side of the Iron Curtain profits came. When the Russian threat was proclaimed contained, they were the first to initiate steps toward peaceful and profitable coexistence. . . .

### Isolationism or Nationalism

The isolationist current was opposed to universalism. On the surface, it seemed to imply doctrines that the United States should not get involved in the wars of other nations unless directly attacked. Historically, it appeared to derive from one of George Washington's basic principles of foreign policy, that the new United States must avoid "entangling alliances." In fact, isolationism was a form of American nationalism clearly expressed in its favorite slogan: America first.

Much has been written on the diverse interests and attitudes isolationism represented. Yet, as James MacGregor Burns wrote, what was common to all isolationists was the view "defense, yes; aid to the Allies, perhaps; but foreign wars—never." [1] The isolationists, except for their transient left-wing fringe, believed in American military power. Their congressional representatives voted eagerly for defense build-ups and displayed a typically nationalist admiration for the flag propped up by guns. They believed fervently that America should defend its interests by military force where threatened. Since those interests were obvious in Asia and Latin America, they were more prepared to challenge Japanese expansionism than that of Germany in Europe, and Mexico's nationalization of United States-owned oil companies aroused an angry furor. What they could support in Roosevelt was his espousal of a strong navy, but they distrusted the uses to which he was going to put American military power. The key issue of debate was the European war.

The isolationists were anti-imperialist, which, in the 1930s and 1940s, meant being against the *only* world imperialism of the time, the British Empire. They regarded it as a global conspiracy on the part of vast financial interests centered in London abetted by similar interests in New York to dominate the world economy. The ultimate aim of Britain, they believed, was to create a world economic and political monopoly which would stifle the natural expansionist desires of latecomer powers, such as America. The isolationists were indeed expansionists, the true heirs of "manifest destiny." They saw a glorious future for America beyond its borders, but not particularly in Europe or Africa or Western Asia. They looked westward to East Asia and southward to Latin America. They believed in laissez-faire capitalism and were hostile to big government, whose only result could be to suppress freedom, the natural right of every individual to deploy his enterprise in the pursuit of his own interests. They believed in the individual, particularly the individual who decided to rise above the masses by acquiring wealth. They had a classical commitment to freedom, to a society subject only to minimal governance. Above all, they saw themselves as Americans, a definite, distinct, and proud nationality with a mission in the world. American, in the understanding of the day, meant white, Protestant, and male.

One can get a sense of the social nature of the isolationists by looking at the Americans who expanded into the Pacific during the late nineteenth century and on into the twentieth. There were three types: merchants, soldiers, and missionaries. Nowhere else in the world, save in Central America, could one find comparable numbers of such Americans. American traders found lucrative new enterprise in Hawaii, the Philippines, China, and in the interstices left open by other empires. Since the Spanish-American War, America had acquired major military bases throughout the Pacific. Missionaries were everywhere in the region preaching more by example than by word the superior nature of American man. Free enterprise in Hawaii showed what honest enterprise could achieve. By the end of the nineteenth century, a few American families, largely of missionary origin, had developed vast sugar and pineapple plantations, recruited Asians to work them, and made immense fortunes. All this occurred under conditions of "freedom" granted to them by the Hawaiian monarchy and then further assured by a beneficent American takeover. Through the Navy, the American military began to develop imperial qualities in the Pacific, most evident in the Philippines, which was run pretty much as a military domain. The effort of the missionaries was ideological, the preaching of Protestant Christianity. Nowhere else in the world did America assume such an ideological role. Europe was regarded as hopelessly corrupt, Latin America as lost to the Catholic Church, and Africa of little interest. Only Asia with its billion heathen seemed within the reach of conversion to Christianity. China, in particular, was the most ardently pursued target for full conversion.

The dreams and visions that the Pacific engendered were not greatly appreciated in the pro-European parts of the American east coast. The westward expansion of the United States was taken for granted, and, of course, America should pursue its interests in the Pacific. But the highly educated men of the Eastern Establishment could not understand the passion which motivated these dreams and visions, and hatreds which arose when they were thwarted. The Pacific symbolized a general American expansionism which in the 1920s appeared to have scored fantastic successes. In 1919, America rejected internationalism, returned to pursue its own narrow interests, and enjoyed an unprecedented boom. By 1930, the boom had collapsed. The expansionists saw the crash of the stock market and the subsequent breakdown of the international monetary system as conspiracies aimed at destroying them. When unions began to organize with the active support of the patrician Roosevelt, the expansionists saw an even greater conspiracy between the mighty of the Eastern Establishment and the communist-inspired labor unions to crush them in the middle. They saw themselves as the real driving force in America, the people who created enterprise and made the wealth which others, bankers and organized labor, then usurped. Expansionism and nationalism were identical in the minds of those who took the isolationist stance prior to 1941; the history of America in the Pacific had forged that identity.

If the nationalists saw expansionism and nationalism as identical, they pretended to see a similar identity between internationalism, communism, and imperialism. The big bankers of Wall Street were internationalist—so were the communists with their Marxist doctrines, and so were the British with their empire. Moreover, the growing alliance between the Roosevelt-led administration and the unions seemed to indicate a real alliance between the forces of international capital and their ostensible enemies, the revolutionary proletarians. All this could only be aimed at capitalism, as the nationalists saw it. The expansionist image of capitalism was that of the National Association of Manufacturers, which saw the corporation, producing and marketing things, and not the banks as the core of free enterprise capitalism. Socialism to them meant monopoly domination of the economy whether by immense finance capital, big government, or communist revolutionaries. When Hitler began to preach that an international conspiracy of capitalists, Jews, and Bolsheviks was trying to crush the expansionist drive of the German nation, many in the United States understood and sympathized. By the late 1930s, the Roosevelt-labor union alliance had expanded to include an emerging British-American alliance to oppose Germany. And after June 22, 1941, the archenemy of mankind, Bolshevik Russia, had joined. The conspiracy became horrifyingly real both domestically and internationally. At home, an Eastern Establishment-dominated administration was colluding with labor unions and Red-sympathizing intellectuals to establish an American socialism. Abroad, an alliance between America, imperial Britain, and Bolshevik Russia was developing against Germany, a country that was nationalist, expansionist, and capitalist in the best sense of the word. A climax was reached in the great lend-lease debates when Roosevelt was ready to turn over a significant number of American warships to Britain, which the isolationists construed as a weakening of American military power, an infringement on American sovereignty, and involvement in a war whose only favorable outcome could be a victory for British international bankers and Russian Bolsheviks.

American nationalism remained isolationist until December 7, 1941. When Japan attacked America, militant nationalism immediately joined the fray. Japan was a welcome enemy for the nationalists. It was a nonwhite power threatening American interests in the Pacific. It was already at war with America's special responsibility in the Far East, China. It was not at war with Bolshevik Russia, thus precluding Russian-American collaboration in the Far East, and, above all, the Japanese had the effrontery to attack their most admired symbol of American military power, the Navy. Hitler's declaration of war against America completed the picture of an attack on two fronts, and war against both Germany and Japan was accepted by all American nationalists.

Prior to December 7, 1941, the interventionists wanted war in Europe and the isolationists opposed it. War against Japan, however, was acceptable to both. It can be argued that the multifaceted Roosevelt was a nationalist and expansionist in the Far East but an internationalist and imperialist in Europe. Roosevelt was a Navy man, and believed in America's pre-eminent role in East Asia. The war in the Pacific was run along nationalist lines on the American side. Unlike the European theater where America and Britain had to conduct a joint war, the war in the Far East, except for Burma, was a strictly American affair. The Americans carried out their special relationship with China without benefit of British advice, and where, as in Burma, British and American actions came into contact, the relationships were bad, such as those between Stilwell and Mountbatten. Roosevelt easily assumed that British power had been shattered in the Far East and only America was able to oppose Japan. The nationalism of the war against Japan was evident, for example, in the racism that accompanied it. While there was deep ideological revulsion against the Germans, there was little anti-German feeling in a racial sense, as in World War I. But the Japanese were hated as an upstart race. Japanese, but not Germans and Italians, were interned in concentration camps in the United States. Japanese captives in the Pacific were much more cruelly treated than German captives.

Whereas the core belief of the internationalist current was the need for international systems, particularly economic, that of the nationalist current was the need for pre-eminent American military power. In a dangerous world, this was the only guarantee for American safety, for the defense of America's interests, and, in particular, for the assurance of the ever-continuing outward expansion of American enterprise. America must have a powerful navy and develop new technologies, such as air power, to the hilt. It must have a powerful army, although the nationalists were always suspicious of universal military service. . . . The nationalists regarded military power as the main force supporting expansionism. It was, therefore, legitimate and necessary to destroy the military power of countries threatening America, such as Japan and Germany, and to do everything possible to prevent new military powers from arising which could threaten America, such as Russia.

## Contradictions Between Internationalism and Nationalism

The debate over America's role in the postwar world found both internationalists and nationalists making expected arguments. The internationalists wanted international systems which would guarantee a world market based on free trade, monetary stability, and political responsibility. The nationalists cared for little else beyond the assurance of American power, particularly military, in the postwar world. In 1919, these two currents had clashed and nationalism won out, although internationalism resurfaced with the Dawes and Young plans. During World War II, they clashed again. This time the outcome was not a synthesis or a compromise but something new—an American imperialism, which neither internationalists nor nationalists had envisaged.

The practical internationalists still thought in pre-1914 terms of a world led by the key powers, America and Britain, working closely together, with Russia's role to be worked out in a manner satisfactory to the world market system. The nationalists believed neither in "one world" nor in the Anglo-American partnership, and felt that America would only get into trouble if it departed from the sound utilitarian principle of self-interest first. Roosevelt's vision of a Pax Americana was in many ways a reincarnation of Wilson's earlier vision, but, unlike Wilson, Roosevelt had the good fortune to appear as a nationalist (in the Pacific), an internationalist (in Europe), and, above all, a popular leader spreading revolutionary ideas to the downtrodden masses of the world.

Both internationalism and nationalism, when stimulated or attacked, generated ideologies of their own, as we shall see. In the postwar period, they became prominent on the left and right of the American political scene. But they were not creative ideologies, and in themselves launched no new vision or policies. Internationalism was too elitist to elicit much popular response except where it coincided with left-wing internationalism. And left-wing internationalism had too little support within the American people to constitute a powerful popular ideology. The popular weakness of both forms of internationalism made them easy targets for nationalism, particularly when it assumed virulent anticommunist forms. Nationalism achieved its own greatest popular success during the McCarthy period, but as an ideology it collapsed when McCarthy began hitting too close to the Establishment. While internationalist and nationalist sentiments are deeply grounded in the American people, the ideologies they generated have remained confined to the left and right extremes of the political spectrum. Since Roosevelt's time, the dominant ideology in America has been one or another form of liberalism, and Roosevelt's role during the 1930s and during World War II was crucial in its fashioning.

A question widely discussed among historians is, Why did the cold war begin? A more appropriate question, in the light of my discussion, is, Why did American imperialism arise? Even Establishment journals such as *Fortune,* musing over the great changes coming over the world in the 1970s, speak of a Pax Americana that governed the world in the post–World War II period. It is my contention that the cold war erupted as a result of America's decision to create an empire, not the reverse. Inspired by Roosevelt's vision, America began to plan a postwar order in which it would be the dominant, guiding force and the source of morality. Russia did not or could not or appeared not to go along with this new order, and, *therefore,* the cold war began. Assuming the burdens of empire is a task not to be taken lightly, and virtually nothing in America's tradition, not even its expansionism, prepared it to assume responsibility for the entire world. Roosevelt did not propose that America join a new League of Nations, but that instead a United Nations be conceived and located on American soil and other nations be invited to join. The United Nations was an American creation which other nations joined largely out of the simple power-political realization that World War II had made America the mightiest nation on the globe. What, then, impelled Roosevelt and his closest advisers to undertake such a novel task? The simplest answer is fear—fear that the world would again degenerate into bloody conflicts, fear that civil wars would erupt, fear that economic and political systems would disintegrate not only from revolutionary pressures but perhaps even more from bitter conflicts within ruling classes themselves. Roosevelt's most profound experience from the American Depression was the vision of America's ruling classes turning against each other with a violence reflected in the bitter struggles waged in and around Congress during the 1930s.

There has been a current in revisionist scholarship that sees the determination of the United States to suppress revolution as the key moving force behind the development of the cold war. While there is much truth to this notion, it overlooks some of the basic fears weighing upon the men who ruled America during the 1940s. If the phenomenon of Bolshevik Russia was loathsome to them, equally if not more loathsome and frightening was the phenomenon of Germany. How could a country in the forefront of civilization and eminently successful in capitalist enterprise have turned into a barbaric monstrosity which showed little hesitation at plunging the world once again into a war? The internationalists were convinced that virulent nationalism was as deadly an enemy of capitalism as Bolshevik Russia. Twice within the century that had not yet reached its halfway point, German nationalism had attacked the world market system, turning what could have been a viable international order for keeping the peace, assuring economic stability, growth, and profits, and allowing the international elites to resolve their countries' problems, into a cauldron for unbelievably destructive war. How to prevent a new Germany, either Germany itself or some other nation, from arising was the central problem for the internationalists during the post–World War II period. . . .

That internationalism and nationalism were contradictory currents in America is evident from the great conflicts that rent the country between 1945 and 1950. The most general form this conflict took was "Europe-first" versus "Asia-first." The word "first" implied a conflict not just of priorities but of different world views. By and large, the pre-1941 interventionists emerged as Europe-firsters and the isolationists as Asia-firsters. The Europe-firsters believed that a healthy Western Europe was the major prerequisite for American security, and demanded that considerable monies be spent to bring this about. The Asia-firsters, who were mainly in the Republican opposition, saw the vast spending that such a program entailed as another New Deal measure to soak business for obscure international purposes whose end result would be only to create an even more powerful and dictatorial federal government. Meanwhile, legitimate American interests were being threatened by communism in Asia, chiefly China. To the Asia-firsters, the Democratic administration's tolerance of communism in Asia was an ominous replay of the worst features of the Roosevelt Administration. Here again, the American people were called on to bail out "Britain" in the West while in the East "Russia's" tentacles, in the form of Chinese communism, were painted as "agrarian reformers," movements of the poor for justice, to be accepted as legitimate forces. In the period 1945–1950, "Asia," especially "China," became the symbol of American nationalism. Senator William Knowland's advocacy of Chiang Kai-shek, so intense that he was nicknamed the Senator from Formosa, would seem ludicrous in retrospect except for the fact that Chiang Kai-shek had become much more than the symbol of determined anticommunism. Methodist by religion and married to an American-educated woman, a leader viewed by them as determinedly loyal to America, he was more American than most Americans. Like General Douglas MacArthur, America's most shining examplar of militant nationalism, Chiang was a beleaguered fighter struggling against an international communist conspiracy directed against him not only by Moscow and its Chinese tools but by Washington, New York, and Harvard as well. In that great conflict, the nationalists felt on the defensive, finding themselves threatened by a range of powerful forces intent on doing away with American nationality and sovereignty. The backlash of McCarthyism indicates how violent the conflict had become.

The bitter conflict for which McCarthyism was more symbol than substance eventually ebbed away in the 1950s for one major reason— "bipartisanship in foreign policy." Spearheaded by Senator Arthur Vandenberg's wartime rallying to Roosevelt's conception of a United Nations, the "liberal" wing of the Republican party accepted the premise that consensus must prevail over the basic issues of foreign policy.

That they were able to force bipartisanship on the party against the opposition of conservatives like Robert Taft was manifest in their candidates in 1948 and 1952: the New York liberal Thomas Dewey and the wartime commander of Allied forces in Europe, Dwight Eisenhower. If bipartisanship had not been achieved in the postwar years, it is likely that the Republican party as the chief political vehicle of American nationalism would have mounted an even greater attack on the Democratic internationalist liberals, which could only have resulted in a foreign policy much different from the Pax Americana, which the United States succeeded in constructing.

A new ideology, different from both internationalism and nationalism, forged the basis on which bipartisanship could be created. The key word and concept in that new ideology was *security*.

### Security as an Operational Idea

No word better characterizes the New Deal of the 1930s than security, just as no word better characterizes the climate of that Depression period than fear. The institution of Social Security for the aged by Roosevelt's Administration typified the New Deal's ideology: unless people had assurance that they would not remain destitute victims of unpredictable business cycles, society would disintegrate into chaos. Only one institution in society, the government, could provide that assurance. If wealth had to be redistributed so that security could be achieved, the more affluent had to pay the price, lest by not doing so they lose everything. An important corollary to these Social Security policies was that injecting money into the economy to "prime the pump" would stimulate a business upturn. What appeared to be waste in order to calm people's fears was essentially similar to private investment, spending in order eventually to produce more income. It would be wrong, however, to see Social Security, loans and payments to farmers, relief measures, small business loans, and so on as simply devices to get corporate capital functioning again. There were twenty-five million unemployed in the 1930s, and class war in the form of militant industrial union organizing threatened to tear the country asunder. The crash providing of even a small degree of economic security was viewed as essential to prevent matters from getting worse. This ideology of security, deeply implanted in the administration, gave rise to an entire range of social legislation, most notably the Wagner Labor Relations Act, which gave unions unprecedented protection under the law. Unions were perceived as a form through which security could be achieved for the most dangerous element of the population, the blue-collar workers. The union meant protection.

The fear that gripped America in the 1930s was domestic. By the 1940s, it had become external as well. In 1941, American soil was attacked by a foreign power for the first time since the War of 1812. Moreover, German and Japanese armies were threatening to take over the entire Eastern Hemisphere, leaving America alone and isolated in the Western Hemisphere. Later as postwar planning proceeded in Washington, the concern for security became the dominant theme, uniting the universalists in the State Department, the ex-isolationist nationalists in the Republican party, and, of course, the key Rooseveltian liberals in the Treasury Department. Whatever form the postwar order took, above all, it had to provide security for the United States against another threat arising such as had provoked World War II. While the talk of security still roused the hackles of conservatives, who saw in it just another cloak for New Deal big government, the great majority of the people responded to it. They finally realized that the world was fundamentally chaotic, something few people had accepted in the nineteenth century. War and depression were endemic to people's existence unless active measures were taken to curb them. If "struggle" is the word most characteristic of Maoism and symbolic of its world view, then security and fear were symbolic of the major world view that governed the United States at the end of World War II—chaos produced fear which could only be combatted with security.

It has been said many times that Roosevelt's vision of the postwar world was an extension of his New Deal to the world as a whole. The United Nations was to become the nucleus of a world government which the United States would dominate much as the Democrats dominated the American Congress. The essence of the New Deal was the notion that big government must spend liberally in order to achieve security and progress. Thus, postwar security would require liberal outlays by the United States in order to overcome the chaos created by the war. It is not accidental that the most ambitious New Dealish schemes for the postwar period came out of the Treasury Department, which was more Rooseveltian in ideology than any other governmental bureaucracy. But even when its plans assumed absurd forms, as in turning the Germans into a nation of farmer/herders, the Treasury most closely expressed Roosevelt's own ideas. It proposed the destruction for all time of the world's most virulent nationalism, that of Germany. If German and to a lesser extent Japanese nationalism were destroyed, the world would never again have to fear that an advanced capitalist nation would threaten the international system. Aid to Russia and other poor nations would have the same effect as social welfare programs within the United States—it would give them the security to overcome chaos and prevent them from turning into violent revolutionaries. Meanwhile, they would be drawn inextricably into the revived world market system. By being brought into the general system, they would become responsible, just as American unions had during the war. Helping Britain and the remainder of Western Europe would rekindle economic growth, which would stimulate transatlantic trade and, thus, help the American economy in the long run. America had spent enormous sums running up huge deficits in order to sustain the war effort. The result had been astounding and unexpected economic growth. Postwar spending would produce the same effect on a world-wide scale. By destroying Germany and paying off Russia, America and the world would achieve security from their two greatest fears—nationalist aggression and violent revolution.

By portraying America as an aggressively imperialist nation since the end of World War II (if not before), revisionist scholarship has washed away one of the most important factors that made American imperialism possible—the tremendous ideological appeal of New Deal doctrines of security. Wilson's Fourteen Points aroused widespread response from peoples throughout the world seeking national self-determination, much to the chagrin of the Versailles peacemakers. But Roosevelt's appeal was of a different order. America was the liberator with the power and money this time to prevent war from recurring. While American anticolonialism was to have a great impact on the Third World countries, the biggest impact on Europe was the American ideology personified by Roosevelt and his New Deal. Virtually the entire communist movement from America to Russia to the European and Asian parties believed that America was coterminous with Roosevelt and the New Deal. Ho Chi Minh was so taken with America that he made the American Declaration of Independence the model for Vietnam's own declaration of independence from France. At the end of World War II, the dominant sentiment in the advanced countries was a yearning for peace and security, not for revolution. Nor was it different in a poor country like China. The Chinese Communists looked to America for some support in their efforts to secure a coalition government with Chiang Kai-shek so that they could cease at last the wars that they had been fighting since 1927. They wanted security from Kuomintang attack, which, when it came in 1946, impelled them back onto the path of revolution. America in 1945 held a virtual ideological monopoly in the world. "Communism" as a global ideology had withered as the result of defeats in Spain, the Nazi-Soviet pact, the disbanding of the Comintern and the American Communist party, the growing awareness of Stalin's purges of Russian and foreign Communists, and the obvious national character of the Russian resistance to the Germans during the war. At the end of World

War II, people did not yearn for class struggle but for an end to struggle. War was so horrible an evil that nothing could be worse. No other nation seemed so dedicated to and capable of providing the security that the world wanted than America. The ideological power that this gave America was one of the most important weapons it wielded in the postwar period, and was decisive in enabling it to construct the Pax Americana, its own imperialism. . . .

## Containment

By the summer of 1947 a new current in American foreign policy became evident, symbolized by the word "containment." This doctrine ostensibly derives from George Kennan, who, from his post as ambassador to Russia, wired home dire cables about the inexorable character of Russian expansionism. Russia might be communist in ideology, he noted, but the real force for its expansionism was nationalist and went far back into Russian history. Unless the free nations put up powerful walls to contain this expansionism, Russian power would ooze out over Western Europe and Asia, and before long America and its allies would be faced with a threat as great as that from Nazi Germany. Kennan's "cable from Moscow" came a little less than a year after former Prime Minister Churchill had given his famous Iron Curtain speech at Fulton, Missouri, in March 1946. Throughout 1946 there was no lack of voices within America speaking of the growing danger emanating from Russia. That a case could be made for Russian expansionism is obvious. Stalin had concluded that great power cooperation was no longer feasible and he might as well fasten his hold on Eastern Europe, as well as on the Soviet zone of Germany. The great atomic test at Bikini on July 1, 1946, was a bad sign, indicating that America was pushing the development of new atomic bombs to the hilt with the ever-present threat that they might be used against Russia. Negotiations for a coalition government in China had broken down, making civil war a certainty. Everywhere Russian-American relations were getting worse. In the euphoric days after Yalta, Stalin had been in the mood for concessions to the British and Americans, but as the months of the Truman Administration passed, he realized that concessions were always followed by more demands. Undoubtedly remembering his experiences with Hitler, Stalin decided that the only language the capitalists understood was power, and moved to consolidate Russia's control over its front entrance in Eastern Europe.

Whether Russia was or was not expansionist is not vital to understanding why the new foreign policy current of containment arose. The facts marshaled by such eminent experts as George Kennan served an already existing ideological need in Washington. The allegedly electrifying impact of his cable of February 1947, and later his "Mr. X" article in *Foreign Affairs,* was hardly due to their analytical brilliance. The rising national security bureaucracy clustered around the White House needed a view of the world that would fit the policies they were beginning to develop.

Kennan's cables and articles, while meant for the bureaucracy rather than the public, had the same ideological impact as *Mein Kampf* had earlier in showing a nation bent on eating up the entire world. Kennan's portrayal of Russia in terms reminiscent of Germany was more welcome to Washington than the rising theme of an international communist conspiracy. Then in the forefront of an effort to uplift, liberate, and reform the world, Washington had no stomach for an anticommunist crusade which would line it up with the international right wing. But an expansionist Russia could allow for the same kind of global united front that was mounted to resist German and Japanese expansion.

The Democrats who ruled Washington in the postwar years were committed to the notion that the American government had the key role in bringing security, peace, and progress to the world. But they did not yet have an operational ideology for America's new role in the world comparable to New Deal ideology on the home front. The nationalists and the internationalists already had world views that envisaged a definite external role for America. For the nationalists, what mattered was dealing with other nations on an *ad hoc* basis for one purpose: serving American interests. To make sure that those interests were respected, America had to remain strong, and what better way to remain supreme than to keep and enforce its own atomic monopoly. The internationalists wanted an economic world based on trade and free enterprise with threats and opportunities handled in utilitarian terms. What Kennan's contributions made possible was the elaboration of a world view that gave the government—not the military or the corporations—the leading role in the new adventures abroad.

The origin of these imperialist policies cannot be dissociated from the Anglo-American alliance which developed at this time and proved to be closer and more harmonious than it was during the war. Laborite Britain, which had aroused feelings of horror among American free enterprisers, turned out to be America's staunchest ally in the development of its imperialist policies. During the war, America and Britain collaborated mainly in the campaign against Germany. Elsewhere in the world, the two nations went their separate ways. In fact, to Churchill's fury, Roosevelt even showed inclinations to break up the British colonial empire. But after the war, America and Britain became close collaborators not just in Western Europe but throughout the world. Britain was in a precarious position when the war ended. It was heavily in debt not only to the United States but to many of its colonies as well, notably India. Moreover, with the Laborite victory in August 1945, Britain launched the welfare state, which imposed a new drain on its limited resources. Most significant of all, the tide toward independence from colonial rule seemed irresistible. The Laborites were more prepared ideologically than the Tories to grant political independence to the colonies, but they were still faced with the heavy burden of maintaining military forces in faraway places. Where "responsible governments" (mainly British-trained elites) would assume political leadership, London was usually glad to grant independence, since this did not involve jeopardy to British economic interests and political influence (after all, the newly independent countries elected to remain within the Commonwealth). But in too many parts of the world either there were no such responsible governments or real threats demanded the continued presence of British military force, at great cost.

In the five years following 1945, Britain had to keep a powerful military presence in Greece, Malaya, the Suez Canal, Jordan, and Iraq, and had to maintain far-flung naval and air units to preserve its credibility as a world military power. In addition, it had to maintain occupation forces in Germany and other parts of Western Europe. In Greece and Malaya, Britain fought Communist revolutionary movements which threatened to bring into power governments that could not be counted on to cooperate with Britain. In the Middle East (which included Greece), nationalist unrest and Arab-Jewish conflict threatened to spill over into regions from which most of the world's oil came. Iran was turbulent because of a left-wing government in Azerbaijan. Rebellious Kurds threatened the Mosul oil fields. King Farouk's rule in Egypt was unstable. Southeast Asia had the same kind of turbulence. Indonesian nationalists were threatening Dutch rule and Vietnamese insurgents would not let the French back into Indochina.

The British feared that the chaos that had beset Europe after the First World War would this time erupt in Asia and the Middle East. Almost everywhere in Asia, civil wars were threatening: between Hindus and Muslims in India, between Jews and Arabs in Palestine, between procommunist Turks and proroyalist Persians in Iran, and between procolonialist and anticolonialist elements in Indochina, Malaya, Indonesia, and Burma; in Greece, the struggle was between Communists and anti-Communists. The Laborites did not share the Tories' confident assumptions that a few staunch British soldiers could easily restore law and order. In fact, they suspected old empire loyalists in India and Palestine of causing more trouble than was necessary. The Laborites shared one attitude with the Tories: they were deeply anti-communist. Like Walt W. Rostow two decades later, they believed that the communists were trouble exploiters who misused natural class and racial conflicts to obtain power. They regarded them as a naked organizational force blindly loyal to Moscow, from whom they expected moral and material support. Like their American labor counterparts, the British Laborites had had considerable experience fighting communists in the labor movement. Bevin criticized Churchill's easy-going friendliness with Stalin and himself preferred to spit in Molotov's face. In Greece, the Communists were receiving weapons from Tito, Moscow's loyal ally in the Balkans. In Iran, the communist Tudeh movement was headed by an out-and-out Soviet agent, Pishavari. In Malaya, Chin Peng was a Moscow-oriented Communist. Thank God that the Communists were still weak in India, where responsible socialists like Jawaharlal Nehru or Islamic nationalists like Muhammad Ali Jinnah could assume power from the British. And while the Glubb Pashas favored the Arabs in Palestine, London knew that Ben-Gurion was a socialist Zionist who could be expected to keep the communist virus out if a Jewish state came into being.

The postwar Anglo-American alliance had several facets. One was the cooperation that flowed naturally out of Bretton Woods where, despite strong disagreements about the postwar monetary system, America and Britain assumed joint responsibility for maintaining the dollar and sterling as key world currencies. Anglo-American cooperation was vital for the resolution of the German question and the eventual creation of a separate Western zone ("Bizonia") out of which the German Federal Republic emerged. Anglo-American cooperation was further necessitated by the fact that the British, even without American know-how, were developing an atomic bomb. These and the many other strands of the alliance naturally facilitated cooperation on the most difficult problem facing Britain: how to extricate itself from its outmoded empire without going bankrupt, while assuring an orderly transition of power to "responsible" governments. The Laborites were opposed to empire but committed to the Commonwealth. With the enormous economic burdens weighing on Britain, London could not afford to lose its share from participation in a world market system that it enjoyed by virtue of far-flung foreign investments, from its central role as a capital market and banking center, and from access to markets in the sterling area.

While Britain felt it could still mount the military power to protect the emerging Commonwealth, it lacked the economic means to do so. If the Commonwealth, comparable formations like the "French Union," and sundry new nations were to be kept afloat, vast sums of money would have to be spent. The only source of such monies was the United States. With a combination of British (and French) military power and American money, the West would be able to maintain control over the emerging countries even while granting them political independence. For over a year after the war, Britain tried to struggle along with monetary infusions from the United States and Canada, but by early 1947 it was facing economic collapse. The British informed Washington then that Greece was on the verge of being taken over by the Communists, which, if it happened, would inevitably produce a domino effect in the fall of Turkey. Truman rose to the challenge and proclaimed his Truman Doctrine for Greece and Turkey. This was the first and most important policy action expressing the new doctrine of containment. It drew a line along the Greek and Turkish borders with Russia and its allies in Eastern Europe. In subsequent years, containment would pursue its line-drawing policies over the entire globe, each time proclaiming the line of demarcation an inviolable frontier. With the proclamation of the Truman Doctrine on March 12, 1947, the United States formally became an imperial power by assuming the mantle of empire from faltering Britain.

Assuming that mantle required, above all, an American commitment to provide the military means necessary to prevent threatened parts of the empire from falling into hostile hands. Defending the empire demanded military means of a particular nature: *conventional* forces (troops, ships, and planes) which could establish bases in threatened regions, engage in ground combat where necessary, or be introduced in sufficient numbers to prop up threatened regimes. As America found out during the Second World War and as it was to rediscover during the Korean and Vietnam wars, conventional forces are exceedingly costly. In contrast to strategic weapons whose initial heavy costs for research and development subsequently decline, conventional weapons, particularly troops, require constant or increasing outlays. By demobilizing its vast armies just after World War II, Washington was able to effect drastic cuts in its budgets. Aside from occupation forces in Germany and Japan, it no longer needed to maintain large standing forces. Britain, on the other hand, was unable to make a similar cutback in its budgets. Along with the increased burden of welfare spending, it was faced with the crushing costs of maintaining occupation armies in Europe and fighting forces in Malaya, the Middle East, and Greece, as well as vast naval installations throughout the world. To make things even worse, Britain also was committed to developing its own atomic capability. In March 1947, Britain formally requested America to take over this burden and Truman responded with alacrity. The Truman Doctrine on Greece and Turkey aroused vigorous opposition within the United States, from both nationalists and internationalists. But when Truman invoked the specter of Russian expansionism, the voices were silenced and "bipartisan" support was given to America's new global imperial role.

Without the Russian threat, neither the nationalists nor the internationalists would have so meekly accepted the new American imperialism. The nationalists were horrified by the vast new spending which these commitments brought with them. They wanted to concentrate on strategic weapons, to maintain the American atomic monopoly, and to enforce that monopoly by a preventive strike against Russia if necessary. When the issue of universal military training was raised, the nationalists opposed it bitterly. They saw it as a device for creating a federal dictatorship which would bankrupt corporate enterprise and usher in a *de facto* socialism, while involving America in a whole range of conflicts where basic American interests were not threatened. America had no real interests in Greece worth defending, and money spent there was designed only to pull Britain's chestnuts out of the fire—*except* that the Greek Communists were Moscow's instrument. The extension of Russian power anywhere in the world was viewed by the nationalists as a threat, and so grudgingly they accepted the Truman Doctrine. But the Truman Doctrine involved more than providing American military protection to Greece and Turkey. Truman announced a vast program of economic and military assistance (foreign aid) to both countries, which set a precedent for the entire range of foreign aid programs which soon followed. Foreign aid to India and Pakistan could then easily be justified as preventive actions designed to avoid the creation of Greek-type insurgencies which would require even more costly military intervention (an analogy originally applied to Turkey).

The internationalists were primarily interested in Western Europe's economic recovery and wanted large-scale infusions of money into the European countries. Though inflation-conscious and not Keynesians, they did not regard these monetary infusions as waste. Economic recovery in Europe would lead to American loans being repaid, a stimulation of world trade which could only benefit America, and a climate of general economic stability which would incur new enterprise. They were as conscious of the Russian threat as the nationalists, but in a different way. The three countries of the emerging "Catholic Union" (France, Germany, and Italy) contained large, powerful Communist and Socialist movements. Italy voted to become a

republic by ousting the monarchy which the American conservative
internationalists regarded as a stabilizing force (like the Japanese Emperor). Communists and left-wing Socialists were growing so fast in
Italy that a left-wing electoral triumph was a distinct possibility. In
Germany, Adenauer's Christian Democrats were not threatened so
much by Communists as by Social Democrats. True, Kurt Schumacher and Erich Ollenhauer were anticommunist and anti-Russian,
but a Socialist assumption of power in West Germany was very disturbing. Socialist programs in Germany could wreck the emerging
revival of free enterprise capitalism with damaging effects on the
international market system. So also in France, where the Communist and Socialist threats were great and could oust de Gaulle from
power. Socialism of any variety in the three great Western European
countries would forever smash the dreams of a European economic
union, since socialist governments would be forced to follow nationalist economic policies in order to pay for the vast social welfare
schemes they wanted to introduce. The best European spokesman
for this conservative internationalist current was Konrad Adenauer,
who loathed Marxism, socialism, and Russia as essentially the same
phenomena. Adenauer was not a "revanchist," the Russian term applied to post-Hitlerian Germans who wanted to retake lost eastern
territories. He wanted to keep Russia or Russian influence out of
Western Europe. If the Truman Doctrine on Greece and Turkey
resulted in the United States committing itself more solidly to conservative Europe through money and troops, it was to be loudly
welcomed.

*Russian expansionism* was the key to the acceptance within the
United States of the Anglo-American program for the transfer of
empire onto America's shoulders, the launching of the Marshall Plan
to revive Western Europe, the institution of world-wide foreign aid,
American rearmament, and especially the American government's new
policy of peacetime fiscal expansionism. If Russia was expanding,
that constituted a threat. A preventive nuclear strike, which the
nationalists advocated, was too risky, because in the long run it would
create even more chaos in the world and provide favorable conditions
for anticapitalist movements. The threat could also be ignored or attempts be made to negotiate arrangements with the Russians to
minimize it by mutual accord. But negotiation with the Russians was
believed to be futile, inasmuch as they would not budge on opening
the doors of their country to on-site inspection and control. So long
as Russia was unwilling to join the international community on American terms, there was no way to convince the nationalists or the internationalists that it was becoming "responsible." The only solution was

*containment,* the spirit of which is best captured in the French rendering of the word, *"endiguement." Endiguement* means building a network of dikes to hold in onrushing flood waters. Dike systems are costly, widespread, and must be hermetically sealed at even the most remote point. They not only protect populations from floods, but allow the working of fields so that wealth can be produced. Containment would not only protect the free world but allow the new world order based on the Pax Americana to flourish. It was the best possible doctrine to allow the formation of a peculiarly American type of empire. . . .

The authors of United States containment policy saw three great sources of danger. First, they were convinced that Russian development of atomic weapons and build-up of conventional forces posed a supreme danger. If the balance of power tilted away from the United States, pressures would rise from American nationalist circles and from countries contiguous to the Russian-controlled parts of the world to redress the balance, by anything ranging from a first strike against Russia to vast new military deployments or political and economic commitments. Secondly, they were convinced that any trouble in areas where Russian and American interests collided could have a Serbian effect leading from minor incidents, in domino fashion, to full-scale war. And thirdly, "chaos" in the free world could lead to changes in the geographical balance of power between Russia and America which, again, would bring pressures from within the United States and the threatened countries to redress the balance by forceful military action.

Their response to these three dangers constituted the core and essence of containment policy. First, failing any chance of achieving enforceable accords with the Russians on nuclear weapons, the United States had to undertake a crash program to develop weapons of such scope and quantity and so speedily that no matter what the Russians did, they would never be able to catch up. Furthermore, control over nuclear weapons and energy had to be removed from the military and placed in the White House. Secondly, to eliminate any doubts from the minds of the Russians as to what areas America considered part of its empire and what areas it conceded to Russia, it undertook to draw demarcation lines which eventually encircled the Soviet Union from northern Norway to the 38th parallel in Korea. And thirdly, to prevent chaos, America undertook a vast program of foreign aid to promote economic development, first in Europe, and then in a whole array of poor countries, particularly those "threatened by communism."

Russia, of course, was the common denominator of each of these fears and the responses to them. It was the only power capable of matching the United States militarily. The world's major trouble spots —Berlin, Greece, Iran, and Korea—were in areas where Russia collided with the newly emerging American empire. And the most threatening form of "chaos" came from communist revolutionary movements in such countries as Greece, Azerbaijan, the Philippines, Malaya, Korea, Indochina, and, of course, China. Cultivated gentlemen like Acheson and Kennan, machine politicians like Truman, tough lawyers like Forrestal and Dulles, all shared an overwhelming fear born of two world wars and a great depression. The only way to banish that fear was to have total security or, as James Forrestal said in December 1947: "We are dealing with a deadly force and nothing less than 100 percent security will do." [2] Russian paranoia was easily matched by American paranoia, and both countries opted for the same solution: control, control, and more control.

### The World View of Containment

. . . The world view of containment made it possible to build up the realm of ideology. Concretely, that realm took the form of the enormously expanded executive branch of the United States government. Its material basis was the federal budget, in which the foreign affairs and national security component played an ever-increasing role until by the early 1960s, it constituted not only the bulk of the budget but one-tenth of the gross national product of the United States. The executive branch acquired a monopoly over "national security policy." Constitutionally, this seemed to derive from the President's role as commander-in-chief. In times of peace, foreign affairs were to be conducted with the advice and consent of the Senate, which had to approve by two-thirds vote any treaties the President entered into. But the world view of containment enshrined a new doctrine, that of the cold war. The cold war was war, and even if not formally declared by Congress, "bipartisanship" in foreign policy signified acceptance of that war. This meant that, as in times of war, foreign affairs were virtually equivalent to national security affairs. More particularly, those foreign affairs that were construed as relating to the conflict between America and Russia were considered to be within the realm of national security. The executive branch thereby acquired a monopoly over all policies relating to national security, which ensured the President a minimum of interference in his national security policies from both the nationalists and the internationalists. Nationalists were strongly represented in Congress and in the military; internationalists were also strongly represented in Congress, with the State Department as their chief bureaucratic vehicle in government.

Presidential monopoly over national security affairs, over time, produced a range of bureaucratic institutions which were direct emanations of presidential power, such as the Central Intelligence Agency (CIA), the National Security Agency, the Atomic Energy Commission, and the various agencies concerned with foreign aid and information. In addition, it led to the creation within existing bureaucracies of top-level policy-making bodies concerned with foreign policy and national security affairs. This was to become most apparent in the Defense Department under Kennedy, where the International Security Agency (ISA), ostensibly a body that advised the Secretary of Defense on foreign affairs aspects of national defense, became a virtual "State Department." The ISA, as the Pentagon Papers reveal, was closer to the White House than to the military services over which the Secretary of Defense presided. It was concerned with "policy," whereas the services, by statute, were supposed to be concerned solely with "operations," that is, implementing policy.

The presidential monopoly over national security policy was the most important achievement of the government during the postwar period—an achievement constantly in danger of assault from nationalist and internationalist currents, which were excluded from the monopoly. Policy, as I have pointed out, means goals, direction, and methods. It specifies what is to be achieved; and by what routes; and it lays down the kinds of "capabilities" (in ordinary language, political, economic, military, and other weapons) to be used. Or, in the words of Samuel P. Huntington, policy means strategy and structure. The world view of containment reserved to the supreme leadership of America a very special kind of policy-making function. Since the American-Russian relationship was the most critical matter in America's foreign relations, since nuclear weaponry had created a *de facto* global unity, and since even minor actions in faraway places (Laos, for example) could have a direct bearing on the American-Russian relationship, only that body of the American political structure which had total and comprehensive knowledge of the entire global picture could make national security policy. Congress or old established bureaucracies like the military services or the State Department, which represented particular interests, could not make national security policy because they were moved primarily by those interests and not by a disinterested awareness of the entire picture. Obviously, only the President and his national security bureaucracy could make national security policy for, by virtue of the great new intelligence agencies which surrounded them, only they had all the knowledge, all the facts, all the necessary wisdom.

Containment ideology envisioned an active role for America. The President was to be not just an arbiter who would decide from among various "options" presented to him by interest groups within the bureaucracy, a phenomenon of presidential decision-making power that was to become apparent (or seemingly so) under the Johnson and Nixon administrations. The duty of the President was to assure America's security and that of the free world primarily by creating conditions that would make it impossible for World War III to break out while preserving the interests of America and its free world clients and allies. Whether or not others shared that commitment either abroad or within the United States did not matter. The supreme criterion for judging the success of a national security policy was the fact that World War III had not occurred. If anyone argued that the fear of nuclear war was excessive and paranoiac (as Mao Tse-tung was alleged to have done), then the facts of nuclear destructive power could be presented to show that the madness was really on the side of the doubter. If a person feels threatened by an impending catastrophe of uncertain source, he will feel justified in fortifying his house and his grounds, stockpiling supplies, and keeping his family in a constant state of readiness. If the catastrophe should not occur, he can point to all the power, wealth, and internal discipline that this effort brought about. It was in this way, through the fears that nuclear weaponry generated, that the American empire came about. Abroad, the empire resulted in a degree of global organization that never before existed. At home, it created a vast American governmental power whose role is crucial to the maintenance of the economy and all other major social and political institutions in the country.

### Notes

1. James MacGregor Burns, *Roosevelt: The Soldier of Freedom*, p. 42.
2. Fleming, *The Cold War and its Origins*, vol. 1, p. 487.

# 3

**Radomír Luža**

# Czechoslovakia Between Democracy and Communism, 1945-1948

*The nations of Eastern Europe were both the source and the
principal victims of the Soviet-American antagonism. In modern times
these small lands remained subject to heavy foreign influence even
after they had won their right to exist as states at the close of World
War I. With the collapse of German power in 1944–45 and the
advance of the Red Army, it was unlikely that they could escape deep
infringement of their newly recovered independence.*

*Nonetheless, it was not foreordained that they must be communized.
In Czechoslovakia a precarious independence was maintained for
almost three years. And even today Finland provides the example of a
country that has preserved a democratic political life while clearly
accepting an international role that respects Russian interests. Was
"Finlandization" excluded for the East European nations? Stalin's own
thinking remains hard to reconstruct. On the one hand, he reportedly
told the Yugoslav communist, Milovan Djilas, that the country that
sent its troops into a liberated area would also inevitably impose its
own social system. On the other hand, he allegedly reassured the
Czech leader Edvard Beneš (among others) in regard to his intentions
toward Warsaw that "communism fit Poland like a saddle fits a cow."
Perhaps the Russian leader never intended to allow a free choice of
regimes in Eastern Europe, or perhaps he interpreted the formulae of
democratic governments and free elections, which he accepted at
Yalta, as being tantamount to a choice for communism. At the least
he expected a strong communist role in Hungary and Czechoslovakia
and worked to assure a preponderant communist influence in Poland
and Rumania from late 1944 on, if not earlier. And even if the final*

*totalitarian result were not planned at the outset of the process, the logic of conflict with Washington meant that every dispute between the two great powers led to further repression in Eastern Europe and thus to more irreconcilable Soviet-American polarization.*

*But what were the United States' stakes in this relatively distant area? Our economic intercourse with Eastern Europe was minimal, although neo-Marxist critics assert that if Washington was to assert the "open door" as its general stance, it had to fight for this right in Eastern Europe as well. More plausible a factor in my judgment was the ideological commitment generated within America as part of the national mobilization for World War II. After waging a messianic struggle on behalf of oppressed peoples, how could American leaders simply surrender the region where World War II had begun to a new repression? (This was all the less likely in view of the millions of votes in major industrial states that the ethnic groups from Eastern Europe represented.) "Realist" critics of American foreign policy could well answer that we ended up surrendering the region in any case and that it was illusory to believe there was an alternative. By refusing to recognize Soviet preeminence, and likewise failing to develop credible threats to deter it, we both "lost" the area to communism and envenomed relations with Moscow. Nonetheless, the wisdom of renunciation is not usually learned without difficulty. At the end of Roosevelt's war, acquiescence in the division of Europe would have demanded an implausibly rapid psychological re-education of Americans—even apart from the moral elements involved.*

*Most accounts of Eastern Europe in English focus upon the region as part of the larger Soviet-American struggle. For an able summary of East European developments in terms of their ramifications upon American policy, the student might well employ Bennett Kovrig's,* The Myth of Liberation: East-Central Europe in United States Diplomacy and Politics since 1914 *(Baltimore, Md.: The Johns Hopkins University Press, 1973). The essay included here offers a different perspective— namely a focus upon the difficulties of the Czechoslovak republic from the viewpoint of Prague. Czechoslovakia was the country of Eastern Europe most akin to the West in terms of social and economic structure; it had enjoyed the greatest success between the wars in maintaining democratic government; it was least ravaged by the war itself; and it was the most successful in combating postwar inflation. It gave the greatest promise of being able to preserve friendly relations with Moscow and a pluralist regime at home. Thus its communization in early 1948 especially dismayed Westerners, convincing them of the gravity of the cold war much as the fall of France had pressed home*

*the earnestness of the Second World War. But the account instructively
highlights the burdens placed upon Czech democracy from its own
internal problems. And it also suggests that failures of will and resolve
also played a crucial role—in short, Czechoslovaks made history as
well as suffered from it.*

*Radomír Luža teaches history at Tulane and with Victor S.
Mamatey is the editor of the volume,* A History of the Czechoslovak
Republic, 1914–1948, *from which this essay is taken with the
permission of Princeton University Press and the author. Professor
Luža has also written* The Transfer of the Sudeten Germans: A Study
of Czech–German Relations, 1933–1962 *(New York: New York
University Press, 1964) and* Austro-German Relations in the Anschluss
Era *(Princeton: Princeton University Press, 1975).*

### The Government of the National Front

The fate of postwar Czechoslovakia, like that of other small nations
of East Central Europe, did not depend on the will and actions of her
people alone. It was also affected by the actions of the great powers
and their postwar relations.

In the winter of 1944–45, while the Red Army was fighting its way
to Prague, Vienna, and Berlin, the Soviet Union, the United States,
and Britain were making final preparations for the meeting of their
leaders at Yalta. They were aware that the presence of the Soviet military might in Poland, Rumania, Bulgaria, Hungary and Czechoslovakia
meant a basic shift of power in Europe. Nonetheless, both East and
West still clung to the concept of postwar coalition and were exploring
the basis for a series of agreements on European and Far Eastern
problems.

The policy of President Edvard Beneš, developed while he was in
exile in London, had been to restore Czechoslovakia to her pre-Munich
territorial integrity and reinstitute her democratic institutions. The
success of this policy depended on the continued cooperation of the
Allied Powers, not only until the end of the war but afterward. Only
in these circumstances could Czechoslovakia hope to recover her independence and territorial integrity and restore her traditional parlia-
mentary-democratic system. Throughout the war, therefore, Beneš had
tried to promote a cooperative effort of the anti-Nazi alliance to find a
permanent settlement in Europe. Alone among the exiled leaders of
East Central European countries he sought both the support of the
Western powers and an accommodation with the Soviet Union. The
signing of the Soviet-Czechoslovak alliance treaty in Moscow in

December, 1943, was conclusive proof of his determination to come to terms with Moscow, and appeared to be a guarantee of the success of his policy.

Beneš was, therefore, deeply disappointed and even shocked when reports reached him late in 1944 that Soviet authorities were promoting a movement in Ruthenia (Carpathian Ukraine)—which had been the first Czechoslovak province liberated by the Red Army—for its secession from Czechoslovakia and its attachment to the Soviet Ukraine. As early as 1939, in conversations with Ivan Maisky, the Soviet ambassador in London, Beneš had voiced his willingness to solve the question of Ruthenia in full agreement with the Soviet Union,[1] and had reiterated this view in his last talk with Stalin in Moscow in December, 1943. At the time the Soviet leaders did not regard the question as pressing, but they now apparently were determined to force a solution favorable to the Soviet Union. Czechoslovak complaints lodged with the Soviet government against Soviet activity in Ruthenia during December, 1944, proved to be of no avail.

At the same time Beneš became alarmed about the ultimate fate of Slovakia, which had been partially liberated by the Soviet army. Although the Communist Party of Slovakia (KSS) had abandoned its earlier agitation for a "Soviet Slovakia," it continued to press—with the approval of the leadership of the Communist Party of Czechoslovakia (KSČ) in Moscow—for a loose federation between Slovakia on one hand and Bohemia and Moravia on the other.

Beneš's tense concern was ended by a personal letter from Joseph Stalin on January 23, 1945, assuring the Czechoslovak government of his full support. The Soviet leader suggested, however, that the problem of Ruthenia should be solved by negotiations between the two countries that would take into account the desire of the province's Ukrainian population to join the Soviet Union. The underlying concern of Beneš, that the Soviet Union would use its control of Czechoslovak territory in disregard of its commitments, was thus relieved.[2] Soviet-Czechoslovak relations had for some time been regarded as an index of Soviet-Western relations. Undoubtedly, Stalin's decision to ease Beneš's fears on the eve of the Yalta conference was motivated, in part, by a desire to dissipate the suspicions of President Franklin D. Roosevelt and Prime Minister Winston S. Churchill, already aroused over Soviet designs in Poland and the other countries of East Central Europe occupied by the Soviet army.

Just before writing his letter to Beneš, Stalin discussed with Klement Gottwald, the exiled Czech communist leader in Moscow, the policy the KSČ should follow during and after the liberation of Czechoslovakia. Stalin advised Gottwald to accept Beneš as president, and to come to an understanding with him and his government.[3] This flexible Soviet policy essentially reflected the line set forth in the Comintern declaration of 1943, which asserted that "the great differences in the historical development of individual countries determine the differences of the various problems that the workers' class of every country has to cope with." Until the next reexamination of communist strategy in the summer of 1947, Stalin set the stamp of his approval on this thesis of national roads to socialism: "In private he even expressed the . . . view that in certain instances it was possible to achieve socialism without the dictatorship of the proletariat." [4]

During its Moscow exile the top echelon of the KSČ (Gottwald, Rudolf Slánský, Jan Šverma, and Václav Kopecký) worked out a policy line in terms of a special Czechoslovak road to socialism.[5] After broadening their reexamination to include a review of past mistakes, they determined that the party should lead and organize the national liberation struggle of the Czech and Slovak people against Nazism. In thus assuming the role of a responsible mass movement, the party acted upon the belief that after the end of the occupation it could win popular confidence under the banner of national independence.[6] In short, the communist leadership in Moscow envisioned liberation as a means of winning a predominant share of power. The irony of such an approach was that it visualized economic and social reform as being subordinate to the achievement of the primary political task: becoming the leading political force in the country. In conformity with this aim, the party tended to move cautiously. It set up broad national and democratic—instead of narrow socialist—demands. In fact, the program of the Czech home resistance—nationalization of industry, banks, and insurance companies—was much more far-reaching than the initial communist platform, which merely involved confiscation of the property of Czech and Slovak traitors and hostile Germans and Magyars.[7]

During the war the principal Czech and Slovak political forces at home and abroad held lively discussions on the future form of the country. In the winter of 1944–45, as the Soviet army overran a large part of Czechoslovakia, the balance of the pendulum between the democratic parties represented by Beneš in London and the communists led by Gottwald in Moscow swung in favor of the communists. It was a foregone conclusion that, at the end of the war, the London cabinet would be replaced by a new government with strong communist participation.[8] In 1945, with the Soviet armies advancing across Czechoslovakia, it became urgent for Beneš to implement this agreement and to return to the liberated part of the country with a newly constituted cabinet. To determine the composition of the new government and adopt a program, it was decided to hold a conference of

Czech and Slovak political parties in Moscow. The choice of Moscow rather than London for the conference was undoubtedly motivated by the fact that the Czechoslovak government needed the consent and assistance of the Soviet government to return to its homeland. It also gave the communists a considerable advantage in the ensuing negotiations.

After taking leave of Churchill and Anthony Eden on February 24,[9] Beneš, accompanied by some members of his cabinet, left London for Moscow, where he arrived on March 17. A delegation of the Slovak National Council (SNR), composed equally of Slovak Democrats and Communists, also arrived in Moscow from the liberated parts of Slovakia. However, since Bohemia and Moravia were still firmly in the grip of the Germans, the Czech home resistance was unable to send representatives. Altogether, the Czech Communist (KSČ), National Socialist, Social Democratic, and People's parties and the Slovak Democratic and Communist (KSS) parties were represented. All other prewar political movements were excluded from the conference, primarily because of their past anticommunist attitude.

Gottwald assumed the initiative at the conference, which opened on March 22 and lasted eight days, with the presentation of a draft program as the basis of the negotiations.[10] Beneš did not take part in the meetings, on the ground that as a constitutional president he stood above parties.[11] This left the London democratic exiles leaderless, since they were used to deferring to him in London, even in minor matters. It also weakened their position, because Beneš enjoyed tremendous prestige, particularly in the Czech provinces. Out of fear of arousing "suspicion on the part of the communists,"[12] they discarded any joint political platform to counter the communist program. To the bewilderment of the disunited democratic camp, it soon became apparent that the negotiations were a controversy between two political groups, one based in London and the other in Moscow: "Here for the first time there was joined the battle of two political worlds."[13] What started out as negotiations for a governmental blueprint broadened into a survey of a program of action that would change almost every aspect of Czechoslovak life.

The democratic leaders received some satisfaction from the fact that the communist draft, to some extent, incorporated points agreed upon during previous exchanges of opinion between the parties. In the main, it reflected Gottwald's conception of the necessity for agreement with the democratic parties and articulated some of the aspirations of the Czech and Slovak people. Although the democratic and communist leaders clashed on many points, in the end their common interests proved strong enough to produce a final text that was not very different from the original draft.

The sharpest controversy during the negotiations occurred between the London group and the Slovak delegation, in which Gottwald assumed the role of benevolent arbiter.[14] The Slovaks brought to Moscow a resolution passed by the SNR on March 2, which demanded what amounted to attributes of sovereignty for Slovakia: a Slovak government, parliament, and distinct army units. The London group rejected this demand. It based itself on Beneš's speech of February 23, 1945, in which the president had recognized the special needs of the Slovaks but had insisted that the definition of Slovakia's place in the Czechoslovak state—like, indeed, all constitutional questions—should be left to the elected representatives of the people at home to decide after the war.[15] In the end the Slovaks yielded and accepted as a compromise a somewhat ambiguously worded statement proposed by Gottwald, which he later called grandly the "*Magna Carta* of the Slovak Nation."

In the negotiations to form a new government, the communists likewise imposed their will, but managed skillfully to camouflage their victory in a seeming compromise. They did not claim the premiership or a majority of posts in the cabinet. Instead, Gottwald proposed, and the other party leaders agreed, that the government should represent a "broad National Front of the Czechs and Slovaks." In strict conformance with the rules of parliamentary arithmetic, this decision was implemented by awarding three posts in the cabinet to each of the six parties participating in the conference. The prime minister and five vice-premiers, who were the heads of the six parties, were to form an inner cabinet to direct and coordinate the government's activities. It was further decided to give posts to four non-partisan experts and to create three state-secretaryships, thus bringing the total membership of the cabinet to twenty-five.

Upon the conclusion of the Moscow conference, President Beneš and the party leaders departed for Košice, a modest eastern Slovak town recently liberated by the Red Army. They arrived there on April 3 and stayed until after the liberation of Prague on May 9. On April 4 the new government was formally installed and the next day it announced its program, which, despite its origin in Moscow, came to be known as the "program of Košice." [16]

The Košice program proposed no radical transformation of Czechoslovak society along socialist lines. It was quite free of characteristic Marxist language. On the other hand, unlike the Czechoslovak declarations of independence issued in Washington and Prague in 1918, which had been idealistic professions of faith in democracy, it said little about freedom. Its tone was sober. It threatened more than it promised.

The program opened with a government tribute to the Soviet Union and a pledge to support the Red Army until final victory. For this purpose the government announced the formation of a new Czecho- slovak army, trained, organized, and equipped on the model of the Red Army, with Czech and Slovak units under a unified command, and educational officers introduced into all units to extirpate fascist influences. Czechoslovak foreign policy, it said, would be based on the closest alliance with the Soviet Union on the basis of the 1943 treaty and on practical cooperation in the military, political, economic, and cultural fields, as well as in questions concerning the punishment of Germany, reparations, frontier settlements, and the organization of peace. It promised to maintain friendly relations with Poland, Yugo- slavia, and Bulgaria on the "basis of Slavic brotherhood," to seek reconciliation with a democratic Hungary (after correction of in- justices), and to promote a rapprochement between Hungary and Austria and their Slavic neighbors. Finally, almost as an afterthought, it thanked Britain for the aid extended during the war and promised to consolidate relations with her and the United States and promote close relations with France.

In the field of domestic policy the government pledged to hold elec- tions at the earliest possible time for a national constituent assembly that would determine the precise form of the Czechoslovak govern- ment. In the meantime, the government guaranteed the people their political rights and set up new administrative machinery, in the form of popularly elected national committees, to administer public affairs at the local, district, and provincial levels.

The Slovaks were recognized as a distinct (*samobytný*) nation and the SNR as their legal representative and "carrier of state power in Slovak territory." The question of Ruthenia was to be settled as soon as possible according to the democratically expressed will of its people. The German and Magyar minorities were given the right of option for Czechoslovakia, with the understanding that disloyal German and Magyar citizens would be removed. The property of those who had "actively helped in the disruption and occupation of Czechoslovakia" was to be placed under national control pending a final disposal by the legislative authorities. Their land would be placed in a National Land Fund and distributed to deserving Czechs and Slovaks.

Czech and Slovak collaborators were to be deprived of voting rights and barred from all political organizations. The former agrarian party and all prewar parties not represented in the new National Front were accused of collaboration and proscribed. War criminals, traitors, and "other active, conscious helpers of the German oppressors" were to be punished without exception. President Emil Hácha and all members of the Protectorate government, as well as Jozef Tiso and all members of the Slovak government and parliament, were to be charged with high treason and brought before a "National Court." Finally, the Košice program provided for a broad system of social welfare.

In the new cabinet, according to a communist participant at the Moscow conference, the communists captured "positions which were a starting point for the assault on the actual fortress of capitalism. . . . The balance of power was such . . . from the beginning of the liberation, that the influence and weight of . . . KSČ was predominant and decisive." [17] At the Moscow conference, the communists had successfully promoted Zdeněk Fierlinger, a left-wing Social Democrat, as prime minister. From their point of view, the choice proved an excellent one. As wartime ambassador to Moscow, Fierlinger had won the confidence of the Soviet government by his display of an uncritically pro-Soviet and anti-Western attitude. As premier, he collaborated with the communists so closely that he won the popular epithet of "Quislinger."

Thanks to separate representation, the combined KSČ and KSS held eight seats in the cabinet and controlled the ministries of interior, information, education, agriculture, and social welfare.[18] The police, security, and intelligence services were in their hands. The Ministry of Defense was entrusted to Gen. Ludvík Svoboda, commander of the Czechoslovak army in Russia, as a nonparty expert. (Although a noncommunist at that time, Svoboda was a loyal friend of the Soviets.) As a concession to the democratic parties, the communists agreed to the reappointment of Jan Masaryk as minister of foreign affairs. A genuinely nonpartisan personality, dedicated only to the defense of his country's interests, the son of the first president of Czechoslovakia was by family tradition, education, and experience a thoroughly Western man. Therefore, as Masaryk's assistant and watchdog the communists insisted on appointing Vlado Clementis, a Slovak communist, to the newly created post of state-secretary of foreign affairs.

Thus far the "circumspect and purposeful course of the KSČ" [19] proved to be of particular advantage to the Communist party, whose chairman, Klement Gottwald, had given proof of his political maturity and craftsmanship. The less colorful democratic leaders let themselves be outmaneuvered. Since the central issue was one of power, it is surprising that neither Beneš nor his colleagues found it advisable to prevent the communists from assuming control of the police and security organs. A reasonable compromise on this question would have helped those forces in both camps who were willing to face up to

problems affecting their common commitment to a democratic Czechoslovakia. Despite some apprehensions, however, the democratic leaders
had no reason to contradict Fierlinger's observations before their
departure from Moscow that "It is an immense achievement that we
can return home united. . . . The ideological borderline between Moscow and London has been removed. I am aware of the fact that not
a few would criticize the composition of the new cabinet . . . but I
consider it an immense success that unlike other emigrations . . . we
are the first to be able to put order into our affairs abroad." [20] Neither
side regarded the Moscow agreement as a final settlement; both were
aware that the final battle was yet to come—at home after the war.

In the Czech provinces the approaching end of the war coincided
with a rising tide of guerrilla activities. Early in 1945 the largest resistance group—the Council of the Three—the illegal trade unions, and the
underground KSČ established the Czech National Council as the center of Czech resistance. The council was strengthened during the first
days of May by a spontaneous popular uprising that spread through
those parts of the country still occupied by the Germans. The movement reached Prague on May 5, where a fierce battle broke out with
German army and SS units that raged even after the official dates of
German surrender at Rheims and Berlin (May 7 and 8, respectively).
In the early morning hours of May 9 the first Soviet tanks arrived in
Prague. On May 10 the government returned to Prague. It was followed by President Beneš amid frenetic acclamation on May 16.

The Nazi occupation was terminated. The war was over.


### Between Democracy and Cominform, 1945–1947

On its return to Prague, the Czechoslovak government took quick
and firm hold of the levers of command. Under the Moscow agreement President Beneš had been given emergency powers to issue
decrees with the validity of laws, at the request of the government,
until the convocation of the National Assembly. These powers were
first used to assert government authority throughout the country. The
Czech National Council was dissolved.[21] The Slovak National Council,
on the other hand, continued to function at Bratislava.[22] It soon
became apparent, however, that it was necessary to define its jurisdiction and the basis of its relationship to the central government at
Prague, a matter that the Košice program had noted only in very
general terms. The SNR took the initiative in the matter. On May 26
it adopted a proposal for the fundamental organization of the republic,
in the drafting of which both Slovak communist and democratic
leaders shared. The proposal envisaged a dualistic, symmetrical organi-

zation of Czechoslovakia into two federated states—Slovakia and Bohemia-Moravia—each with a government and diet of its own. A federal government and parliament were to be centered in Prague.

The previous Czechoslovak experiment in federalism—the ill-fated Second Republic in 1938–39—had not been a happy one. The proposal of the SNR therefore encountered opposition from the Czech parties, both communist and democratic. On May 31, just before the government at Prague began a discussion of the SNR proposal, the leaders of the KSČ invited the KSS leaders to a meeting at which the KSS submitted to the "unified leadership" of the KSČ and agreed to abandon the SNR plan.[23] At the cabinet meeting on May 31 and June 1, only the Slovak Democrats defended the proposal for federalization, while the Czech National Socialists and Populists pressed for the restoration of the republic's pre-Munich centralist organization; the KSČ and KSS adopted a halfway course. The discussions ended in a compromise. Federalism was discarded, but Slovakia's autonomy was assured. The resulting "First Prague Agreement" both defined and circumscribed the jurisdiction of the SNR.[24]

The government delayed a full year before implementing its pledge, given in the Košice program, to hold general elections for a constituent assembly at the earliest possible time. Meanwhile it covered the naked strength of its power in a temporary constitutional garb. On August 25, 1945, a presidential decree provided for the formation of a single-chamber, 300-member provisional national assembly. It was to be chosen not by general elections but by a complicated system of three-stage elections through the local, district, and provincial national committees—thus allowing the parties of the National Front to determine its composition.[25] The Provisional National Assembly met for the first time on October 28, 1945, the national holiday, and confirmed President Beneš in his office. In the next few days the cabinet was formally reorganized, but no significant changes were effected in its composition.

The Provisional National Assembly's initiative remained limited. Usually, it approved unanimously and without discussion the decisions made by the party leaders at meetings of the National Front. Thus on February 28, 1946, it approved, also unanimously and without discussion, the ninety-eight presidential decrees issued from May to October, 1945, many of which affected the fundamental structure of the Czechoslovak state and society.

The delay in holding elections, however, did not indicate indifference on the part of the party leaders to public opinion. Quite the contrary. After the overthrow of Nazism all of Europe was swept by an intense popular demand for immediate reform and a certain disillusionment, or impatience, with constitutional procedures when they threatened to delay reform. Under these circumstances, to defer the pressing tasks of reconstruction and reform in order to engage in an electoral contest appeared almost frivolous to the Czech and Slovak party leaders. Their decision to preserve the interparty truce offered by the National Front and "get to work" had full public approval.

Air attacks, military operations, and the German occupation had made World War II more destructive for the Czechs and Slovaks than any previous conflict. According to an official government estimate 250,000 persons had died. In Bohemia, 3,014 houses were destroyed and over 10,000 were badly damaged; in Moravia the respective figures were 11,862 and over 19,000. In Silesia 34,986 buildings were ruined. Slovakia, because of the prolonged fighting in 1944–45, was the most seriously hit.[26] In the Czech provinces the total war damage per person was estimated at 17,000 Czechoslovak crowns (about $2,400), but in Slovakia it amounted to 35,000 crowns (about $4,900).[27] In eastern Slovakia alone 169 villages were razed and 300 damaged; 24,000 buildings were ruined or heavily damaged. The transportation system was seriously dislocated. Almost all the large factories had been badly bombed.[28] Livestock suffered heavily. Nevertheless, a large amount of food and raw materials stockpiled by the Germans during the occupation remained in the country.

The end of the war closed a struggle for the Czech nation's very existence. Since 1938 the Czechs had been humiliated and persecuted. They had also suffered from Nazi cruelties and the bloody fighting of the last days of the war. The radical mood of the country transformed resentment against the Nazis into demands for the permanent removal of all Germans. Popular support for the idea of expelling the Sudeten Germans caught even the Communist party by surprise. However, it swiftly went beyond the Košice program and espoused popular demands. A presidential decree on June 21, 1945, provided for the expropriation without compensation of the property of the Germans and Magyars as well as that of Czech and Slovak collaborators and traitors. The land that came within the scope of the decree involved about 270,000 farms covering 6,240,000 acres, which provided the communist minister of agriculture with a rich pork barrel from which to reward those who were willing to serve the party. By the spring of 1948 some 1,500,000 people had moved to the Czech borderlands left vacant by the Sudeten Germans, who had been removed to the American and Soviet zones of occupation in Germany in accordance with the mandate given Czechoslovakia by the Allied powers at Potsdam. After June 15, 1949, only 177,000 Germans were left in the Czech provinces.[29] This national adjustment wrought a profound change in the economic and social structure of the country. There was much disorder and violence—yet this is present in every revolutionary process. In the final analysis, the expulsion of the Sudeten Germans was a Czech national response—neither communist nor Soviet inspired —to a situation created by Nazi war policy and the Sudeten Germans themselves.

The Slovaks, led by the KSS, pressed for a similar removal of the Magyar minority from Slovakia. But it was one thing to press a claim against the Germans, who at that time were regarded as outlaws in all of Europe, and quite another to press one against the Hungarians, who were regarded as minor culprits. The Soviet Union tended to regard Hungary as a future satellite, like Czechoslovakia, and was not anxious to complicate its tasks by contributing to dissension between two of its prospective clients. At the Potsdam conference it failed to back the Czechoslovak demand for the removal of the Magyar minority. The matter was left to bilateral Czechoslovak-Hungarian negotiations. Under a mutual exchange agreement concluded between the two countries on February 27, 1946, 68,407 Magyars out of some 500,000 did leave for Hungary and a somewhat smaller number of Slovaks returned to Slovakia.[30] No large fund of land comparable to that in the Czech borderlands became available in Slovakia, a factor that had important repercussions in Czechoslovak politics.

Partly for this reason, the Czechoslovak delegation at the Paris Peace Conference in 1946 raised the demand for authorization to remove 200,000 Magyars from Slovakia. But by then, the Western powers were adamantly opposed to any further population transfer, and the matter was dropped.[31] They did, however, accede to the Czechoslovak demand for a small enlargement of the Bratislava bridgehead on the south bank of the Danube River at the expense of Hungary.[32]

Meanwhile, in June, 1945, the Poles suddenly reopened the Těšín (Teschen) question. On June 19 Polish troops under General Rola-Zymierski moved up to the city of Těšín. Possibly the Poles were encouraged to revive this old thorn in Polish-Czechoslovak relations by the Soviet government, which was anxious to prod Czechoslovakia into settling the Ruthenian question. In any event, on the same day the Soviet government invited Czechoslovakia and Poland to send delegations to Moscow to discuss outstanding questions affecting their relations. On June 29, after a week of discussions, the Czechoslovak and Soviet governments signed an agreement formally transferring Ruthenia to the Soviet Union.[33] When the Czechoslovak delegation returned to Prague, Prime Minister Fierlinger announced that the Polish-Czechoslovak discussions had been indefinitely adjourned. Apart from the loss of Ruthenia and the enlargement of the Bratislava bridge-head, the pre-Munich boundaries of Czechoslovakia remained intact.

The internal position of Czechoslovakia appeared to be fully consolidated. The withdrawal of Soviet and United States troops from Czechoslovakia as early as November and December of 1945 heralded a return to normalcy. By the fall of 1945 the country had also made considerable progress in economic reconstruction. Almost everyone agreed that it had bright prospects, provided that the wartime grand alliance and the internal balance between the communist and democratic forces could be maintained.

Since it had to compete with the democratic parties, the Communist party sought to be a mass party. The KSČ readily admitted members of former parties, drawing a line only at admitting former fascists and collaborators who, in Czech opinion, stood beyond the pale. The KSS, on the other hand, readily admitted even members of the former Hlinka People's party—indeed, it strenuously courted them. It posed as a Slovak nationalist party and did not hesitate to exploit religious prejudice by pointing out to the Slovak Catholic majority that the leadership of its competitor, the Slovak Democratic party, was largely Protestant. At the end of 1945 the KSS claimed a membership of 197,000, while in March, 1946, the KSČ claimed to have over 1,000,000 members.[34]

The growing strength of the Communist party was reflected in its high moral and internal consolidation. Between 1945 and 1948 the leadership of the KSČ (with Klement Gottwald as chairman and Rudolf Slánský as secretary-general) remained remarkably stable, and the party was unusually free of factional strife. The KSS experienced some internal stress, however, as its nationalist posture came into conflict with the strategy of the parent party, the KSČ. At a joint meeting of the central committees of the KSČ and KSS in Prague on July 17–18, 1945, the Czech communists sharply criticized their Slovak comrades for viewing the development from a "nationalist," instead of a "class," point of view and for allying themselves with the "reaction" in the SNR, that is, the Slovak Democrats. A resolution, passed at the meeting, demanded that the "policy of the KSS must not be to separate but to orient the party towards the progressive forces in the Czech provinces and in the central government" and delegated Viliam Široký, a dour internationalist communist, to take charge of the KSS.[35] The separation of the two parties, which was maintained for tactical reasons, thereafter became nominal.

While the Communist party was united, the Czechoslovak Social Democratic party (chairman: Zdeněk Fierlinger; secretary-general: Blažej Vilím), which had a long and distinguished history of defending the cause of the Czech working class, was increasingly rent by a tug-of-war between its right and left wings, representing its liberal-democratic and Marxian-socialist traditions, respectively. The Czech National Socialist party (chairman: Petr Zenkl; secretary-general: Vladimír Krajina), which claimed to be a socialist but non-Marxist party, suffered from no such dilemma. It came increasingly to the fore as the most resolute adversary of the communists among the Czech parties. The Czech Populist party, under the leadership of Msgr. Jan Šrámek, the wartime premier in London, was a progressive Catholic party that before the war had received its greatest support among Czech peasants, especially in Moravia. After the war it had difficulty in finding its bearings in the radical atmosphere, which affected even the countryside. The Slovak Democratic party (chairman: Jozef Lettrich; secretary: Fedor Hodža), which was largely a continuation of the Slovak branch of the proscribed agrarian party, suffered from the polarization of Slovak opinion after the war between the radical revolutionary movement and the conservative Catholic anticommunist movement. It could not compete with the communists in appealing to the former and found it distasteful and dangerous to appeal to the latter, for fear of exposing itself to the charge of catering to cryptofascists.

In retrospect it is clear that the prolongation of the provisional regime benefited the Communist party more than the democratic parties, by allowing an unusual measure of influence in public affairs to various extraconstitutional mass organizations, such as worker, peasant, youth, resistance, and other nationwide associations, that sprang up after the liberation of the country. The general European "swing to the left" immediately after the war undoubtedly helped the Communist party gain a preponderant influence in these organizations. No instrument was more important to it than the united Revolutionary Trade Union Movement (ROH) and workers' factory councils (závodní rady). This was true at least in the Czech provinces. In Slovakia, where the working class did not have the same importance,[36] the Communist party relied more on its influence in the resistance organizations, especially the association of former partisans.

The communist plans had emphasized the necessity of gaining leadership of the working class, a traditional domain of the Social Democratic movement. In the first postwar days the communists occupied positions of power in the ROH and the workers' councils in all large factories. In this situation, the predominant influence of the Communist party with the working class,[37] combined with its control of important levers of the state apparatus, became the central fact of politics.

After the party consolidated its grip on the political structure in the early summer of 1945, its initial moderation in economic affairs began to fade. President Beneš and the two socialist parties viewed the nationalization of the principal industries, banks, and insurance companies as inevitable. Moreover, the corresponding pressure exerted by the workers found widespread popular support. Under these circumstances the expropriation of German capital evolved into a wider trend that reflected a consensus of all responsible political forces. Thus, the first postwar measure of large nationalization in Europe [38] became a demonstration of a common resolve to establish collective ownership and direct state control over the chief means of production. The presidential decrees of October 24, which were mainly prepared by the Social Democratic controlled Ministry of Industry, resulted in the creation of a nationalized sector containing 61.2 percent of the industrial labor force.[39]

The nationalization decrees were the last great measures adopted without parliament's authorization. After the convocation of the Provisional National Assembly four days later, the democratic parties sought to limit the influence of the ROH and other extraconstitutional mass organizations and to confine policy-making to parliament. This encountered the opposition of the communists, who had found it advantageous to promote their aims through these organizations. They lent themselves more easily to manipulation than did the parliament, which had an orderly procedure and in which, moreover, they were a minority. The National Front began to experience increasing strains, and early in 1946 it was decided to hold general elections for the constituent assembly. May 26 was set as the date for the elections.

All parties committed themselves to maintain the National Front and the Košice program. This seemingly left no divisive issues. The electoral contest was nevertheless lively, though orderly. The difference between the parties lay in the accent they placed on specific aspects of the common program. The communists and Social Democrats stressed its social aspects and hinted that there were more to come. The democratic parties, on the other hand, maintained that the social goals of the program had largely been attained and placed a greater accent on freedom and democracy.

In Slovakia two new parties came into existence. Some of the old Slovak Social Democrats regarded the fusion of their party with the Communist party during the Slovak uprising in 1944 as a shotgun marriage, and now wished to go it alone. In January, 1946, with the assistance of the Czech Social Democrats, they formed the Labor party.[40] The other new party, the Freedom party, came into existence as a byproduct of electoral strategy by the Slovak Democratic party (DS). On March 30 Lettrich, the chairman of the DS, concluded an agreement (incorrectly known as the "April Agreement") with the Catholic

leaders under which the Catholics were promised representation in all
organs of the DS in a ratio of 7:3 in their favor.[41] The April Agreement promised to bolster the electoral strength of the DS, because the
Catholic clergy had a powerful influence in Slovakia, especially in the
rural areas, but it was fraught with dangers for the party. Many Catholic politicians were unreconstructed l'udáks. Their entry pulled the party
sharply to the right and proved more than some of its leaders could
stomach. The dissidents, among whom was notably Vavro Šrobár,
formed the Freedom party on April 1.[42] Even more important was the
communists' reaction to the April Agreement. In direct retaliation for
its conclusion, the KSČ, with the concurrence of the Czech parties and
the KSS, pressed through a further limitation of SNR prerogatives.
Under the "Second Prague Agreement" on April 11, 1946, the SNR
was deprived of the important power of making personal appointments
without the approval of the Prague government.[43]

While the United States remained studiedly aloof during the electoral campaign, the Soviet Union gave a pointed reminder of its interest. On May 22, almost the eve of the elections, it was announced
the Soviet troops would be moved across Czechoslovak territory from
Austria and Hungary to the Soviet zone of occupation in Germany. At
the outcry of the democratic leaders over this crude attempt at intimidation, the troop movement was postponed, but its psychological purpose had already been attained—it reminded the Czechs and Slovaks
that the Soviet army was close by and could return on short notice.[44]

The communists approached the elections with confidence. They
hoped to win an absolute majority, but were not worried if they did
not. On February 4, at the outset of the campaign, Gottwald assured
the party workers: "Even if it should happen, which is improbable,
that we should not gain a favorable result . . . the working class, the
party, and the working people will still have sufficient means, arms,
and a method to correct simple mechanical voting, which might be
affected by reactionary and saboteur elements." [45] In other words, if
the results of the election were favorable to the communists, they
would be accepted; if not, they would be "corrected."

The elections on May 26, which proved to be the last free Czechoslovak elections, passed without incident and, according to foreign
observers, without any attempt at intimidation or manipulation. The
ballot was secret. All citizens over eighteen years of age, except
political offenders, were not only allowed, but were obliged to vote,
thus assuring a heavy turnout. The results did not basically alter the
existing party balance. In the Czech provinces the KSČ obtained 40.1,
the National Socialists 23.5, the Populists 20.2, and the Social Democrats 15.6 percent of the vote. In Slovakia the DS obtained 62, the KSS

30.3, the Freedom party 3.7, and the Labor party 3.1 percent.[46] In the whole country the communists (the combined KSČ and KSS) secured 37.9 percent of the vote. This fell short of their hopes but was still impressive. The most surprising development was the failure of the Social Democratic party, which had at one time been the largest party in Czechoslovakia but was now the smallest. Its Slovak branch, the Labor party, likewise made a poor showing. During the electoral postmortem the democratic wing blamed the defeat on the campaign strategy of the party leadership, which had adopted an almost identical position on many issues as the communists, and demanded that in the future the party follow an independent course of action.

The most impressive gains were made by the Slovak Democrats. There is no doubt, however, that the large vote cast for the DS represented less a show of confidence by the Slovak electorate in the DS than a rebuke to the KSS. Several factors accounted for the communists' modest showing in Slovakia compared with their good record in the Czech provinces: the relative unimportance of the Slovak working class; the absence of a large reserve of confiscated land with which to entice the land-hungry peasantry, such as existed in the Czech borderlands; the greater war damages in Slovakia and consequently greater problems of reconstruction (in the winter of 1945–46 there were acute food shortages in the province); the influence of the conservative Catholic clergy, who did not hesitate to warn in their sermons against the perils of "godless" communism; and the bitter memory of the many excesses committed against the civilian population by the Red Army during its operations in Slovakia in 1944–45, for which the injured took revenge by voting against the "Russian party," that is, the communists.[47]

The communists did not mistake the fact that the large vote for the DS was really a vote against them, and at once took steps to correct the situation. "We have not won yet, the struggle continues," said Gottwald in reporting the results of the election to the central committee of the KSČ on May 30,[48] and he made it clear that the first target in the continuing struggle must be the DS. In order to limit its influence, Gottwald proposed to abolish what was left of Slovak autonomy—"even if we thereby violate formal national rights or promises or guarantees. . . . The Slovak comrades will no doubt understand." [49]

For the assault against the DS, Gottwald proposed four concrete steps: to limit further the prerogatives of the SNR, to launch a drive against the l'udáks camouflaged in the DS, to punish Jozef Tiso, and to take steps against the Slovak Catholic clergy, for the adoption of which the KSČ secured the concurrence of the National Front of the

Czech parties on June 12 and the National Front of the Czech and Slovak parties two days later.[50] The first step was implemented in the "Third Prague Agreement" on June 27–28, 1946, which placed the legislative powers of the SNR under government control and the Slovak commissioners under the appropriate ministers in Prague.[51] In practice, Slovakia reverted to the position that it had held before the Munich agreement in 1938: that of a simple administrative unit, like Bohemia and Moravia. This latest advance of centralism placed added strains not only on the relations between the KSS and DS but also—since it was supported by all Czech parties—between the Czechs and Slovaks as a whole.

The National Front had been somewhat shaken by the electoral contest. However, all parties still professed loyalty to it and it was continued. The Eighth Congress of the KSČ in March, 1946, had endorsed the strengthening of the National Front and had directed the party to implement further the national and democratic revolution.[52] (The KSČ never failed to stress that whatever the future model of the republic, it would correspond closely to special Czech and Slovak conditions.[53]) On July 2 the cabinet was reshuffled to conform with the results of the elections. Fierlinger yielded the premiership to Gottwald, as the representative of the largest party. Of the twenty-five cabinet posts, the KSČ received seven, the KSS one and one state secretaryship, the National Socialists four, the DS three and one state secretaryship, and the Czech Populists and Social Democrats three posts each.[54]

The parties were impelled to maintain a solid front by, among other things, the opening of the Paris Peace Conference on July 29. Three days earlier Gottwald and a delegation had returned from Moscow with the good news that the Soviet government had not only promised to support Czechoslovak claims at the conference but had also waived the provision of the Potsdam agreement that entitled it to claim German "external assets" in Czechoslovakia. Moreover, Gottwald revealed that the Soviet government had promised to support Czechoslovak economic plans by concluding a long-term trade treaty. On the other hand, the United States government had granted Czechoslovakia a credit of $50 million in June to buy American surplus war supplies in Europe. However, in September, before the credit was exhausted, the United States abruptly suspended it because the Czechoslovak delegates at the peace conference had applauded the Soviet delegate when he inveighed against American "economic imperialism." [55]

Czechoslovakia had been caught in the first cross fire of the cold war. On July 10, Soviet Foreign Minister Vyacheslav Molotov fired the first shot in the East-West struggle for Germany, by calling for the formation of a German national government and questioning the French right to the Saar. United States Secretary of State James F. Byrnes replied in his famous Stuttgart speech on September 6, by also calling for a German national government and by repudiating—in effect —the Potsdam agreement on the Oder-Neisse boundary and thus, by implication, reopening the whole question of the eastern settlement. Czechoslovak isolation from the West and dependence on the East had increased.

This development boded ill for the first important measure of the Gottwald government—the Two-Year Economic Plan for 1947–48, which the National Assembly approved on October 24.[56] The plan, which proposed to raise the standard of living ten percent above the prewar level, was oriented toward the long-range coexistence of the private and nationalized sectors of the economy and was predicated on the assumption that Czechoslovakia's traditional trade ties with the West would continue. At that time the Soviet Union faced gigantic problems of reconstruction and was in no position to provide economic aid to Czechoslovakia or to furnish, in exchange for Czechoslovak exports, the kind of goods and services she needed to realize her economic plans. The promised Soviet-Czechoslovak trade pact did not materialize until December, 1947.

The next important measure of the Gottwald government was political: it staged the trial of Monsignor Tiso as a deterrent to Slovak separatists. The trial, which opened in Bratislava on December 3, 1946, ended in March of the following year with Tiso's conviction of treason and a sentence of death. As calculated by the communists, the sentence placed the DS in a difficult position. The leaders of the party, chairman of the SNR Lettrich and Vice-Premier Ján Ursíny, were Protestants and former agrarians. They had led the Slovak resistance against Tiso's government during the war and had little sympathy for him, but they were put under pressure by the party's Catholic wing to save him. When the government considered Tiso's appeal for mercy on April 16, the DS ministers moved to commute the sentence to life imprisonment. They were seconded by the Czech Populist ministers, who demurred at hanging a fellow priest. However, the other ministers held firm for execution.[57] On the recommendation of the cabinet, President Beneš declined the appeal for mercy, and on April 18 Tiso was hanged.

Since the removal of the Sudeten German minority the "Slovak question," that is, the problem of satisfactorily adjusting relations between the Czechs and Slovaks, had become the foremost internal question in the country. The trial of Tiso, by deeply offending conservative Catholic opinion in Slovakia, aggravated this concern. It was to trouble the Third Czechoslovak Republic until its end—and, indeed, continued in a different form afterward.

In the spring of 1947 the Communist party adopted the goal of winning at least fifty-one percent of the votes in the next elections and thus gaining a majority in the National Assembly. This angered the other parties, but it did indicate that the communist leadership did not yet wish to take over all power, but was committed to the maintenance of the National Front. There were radical elements in the party that criticized the leadership for not following the Bolshevik way. Simultaneously, there were anticommunist groups in the country, biding their time. Both segments, however, represented politically insignificant forces. The predominant majority of the people wholeheartedly endorsed the objectives of the National Front to liberate men from economic and social domination within a democratic society.

These hopeful expectations, predicated on the belief that Czechoslovakia could eventually become the show window of a new, more humane system and the bridge between East and West were shattered in the summer of 1947 by Stalin's new policy line,[58] which called for consolidating the Soviet hold on Eastern Europe and drawing clear lines of combat with the West. On June 5, at Harvard University, U.S. Secretary of State George C. Marshall made his historic offer of American aid to Europe. Czechoslovakia was eager to share in the American aid, which it needed to complete the Two-Year Economic Plan successfully. On July 4 and 7 the cabinet and inner cabinet, respectively, voted unanimously to accept an invitation to sent a delegation to a preliminary conference of European states in Paris to discuss the Marshall Plan.[59] Immediately after the cabinet made its intention known, a government delegation led by Premier Gottwald left for Moscow where it was scheduled to negotiate mutual trade problems and to discuss the possibility of concluding a Franco-Czechoslovak treaty. When the delegation arrived in Moscow on July 9, it was given an ultimatum by Stalin to choose between East and West. On the following day the Prague government reversed its decision to send a delegation to Paris.[60] It had chosen the Soviet alliance.

At the end of September, the Information Bureau of the Communist parties (Cominform), including the KSČ, was founded at Szklarska Poreba in Poland as the institutional device of the communist international control system.[61] The delegates aimed "to apply the final touches to a general plan for easing the 'National Front' allies out of power and establishing a Communist dictatorship" in Eastern Europe.[62] The Cominform, then, was founded at the moment when "the Soviet Union had finally decided to take under her direct control a number of East European states," particularly Czechoslovakia.[63] The secretary general of the KSČ, Rudolf Slánský, informed the conference that the first task of the party was "to deal a death blow to reaction in Slovakia," [64] and added ominously: "It will be necessary to throw reactionary forces out of the National Front." [65] The road was opened for the Stalinist takeover in Czechoslovakia.

## From the Cominform to the Prague Coup

By the fall of 1947 the struggle for power in East Central Europe was almost decided. Czechoslovakia remained the sole exception. It still had a coalition government. During the summer her hitherto favorable economic development suddenly ceased. A severe drought caused the harvest to fall to one-half of its normal level. As the leading party in the government, the communists received the major blame for the deteriorating economic situation. Feeling that the tide of public opinion was turning against them, they sought to postpone the elections that they had proposed in the spring. The democratic parties, on the other hand, aware that their chances in an electoral contest had improved, pressed for holding them at an early date. After much bickering it was decided to hold them in May, 1948.

As the parties girded for another electoral struggle, the communists displayed a wide arsenal of political and psychological weapons. In August they proposed that the owners of property in excess of one million Czechoslovak crowns pay a 'millionaires' tax" to provide aid to the ailing rural districts. Millionaires had never been numerous in Czechoslovakia and their ranks had been further reduced by the war and the subsequent expulsion of the German minority. Even the Social Democrats demurred at supporting so demagogic a measure. However, when communist propaganda succeeded in arousing popular support for it, the Social Democrats hastened on September 11 to conclude an agreement with the KSČ providing for their cooperation. The social democratic leadership thus sought to bind the KSČ to their own democratic practices. However, a large number of party members sharply criticized the agreement and Minister Václav Majer even tended his resignation.[66]

A strident note crept into communist propaganda. The communist press began systematically to impugn the loyalty of the other parties to the republic and to vilify their leaders. The public was shocked by the revelation on September 10 of an abortive attempt on the lives of noncommunist ministers Jan Masaryk, Petr Zenkl, and Prokop Drtina, who had received parcels containing bombs. The communist Minister of Interior Válav Nosek and the communist-dominated police showed a curious lack of interest in the case. Instead, with much fanfare, the

Slovak Commissioner of Interior, Mikuláš Ferjenčík, announced on December 14 the discovery of a plot by the ľudák underground to assassinate President Beneš and overthrow the republic. Subsequently, the police linked the alleged plot to the ľudák exiles Karol Sidor and Ferdinand D'určanský. Widespread arrests, ultimately of more than 500 persons, followed. Among the arrested were three DS members of the National Assembly and a secretary of Vice-Premier Ján Ursíny. Although Ursíny himself was not implicated in the plot, he was forced to resign from the cabinet.

The affair served as a smoke screen behind which the communists prepared to purge the Slovak board of commissioners of its DS majority and to restructure the National Front of Slovak parties to make it more responsive to their wishes.[67] To set the stage for this coup, they arranged for the Slovak Trade Union Council (SOR—the Slovak counterpart of ROH) to meet in Bratislava on October 30 and for the Slovak Peasant Union to meet there two weeks later. At its October 30 meeting the SOR passed a resolution blaming the board of commissioners for the breakdown in food distribution and a failure to safeguard the security of the state and calling for its dismissal. Another resolution called for the reorganization of the Slovak National Front to include trade union, resistance, and peasant organizations. On the following day, in response to this "voice of the people," the communist chairman of the board of commissioners, Husák, four other communist commissioners, and the nonparty Commissioner of Interior Ferjenčík resigned from the board. Husák declared that the board was thereby dissolved and opened negotiations with the minute Freedom and Labor parties, until then unrepresented on the board, to form a new one. The DS leaders naturally protested against this novel constitutional concept whereby a minority could dismiss the majority from the caginet. They refused to resign from the board or to admit the mass organizations into the National Front.

The government in Prague then stepped into the situation, but to the dismay of the communists the National Socialists and Populists refused to associate themselves in a communist measure of coercion against the DS. On November 18, after prolonged negotiations, a new board of commissioners was formed in which the DS was deprived of its majority and the Freedom and Labor parties received representation.

The Slovak "November crisis" proved to be a dress rehearsal for the Prague "February crisis." The communists had effectively used their control of the police and mass organizations and had ruthlessly exploited every weakness in the ranks of the DS to achieve their objective. The democratic parties were alerted to what was in store for them. An early symptom of their reaction was the reassertion by the Social

Democratic party of its independence of the KSČ. At its congress at Brno on November 16 the procommunist Fierlinger was removed as chairman of the party and replaced with centrist Bohumil Laušman.[68] The democratic parties were encouraged by this development to believe that the Social Democratic party would cooperate with them. Laušman, however, personified the inability of the party to decide whether to fight on the side of the Communist party for social demands or on the side of the democratic parties for democracy. Under his leadership the party wavered in Hamlet-like indecision between the communist and democratic parties.

The communists increased their pressure on the other parties through the winter of 1947–48, with each issue exacerbating the political atmosphere and widening the divergences between the two camps.[69] The noncommunist parties made common complaint about police use of false confessions and *agents provocateurs*. Accusations levelled at the KSČ for attempting to monopolize control of the police engendered popular demands for the preservation of basic democratic freedoms. The time remaining for any possible settlement was running out. In November, 1947, the upper echelons of the KSČ began concerted action according to a plan based on their experience in the Slovak crisis. This involved a call by the ROH for a meeting of the workers' factory councils and peasant committees to formulate new popular demands. The party would then endorse their program, which would be adopted subsequently by all the mass organizations and those personalities within the existing parties who had secretly been won over by the communists. The ensuing "renovated" National Front would draw up a unified list of candidates for the elections.[70] The new alliance would then mount an electoral campaign aided by the mass media of communication, national committees, and police machinery— all controlled by the party.[71]

On February 12, 1948, the ROH issued a call to the workers' factory councils to meet in Prague on February 22, an action that convinced the democratic leaders that the communists were about to move. In a cabinet meeting the following day, the National Socialist ministers precipitated a crisis by protesting against the demotion and transfer of eight high noncommunist police officers by Minister of Interior Nosek. All ministers except the communists approved a motion introduced by the National Socialists to instruct Nosek to reinstate the police officers and desist from further personnel changes in the police forces. The communists were placed in a minority position in the cabinet and appeared isolated. Encouraged by their success, the National Socialists decided to take the offensive against them and try to upset their timetable. On February 20 the National Socialist ministers, followed by the Populist and Slovak Democratic ministers, resigned from the cabinet in protest against the failure of Nosek to carry out the cabinet decision of February 13 in the police matter. The "latent crisis" was thus transformed into "open crisis." [72]

The dramatic return of two old adversaries, U.S. Ambassador Laurence A. Steinhardt and Soviet Deputy Minister of Foreign Affairs and former ambassador to Czechoslovakia Valerian A. Zorin, to Prague on February 19 appeared to give the crisis an international dimension. Steinhardt declared to the press that the door to the Marshall Plan was still open to Czechoslovakia.[73] Zorin arrived ostensibly to expedite deliveries of grain, which the Soviet government had promised in December to alleviate the food shortage. The Western press speculated widely that he had really come to Prague to direct the communist takeover. Actually, no evidence ever turned up indicating that he had directly intervened in the crisis.[74] He did not have to. Gottwald and his associates had matters well in hand.

The ministers who had resigned constituted a minority, since neither the Social Democrats nor nonparty ministers Jan Masaryk and Ludvík Svoboda had been consulted and thus had not resigned. Consequently, Gottwald remained legally in power. The ministers who had resigned counted on President Beneš to refuse to accept their resignations. In that case, they would compel Gottwald either to call new elections or to carry out the decision of the cabinet in the police matter. They thought in strictly parliamentary terms, regarding their resignation as a mere cabinet affair, and called on their supporters "to remain calm under all circumstances." But the communists refused to abide by the rules of parliamentary democracy. While the democratic ministers and parties passively awaited Beneš's decision, the communists used their control of mass organizations and the police to take over power.

On the morning of February 21 Gottwald addressed an organized mass meeting in the Old Town Square in Prague. He accused the resigned ministers of having formed a "reactionary bloc" in the cabinet to obstruct the popular policies of the communists. They had precipitated the crisis, he alleged, to prevent the holding of elections, the outcome of which they feared. By their action they had "excluded themselves from the National Front," and the communists could have no further dealings with them. They would be replaced "with new people, who had remained faithful to the original spirit of the National Front." Gottwald put his proposal for the "renovation" of the cabinet into a resolution that was approved by acclamation, and on the spot a workers' delegation was "elected" to carry this expression of the "will of the people" to the president.

At the same time the communists deployed the instruments of their takeover—party activists, workers' militia, the police, and "action committees"—in Prague and outside it, according to a carefully prepared plan. On February 24 armed workers lent Prague a certain spurious aura of Petrograd in 1917, but their military value was slight, if any. In the event of an armed conflict with the other parties, the communists relied on the police, particularly on specially trained police regiments composed exclusively of communists. On the morning of February 21 the police assumed guard over the Prague radio station, post and telegraph offices, and railway stations. The most original instrument of the communist takeover was the action committees, which had been secretly organized earlier among men within and outside the KSČ whom the party could trust. Action committees sprang up in every government bureau, factory, and town—in fact, in every organized body in the country—and proceeded to purge them of democrats.[75]

By mass demonstrations centered on Prague and the mere threat of violence, the communists isolated and silenced the democratic parties, split the Social Democratic party, and awed the president. In such an unprecedented situation, naturally, the majority of the population expected word from Beneš—word that never came. After resisting the communist demands for five days, Beneš yielded. On February 25 he accepted the resignation of the democratic ministers and simultaneously appointed a new cabinet handpicked by Gottwald, which—in addition to communists and Social Democrats—included some members of the National Socialist, Populist, and Slovak Democratic parties, who had secretly agreed to cooperate with the communists. The façade of the National Front was thus maintained.

The only force that could have prevented the communist takeover was the army. But the army under General Svoboda, a friend of the communists, remained neutral throughout the crisis. In any event, Beneš never considered opposing force by force. The behavior of the noncommunist party leaders was, if possible, even worse. While the communists were brilliantly using the instruments of power, "the non-Communist parties . . . had no organization, no plan"[76] and finished in complete disarray, despite the support they enjoyed from the helpless and baffled majority of the Czech and Slovak people. By their precipitate and ill-considered resignation, the democratic ministers had made it possible for the communists to take over power by constitutional means. They were not forced out of the government by the communists; they had walked out of it.

Meanwhile, the zealous Husák had anticipated Gottwald's coup at

Prague with one of his own at Bratislava.[77] But the events in Bratislava lacked the drama of those in Prague, because they constituted, more or less, only a mopping-up operation, designed to complete what had been left undone in November. Unlike Gottwald, Husák did not have to contend with Beneš. Moreover, while Prague was swarming with foreign correspondents who had come to observe and report on the death of Czechoslovak democracy, none troubled to go to the provincial backwater of Bratislava. Husák, therefore, dispensed with the elaborate *mise en scène* that Gottwald felt compelled to arrange at Prague. Unlike the DS ministers in Prague, the DS commissioners in Bratislava did not resign; they had to be expelled from the board. On February 21, without awaiting the outcome of the cabinet crisis in Prague, Husák wrote them that the resignation of the DS ministers from the central government bound them to resign too, and against the eventuality that they might dispute this ruling he posted policemen at the doors of their offices to turn them away. They did not choose to resist, for the DS had been emasculated and cowed in November and had nothing left with which to fight. The communists took a majority of seats on the board (eight out of fifteen), and distributed the rest among the other parties (including two pliant DS members) and representatives of the communist-controlled mass organizations. Action committees completed the mop-up.

After appointing the new government on February 25 and receiving its members when they were sworn in on February 27, Beneš retired to his country residence at Sezimovo Ústí. On June 7 he resigned and withdrew from further participation in the conduct of state affairs. The communists were left the sole masters of the republic—free to reorganize it according to their beliefs and concepts.

## Notes

1. Edvard Beneš, *Memoirs: From Munich to New War and New Victory* (Boston, 1954), p. 139.

2. See the account of Eduard Taborsky, Beneš's former secretary, "Benešovy moskevské cesty" ["Beneš's Trips to Moscow"], *Svědectví*, 1, Nos. 3–4 (1957), 203ff. Taborsky stated that in his wartime conversations with Soviet leaders Beneš held that Ruthenia should belong either to Czechoslovakia or to the Soviet Union. "As much as he wished" this area "to be Czechoslovak again, he was by no means ready to insist on it as the price of Soviet friendship" (p. 207). On March 24, 1945, Soviet Foreign Minister Vyacheslav M. Molotov asked Beneš to repeat in writing his acceptance of the loss of Ruthenia (p. 212).

3. Gustáv Husák, *Svedectvo o Slovenskom národnom povstaní* [*Testimony about the Slovak National Uprising*] (Bratislava, 1964), pp. 554–55; Zdeněk Fierlinger, *Ve službách ČSR* [*In the Service of the Czechoslovak Republic*] (2 vols.; Prague, 1947–48), II, 599ff.

4. See Miroslav Soukup, "Některé problémy vzájemných vztahů mezi kommunistickými stranami" ["Some Problems of the Mutual Relations between the Communist Parties"], *Příspěvky k dějinám KSČ*, IV (Feb. 1964), 13ff.

5. Gottwald's report to the central committee of the KSČ, September 25–26, 1946.

6. Milan Hübl, "Lidová demokracie V 1946" ["Popular Democracy in 1946"], *Slovanský přehled*, No. 2 (1966), 65–70.

7. See Karel Kaplan, *Znárodnění a socialismus* [*Nationalization and Socialism*] (Prague, 1968), *passim*. This tendency was discernible in other European communist parties, notably in France and Italy.

8. See the discussion Beneš had with Gottwald and other communist exiles in Moscow in December 1943, in Beneš, *Memoirs*, pp. 268–75, and, from the communist point of view, Bohuslav Laštovička, *V Londýně za války* [*In London during the War*] (Prague, 1960), pp. 310–30.

9. See Libuše Otáhalová and Milada Červinková, eds., *Dokumenty z historie československé politiky 1939–1943* [*Documents on the History of Czechoslovak Politics 1939–1943*] (2 vols.; Prague, 1966), II, 750–51.

10. For the minutes of the negotiations see Miloš Klimeš *et al.*, eds., *Cesta ke květnu* [*Road to May*] (2 vols.; Prague, 1965), I, 380–453. For accounts see Laštovička, *V Londýně*, pp. 496–553, and Husák, *Svedectvo*, pp. 578–89.

11. Josef Korbel, *The Communist Subversion of Czechoslovakia, 1938–1948* (Princeton, 1959), p. 114. Korbel rightly blames Beneš for his withdrawal from what the President wrongly considered to be a matter of party politics. For revealing conversations between President Beneš and U.S. ambassador in Moscow, W. Averell Harriman, on March 22 and 31, 1945, see U.S. Department of State, *Foreign Relations of the United States. Diplomatic Papers 1945*. Vol. IV: *Europe* (Washington, 1968), pp. 427–29 and 430–33.

12. Korbel, *The Communist Subversion*, p. 114.

13. Minister Jaroslav Stránský's recollections, ibid., p. 114.

14. Jaroslav Opat, *O novou demokracii, 1945–1948* [*For a New Democracy, 1945–1948*] (Prague, 1966), pp. 44–48; Jozef Jablonický, *Slovensko na prelome* [*Slovakia in Transition*] (Bratislava, 1965), pp. 227–85; Jaroslav Barto, *Riešenie vzťahu Čechov a Slovákov, 1944–1948* [*Solving the Relations Between the Czechs and the Slovaks, 1944–1948*] (Bratislava, 1968), pp. 30–34; and Samo Falt'an, *Slovenská otázka v Československu* [*The Slovak Question in Czechoslovakia*] (Bratislava, 1968), pp. 186–200.

15. Edvard Beneš, *Šest let exilu a druhé světové války. Řeči, projevy a dokumenty z r. 1938–45* [*Six Years of Exile and the Second World War: Speeches, Declarations, and Documents in 1938–45*] (Prague, 1946), pp. 423–24.

16. The full text of the Košice program may be found in *Za svobodu českého a slovenského národa: Sborník dokumentů [For the Freedom of the Czech and Slovak People: a Collection of Documents]* (Prague, 1956), pp. 368–90, published by the Institute for the History of KSČ in Prague. For an English translation of point six of the program dealing with the Slovaks, see Jozef Lettrich, *History of Modern Slovakia* (New York, 1955), pp. 317–18.

17. Bohuslav Laštovička, "Vznik a význam košického vládního programu" ["The Origin and Importance of the Košice Government Program"], *Československý časopis historický*, VIII (August 1960), 465.

18. For the negotiations leading to the formation of the government and its composition, see Opat, *O novou demokracii*, pp. 48–50. In the SNR and its executive organ, the board of commissioners, the Communist party of Slovakia (KSS), and the Democratic party (DS) continued to share power equally.

19. Laštovička, "Vznik," p. 463.

20. Klimeš, *Cesta*, I, 447.

21. During the war both the Moscow and London exiles emphasized the primary importance of the home front. Upon returning to Prague, however, both united in refusing to offer the Czech resistance leaders any representation in the cabinet. See Josef Belda et al., *Na rozhraní dvou epoch [On the Frontier of Two Epochs]* (Prague, 1968), pp. 40–41.

22. Apart from the fact that the SNR was recognized in the Košice program, it had functioned continuously since February, 1945. By the time the government was established in Prague in May, the SNR was well entrenched and carried on as a quasi-government.

23. Falťan, *Slovenská otázka*, pp. 206–207; Barto, *Riešenie*, pp. 54–58.

24. Barto, *Riešenie*, pp. 67–79; Falťan, *Slovenská otázka*, pp. 207–12; Belda, *Na rozhraní*, p. 43.

25. The four Czech parties received forty seats and the two Slovak parties, fifty seats each. The remaining forty seats were distributed among representatives of mass organizations.

26. Radomír Luža, *The Transfer of the Sudeten Germans* (New York, 1964), p. 262.

27. V. Jarošová and O. Jaroš, *Slovenské robotníctvo v boji o moc, 1944–1948 [The Slovak Workers in the Struggle for Power, 1944–1948]* (Bratislava, 1965), p. 69.

28. Luža, *The Transfer*, p. 262.

29. Ibid., pp. 271, 291; Karel Kaplan, "Rok československé revoluce 1945" ["Year of the Czechoslovak Revolution"], *Sborník historický*, 15 (1967), p. 115.

30. Juraj Zvara in *Historický časopis*, No. 1 (1964), 28–49, and in *Příspěvky k dějinám KSČ* (June 1965), 409–27.

31. U.S. Department of State, *Foreign Relations of the United States 1946*. Vol. IV: *Paris Peace Conference: Documents* (Washington, 1970), 727–28; A. C. Leiss and R. Dennett, eds., *European Peace Treaties after World War II* (Boston, 1954), pp. 93–96.

32. For Article I of the Hungarian peace treaty, defining the bridgehead, see ibid., p. 274.

33. F. Němec and V. Moudrý, *The Soviet Siezure of Subcarpathian Ruthenia* (Toronto, 1955), pp. 251–53. For the text of the Soviet-Czechoslovak treaty of June 29, 1945, on the cession of Ruthenia, see *British State and Foreign Papers*, Vol. 145 (1943–45) (London, 1953), pp. 1096–98.

34. Opat, *O novou demokracii*, p. 69. For a good survey of the strength, aims, and leadership of the KSČ and all parties after liberation, see Belda, *Na rozhraní*, pp. 22–39. For the KSČ, see Zdeněk Eliáš and Jaromír Netík, "Czechoslovakia," in William E. Griffith, ed., *Communism in Europe. Continuity, Change, and the Sino-Soviet Dispute* (Cambridge, Mass., and London, 1966), II, *passim*.

35. Barto, *Riešenie*, pp. 98–100; Jarošová and Jaroš, *Slovenské robotníctvo*, p. 97. The resolution was implemented at a conference of the KSS at Žilina on August 11–13, 1945, when Široký replaced Karol Šmidke as chairman and Štefan Bašťovanský replaced Edo Friš as secretary of the party. Neither Šmidke nor Friš was a Slovak nationalist but both had been swept along by the nationalists since the Slovak uprising. Široký had not participated in the uprising, being in prison at the time. Of Slovak origin but a Magyar by education, he was a bitter enemy of Slovak nationalists whether in or out of the party. The true spokesman of the nationalists in the KSS, Gustáv Husák, saved himself, for the moment, by abjuring nationalism—also for the moment—and turning on his wartime nationalist allies, the Slovak Democrats.

36. In Slovakia 25.58 percent of the population derived an income from industry, mining, and the trades, compared to 39.5 percent in Bohemia and Moravia. On the other hand, 52.59 percent of the Slovak population worked in agriculture, forestry, and fisheries, while only 20.37 percent of the population of the Czech provinces did. See Jarošová and Jaroš, *Slovenské robotníctvo*, p. 65.

37. June, 1945, the prominent communist trade unionist Antonín Zápotocký became chairman of the ROH. The membership amounted to 2,249,976 on December 31, 1947. See V. Pachman, "Boj o odborovou jednotu v letech 1945–1948" ["Struggle for the Unity of the Trade Union Movement in 1945–1948"], *Československý časopis historický*, VIII, No. 6 (1960), 810.

38. Czechoslovakia was the second state after the U.S.S.R. to nationalize its industry and banks.

39. Opat, *O novou demokracii*, p. 115; Kaplan, *Znárodnění*, pp. 7–58.

40. Marta Vartíková, *Od Košíc po február* [*From Košice to February*] (Bratislava, 1968), p. 71. Jaroslav Nedvěd, "Cesta ke sloučení sociální demokracie s komunistickou stranou" ["The Road to the Merger of the Social Democratic and Communist Parties"], *Rozpravy Československé Akademie věd*, No. 8 (1968), 46–48.

41. Opat, *O novou demokracii*, pp. 162–66; Belda, *Na rozhraní*, p. 70; Vartíková, *Od Košíc*, p. 78.

42. Vartíková, *Od Košíc*, pp. 74–77.

43. Barto, *Riešenie*, pp. 138–47; Falťan, *Slovenská otázka*, pp. 216–17.

**103   Charles S. Maier**

44. Hubert Ripka, *Le Coup de Prague: Une révolution préfabriquée* (Paris, 1949), p. 39.
45. Belda, *Na rozhraní*, p. 60.
46. Ibid., pp. 72–73; Opat, *O novou demokracii*, pp. 178–89.
47. The same factors operated against the communists, to a smaller extent, in Moravia. The communist share of the vote in Moravia was 34.5 percent as against 43.3 percent in Bohemia.
48. Belda, *Na rozhraní*, p. 74.
49. Vartíková, *Od Košíc*, p. 80; Jarošová and Jaroš, *Slovenské robotníctvo*, p. 157; Barto, *Riešenie*, p. 159.
50. Barto, *Riešenie*, p. 160; Belda, *Na rozhraní*, p. 80.
51. Belda, *Na rozhraní*, p. 83; Opat, *O novou demokracii*, pp. 193–95; Barto, *Riešenie*, pp. 170–71; Falťan, *Slovenská otázka*, p. 222. For the Czecho-Slovak negotiations in the National Front, see the informative article by Miroslav Bouček and Miloslav Klimeš, "Národní fronta Čechů a Slováků v letech 1946–1948" ["The National Front of the Czech and Slovaks in the Years 1946–48"], *Sborník historický*, 20 (1973), 207–14.
52. Opat, *O novou demokracii*, pp. 135–36.
53. Gottwald on July 8, 1946, in presenting the "construction program" of his new government to the National Assembly. See Opat, *O novou demokracii*, pp. 197–200. Also in September, 1946, and on October 4, 1946.
54. Ibid., pp. 191–96; Belda, *Na rozhraní*, pp. 84–86. While claiming the premiership and a proportionate share of posts in the central government, the communists were extremely reluctant to accept the results of the elections in the Slovak National Council and the board of commissioners. It was not until August 7, after bitter wrangling between the KSS and the DS, that the DS was allowed to take 60 percent of the seats in the SNR and 9 out of 15 posts on the board of commissioners. The communists fought tooth and nail against relinquishing the commissariat of interior, which controlled the police. In the end they agreed to relinquish it, not to a DS member but to a nonparty expert, Gen. Mikuláš Ferjenčík. Moreover, contrary to the principle that the strongest party should get the chairmanship of the board, which Gottwald had invoked to claim the premiership, this important post was retained by the communist Husák. See Vartíková, *Od Košíc*, pp. 109–11; Jarošová and Jaroš, *Slovenské robotníctvo*, p. 163.
55. James F. Byrnes, *Speaking Frankly* (New York, 1947), pp. 143–44; Ripka, *Le Coup*, p. 41. In addition to the insult at the peace conference, the Americans were angered by a Czechoslovak deal with Rumania, under which Prague resold American goods to the Rumanians at a profit, and by the Czechoslovak failure to compensate American citizens for the loss of property in Czechoslovakia through nationalization. The American rebuff was a great blow to Masaryk, who had to explain it in a secret cabinet meeting on October 7. See Belda, *Na rozhraní*, pp. 120–21; U.S. Department of State, *Foreign Relations of the United States 1946*, Vol. VI: *Eastern Europe: The Soviet Union* (Washington, 1969), pp. 216, 220ff.
56. Belda, *Na rozhraní*, p. 95; Opat, *O novou demokracii*, p. 204.

57. Belda, *Na rozhraní*, pp. 172–73.

58. Jaroslav Opat, "K metodě studia a výkladu některých problémů v období 1945–1948" ["On the Method of Study and Explanation of Some Problems in the Period of 1945–1948"], *Příspěvky dějinám KSČ* (February, 1965), 65–83.

59. Belda, *Na rozhraní*, pp. 121–22; Opat, *O novou demokracii*, pp. 236–38.

60. Ripka, *Le Coup*, pp. 51–55. Apparently, the Czechoslovak acceptance of the invitation to go to Paris was in part a result of a misunderstanding brought about by Soviet inefficiency. Masaryk sought advance Soviet approval for accepting the invitation, but Bodrov, the Soviet chargé d'affaires in Prague, lacked instructions. Failing to get a reply from Moscow in time, the Czechoslovak government announced its acceptance—only to be told by Moscow that it must not go to Paris. See Belda, *Na rozhraní*, pp. 122–25. Masaryk, who clung to relations with the West, was crushed by the humiliation. For more information see Josef Belda et al., "K otázce účasti Československa na Marshallově plánu" ["On the Question of the Czechoslovak Participation at the Marshall Plan"], *Revue dějin socialismu*, VIII (1968), 81–100.

61. *For a Lasting Peace, for a People's Democracy*, November 10, 1947.

62. Eugenio Reale, who participated at the conference as the delegate of the Communist party of Italy, in Milorad Drachkovitch and Branko Lazitch, eds., *The Comintern: Historical Highlights* (New York, 1966), p. 260.

63. Vladimir Dedijer, *Tito* (New York, 1953), p. 292.

64. The minutes of E. Reale in Drachkovitch and Lazitch, *The Comintern*, p. 254; Jarošová and Jaroš, *Slovenské robotníctvo*, p. 232.

65. Conference of the Nine Communist Parties, p. 118, quoted in Korbel, *Communist Subversion*, p. 186.

66. Nedvěd, "Cesta ke sloučení," p. 56; Belda, *Na rozhraní*, pp. 154–67; Opat, *O novou demokracii*, pp. 242–45.

67. For the Slovak November crisis see Jarošová and Jaroš, *Slovenské robotníctvo*, pp. 221–52; Vartíková, *Od Košic*, pp. 147–62; Lettrich, *History*, pp. 249–51. For Gottwald's formula to solve the crisis, see Václav Král, ed., *Cestou k únoru* [*The Road to February*] (Prague, 1963), p. 270.

68. Nedvěd, "Cesta ke sloučení," pp. 58–59.

69. The KSČ raised demands for the nationalization of private trade and for new land reform. In February, 1948, it was defeated in an attempt to prevent an increase in the salaries of public servants. It continued to use the security apparatus to increase pressure, and managed to hush up an investigation of the attempt against the lives of three democratic ministers.

70. According to a confidential survey of public opinion taken by the communist-controlled Ministry of Information, the KSČ faced a loss of eight to ten percent in the next election. See Ripka, *Le Coup*, p. 190.

71. Miroslav Bouček, *Praha v únoru* [*Prague in February*] (Prague, 1963), pp. 25, 149; Karel Kaplan in *Historica* (Prague, 1963), V, 241.

72. The literature on the February crisis is quite extensive. Among the communist accounts and documentary collections are: Belda, *Na rozhraní*, pp. 223–62; Bouček, *Praha*, pp. 143–254, and *Únor 1948: Sborník doku-*

*mentů* [*February 1948: A Collection of Documents*] (Prague, 1958); Král, *Cestou,* pp. 329–410; Miroslav Bouček and Miloslav Klimeš, *Dramatické dnú února 1948* [*The Dramatic Days of February, 1948*] (Prague, 1973), *passim;* Jiři Veselý, *Prague 1948* (Paris, 1958), pp. 71–190, which is a French adaptation of his *Kronika únorových dnů* [*Chronicle of the February Days*] (Prague, 1958); and Alois Svoboda *et al., Jak to bylo v únoru* [*What Happened in February*] (Prague, 1949), *passim.* A Czech National Socialist account may be found in Ripka, *Le Coup,* pp. 201–316, of which there is an English translation, *Czechoslovakia Enslaved* (London, 1950), and a Social Democratic one in Bohumil Laušman, *Kdo byl vinen?* [*Who is to Blame?*] (Vienna, n.d.), pp. 108–54. President Beneš's side of the story is told in detail by the head of his chancellery, Jaromír Smutný, in "Únorový převrat 1948" ["February Revolution, 1948"], *Doklady a Rozpravy,* Nos. 12 (1953); 19 (1955); 21 (1955); 25 (1956); and 28 (1957); published by the Institute of Dr. Edvard Beneš in London. For Steinhardt's report of the February coup, see *Foreign Relations of the United States, 1948,* 9 vols. (Washington, 1974), IV, 738–756. Accounts by Western scholars may be found in Korbel, *Communist Subversion,* pp. 206–35, and Paul E. Zinner, *Communist Strategy and Tactics in Czechoslovakia, 1918–1948* (New York, 1963), pp. 204–16. The most recent analysis was given by Pavel Tigrid, "The Prague Coup of 1948: The Elegant Takeover," in Thomas T. Hammond, ed., *The Anatomy of Communist Takeovers* (New Haven and London, 1975), pp. 399–432. Among the numerous accounts by Western journalists, perhaps the best may be found in Dana Adams Schmidt, *Anatomy of a Satellite* (Boston, 1952), pp. 108–21.

73. Report of ČTK, the Czechoslovak News Agency, in Král, *Cestou,* p. 347. Steinhardt informed Czechoslovak officials that the United States would consider favorably an application for a credit of $25 million to purchase American cotton. See Schmidt, *Anatomy,* p. 110. Although Czechoslovakia experienced great economic difficulties at the time, the economic weapon was quite inadequate to affect the crisis.

74. According to Belda, *Na rozhraní,* p. 265, Zorin assured Gottwald that "the Soviet Union would not allow Western powers to interfere in the internal affairs of Czechoslovakia." Since, however, none of the Western powers intervened in the crisis, the Soviet Union did not have to do so either. Although the crisis had international repercussions, it was a purely internal one.

75. The purge involved some 28,000 persons. See Karel Kaplan, *Utváření generální linie výstavby socialismu v Československu* [*The Formation of the General Line of the Construction of Socialism in Czechoslovakia*] (Prague, 1966), p. 27.

76. Kaplan, *Historica,* V, 250ff.

77. For the Slovak side of the crisis see Vartíková, *Od Košíc,* pp. 181–84; Jarošová and Jaroš, *Slovenské robotníctvo,* pp. 265–67; Lettrich, *History,* pp. 259–60.

# 4

**Daniel Yergin**

# Shattered Peace: The Origins of the Cold War and the National Security State

*Daniel Yergin's recent study of cold-war origins is one of the most rewarding narrative syntheses since the stately work of Herbert Feis—* Churchill-Roosevelt-Stalin *(Princeton, 1957);* Between War and Peace: The Potsdam Conference *(Princeton, 1960); and the lesser* From Trust to Terror *(New York: Norton, 1970)—and William H. McNeill—* America, Britain, and Russia: Their Cooperation and Conflict, 1941–46 *(New York: Oxford University Press, 1953). Yergin enjoyed the advantage of access to British and American documentary collections that were closed to McNeill and only partially available to Feis. On the other hand, the earlier authors still convey a solidity and massiveness that Yergin's focus on personality and anecdote cannot rival. Admittedly the very colorfulness of Yergin's narrative can be misleading. In other chapters of his book Yergin dissects the bureaucratic and not merely personal inputs to American policy: the long-ripening "Riga axioms" within the State Department that predisposed U.S. policy toward distrust of Moscow, or the pressure of the aviation industry and the Air Force for a remilitarized United States. Further historical work must now focus even more carefully on these organizational determinants of United States conduct.*

*Yergin's political judgments are also nuanced. By his critical focus on American policy the author naturally conveys a revisionist stance. Nevertheless, he realizes that Soviet sources might suggest a different story, and he constantly stresses the repressiveness of Stalin's regime— in part perhaps to disarm orthodox critics, in part because he believes the Soviets might well have been repressive without being expansionist. The question remains whether a dictator who sought such oppressive*

*security at home would really have remained tolerant of the ambiguity
of pluralist regimes on his borders. The story is still ex* parte, *although
it is illusory to believe that even if we someday have Soviet archives
open to us, questions of intention can be fully resolved.*

*Daniel Yergin is a researcher with the Harvard Center for
International Affairs and the Harvard Business School. In addition to
his historical work, he writes frequently on international economic and
political affairs. This selection, chapter 12 of* Shattered Peace, *"The
Margin of Safety," is reprinted with his permission and that of his
publisher, Houghton Mifflin Company.*

### The Margin of Safety

JAMES RESTON: The only weakness in what was otherwise a magnificent statement of the President—namely, that he gave the impression, rightly or wrongly, that the people who were going to
get help were the people who were in desperate straits and who
had an armed minority at their border; whereas I would like to
have seen him indicate that you can fight Communism in other
ways—in economic ways.

JAMES FORRESTAL: The core of the thing is are you going to try to
keep Germany a running boil with the pus exuding over the rest
of Europe?

Telephone conversation, March 13, 1947 [1]

Even as U.S. policymakers were formulating the Truman Doctrine,
they saw before them in Western Europe an economic crisis with
momentous political ramifications. Their response took the form of a
policy that answered several questions at once—what to do about
Germany? what to do about Western Europe? what to do about the
Soviet Union? The goals were several as well—the economic revival
of Western Europe, the creation of an environment hospitable to
democracy and capitalism in Western Europe, the maintenance of the
balance of power on the European continent, and the "containment" of
the Soviet Union and communism. The industrial might of western
Germany was presented as essential for the recovery of its noncommunist neighbors. In this way, with its firm entrenchment in a Europe-
wide framework, a reconstituted West Germany would become politically acceptable throughout the rest of Western Europe.

The chosen instrument for achieving these various goals was American economic power. "It is necessary," Harry Truman reminded
members of the Associated Press in April 1947, "that we develop a
new realization of the size and strength of our economy." [2] The

realization involved a subordination of international economics to international politics, an essential feature in the rise of the national security state. Prior to 1947, economic matter (involving trade as well as reconstruction) and political questions were usually dropped into different boxes, although that separation had eroded somewhat by 1946.

Official thought on international economic matters, coming out of the Second World War, had been obsessed with preparing for a multilateral world—that is, an open international trading system, free of tariffs and other restrictions, and unhindered by bilateral trade agreements. Despite disagreement about the importance of foreign trade to the postwar American economy, many assumed that the trade barriers of the 1930s had helped pave the way to the Second World War, and they wanted to avoid a rerun. Dominating the planning was a curious kind of optimism about how easy it was going to be to pass through what was loosely referred to as the "post-war transition" and get on to the main business of constructing the new multilateral trading world.

This is not to say that American officials ignored the damage done by war. In his diary, for instance, Henry Stimson recorded his shock at the "powerful picture of the tough situation" that John McCloy brought back from a trip to Germany in April 1945—a scene of devastation that suggested itself as "worse than anything probably that ever happened in the world."

In general, however, the officials in Washington who managed policy at the conclusion of the war and immediately afterward tended to discount the pressing problems symbolized by the urban rubble, which, like graveyards, dotted the Continent. Those who worked abroad, in public and private capacities, took more seriously the effects of the wartime trauma and the depths of the postwar problems. In February 1946, Colonel Sosthenes Behn, founder of International Telephone and Telegraph, wandered into the offices of his New York bank, J. P. Morgan, "very blue about the foreign outlook." Behn said that he "liquidated every foreign property that he could as fast as he could." His hope—"to build up a big domestic company." [3] A couple of months later, E. F. Penrose, an American economics official based in London, was struck on returning to Washington by "the attitude of rather casual and easy optimism about European revival in many Washington circles." In 1946, the State Department put more attention and more staff to work on an international trade charter and tariff reduction than on relief and reconstruction. The Administration was relieved to be done with UNRRA, the United Nations relief organization, which was too independent of Washington and too controversial with many congressmen. Also, perhaps, a strong element of wishful

thinking influenced the tendency to underestimate the task of reconstruction; for even before the war was over, officials had already
concluded the postwar assistance programs would arouse considerable
domestic opposition.[4]

At the end of 1945, an unexpectedly grave food crisis gave the
first major signal that the "post-war transition" might prove much
more treacherous than the blueprints had allowed. By early 1946,
more than 125 million Europeans were subsisting on no more than
2000 calories a day; many of those millions, on no more than 1000—
in grim contrast to the 3300 calories a day that was the average in the
United States.[5]

In response, Truman, in the spring of 1946, sent Herbert Hoover
on another of the former President's regular spring forays into foreign policy, this time to survey famine conditions abroad. After World
War I, Hoover had proved himself not only an expert famine relief
administrator in Europe, but also an excellent strategist in using food
to contain communism, and he was welcomed back into policy councils with something like religious awe. Foreshadowing what was to
become a common theme in the next year, he argued, both publicly
and privately, not only in Washington but also as he toured abroad,
that economic distress should be evaluated in terms of conflict with the
Soviet Union. Like Forrestal, he even felt the need to warn the Pope
that "Catholicism in Europe was in the gravest danger from the Communist invasion, the gates of which would be wide open from starva-
tion." Hoover sketched a similar scene for Attlee, but was somewhat
disappointed when the only response from the British Prime Minister
was, "This has been very interesting" and "I shall be seeing you at
lunch." [6]

The food crisis eased later in 1946, temporarily at least, and optimism quickly returned to American leaders. Industrial production
picked up in Europe—for instance, by 1947, Holland had exceeded
prewar averages—and officials on both sides of the Atlantic were sure
that the worst was past. On October 5, 1946, Hugh Dalton noted
that he and Will Clayton "are agreed that UNRRA must definitely
stop, as arranged, in the next year, and that, apart from the Germans,
only Italy, Austria and Greece should rank for further doles from
either the U.S. or U.K." [7] Then came a crisis so serious that, in
itself, it pushed the polarization between East and West to the point
of virtual partition of Europe.

The crisis had been pending, brought on not only by the visible
destruction—the dead and injured, the apartments burned out, the
factories flattened, the railway bridges destroyed—but also by invisible
devastation. Capital equipment was obsolete and worn out. The labor

forces in Europe were exhausted, undernourished, and disorganized. Technical skills had been lost. Such reconstruction as had taken place created a great hunger for American goods, and so aggravated the problems. And then the weather—droughts in the summers of 1946 and 1947 and what has been called a Siberian winter in between— brought conditions to a crisis point. The weather, to be sure, was not the cause of this crisis, but rather, the precipitant.

For clarity's sake, we might see the picture in three panels. The first was the food and raw materials crisis that had been mounting through 1946. Western Europe was no longer able to obtain food stores from traditional sources in Eastern Europe and the Far East. In Western Europe, soil fertility had declined markedly, and the traditional market links between town and country had been sundered. European wheat production in 1947 fell to less than half of what it had been in 1938. British coal production in 1946 was 20 percent lower than it had been in 1938; in the western parts of Germany, the output of coal was only two-fifths of what it had been in 1938.

Second, the war had broken established habits and patterns of economic activity within Europe and between Europe and the rest of the world. The Europeans were not able to sell to former customers abroad. American efforts to penetrate the sterling bloc of the British Empire aggravated Britain's economic problems. The successful insistence by the U.S. that the British make the pound convertible in the summer of 1947 created an immediate, massive, and worldwide rush from pounds to dollars, and so made matters much worse. The most important of all the economic dislocations involved the collapse of Germany, which had formerly played a central role in Europe as both importer and exporter. Before the war, the three Western zones alone had been the source of one-fifth of all industrial production in Europe; in the immediate postwar years, production there barely reached a third of those prewar levels.[8]

But, in 1947, the heart of the problem was a financial crisis. Part of the problem was inflation—wholesale prices had risen 80 percent in France during 1946. Such inflation led to strikes and promoted instability. Even more important was the need to find a way to finance both the equipment necessary for reconstruction and the food and other raw materials that Europe needed to obtain from the United States. The trade balance between the United States and Europe was not at all in balance. In 1947, the United States exported to Europe almost seven times as much as it imported from Europe. This seemed to indicate a worsening trend, for U.S. imports from Europe had actually declined between 1946 and 1947, while the demand for U.S. exports—both manufactures and commodities—was increasing.

Meanwhile, inflation in the United States, which Washington started to see as a serious problem in March 1947, widened the gap. Wholesale prices in the United States rose 40 percent between June 1946 and September 1947. By the second quarter of 1947, the U.S. export surplus was running at a staggering annual rate of $12.5 billion.

How could Europe finance its vital purchases from the United States? Lend-lease had long since ended; UNRRA would cease in mid-1947; other credits were being drawn down. The foreign assets of the European countries were disappearing; and they had lost a very substantial part of the invisible earnings that had formerly flowed in from overseas investments, shipping, insurance, and so forth. They were unable to sell goods to traditional markets elsewhere in the world and indeed these former markets themselves were now lining up in competition with the Europeans for the product of the American machine.

The result became known as the "dollar shortage" or the "dollar gap." The only way the Europeans could continue to buy was if the U.S. financed the purchases in some fashion.[9]

"The dollar shortage is developing everywhere in the world," British Chancellor Hugh Dalton complained in the spring of 1947. "The Americans have half the total income of the world, but won't either spend it in buying other people's goods or lending it or giving it away on a sufficient scale. The Fund and the Bank still do nothing. How soon will this dollar shortage bring a general crisis?" [10]

When the Americans finally perceived the crisis, they responded with alacrity, driven at times by something akin to panic, especially as they measured the problem against what they perceived as Soviet intentions. "I am deeply disturbed by the present world picture, and its implications for our country," Will Clayton noted, a week before the Truman Doctrine speech. "The reins of world leadership are fast slipping from Britain's competent but now very weak hands. These reins will be picked up either by the United States or Russia." But the United States could not assume this leadership "unless the people of the United States are shocked into doing so." He was not suggesting that they be deceived, but only that they be led to see the "truth" as seen by Administration officials and as reported "in the cables which daily arrive at the State Department from all over the world. In every country in the Eastern Hemisphere and most of the countries of the Western Hemisphere, Russia is boring from within." The key lay in providing the dollars necessary to finance recovery and thus underwrite political stability.[11]

By this point, the Americans were consciously turning away from trying to make the Great Power consortium work. Dean Acheson made this point on April 18 (while Marshall was still in Moscow) when he explained that diplomacy and negotiations, what he called the first of the country's instruments for carrying out its foreign policy, had not succeeded in building "with the Soviet Union that mutual trust and confidence and cessation of expansionism which must be the foundation of political stability. We have concluded, therefore, that we msut use to an increasing extent our *second* instrument of foreign policy, namely, economic power, in order to call an effective halt to the Soviet Union's expansionism and political infiltration, and to create a basis for political stability and economic well-being." [12] In other words, Acheson was saying that the Rooseveltian approach had failed; containment, economic to begin with, was the appropriate course.

George Marshall arrived at a similar conclusion three days before Acheson's speech. As a result of his April 15 meeting with Stalin, the Secretary became convinced that the Russians were stalling, waiting for an easy victory in Europe. On his way home from Moscow, Marshall stopped for two hours at Tempelhof Airport in Berlin. There he instructed Clay to push economic revival in Bizonia. Back in Washington, the Secretary met a few journalists in an off-the-record session. "Marshall kept talking about Western Europe, especially France and Germany," James Reston noted.

Marshall ordered that more effort in the State Department be put into the staffwork for a new kind of aid program that would become known as the Marshall Plan. It was to be continental in scope (or at least half-continental), a point he had emphasized as early as February. And it was to cover the entire range of European economic problems. "We can no longer nibble at the problem and then nag the American people on the basis of recurring crises," observed Robert Lovett, who succeeded Acheson as Undersecretary in early summer. He added, "It is equally apparent that the Congress will not make funds available unless there is some reasonable expectation that the expenditure of these funds will produce more visible results; or alternatively, unless it can be shown that the failure to expend these funds will produce calamitous circumstances affecting our national security and our economic and social welfare." [13]

The Marshall Plan had two basic aims, which commingled and cannot really be separated—to halt a feared communist advance into Western Europe, and to stabilize an international economic environment favorable to capitalism. It was not much tied to any concerns about an impending American depression, which was what the Russians claimed at the time, and as some recent writers have argued. Such a case exaggerates both the importance and the general need that was felt for overseas markets. For instance, the export surplus of the United States with Europe in 1946 and 1947 accounted for just 2 percent of the U.S. gross national product. In fact, influential leaders like Harriman and Hoover explicitly supported increasing the output of the German steel industry so that the American steel industry would not become too dependent on the export market. The Council of Economic Advisers reported to President Truman in October that foreign aid, insofar as it financed exports, provided both "a temporary prop to the domestic market" and "an additional strain." [14]

As should be clear, the anticommunist consensus was, by this time, so wide that there was little resistance or debate about fundamental assumptions. One State Department official, for instance, described the "departmental frame of mind" as follows: "The failure to reach agreement on Germany at Moscow was due primarily to Soviet anticipation of continued deterioration in France, Italy and Western Germany plus hope for a U.S. depression. It was essential to improve the Western European situation in order to prevent further weakening in our bargaining power."

Here was a focus for the expansive doctrine of national security. Under George Kennan, the new Policy Planning Staff came to general agreement on May 15 "that the main problem in United States security today is to bring into acceptable relationship the economic distress abroad with the capacity and willingness of the United States to meet it effectively and speedily." American officials worked in an atmosphere of increasing tension. Ambassador Walter Bedell Smith, home on leave, told senior military intelligence officers in the War Department on May 16; "There are no limits to the Soviet objectives. Statements made by Lenin to the effect that a great struggle between Communism and capitalism will take place and that one or the other must go down are still being reiterated by Stalin." He added, "They have no inhibitions." Officials were more and more worried.[15]

Similar fears were becoming increasingly common outside government. Unless something were done soon to arrest the decline in confidence, businessmen would clearly make individual decisions that, in sum, would only speed Europe toward a collapse. "Everything I heard and read—and I hear and read a lot—points to the gravity of food, fuel, finance and communism impending in France," wrote Russell Leffingwell of the Morgan Bank in May. "It is a matter of great practical business importance to this bank. We cannot afford to have the Paris officers and directors living in an unreal Pollyanna dream, and we think it most important they should understand the gravity of the risks, and conduct their business accordingly."

No encouraging signs appeared in May. So short was the food supply in Germany and Austria that rations had fallen below the official level of 1550 calories—down to 1220 in some regions, even to 900 in others. "We do not see why you have to read *The New York Times* to know the Germans are close to starving," General Clay angrily cabled the War Department in May from Berlin. "The crisis is now, not in July."

The Americans feared that the Soviet Union would exploit the economic crisis to extend its political control over the rest of Europe.[16] But was this truly Moscow's goal? It seems unlikely. Certainly, the Truman Doctrine had been read and annotated very carefully in Moscow. Yet, despite its evangelical tone, its clear promise to use American economic power for explicit American political goals, and its establishment of American military power close to the Soviet periphery in Turkey, it was obviously understood by the Russians to be confined in operation chiefly to Greece, which was an area Stalin had deeded to the West. Stalin still seemed interested in maintaining the consortium, and his public statements represented that interest. If he could have at low cost pushed communism—or, to be more precise, extended *his* power—into Western Europe, no doubt he would have done exactly that. But he always had a tendency to exaggerate the strength of his enemies. Within the Soviet Union, where the balance of forces was in his favor, he had destroyed them; in international politics, where the balance was at best uncertain, he respected their power and tried to bluff and do business with them, and consolidate his own position, all at the same time. Perhaps he was more impressed by American power in the immediate postwar years than were the anxious American policymakers. Not only did the United States wield enormous economic strength, but its air power and the atomic bomb made up at least in the short term for the absence of a large American land army in Europe. He no doubt recognized that a major communist military or political assault in Western Europe would have generated an all-too-strong and unpredictable reaction in the United States. After all, the Americans had just intervened in Europe for the second time in less than three decades over the question of the balance of power on the Continent. Stalin presumably did not take too seriously the talk in the United States of preventive war, though no doubt he did take note of it. He also knew that, if circumstances changed, it could become a more immediate topic. In ordering the Yugoslavs to end their assistance in the Greek civil war, Stalin declared, as already noted, that Britain and the United States—"the United States, the most powerful state in the world"—would never permit their lines of communication in the Mediterranean to be broken. What he said about the American reaction to a communist victory in Greece could have been multiplied by ten for communist moves in France or Italy.[17]

Similarly, Stalin was not going to relinquish his sphere. The wartime Grand Alliance had been an international popular front. As its legacy and mirror, it had left behind national popular fronts, coalitions of communists and noncommunists. This was the case in Western Europe, in France and Italy, and also the case, although in far more difficult circumstances, in Eastern Europe, to varying degrees in Czechoslovakia, Hungary, even Poland. As the Grand Alliance fissured, such coalitions became anomalies, and coalition members on one side of the dividing line in Europe who were allied to forces on the other were regarded as fifth columnists, traitors-in-place. So strong was the memory of the Comintern that the Americans could not see clearly the advantages of dealing with national communist parties, of recognizing them as entities independent of Moscow, of using U.S. economic power to build a bridge across the chasm.

The worsening economic situation made the coalitions in Western Europe increasingly unstable.* Washington explained to the French and the Italians that economic aid was much more likely if (as the American ambassador in Italy put it), they "would find the means of correcting the present situation." Correction followed. The communists, though fighting hard to remain in the French and Italian governments, were pushed out of both in May 1947. A couple of days after the exclusion of the communists in France, John McCloy, the new president of the World Bank, announced a major loan to France.[18]

Stalin's answer came at the end of May—though it is still unclear whether this was a genuine response, a coincidence, or whether the Russians cynically used the changes in France and Italy as a pretext for their own purposes. In late 1945, under Soviet tutelage, the Hungarians had elected a noncommunist majority, with the leading role played by the Smallholders party. The country was governed by what the State Department privately called "a moderate coalition cabinet." The situation did not last. In February 1947, the former secretary-general of the Smallholders was arrested, allegedly confessed to espionage, and disappeared. Many in Hungary took as a very important signal the fact that his arrest had been carried out not by local security forces, but by the Red Army itself. In May, Premier Ferenc Nagy was impli-

---

* Of course, having communists in the Western European coalition governments did create problems. "We can't carry on a discussion between two Great Powers," Bevin had complained to Bidault, "with a third Great Power in the cupboard with a listening device."

cated in the "confession," chose exile, and the communists very much tightened their control over the Hungarian government. This was only the most obvious example of how the Soviets were now consolidating their hold over Eastern Europe in the context of international polarization. Poland, for instance, had been the first issue to seriously divide the members of the Grand Alliance, long before the war's end. In January 1947, it was resolved, in a fashion. That country had remained in a very unsettled domestic condition since the German defeat. As election day approached, the communists became ruthless against their opponents, the elections themselves were fraudulent, and the communist-dominated "Democratic Bloc" won an overwhelming majority in the parliament.

Polarization was having its influence in the West, as well, but there the now-excluded communist parties continued to function, protected by law. In Hungary, as elsewhere in Eastern Europe, terror was added to expulsion, with the consequent destruction not only of the noncommunist parties, but also of noncommunist politicians.

Most American officials saw the takeover in Hungary as further proof of Soviet expansionism. "You no doubt realize the extent to which this issue has rocked the Department," Harold Vedeler of the Central European Division wrote in August 1947 to Ambassador Steinhardt in Prague. "At the time the coup occurred many meetings and extended discussions were required before the Department was able to come to a conclusion on sending a note of protest rather than to take the matter to the Security Council at once." One of the reasons for not going to the Security Council was a desire to "concentrate on our Greek policy." Another was that if the Americans sought to have the Russians censured "for unilateral actions" in the Allied Control Council in Hungary, then "the Soviets might level counter charges against us concerning MacArthur's actions in Japan."

One could have viewed the events in Hungary in a less alarmist fashion—while not minimizing the internal consequences, still seeing it as a defensive, even conservative move on Stalin's part. Within the State Department some tried with no success to make that argument. "The Communist coup in Hungary is not 'a critical act of the struggle of Communism and Western Democracy for the control of Europe' but is rather a routine and anticipated move on the part of the USSR to plug an obvious gap in its security system," suggested H. Stuart Hughes, head of the Division of Research on Europe in the State Department. "It was not the democratic character of the Hungarian government that brought down upon it the wrath of the Soviet Union. It was its foreign policy of cultivating the favor of the Western democracies, particularly the United States. The Hungarian statesmen of the

Smallholders Party simply refused to do as the Czech leaders had done and to recognize the geographic and strategic realities that had placed their country within the Soviet sphere of influence and the consequent suicidal character of a pro-Western foreign policy." Hughes added that, if nothing more, "the Truman doctrine accelerated the process" of communization, for "the removal of the Communist ministers from the governments of France and Italy indicated that this doctrine was receiving a practical political interpretation in the West." [19]

As they devised this ambitious program of economic assistance for a prostrate polarized Europe, the Americans saw four challenges: first, to get the Europeans to create a cooperative plan that would move beyond relief to revitalization; second, to avoid the kind of criticism that had accumulated around the Truman Doctrine, of being too negative and too nakedly anticommunist; third, to keep the Russians out of the program; and, fourth, to get the Congress into the plan by winning its approval.

Marshall unveiled the concept in a speech at the Harvard Commencement on June 5, 1947. With his remarks, the State Department forestalled some of the sort of criticism that had hurt the Greek-Turkish program. Marshall sketched the picture of European collapse; called for a program of reconstruction, not relief; asked the Europeans to take the initiative; and invited all nations to participate, which meant that the Soviet Union was implicitly included in the invitation.[20]

The open invitation, however, was a ploy. The prospect that Russia might actually accept greatly alarmed the Americans, who had already written off the Economic Commission for Europe because of Soviet participation. But they had not wanted to bear the onus of excluding Russia from the proposed program. That would have created political problems in Western Europe. The U.S. might have been viewed as the power that had partitioned Europe. (Onus-shifting was one of the main goals of diplomacy and propaganda in these years, with each side trying to convince the international galleries that all blame for dividing the Continent lay with the other.) On the other hand, the Americans were hardly disposed to grant any aid to Russia for fear that it would try to immobilize any program it did join, and they were also convinced that Soviet participation would be the quickest way to assure congressional rejection. As Bohlen put it a few years later, they had taken "a hell of a big gamble" in not explicitly excluding Russia.

Their concern mounted when Molotov arrived in Paris at the end of June with upward of a hundred advisers, to join Bevin and Bidault in preliminary discussions on a European program. "I am deeply concerned about the next six months," Forrestal said on July 2, "and I've got one eye on what's going on in Paris and what I think will be the alternative if the result I hope eventuates from that—namely—that the Russians don't come in. I think the most disastrous thing would be if they did." [21] But the Americans could have been more confident than they were. The odds were in their favor. "In the discussion of any concrete proposals touching on American aid to Europe," read the internal instructions for the Russian group, "the Soviet delegation shall object in terms of aid that might prejudice the sovereignty of the European countries or infringe upon their economic independence." What that meant became evident when Molotov offered his own plan in the preliminary discussions: each country to draw up a list of its needs, and then ask the United States to come up with the requisite money. But it was clear to all the delegates in Paris that in exchange for aid the United States would insist on inspection, considerable disclosure, and cooperation, and that both the British and the French would agree to that approach, and that the Russians would not. As we shall see, the Russians were also concerned about the effect of such a program on their hold over Eastern Europe, and they realized that it would almost certainly deny them reparations from the Western zones of Germany. Moreover, in the American scheme the Russians might actually have been required to provide raw materials to Western Europe.

Molotov, according to Djilas, considered accepting an invitation to the follow-up planning conference, so that he could then stage a walk-out, but was overruled by Moscow; and so, on July 2, Molotov and his delegation packed up and speedily departed Paris and the preliminary meeting, blasting American imperialism on the way out.[22]

The Americans had hoped, however, that some of the Eastern European countries would participate in the program. In this regard, the Marshall Plan was the last great effort, using the powerful and attractive magnetism of the American economy, to draw these countries out of the Soviet orbit. The effort represented a reversal. In 1946, Washington had very consciously restricted and tightened aid and refused to give credits in an ill-conceived attempt to force those countries to break formally with the Soviet Union on foreign policy issues.[23]

Responding to Marshall's speech, Poland indicated that it might attend the Europe-wide conference that was to open in Paris on July 12. Certainly Poland's needs were great. UNRRA had estimated that, after termination of its own program, Poland would require almost $300 million in relief in 1947 just to satisfy such basic needs as "the health and growth requirements of her children and mothers." In the middle of 1947, 80 percent of Warsaw remained in rubble; up to 30,000 corpses still lay buried beneath the ruins of the Warsaw Ghetto. Polish officials made clear that they wanted to trade with the West. And in fact Poland was still trying, under its communist leaders to pursue a path somewhat independent of Moscow. Wladyslaw Gomulka, secretary-general of the Polish party, was not following the Soviet model. He even went so far, in May 1947, as to declare that Marxism "does not give us any ready, universal indication or recipe which can be made use of with an identifiable result, without regard to time, place, and the existing conditions." [24] More obviously than Poland, Czechoslovakia was trying to maintain an independent course. Foreign Minister Jan Masaryk was a guest on the yacht of the Norwegian foreign minister when word came through that Molotov had agreed to go to Paris. "Never in my life have I seen a man so happy as Masaryk," remembered the Norwegian minister. [25]

After their Paris walk-out, the Russians would hardly allow the nations of Eastern Europe to participate in the American scheme. The Poles abruptly announced on July 9 that they would not attend the follow-up conference that was to open three days later. For the Czechs, matters were more complicated. They had already said that they would attend the second meeting. Masaryk and the communist premier Klement Gottwald, in Moscow on other business, were suddenly summoned to the Kremlin. Stalin and Molotov, expressing "surprise" at the Czech intention, indicated that they understood at least part of the purpose of the Marshall Plan; for they reportedly "emphasized their conviction that the real aim of the Marshall Plan and the Paris Conference is to create a western bloc and isolate the Soviet Union . . . Even if the loans should be granted sometime in the future by America they would not be without decisive limitations on the political and economic independence of the recipients." Thus, said the Soviet leaders, Czech participation would be interpreted "as an act specifically aimed against the USSR."

The Czechs renounced their acceptance. [26]

The most important reason for the Soviets' rejection of the plan would seem to have been their fear that it would disrupt their sphere in Eastern Europe. Second, they saw the Marshall Plan as an alternative to reparations—but an alternative that might be of no benefit to them. It was less important that American economists would poke around in Soviet production statistics. And because the Russians rejected the plan, so did the Eastern Europeans.

"Perhaps in view of the manner in which the incident dramatically revealed the real position of Czechoslovakia in international affairs, there could be detected a certain sympathy in the Department for this country, or at least the moderates, which had not been apparent since the summer of 1946," commented Harold Vedeler of Central European Affairs. But the Czech "trip to Canossa," as Vedeler called it, also created an odd kind of pleasure in American policy councils, in effect, further proof of malignant Soviet intentions. "Russians smoked out in their relations with satellite countries," Kennan noted to Marshall. "Maximum strain placed on those relations." The Americans did not see the Soviet reaction to the Marshall Plan as a defensive move by a country that could hardly compete with the United States economically, but rather as a further indication of aggressive designs. "The Czechoslovak reversal on the Paris Conference, on Soviet orders, is nothing less than a declaration of war by the Soviet Union on the immediate issue of the control of Europe," commented Ambassador Smith in Moscow. "The lines are drawn." [27]

The most important line on the European map had been drawn two years before, in 1945. It divided Germany between East and West. This line was supposed to be temporary, in pencil, as it were. But now, in 1947, it was about to be permanently inked in. For the Marshall Plan also provided a solution to the vexing problem of what to do about Germany. The basic question had remained unanswered. Were the Four Powers (but principally the United States and the Soviet Union) to cooperate in policing and punishing the former Reich, or were the occupation zones in the former Reich to become potential allies for one side or the other in the developing confrontation? For many months, American opinion on Germany had been shifting steadily away from favoring cooperation with the Russians. The failure to agree on common policies with the Russians and the expenses and difficulties of the occupation encouraged the trend. Moreover, as Europe failed to revive economically, the conviction grew in the West that Germany would have to play a central role in Western European reconstruction.[28]

In the autumn of 1946, Americans had taken a step toward partition when they amalgamated the British and American zones to form Bizonia. The initial emphasis was on economic problems alone. The Americans studiously avoided giving Bizonia a political coloration, because, explained General Clay in September 1946, "We believe it would widen the gap between west and east." [29] But by the end of 1946, Americans, at least those within policy councils, were tending to see Germany as a battleground between East and West. In December, former general John Hilldring, now Assistant Secretary of State for Occupied Territories, provided the double rationale for Bizonia: "It will serve the purpose of getting the United States government out of the red in three years in Germany, and it will give us a climate in which to plant our political ideas in Germany." He added, "We are fighting all totalitarian concepts in Germany, Nazism and Communism."

The break-up in April 1947 of the Moscow Council of Foreign

Ministers meeting with no progress on Germany provided the impetus for the Americans to take the next steps. As Clay noted in early April, "My three weeks at Moscow convinced me that nothing of import will come from this conference other than to bring the issues squarely on the table." [30]

We must recognize, however, that "success" at Moscow might well have disturbed the Americans more than failure, for many feared that any compromise that maintained Four-Power unity would open the door to Soviet domination of Germany and the rest of Europe. "The present zonal basis will continue, which, I think, is good," Dulles wrote to Vandenberg during the Moscow Council. "It is useful to have more time to consolidate the Western zones and not expose them yet to Communist penetration." [31] Upon Marshall's return from Moscow, the reorientation of U.S. policy speeded up. The Americans put more emphasis on raising the level of industry and restoring production in Germany, and thought more about the possibilities of a West German state.[32]

But the efforts to push economic recovery in Germany continued to encounter already familiar obstacles. While the overall thrust was clear, implementation created conflict and confusion between the State and War Departments. Clay frequently became so riled that he almost habitually announced his imminent resignation. An ongoing controversy between the British and Americans over the "level of industry" and socialism in the Ruhr coal mines hindered the development of Bizonia. Moreover, the very idea of economic recovery generated much resistance, for the future of Germany remained a volatile issue. The Russians, of course, remained adamant on the subject of reparations and obsessively fearful of a revivified Germany. But U.S. encouragement of German recovery also stirred much opposition in Western Europe, especially France. In addition, the Western Europeans wanted their reparations from Germany. "We have had a stop order in effect on reparations from our zone since May 1946," John Steelman, a senior White House adviser, informed the President in the spring of 1947. "As a result, we are getting a great deal of the blame for the inability of many western European nations to restore their capital goods structure. Moreover, much of the German plant is standing idle and some is rusting away."

The apprehension about German recovery was also widespread in the United States, and reached some who were close to the President, such as Edwin Pauley, Truman's reparations adviser. In March 1947, Herbert Hoover, returning from a survey of Europe for the Administration in one of his annual forays into foreign policy, wrote a report urging that German recovery be given the highest priority. Hoover's proposals outraged Pauley, who warned the President that they "would restore Germany to the same dominant position of industrial power which it held before the war . . . I cannot avoid looking into the future and contemplating the Germany which this plan would produce—a Germany not merely as powerful industrially as the Germany of Hitler, but *more* powerful because of the incredible advances of science." No one doubted, of course, that *something* had to be done about Germany —and quickly. "We are reaching a point," John Steelman told the President, "where almost any action would be an improvement." But he added, "There must be other approaches to these problems than the revival of a German colossus along the lines suggested by Mr. Hoover." [33]

The Marshall Plan was that other approach, an alternative solution to the German problem. It reduced the tension over German recovery by placing that nation at the center of a Continent-wide effort. Without Germany, it was argued, Europe could never recover, and the Americans made clear to jittery Europeans that success in the Marshall Plan depended upon an economically vital Germany. Aid from the United States would compensate the Western Europeans for the reparations they would not be getting from Germany. Meanwhile, economic recovery would keep most of Germany looking to the West, and so integrated into a Western system. Here, then, were the central and double aims of the Marshall Plan—economic recovery and economic containment. Here, also, was a solution to the German Question. But, while the American occupation authorities had a plan for the political fusion of Bizonia that they had informally discussed with the British by August 1947, they were reluctant to go the whole distance and commit themselves to the establishment of a separate government in Western Germany, at least until after the next Council of Foreign Ministers meeting.[34]

By the terms of Marshall's offer, the Europeans (albeit abetted by American "friendly aid in the drafting") were to draw up the actual plan themselves. This they did, though not without difficulty. There was a certain degree of suspicion of American intentions. The British believed that the U.S. was trying to interfere with the Labour Party's welfare state program, and they also thought Washington had aggravated England's financial problems. Galloping inflation in the U.S. had certainly compounded the dollar shortage. Britain was "being rooked" by the Americans, Dalton complained at the end of July. "We should tell them that we were going to *stop buying* and keep them guessing for how long . . . The result of this would be to bring prices down." The French opposed a concentration on German recovery for powerful emotional, as well as strategic, reasons. It was feared that this issue, highly explosive in French domestic politics, could topple the government. In addition, France had hopes of replacing German steel production with its own.

There was a good deal of conflict within the American government, as well. The State Department needed to convince the War Department to integrate Bizonia formally into the planning for the Marshall Plan. At the end of August, Charles Bonesteel, who had moved over from War to State, provided Undersecretary Lovett with a script for a conference meant to persuade top-level War Department officials that Bizonia should become part of the Marshall Plan. In Bonesteel's dialogue and stage directions, we again see how officials polished their own beliefs, rather than fabricating fake ones, to sell policies: "Our approach should be more educational, with a slight dictatorial flavor . . . Chip and yourself present the broad global picture, bringing out the two-world assumption and the need to work on a tighter organization of the Soviet world. The importance of treating Europe west of the Iron Curtain on a regional basis should then be emphasized." After advising that "the budgetary nettle" be firmly grasped, Bonesteel moved to his climax. "We should then put forward the requirement that the German economic matters be discussed at Paris . . . Emphasis should be laid on the security aspect of drawing more closely to us the nations of Western Europe now wavering between communism and us. Throughout the presentation the strategic and security aspects should be underlined and emphasized at every opportunity."

As the Marshall Plan discussions proceeded, there was also disagreement within the State Department. Washington became unhappy with the excessive zeal applied to tariff reductions by one of the American officials who was helping to provide "friendly aid" by sitting in on the negotiations among the Europeans. Will Clayton—"Doctrinaire Willie," as Dalton had taken to calling him—was, in Washington's view, giving rather too much attention to reducing trade barriers, and U.S. officials exerted pressure "to bring Mr. Clayton fully in line with the departmental position." [35]

In mid-September, the sixteen Western European nations completed a proposal—with provisions to increase production and exports, create financial stability, and provide for increased economic cooperation. They forwarded it to the United States, and asked for twenty billion dollars over the next four years to pay for imports from America.

Despite efforts to deflect possible criticism of the proposal in Europe and the United States, American policymakers thought of the Marshall Plan as "a Truman Doctrine in Action" (in George Elsey's words).

That is, it was a countermove to Soviet expansionism. "The problem is Russia," War Secretary Robert Patterson wrote to a newspaper publisher in June 1947. The "real menace," he said, was "the basic belief of the ruling group in the USSR that a communist state cannot exist in the company of democratic states." He also noted how he had shifted from the Yalta to the Riga outlook: "I thought during the war that the belief had been abandoned, but apparently it is still part of the creed. It means aggression, of course." [36]

What Patterson was expressing, of course, was the shared view of the men within the Executive who were making U.S. foreign policy. But now their common outlook was given formal, public, and even elegant statement. The prestigious journal *Foreign Affairs* published in its July issue an article entitled "The Sources of Soviet Conduct." Its author was a certain Mr. X. Appearing just as Molotov was sitting down in Paris with Bevin and Bidault to discuss Marshall's offer, the article undoubtedly strengthened the Kremlin's conviction that the Marshall Plan was primarily an anti-Soviet device. This Mr. X, author of what is arguably the single most famous magazine article in American history, was soon revealed to be none other than George Kennan—at this point head of the State Department's Policy Planning Staff and one of the major authors of the Marshall Plan. The article would forever link Kennan's name to the policy of containment.

The godfather of the article was James Forrestal, who for many, many months had been asking in one form or another that same question—whether the United States was facing a traditional nation-state or a militant religion. Forrestal personally had few doubts but that it was the latter. It will be recalled that he had commissioned an analysis on the subject by a Smith College professor, Edward Willett, who had explained Soviet foreign policy almost entirely in terms of ideology. Forrestal had been distributing Willett's various drafts to a decidedly mixed reaction. "I question the adequacy of an analysis of Russian foreign policy based mainly upon deductions from dogma," Robert Strausz-Hupe of the University of Pennsylvania informed Forrestal. Philip Mosely of Columbia University commented, "I cannot agree in drawing the conclusion that the Soviet government operates blindly on the basis of philosophical assumptions. It is only one element which enters into an immediate and concrete decision or into a program of, say, ten years of policy as sketched out for the future when they envision it." [37]

And, of course, Forrestal had sought the opinion of George Kennan, who, instead of commenting, presented at the end of January his own paper on "The Psychological Background of Soviet Foreign Policy." Virtually unchanged, it found its way as the Mr. X article into the July issue of *Foreign Affairs*.[38] Kennan had been asked to comment on a paper stressing the role of Soviet ideology, and this, as he himself said afterward, undoubtedly affected the thrust of his own piece. But Kennan was also continuing the line of argument of the Long Telegram as he here made the case that the United States was dealing not with a Great Power pursuing imperial goals, but principally with a messianic religion, an ideological force, for which coexistence was always a threat.

"Its political action," Kennan wrote, "is a fluid stream which moves constantly, wherever it is permitted to move, toward a given goal. Its main concern is to make sure that it has filled every nook and cranny available to it in the basin of world power. But if it finds unassailable barriers in its path, it accepts these philosophically and accommodates itself to them." The appropriate response, Kennan called "containment"—"the adroit and vigilant application of counterforce at a series of constantly shifting geographical and political points, corresponding to the shifts and maneuvers of Soviet Policy." He expressed some exultation over the challenge and "a certain gratitude to a Providence which, by providing the American people with this implacable challenge, has made their entire security as a nation dependent on their pulling themselves together and accepting the responsibilities of moral and political leadership that history plainly intended them to bear."

The article, reiterating the Riga outlook in a bipolar world, did express the outlook of the Truman Administration. It provided a name—"containment"—to describe this thrust in American foreign policy. But it should be noted that Kennan meant to admonish not only those whom he considered still blind to the inevitable challenge, but also those whose alarm had run wild. To that latter group, he was saying that the confrontation should not be seen in military terms, that hostilities need not be imminent, and that preventive war was unnecessary.

"The Sources of Soviet Conduct," by Mr. X, received wide attention. The article was quoted and cited, it seemed, almost everywhere in the American press. Both *Life* and *Reader's Digest* excerpted it. "I thought you might be interested in having a copy of the article by 'X' in the July issue of *Foreign Affairs* and have therefore arranged to get some reprints, one of which I enclose," a State Department official wrote to the American ambassador in Czechoslovakia. "I give you one guess on whom the author is . . . We leave it to you to make such distribution on a personal basis in your area as you may consider appropriate." [39]

By the summer of 1947, the "two-world assumption" had completely displaced any notions of cooperation. From Moscow, Ambassador

Smith described the Czech reversal on the Marshall Plan as a Soviet declaration of war for the control of Europe. It is probable in turn that the Russians saw the Marshall Plan as a declaration of war by the United States for control of Europe. Although clothed in generous language, it capped a process of reorientation for Washington, away from relief and reconstruction per se to relief, reconstruction, *and* anticommunism. American aid would no longer be used to create links and bridges, but rather to isolate communists. The Russians now assumed that the United States would use its great economic power for the specific goal of isolating the Soviet Union, and that American leaders had lost all interest in the Great Power consortium. The Marshall Plan precipitated a dramatic shift in Soviet foreign policy. That the Cezchs and even the Poles would consider participating in the Marshall Plan despite Soviet displeasures indicated to Stalin that a dangerous diversity existed within his sphere. This he would no longer tolerate in a changing international environment. For Stalin, spheres of influence would no longer mean a process of mutual accommodation but rather one of hostile confrontation.

In December 1947, Laurence Steinhardt, the American ambassador to Czechoslovakia, gave his own testimony as to the change that followed the Czech acceptance and then renunciation of the invitation to discuss the Marshall Plan: "It is no mere coincidence that the rather benign attitude of Moscow toward the Czech government suddenly hardened after the acceptance. By benign I mean that up to that time the Russians had not exercised much pressure on them. They had made a few suggestions here and there in connection with their political and commercial decisions, but not much more than other governments make to one another, and they had not, as far as we could see, directly interfered or given any orders." [40] Perhaps by December of 1947, U.S. policymakers were feeling some nostalgia for the ambiguity that had characterized the Czech position in 1946 and into 1947.

The first public reaction to the Marshall Plan by the Russians was a hastily improvised series of trade treaties with Eastern Europe, called, with some exaggeration, the Molotov Plan. This, however, was only the beginning of the Russian efforts to consolidate a new empire.

If there was any turning point in Soviet policy toward Eastern Europe and the West, it was the organizing conference of the Cominform—the Communist Information Bureau—held in September 1947 in a manor house that was now a sanitorium belonging to the Polish State Security Service. Not a lineal descendant of the Comintern, and of considerably more exclusive membership, the Cominform advertised itself as a coordinating body for national communist parties in the Soviet Union and Eastern Europe, along with those of France and

Italy. It was totally dominated by the Soviets, and was to be used to tighten the Soviet hold on Eastern Europe. It was also the mechanism for directing the Italian and French Communist parties to begin those disruptive activities in which, Washington thought, they were already engaged.

The Cominform was a device for restoring ideological unity to the communist parties, but this was ideology not in the service of Marx, but of the Soviet state. At the meeting in Poland, Andrei Zhdanov, already identified as a keeper of ideological purity in the USSR, proclaimed the division of the international system into two camps—that of "imperialist and anti-democratic forces" and that of "democratic and anti-imperialist forces." Curiously, he said that Soviet foreign policy continued to be based on the possibility of coexistence between capitalism and communism, but now the United States was creating a hostile bloc against the socialist states—that is, against the Soviet Union. The United States, he said, was an expansionist power, as evidenced by the network of military bases it was establishing around the world, and by the use of its economic power to create a sphere of influence over Western Europe and over Britain and its empire. There was some degree of truth in what Zhdanov said, although the Americans hardly saw it. Nor could the Russians admit that American policy was in part in response to a perceived threat of Soviet power and influence. Zhdanov was obviously deeply concerned about the revitalization of the Western zones in Germany and their integration into a Western political and economic system.

The Soviets were responding in kind, and with a vengeance, to the drawing together of such a Western bloc. The cynical Russians, joined by the enthusiastic Yugoslavs, denounced the French and Italian parties for their parliamentary reformist course, their popular-frontism —the very line approved in the last meeting of the Comintern in 1943, and, more important, mandated by Stalin himself during and immediately after the war. "While you are fighting to stay in the Government," Zhdanov now taunted the French communists, "they throw you out." He ridiculed the Italians: "You Italian comrades are bigger parliamentarians than de Gasperi himself. You are the biggest political party, and yet they throw you out of the Government." Jacques Duclos, the representative of the French Communist Party, went into shock; he sat by himself in the park swinging his legs, talking to no one. He literally cried in rage. The Italian and French parties left the meeting in Poland with their marching orders: to intensify the class struggle, to go over—as they did with disruptive strikes—into opposition against the Marshall Plan and American influence.

In Eastern Europe, political diversity was to come to a quick end.

Zhdanov criticized "national communism." This was an attack on Gomulka, who had defended a "Polish way to socialism," which was wide enough to accommodate the small entrepreneur and farmer. In fact, Gomulka had resisted the whole idea of a Cominform, but he was forced to accede to the Russian demand that the Cominform endorse collectivization (on the Soviet model) as the only appropriate path to socialism. In Berlin at the same time, East German communists were instructed that there was no longer a separate German road to socialism. The Cominform meeting marked the beginning of the Stalinist reign of terror in Eastern Europe, although the worst was yet to come. In the autumn of 1947, there was still a coalition in Czechoslovakia, although it seemed more and more like an archeological remnant, a relic of another time and spirit.[41]

Meanwhile, in Washington, the Truman Administration was very worried that Congress would not approve the Marshall Plan, even though the $20 billion proposed by the Europeans had been pared to $17 billion. Policymakers were sure that a congressional rejection would lead to the collapse of Europe. Budget-conscious Republicans, now in the majority on Capitol Hill, and highly suspicious of liberal "give-aways," were vocally resistant to the idea of further aid. They complained, as they added up the host of programs approved or pending, that (in the words of Representative John Taber) "there seem to be no grasp of any business principles in connection with this situation." There was also resistance on procedural grounds, a continuing resentment of the dramatic manner in which the Truman Doctrine was introduced, which had seemed to preclude any real debate.[42]

To deflect such criticism, the State Department drew Vandenberg deeply into the development of the Marshall Plan. A few years later Marshall would recall that he and the Michigan senator "couldn't have gotten much closer together unless I sat in Vandenberg's lap or he sat in mine." The Administration put considerable effort into selling the plan to Congress and the public. Hosts of special committees—some presidentially appointed, some congressional, some composed of leading laity like the now-retired Henry Stimson—studied the matter. All of them reported that the Marshall Plan was essential to the national security, and that it would help, not hurt, the United States economically. Even so, the winning of congressional approval was difficult.

An important point must be made here. As with the Truman Doctrine, the Executive was consciously trying to "educate," even manipulate, public opinion. But, again as with the Greek-Turkish aid, it was doing this in order to bring the public around to accepting its own worried world view. The arguments that the Administration used to present the issue to the public were congruent with the concerns expressed privately within policy councils. In their attempt to educate public opinion American leaders may have confused two things—the Soviet Union as the alleged perpetrator of economic distress in Europe, and the Soviet Union as likely beneficiary of that distress. But, then, that distinction was blurred in their own minds. When Marshall left Moscow in April 1947, he was convinced that the Soviet Union was deliberately retarding European recovery to achieve its own political goals.[43]

The sense of urgency among U.S. policymakers, high from the beginning, kept increasing, as it became more and more apparent that they had continued to underestimate the depth of the crisis. "At no time in my recollection have I ever seen a world situation which was moving so rapidly toward real trouble," wrote Undersecretary Lovett at the end of July, "and I have the feeling that this is the last clear shot that we will have in finding a solution." A few weeks later, Henry Ford II, as a member of a presidential air policy commission, went to see Lovett. "He was even more pessimistic than were the Joint Chiefs of Staff," Ford reported, "and felt that war could come at any time and that there were at least two crises a day in the State Department." The President himself was feeling the same way. "The British have turned out to be our problem children now," Truman wrote to his sister in August. "They've decided to go bankrupt and if they do that, it will end our prosperity and probably all the world's too. Then Uncle Joe Stalin can have his way. Looks like he may get it anyway." [44]

Bad news followed bad news in August and into September. The smallest wheat crop in France in 132 years. Extra rations distributed to Ruhr coal miners in a desperate bid to encourage higher production. Near-exhaustion of dollar reserves in France and Italy, while U.S. prices kept rising. Many European countries cutting back on the purchases of essential U.S. goods. And massive strikes—the communist parties in the West now clearly bent on a policy of opposition and disruption.[45]

The State Department's Policy Planning Staff summed up the situation: "The margin of safety in Europe, both from an economic and political viewpoint, is extremely thin." U.S. leaders concluded in early autumn 1947 that a Marshall Plan approved and appropriated by Congress in mid-1948 would be too late unless stopgap aid were provided immediately.[46]

At the end of September, Truman hosted a small group of congressmen in the Cabinet Room at the White House.

"I do hope that we can reach some decision on this and get things started," Truman said. "General Marshall has reviewed the trouble he is having with Russia in the United States, and Bob Lovett has given you the detailed picture. We'll either have to provide a program of interim aid relief until the Marshall program gets going, or the governments of France and Italy will fall, Austria too, and for all practical purposes Europe will be Communist. The Marshall Plan goes out of the window, and it's a question of how long we could stand up in such a situation. This is serious. I can't overemphasize how serious."

"I had hoped very much, Mr. President, there would be no special session of Congress," said Sam Rayburn. "Can't something be worked out?"

"It doesn't seem we can get the money any other way, Sam," replied Truman. "Congress has got to act."

"That is just the situation," added Lovett.

"Then the plan had better be well worked out, right down to the details, and everything ready so that we can get right to it the minute Congress meets," said Rayburn.

"Communism has started its campaign of aggression," said Charles Eaton, the Republican who was chairman of the House Foreign Affairs Committee. "We have already met the challenge in Greece and Turkey. We've got to stop Communism, and I'm ready to work with Senator Vandenberg."

But Majority Leader Charles Halleck had a word of caution: "Mr. President, you must realize there is a growing resistance to these programs. I have been out in the hustings, and I know. The people don't like it."

On October 15, Clark Clifford summarized the reasons for calling a special session of Congress: "Two most important issues today are high prices and aid to Europe. They are inevitably bound together. The situation in each instance is getting worse . . . In France the subway and bus strike is spreading and we can expect serious trouble. The President must have a plan. It must be thought through now so it can be quietly set in motion." [47] On October 23, Truman announced that he was calling the special session. The campaign for foreign aid continued. "The people can never understand why the President does not use his supposedly great power to make 'em behave," Truman wrote to his sister on November 14. "Well all the President is, is a glorified public relations man who spends his time flattering, kissing and kicking people to get them to do what they are supposed to do anyway." Three days later, he presented to a joint session of Congress his proposal for almost $600 million in interim aid for France, Italy, and Austria. A month later, after more debate and more flattering, kissing, and kicking, he was able to sign the bills providing the emergency assistance.[48]

Between Truman's message and the approval of interim aid, there occurred the last act, the anticlimax, of the Yalta approach—the London Council of Foreign Ministers meeting. As in Moscow the preceding spring, the issue again was how to proceed on a German peace settlement and what to do—or not do—about reparations. No optimism remained; polarization had gone too far. The Americans, British, and French all thought in advance that this Council would almost certainly fail, that they would not be able to work out a German settlement with the Russians, and that therefore they should go ahead and consolidate the Western zones. The Russians, for their part, expected to face a united Western front, which was planning to establish a Trizonia, and they were extremely bitter about the steps toward fusion that had already taken place.[49]

In October, looking ahead to the Council, Robert Murphy laid out Administration thinking on Germany. "We have maintained the position until there is either a break-down of the Four-Power relationship in Germany, or a solution of it, that we would not admit having established a political structure." However, if the London meeting did not lead to a resolution, "shortly thereafter we would be obliged to develop a political organization in Western Germany." He added, "Naturally, this is a serious step." The United States would be accused of splitting Germany, but Murphy was not too much concerned about this. "We will have to meet that charge when we get to it and we are prepared to do so."

He did foresee one danger—Berlin—"an island in the heart of the Soviet zone." The Russians, he explained, "could easily make our lives unbearable and we would eventually have to leave Berlin. But we have no intention of doing so."

There was something paradoxical in the American stance. Expecting failure in London, the Americans, along with the British, were at work on the foundations of a new West German state as an alternative to a Four-Power occupation. But such preparations in themselves were sure to increase Soviet suspicion and obstructionism and thus would guarantee the very failure that the Americans and British were convinced was at hand. On balance, however, it must also be said that the deterioration of the Four-Power occupation had proceeded apace, day by day, over many months. By the time of the London meeting, the Americans had had just about enough of any effort toward a Four-Power German settlement. Indeed, they feared it.* [50]

So, there were charges and countercharges at the London meeting, which opened on November 25, 1947, but little of substance—save for what happened when the meeting ended. France left no doubt that it now belonged to the Western bloc; indeed, the French even encouraged secret meetings during the London Council among the three Western foreign ministers to discuss other possible solutions to the German question.

Knowing that he was isolated, Molotov responded with unyielding intransigence and acid propaganda. In 1933, it may be recalled, William Bullitt had marveled at what he called Molotov's "magnificent forehead" and was reminded of a "first-rate French scientist, great poise, kindliness and intelligence." But now all that Westerners noticed on Molotov's forehead was a bump that swelled when he felt pressured.[51] He was certainly under such stress in London, as he tried to find some way to stop the movement toward unification in the Western zone. But his violent language only strengthened the determination of the Western powers to proceed.

The two sides debated back and forth on reparations. The Russians still sought reparations valued at ten billion dollars, to be delivered by 1965. To this, the British were somewhat more responsive than the Americans, perhaps because they were more sensitive to the war ravages of the Nazis. But both nations rejected any compromise with the Russians on this issue. The State Department believed that Congress would not vote aid for Europe were the Soviet Union to receive German reparations.

On December 3, Bevin told Harold Nicolson about his strenuous efforts, the day before, to have a real heart-to-heart talk in his own flat with Molotov.

"You cannot look on me as an enemy of Russia," Bevin had said to the Soviet foreign minister. "Why, when our Government was trying

---

* On November 6, Marshall told the Cabinet that all he expected from the Russians at the next Council of Foreign Ministers meeting were "various ruses . . . to try to get us out of western Germany under arrangements which would leave that country defenseless against communist penetration." He explained, "The world situation is still dominated by the Russian effort in the post-hostilities period to extend their virtual domination over all, or as much as possible, of the European land mass." He said that the Americans would resist the Soviet moves at the foreign ministers meeting and instead "see that [Germany] is better integrated into Western Europe" and press the other Western European countries to so accept Western Germany.

to stamp out your Revolution, who was it that stopped it? It was I, Ernest Bevin. I called out the transport workers and they refused to load the ships. I wanted you to have your Revolution in your own way and without interference. Now again I am speaking as a friend. You are playing a very dangerous game. And I can't make out why. You don't really believe that any American wants to go to war with you—or, at least, no responsible American. We most certainly do not want to. But you are playing with fire, Mr. Molotov . . . If war comes between you and America in the East, then we may be able to remain neutral. But if war comes between you and America in the West, then we shall be on America's side. Make no mistake about that. That would be the end of Russia and of your Revolution. So please stop sticking out your neck in this way and tell me what you are after. What do you want?"

"I want a unified Germany," replied Molotov.

That was virtually all Bevin could get out of him.[52]

But a bit of explication is needed. A "unified" Germany meant treating Germany as an economic unit so that the Russians could obtain reparations from the Western zones. It also meant preventing the birth of a strong, Western-oriented West Germany.

Meanwhile, strikes, in part led by the communists to protest the Marshall Plan, were spreading in France. With Marshall's permission, John Foster Dulles left London on December 4 for a firsthand survey of the French situation. He brought back an alarming report—utilities running only intermittently in Paris, his own train rerouted because tracks had been blown up, industry at a standstill. The impression was widespread that Europe was rolling toward the precipice while the conference dragged on. *New York Times* correspondent C. L. Sulzberger wrote in his diary that he had come to Brussels "mainly to organize an emergency system in case the strike wave shuts off communications with New York; or even worse, in case it becomes a real political menace and a Communist bid to take over in Europe . . . am also distributing large chunks of money to correspondents in France, Belgium, Italy, Spain so they can get out their families if necessary, amid chaos." [53]

By December 6, Bevin and Marshall were privately planning how to bring about a breakdown in the Council.

"We ought," said Bevin, "to force the debate on the main outstanding economic questions and also possibly indicate our requirements for the political organization of Germany in a way to bring out that the Soviet objective was a Communist-controlled Germany."

"Quite frankly," replied Marshall, "what would be popular in the U.S would be that I should break off and tell the Russians to go to the devil." But he feared that such popular approval would not last. "It might be wise to indicate the differences on matters of real substance and to suggest that unless agreement could be had on them we would have to proceed—always making it clear, however, that we were not permanently breaking. It was important, of course, to choose our ground carefully and to time it to the best possible advantage."

Marshall, who had no intention of sitting through a long conference, concluded that the meeting could serve no further use. On December 11, he reported to Washington: "It is plainly evident that Molotov is not only playing for time but is consistently, almost desperately, endeavoring to reach agreements which really would be an embarrassment to us in the next four to six months rather than true evidence of getting together."

"We are all with you," Truman wired Marshall.[54]

During the weekend of December 13 and 14, the American delegation reached the decision to end the session. And so at the seventeenth session on Monday, December 15, after a last debate on reparations, Marshall called for adjournment. "No real progress could be made because of Soviet obstructionism," he said.

Denying responsibility for the impasse, Molotov accused Marshall of seeking adjournment "in order to give the U.S. a free hand to do as it pleased in its zone of Germany."

The Council, said Bidault, "should adjourn rather than further aggravate relations between the Four Powers." On that, at least, the foreign ministers could agree, and adjourn they did, without fixing a date for another meeting.

There was a certain relief in the break-up. "The Russians had at last run against a solid front," said Marshall three days later, with some satisfaction. But the ministers also recognized the gravity of the situation. Bidault privately worried that there might be a rupture in French-Soviet diplomatic relations, and that a coup was imminent in Czechoslovakia.[55]

The Council led to two specific outcomes. First, the Western powers agreed among themselves to move further toward the creation of a new West German political state, although trying to avoid, as Robert Murphy put it, "unseemly haste." There would be one more try at a united Germany, and if that did not work, then Bizonia would become the basis of this new state, along with, it was hoped, the French zone. They committed themselves to a German currency reform, an economic move to counter inflation, but also of great political significance if done without the Russians. The Western countries would carry it out by themselves if necessary, although Clay believed that it was not "absolutely impossible" to get the Russians to go along on a new currency.

Second, Bevin and Marshall decided that some kind of Western alliance was required. "The issue," Bevin said, "was where power was going to rest." He elaborated: "We must devise some western democratic system comprising the Americans, ourselves, France, Italy, etc. and of course the Dominions. This would not be a formal alliance, but an understanding backed by power, money and resolute action. It would be a sort of spiritual federation of the west."

There was no choice, Marshall replied. Events had to be taken "at the flood stream." [56]

Just before the Council session had opened, Edwin Pauley, occupying what was by then the largely ceremonial post of special adviser on reparations, had written to Marshall: "The forthcoming CFM meeting will be one of transcendental significance. It will constitute one of the Great Divides of American policy in this era."

Pauley was right. The London Council marked the end of the approach to postwar relations with the Soviet Union that Roosevelt had so optimistically, yet tentatively, outlined in the midst of the war. Such an approach had failed, ending in a dismal parody of diplomacy. We might be more precise and say that the Yalta axioms had died some months earlier, at Moscow in the spring of 1947. At London, they were buried. The Americans now looked in other directions.

Nations try to live less dangerously, to find some security, and so the Americans responded in kind to what they feared—to the threat of war by preparing themselves for war. The aging Admiral Leahy expressed the consensus among U.S. leaders when he wrote, the day after the break-up—in the course of noting in his diary that the impasse on Germany had resulted from Soviet insistence on reparations—that the consortium was finished. "No proposal was made by any of the Foreign Ministers for another meeting and it appears now that some other method of arranging a peace in Europe must be found." One step, he said, was a separate treaty with a Western-oriented West Germany, although "the Soviet Government would offer violent objection to such, even to the extent of using military power if necessary." Indeed, he feared that Russia would decide "to start its 'inevitable' war without delay." There was no choice in Leahy's mind— American foreign policy had to be militarized.

"In view of the very menacing situation that confronts western civilization," wrote the admiral, "I believe that the United States should begin a partial mobilization of forces of defense without any delay." [57]

## Notes

1. Telephone transcript, March 13, 1947, Joseph M. Jones papers, Harry S. Truman Presidential Library, Independence, Mo.
2. *Harry S. Truman Public Papers: 1947,* p. 212. Also see Elsey to Freeland, May 11, 1967, George Elsey papers, Truman Library.
3. Colonel Behn in Wasson to Lamont, February 25, 1946, Thomas Lamont papers, Baker Library, Harvard University. Henry Stimson diary, Yale University, April 19, July 25, 1945. For another eyewitness reaction to Europe's dislocation, see Lane to Dewey, August 14, 1945, Lane to Durbrow, August 3, 1945, Arthur Bliss Lane papers, Yale University. The studies of multilateral planning are many, for instance, Richard Gardner, *Sterling-Dollar Diplomacy* (Oxford, 1956), and Richard M. Freeland, *The Truman Doctrine and the Origins of McCarthyism* (New York, 1972).
4. E. F. Penrose, *Economic Planning for Peace* (Princeton, 1953), pp. 321–33; Edward Mason oral history, Truman Library, pp. 29–31. For the concern on U.S. public opinion and international relief, Lubin to Hopkins, January 6, 1944, and report to Lubin by Cantril and Lambert, November 15, 1943, Post-War Planning file, Harry Hopkins papers, Franklin D. Roosevelt Presidential Library, Hyde Park, N.Y.
5. War Council minutes, November 7, 1945, Box 23, Robert Patterson papers, Library of Congress; Penrose, *Economic Planning,* p. 320; Francis Williams, *Twilight of Empire: Memoirs of Prime Minister Clement Attlee* (New York, 1962), p. 136; Harry Truman, *Year of Decisions* (Garden City, 1955), p. 236; Byrnes quoted in *FRUS, 1946,* I, p. 1441; Clayton-Wallace telephone conversation, April 15, 1946, Wallace papers, University of Iowa.
6. John Morton Blum, *The Price of Vision: The Diary of Henry A. Wallace* (Boston, 1973), p. 554; memo on world trip, May 7, 1947, Gibson memorandum, February 21, 1947, Box 220, Herbert Hoover papers, Herbert Hoover Presidential Library, West Branch, Iowa. War Council minutes, May 16, 1946, Box 23, Patterson papers.
7. Hugh Dalton diary, October 5, 1946, London School of Economics.
8. United Nations, *Economic Report: World Economic Situation 1945–47* (New York, 1948), pp. 123–25; Ingvar Svennilson, *Growth and Stagnation in the European Economy* (Geneva, 1954), pp. 253, 246; United Nations, *A Survey of the Economic Situation and Prospects of Europe* (Geneva, 1948), p. 5. Also see Richard Mayne, *The Recovery of Europe, 1945–1973* (Rev. ed., New York, 1973), pp. 117–18, and *Business Week,* August 2, 1947.
9. United Nations, *Situation and Prospects of Europe,* pp. 53–55, 62–74, 144; Harry Bayard Price, *The Marshall Plan and Its Meaning* (Ithaca: Cornell University Press, 1955), pp. 29–32; Dirk Stikker, *Men of Responsibility* (New York, 1966), pp. 163–65; Nourse to Truman, May 7, 19, October 18, 1948, Nourse papers; "Some Aspects of Foreign Aid Program," October 18, 1948, Salant papers, both in Truman Library.
10. "Overseas Deficit," May 2, 1947, III–4, miscellaneous papers, Dalton

papers. Also see memorandum to Mr. Rowen for Prime Minister, July 29, 1947, Attlee papers, University College, Oxford, England.

11. Frederick J. Dobney, *Selected Papers of Will Clayton* (Baltimore: Johns Hopkins Press, 1971), p. 198; Cleveland to Jones, July 2, 1947, Jones papers. Also see Salant to Clark, May 12, 1947, Salant papers. *FRUS, 1947, III*, pp. 210–11. Freeland argues (*Truman Doctrine,* p. 154) that plans for aiding Europe had been deferred for domestic political reasons. On the contrary, policymakers did not recognize the economic problems until the winter and spring of 1946–47.

12. Acheson speech, April 18, 1947, Box 1, Jones papers.

13. Bohlen and Marshall interviews in Harry Price oral history collection; Gimbel, *The American Occupation of Germany: Politics and the Military, 1945–49* (Stanford, 1968), pp. 123, 150; Lovett to Lamont, July 31, 1947, Lamont papers; James Reston notes, vol. 1, Black Book, Krock papers. For Marshall's early emphasis upon Europe-wide approach, see Marshall to Bowles, February 17, 1947, Bowles papers, Yale University. Kennan, in charge of drawing up the program as head of the Policy Planning Staff, had been keenly interested in a Europe-wide approach for some time. In 1942, he had suggested, "We endeavor to take over the whole system of control which the Germans have set up for the administration of European economy, preserving the apparatus, putting people of our own into the key positions to run it, and that we then apply this system to the execution of whatever policies we may adopt for continental Europe, in the immediate postwar period." Two years later he observed that European integration, in the form of some kind of federation, seemed to be the best solution to the problem of Germany and "the only way out of this labyrinth of conflict which is Europe today." Kennan to Burleigh, June 18, 1942, remarks to staff at Lisbon, June 1944, Kennan papers, Princeton University.

14. United Nations, *Situation and Prospects of Europe,* p. 61; Council of Economic Advisers, "Third Quarter Review," October 1, 1947, Nourse papers; Harriman and Hoover cited in Forrestal diary, April 9, 1947, pp. 1566–67, Princeton University. The Kolkos mistakenly argue: "As a capitalist nation unable to expand its internal market by redistributing its national income to absorb the surplus, the United States would soon plunge again into the depression that only World War II brought to an end. The alternative was to export dollars, primarily through grants rather than loans" *The Limits of Power: The World and United States Foreign Policy, 1945–54* (New York: Harper & Row, 1972).

15. *FRUS, 1947, II*, p. 240, *III*, p. 220; Dobney, *Clayton,* p. 202. Smith talk in F.P.M. to Peterson, May 16, 1947, ASW 091 Russia, RG 107, Modern Military records, National Archives. "I agree with the general object of the Marshall Plan to help maintain the Western European countries in their battle against Communism," Taft wrote on November 28, 1947, to Harry Bannister, Box 786, Robert A. Taft papers, Library of Congress.

16. Leffingwell to Lamont, May 21, 1947, Lamont papers; Jean Edward

Smith, ed.; *The Papers of General Lucius D. Clay: Germany 1945–49,* 2 vols. (Bloomington: Indiana University Press, 1974), pp. 356, 361; Keyes to Hoover, May 21, 1947, Hoover papers.

17. Djilas, *Conversations with Stalin* (London: Pelican, 1969), p. 141.

18. Dalton diary, September 10, 1946; *FRUS, 1947,* III, p. 894.

19. Kolko, *Limits of Power,* pp. 212–15; Hugh Seton-Watson, *The East European Revolution* (New York: Praeger, 1956), pp. 190–202; Vedeler to Steinhardt, August 12, 1947, Box 55, Steinhardt papers, Library of Congress; Hughes to Booth, June 11, 1947, H. Stuart Hughes papers. For "moderate coalition," "Secret Summary for Secretary," June 2, 1947, with Marshall to Truman, June 2, 1947, Box 180, President's secretary's file, Truman papers.

20. *FRUS, 1947,* III, pp. 224–25, 237–38; memorandum on June 5, 1947, speech, Jones papers.

21. Marshall and Bohlen interviews, Price oral history collection; Forrestal conversations with Ploesser, July 2, 1947, Box 92, Forrestal papers. For the writing off of the Economic Commission for Europe, see George Kennan, "Problems of U.S. Foreign Policy," Lecture, Washington, D.C., May 6, 1947.

22. B. Ponomaryov, *History of Soviet Foreign Policy, 1945–70* (Moscow: Progress, 1974), p. 163; Bohlen interview in Price oral history collection; Price, *Marshall Plan,* pp. 26–29; Djilas, *Conversations,* pp. 99–100.

23. *FRUS, 1947,* III, p. 235; Hickerson to Acheson, April 11, 1947, Hickerson to Labouisse, April 5, 1947, Winiewicz-Thompson conversation, April 3, 1947, Box 3, Hickerson files, State Department papers, National Archives; Thomas Paterson, *Soviet-American Confrontation* (Baltimore: The Johns Hopkins University Press, 1973), pp. 210–11; Robert Elson, "New Strategy in Foreign Policy," *Fortune,* December 1947, p. 222.

24. *FRUS, 1947,* III, pp. 260–61; notes on Poland, September 10, 1947, Christian Herter papers, Howard University; Pate to Lane, March 21, 1947, with UNRRA memo, Lane papers. Gomulka quoted in Nicholas Bethell, *Gomulka* (London: Penguin, 1952), p. 135; Karel Jech, ed., *The Czechoslovak Economy, 1945–48* (Prague: State Pedagogical Publishing House, 1968), p. 54. For the initially keen Polish interest in the Marshall Plan, also see Eugen Loebl, *Sentenced & Tried: The Stalinist Purges in Czechoslovakia* (London: Elek, 1969), p. 25.

25. Interview with Halvard Lange, Price oral history collection.

26. *FRUS, 1947,* III, pp. 318–22; Ripka, *Czechoslovakia Enslaved* (London: Victor Gollancz, 1950), pp. 56–71; Jech, *Czechoslovak Economy,* pp. 55–56.

27. Vedeler to Steinhardt, August 12, 1947, Box 55, Steinhardt papers; *FRUS, 1947,* III, pp. 335, 327.

28. Eisenhower to Clay, March 1, 1946, Clay folder, Eisenhower papers, Eisenhower Library, Abilene, Kansas.

29. Clay to Warburg, September 21, 1946, Box 26, James F. Warburg papers, John F. Kennedy Presidential Library, Waltham, Mass. War Council minutes, November 7, 1946, Box 23, Patterson papers.

30. John Hilldring, Lecture, Washington, D.C., December 5, 1946; Clay to Dodge, December 23, 1946, Joseph Dodge papers, Detroit Public Library; Clay to Hoover, April 7, 1947, Hoover papers.

31. Memorandum of Hoover-McNeil conversation, February 20, 1947, Hoover papers; Dulles to Vandenberg, March 29, 1947, John Foster Dulles papers, Princeton University.

32. Forrestal diary, April 28, 1947, pp. 1600–1601; Hoover to Taber, May 26, 1947, John Taber papers, Cornell University.

33. Smith, *Clay Papers,* pp. 387–91, 345, 372, 375, 412–13; Clay to Hoover, June 8, 1947, Hoover papers; Gimbel, *American Occupation,* pp. 156–58, 170; Forrestal diary, May 17, 1947, p. 1618; Pauley to Truman, April 15, 1947, Steelman to Truman, n.d., Box 133, President's secretary's file, Truman papers, Truman Library. For Hoover's report, see Gimbel, *The Origins of the Marshall Plan* (Stanford: Stanford University Press, 1976), pp. 182–84. Bizonia clearly posed a policy dilemma for the British. For their effort to balance off their heavy financial burden in Germany against the fears that the U.S. would undercut their plans for socialization of heavy industry in the Ruhr, see CAB 128/6, pp. 45, 126–28, Cabinet papers.

34. Royall to Taber, August 8, 1947, Taber papers; Smith, *Clay Papers,* p. 416; Gimbel, *American Occupation,* p. 195. In his excellent new study, *The Origins of the Marshall Plan,* John Gimbel argues that the "American economic dilemma in Germany" provided "the primary motivation for the Marshall Plan" (p. 279). Only by linking Germany to an overall Western European recovery could the U.S. overcome French resistance to a revivified Germany. He convincingly documents that, contrary to later memories, the Four-Power occupation broke down because of French obstructionism—not the Soviets'. See pp. 33–34, 48–49, 85–97, 112, 127–31, 138–39. In effect, he rightly says that the history of the German occupation in 1945 and 1946 was rewritten in 1947 and thereafter. He gives serious attention to the reparations issue and the role of "hidden reparations" from the Western zones. He also puts emphasis on the continuing clash between the State Department, worried about France and the rest of Western Europe, and Clay and the War Department, anxious to get out of the occupation business by getting Germany back onto its feet. Despite my agreement with his thesis that the Marshall Plan provided a "solution" to the German problem, as well as the considerable skill and care with which he makes his argument, I find his focus too narrow. The Marshall Plan was an effort to cope with the "problem" of Europe, which had three dimensions—Germany, the Western European economy, and the Soviet Union. Gimbel is right that an incorrect interpretative framework—what I have called the Riga axioms—was applied to Germany. Nevertheless, the fears and misperceptions of the Soviet Union among U.S. policymakers were very genuine. Second, their alarm about the German economy was more than matched by their alarm about what was happening in the economy of the rest of Western Europe, and he pays practically no attention to the latter. Finally, in developing his State-War controversy, he overlooks the significance of the close personal relationship between Byrnes and Clay.

And it is not surprising that he finds no "plan" in the spring and summer of 1947. What existed—and from this emerged the plan—was a perception of crisis, a sense of danger and responsibility, and some general intentions and some thoughts about the need for a comprehensive response. All this said, Gimbel's book is a major addition to the literature, and is important for directing attention to the way in which the Marshall Plan was meant to provide a solution for Germany. But neither in the minds of its originators nor in fact was the plan separated from the confrontation with the Soviet Union.

35. Dalton diary, July 30, June 26, 1947; Bonesteel to Lovett, August 27, 1947, 740.00119 Control (Germany) 8–2747, State Department papers, National Archives; for "friendly aid" and Clayton, *FRUS, 1947*, III, pp. 223–30, 370; for France, Gimbel, *Marshall Plan*, pp. 252–54. On June 23, General Albert Wedemeyer, in reporting on a trip to Europe the previous month, observed that he had noted "restrained anti-American feeling" in Britain. "Lew Douglas the ambassador confirmed this. It is understandable—no people feel friendly toward creditors and may look to us as Shylocks. Life is very austere." Wedemeyer added, however, "There can be no doubt about the almost universal British desire to remain close to America in a political, economic and military sense." Attached to memo by Humelsine, July 15, 1947, FW 740.00119 Control (Germany) 7–749, State Department papers. The disastrous five weeks between July 15, when the British made the pound convertible in accord with the Anglo-American loan agreement, and August 20, when Britain suspended convertibility, fueled British antagonism. See R. Gardner, *Sterling-Dollar Diplomacy*, pp. 306–25, 337–42.

36. Elsey quoted in Paterson, *Soviet-American Confrontation*, p. 207; Patterson to Hoyt, June 23, 1947, Patterson papers.

37. Forrestal to Lippmann, January 7, 1946, Mosely to Forrestal, October 14, 1947, Box 70, Strausz-Hupe to Forrestal, March 14, 1946, Box 71, Forrestal papers; Forrestal diary, October 15, 1946, p. 1301.

38. Kennan, "Psychological Background," Box 18, O'Connor memo, October 7, 1946, Box 68, Forrestal papers; Kennan, *Memoirs 1925–50* (Boston: Atlantic Little-Brown, 1967), pp. 373–76.

39. George Kennan, "The Sources of Soviet Conduct," *Foreign Affairs*, July 1947; Riddleberger to Steinhardt, August 29, 1947, Box 55, Steinhardt papers.

40. Vandenberg to Roberts, August 12, 1947, Arthur Vandenberg papers, University of Michigan; Laurence Steinhardt, Lecture, Washington, D.C., December 1947.

41. See Vladimir Dedijer, *Tito Speaks* (London: Weidenfeld & Nicolson, 1954), pp. 302–6; Bethell, *Gomulka*, pp. 135–38, 146–47; Djilas, *Conversations*, pp. 99–101; Marshall D. Shulman, *Stalin's Foreign Policy Reappraised* (Cambridge, Mass.: Harvard University Press, 1963), pp. 14–17, 84; Alexander Werth, *Russia: The Post-War Years* (New York: Taplinger, 1971), pp. 294–326; A. I. Sobolev, *Outline History of the Communist International* (Moscow: Progress, 1970), pp. 512–15; Adam Ulam, *The Rivals*

(New York: Viking, 1971), pp. 131–34; for the German communists, see Wolfgang Leonhard, *Child of the Revolution* (Chicago: Henry Regnery, 1958), pp. 458–61; for a Western survey of the Polish road, John Scott, "Report on Poland," June 1, 1947, Box 55, Steinhardt papers.

42. *FRUS, 1947,* III, pp. 350–51; Taber to Hoover, May 21, 1947, Hoover papers; Taft to Bannister, November 28, 1947, Box 786, Taft papers; Hinshaw to Aldrich, October 27, 1947, Box 82, Winthrop Aldrich papers, Harvard University.

43. Marshall interview in Price oral history collection; Vandenberg to Roberts, August 12, 1947, Arthur Vandenberg papers.

44. Forrestal diary, July 26, 1947, p. 1751; Lovett to Lamont, July 31, 1947, Lamont papers; Ford to Johnston, Air Policy Commission papers, Truman Library; Margaret Truman, *Harry S. Truman* (New York: Morrow, 1973), p. 352.

45. Southard to Snyder, August 12, 1947, Snyder papers; "Notes on Boat Trip Coming Over" and London, September 3, 1947, Herter papers; Lovett to Taber, September 21, 1947, Taber papers; *Business Week,* August 9, 1947, p. 86, September 6, 1947, p. 102.

46. *FRUS, 1947,* III, pp. 344–46, 361, 470–71, 475–76; Leahy diary, September 29, 1947, Library of Congress; Margaret Truman, *Truman,* p. 354.

47. For the dialogue, McNaughton file to Bermingham, October 4, 1947, Frank McNaughton papers, Truman Library; memorandum, October 15, 1947, Box 4, Clark Clifford papers, Truman Library.

48. Truman, *Truman,* p. 356; *Truman: Public Papers, 1947,* pp. 475–76, 492–98; Leahy diary, November 17, 1947.

49. *FRUS, 1947,* II, pp. 684, 680, 687, 713.

50. Robert Murphy, "The Current Situation in Germany," Lecture, Washington, D.C., October 1947; Smith, *Clay Papers,* pp. 351, 440, 448, 458–60, 463–64, 491; Marshall's presentation with Humelsine to Secretary of Agriculture, November 12, 1947, 711.61/11–1247, secret file, State Department papers, National Archives.

51. *FRUS, 1947,* II, pp. 732, 738, 749, 756; *FR:USSR,* pp. 57–60; Dean Acheson, *Present at the Creation* (New York: Norton, 1970), p. 313.

52. *FRUS, 1947,* II, pp. 731, 757, 759, 817–18; Harold Nicolson, *Diaries and Letters, 1945–62* (London: Fontana, 1971), pp. 107–8.

53. John Foster Dulles, *War or Peace* (New York: Macmillan, 1950), pp. 106–7; C. L. Sulzberger, *A Long Row of Candles* (New York: Macmillan, 1969), p. 373.

54. *FRUS, 1947,* II, pp. 751–73, 764–65. On Marshall's lack of patience, see John Hickerson interview, Dulles oral history interviews, Princeton University.

55. *FRUS, 1947,* II, pp. 769–72, 826, 812.

56. Ibid., pp. 819, 823, 827, 815–17. Smith, *Clay,* pp. 501–2 (misdated).

57. Pauley in *FRUS, 1947,* II, p. 715, Clay to Patterson, December 23, 1947, Box 30, Patterson papers; Leahy diary, December 16, 1947.

# 5

## John Gimbel

# The Origins of the Marshall Plan

*John Gimbel's prior works on Germany (see Introduction) have
consistently argued that postwar occupation arrangements broke down,
not because of Soviet intransigence but because of French resistance.
The conventional history written in the light of the Cold War and
buttressed by the recollections of General Lucius Clay, head of the
U.S. military government, maintained that Germany became a Soviet-
American battleground when the Russians refused to follow through
on agreements for administering all four occupation zones as one
economic unit. Carefully reexamining the documents, Gimbel found
the French to be the major impediment to Allied cooperation on
Germany. Only as Soviet-American cooperation chilled over other
issues did American policymakers choose to soft-pedal disagreement
with the French and displace the confrontation upon the Russians.*

*In his new study,* The Origins of the Marshall Plan, *Gimbel resumes
this argument and takes up again another earlier theme: namely, the
bureaucratic conflicts between the U.S. State Department and the War
Department (supporting Clay). The War Department was entrusted
with administering our occupation zone and had to win the needed
funding from Congress. It wished to minimize the tax burden involved
in supporting the ravaged German economy, hence it moved consistently
to allow the Germans to rebuild their industry. The State Department
was sensitive to Germany's neighbors, still battered from 1940–45,
if not 1914–18, and worked to slow up German reconstruction. In his
new book, Gimbel suggests the Marshall Plan was designed to reconcile
all these conflicting priorities.*

*Gimbel is probably the leading expert on the huge archives left by* *the United States Office of Military Government in Germany (OMGUS). He has valuably demonstrated that while the German question became central to the Cold War, it was not at the root of the antagonism. Nevertheless, my own evaluation is that Gimbel's account may excessively polarize historical issues. He argues strongly in his recent study that the Marshall Plan of 1947 was no plan at all—granted, but the word "plan" need not be taken so literally. And by the time the initiative emerged fully clad in 1948 as the European Recovery Program—to which the name Marshall Plan is also commonly ascribed— it certainly had scope and coherence. Likewise, the fact that the French were the major early irritant in Germany need not exclude a growing dispute with the Soviets. In the fall of 1946 John Kenneth Galbraith caught the complexity of the problem when he wrote, "In the last analysis unification of Germany will depend not on France but on Russia. The French opposition so far has, in a measure, served as a cover for Russian intentions."* ***

*My reservations, however, should not detract from the significance of Gimbel's work in demythologizing the German issue. For this selection I have chosen chapter 19, "Germany and the Marshall Plan," and portions of chapter 20, "Of Myths and Realities," from* The Origins of the Marshall Plan. *They are reprinted with the permission of the author and publisher, Stanford University Press, and the trustees of the Leland Stanford Junior University.*

### Germany and the Marshall Plan

The complicated negotiations with Britain, France, and the Army on the bizonal level of industry and the Ruhr coal-management plan finally convinced the State Department that it would eventually have to assume administrative responsibility for the policies it wanted implemented from the American base in Germany. Faced with the financial responsibilities that accompanied administrative responsibilities in Germany, the State Department moved toward a position it had prevented the Army from taking for more than two years: it became more critical of France's aims and objectives regarding Germany and the future of Europe, and it finally concluded that France's territorial and economic demands were, in fact, incompatible with any program that would have Germany achieve a viable economy in the future.

* John Kenneth Galbraith, *Recovery in Europe,* National Planning Association Pamphlet No. 53 (October 1946), p. 31.

Though much has been written about the continuing influence of a Morgenthau-plan mentality on American policy in Germany, the issues were much more complex than that.[1] Riddleberger had, in fact, outlined the American dilemma in Europe as early as November 24, 1945, when he discussed the pitfalls of a policy that would try to destroy Germany's industrial war potential on the one hand and prevent the creation of a "soup kitchen" economy on the other.[2] Essentially, the problem was and remained one of achieving balance, moderation, and a "golden mean," which—as I have shown—the French would not discuss, much less consider; which the State Department would not further unless France was satisfied; and which the Army would not pursue, in part because it wanted to promote sufficient economic recovery to make a case for relief from the civil-political responsibilities of the occupation and in part because it was out of sympathy with the State Department's broader politico-economic mission in Europe.*

Late in April 1947, when Marshall learned from Clay and from his own advisers what the political and economic consequences of his and Bevin's Moscow decisions on Germany were likely to be, he instructed Kennan and the PPS to initiate studies that would, in effect, look toward a balanced solution of Europe's economic problems, rather than toward the unilateral rehabilitation of the bizone which the Army, the British, Herbert Hoover, and the Eightieth Congress seemed to prefer. As noted previously, the PPS divided the problem, recommending a

---

* Interestingly, the Russians made specific proposals that would have had the effect of achieving a balance between reparations, exports, and imports, and German consumption, and they did so repeatedly—at Potsdam, during the Clay-Sokolovsky discussions in Berlin late in 1946, and at the Moscow CFM in 1947. See *FRUS, 1945*, Potsdam II, 810, for the Soviet proposal of July 23, 1945, which said: "In working out the economic balance of Germany the necessary means must be provided for payment for imports approved by the Control Council. In case the means are insufficient to pay simultaneously on reparations account and for approved imports, all kinds of deliveries (internal consumption, exports, reparations) have to be proportionally reduced." See *FRUS, 1945*, Potsdam II, 276–81, for a discussion of the Russian proposal, and Clay to War Dept., for Echols, Oct. 11, 1946, RG 165, file WDSCA 387.6, Sec. IV, Box 351, NA, for the Russian proposal in the fall of 1946, a proposal that Clay considered to be "a reasonable basis for discussion." Clay's judgment that the Soviet proposal violated neither the Potsdam Agreement nor the level-of-industry plan may be found in Clay to War Dept., for Noce, Jan. 22, 1947, RG 165, file WDSCA 387.6, Sec. VIII, Box 354, NA. See SecState to the President and ActgSecState, March 19, 1947, *FRUS, 1947*, II, 264, for the statement that at Moscow Molotov "insisted that German industry must be set at a level to insure her internal needs, payments of imports, and reparations."

limited German recovery program (the Coal for Europe plan) and a long-term European program to be developed by the Europeans themselves, albeit with American "friendly aid in the drafting." [3] Both recommendations were essential elements of the Marshall Plan, the first one to pacify the Army and the second one to pacify the Europeans and the State Department.

The Marshall Plan emerged issue by issue during 1947, but in conformity with the PPS's two major recommendations and with remarkable clarity and consistency. A limited amount of general German economic recovery would have to occur as an essential component of the Coal for Europe program, and perhaps to satisfy the Army, the British, the Congress, and the American public. But Germany's recovery would have to be controlled in such a way as to satisfy the political interests of Bidault and to ensure the prior recovery of Germany's neighbors and provide for their security.[4] In the interests of better control, neither the American Army, nor the British, nor the German Socialists would be permitted a free hand in the Ruhr and the Rhineland. Furthermore, the announcement of German recovery programs, such as those provided for by the Bevin-Marshall decisions in Moscow and detailed in the Clay-Robertson level-of-industry plan, would have to be coordinated with the long-term program for European recovery; their implementation would have to be delayed until the Europeans agreed upon a common recovery plan, and—if necessary —those aspects of the German recovery program that were ready for implementation before the common plan could be developed would have to be kept under wraps until it was politically opportune to reveal them to Germany's neighbors or to make them public.

As Kennan's committee had recommended, the German-recovery phase of the PPS report (the Coal for Europe program) went forward immediately, even while the long-term program was still very much in its embryo and developmental states, and long before the Americans had a clear conception of the general European plan. That condition produced the events and situations already described: the British-American coal talks, the wrangling over the coal-management plan and socialization, the dispute about the export price of coal, and the conflict between Berlin and Washington on the bizonal level-of-industry plan. The condition also confronted the State Department with the task of reconciling its limited German recovery program—which was moving ahead more rapidly than the general European recovery program—with its own priorities and with France's demands for security, territory, coal, a decimated German economy, and a decentralized German political structure. The latter remains to be described.

Early in June 1947 the State Department urged OMGUS to proceed rapidly with the British to develop a coal-production program in Germany. Later in June the Committee of Three asked Clay and Murphy to report on what was needed to permit the German economy to contribute actively to European recovery and to bizonal self-sufficiency.[5] On July 2, 1947, the State Department instructed Clay to make sure that the level of industry being planned for the bizone would provide for a self-supporting German economy, but also to make sure that substantial reparations deliveries from Germany would occur, even though doing the latter might be at the expense of Germany's future standard of living.[6] One day later the Committee of Three combined these and other instructions and adopted a policy statement on Germany and the Marshall Plan:

1. The United States would make known publicly its willingness to have its zone of Germany collaborate in the European recovery program, but no initiative was to come from Berlin even though "the occupied area must be represented when European recovery plans are being prepared."

2. If the restoration of European international commercial relations required an increase in American expenditures in Germany, or if such restoration would set back German self-sufficiency, American expenditures in Germany would be increased, or the German economy would be compensated by provision of American relief monies to the country or countries benefiting from Germany's trade so as to enable them to pay Germany.

3. The American commander in Europe would consult with European countries and international organizations regarding German production and trade and ensure that emphasis was given to the export of German goods needed by the European countries for their economic recovery and rehabilitation.

4. Transactions of a substantial nature, or those which resulted in trade exchanges between Germany and other European countries—but not in conformity with the three preceding principles—were to be referred to Washington for decision.[7]

According to Petersen, who sent the policy statement to Clay on July 10, 1947, paragraph 2 was a frank admission that United States policies and programs in the interests of general European recovery might delay a self-sustaining German economy and require an increase in funds for Germany or for other countries so they could pay Germany for her exports.[8] That paragraph was, in fact, a hasty and uncoordinated reversal of previous policy, and when it was grafted onto the draft of JCS directive 1779 on July 11, 1947, it stood there in flat contradiction of another section of the same directive, which stated that the United States would "not agree to finance the payment of

reparation by Germany to other United Nations by increasing its financial outlay in Germany or by postponing the achievement of a self-
sustaining German economy." [9]

The flow, the content, and the contradictions of the policy instructions and directives that went from Washington to Berlin in June and
July 1947 testify to the State Department's attempt to reconcile the
irreconcilable: German recovery to self-sufficiency and France's demands for coal, security, and economic advantage. Matthews, who
had worried similarly to McCloy in 1945, warned Lovett on July 11,
1947, that "conversations looking toward the level of increase in
German industry are about to result in an agreement between the
British and ourselves with benefit to the economy of Germany," that
German coal exports would be reduced, and that unless France received compensating benefits the French government would face serious political problems.[10] On the same day, Clayton and Caffery
heard from Ramadier and Bidault that France had not changed its
German policies and demands, and that if France could not be ac-
commodated there would be no Marshall Plan. They advised Marshall
immediately to use "extreme care . . . in dealing with this matter." [11]

Neither extreme care, nor caution, nor attempts at rational argument
or persuasion were enough to allay France's fears, and Bidault's
warnings of impending doom for France, the Marshall Plan, and
Europe increased with multiplier effect as he received more and more
information about the British-American plans for the bizone. Bevin,
who was in Paris, warned that publication of the level-of-industry
plan "would be a tragic mistake." The Army ordered Clay to hold
up everything for the time being. Harriman, who "found Bidault in a
hysterical condition," tried to convince him of the absolute necessity
for a new level of industry in the bizone and claimed "that the point
had been reached where measures had to be taken." But Bidault had
already told him he was "very alarmed about developments in Germany," and he warned that "he would be compelled to protest" if the
Americans went ahead with their plans.[12]

Marshall finally capitulated and advised Bidault on July 21, 1947,
that no further action on German recovery plans would be taken until
"the French Government has had a reasonable opportunity to discuss
these questions with the United States and United Kingdom Governments." [13] Marshall had been influenced by a personal plea from Bidault, by official demands from the French government, by suggestions from Bevin, and by advice from Kennan to hold tripartite talks
and use the occasion to "place squarely before the French the choice
between a rise in German production or no European recovery financed
by the U.S." [14] Marshall's sensitivity to the political tightrope on which

he was walking is revealed most clearly in a memorandum he wrote to Secretary of Agriculture Anderson on July 22, 1947. Anderson had been in Europe from July 1 to 14, 1947. Upon his return he wrote a report for Truman and asked the State Department for advice on its possible publication. In reply, Marshall assured Anderson that he had been "tremendously impressed" with Anderson's report to the cabinet, but that recent French reactions to the level-of-industry plan for Germany had "produced a very delicate situation, particularly with regard to the development of the meetings of the sixteen nations in Paris." Under the circumstances, Marshall said, the publication of Anderson's report would be unwise "for the reason that it stresses the economic reconstruction of Germany virtually to the exclusion of any mention of our interest in the reconstruction of the liberated areas—which is the basis of the Paris conference." In other words, Marshall liked the report but feared that its publication would "add fuel to the flames now raging by reason of the agreement negotiated between General Clay and General Robertson." [15]

### TRIPARTITE TALKS ON GERMANY AND THE MARSHALL PLAN

As noted previously, Marshall agreed to discussions on Germany with the French for political reasons, and he did so before the Americans and British had agreed on what they would discuss. What the two powers finally discussed with France is conveniently summarized in the State Department's instructions of August 12, 1947, to Ambassador Douglas, who was the American delegate and the chairman of the London tripartite discussions. The French were to be given every opportunity to make a full statement, but Douglas was to "make it clear that in the absence of a fusion of the French zone with the US and UK zones, the US and UK are responsible for and will take final decision on all matters regarding the bizonal areas." Douglas was to defend the Clay-Robertson plan vigorously against modification, but "if in your judgment there is a genuine threat to the success of the European economic plan or if democracy in France will be threatened unless changes are made," the issue was to be referred to Washington for further instructions. Douglas was to discuss neither the resumption of reparations nor the rate of reactivation of Germany industry. If the French raised the Ruhr management issue, Douglas was to tell them that "acceptance" was not involved, but that the matter could be discussed in the CFM scheduled for November. If France raised the question of the French zone's union with bizonia, Douglas was to make clear that the United States desired such union, but that it would not hold up the new level-of-industry plan pending a French proposal and its discussion. If France wanted to discuss the Saar, Douglas was to say that he had no instructions and that the matter was being dealt with through diplomatic channels.[16]

As Clay had predicted in July, the French made clear in London that their major objection to the bizonal level-of-industry plan was that it threatened the Monnet Plan's projected steel production figure of 12 million tons per year. At issue were France's plans to replace German steel production with French steel production, ostensibly to ensure permanently France's economic and political security. The French said they could not accept the plan in the absence of a prior agreement that made certain Germany would have to export "sufficient coal and coke to insure that German steel production will not absorb so much German coal as to hamper the steel production of other countries, particularly French Monnet plan." [17] Before the London talks were over, the United States instructed Douglas to advise the French of American willingness to discuss the matter and to "give sympathetic consideration" to the proposal for a Ruhr authority which would assure "that access to production of the Ruhr shall not in the future . . . be subject to the will of Germany." According to Douglas, the British were prepared to cause trouble on the issue, and he there-fore decided to take a chance and try to get France to approve the final communiqué without using the policy statement.[18] He hardly needed to do so, since he, Clayton, and Caffery had already told Bidault on August 19, 1947, that they had instructions to postpone further informal discussion with the French on the question of an international board for the Ruhr, but that they "were authorized to say . . . that at some more appropriate time we would be glad to give sympathetic consideration to the French position on the Ruhr." [19] Although Bidault was disappointed, "even" chagrined, and threatened once again that "no French Government, neither the present one nor any succeeding one, could ever agree to a revised level of industry for Germany, without some assurances as to French security and access by Europe to the products of the Ruhr," he finally became reconciled—partic-ularly after the three Americans said they would recommend that discussions be held on the issues immediately after the London tripartite talks.[20]

The political considerations that were so important to the decision to hold the tripartite talks on Germany also dictated the content and the emphasis of the final communiqué. The communiqué covered up disagreements, played down the many issues that had not been re-solved, and failed to make clear that France continued to object to the level-of-industry plan and its implications.[21] The talks and the communiqué nevertheless gave both sides what they wanted: Bidault got the political leverage he said consultations would give him to fore-stall political crisis and to remain in control in France. The British and Americans could now publish the Clay-Robertson bizonal level-of-industry plan and use it officially as the basis for Germany's con-tribution to the Marshall Plan for European economic recovery.

The issues that were not agreed upon during the London tripartite talks were the subjects of continuing discussions and negotiations in Berlin, Paris, London, and Washington throughout 1947 and on into 1948. For example, the military governments in Berlin negotiated agreements on the Saar, coal, coke, and the Moscow sliding scale for German coal exports.[22] In Paris, Clayton, Caffery, and Douglas—seconded by Kennan and Charles H. Bonesteel (a colonel on the War Department General Staff, on assignment with the State Depart-ment)—initiated informal talks with the French on the international board for the Ruhr, thus laying the basis for the final agreement on a Ruhr coal and steel authority, which came out of the London six-power talks of 1948.[23]

Interesting and significant though the continuing negotiations are, they are beyond the scope of this study. Once the Americans had reasonable assurances that the French would not (could not, since they had been consulted) *openly* and *publicly* protest the Ruhr coal-man-agement plan, the price of export coal, and the Clay-Robertson level-of-industry plan, they concentrated on giving "friendly aid" to the CEEC in Paris on the form, structure, technicalities, and nature of the European recovery program. In the end, they made sure that the Ger-man decisions that Marshall and Bevin had made in Moscow would be implemented.

### Germany and the CEEC

A convincing body of evidence now available makes clear that the Americans conceived and developed the Marshall Plan as a method for resolving the United States economic dilemma of the German occupa-tion. There are, for example, Marshall's and Dulles's reports on the Moscow CFM;[24] the PPS's report of May 23, 1947, with its empha-sis on German coal for Europe; and the SWNCC message of June 19, 1947, to Clay, which said that "any program of European reconstruc-tion must necessarily take Germany into account." There is a record of Clayton's remarks to Bevin and the British cabinet members that "a radical change is needed in approaching the German coal problem as *sine qua non* to any consideration of the over-all European problem." Finally, there is the Committee of Three's policy decision of July 2, 1947, which said that "the occupied area must be represented when European recovery plans are being prepared." [25]

Kennan's recommendation that the Europeans themselves develop the long-term program of European recovery, together with the political decision to have them do so despite Clayton's vigorous protests that *"the United States must run this show,"* and the continuing public posture taken by Marshall and others that the United States would limit its role to "friendly aid," all made it difficult for the Americans to get the kind of German program they wanted and needed. Interestingly, Molotov seems to have sensed that there was more to the Marshall invitation than met the eye, for he asked Bevin and Bidault in Paris whether they had additional information from the Americans.[26] Though I have no way to demonstrate the conclusion, Molotov's performance at Paris late in June and early in July 1947 makes sense if one assumes that the Soviets detected either duplicity or a political-economic trap in the Marshall Plan. Why else would Molotov ask, as the first order of business, whether Bevin and Bidault had "inside" information from the United States or whether they had made any "deals" among themselves? Why would he ask the two unanswerable questions he proposed they send to Washington: How much money was the United States prepared to spend on European recovery, and would the Congress vote to approve the credits? Perhaps Molotov knew from Russia's own experience with economic planning that the grand plan implied by Marshall's invitation was impossible to achieve—either because the capitalistic economic systems would refuse to stand still for that, or because the various nations would not attempt the encroachments on their national sovereignty implied in the program, or because of the sheer *technical* impossibility of constructing the economic input-output tables that would be required for the task. Since its economic objectives were either unbelievable or impossible to achieve, Molotov's assumption that the Marshall Plan was essentially a political program, not unlike the imperialism that Marxist-Leninists were inclined to see, has a certain logic.

Molotov's departure from Paris on July 3, 1947, undoubtedly helped to narrow the range of political disagreement after that, but it did not pave the way for the kind of German-based European recovery program the Americans had in mind. On July 20, 1947, Caffery reported on the first week of the CEEC's Marshall Plan talks in Paris, concluding that the "French, of course, have not abandoned outwardly their . . . 'pastoral' approach to [the] German problem and contend that security lies in 'pulling heavy industrial teeth' of Germany." [27] On August 6, 1947, after a three-day round of discussions on the progress of the CEEC and on the latest PPS paper (of July 23, 1947), Clayton, Caffery, Douglas, Murphy, and Paul H. Nitze (the Deputy Director of the Office of International Trade Policy, State Department) recommended formally that it was time to give "friendly aid" to the Paris conference. The recommendation produced considerable discussion in Washington and Paris on how to give "friendly aid" without facing charges of dictation and on how to develop a "united front" in Washington to ensure against contradictory "friendly aid" from the War Department and the State Department.[28] On August 14, 1947, the State Department sent guidelines to Paris for Clayton's and Caffery's use in "informal talks with appropriate committee chairmen and others."

These guidelines were vague and cautious on details, but firm on principles that would require effective German participation in European recovery. The guidelines said the participating countries were paying too little attention to Marshall's call for self-help and mutual aid. "An itemized bill summing up prospective deficits against a background of present policies and arrangements will definitely not be sufficient." The Americans expected the production programs of participating countries to be based not only on their own needs, but also on fulfilling the needs of the other participating countries. Apparently to ensure that Germany would be included as a full participating country, the guidelines concluded by stating that "further aid can be given [regarding the] role of western Germany." [29] The importance of the latter emerged in future exchanges.

Clayton and Caffery reported on August 20, 1947, on their "friendly aid" in Paris, noting—as one example of a fundamental problem—that the combined steel-production figures submitted by the bizone and France would require more coke than would be available anywhere.[30] Douglas believed that the "French must be persuaded to abandon [their] present position that original Monnet plan must be accepted practically unchanged no matter what the cost to US or to general recovery," and he thought the United States would have to be represented in Paris to defend the bizonal production plans against the competing demands of the Monnet Plan. Though the United States need not take the lead, Douglas said, "neither should we hang back." [31]

Meanwhile, in Washington, further discussion within the State Department produced the consensus "that sufficient friendly aid is not being given." Two days later, Lovett cabled Marshall (who was attending an inter-American conference on peace and security at Petropolis, Brazil) that the CEEC was scheduled to produce a report within a week, and that the news was all bad. The CEEC was going to come out with sixteen shopping lists that would require an unreasonably large grant of American aid and that would in the end fail to establish European self-sufficiency by 1951. Lovett said the conference had gone ahead despite Clayton's and Caffery's instructions of August 14. The United States had "pointed out [the] necessity for primary emphasis on efficient utilization of existing capacity rather than on capital development," but "adequate results have not ensued." According to Lovett, "the time has now arrived for us to give some indications that the present plan is not acceptable and to do so promptly." He recommended that Clayton and Caffery be instructed to press for a European plan based upon self-help and mutual aid rather than on long-term capital improvements in the individual nations. They should "emphasize the breaking of specific bottlenecks well known to them and to us." [32]

Lovett talked about shopping lists, costs, and principles, but he also alluded to the fundamental issues at stake. The "specific bottlenecks well known to them and to us" referred to the Ruhr and the Rhineland, to the PPS's Coal for Europe program, and to the limited rehabilitation of transportation and of steel and machinery production that was needed in Germany to implement the coal-recovery program. Lovett's insistence on self-help and mutual aid rather than on long-term capital improvements referred to the conflicting demands for coal, coke, steel, manpower, and other factors of production between the Monnet Plan and the Clay-Robertson bizonal level-of-industry plan. Finally, his note that the Americans wanted "primary emphasis on efficient utilization of existing capacity rather than on capital development" meant that the Americans had opted for the Clay-Robertson plan for Germany rather than the Monnet Plan for France; for European recovery that would include substantial German recovery rather than for European recovery that would, in the first instance, benefit France. It was well known that the greatest source in Europe of idle or underutilized capital equipment—on which the Americans wanted to put "primary emphasis"—was in Germany. The Harriman Committee, for example, referred to that knowledge when it observed that "over-all production in some European countries has shown remarkable recovery, [but] it is still true that Europe's total production, *especially when Germany is taken into account,* is well below prewar levels, with the critical item of coal a prime example." [33] Marshall himself referred to it in a speech he made to the Chicago Council on Foreign Relations on November 18, 1947: "The truth is that far from being accorded a preference over any Allied country, German recovery has lagged so far behind that of the other countries of Europe as to retard the whole effort for European recovery. At the present time industrial production in Western Germany is less than one-half that of pre-war." [34]

Armed with a State Department policy statement of August 26, 1947, and assisted by Charles H. Bonesteel and Kennan (who supplied additional, oral instructions "relating to general political situation"), the Americans in Paris, with Marshall's approval, told the CEEC what they wanted. The fundamental objectives of the program were "to move entire area" toward a "working economy independent of abnormal outside support." To do that "participants must . . . foster European recovery as a whole, and . . . make national contributions to this common goal." In order to maximize self-help and mutual aid, the "program must . . . concentrate initially on elimination of bottlenecks and [on] other opportunities for greatest immediate recovery at lowest cost in scarce resources," and—as if to nail down the German contribution firmly—the "program must be directed primarily toward short-run recovery rather than long-run development; full use of existing or readily repairable capacity and restoration of normal domestic and intra-European intercourse therefore have priority . . ." Clayton and his colleagues in Paris translated their instructions into seven "conditions," which they presented to the leadership of the CEEC on August 30, 1947. The "condition" providing specifically for Germany's recovery stated that "long-run development projects should not be allowed to interfere with the reactivation of the most efficient existing productive facilities. The latter must have first priority." [35]

AMERICAN STRATEGY AND THE CEEC

The State Department's strategy was to dovetail German rehabilitation with the general European recovery program and to present to the United States Congress a single foreign-aid package. To do that, it sought acceptance in Paris of a set of broad, general principles that would permit implementation of the level-of-industry plan for the bizone and allow a rate of reactivation of German industry that would also be acceptable to the Army, the British, the Congress, and ultimately the American public. The strategy, to be followed on three fronts, was outlined in detail by Charles Bonesteel in a memorandum of August 27, 1947, to Robert Lovett.

In Paris, "the United States will state to the participating countries that it is our intent to meet their views with regard to bizonal matters in so far as is possible, consistent with our responsibilities as the military governors. This intention to be based clearly on the assumption that the Paris conferees give assurances of an equal intent with regard to their national programs, and further demonstrate this intent by their actions at Paris. The demonstration of their intent requires, in effect, that discussions of the German zones are part of a broader discussion of all national programs."

In London, Douglas would consult with the British to get them to agree to the proposed discussions in Paris.

In Washington, the difficult assignment of satisfying the Army would go to Lovett, Bohlen, and Saltzman, who would meet with Royall, Eisenhower, Draper, Lauris Norstad (the Director, Plans and Operations Division), "and no others," if that could be arranged. According to Bonesteel, the State Department approach to the Army should be "educational, with a slight dictatorial flavor." Lovett and Bohlen could "present the broad global picture, bringing out the two-world assumption" and emphasizing the need to counterbalance the "Soviet world" and to treat "Europe west of the Iron Curtain on a regional basis." With respect to budget and finances, the State Department might assure the Army that it was committed to obtaining "considerably greater sums for Germany as part of the regional program." Last, the Army should be told of "the requirement that the German economic matters be discussed at Paris," emphasizing the "security aspect of drawing more closely to us the nations of Western Europe now wavering between communism and us." [36]

### Implementing the Strategy

*The Army.* The State Department's grand strategy proved difficult to implement, even though the Army and the Harriman Committee (the President's Committee on Foreign Aid) fell into line readily. The Army accepted the strategy and agreed to discussions in the CEEC regarding integration of the bizone into the European recovery program. Clay accepted the decision taken in Washington, but he apparently did so on the assumption that he was leaving, for he later made clear that "no self-respecting man would continue to operate with the degree of interference he had experienced" and that he "would not be willing to continue under these conditions for another year." [37]

*The Harriman Committee.* Convincing the Harriman Committee was easy. Harriman had endorsed Herbert Hoover's report on Germany in March 1947, and he had been promoting Hoover's recommendations since then. After Truman created the Committee in June 1947, Harriman arranged for it to hear reports from Marshall, Kennan (on the political background of the Marshall Plan), Eisenhower (on economic stability and national security), and others.[38] The records of an August

15 meeting of the subcommittee for economic and financial analysis —whose membership included Calvin B. Hoover, former Chairman of the German Standard-of-Living Board in Berlin—reveal a strong bias in favor of stimulating coal production in the Ruhr and Rhineland, increasing the bizonal level of industry, and (in the interests of speedy European recovery) reactivating plants that were in excess of those needed by the German economy under the level-of-industry plan.[39] On September 10 and 11, 1947, the full Harriman Committee heard speeches and reports by several government functionaries, including Kennan, Bonesteel, and Lovett. Lovett reviewed the developments in Paris, summarized the State Department's August 14 guidelines, "which will not be compromised," and described the Clayton-Kennan-Bonesteel attempt to get the technical experts in Paris to modify the requirements for American aid. He concluded that the current CEEC documents and reports could not be translated into a workable program, and he observed that "the Department of State desires that the work to date not be considered as constituting a program." [40]

The message the Harriman Committee got on September 10 and 11, 1947, is described in a letter of September 12, from Owen D. Young, the chairman of the subcommittee on economic and financial analysis, to Harriman. It said, in part:

> I share fully the apprehension of the State Department that if we fail to meet the present food and fuel emergency which faces the German people and if we fail to help them develop promptly a long range program of rehabilitation, which will enable them to support themselves, there is grave danger that western Germany will become communistic and will be taken over by Russia. If Russia could supplement her present vast resources of raw materials and manpower with the creative, productive and organizing capacity of the German people, she would become shortly the most powerful nation in the world. The result very likely would be that all of Western Europe would be forced to accept a communistic program. The United States would then be faced with a menace which would make the Hitler threat in perspective look like child's play.[41]

It is needless to push the point further, for the published report of the Harriman Committee is filled with statements and allusions attesting to the Committee's acceptance of the State Department's strategy and policy. There is, for example, the statement that "the amount of aid allotted to Germany may have to be higher than was set at Paris." Further: "In the opinion of the Committee . . . it is the policies pursued in Germany by our own Government wihch are of all-importance to the success of any aid program." In addition: "It cannot be too strongly emphasized that the producing and purchasing power of Germany, and, through Germany, the producing and purchasing power of all Central Europe, is indispensable to the recovery of Western Europe." Finally, there is the entire section entitled "Report on the Special Position of the Bizone." [42]

*The British.* The British initially rejected Washington's proposal to have the CEEC discuss the integration of the bizone into the European recovery program, and the Americans eventually had to seek Britain's support by roundabout means. Perhaps the British agreed with Murphy, who warned on September 8, 1947, that if Germany were discussed in the CEEC the European countries would try to obtain indirect financing from the United States through Germany.[43] Upon hearing of the British rejection, Marshall cabled Douglas to impress upon Bevin the seriousness with which he regarded the British opposition. Marshall noted that "the force of US pressure" to get a cooperative, regional approach at the expense of national programs such as the Monnet Plan "is seriously weakened if the one European area in which the US has direct responsibility abstains." He argued that Germany had not been adequately included in the CEEC reports, and he noted as evidence that the bizone's CEEC questionnaire had reported that mining-machinery production would reach about $1,000 million in 1951, but that the CEEC experts had planned for *only* $13 million in mining-machinery exports from Germany between 1948 and 1951. Further, he noted, the CEEC reports contemplated *no* net steel exports from Germany after 1947.[44]

Douglas was unable to turn Bevin and the British around. Harried by problems in Paris, confronted with the CEEC delegates' resistance to excessive American "friendly aid," and warned by Bevin that direct United States interference would delay the CEEC reports, Douglas asked the State Department to go more slowly. On September 12, 1947, he reported that he had not brought up the bizonal-inclusion question with the British because of the other difficulties he and Clayton were having in Paris. He and Clayton suggested that it might be "more appropriate to ask for the inclusion of the bizonal areas when the conference is reconvened after the submission of the 'provisional' or 'first report.' " [45] Five days later Douglas repeated his advice, saying that the United States could press for inclusion of the bizonal areas after the first CEEC report had been received by the United States government "and when, should it be necessary, the conference is reconvened for the purpose of modifying the first report or preparing a second." [46] In the end, Britain accepted the State Department's strategy and policy on Germany during the broader negotiations in the CEEC and in Washington.

*The CEEC.* Irony of ironies—in view of what had happened since

1945—as the Marshall Plan talks progressed in 1947, the State Department began to press actively for German recovery over the objections of the liberated countries. It apparently did so roughly in correspondence to its accumulating knowledge of the costs of a European recovery program unless something more was done in Germany than to implement Kennan's Coal for Europe program. Late in August 1947, after Clayton and others had reviewed the draft CEEC reports being prepared in Paris, Clayton advised Sir Oliver Franks, the President of the CEEC in Bevin's absence, that the $28.2 billion Marshall Plan aid figure that was emerging "was out of the question." He reported to Washington that he was "convinced there is no other way to deal with this situation than to impose certain necessary conditions." [47] The State Department responded with a flurry of activity, much of which mocked the concept of "friendly aid."

On August 26, 1947, the State Department sent Clayton and Caffery a policy statement listing certain fundamental objectives and conditions, which have been summarized previously. It also outlined a procedure for informal and formal American review of the CEEC reports with respect to "both general policy matters and technical questions." It said Germany was to be "covered fully into program" with the revised bizonal level-of-industry plan as the basis. The latter might be changed in the interests of general European recovery as "recommended by conference on same basis that conference makes similar recommendations for changes in Monnet or other national plans." [48] On August 30, 1947, Clayton and Caffery presented the American "conditions" to the Executive Committee of the CEEC. They told the Committee that the preliminary materials and reports they had examined were "disappointing," that the $29.2 billion preliminary aid figure was "much too large." They insisted that the CEEC had to develop a common, regional approach rather than simply add up the uncoordinated national requests. Significantly, the Americans illustrated their arguments from the example of coal and steel, remarking that the CEEC report on steel assumed that all existing steel plants in the sixteen nations would operate at full capacity from 1948 on, even though there was insufficient coal and transportation for this purpose. Confronted with the "conditions," and advised of Clayton's opinion that the existing conclusions of the CEEC "might, if formally advanced, prejudice the success of the entire Marshall program," the Executive Committee gave up "any idea of completing the report by September 1." [49]

A MISSIONARY'S REPORT

Kennan and Bonesteel—who had been present when the "conditions" were discussed with the CEEC Executive Committee in Paris—reported independently to Lovett. They endorsed the official Clayton-Caffery-Douglas "suggestion that the time has come to present our views to [the] governments directly," [50] and Kennan filed a personal, fascinating analysis of the reasons for the failure of the Paris Conference to develop a satisfactory European recovery program.

Kennan concluded that the United States "must not look to the people in Paris to accomplish the impossible. . . . No bold or original approach to Europe's problems will be forthcoming. . . . Worst of all: the report will not fulfill all of the essential requirements listed by Mr. Clayton . . . on August 30." None of the CEEC delegates was a strong political figure at home, Kennan said, and none could afford to "take extensive liberties with the anxious reservations of the home governments." Furthermore, since the Russians were not present, "the gathering has reverted, with a certain sense of emotional release, to the pattern of old-world courtesy and cordiality in which many of the participants were reared and for which they have instinctively longed throughout the rigors of a post-war diplomacy dominated by the Russian presence." That condition had "practically ruled out any critical examination of the other fellow's figures—particularly as most of the delegates must have lively doubts as to the entire validity of some of their own, and cannot be eager to enter a name calling contest between pot and kettle." At bottom, however, the CEEC delegates' difficulties were compounded by three basic problems and conditions, none of which "can be corrected within the brief period of grace which still remains." Britain's sociopolitical sickness was one of the basic problems. Another was the failure to integrate Germany into the European program. The third was the general political weakness of the participating governments.

According to Kennan, Marshall's Harvard speech had put the European nations to a test, which they had failed. The United States could let things ride, "receive a report which will not really be satisfactory, review it and reject it in due course, making no further effort to aid." Another alternative—"the one we should adopt"—would be for the United States to "make efforts to have the report presented in such a way as to avoid any impression of finality; let it come to us on the understanding that it will be used only as a basis of further discussion; try to whittle it down as much as possible by negotiation; then give it final consideration in the Executive Branch of our Government and decide unilaterally what we finally wish to present to Congress. This would mean that we would listen to all that the Europeans had to say, but in the end we would not *ask* them, we would just *tell* them what they would get." That, according to Kennan, was "what some of the more far-sighted of the Europeans hope we will do." [51]

Three days after Kennan's report, and on Caffery's renewed request for "vigorous and direct representations" to the governments concerned, Lovett sent a circular telegram to the American representatives accredited to the CEEC nations. He instructed them to see the respective foreign ministers or prime ministers as soon as possible and to say that the CEEC plan had "numerous deficiencies" that would make it "unacceptable" to the State Department, "undoubtedly evoke strong criticism" in the United States, and "endanger" the entire program. The amount of aid to be requested was too high, Lovett continued, and the "whole program shows little more than lip service to principles of European self help and mutual help." The telegram summarized the American "conditions," generally went on in the same uncompromising way, and closed with the information that the State Department was trying to get the British to agree to an American proposal to discuss the bizonal plans in the CEEC and integrate Germany into the recovery program.[52]

A footnote in *Foreign Relations* states that "replies from the American missions indicated that these views received sympathetic consideration by the various foreign ministers." But if the British response is indicative, and if Bevin's conclusions are accurate, the footnote is a pure fabrication. Bevin, Sir Edmund Hall-Patch, and Roger M. Makins told Douglas that the seven "essentials" were not new to them, that it was impossible to postpone the scheduled date for the CEEC's report in order to meet the American demands, that the participating countries had already cooperated as much as was possible, and that "any effort to press further would . . . so impair national sovereignty that many countries would rebel." In reporting these things to Washington, Douglas noted that "in view of the foregoing, it would have been futile to press for a decision" on CEEC discussion of the bizone and its integration into the general plan.[53]

The American effort to have the CEEC report delayed and revised failed also. The Executive Committee told Clayton and his colleagues on September 10, 1947, that "to meet entirely the US conception of a program would require a change in the terms of reference and this would mean a new conference." There was, in fact, "no possibility of the present Conference agreeing on an integrated plan." The most the Executive Committee would agree to do was to label the CEEC's report as "provisional," with the understanding that they would go to Washington—along with selected technical experts—to review the program there.[54]

While Marshall tried to arouse British sympathy for the American approach and expressed a veiled threat to take unilateral action regarding the bizone, Clayton and his colleagues tried again to move the Executive Committee in Paris. They finally reached an understanding to delay the CEEC's report for about a week and to let American technical experts work *directly* with the CEEC technical committees in Paris to improve the report. Meanwhile, the Americans and the Executive Committee would continue to discuss what further actions would be taken after the provisional report was issued. At this point Bevin asked Douglas to advise Marshall of his earnest "hope that the United States Government, having made its views known, will now allow the Conference to work upon them and complete its report in an atmosphere of calm and without any feeling of external pressure." It is also the point at which Clayton and Douglas decided not to push the question of German discussions in the CEEC and to advise Washington that "it would be more appropriate to ask for the inclusion of the bizonal areas when the conference is reconvened after the submission of the 'provisional' or 'first report' and press for inclusion during the remaining 8 days of the present phase of the work of the conference." [55]

The final result of all these things was the adoption of a procedure remarkably similar to the one Kennan had outlined on September 4, 1947. The CEEC issued a "first report" on September 22, 1947, and sent it to Washington as the European plan called for in the Harvard speech. In Washington the Advisory Steering Committee on European Economic Recovery reviewed the report. The committee had been established late in August when the decision to offer more "friendly aid" was made. It met for the first time on September 9, 1947, under tight secrecy and security rules. At one time it seems to have had about a third of the personnel of the State, Commerce, and Treasury Departments working for it.[56] The Advisory Steering Committee coordinated the CEEC reports with the Harriman Committee and other groups, and it finally met with the CEEC Executive Committee and selected technical experts in Washington in October and November to work out the outlines of the proposal that would be presented by the administration to the Congress.[57]

According to Ernest H. Van Der Beugel, a Dutch foreign affairs expert who participated in the Washington meetings, the discussions in Washington were largely technical but highly informative to the Europeans for what they revealed about the way the American system worked. The Americans, he said, used the Europeans as "part of a team charged with the difficult task of making the Paris Report as attractive as possible for the presentation to Congress." In the process, Van Der Beugel continued, "there was an inclination on the part of the Administration to change accents, to color presentations, to minimize some problems and overemphasize others, to hide existing shortcomings and to applaud practically non-existing achievements, in its efforts to win Congressional approval. . . . The aim was Congressional approval for a program created solely for the benefit of the Europeans. It was no wonder . . . that [the Europeans] had some difficulty, not only in adjusting . . . to this situation, but suddenly becoming part of this process." [58]

What the administration did—in fact needed to do—is perhaps illustrated best by quoting portions of an exchange between Vandenberg and Marshall during the Senate Foreign Relations Committee hearings on the European recovery program. According to Vandenberg, the first question he wanted to ask Marshall was also the one he considered to be most basic—too important to be left to Royall, who would appear before the Committee later for the Army.

*Vandenberg:* What I want to ask you is for your comment as to whether there is any dependable hope for this program without a restabilization and integration of western Germany into the program.

*Marshall:* The inclusion, or integration, of western Germany into the program is essential. Coal alone provides one of the great essentials to the recovery program, and Germany is a major source of coal. I merely say that it is essential that western Germany be considered an integral part of the program.

*Vandenberg:* That does not quite go far enough. . . . I would think that it was just as essential that we had a rather definite and hopeful program for the stabilization of western Germany without too long a delay as it is to have a program for any of the rest of these countries, and to whatever extent you are able to make the statement I should like your comment as to the progress that is being made in that direction, and what the prospects are.

Marshall talked then in rather vague and general terms about coal, about conversations with the French, about administrative reorganization in Germany, and other things.

*Vandenberg:* To get down to the bare bones of the thing, would it be fair to say that within the limitations of whatever four-power agreements are binding upon us, we are no longer proposing to await decisions of the Council of Foreign Ministers in respect to the mutual integration of the three other zones . . . and that we are now proceeding . . . without waiting for programs from the Council of Foreign Ministers, always intending . . . to leave our programs open to any who wish to subscribe?

*Marshall:* That is correct, Senator. We are going ahead exactly on that basis. [59]

## Of Myths and Realities

The background and origins of the Marshall Plan for European economic recovery described in this study suggest that neither the official and orthodox interpretations of its inception and purposes nor the ones offered by the revisionists are complete and credible.

CONTAINMENT

It would be ridiculous indeed to deny that the doctrine of containment and the hope for a Communist rollback were features of the discussion and debate on the European recovery program.[60] Kennan's chairmanship of the PPS would have been an anomaly if it had been otherwise. But Kennan and the PPS actually recommended on May 23, 1947, that "immediate measures be taken to straighten out public opinion on some implications of the President's message on Greece and Turkey." The PPS did not see "communist activities as the root of the difficulties of western Europe," and it wanted "to clarify what the press has unfortunately come to identify as the 'Truman Doctrine,' and to remove in particular two damaging impressions which are current in large sections of American public opinion." The two impressions were, first, "that the United States approach to world problems is a defensive reaction to communist pressure and that the effort to restore sound economic conditions in other countries is only a by-product of this reaction and not something we would be interested in doing if there were no communist menace," and second, "that the Truman Doctrine is a blank check to give economic and military aid to any area in the world where the communists show signs of being successful." [61]

But, as it turned out, there was no containing the doctrine of containment, to which Kennan himself contributed with his article in *Foreign Affairs*.[62] The State Department could not carry out the PPS's recommendation, because to do so effectively would have required a forthright discussion of German recovery, which was so essential to the Marshall Plan. As I have shown, a forthright discussion of the German problem aroused Bidault and threatened the political stability of France. Closer to home in the State Department, a forthright discussion of Germany would have called into question the "official" explanations for the difficulties in Germany since 1945. It would have called into question Byrnes's explanations of his failures in the CFM and of the origins of the bizone. It would have called into question the State Department's interpretation of Clay's reparations suspension, and it would inevitably have opened the subject of "hidden reparations." It would have called into question Marshall's explanations of the failure of the Moscow CFM, and it would have challenged the credibility of other pronouncements, releases, and statements—all of which were public knowledge. In a sense, Kennan, Acheson, Matthews, Cohen, Bohlen, and others in the State Department lived to reap the fruits of their own suspicions and of the various tests they had devised and used to frustrate the Russians and keep Clay and the Army off France's back in 1945 and 1946.

An effort to contain the doctrine of containment in 1947 and 1948 would also have flown in the face of a broad spectrum of opinion in the newly elected Eightieth Congress, where the State Department's wartime and immediate postwar stewardship was already under attack for "appeasement" of Russia. Scaring hell out of the Congress and the American people and emphasizing the Communist menace to promote the Greece-Turkey aid bill had paid off, as Joseph Jones pointed out so clearly.[63] In any case, the State Department took a pragmatic approach, rather than follow the PPS's recommendation to correct the anti-Communist emphasis of the Truman Doctrine. It chose to ride the Marshall Plan home safely on the high tide of anti-Communist rhetoric and opinion (which it had helped to further), rather than to risk the plan's defeat and the consequent rehabilitation of Germany by the Army and the Congress on the advice and recommendations of Herbert Hoover—or according to some other "bright and unworkable ideas," as Marshall put it.[64] Naturally, the flow of events themselves contributed to the State Department's option. How would it have been able to abandon the anti-Communist line and reconcile that with Molotov's behavior in Paris in June and July 1947; with the Soviet Union's pressure on Poland and Czechoslovakia not to participate in the Marshall Plan; with the creation of the Cominform in October 1947; and with the coup in Czechoslovakia in 1948?

OPEN-DOOR DIPLOMACY

It would be futile to deny that the concepts that have been described as characteristic of the diplomacy of the open door influenced and guided American policymakers in the inception, discussion, debate, and passage of the European recovery program. But to conclude, as William A. Williams did for example, that "the problem was to coerce the Russians, help western Europe, and thereby establish the reality of an open door system throughout the world" is to ignore the evidence and resort to a secular devil-theory of historical causation designed, perhaps, to bolster those already converted and to spread the gospel among the gullible and the naive.[65] Politicians, along with other mortals, never stand naked of the robes of the past as they make their way toward decisions; they do not go from day to day and issue to issue with an ideological blank slate. In other words, unless one expects miraculous conversions or a revolution, one can hardly expect the policymakers of 1947 to have forgotten or rejected Cordell Hull, Woodrow Wilson, and a host of others as they moved toward resolution of one of the major postwar problems with which they were faced: making peace with Germany and reconstructing war-torn Europe.

In any case, if published analyses and public rhetoric are reliable, there is little doubt that the American policymaking establishment was imbued with, permeated by, and committed to the private-enterprise economic system. American leaders wanted to create and preserve the forms of political and social organization and the patterns of international trade (multilateralism) most conducive to the free-enterprise economic system. They wanted an interlocking, worldwide system of production and consumption, and they apparently believed that that was the most efficient, effective, and just foundation for peace, prosperity, and a rising standard of living for all.[66] The "conditions" laid down by the Americans in Paris late in August 1947 included demands that the participating countries undertake internal financial and monetary reforms, stabilization of currencies, the establishment of proper rates of exchange, as well as "steps to facilitate the greatest practicable interchange of goods and services among themselves, adopting definite measures directed toward the progressive reduction and eventual elimination of barriers to trade within the area, in accordance with the principles of the ITO Charter." [67] The American determination to achieve these and other objectives in Europe helps to explain the progressive shift from the *invitation* of June 1947 to the *dictation* of October 1947: the progressive shift from letting the Europeans draft their own recovery program, to "friendly aid in the drafting," to Clayton's personal missionary work in the capitals of Europe in June and July, to the more stringent (but informal) advice and requirements of mid-August, to the presentation of "conditions" and "essentials" to the CEEC in Paris late in August and to the governments themselves early in September, and finally to the outright intervention in the development of the CEEC's program in September, October, and November. But, as I have shown in the analysis, the progressive shift from the *invitation* of June to the *dictation* of October was also heavily influenced and conditioned by the immediate objective of ensuring Germany's rehabilitation, which was to be dovetailed with the larger European program. In fact, it can be argued that the attempt to resolve the German dilemma was the occasion for calling forth the principles of the open door, rather than the reverse.

Significantly, Kennan—who had insisted in May (over the fierce protests of Clayton) that the Europeans themselves draft the plan—was the one who marshaled the major arguments in September for United States dictation of the final program of European recovery. In the end, he said, the United States should not ask the Europeans, but should just tell them what they would get. Kennan's reversal suggests that there was no clear "open door" plan when Marshall spoke in June, and it supports the idea that bureaucratic tinkering to solve the economic dilemma in Germany gave rise to the Marshall Plan. . . .

## MARSHALL'S PLAN

Current interpretations of the Marshall Plan are all predicated, in some respect or other, on the assumption that there existed a rational plan or policy for European recovery in June 1947. But Marshall later denied that he had a plan at the time, and my study has demonstrated that his statements were accurate. When he spoke at Harvard on June 5, 1947, Marshall had no plan for European recovery, for containment, for creating a multilateral trade world, for promoting the open door in Europe, for forestalling a postwar American depression. He had a practical problem that he thought would have to be resolved, for its own sake and before someone with "all kinds of bright and unworkable ideas" tried to do it. With that in mind, the origins of the Marshall Plan may be reviewed.

Faced with the post-Potsdam impasse in Germany caused by France's actions, and appalled at the high cost of the occupation in appropriated dollars, the Army and Clay maneuvered for two years to try to bring France around. But the State Department refused either to apply sanctions against France or to admit publicly that France was indeed the major problem in Germany. Instead, State Department functionaries expressed suspicions about Russian intentions and long-range objectives, and they did so despite the Army's protests, despite the Army's evidence that the Russians were cooperating in Berlin to fulfill the terms of the Potsdam Agreement. Eventually, the State Department devised tests of Russian intentions, and finally its officials asserted openly that Russia had violated the Potsdam Agreement and other things. Meanwhile, the Russians went their own way in their zone. The British, who agreed with the Army on the need to reduce occupation costs in Germany, threatened several times to adopt unilateral policies in their zone. In July 1946 Bevin outlined a British plan to promote a self-sufficient economy in the British zone, which included the Ruhr. Searching for an alternative to Britain's plan for unilateral action in the Ruhr, Byrnes invited all the occupation powers to join their zones with the American zone in economic unity. Britain eventually accepted Byrnes's invitation, but France and Russia did not. Britain and the American Army expected zonal union to result in substantial reductions in the financial burdens of the occupation, and the two military governments developed a three-year plan to make the bizone economically self-supporting by 1949. But the State Department, which made policy for the United States in Germany, would not agree to economic policies in bizonal Germany that impinged on its plans for rehabilitating liberated Europe first. Neither would the State Department accept bizonal policies and practices that threatened France's political stability or left France's expectations for German coal exports unfulfilled.

Early in 1947 the Army and the British got an ally. The Republican leaders of the newly elected Eightieth Congress were determined to cut costs and to wrest power from the Executive Branch, from the Democratic administration. Some of them were prepared to conduct an investigation into the causes of the "failure" in Germany; some were prepared to review the State Department's wartime and postwar stewardship of American foreign policy; many of them were spoiling for a political showdown with the party of the New Deal. The combination of Congress's inclination to intervene in the German occupation, the Army's restlessness, the CFM's failure to make progress on a German settlement in Moscow, a British decision to increase German production, and Marshall's steady hand in the State Department finally broke the post-Potsdam impasse and inspired the Marshall Plan.

At the Moscow CFM in April 1947, Marshall agreed privately with Bevin to reorganize the British and American zones, to raise the German level of industry, and to make the two zones economically self-sustaining by 1949. Marshall was relatively new to his job at the time. He was burdened with the normal demands of bringing order to the shambles of policy left by Byrnes, who reportedly had carried the State Department around the world in his briefcase. Marshall's well-developed sense of procedure, order, and harmony was heavily taxed by the Greece-Turkey aid bill, the Austrian treaty, the Truman Doctrine, and the CFM in Moscow. He was pushed and pulled by advice from the State Department, the War Department, Dulles, and OMGUS; by France's demands for coal and other concessions; by Britain's initiatives to reduce Britain's dollar costs in Germany; and by Herbert Hoover's "independent" actions regarding German policy. But he was also mindful of the political currents in the United States that had brought forth the Eightieth Congress, pledged to economy in government; to reducing the power of the Executive Branch; to fighting communism at home and abroad; to turning around the diplomacy that had produced Yalta, Potsdam, the changes in Eastern Europe, and the "failure" in Germany. Instinctively sensing that the Moscow decisions on Germany would cause trouble, Marshall prevailed upon Bevin to agree to a six-week delay in announcing them. Upon further reflection, and after consultations with Dulles, Clay, and his State Department advisers, he concluded that the Moscow decisions on Germany were politically dangerous and economically unwise. Although they might solve the German problem, they would do so at economic and political costs that his own department would not accept, and that would be virtually impossible to justify to potential critics who would charge the United States with rehabilitating its recently defeated enemy ahead of its friends and allies. The Moscow decisions on Germany threatened to cause political disaster in France. They would certainly bring heavy criticism from France, from Russia, from German hard-liners in the United States (such as Henry Morgenthau and the Society for the Prevention of World War III), from the liberal press in the United States (such as *PM* and the *New Republic*), and from leftists and Communists everywhere. Marshall decided that his commitment to Bevin would have to be modified, and that the Army's, Hoover's, and the Congress's plans for German recovery would have to be headed off.

True to his training and experience—and perhaps to his instincts as well—Marshall called for the equivalent of military staff studies on his problems. Immediately upon his return from the Moscow CFM he instructed Kennan to activate the Policy Planning Staff in the State Department and to prepare the studies that eventually became the basis for the Marshall Plan. Kennan and the PPS tried to resolve Marshall's post-Moscow dilemma by recommending a short-term program (Coal for Europe) that would do in Germany much of what he and Bevin had already decided in Moscow to do, and a long-term program of European economic recovery to be developed by the Europeans themselves. The short-term program would be merged with the long-term program and thus diffuse domestic criticism of Germany's recovery and help to ensure against the economic and political disaster that a "Germany first" program threatened to call forth, particularly in France, but not exclusively there. The PPS proposal of May 23, 1947, was in fact a plan to implement and gain acceptance for the German decisions that Marshall and Bevin had already made; decisions that raised the specter of a restored Germany equipped with the manpower, the resources, and the technical facilities that Germans had used with such profound effect in the past.

As Marshall said over and over, and as I have demonstrated, there was no "Marshall Plan" in June 1947. When Clayton went to Europe for consultations late in June, he had specific instructions about a

German-based Coal for Europe program and about socialization, but he had only very general and vague conceptions of what was to become the European recovery program. What he did in the capitals of Europe with respect to the latter eventually caused much concern in the State Department. The minutes of a round of discussions in the State Department in August 1947 show a "consensus that Mr. Clayton, while generally aware of departmental thinking with regard to the 'Plan,' holds fundamental divergent views on some aspects." The minutes also make clear that "a comprehensive departmental position has not been officially approved," and they show that "the time has come to firm up the overall departmental position." [68] The upshot was a formal policy statement, which was sent to Clayton and Caffery on August 26, 1947, nearly three months after the Harvard speech. But the "plan" was still incomplete, for Kennan and Bonesteel were dispatched to Paris personally to deliver oral instructions and policies regarding the "general political situation." [69] In short, what existed in the summer and fall of 1947 were the Bevin-Marshall decisions taken at the Moscow CFM, decisions that raised a spectrum of actual and potential domestic and foreign problems that would have to be resolved, defused, and—if necessary—kept from the arena of public discussion and debate, at least for a time.

Perhaps typical of the system that gave rise to it, the Marshall Plan was actually a series of pragmatic bureaucratic decisions, maneuvers, compromises, and actions. Typically also, contemporaries, commentators, and historians have construed the entire series as a plan for purposes of communication and rationalization (and maybe for other reasons). The questions that bureaucrats struggled with included the following: How could they sell a European recovery program to the American public and to an American Congress publicly committed to economy and reduced government spending? How could they explain a new foreign aid program to members of Congress who had already criticized wartime lend-lease and postwar United Nations (UNRRA) aid? How could they reconcile the fundamental differences between the Army and the State Department regarding the purposes, objectives, and length of the American presence in Europe? How could they reconcile the demands of France for German coal to implement the Monnet Plan and the demands of the American and British military governments for coal to provide a self-sufficient German economy? How could they increase coal production in the Ruhr and prevent the British and the German Social Democrats from alienating the American Congress and others by nationalizing the German coal industry? How could they reconcile the conflicting demands of the victorious powers for German reparations and of the military governments for a

German industrial base with which to achieve self-sufficiency for the bizone? How could they reconcile the conflicting demands of Germany's neighbors for cheap German imports and of the military governments for sufficient German export proceeds with which to pay for needed food and raw materials imports, and for previous outlays for such imports?

The series of pragmatic bureaucratic decisions and compromises that became the Marshall Plan included the decisions to do something about German recovery. Neither the Army, nor the British, nor the Congress would settle for less. It included the maneuvers to prevent socialization or nationalization in the Ruhr, and perhaps in all of Germany. Neither the Army, nor Forrestal, nor the Congress would settle for less. It included the actions and maneuvers to restore France and maintain Bidault in power—at least to prevent a leftist United Front in France, and definitely to forestall Communist ascendancy there. Neither the French government nor the State Department would settle for less. It included actions to rehabilitate the liberated nations and Germany's neighbors other than France, some of whom (especially Belgium, Luxembourg, and the Netherlands) were sympathetic to the economic rehabilitation of Germany while mindful of the need for continued security. It included a decision to reduce Germany's economic potential for war by resuming dismantling and reparations, a decision that was in turn countered by actions to rehabilitate Germany's coal, steel, transport, and other industries in the interests of short-term, speedy, and less costly European recovery, and of creating or promoting the eventual formation of a Western European economic and perhaps political union. The series included maneuvers to satisfy France's demands for coal, coke, security, and territory, but there were also actions that forestalled complete satisfaction of France's demands. It included compromises to satisfy Congressional demands for economy and an end to foreign aid, but there were also requests for billions of dollars of foreign assistance that somehow had to be made acceptable to the Congress. To satisfy the Congress and the public, the Truman administration talked about the advantages of multilateral trade and the free flow of goods which foreign aid would stimulate. It talked about the immediate effects of bad crops in Europe; about the hardships caused by the blizzards and the hard winter of 1946–47. It talked about the Marshall Plan as a one-shot deal,[70] as an experiment in pump priming, as a means to forestall a postwar recession, as a humanitarian act, as an economic effort that would reduce the need for military preparedness, as a measure for ensuring access to strategic resources, and as a hard-headed venture in the promotion of peace and security.[71] But the State Department also resorted to a practice it had used with effect before: it described and analyzed "the broad global picture" by emphasizing "the two-world assumption," the need to counterbalance the "Soviet World," and the desirability of "treating Europe west of the Iron Curtain on a regional basis." [72]

Interestingly, Bidault's and Molotov's actions in 1947 show that both France and Russia understood the primary motivation for the Marshall Plan to have been the American economic dilemma in Germany. Typically, the French would not even discuss Germany at first. When Bidault learned from Clayton and Harriman about the plans the Americans had for increasing coal production in the Ruhr and raising the level of industry of the bizone, he threatened to sabotage the Paris Marshall Plan talks and warned that if he did so there would be no Europe. As I have shown, Bidault and the French eventually bowed to the inevitable, but only after they realized that the State Department was as determined in 1947 to solve the German problem as the Army had been in 1945 and 1946. Unlike the Army, however, the State Department gave Bidault an opportunity to compromise and retreat without loss of face and power. As a result, the French modified their demands for separation of the Ruhr and Rhineland from Germany, and they agreed to negotiate on reparations, restitutions, and other economic questions arising from French annexation of the Saar. In turn, the State Department advised France that the United States supported in principle some form of international board that would control and allocate the basic production of the Ruhr. Molotov—also typically—protested the Marshall Plan procedures, probably for substantive reasons. He objected to making decisions on Germany outside the organized Council of Foreign Ministers. The State Department never gave *him* an opportunity to retreat gracefully or politically, and he apparently tried to find out what the Americans had promised Bidault and Bevin as a *quid pro quo* for their support of the Marshall Plan. He asked Bidault and Bevin directly whether they had inside information on the plan, he warned them of the serious consequences of any independent actions they might take in concert with the Americans, and then he left the Paris talks on the Marshall Plan early in July 1947. He interpreted Marshall's initiative in terms of the Marxist-Leninist dialectic, and, after he left Paris, he apparently contributed to the decisions in Moscow to establish the Cominform, to implement the so-called "Molotov Plan," and to organize and mobilize the vanguard that would lead mankind into the future.

### Notes

1. See Lucius D. Clay, *Decision in Germany* (Garden City, N.Y., 1950),

p. 109, for a comment on the lingering sentiment in the United States for a "scorched earth" policy.

2. James W. Riddleberger, "United States Policy on the Treatment of Germany," State Dept. *Bulletin,* XIII (Nov. 25, 1945), 841–49.

3. Kennan to Acheson, May 23, 1947 *FRUS (Foreign Relations of the United States),* 1947, III, 223–30. [PPS: Policy Planning Staff.]

4. See Memorandum of Conversation, Ernest Lindley (*Newsweek*) and Mr. Williamson and Mr. Fuller, Aug. 11, 1947, RG 59, file 740.00119 Control (Germany)/8–1147, NA (National Archives, Washington), for the statement that "the Department was confronted with the necessity of rebuilding [the] German economy in such a manner as not to jeopardize the interests of European and world security."

5. War Dept., from SecWar, SecState, and SecNavy, to Clay, June 19, 1947, RG 107, file ASW 091 Germany, Book 2, Box 26, NA.

6. War Dept. to OMGUS, July 2, 1947, RG 107, file ASW 091 Germany, Book 2, Box 26, NA.

7. Minutes, Meeting of SecState, SecWar, and SecNavy, July 3, 1947, War Dept. Papers, SecWar, Office of Special Assistant, 334, Committee of Three, Jan. 1947– , NA.

8. Petersen to Clay, July 10, 1947, RG 107, file ASW 091 Germany, Book 2, Box 26, NA.

9. See JCS 1779, V, 18c and V, 16c, in U.S. Dept. of State, *Germany, 1947–1949,* Pub. 3556 (Washington, 1950), pp. 37–38.

10. Memorandum, Matthews to Lovett, July 11, 1947, *FRUS,* 1947, III, 717–22.

11. Caffery to SecState, July 11, 1947, *FRUS,* 1947, II, 983–86.

12. BrEmbassy to SecState, *Aide-Mémoire,* July 15, 1947, *FRUS,* 1947, II, 986–87, and note 16; Petersen to Clay, July 15, 1947, RG 107, file ASW 091 Germany, Book 2, Box 26, NA; Caffery to SecState, July 17, 1947, as noted in *FRUS,* 1947, II, 997, note 29; Caffery to SecState, July 20, 1947, *ibid.,* 997–99.

13. SecState to Bidault, July 21, 1947, *FRUS,* 1947, II, 1003–4.

14. Memorandum, by Director of PPS (Kennan), July 18?, 1947, *FRUS,* 1947, III, 332–33.

15. Clinton Anderson to Truman, July 18, 1947, Anderson Files (Germany Trip), Box 8, Truman Library; Marshall to Anderson, July 22, 1947, *FRUS,* 1947, II, 1154, note 56, 1156–57.

16. Marshall to Douglas, Aug. 12, 1947, *FRUS,* 1947, II, 1027–29.

17. Douglas to Lovett, Aug. 22, 1947, *FRUS,* 1947, II, 1047–49.

18. ActgSecState to AmEmbassy, London, Aug. 27, 1947, *FRUS,* 1947, II, 1063–64; Douglas to SecState, Aug. 27, 1947, *ibid.,* 1064–66. The record shows, however, that Douglas advised the French delegate (Massigli) informally of the U.S. position, which Douglas and his colleagues had passed on to Bidault in Paris on Aug. 19, 1947.

19. See Memorandum, Hickerson to Lovett, Aug. 23, 1947, *FRUS,* 1947, 1050–54, for a judgment that the American and British unwillingness to discuss with the French an international board for the Ruhr was a "negative

policy," and a prediction that "a serious crisis will be precipitated if we insist on the . . . negative position."

20. Caffery to SecState, Aug. 19, 1947, *FRUS*, 1947, II, 1041–42. But see Memorandum of Bonnet-Lovett Conversation, Aug. 21, 1947, *ibid.*, 1046–47, for the record of Bonnet's efforts to get a commitment on a Ruhr authority from Lovett.

21. The communiqué is in U.S. Dept. of State, *Germany, 1947–1949*, pp. 356–59. See also AmEmbassy, London, to SecState, Aug. 27, 1947, War Dept. Papers, file WDSCA 014 Germany, Sec. XXV, NA, and Hickerson to James C. H. Bonbright, Aug. 30, 1947, RG 59, Hickerson Papers, folder B, Box 4, NA, for the observation that "your clients [the French] behaved badly but I suppose no more badly than usual."

22. Murphy to Douglas, Sept. 5, 1947, *FRUS*, 1947, II, 1089–90; Murphy to Hickerson, Oct. 1, 1947, *ibid.*, 1096–98; OMGUS, from Clay, to TAG, for Noce, Sept. 30, 1947, RG 165, file WDSCA 463.3, Sec. VI, NA; OMGUS, from Wilkinson, to C/S, U.S. Army, for Clay, Oct. 10, 1947, *ibid.*; Draper to Clay, Nov. 22, 1947, *FRUS*, 1947, II, 725–26; OMGUS, from Hays, to Draper, CC 2392, Nov. 24, 1947, War Dept. Papers, file SAOUS 463.3 Germany, NA; CC 2510, Dec. 6, 1947, *ibid.*; Memorandum, William C. Baker, CAD, to Chief, CAD, Dec. 10, 1947, War Dept. Papers, file CSCAD 014 Germany, Sec. 29, NA.

23. See Douglas to Lovett, Sept. 2, 1947, *FRUS*, 1947, II, 1068–69; Caffery to SecState, Sept. 16, 1947, *ibid.*, 1072, and note 40; Memorandum of Marshall-Bidault Conversation, Nov. 28, 1947, *ibid.*, 739, note 74; *ibid.*, 1097; and John Gimbel, *The American Occupation of Germany* (Stanford, Calif., 1968), pp. 198ff, 208–9.

24. Marshall, Report on Moscow CFM, April 28, 1947, U.S. Dept. of State, *Germany, 1947–1949*, pp. 57–63; Dulles, Report on Moscow Conference, April 30, 1947, *Vital Speeches*, XIII (May 15, 1947), 450–53. Dulles said that "as we studied the problem of Germany in its European setting, we became more and more convinced that there is no economic solution along purely national lines." [CFM: Council of Foreign Ministers.]

25. War Dept., from SecWar, SecState, SecNavy, to Clay, June 19, 1947, RG 107, file ASW 091 Germany, Book 2, Box 26, NA; Clayton to SecState, June 25, 1947, *FRUS*, 1947, II, 932–33; Minutes, Meeting of SecState, SecWar, and SecNavy, July 3, 1947, War Dept. Papers, SecWar, Office of Special Assistant, file 334, Committee of Three, Jan. 1947–, NA. [SWNCC: State, War, Navy Coordinating Committee.]

26. Clayton, "The European Crisis," *FRUS*, 1947, III, 230–32; Caffery to SecState, June 28, 1947, *ibid.*, 297–99; Douglas to Marshall, June 28, 1947, RG 59, file 840.50 Recovery/6-2847, NA. [CEEC: Committee on European Economic Cooperation.]

27. Caffery to SecState, July 20, 1947, *FRUS*, 1947, III, 333–35. See Caffery to SecState, July 27, 1947, *ibid.*, 338–39; July 29, 1947, *ibid.*, 339–41, for further reports of French objection to German recovery.

28. Hickerson, Memorandum, Aug. 11, 1947, *FRUS*, 1947, III, 351–55,

said: "The United States must present a united front when talking to other powers. It would be undesirable to have two independent groups of U.S. representatives, one representing our interests in the over-all European recovery and the other representing our interests in Germany alone." Naturally, Hickerson thought the State Department should do it. See also SecState to AmEmbassy, Paris, Aug. 11, 1947, *ibid.,* 350–51; Caffery to SecState, Aug. 12, 1947, *ibid.,* 355–56; Memorandum Prepared by PPS, Aug. 14, 1947, *ibid.,* 360–63.

29. Lovett to Clayton and Caffery, Aug. 14, 1947, *FRUS,* 1947, III, 356–60.

30. Caffery to SecState, Aug. 20, 1947, *FRUS,* 1947, III, 364–67.

31. Douglas to SecState, Aug. 21, 1947, *FRUS,* 1947, III, 368–69.

32. Minutes of Meeting on Marshall "Plan," Aug. 22, 1947, *FRUS,* 1947, III, 369–72; Lovett to SecState, Aug. 24, 1947, *ibid.,* 372–75.

33. The President's Committee on Foreign Aid, *European Recovery and American Aid* (Washington, 1947), pp. 22–23 (emphasis added). For statistics on the comparative lag in German production see *ibid.,* p. 117; U.S. Congress, Senate, Committee on Foreign Relations, 80th Cong., 2d Sess., *Hearings . . . on United States Assistance to European Economic Recovery* (Washington, 1948), pp. 249–50; and Bert F. Hoselitz, "Four Reports on Economic Aid to Europe," *The Journal of Political Economy,* LVI (April 1948), 112–13.

34. Marshall, "Problems of European Revival and German and Austrian Peace Settlements," Nov. 18, 1947, in U.S. Dept. of State, *Germany, 1947– 1949,* p. 13.

35. *FRUS,* 1947, III, 375, note 5; Lovett to Clayton and Caffery, Aug. 26, 1947, *ibid.,* 383–91; Clayton to SecState, Aug. 31, 1947, *ibid.,* 391–96.

36. C. H. Bonesteel to Lovett, Subj: Discussion of Bizonal Economic Plans at Paris Conference, Aug. 27, 1947, RG 59, file 740.00119 Control (Germany)/8-2747, NA.

37. War Dept., from Noce, to OMGUS, Sept. 3, 1947, RG 165, file WDSCA 334 EECE, Sec. II, Box 319, NA; SecState to Douglas, Sept. 5, 1947, *FRUS,* 1947, III, 409–10; Memorandum of Conversation, Lovett, Saltzman, Draper, Clay, and Gordon Gray, Oct. 18, 1947, RG 59, file 740.00119 Control (Germany)/10-1847, NA.

38. ActgSecState to SecState, March 20, 1947, *FRUS,* 1947, II, 394–95; Meeting of the Non-Partisan Committee of Nineteen Distinguished Citizens, July 23, 1947, Records of the President's Committee on Foreign Aid, 1947, file PCFA—Minutes & Meetings, Box 1, Truman Library.

39. Minutes of the Meeting of the Subcommittee on Economic and Financial Analysis in Hanover, N.H., Aug. 15, 1947, Records of the President's Committee on Foreign Aid, 1947, file Subcommittee—Economic and Financial Analysis, Box 6, Truman Library. Calvin Hoover, it will be recalled, had been the Chairman of the OMGUS German Standard-of-Living Board in 1945 and had left Germany disappointed and unhappy with existing policy and with Germany's economic prospects for the future.

40. Minutes of the President's Committee of Nineteen on Foreign Aid,

Sept. 10–11, 1947, Records of the PCFA, 1947, file PCFA–Minutes & Meetings, Box 1, Truman Library; Notes for Press Conference, 9/11/47, *ibid.;* Interdepartmental Committee on Marshall Plan, Minutes, Sept. 9, 1947, Clifford Papers, file ERP–ECA Miscellaneous, Truman Library.

41. Owen D. Young to Harriman, Sept. 12, 1947, Records of the PCFA, 1947, file Member–Owen D. Young, Box 2, Truman Library.

42. The President's Committee on Foreign Aid, *European Recovery and American Aid,* pp. 3, 7, 33–34, 117–22, and *passim.*

43. SecState to Douglas, Sept. 5, 1947, *FRUS,* 1947, III, 409–10; Sept. 8, 1947, *ibid.,* 410, note 2, and 418–19.

44. SecState to Douglas, Sept. 8, 1947, *FRUS,* 1947, III, 418–19.

45. Douglas to SecState, cable number 4950, Sept. 12, 1947, *FRUS,* 1947, III, 428–29; cable number 4951, Sept. 12, 1947, *ibid.,* 429–30.

46. Douglas to SecState, Sept. 17, 1947, RG 59, file 840.50 Recovery/9-1747, NA.

47. Clayton to Lovett, Aug. 25, 1947, *FRUS,* 1947, III, 377–79.

48. Lovett to Clayton and Caffery, Aug. 26, 1947, *FRUS,* 1947, III, 383–89.

49. Clayton to Lovett, Aug. 31, 1947, *FRUS,* 1947, III, 391–96.

50. Lovett to Marshall, Aug. 31, 1947, *FRUS,* 1947, III, 396–97.

51. Kennan, Situation with Respect to European Recovery Program, Sept. 4, 1947, *FRUS,* 1947, III, 397–405.

52. Caffery, from Dept. Economic Advisers, to Lovett and others, Sept. 5, 1947, *FRUS,* 1947, III, 405–8; ActgSecState, Circular Telegram to Representatives Accredited to CEEC Nations and Murphy, Sept. 7, 1947, *ibid.,* 412–15.

53. *FRUS,* 1947, III, 415, note 3; Douglas to SecState, Sept. 9, 1947, *ibid.,* 420.

54. Caffery to SecState, Sept. 11, 1947, *FRUS,* 1947, III, 421–23.

55. Caffery to SecState, Sept 12, 1947, *FRUS,* 1947, III, 425–28; Douglas to SecState, cable number 4950, Sept. 12, 1947, *ibid.,* 428–29; cable number 4951, Sept. 12, 1947, *ibid.,* 429–30. See also Douglas to SecState, Sept. 17, 1947, *ibid.,* 435, for a repetition of the advice to press for inclusion of the bizone *only after* the first report had been received.

56. Editorial Note, *FRUS,* 1947, III, 439–41; SecState to AmEmbassy, London, Nov. 5, 1947, RG 59, file 840.50 Recovery/11-547, NA; Frank A. Southard to Secretary Snyder, Oct. 3, 1947, Snyder Papers, file Congress –Interim Aid Program, 1947–48, folder 1, Truman Library; U.S. Congress, Senate, *Congressional Record,* 80th Cong., 2d Sess., March 11, 1948, pp. 2528–31.

57. Record of a Meeting Between Members of the Advisory Steering Committee and the CEEC Delegation, Nov. 4, 1947, *FRUS,* 1947, III, 463–70.

58. Ernst H. Van Der Beugel, *From Marshall Aid to Atlantic Partnership: European Integration as a Concern of American Foreign Policy* (Amsterdam, 1966), esp. pp. 77–93. See also Arthur Krock, in *New York Times,* Oct. 5, 1947, DNC Clippings, Box 24, Truman Library; Sir Hubert

Henderson, "The European Economic Report," *International Affairs,* XXIV (Jan. 1948), 19–29; and Michael Straight, "The Betrayal of the Original Concept," *The New Republic,* 118 (Jan. 12, 1948), 9–11.

59. U.S. Congress, Senate, Committee on Foreign Relations, 80th Cong., 2d Sess., *Hearings . . . on . . . European Economic Recovery,* Jan. 8, 1948, pp. 11–12.

60. See, for example, U.S. Congress, House, Committee on Foreign Affairs, 80th Cong., 1st Sess., *Hearings . . . on European Interim Aid . . .* (Washington, 1947), pp. 121–22, for a discussion on Nov. 13, 1947, about using an economic pistol on the Russians and forcing a change in the Soviet Union, as well as the prospects of a successful program to roll back Communism behind the iron curtain.

61. Kennan to Acheson, May 23, 1947, *FRUS,* 1947, III, 223–30.

62. George F. Kennan, [Mr. X], "The Sources of Soviet Conduct," *Foreign Affairs,* XXV (July 1947), 566–82.

63. Joseph M. Jones, *The Fifteen Weeks* (New York, 1955), esp. pp. 138–40, 150–51, 175–76.

64. See George F. Kennan, *Memoirs, 1925–1950* (Boston, 1967), pp. 325–26; Jones, pp. 223–24.

65. William A. Williams, *The Tragedy of American Diplomacy,* rev. & enlarged ed. (New York, 1962), p. 268.

66. See, for example, Thomas C. Blaisdell, "The Foreign Aid Program and United States Commercial Policy," *Proceedings of the Academy of Political Science,* XXIII (Jan. 1950), 397–407.

67. Caffery to SecState, Aug. 31, 1947, *FRUS,* 1947, III, 391–96.

68. Minutes of Meeting on Marshall "Plan," Aug. 22, 1947, *FRUS,* 1947, III, 370.

69. Lovett to Clayton and Caffery, Aug. 26, 1947, *FRUS,* 1947, III, 383–89.

70. U.S. Congress, Senate, Committee on Foreign Relations, 80th Cong., 2d Sess., *Hearings . . . on . . . European Economic Recovery,* Jan. 8, 1948, esp. p. 4.

71. See, for example, Marshall's and Lovett's remarks, respectively, in U.S. Congress, House, Committee on Foreign Affairs, 80th Cong., 1st Sess., *Emergency Foreign Aid. Hearings . . . ,* Nov. 10, 1947, esp. p. 3; Nov. 12, 1947, esp. p. 44.

72. C. H. Bonesteel to Lovett, Memorandum, Subj: Discussion of Bizonal Economic Plans at Paris Conference, Aug. 27, 1947, RG 59, file 740.00119 Control (Germany)/8-2747, NA.

# 6

**Hadley Arkes**

# Bureaucracy, the Marshall Plan, and the National Interest

*The following selection is the work of a political scientist and is included here for a purpose different from that for which it was written. Arkes' book is an effort to discuss the origins and administrative structure of the European Recovery Program—with its managing body, the Economic Cooperation Administration (ECA)—to make an argument about political philosophy. For Arkes the evolution of the Marshall Plan as an administrative entity represented a healthy application of national interest. By national interest the author does not mean the geopolitical requirements of a state, but its very regime, i.e., its constitutional order and the core values that support its political and economic system. At each stage of its development, Arkes argues, the Marshall Plan forced American policymakers to articulate what they believed their country should be trying to achieve in light of its basic regime and values. Even more specifically it forced Congress to confront a problem that was both administrative and political, to take full acount of the consequences of its legislation in terms of an ongoing program and not merely to design a scheme for aid that would then escape its responsibility. In short, the Marshall Plan was allegedly a process of education for Americans. Although it was not unselfish, it was nonetheless elevating by virtue of its incentive for civic reflection.*

*I have chosen Arkes' chapter 14, "Theory and Coercion in the ECA," to illustrate another aspect of the program. Through the material in this segment the student can think about what political intervention in Europe was likely to accompany economic aid. Americans sought to make a distinction between political intervention and economic advising and Arkes documents their effort. Still, the*

*distinction was often naive, and as the chapter shows, they often failed
to concede how much political influence was exerted. Nor, I would
argue, does this selection even get into the major intervention behind
the Marshall Plan. The program itself was based on winning the
cooperation of those politicians, businessmen, and labor leaders abroad
who believed in economic growth and were prepared to subordinate
any aspirations for redistributing power within a capitalist system. The
very process of offering aid and inviting Europeans to work out its
application tended to bring into coalition socialists and centrists and
conservatives in Europe and exclude the communists, as Yergin's earlier
chapter also suggests. Thus political intervention was not really
necessary once the European Recovery Program had been put into
place and started functioning. The major political exclusion had already
taken place. Arkes' discussion, however, remains a careful examination
of how United States officials sought to work out economic aid as a
problem in itself and not merely as an anticommunist measure. In their
day-to-day operations Americans involved in the European Recovery
Program saw their efforts as a politically neutral crusade on behalf of
productivity and technology and growth, and the crusading vigor they
demonstrated in this cause is worth recollecting. The passage is reprinted
with the permission of the author and Princeton University Press.*

### Theory and Coercion in the ECA

I

To say that the ECA was not running the economies of the Marshall
Plan nations was not to say, however, that the agency had no important influence on the internal decisions of the ERP countries. The manipulation of aid that could represent some 3 to 5 percent of a national
budget would inevitably have some bearing on the choices available
to the national governments. But the "intervention" in this case had a
remote quality that was far more characteristic of the ECA. It inhered
a continuous pressure on the Marshall Plan countries for basic investment (as opposed to consumption), and this pressure in turn emanated
from the antibureaucratic features of the ECA—more specifically,
from the basic commitment of the ECA to cut back its program with
each successive year.

What we have called the "debureaucratization" features of the ECA
referred to the preferences for a decentralized agency that would complete its temporary assignment on schedule and leave no bureaucratic
vestiges behind. There was an attendant theory here, also, which sug-

gested that the prospect of a permanent foreign assistance program might undermine the ends of the Marshall Plan. Principally, it was feared that the Europeans would have less incentive to make hard domestic decisions if they thought American aid would always be available as a crutch. As the program wore on, this theory acquired a force of its own, and the debureaucratization theme assumed the weight of a primary commitment or an independent policy value.

When rumors arose in 1949 that the United States might continue the Marshall Plan after 1952, Hoffman declared: "I can think of nothing that will interfere more with achieving the aims of this act than to have the impression get out that this act will be extended. I think this particular activity must end on June 30, 1952." Senator Connally thought the "virility" would be taken out of the program, and Hoffman agreed that "the immediate effect would be to damp the efforts of the people who are really trying to make a success of it. They might slow up." [1] To a surprising degree, this question arose repeatedly in the Congressional hearings, as though Congressmen had to be assured again and again. The ECA reiterated the theme in its official reports, and the executives in the agency continued to affirm the theory.[2]

But what were the *operational* commitments of debureaucratization, and on what basis could we say that this feature achieved the status of an independent or primary value in the program? Here it is possible to identify at least two important empirical standards for the debureaucratization theme: (1) the basing of aid on 1938 consumption levels, and (2) the presumption in favor of standard annual reductions in the country programs of 15 to 25 percent.

Hoffman told the Senate Appropriations Committee in 1950 that the ECA had an "informal" understanding with the Marshall Plan countries that the United States would not underwrite programs that allowed *per capita* consumption to rise above the figures of 1938.[3] For the precise implications of that decision one has to go back a bit further, to the ECA's first annual report, *Recovery Progress and United States Aid*. To arrive at some consistent standard for the allocation of aid, the ECA needed a reliable forecast of investment and consumption in each country. The policy was to finance only that very basic capital investment that a country could not finance for itself, either with its own export production or with diversions from present consumption. But these tests, it was admitted, "could not be applied with precision," and so the ECA was faced with one of those "two-handed" matters of judgment. On the one hand, if standards of living rose above 1938 levels, American financing might simply be used to support more consumption. On the other hand, if consumption were repressed and goods were diverted from the home market into the export trade, there was the danger of a domestic inflation that could wipe out the previous gains and ultimately raise the cost of those export goods themselves. Thus, either alternative had its pitfalls. What the ECA was forced to do was adopt some stable preference in the form of a working rule of thumb:

> There is no easy criterion by which to judge the adequacy of living standards or rates of investment. Nevertheless, wherever there was an indication of an excessive use of resources, actual or proposed, in one of these major categories, the inference was drawn that fewer were needed, that the country could export more or import less, and that the requested volume of ECA aid was larger than necessary.[4]

That is, if living standards rose to such a level that the country seemed able to support more investment, it was *presumed* that it could indeed finance that investment, and that American aid could be diminished. Now, in taking the 1938 figures as the standard, Hoffman had a more precise test. By gearing American aid to the prewar levels of consumption, the ECA hoped to reduce the possibility that Marshall aid would be used to finance the importation of such goods as automobiles, furs, oranges, and bubble gum.

With production rising in the ERP countries, the 1938 standard provided some reasonably intelligible grounds for the future reductions in aid. But in 1949 Hoffman and ECA took an even more drastic step, and here they added a second empirical commitment to their pledge of debureaucratization. It was decided to give the British a 25 percent cut in aid, and lower the allocations to all the other ERP countries by 15 percent. Thomas Finletter, the head of the ECA mission in Britain, thought that "the British themselves took the initiative in whittling down the figure," and so he told the Senate Foreign Relations Committee. But he was apparently misinformed, and Hoffman stepped in to correct the record.

> MR. HOFFMAN. . . . I think I can add a little light on this. In July, when I first met Mr. Stafford Cripps [the British Chancellor of the Exchequer], we were talking about the second year's program. I told him I thought it should be understood that the Americans were very insistent that the second year's program be less than the first year's program, and he asked what amount of cut I had in mind.
>
> "Well," I said, "I think that as it is to be a 4-year program, it would be a good thing to aim at a 25-percent cut."
>
> What figure he had in mind up to that time I do not know. He came out with a 24-percent cut.

SENATOR TYDINGS. What did he say in response to your suggestions?
MR. HOFFMAN. He said, "That is a very drastic downward revision."
I said, "Nothing less than a marked revision will convince the
Americans that the Europeans are really serious." [5]

The decision was not based on an analysis of projects or a calculation of dollar balances. It flowed exclusively from the presumption in
favor of debureaucratization, and it was now the chief operational expression of that commitment. In the next year the British formula was
applied across the board, and as Hoffman reported, "instead of asking
each country to submit a program for the coming fiscal year based
upon its needs for dollars, we asked each country to submit a program
based on the assumption of a 25 percent reduction from the aid it will
have received in fiscal 1950. . . ." [6]

If Hoffman was able to afford frankness in 1950, it was because
the steps had already been taken that subordinated the balance of
payments and the dollar theories. When the ECA introduced condi-
tional aid (with "drawing rights") what it did, in effect, was replace
the balance of payments as a guideline for aid. From that time forward
the amount of assistance that any country would receive would not
depend on its overall balance of payments deficit, but on its deficit with
the dollar area; and in the latter part of 1949, the ECA freed itself
from the dollar theory as well. It was felt that the system, as it stood,
provided little incentive for the ERP nations to correct their deficits,
for the larger the deficit, the greater was the claim, supposedly, for
American aid. Therefore the arrangement posed a fundamental
dilemma. If Marshall aid rose or fell in response to fluctuations in the
balance of payments, then it might grow larger in succeeding years
rather than smaller, and there could be no assurance at all that it
would end by 1952. Yet, if the dollar theory was abandoned, what
would one use for standards?

What the ECA finally did was to take the 1949 allocations as a base.
From that point it would progressively reduce the allocations with each
succeeding year as it moved toward 1952. Henceforth, as Howard Ellis
commented, "the incurring of a larger deficit would not establish a
presumption in favor of increased aid." [7] The state of the balance of
payments or dollar reserves, then, would not be allowed to determine
the life or magnitude of the Marshall Plan. Instead, it was the duration of the ECA that would determine the size of the program. Debureaucratization had now achieved the dominance of an independent
policy commitment; it was Marshall aid itself that was thrust into a
dependent position as a function of the administrative schedule.

As if to firm up that relation as unalterable, the commitment to debureaucratization began to shape now the kind of social science the ECA would use. Conventionally, our discussion of theory in the social sciences follows the categories of prescriptive and descriptive, ethical and empirical. But it is possible that there is variant between the two that might be called a "contingent" theory. That is to say, we may find ourselves in a situation where either one of two descriptive theories, or two sets of empirical assumptions may be equally valid, and yet there may be no means of deciding between them on empirical grounds. There is of course the old question, for example, whether the glass is half full or half empty, or whether the dominant pattern in society is one of conflict or cooperation.

For certain refined purposes of theory-building we might conditionally adopt one assumption rather than another. We might assume, for instance, that conflict is the dominant characteristic of social life, and we might go on from there to draw out some propositions about the management of conflict or the transformation of conflict in an industrial society. The kind of theory I have in mind here would be something like that, but it would also have certain slight differences. It would begin by recognizing that any one of several descriptive theories may be equally accurate or inaccurate, and we would forswear at the outset any effort to decide the issue on empirical terms. Instead, we would choose an "appropriate" descriptive theory on the basis of some intervening value judgment or consideration of policy.

Strange as it might appear on the surface, something of this nature seemed to be at work in the ECA. As we noted earlier, the ECA was faced with some staggering problems in managing its own empirical subject matter. To estimate the balance of payments for the OEEC countries, the economists in the ECA had to forecast the precise direction and volume of trade in various commodities, and the approximate proportions of investment in all the member countries. The result, as they realized, was highly problematic. But even so, there was always something else coming along to throw off the estimates—like the maneuvering that took place before the British devalued in the fall of 1949, or the inventory buildups and the rush for raw materials that followed the outbreak of the Korean war. And yet, admitting all these difficulties, the ECA still had to distribute aid, and it had to find some minimally rational standards by which to do it.

The strategy finally adopted was to construct models based on the most favorable assumptions. Before putting all the estimates together and proceeding "from the diagnosis to an estimate of aid . . . it was necessary *first* to assume that the country in question would achieve self-support status as rapidly as could reasonably be expected, and *then* to forecast what its balance of payments would be." [8] In the early period there seemed to be nothing rigid in this posture. No one's model was better than anyone else's, so it was as reasonable to use an optimistic model as a conservative one. Besides, the ECA seemed to imply that the model was largely hypothetical anyway, and the specific model chosen was far less important than the fact that some model—any model—was used. But it became evident after a while that the commitment to the model was much harder than anyone might have supposed—that it was a reflection, in fact, of the basic commitment to end the program by 1952. Thus, when a sharp difference arose between the ECA and the OEEC in estimating the Europeans' deficit on current account, and it was suggested that the figures of the ECA might have been unrealistic, the ECA tended to dismiss the criticism, not for being wrong so much as irrelevant. The justification of the ECA surely must have been one of the oddest statements that the people at the OEEC had ever encountered. As the Marshall Plan agency "explained,"

> The ECA has throughout adopted favorable assumptions on economic trends in the participating countries. It believes that the reduction in the over-all deficit on current account in 1948/49 from the level of about $6.04 billion forecast by OEEC to a level of about $5.07 billion, or a reduction by one-sixth, is possible of attainment while maintaining, though not improving, living standards. *It is very important that the over-all deficit be steadily reduced for this is the measure of the ability of the participants to move progressively toward self-support.*[9]

To translate, the OEEC figures suggested that the ECA might be wrong in its empirical estimates. The ECA replied that it could not be wrong, because these were the only estimates that were consistent with its premises: The figures simply had to be correct if the ECA was to reduce the program progressively. Since there was no question that the ECA was going out of business by 1952, there could be no question about the estimates either. If one happened to believe, in addition, that the Europeans would act decisively only if the Marshall Plan was certain to end by 1952, then the lower allocations could also present a self-fulfilling prophecy. If the Europeans believed it, they would have to become more active on their own behalf, and they might even achieve those projected improvements in the balance of payments. If the choice of the more ambitious estimates would actually succeed in prodding the Europeans and bringing about the desired end, then who was to say that these estimates were not, in the final analysis, the most accurate of all?

And happily enough, the dollar deficit of the OEEC nations did decline, dropping from $8.5 billion in 1947 to $1 billion in 1950. In

1951 Richard Bissell could tell a joint Senate committee that the problem of the European dollar deficit with the United States "has largely ceased to exist." [10] By that time, of course, Korea had superseded the questions of debureaucratization and the dollar deficit. Military production was on the rise, and American soldiers were coming to Europe with dollars. The Marshall Plan would be put in the service of the rearmament program, and the ECA itself would end on December 31, 1951, instead of June 30, 1952. The foreign aid program would be continued but with a different emphasis, as reflected in the title of the successor organization, the Mutual Security Agency. But in 1949 and early 1950 it was the commitment to debureaucratization that was still dominant. Hoffman could still tell Senator Fulbright—with no trace of apology—that the program would end by 1952, even though several of the ERP countries could not hope to be fully self-supporting by that time.[11] The ECA could go steadily on its way, then, making annual reductions of 25 percent. In 1950, however, Senator McCarran and the watchdog committee began to catch on to what was happening. They recognized that the ECA was using only a rule of thumb in making its reductions, and that the allocations had lost much of their foundation in economic fact. McCarran's reaction was in part a lecture to the ECA, but in part, also, an exercise in his own expanding recognition of what should have been evident to him for some time:

> When people were near starvation you could calculate requirements for calories, translate them into dollars, and feel some confidence that you had the answer. When factories were idle you could make an estimate of the quantities of copper, coal, and machinery to get them into operation, and you were proved correct if the result was that the factories got into operation. . . . [But] today those objectives have been reached and . . . the problem of determining how much money it is necessary for us to supply . . . is much more difficult.[12]

If the estimates lost their relation to precise standards, McCarran could be forgiven for wondering why Europe needed 25 percent less aid, rather than 50 or 40 or 15 percent.[13] The ECA could respond only by reciting the old slogan of a "cure rather than a palliative," but by this date it failed to convince anyone. The fact was that the ECA was now disarmed; it had no defense beyond the bare logic of its promise to end the program by 1952. If that seemed to make little sense as a basis for allocating aid to Europe, what sense did it make, after all, as a rule governing the size and resources of the agency itself? The ECA was pressed to show consistent decreases in administrative expenses and personnel; and yet the functions of the agency were not decreasing, but enlarging. Congress had been adding programs rather than deleting them, and in 1950, when the ECA was planning sharp cuts in administrative expenses, it was scheduled to increase its efforts in technical assistance, information, and end-use checking. Also, conditions had changed since that early period when the ECA was shipping large bulk commodities such as wheat. At that time the average ECA voucher was for $143,000. But now that it was shipping items like machine tools, which came in smaller packages, its average transaction was only $12,000 to $13,000. The overall value of American assistance had declined, but the volume of transactions had actually multiplied.[14] In short, the ECA had more to do, not less. Neither the reduction in the ECA nor the drop in the assignments of aid had any relation, then, to the substantive needs of European recovery. They had their origin in another value, and a prior commitment.

This was a logic that might have baffled Alice and the White Queen, but it had its uses. Hoffman was determined to convert the squeeze on resources into a form of pressure on the ERP countries. And in some respects it was a rather apt method for an agency like the ECA that disclaimed any intention of interfering in the decisions of the ERP countries, and which lacked the leverage for major interventions anyway. Thus Hoffman could say, with sincerity, that questions of nationalization were matters exclusively for the local government. Nor did he think it proper, for example, that the United States should refuse textile machinery to Britain for fear of competition.[15] But the concern for economic rationality could also give him the basis for some fine distinctions:

> I have had this [matter of nationalization] out with the British. I have said, so far as we are concerned what they do with their economy is their business, and what we do with our dollars is our business and if they start playing ducks and drakes with their economy to such a point that they cannot recover and our investment is not worth while, we are going to hold up the investment. . . .[16]

How the British happened to regulate the butchers and the bankers, Hoffman insisted, was no concern of the ECA. However, "they should not use our dollars to engage in social experimentation . . . [but] only for essential imports needed for recovery, and that has been the test." With that line of reasoning he could feel perfectly justified in cutting British aid if he suspected them of social experimentation, while at the same time he could find nothing inconsistent with his professions of noninterference. When more cotton goods began to appear on the consumer market in Britain, Hoffman found it appropriate to cut the British cotton imports by $60 million. Was the government entering the field of housing construction? Then $25 million might be shaved off the Marshall Plan exports of lumber.[17] And this was all compatible with the presumption in favor of basic investment. If the local government could divert funds to consumption, then Marshall aid could be eliminated proportionately. It was not surprising, therefore, that the British Labour Government found some difficulty in maintaining the pace of its social welfare programs. After the first year of the Labour Government, government consumption took 26.2 percent of the resources available for domestic use. By 1948 that figure had been reduced to 18.2 percent. With cuts in the programs for housing, health, and education, that figure was being pushed steadily downward. Projecting the trend, the proportion was expected to decline to 16.8 percent by 1952;[18] and as a result, in part, of these restrictions on welfare and consumption, the British managed to keep investment close to the ECA's target figure of 20 percent of the gross national product.

Still, if influence was to be exerted, it *was* more fitting for an agency with a pluralist orientation that its interventions remain more subtle and indirect. If it had to interfere at all, it was more appropriate for the ECA to do that by arranging incentives rather than dictating policies. Perhaps the ECA staff expressed it best in its first annual report:

> We are not seeking to impose on other countries any specific economic pattern. The degree to which other governments find it necessary and desirable to exercise direct controls over economic processes is a matter for them to decide. The United States is simply following a common-sense policy which will, if it is successful, reduce the insistent economic pressures that compel governments to ration, to control, and to regulate. . . .[19]

Thus, even where there were conscious goals for directing the Europeans, the ECA was still wedded to a liberal position, and even the irony of its intervention was characteristic: The most effective tool of coercion it had—the pressure of a continuing cutback in program funds—was a product of its own weakness as an agency.

II

We speculated earlier that several themes in the intellectual origins of the Marshall Plan might have converged to create an operating presumption in favor of deemphasizing political considerations. That is, the ECA was to concentrate on economic criteria; it would not (according to our hypothesis) attribute political motives where some other construction was possible, and it would not bring disagreements immediately to the level of overt political contest. Among the various themes these decision rules might have summarized were the following:

—that the ECA would represent a peculiar expertise for dealing with operations of a "business-like" nature, that it possessed a distinct legitimacy based on the perspectives of business management and economic rationality;

—that the preference for "a cure rather than a palliative" in Europe prescribed a full rein for the criteria of economic rationality;

—that nothing more had been decided on the national interest in Europe than the approval of an *economic* aid program—and by implication, if there were any larger political decisions to be made, they were to be reserved for another time and settled on their own terms, rather than simply precipitated by the decisions of the ECA;

—that the United States should confine its intrusions overseas by concentrating on the problem of reconstruction and avoiding, as much as possible, any involvement in domestic political decisions; and it should observe these limitations because, for one thing, it was more proper, but also because interventions would tend to confirm the propaganda of the Communists.

Unquestionably, the decisions of the ECA in cutting aid allotments could seriously restrict the policy choices open to the Europeans, and Paul Hoffman was one of the first to acknowledge that. Yet, as the passages above make equally clear, he saw nothing in the record that might have contradicted his own frequent insistence that the ECA would avoid any meddling in the internal decisions of the ERP countries. What removed the contradiction for him, apparently, was the belief that the ECA was doing something fundamentally different from political work. The agency was concentrating on economic decisions, and it would dispute the Europeans only on matters relating to the use of American aid. The British could nationalize industry or do anything else with their economy, and it was their business alone. However, if the British succeeded only in damaging their economy as a result of these adventures, they would threaten the usefulness of American aid, and it was at least legitimate at that point to consider the case for reducing American grants. Implicitly, it would not be an issue of intervention anymore, but something closer to a salvage operation for American resources.

But did Hoffman and his colleagues really believe in this distinction, and did they act upon it? It so happened that the annual Senate hearings furnished one of the most precise and thorough tests on this point, thanks in large measure to the persistence of Senator Fulbright. When the legislation was first considered in 1948, Fulbright maintained that the goal of economic integration was insufficient; political integration was the key to peace and the prerequisite to an integrated economic market. Fulbright continued to believe, for that reason, that the Marshall Plan would fail in its objectives so long as the ECA refused to push for political federation in Europe. Moreover, his challenge did not end in 1948 with the passage of the legislation. He used the hearings in the succeeding years to pick away at the performance of the ECA as a method of advancing his thesis. An important part of that argument over the years was to point out to Hoffman and his assistants that their decisions carried important political implications. If the top executives in the ECA could have been made to admit that they were involved in politics after all, then they might have been convinced to go all the way and seek a political solution. But interestingly enough, as doggedly as Fulbright would press the point, the ECA people would continue to resist; and they consistently failed to be persuaded.

When Fulbright asked Hoffman in 1949 why the ECA did not promote political integration instead of merely encouraging the movement of goods, Hoffman replied, "I am an ECA administrator, sir."

SENATOR FULBRIGHT. Do you feel that because there was nothing in the authorization of the ERP regarding political matters that therefore your jurisdiction is limited to economics? That it would not be within the contemplation of the law that you have anything to do at all with the political pattern in Europe?

MR. HOFFMAN. I think the Congress was very wise in limiting ECA to the economic field. I think that the State Department has an agency set up to deal with the political field. I think that we can do our job with the economic field, because we are an independent agency, perhaps better than could be done as part of a regular Government department. . . . I am certain we do not belong in the political field.[20]

Fulbright found the same resistance as he confronted one after another of the prominent officials in the ECA. At the time of the hearings there were reports in the press about the efforts to form a Council of Europe as a step toward the building of common political institutions. Fulbright was astonished then when Averell Harriman, as the Special Ambassador in Europe, professed to know nothing more about the development than what he read in the press. "I am not involved in the political aspect," Harriman explained, "I am very much involved in the development of cooperation in OEEC." [21]

As Deputy Chief of the ECA mission in Germany, N. H. Collison once withheld American aid until the directors of the German national railways agreed to balance their budget. But since that was obviously an "economic" problem, he too had little reason to suppose that he ever involved himself in politics. "My contacts," he told the Senate committee, "have been on economic matters rather than political matters. I do not recognize that I have any mandate or any responsibility politically under that law. I do have economic responsibility." [22]

On one revealing occasion in the hearings, Fulbright's hammering at the ECA finally moved Chairman Connally to step in:

> May I intervene right there? I want to suggest that under this bill, *which deals only with economics,* I would feel disposed to take disciplinary action against anybody in the ECA who exceeded his authority and began to meddle with the political situation in Europe. It is not the purpose of this bill to deal with the politics of Europe, either for a union or against a union or halfway between them. [23]

Coming as it did from one of the key Senate leaders who guided the original bill through Congress, this support for the peculiar approach of the ECA seemed particularly authoritative.

Was it fair to say, then, that the ECA people denied the presence of political overtones in their decisions, or that in some naïve way they were determined to make economics out of politics? The record would show, on the contrary, that they were not so simpleminded. It would demonstrate, rather, that their understanding followed the sense of our hypothetical operating rules. Hoffman never contended that there was a complete separation between politics and economics. He warned the Senate committee once that "life cannot be neatly divided into economic, political, social, and military compartments. Europe's problem cannot be attacked simply in terms of economics nor solved by our handing over a carefully computed number of dollars. . . ." [24] And after he had time for further reflection, he was able to respond to Fulbright in language that conveyed the essence of our operating rule:

> I do not think I have ever felt there is any real difference between yourself and myself on what should transpire in Europe. We have both agreed, I think, that there must be a greater unity among the free nations of western Europe. *The whole difference is a question of method,* and I felt quite certain that *as far as ECA was concerned, the Congress intended us to deal on the economic front* and intended us also *to so restrict our efforts* with the clear understanding that you cannot operate in an airtight compartment. What we do has political repercussions and vice versa. [25]

What made this distinction practicable was that the idiom of economics was entirely sufficient to the needs of the ECA. Political judgments were so naturally entangled with the economic, that there was enough to do simply in arguing about these so-called "economic" decisions. The ECA might believe, for example, that British competitiveness was undermined by labor practices that raised costs and retarded modernization. It could feel that the Labour Government was taking too soft a view toward labor, that its acceptance of overly full employment was inhibiting the reforms that were needed for a thorough recovery. But at the very least the British deserved to have that critique documented, for even some of the more articulate critics of the government could not subscribe to that thesis. The government could argue, in return, that the British problems were rooted in the structural changes brought about in the international economy by the war. It could point to the liabilities involved in managing sterling, and it could cite a pattern of neglect for capital investment that started early in the twentieth century. Surely there was enough to argue about in all these issues without flying to the conclusion that the British and American governments were divided on fundamental grounds of principle.

There was actually a coincidence of interests here. Both a decent respect for the British government and a concern for making the wise substantive decision would have suggested the propriety of exploring the factual matter at greater length before the disagreement was brought to the political level. At times, the mere challenging of a decision was enough, because it faced the recipient government with the burden of making a more coherent justification. If the government in question could cite some reasonable economic grounds for the decision, then that was as much as the ECA could legitimately expect, and as far as the Marshall Plan agency was concerned, that was enough in itself to make the decision considerably better. If there was still room for the play of political criteria, then that was the business of the local government; the ECA had done all it could on behalf of its own criteria. Was there something suspect in the location of two steel plants in France that were built with ECA funds? Then that was the concern of the French government, and it was better not to inquire too deeply into certain things. For was the steel not being produced, and was the production not contributing to the overall plan that measured European recovery?

By following these rules on the use of political criteria, the administrators not only made their own actions more consistent with the pluralist ethic conveyed by Marshall in his address at Harvard; they also contributed something that would last far beyond the life of their own agency: They prevented their own intrusions, which were occasioned by crisis conditions, from achieving the level of principle. The nonintervention doctrine would emerge from the Marshall Plan substantially intact. And thus, Donald Stone, who served throughout the program as the ECA Director of Administration, would consistently refer to the American operation in Greece as a "special case."

Few people were as intimately involved in the administration of the Marshall Plan as Stone was, and yet he never saw intervention as the typical form of ECA practice. It was always a matter of some importance to him to maintain the consciousness of the Greek venture as a noticeable exception to a general pattern of conduct.

If the operating presumptions in favor of economic criteria had not been held sincerely, it would be hard to account for the process by which the Marshall Plan was generalized from a limited European assistance effort to a permanent foreign aid program with universal application. In 1951 the Marshall Plan had been converted into an economic support program for the European rearmament effort. For many in the ECA the change was not merely one of emphasis, but an alteration that destroyed the very meaning of the Marshall Plan. Two months before the ECA was scheduled to close itself out, Donald Stone entered his own dissent in an almost emotional memorandum (he admitted in the preface that he was "all steamed up" when he wrote it). Stone objected to the new concept of aid, which subordinated economic assistance to military production. He still believed in the organizational decision of 1948—that the Marshall Plan was an autonomous program, with its own distinctive ends. Those ends, he declared, were in making a better life for the citizens of the recipient countries, to show them that democracy was an effective and worthwhile alternative to communism. It was a humanitarian program that demonstrated to the people of Europe that the United States was concerned with them as individuals and wanted to see them improve their lives. But this new program, according to Stone, would hold up a different meaning to the world. It would tell the Asians, for example, that the United States was "not really interested in improving conditions of life, that we are interested only in *their help* for *our defense* against communism." (Stone's emphasis.) What the new program was doing was throwing overboard what Stone saw as the theory of postwar foreign policy since 1947, "that security, peace, and in fact victory in our contest with communism, must be built upon sound economic foundations. . . ." There was a connection in Stone's mind between the goal of world peace and the commitment to economic welfare programs. Peace would come "only when enough government leaders and other important people . . . reflect in their personal lives those moral values which produce stable and democratic institutions." In turn, those values were acquired "when a sense of individual and national responsibility begins to be felt for human misery wherever it may be found. . . ." [26]

That same year, Paul Hoffman (now retired as Administrator of the ECA) published his own book, *Peace Can Be Won*. In it, Hoffman had the chance to give an account of his own work in the Marshall Plan and express his own understanding of the foreign aid program. Characteristically, he fell back on the old liberal cliché of commerce as a great healer. The Marshall Plan raised production, diffused prosperity, and in this way helped to prevent totalitarian revolutions in Europe.[27] In one of those strange conversions that occurs in public life, the practical man of affairs had become very much a man of theory. For the difference between a practical and a theoretical man must surely lie in a certain sensitivity to the detail and texture of particular cases, and to the circumstances that make some situations truly separate. And yet what practical man of affairs, having administered the Marshall Plan, would write as Hoffman did in 1951, that "We have learned in Europe what to do in Asia"? For where, after all, were the similarities, and what had Hoffman learned?

> While in Europe we concentrated on turbines and tractors, in Asia we are primarily concerned with vaccines and fertilizers. But the political principle remains the same. Only the deeds of democracy can enable the peoples still undecided between the lures of despotism and the life of freedom to make an honest choice.[28]

The principle, apparently, was that democracy got the goods to the people in time. When the minimal needs of the people were taken care of, when desperation was removed, then the people were able to sit back and make a rational choice among the competing political systems. This was the voice of Hoffman, the former used car salesman; it was all, in the final analysis, a matter of consumer's choice.

Yet, what was there in the program these two men administered that led them to such an understanding of the Marshall Plan? To say that the program improved the lives of the people by raising production or serving the "general good" is surely too broad and vague. If these characterizations by Stone and Hoffman meant anything, they had to mean something very close to the picture drawn by Hoffman of an active competition for the favor of the populace. That is, the Marshall Plan would have demonstrated the effectiveness of democracy by bringing dramatic improvement to the standard of living for the vast majority of Europeans. It would have been a form of Tory socialism that lured the workers away from the appeals of radical ideologies, and it would have done it by bribing the people, as it were, with a more egalitarian distribution of material goods. But it would require a wide stretching of the facts to make the record of the Marshall Plan fit this theory. As we have already seen, one of the most basic operating tests used by the ECA was to keep per capita consumption approximately at 1938 levels. The object was to allow additions to consumption only where that was necessary to check a potential inflation. Otherwise resources were to be directed toward investment, and manufactured goods were to be diverted from the domestic economy into the export market.

Hoffman himself admitted in 1950 that the ECA had taken no interest in promoting wage increases or a better standard of living for workers. At this same time he expressed his hope that the policy of transferring resources from consumption to investment "will, *after we have pulled out,* enable them to increase their standard of living considerably." [29] Improvements in the standard of living were to be deferred until *after* the Marshall Plan.

Real wages did in fact rise during this period. But that was not due to any increased assertiveness on the part of labor in demanding a larger share of the national wealth. The general pattern in wages was one of restraint. With the exception of the Netherlands, there was no direct control on wages, but there were some very successful programs of voluntary restraint, which held up until the wage-pull pressures of the post-Korean period, when there was a scarcity of labor. Labor governments were in an especially advantageous position to cajole the unions into restraint, and they backed up their own part of the bargain by a vigorous policy of taxing excess profits. At one point in the Netherlands the unions even accepted a cut in real wages as a contribution to a deflationary policy.[30] Here, as elsewhere in Europe, unions gave their support to austerity programs. As in Italy, workers came to appreciate the fact that their future consumption might depend on a stiff deflationary policy, which could make saving meaningful again. But the benefits in these cases were all in the long run; labor was not bribed into support for the political system with immediate payoffs. In fact, labor acceptance of these arrangements made sense only because the union members were already integrated into their political communities. If the situation was as Hoffman described it, with the population waiting to be sold on entering the political system, it might well have been irrational for the workers to have accepted these sacrifices. Deferring short-term advantages for long-term gains would have made far less sense if the working classes were still without leverage in their respective political systems; for they would have had far less assurance in that case that benefits were really being deferred, and that their governments would indeed make good on their promises later. What made this renunciation of self-interest possible was the fact that the workers were not outside their political communities, but thoroughly committed. One could not account for the behavior of European labor in this period, then, in the familiar terms of a consumers' politics. Instead, the analysis would require some rather traditional and unrevolutionary concepts like party loyalty, enlightened self-interest, or even civic obligation.

Finally, the ECA was bound to a conceptual apparatus that blocked it off from an active interventionist policy. The balance of payments analysis was a rather gross analytical tool, but for an agency that was equipped to do little more than pump goods into Europe, it was good enough. It was sufficient for dealing with advanced industrial nations, when the ECA had to do little more than authorize the procurement of goods. There was practically no need to provide facilities for unloading the materials or distributing them inside the country. It was unnecessary to teach the recipients what to do with the raw materials or how to market them when they were turned into finished goods. Thus, there was really no need for the ECA to inject itself in the production decisions of specific industries, even if it had the capacity to become involved. For this particular program, then, and for this particular set of nations, the balance of payments offered a fairly comfortable analysis. Moreover, the balance of payments had relevance for some of the more sophisticated problems facing these nations in the form of trade imbalances; and besides that, it seemed to do no special harm.

But the limits of the theory became evident in 1951, when an effort was made to mesh the operations of the ECA with the military aid program. In developing estimates for Fiscal 1952, it was found that the ECA was still using a modified balance of payments analysis. What the military required, however, was a very detailed model covering the entire production system. It was essential to have specific information on the total resources available in the participating countries for meeting targets of military production.[31] However, as long as the ECA was operating with the balance of payments analysis, it was incapable of dealing with specific production issues. It was virtually predictable, then, that when a new foreign aid agency moved into the underdeveloped areas and took up the responsibility for an assistance program in Southeast Asia, the balance of payments theory would have to be abandoned. Almost all of these countries had surpluses in dollars or other hard currencies as a result of selling raw materials to the West. Here, instead of providing a rough but useful index of a real economic problem, the theory worked to obscure a fundamental need for development.[32]

Nothing seems more fanciful, therefore, than the notion that an agency like the ECA, operating from afar with the bluntest of tools, could possibly regulate the distribution policies of the ERP countries and direct them toward egalitarian ends. The ECA did nothing to credit some of the early fears among conservatives that the Marshall

Plan would project the New Deal abroad. If, in retrospect, Hoffman and Stone tried to generalize the Marshall Plan as a program of welfare economics, they were misleading themselves.[33] But these were intelligent men, who were in the center of operations. There must have been something in the Marshall Plan that gave even that erroneous explanation some grounding in fact. And what that basis seemed to be was the sense of distinctiveness for the Marshall Plan as an autonomous program with a concentration on economic policy. Stone had difficulty in articulating the philosophy of the Marshall Plan, but there was no doubt in his mind that it was fundamentally different from the military program. From that persuasion it was a shorter step to the view that the Marshall Plan also had its own distinctive ends, which had to be related to the autonomy of its peculiar criteria. But was that not the essential content of Vandenberg's thinking in 1948, when he moved to separate the ECA from the State Department? Yes, but it was dependent also on several other strands of thought in the Marshall Plan, which combined in support of some concrete working rules. It was not simply that the people at ECA *perceived* themselves as separated from the State Department, but that the character of their agency actually made them different in their day-to-day work. Thus, to know how the Marshall Plan came to be generalized after 1951 one would have to account for that unshakable assurance with which Hoffman seemed to understand the exact character and place of his agency—how he could admit so blithely that the decisions of ECA were surrounded with political implications, and yet maintain through it all that in "ERP, however, our attention is focused on economic problems."

### Notes

1. Senate Foreign Relations Committee, *Hearings on Extension of ERP,* 1949, p. 78.
2. See, for example, Howard Bruce in *ibid.,* p. 332; Hoffman in Senate Foreign Relations Committee, *Hearings on Extension of ERP,* 1950, p. 23 (and in almost every hearing at which he testified before the foreign relations committees), and Richard Bissell in Senate Committees on Foreign Relations and Armed Services, *Hearing on Mutual Security Act of 1951* (1951), p. 157.
3. Senate Committee on Appropriations, *Hearings on Foreign Aid Appropriations for 1951* (1950), pp. 172, 241.
4. ECA, *Recovery Progress and United States Aid,* 1949, p. 61.
5. Senate Foreign Relations Committee, *Hearings on Extension of ERP,* 1949, pp. 498 (Finletter) and 499 (Hoffman).

6. Senate Appropriations Committee, *Hearings on Foreign Aid Appropriations for 1951* (1950), p. 172.

7. Howard S. Ellis, *The Economics of Freedom* (New York: Harper and Brothers, 1950), pp. 530–31.

8. ECA, *Recovery Progress and United States Aid*, p. 62. Emphasis added.

9. *Ibid.,* p. 70. Emphasis added.

10. Senate Committee on Foreign Relations and Armed Forces, *Hearings of Mutual Security Act of 1951*, p. 180.

11. Senate Foreign Relations Committee, *Hearings on Extension of ERP*, 1949, p. 61.

12. See Senate Committee on Appropriations, *Hearings on Foreign Aid Appropriation for Fiscal 1951*, pp. 266–67.

13. *Ibid.,* p. 267.

14. See William Foster's testimony in House Subcommittee on Appropriations, *Hearings on Foreign Aid for Fiscal 1951* (1950), pp. 416–17.

15. Senate Foreign Relations Committee, *Hearings on Extension of ERP*, 1949, pp. 48, 59–61, 430.

16. *Ibid.,* p. 61.

17. Senate Foreign Relations Committee, *Hearings on Extension of ERP*, 1949, pp. 502, 507.

18. See the testimony of Thomas Finletter and the accompanying charts in *ibid.,* pp. 160–61.

19. ECA, *Recovery Progress and United States Aid*, p. 2.

20. Senate Foreign Relations Committee, *Hearings on Extension of ERP*, 1949, pp. 85–86.

21. *Ibid.,* p. 147; and see also, pp. 139–40.

22. *Ibid.,* p. 310.

23. Senate Foreign Relations Committee, *Hearings on Extension of ERP*, 1949, p. 198, and see also p. 309. Emphasis added.

24. *Ibid.,* p. 13.

25. *Ibid.,* p. 525. Emphasis added.

26. Donald Stone to F. J. Lawton, "Implications of Mutual Security Act and Requirements for Action," October 6, 1951, Bureau of the Budget, Series 39.27.

27. Paul G. Hoffman, *Peace Can Be Won* (Garden City, New York: Doubleday and Company, Inc., 1951), p. 20.

28. *Ibid.,* pp. 130–31.

29. Senate Committee on Appropriations, *Hearings on Foreign Aid Appropriation for Fiscal 1951* (1950), p. 241. Emphasis added.

30. See UN, *Economic Survey of Europe Since the War*, p. 72.

31. See Bureau of the Budget, *Survey of the ECA,* September 1951, p. 63. Series 39.32.

32. See *ibid.,* pp. 35–36.

33. For some reason there is a tendency to overlook the fact that the ECA subordinated the principle of "need" in 1949 when it decided to take the existing allocations as a base and make proportionate cuts with each

successive year. The matter turned in part on the question of incentives. If aid was reduced when a country's deficit contracted, it would have penalized improvement. Instead, the ECA determined to shift its incentives to reward success, even if it meant that aid might not go where it was most vitally needed. If there was any allocating principle more removed from the premises of a welfare orientation, it would have been hard to imagine. See Ellis, *op. cit.*, pp. 531–32.

# 7

**Lutz Niethammer**

# Structural Reform and a Compact for Growth:Conditions for a United Labor Union Movement in Western Europe after the Collapse of Fascism

*Most studies of Cold War politics focus on nation-states, but in the following essay Professor Niethammer of the University of Essen analyzes comparatively the labor movement after World War II. Organized labor had been a major victim of fascism and German occupation: its cadres smashed, its leaders killed, imprisoned, or driven into exile or underground. With the liberation of Italy and France in 1944 and the defeat of Germany in 1945, labor leaders looked toward reconstruction of their prefascist unions. Since they felt that their earlier divisions between communists, socialists, and Christian trade unionists had prevented labor from organizing effective resistance to fascist trends, there was a strong pressure for trade-union unity. Such unity, however, proved precarious, and by 1947–48, the Western European labor movements had fractured once again.*

*Niethammer examines this brief period of unity and the conditions that enabled it to function. The unified labor movements pressed for nationalization, welfare measures, and sometimes worker control of the plants. But they could not survive earlier bitter differences and the pressures of the Cold War. As the Soviet-American split overshadowed Europe—as the East European regimes were molded into satellite states and the communists were maneuvered out of the party coalitions in the West, as too the United States announced the Marshall Plan and the Soviet Union decided it could not participate—the labor movement was caught in the cross fire. It proved impossible for communists and the non-communist components to work together; indeed American labor observers, such as the AFL and reluctantly the CIO, actively urged the non-communists to secede and form their own unions. In*

*Italy and France, the communists retained control of the federations in being, for they had gained strength and mass support during the resistance to fascism. In Germany because of the East-West split, communism remained dominant in the Soviet zone. Whatever adherents communism enjoyed in the western zones were rapidly thrust to the margin of politics. In all of Europe the schism became a major feature of the sociopolitical polarization that marked Cold War public life. While partially bridged over since the late 1960s, the split still effectively divides the West European labor movements.*

*Professor Niethammer's essay is written from a perspective on the Left that is critical of both the American and communist roles. My own feeling is that the euphemistic slogans of the Left (which often sought to monopolize such terms as "antifascist" or "democratic" for procommunists) are sometimes pressed into service too uncritically, whereas the rhetoric of liberalism is fully unmasked. Perhaps, too, the comparability of British developments with those on the Continent is overdrawn. Nonetheless, this is a highly sophisticated review of the massive literature on the unions, and the author valuably brings out all the inherent difficulties that stood in the way of radical renovation after the war.*

*A note on translation: Although it is cumbersome, I have used the term "political united union" for Niethammer's politische Einheitsgewerk- schaft. By political, the author wished to stress that the post-1945 labor organizations were intended to work in tandem with the affiliated parties of the Left for political and social as well as narrowly economic reform. To this idea he contrasts the idea of the "industrial union," charged with the advocacy of economic interests alone (e.g., wages, perhaps plant organization). The term "industrial union" is not intended here to suggest the American contrast of "industrial" versus "craft" unions (e.g., CIO vs. AFL).*

*For this collection I have omitted a few pages at the beginning and end of the whole essay that address the Germans' own debate on the history and proper role for their own trade union federation (DGB). In these pages the author explains that his comparative approach is designed to rescue the history of the German union federation from too one-sided an analysis in terms of its national background alone; and in his conclusion he assesses both the achievements and the limits of the DGB. Footnotes have been made consistent with the text selections, which has entailed some rearrangement. When Niethammer has used French or English-language works in German translation, I have kept his citation for the sake of simplicity. Miss Rebecca Boehling lent some assistance with the translation. The author has made a few small revisions for this version of his article.*

*The essay has been translated and reprinted with the permission of the author and the publisher, Bund-Verlag of Cologne, from a collection of essays edited by Heinz Oscar Vetter to commemorate the post-1945 German labor leader, Hans Böckler:* Vom Sozialistengesetz zur Mitbestimmung. Zum 100. Geburtstag von Hans Böckler [*From the Law suppressing the Social Democratic Party (1878) to Co-Determination (1950 and after). For the 100th Birthday of Hans Böckler*], *Cologne, 1975. Professor Niethammer is also the author of, among other works,* Entnazifierung in Bayern. Säuberung und Rehabilitation unter amerikanischer Besatzung [*Denazification in Bavaria: Purge and Rehabilitation under American Occupation*], *Frankfurt/Main, S. Fischer, 1972. With Ulrich Borsdorf and Peter Brandt he has coedited* Arbeiterinitiative 1945. Antifaschistische Ausschüsse und Reorganisation der Arbeiterbewegung in Deutschland [*Worker Initiatives 1945: Antifascist Committees and the Reorganization of the Labor Movement in Germany*] *(Wuppertal: 1976).*

### Typology of the Political United Labor Union

The first phase of the international history of the trade unions in the postwar era was characterized by the formation and the collapse of the World Federation of Trade Unions (WFTU).[1] This phase lasted from 1945 to 1947, although in certain countries forerunners of the united union emerged as early as 1943; and later the international schism that resulted from the collapse of the movement went on into 1948–49. The WFTU phase was dominated by the effort to form the most united organization possible, or at least an operational alliance of unions on the national and international level. The attempt sought also to go beyond the various party affiliations of the individual unions; leaders wanted the unions to attain a pivotal position within society as a whole. This task required participation in the antifascist purges. It also meant helping to start up and to increase production so as to overcome the postwar economic crisis by means of rapid growth. It meant institutionalizing a working-class role in economic management by means of state planning and control of monopolies —e.g., by nationalizing heavy industries and establishing factory councils or other forms of worker participation in individual firms or at the industry-wide level. As the concept of a united labor union was worked out, each country's particular background and conditions led to different organizational forms. But the concentration of craft unions into industrial federations and their political consolidation as forms of pressure groups were unmistakable everywhere.

The political core of the united trade unions in the WFTU phase consisted of the effort to form to the greatest degree possible a mass union movement by integrating the prewar unions with the communists, who had greatly expanded in the European resistance against German fascism. In the former fascist countries, especially, where independent unions had been totally shattered and replaced by corporative organs designed to integrate workers and employers, the emerging Christian labor unions, which had also failed to survive as an independent movement, could be worked into a united organization. This new unity was made possible essentially because ever since Stalin had adopted a policy of seeking allies [against Hitler], the communists had accepted a reformist program. This reformist platform included different mixes for each country of partial nationalization, workers' participation, and economic planning. But it remained generally compatible with the concept of "Economic Democracy" that had been advanced by the German Social Democratic trade unions in 1928.* At the same time, giving the unions a broader political assignment—which all the differing labor groups agreed upon as a means of reconstruction and antifascist reform—also would allow more scope for the communist concept. They saw the union as an instrument for mobilizing and educating the proletarian masses, i.e., for extending the influence of the communist leadership. In tactical terms the united trade union enabled the communist cadres to apply the policy of a United Front "from above and from below" [i.e., at the union leadership and plant levels simultaneously]. This was attractive both for the communists in the West who wanted to anchor themselves in powerful positions in the state and economy and for the communists in the East who wanted to eliminate the organized opposition. Simultaneously it appealed to reformist leaders. They wanted not only to strengthen the power of the labor movement by avoiding conflict within the proletariat, but also sought to protect themselves from the possibility that their earlier rivalry with the communists might resume. Renewed rivalry could assume threatening proportions, given the popularity of the Eastern Ally in the lands freed from German occupation or the strength of the communists in the national movements of liberation. The discrediting of the European Right along with the widely held view that socialism was the next item on the agenda of history and was necessary for reconstruction; the confidence in the durability of the coalition against Hitler; and the socialists' par-

* Ed. note: Economic Democracy was a platform that called not for the abolition, but the progressive reform of capitalism—predominantly by increasing involvement of the unions in economic planning and control alongside managers in industry-wide councils.

ticipation in almost all European governments—all produced that optimism with which the united trade union experiment was undertaken in the WFTU phase. The tradition of Economic Democracy thus became the most suitable compromise platform for the united trade union. For the socialists its continuity with prewar *ideology* prevented dwelling on the [ineffective] prewar *practice* of the reformist unions. For the communists, as a partial objective it was compatible with the "antifascist-democratic" transitional strategy of Stalinism. At the same time both partners thought they could rely on the practical efficacy of their own party organizations to hold their own.

### Economic Conditions

The goals of Economic Democracy were appropriate ones not only in view of the paralysis of the European economies, but also as surrogate objectives for the trade unions. For in this period of early social reconstruction, the rapid progress made in organizing the unions contrasted with the restricted role that the unions could play as participants in the struggle over income distribution. In view of this discrepancy the great influx of members into the unions in all the postwar European countries requires explanation; previous research has considered it insufficiently. It obviously drew most generally upon the spontaneous loyalty of the workers to their own organizations—those most identified with the working-class—which fascist and fascist-occupied regimes had deprived of rights. At the same time the unions represented the hope for some sort of socialist alternative for the future. First, however, they had to face more concrete problems.

All the European economic systems were afflicted by negative growth on account of the war: [3] disproportionally developed productive capacities, massive destruction of currencies and capital, plundering, death, the deportation or drafting of a large part of the labor force, collapse of the infrastructure, and extreme limits on international exchange. The postliberation economies were in acute crisis. They required extensive reconversion, and in heavily destroyed areas above all, reconstruction of the infrastructure (e.g., transportation facilities and public utilities). Despite the great losses of human life from war and terror, the Continent faced a growing surplus of labor—some of it overqualified. With few plants functioning, the economies had to absorb expellees, displaced persons, forced labor, and prisoners of war. The need for goods of all sorts vastly exceeded the productive capacity of the system. Thus the crisis had to be overcome by comprehensive reconstruction and by increasing productive capacity (with special urgency in heavy industry and mining, coal mining above all), if sufficient jobs were to be created and the most elementary needs of the population satisfied. In contrast to cyclical economic crises, the problem did not lie in underconsumption or overproduction—except perhaps for armaments, as was the case in part for Germany and the United States—but rather in enlarging and restructuring the productive apparatus. If the unions saw themselves not merely as spokesmen for one of the groups in the productive process, but as advocates of the laboring (or jobseeking) masses, then in order to create jobs and accelerate the flow of goods they had to concentrate their entire energies in the crisis on promoting growth—on increasing production, ensuring labor discipline, avoiding strikes, influencing systematic control of the productive and distributive apparatus. At the same time they had to watch out that reconversion was not carried out at the expense of the workers by mass layoffs in armaments factories, as in the United States and, at first, in Germany. To get production going once again and to increase it, they had to reabsorb all the professions that were indispensable, at least for the time being, to the economic system, especially technically skilled lower-level managers, engineering personnel, and independent small businessmen. These tasks represented, so to speak, an objective economic necessity even though they deviated from the traditional union struggle to reduce the exploitation of labor. And it was precisely these tasks that the united labor unions—including the cadres from each political party—carried out in all European countries, East and West, between 1944 and 1947. Their function of disciplining the labor force for the sake of the reconstruction of society as a whole made them so indispensable that they could demand a lot, especially in the way of structural reforms, from national leaders and from other social groups.

### Alternatives?

Was there a basic alternative? In order to justify the fact that at the end of the war their party and union leaders did not press for an immediate transition to socialism (except in prevailingly agricultural Yugoslavia), communist literature has often argued that the workers' class consciousness had been overwhelmed by fascism and apparently even by the antifascist struggle.[4] But this argument obscures the real reasons. An immediate transition to socialism would have made the economic difficulties sketched above even more acute by setting additional impediments to production: lack of experts, losses of working time, bourgeois sabotage, further crippling of the infrastructure. Just to satisfy the most immediate needs of the working masses forced renunciation of an early revolution. Secondly, Western Europe was filled with American troops instructed to intervene in case of "disease and unrest." Revolution would thus have meant further war, especially if the Soviet Union, herself afflicted by the same acute shortages, had been forced to intervene in so completely uncertain a situation. But since in view of her own crisis she was unwilling to be dragged into any such adventure, she tolerated no such enterprises in her own sphere of influence and discouraged equivalent Communist Party initiatives in western and southern Europe. She favored instead a step-by-step policy, fitted to each country and permitting delay and halts.[5] But even leaving aside the military stabilization of the existing systems by the Americans, it is difficult to ascribe the failure of revolution in a highly industrialized system undergoing wartime collapse solely to a lack of will. To be sure there was a potential force of revolutionary activists, but they were fragmented into regional partisan bands and local committees and were politically uncoordinated. Granted that from the economic viewpoint most European countries still had a large enough stock of capital and a sufficiently skilled labor force to assure a high rate of growth during the reconstruction period, even after socialization of the means of production. The crisis of transition [to socialism] would still have entailed too high a cost. It might have caused food supplies to collapse completely and would not have been able to raise the level of production quickly. Even a revolution needs supplies if it is not to sacrifice its goals out of hunger and terror.

The other alternative, that of immediately liberalizing [i.e., deregulating] the capitalist system by ending the planning apparatus of the war economies can be even more quickly dismissed. This would have shoved the costs of the crisis exclusively onto the shoulders of the workers. Massive state intervention would then have been needed to recover from the postwar economic collapse. In turn it would have meant backing up economic deregulation with a right-wing political dictatorship for which no basis existed in the liberated countries. The workers' movements would have reacted with the support of armed partisans. In no way could this alternative have provided a suitable union strategy.

Thus the question remains: what concrete possibilities remained in the concept of Economic Democracy (to use this as a shorthand for the program of reconstruction); above all, were there any outcomes likely other than failure? To determine any such possibilities more precisely, several variables must be introduced and the constellation of national factors in the most important countries must be compared.

*A United Trade Union and Limited Structural Reform: Italy.* Italian conditions are especially useful to point up the special development of the trade unions in occupied Germany. Certainly Italy had undertaken an opportunistic switch to the Allied side in 1943–44, as one can see from the actions of the Badoglio government [Marshall Badoglio, royal appointee to succeed Mussolini in July 1943] and the country's elite. However, months before the Allied landing in Sicily, the Italian working class had demonstrated its own independent antifascist strength by means of largely spontaneous strikes in the industrial centers of the North. Such political and economic mass strikes were applied repeatedly and with increasingly organization over the next two years against the German occupiers in Northern Italy. They provided an essential backbone for building an armed partisan resistance. They led in the final stage of the war not only to local uprisings and efforts at liberation in the cities and the so-called partisan republics, but also to establishment of worker power in many factories through committees of liberation and agitation. While this struggle resembled that of other liberation movements fighting for national and social objectives in German-occupied Europe, Italy was distinguished by the fact that autonomous mass action arose under conditions of a home-grown fascist regime during the war.[6]

Those Italian experiences most comparable to Germany's, however (at least before the Germans occupied northern Italy), did not so much involve the independent activity of the working class as the political and trade-union organizations. Even the transitional regime of Marshal Badoglio can be compared with the conservative resistance of the 20th of July 1944 [the German conspiracy against Hitler]. As in Germany, the organized resistance of the unions and parties—in contrast to the spontaneous mass action in the final phase of the war—remained weak, isolated, and ineffective. The collapse of the regime led, however, to a rapid reconstitution of the prefascist organizational leadership as major party and union functionaries returned from exile or "inner emigration." As German resistance leaders also planned to proceed, union reorganization under Badoglio began with the assignment of top labor union officials from different parties as commissioners to high positions in the fascist corporative organizations. As in the case of the German Labor Front the Italian corporative bodies were organized by industry. To be sure, the rank and file resisted making use of the fascist organizational forms. But the period between the dismissal of Mussolini and the German occupation [i.e., July 25 to

September 8, 1943] proved too short to see how this emerging dispute over organization would turn out. Nevertheless, even in this brief interval working-class leaders did manage to reach an agreement with industrialists for the election of factory councils. This preempted wildcat strikes in the factories and was supposed to provide an enduring basis for worker representation in the plants. Even these early initiatives revealed how willing the union leadership was to cooperate with the industrialists, if thereby they could immediately secure an extensive trade-union-like organization with a monopoly on labor representation. The same interest marked the 1943–44 concepts of German resistance labor leaders, Leuschner and Tarnow, for a transformation of the German Labor Front into a broad union with compulsory membership.[7]

With the German occupation of Northern Italy and the flight of the Badoglio government from Rome to the Allied-occupied South [September 1943], conditions for rebuilding the unions were transformed. Plans for converting fascist corporativism from the top down into a united union had the ground cut from under them by both the politically inspired resistance units in the North and the Allied powers in the South, who demanded a reconstruction of free trade unions.[8] As a consequence, a dualist system of political and economic working-class organization emerged in Italy. It could be roughly described as a relatively autonomous trade-union structure, organized to exert power at the national level in the South and on the factory level in the North. After liberation it was to prove a national two-tier system of long-term importance. The authority of the trade-union leadership derived from their political role in the antifascist parties; this was quite different from the Western zones of Germany and most comparable to the [Communist] Free German Union Federation [FDGB] in the Soviet zone of occupation. In the South of Italy politically oriented unions were the first to form—one a combined socialist-communist federation, one nonpartisan, and one Catholic. After negotiations between the union representatives of the national party executives, these were consolidated by the Pact of Rome on June 3, 1944, into a united union, the General Italian Confederation of Labor (CGIL). The CGIL aimed at a combined horizontal and vertical structure, whose regional and local components would have the power to overcome opposition from the industrialists' associations—not least because the proportional representation agreed to for local and regional elections would assure the parallel strength of the working-class political parties. In any case, the autonomous local and regional groups who held power in the North during the liberation might be expected to exert considerable influence. As General Secretaries of the united union, a socialist, a communist, and a Catholic each shared equal prerogatives. During the following years, however, the communist element rose to clear predominance because of the contingencies of personnel at the top and the Party's skillful organizational politics.[9]

These successes for communist organizational politics in the CGIL proved of decisive importance for political and economic reconstruction once they were extended to the liberated North. In an extremely flexible policy—Togliatti even entered the Soviet-recognized Badoglio government—the communists set the unions on a firm "antifascist-democratic" course. This included supporting an all-party government to establish a parliamentary republic as well as ideological and personnel purges. It also involved helping to advance economic reconversion and higher production by cooperation with management, by promotion of labor discipline, and by wage restraint. In working out the constitution, extensive planning powers were ceded to the state and apparently made politically secure by virtue of the workers' parties' role in the government. At the same time, provision was made for future enlargement of the nationalized sector of banks, energy concerns, and transformation industries, which Mussolini had already initiated. With its takeover of many state- and local-government positions, the working-class movement appeared to have become an integral part of the system. With the establishment of Chambers of Labor and the formation of joint labor-management committees to oversee many northern industries, the working class won the capacity for codetermination of economic and social issues. These committees had generally arisen during the struggle for liberation and represented the interest that managers as well as plant workers had in protecting industrial plants against destruction by the Germans. In view of the fact that the fascist regime had already greatly expanded the public sector of the economy, this structure of working-class achievements added up to what the program of Economic Democracy envisaged, even if the Italian reforms rested more on *de facto* victories than on statutory enactments. The communist leadership supported the constitution, participated in the cabinets, and despite the shift to the right in 1947 that led to its own dismissal, still sought to return to the government. The PCI could rightfully take pride in its role in sharply curbing national strikes or in limiting them to short, local conflicts.[10]

In fact, this policy failed on all levels. As was the case in Germany, contemporaries sharply overestimated the destruction of Italian productive capacity [and therefore of capitalist vitality]. Once the continuity of private property was recognized in principle, the position of the bourgeoisie grew stronger and stronger. The real problem lay [not in destruction], but in acute aggravation of Italy's chronic underemployment, which decisively weakened the economic position of the working class. Against this background, the division of functions in the government also played a role. Socialists and communists generally took over the administrative apparatus for labor and social welfare, but they left decisive positions over economic and financial policy to the bourgeois parties, in part because they just lacked ideas and experts. These posts were largely taken over by a group of old-laissez-faire economists who effectively intervened with measures to stabilize the middle classes and to continue deregulation of the economic system. At the same time, they used the new planning machinery only to get out of the postwar crisis, and by fiscal measures (lowering progressive taxation, deflating without redistributing the resulting losses or without protecting jobs) made capital accumulation easier.[11]

The CGIL leadership was not able to bridge the gap that separated it from its own rank and file. Because of its stress upon the needs of the economy as a whole and its agreement on reconstruction, the leadership exerted restraint on wages. It also inhibited any protests against the suppression of local resistance organizations by central administrative and parliamentary institutions. Besides the divergence in trade-union development between South and North during the dual occupation that was cited above, different political perspectives and economic conditions were also responsible for the cleavage between leaders and rank and file. Toward the end of the national liberation struggle, socialist and communist partisans made repeated attempts to push the local resistance movements in the direction of a socialist revolution. But the communists' "antifascist-democratic" strategy for Europe, which seemed so compelling while Anglo-American troops were in Italy, actually contributed to the leadership's undercutting all such revolutionary efforts. One example was the Sicilian city of Ragusa, where an attempted communist revolt was suppressed with the approval of the national Party leadership.

During the years 1945–46, the rank and file staunchly worked to preserve the organs created in the liberation struggle, while the strengthened business community sought to undermine the joint manager-employee committees and the state administration won out over the competing committees of liberation. The unions' policy of wage stabilization proved even more constraining since it meant that the postwar inflation and the reconversion of armaments plants cut into the workers' standard of living and reduced employment. While the national leadership of the working-class movement was concerned with avoiding strikes, the country was overtaken by waves of spontaneous or locally organized work stoppages, short in duration and in the nature of social protest.[12] The inability of the leadership to discipline the workers in general, or just to bring their own organizations into line, cost their policy of collaboration with the bourgeoisie its credibilty. On the other hand, the very emphasis the labor leaders placed on this policy underlined their limited capacity to integrate their own workers. In turn, this made popular-front unity fragile indeed. After 1946 anticommunism would serve increasingly as a way to weaken the labor movement.

The pressure for a united front between communists and socialists had already led to social-democratic splinter movements and had raised tension within the united labor unions. Dismissal of the communists from the government and the absolute majority won by the Christian Democrats, who campaigned in 1948 as an anticommunist bulwark against the Communist-Socialist People's Bloc, also split the CGIL. In autumn 1948 a Catholic union emerged, friendly to the government and concerned only with issues of salaries and wages (the LCGIL); later on, segments of liberal and socialist unions followed. The communists' emphasis on the concept of a political union catalyzed the schism. In light of the economic difficulties and the Americans' requirement for a cooperative stance in return for credits, the other union groups backed away, to revert to representation just of their adherents' immediate economic interests. The economic power that the workers had enjoyed in 1945–46 had not been effectively used by the communist-dominated unions to shape durable institutions suitable for political and social struggle. Hence, while the masses might still respond in 1947–48 to the call for a political strike against the Marshall Plan and the assassination attempt against Togliatti, these actions only hastened the collapse of their organization, and they were soon exhausted.[13] Reconstruction of the liberal economic order by continuing low wages and underemployment (and also by the institution of a powerful police apparatus) had melted away the potential for an enduring struggle. Political protest and attainable economic demands increasingly diverged. With the reestablishment of an economic system in which emigration served as ersatz cure for the chronic unemployment that was starkly revealed once again, the united trade union lost its strategic position.

*A Limited United Union and Structural Reform: France.* The development of the united trade-union movement in France deviated from that in Italy—and from that in Germany—because of the essentially different historical conditions that shaped it. The continuity and autonomy of the French parties and unions was not wholly destroyed by a home-grown fascism, nor was their post-liberation course of development supervised at the outset by a British-American occupation. Both these factors exerted only an indirect influence. Nonetheless, there were many similarities with Italy, attributable above all to the parallel behavior of the communists.

In France, too, the communists were the driving force behind the unification of the trade unions and won a predominant role in the union organization by virtue of their tactical superiority. In addition, they were able to credit to their account a massive influx of members as a result of the prestige acquired as a result of their dynamic Resistance combat in the second half of the war. France, too, revealed the split between a leadership pursuing coalition policies and the local, autonomous Resistance groups, especially those in the South, who frequently pushed for a revolutionary restructuring but were repressed by the central institutions of the administration, the parliament, and the interest groups. In France, too, the leaders of the PCF returned from exile in Moscow as the champions within the Left of a return to normalcy. They actively advocated a bourgeois-proletarian pact among the three mass parties (Communists, Socialists, Catholic M.R.P.) on behalf of reconstruction, and they invoked their prestige against local strikes protesting hunger and against other economically motivated, spontaneously ignited labor struggles. As in Italy, even after their dismissal from the government in the spring of 1947, the communists sought to return to the party coalition and for several months continued their policy of cooperation—until the dispute over the Marshall Plan.[14]

Nonetheless, the united trade union experiment encountered resistance from the outset even in the labor movement. Labor's traditions had remained compelling from the Third Republic through the Phony War, Vichy, the Resistance, and de Gaulle's government in exile. Except for Spain, socialists and communists had tried the experiment of a popular front government only in France. At first this experience reinforced the mutual opposition of the two parties, and with the Hitler-Stalin Pact of 1939, the communists were expelled from the General Confederation of Labor (CGT). Here their originally small communist union organization, which had merged during the preparations for the Popular Front, had already won increasing influence during the course of the Blum government to which they gave passive support. The Christian Unions' CFTC—then still merely an insignificant clerical movement—had remained on the sidelines and recruited opponents of the Popular Front.[15] Like the communists, who had adopted a policy of "revolutionary defeatism" during the period of the Hitler-Stalin Pact, some of the socialists who had collaborated with the Vichy regime were heavily compromised in the view of de Gaulle's exile government and the Resistance. Vichy prohibited both the CGT and the CFTC and replaced them with corporative organizations. Both federations, however, preserved considerable cohesiveness while illegal: witness the major strike among miners in Northern France in May 1941. An alliance between the CFTC and the noncollaborationist segments of the CGT thus seemed natural. They united on a common manifesto that attributed responsibility for the defeat of France to capitalism. The political functions of the state were to be separated from the economic ones of the unions, and production was to be directed by compulsory planning.[16] Once the Communist Party was freed from the Hitler-Stalin Pact [through the German attack on Russia] and could bring its own dynamic organization into the Resistance, it sought a rapprochement with the old CGT leadership. This bore fruit with the Perreux agreements of April 17, 1943, which provided for admitting three communists to the eight-man clandestine union leadership. Within the industry-wide as well as locally based unions, the political relationships that had existed before the schism of 1939 were to be restored.[17] In the National Council of the Resistance (CNR), the united CGT was represented by a nonparty member who was close to the communists. The CNR worked out a program whose central economic demands —nationalization of monopolies, of mineral deposits and banks, and state planning for economic reconstruction—reflected the interwar socialist program. The communists demanded only the expropriation of collaborators, a point that was disputed, however, among the Resistance organizations because it lacked precision. Although the communists pressed especially hard, no fusion of the reunited CGT took place with the CFTC. The Christian unions certainly joined the resistance struggle and agreed to a pact for unity of action with the CGT on socioeconomic issues; but they feared that in the case of a merger they could not successfully maintain their religious, educational, and cultural policies in the wake of the CGT, while on matters of organization they would be dragged along by the communists. In contrast to the Church hierarchy, the Christian unions comprised an active component of the Resistance, and they participated in the unions' struggle against the German occupation by means of strikes and sabotage. The agreement for united action proved its worth by the extensive resistance measures during the period of liberation, especially in the general strike called on August 18, 1944, which provided the basis within the city for the liberation of Paris.[18]

After liberation both unions grew mightily. The CGT regained its highest membership figures of the 1936 Popular Front with about 5.5 million adherents; the CFTC attained an absolute peak with three-quarters of a million. Since the CFTC insisted on keeping its own independence as an organization, the movement toward a united union was limited to a pact between socialists and communists. This turned out less cohesive than in Italy, for the French socialists had at least in part preserved their continuity and could resume a more successful and solid tradition. In contrast to the left-wing majority of the Italian socialists, the SFIO kept its distance as an organization from the PCF, and by cooperation in the cabinet with the MRP—then a prevailingly progressive mass party of Catholics—it created a counterbalance to the communist influence. In the long run the united trade union could not overcome the gap continuing between the parties, for the trade union federation served less as an economic interest group in the postwar crisis than as an instrument of political order. The distance between the two currents showed up as early as 1946, as the socialists within the CGT increasingly opposed communist organizational policies and their transformation of the united trade union into a mass political federation. The socialists paid for their ambivalent alliance policies with declining union membership as well as considerable losses at the polls and internal party revolts.[19]

On the other hand, it was the merit of the tripartite governments and of their alliance with the two major unions to transform into reality during 1945–46 a good part of the structural reforms that the National Council of the Resistance had envisioned: nationalization of mineral deposits, of large transportation enterprises, of the largest banks and insurance companies, the expropriation of collaborationists (especially of the Renault works), the establishment of the state's economic planning instruments, the participation of unions and consumer cooperatives in the supervision of nationalized industries, legal protection for factory councils, and extension of social security. Even if the achievement fell short of socialist demands, of all similar efforts to democratize the economies of the West, this came closest to realization.[20]

Structural reforms, however, could not solve the economic and financial problems of reconstruction. Instead, because an effective social redistribution of the costs of the war was avoided and the economy was progressively deregulated, a dichotomy resulted, similar to what had marked the Italian economy with far less pervasive structural reform. On the one hand, there was reconsolidation of the bourgeoisie, and on the other, undernourishment and underemployment of the working class. Even the CPF leaders could not durably resist the pressure from its rank and file—most notably a major strike for higher wages in the nationalized coal mines; and finally the leadership reluctantly had to take over the direction of a spontaneous strike in its own labor stronghold at Renault.[21] The socialist prime minister, who was then negotiating with the United States for economic assistance, took the occasion to dismiss the communists from the government. Although thrust into opposition, the communist leadership still behaved throughout the early summer months of 1947 as if it were a government party. On the other hand, as the American [Marshall Plan] initiative in Europe took shape, French government policies shifted to the Right. The new trend decisively increased the factionalism within the CGT and ended with the secession of the Socialist Force Ouvrière (CGT/FO) once the communists employed the CGT to unleash a political strike against the Marshall Plan, a tactic familiar from Italy. Still, as in Italy the preeminent participation of the French Communist Party in the Resistance and then in the postwar coalitions meant that although the socialist union leaders might secede from the CGT, there was to be no proportional loss of rank-and-file membership. The CGT remained the dominant economic and political interest group representing the French workers, while the FO remained a relatively insignificant faction, even in comparison to the Catholic CFTC.[22]

*A United Movement Without a Unified Organization. Structural Reform Without Codetermination in England.* The English case demonstrates that the movement toward united unions in the early postwar years was perhaps inconceivable without socialist-communist cooperation, but was nonetheless no mere consequence of communist preponderance (as might have been presumed from events in the Latin countries). Admittedly the British Communist Party had emerged from its sectarian isolation after its turn to the Popular Front and especially after 1941, and during the war it achieved control of a group of union locals and some regional federations. However, the disputes over accepting the CP as a corporate member of the Labour Party revealed that the communists and their supporters in 1943 had only a bit over one-third, and in 1946 not even a fifth of the votes at the union-dominated Labour Party conferences; and even of these the actual communist members were only a small minority.[23] Admittedly the communist position in the Trade Unions Congress was stronger, especially since the divisions separating them from other left-wingers were fluid. Nonetheless, communist representation was not the only, or even the immediate, cause for the TUC's major initiative to overcome the schism in the international trade-union movement. This derived instead from the situation of 1941 when only the Soviet Union and Great Britain stood as besieged military adversaries of German fascism and the TUC took the occasion to initiate an Anglo-Soviet trade-union committee. In the following years this first step was extended with the result that a united World Federation of Trade

Unions was formed on May 30, 1945, bringing together communist, independent, and united unions with the exception of the American Federation of Labor.[24] Without the political influence of the left wing of the TUC, which extended far beyond the communists, the great social-welfare progress of the wartime coalition government in Great Britain and of the [post-1945] Labour government would likewise have been brought about only with the greatest difficulty. On the other hand, even these epoch-making reforms in the areas of social insurance, national health service, educational reform, and urban reconstruction were more the products of liberal and technocratic innovation than of socialist or Marxist theory.[25]

Besides the initiative for trade-union unification and the gains for social welfare, few trends attributable to the Left connected the British with the Continental program for the united trade union. What was noteworthy in Britain was the great organizational progress of the TUC, which more than recovered the setbacks of the interwar period. The returning flood of old members into the unions and the additional recruitment was not distributed equally among all regional or factory locals of the fragmented English union movement, but redounded above all to the benefit of the large unions, once again those in the TUC. The average size of the TUC unions was about twice as large in 1945 as in 1930, but the number of unions was down about 10 percent to 192. Their total membership nearly doubled to about six and a half million, of which over half were concentrated in six large unions. The proportion of all union members whose federations belonged to the TUC attained what was to be a high point of 84.7 percent. Even in the five postwar years the concentration in favor of the large unions continued, although the TUC could not extend its own monopolistic percentage share of union members until the mid-1960s. At the end of the Second World War the number of independent unions was half the number of those at the end of the First World War, even if with 780 it remained very high. It is nonetheless clear that given extraordinarily difficult and fragmented conditions, the war and the immediate postwar period brought considerable growth of membership together with decisive progress toward large industrial unions and consolidation of a national union. Thus, along with the wartime "opening to the Left," the political and economic outlines of a united labor union were discernible even under specifically British conditions.[26]

Such progress would not have been thinkable without unified policies. Although spontaneous wage strikes took place more frequently toward the end of the war, ever since 1941 the leadership of the TUC, the Labour Party, and the Communist Party continued to support the efforts of Churchill's government to raise production and stabilize wages. As Minister of Labour, Ernest Bevin, the most prominent union representative in the cabinet, was even able to have organized strikes declared illegal, a ruling that the Labour government extended until 1951.[27] Pressure for increased production, wage stabilization, and avoidance of strikes under conditions of full employment were, however, to become points of conflict between the Labour government and the TUC, also between Right and Left, and between leadership and rank and file in the deepening postwar financial and balance-of-payments crises.[28] The record of workdays lost in the more or less spontaneous strikes that were not organized by the unions is eloquent: 1944, 3.7 million; 1945, 2.8 million; 1946, 2.1 million; 1947, 2.4 million. During the wage freeze of 1948 the number sank below the 2-million mark, to exceed it again only in 1952.[29]

The TUC's attitude toward structural reforms was also characteristic of the tendency to focus the broad united labor movement upon specific trade-union objectives. Great Britain not only developed its state-planning instruments during the reconstruction period, but the Labour government, decisively supported by the TUC, carried out a series of spectacular nationalizations. The government began with the Bank of England, the transportation industries, and other infrastructural key activities such as health and gas and electricity, then moved to strengthen control over public planning and eminent domain for the establishment of new cities, and finally nationalized the coal and steel industries. Certainly these measures did not come to pass because of any communist pressure; they corresponded far more to the technocratic tradition of the intellectual Fabian socialists—indeed it has been questioned whether such partial socialization is really in the interest of the working class.[30] The Labour government's nationalizations, nonetheless, were more extensive than those of any other Western country of the era (even if they were only a way in part of making up for prior backwardness). They exceeded even the short-term goals of the West German labor movement.

But quite in contrast to labor on the Continent, the English union leadership did not want to help direct the nationalized industries unless it was through party and state supervisory agencies. Traditionally the British saw codetermination, on the one hand, as an expression of left-wing syndicalism, much as represented by the shop-steward movement, guild socialism, and workers' control that had arisen to challenge union authority in the factories after World War I. On the other hand, British labor perceived a threat to the unions' capacity for resistance in that consultative committees in the plants might prove friendly to management. Even in the nationalized sector union leaders did not wish to infringe upon the principle of free collective bargaining. In accordance with English democratic tradition they interpreted industrial democracy as an application of the parliamentary conflict between government and opposition to the adversary relationship over salary and working conditions between the worker and management, even the management of the nationalized industries. Union participation in plant management would encourage ambivalent responsibilities, which, in view of the extensive autonomy of the rank and file in the British labor movement, could only produce a crisis of legitimacy for the union leadership. The TUC thus supported nationalization to achieve higher rationality for the national economy, but rejected any participation in the leadership or control of the factories. As a compromise, though, a group of the most important union leaders were summoned to the management boards of the nationalized sectors. In fact, they thus sacrificed their trade-union roles. They were certainly unable to avoid the reproach that they had merely won plums for the union elite, a charge that was levelled as soon as it became clear that wages and working conditions had not really changed by virtue of nationalization of the factories.[31]

*A Flawed United Union and Postponed Structural Reforms in West Germany.* Developments in organization and function certainly allow the united trade union in occupied Germany, especially in the Western zones, to be compared with those in the other large European industrial nations. But the contradiction between the especially restricted political sphere of action and the all-encompassing programmatic expectations of a democratic economic utopia remained characteristically German. The existing scholarly literature runs the risk of assuming that this vision, coupled with the constraints imposed on the rank and file at the time the unions were reorganized, added up to a dynamic socialist potential. Against this potential the repressive occupation powers are posited as a purely exogenous factor. But unless one answers the question why the French and Americans above all were in a position to prevent the rapid reconstitution of a united trade union in Germany as well as partially to prohibit, partially to postpone, its basic programmatic demands, one misconceives the problematic contrast between theory and practice.

Both the opportunities for, as well as the major impediment to, a united trade-union movement in Germany arose from the fact that the working-class movement had been so thoroughly defeated by fascism that it simply disappeared as an organization. The collapse of democratic counterweights—liberal institutions and an organized labor force —was what initially made possible the self-destructive running amok that capitalist society embarked upon in Germany in 1933 under National Socialist leadership. In this respect the loss of national sovereignty at the end of the war, which made the development of parties and unions directly dependent upon the respective interests of the victors, really goes back to the particular and the collective failures of the non-Nazi organizations during the world depression. The self-imposed isolation of the communist union organization and the nonresistance and compliance (*"Gleichschaltung von innen"*) [32] with which socialist and Christian union leaders hoped to preserve their organizations in the Third Reich had precluded their unity and any mobilization of their strength. Deprived of a common combat experience, the working class could not achieve a common effective resistance.[33] Fascist persecution of trade-union and political cadres forced the leadership, if not to imprisonment or death, into the atomization of foreign or "inner" emigration.

Still, the class basis of the union organizations (in contrast to the integrative nature of parliamentary parties) meant that whatever organizational unification of the working-class movement during the transitional period of resistance and emigration was achieved was most successful in the trade-union sphere. The common trend toward organizational and political unification did not mean, however, that the same format and programs were followed everywhere. The initiatives of those German trade-union groups in exile unmistakably reflected the trends in their lands of asylum. Similarly within Germany trade union leaders in the resistance often took the Nazi DAF (German Labor Front) as a starting point for a future democratic union evolution. Three major organizational forms can be distinguished: socialist and Christian labor leaders in the Resistance and in the Swedish emigration wanted a process of democratic transformation that would divest the DAF of its corporative characteristics.[34] The communists advocated a so-called *Eintopf*-[goulasch] union, a united political union borrowed from their experience in the Latin countries in which the political authorities at the local, regional, and national levels were to possess the upper hand over the economic interests of the factory- or industry-wide locals.[35] Finally, the union émigrés in England, influenced by the concept for the World Trade Union Federation, developed a model that laid less stress on central organization. With its emphasis on party neutrality it can be seen more in terms of an invitation to the Christian unions than as a unification of social democrats and communists.[36]

All three models proliferated widely among the groups seeking to found local unions once the Allies occupied Germany. In addition, local variants sprang up, such as shop-steward movements. Former union leaders who were reinstated in their old work resumed their old organization by industry. What proved decisive for implanting these models in the locals that were taking shape, but a factor that scholarly literature has hitherto understressed, was the return of numerous union leaders from abroad with the first Allied troops. The Communist Party groups attached to the Red Army are widely known; in the West, too, there were many delegates of the National Free Germany Committee for the West," who flowed from France, Switzerland, and Belgium into western and southern Germany especially. [The Free Germany Committee had been organized originally among German prisoners of war in the Soviet Union and was thus sympathetic to Russian objectives; the one for the West presumably united sympathizers from the other countries.—Ed.] Finally, there was a group of social democrats from the English emigration who were placed in the most important German cities as collaborators of the American intelligence service, the OSS. Although officially enjoying only an advisory function, they still provided significant help with programs and organization by virtue of their knowledge and connections.[37]

In contrast to this indirect assistance, the Allies also intervened directly in trade-union autonomy. The Soviets advanced the *Eintopf-*union model in their zone, seeking so far as possible an all-German federation with a centralized Party-nominated leadership. In the western zones, as well as in the East, it included a strong communist component and generally took the name Free German Trade Union Federation (FDGB). All the occupation authorities vetoed any effort to convert the DAF into a union, a goal that was sought, for example, by Hans Böckler in Cologne or Markus Schleicher in Stuttgart. The Americans favored organizing unions industry by industry as economic interest groups. The British and Americans imposed a step-by-step plan for organizational reconstruction from the local and factory level up and thus hindered any rapid buildup of trade-union power at the higher leadership levels of the Weimar era, while the French permitted federation at the state (*Land*) level but tenaciously resisted any consolidation of national unions.[38] Besides the influence of the emigration and the military governments, foreign unions also played a role, as they sought —sometimes in cooperation with the occupying power—to win over German colleagues for their own union format and programs. The AFL committed its efforts for the longest period, rejecting the gradualist pattern of union reconstitution that the American military government desired because it feared that this procedure would result in a larger communist influence. Instead, the AFL advocated building up economically oriented industrial unions in the western zones with strong participation on the part of the prewar reformist union leadership. A TUC delegation also played an important role when it made clear to the union leaders of the British zone that the English would never agree to any form of centralized united union whether derived from the DAF or the communist model.[39]

Thus preliminary decisions on organizational questions tended to set the pattern for a highly diverse structure of unions, which in fact tended initially to stagnate at the regional or zonal level. From the outset two paths diverged. The first was the political, centralized united union of the Soviet sphere, which was also represented among those western locals that had a particularly strong communist rank and file. The second included the diverse variants of the already elastic model from the English emigration—now watered down even further—that prevailed in the western zones. The western Allies could look with all the more favor on regional organizational levels retaining their predominance, because this would avoid any repetition of the split between local groups striving for autonomy and the national summit of the labor movement, such as had occurred in Italy under American impetus.[40]

The second basic problem of organization concerned the extent, the interests, and the spontaneity of the potential unions. Reorganization began immediately after the occupation. It was regarded by all participants as more important than the building of political parties, and quickly became a wide-ranging effort.[41] Independent of their immediate interests and their political affiliations, many workers and employees saw joining the new unions as the most natural and direct response to their earlier suppression in the Third Reich, no matter what sort of form they might be taking in their own particular locality. The unions were founded on two different bases at the same time: on the one hand, built around the usual old leaders organized by region; on the other, organized at the plant level.[42] In contrast to Italy, however, neither sort of organization won much power. Regional fragmentation weakened the leadership groups, while the rank and file lacked the experience of conflict and the militance of the national movements of liberation. Without the self-consciousness imbued by a successful resistance, diminished by the large numbers of workers drafted for war service, and demoralized by their own split from the reserve army of forced labor the Nazis had imported, German workers had relatively little spontaneous capacity for political action, especially for carrying out any purge. On the other hand, they demonstrated intense interest in cooperative self-help and union representation in order to resume production, to secure jobs, and to reach a minimal level of welfare. This working class was far readier than, say, the partisans in southern Europe to accept union wage restraint within an overall partnership for growth in order to overcome the postwar crisis. Certainly there were cases in Germany, as elsewhere, of the divergence between union cooperation on behalf of recovery for society as a whole and the immediate interests of the rank and file. Comparatively speaking, however, these discrepancies were mere nuances. The dismantling of Antifa [Antifascist groups that were organized by workers at the time of surrender] and factory committees, then later of factory councils as unions and administrative agencies were reestablished, ran an undramatic course. The same activists frequently just took over a new function. This certainly contributed to democratizing the regional leadership of the emerging union organizations, but at the same time meant subordination to new responsibility and discipline.[43]

Besides labor's own weakness, direct Allied rule and the more serious postwar economic and infrastructure crisis in Germany also contributed to the restraint on "class struggles in the western zones." [44] These conditions diminished the clout and influence of the unions. In a situation where planning and wage freezes were not the work of a national government that needed the support of union leaders, but were instead decreed directly by the military authorities in the different zones, military power replaced the strength of the labor unions in integrating workers into the process of reorganizing and increasing production. To the degree, however, that the unions in Germany were unnecessary for the economic system, they failed to win the positions that would have let them exact social and economic structural reforms or essential social welfare gains as the price of their cooperation. On the other hand, insofar as the bargaining position of the unions was already weak at the start of the occupation, there was less conflict than in other countries with the rank and file, which was itself less active than elsewhere. (The relative position of the grass roots in the unions did benefit, however, from the fact that all social interaction tended to be reduced to the local level during the economic crisis.) Instead the leaders and rank and file both concentrated on the effort just to build a united trade union in the face of Allied restrictions. Thus the early postwar years were dominated by the question of organization. And the unifying tradition that a common resistance against fascism provided elsewhere was replaced by a united resistance to the limitations on union development that the Allies imposed as well as against their industrial dismantling policies.

The situation changed when the occupying powers abandoned efforts to increase coal production by coercive measures. But the new incentives to extract higher output promptly precipitated in 1947 familiar short-term reactions: a campaign for increased output, strikes protesting malnutrition, progress toward codetermination and nationalization.[45] Although the occupying powers prevented the German unions from taking advantage of the general socioeconomic function served by the West European united unions until 1947, and even, in part, through 1949, the unions still sought to play the equivalent social role as elsewhere. They aligned themselves as auxiliaries in the Allied-directed process of reconstruction. For many union leaders believed along with Hans Böckler that the capitalist order at home had been critically weakened with the collapse of Germany's economic potential.[46] This meant that they felt labor could first fulfill its social responsibilities and help with reconstruction, then later could always push through nationalization and other structural reforms. The very social democrats who in 1945 frequently viewed socialism as the task of the hour were now willing to postpone it according to Kurt Schumacher's maxim: *Primum vivere, deinde philosophari* [The first thing is to live; philosophy comes later].[47] In practice this meant following the communist tactic of seeking strength for a future socialist transformation by undergoing a period of testing in the pragmatic work of reconstruction.

Resuming the program of Economic Democracy [48] in the 1945 situation also seemed to mean at first inheriting its greatest disadvantage, namely, the lack of any strategy to compel nationalization, planning, and codetermination. Many advocates believed that these concepts should no longer be fought for, but merely introduced into a receptive economic order by recourse to the ballot. This would supposedly have let the unions inherit a pivotal social role as organizer of a communal economic order. The unions themselves would then become the instrument of social bargaining and compromise while they could downplay their old role, still retained in England, of championing the particularistic interests of the working class in labor struggles. By virtue of the extensive list of nationalizations and the demand for an equal union voice in management, German objectives likewise transcended French goals, even though the CGT occupied a far more favorable strategic position vis-à-vis the reformist political coalition than did the fragmented German unions in respect to the occupying powers. The majority of German union leaders thus faced an unresolved contradiction between an overambitious socialist utopia and their actual partnership for economic reconstruction with the military governments and with the firms and state agencies that had survived and whose very recovery made realization of the union program ever more unlikely. This contradiction resulted from a flawed perception of the international interests in contention, but it also derived from an

abstract union plan for reconstruction that failed to relate the unions'
organization and envisaged function either to each other or to the tactical situation, but only to the expectation of some future socialist
order.

The special role of the communists in the postwar unions still requires explanation. Just as the communists in the Russian zone of occupation sought to establish their own form of the united union by means
of negotiations among the organizational elites in the FDGB,[49] they
similarly cooperated in the unions of the western zones and in their
practical behavior were distinguishable only in nuance. Still, it is inaccurate to claim, as is frequently said about 1945–46, that political
differences played no role in reconstructing the unions. Sufficient
examples can be cited in which former socialist and Christian trade
unionists perceived the growing number of communists in the unions
and especially in the factory councils as a threat and sought to cut
them back.[50] The communists, however, wanted to use union discipline and concerted action to achieve unity and establish themselves.
Tilman Fichter has argued that this method of taking root and
mobilizing a mass base was more realistic than urging socialism as the
task of the day, but that the communists were politically inconsistent in
1947. At that time spontaneous strikes broke out in the Ruhr, as in
France, against a union-supported campaign for increased output even
while food shortages continued. In Fichter's view the communists
failed to develop the socialist mass base that had become, as it were,
capable of action. Instead they domesticated the class struggle and
proved unable to mobilize an equivalent potential with their subsequent
political struggle against the Marshall Plan.[51] Since a more accurate
analysis of the motives and course of these 1947 strikes still remains to
be written, any estimate of their potential must remain uncertain. In
any case the critique completely fails to take into account the limiting
conditions on communist policy of the day. If we bear in mind the
French events of the spring of 1947 as well as the continuing FDGB
efforts at interzonal conferences to achieve a united union throughout
Germany (granted, one that would follow their own pattern as far as
possible) [52] there is no doubt that the communists insisted on a united
union from higher considerations quite independent of the interests of
specific workers. In particular, they wanted to keep developments in
each country during the "antifascist-democratic" transitional phase
parallel and coordinated, and not let themselves become isolated in
terms of Europe as a whole by letting the class struggle break out prematurely in different locations.

## The Schism

The united union movement broke off during 1948 in the West European countries. In France, the socialists, and in Italy, Catholics, liberals, and a segment of the socialists split from the united unions, which thereupon became entirely communist mass organizations. In England a campaign against communist union officials was begun and the TUC withdrew its membership in the WFTU. Anti-communism and adherence to the new International Confederation of Free Trade Unions (ICFTU), which arose out of the WFTU schism, also characterized developments in the West German zones once efforts failed to found an all-German union organization (which alone could have produced a political united union in Germany). These last sections of the article should reveal what factors led to the political split in the unions and what consequences resulted for the changing functions of the rump unions, especially for the German Trade Union Federation (DGB) that was constituted only at this time.

Some reasons for the end of the WFTU have already been given. As worked out in recent research they contrast with accounts of the time that presented the union schism as an expression of a democratic struggle for self-determination against communist subversion.[53] Causes now adduced include the large-scale political and economic initiatives of the United States' European policy after 1947 and AFL support for the European opponents of the united unions.[54] These external factors certainly require closer illumination. On the other hand, external influences could never have proved effective if within the political united unions, and in the relationship of their policies to actual social conditions, the explosive material was not already at hand for American policy to ignite. It is worth analyzing here again the internal problems of the political united union so as to counteract the superficial thesis that manipulation alone was at bottom—as if the vital currents of the European working-class movement could be held back by virtue of diplomatic trickery and a bit of bribery.[55]

*Organizational Reasons.* We have tried to demonstrate here that the typical political united union basically rested on an alliance between social democrats and communists. In the case of the postfascist countries, this was an alliance in which Catholic unions could also participate because once all unions had been shattered and compulsory corporative bodies established, a wider solution had become possible. For the communists the united unions were a means for establishing themselves politically and for carrying out their gradualist "antifascist-democratic" strategy of transition. For the social democrats, the united unions offered a means to integrate the labor movement and then by virtue of its united mass to push through structural reforms along the lines of the Economic Democracy program. The unions would thus become an instrument of rational planning and of compromise among interests for the sake of society as a whole. For both points of departure the national political economy took priority over the traditional function of representing particularistic worker interests, especially in view of the postwar economic crisis, shortages, and the need for growth. On the other hand, the noncommunist labor leaders had been trained precisely in the old unions that had always focused on wage issues. They hardly felt that the goals of Economic Democracy, as they had been worked out in the 1920s by social democratic intellectuals, were their primary task.

Conflict was thus in the offing between a policy on wages and social issues geared to the interests of the membership and a policy of united union cooperation on issues of wage stabilization, growth, and structural reform for the sake of the economy as a whole. Throughout 1945–46 it smouldered in the tensions between local and plant organizations and the top leadership. Only in Western Germany did this conflict fail to produce a clear confrontation because there, reconstruction of the unions was delayed. Even in the other countries it did not initially shatter the organization because in the crisis at the end of the war, cooperation was more important than wage-and-price issues, the future seemed open, and the labor movement was granted, as it were, a vote of confidence in advance. The more the economic system recovered, however, the more important the pay issue became, and the more difficult it grew to secure union cooperation in the campaign for higher production. After the difficult winter of 1946–47, when throughout large areas of Europe energy and food supplies fell to their lowest point, the latent conflict came to a head with massive strikes. The centrist union elites were put under pressure from both the left and right of the working-class movement to reorient the political united union toward more direct advocacy of the workers' immediate economic interests. In France, for example, the AFL delegation found a willing ear among the [noncommunist] opposition with their argument that worker interests should take precedence over political unity and were best represented by industrial unions, even if they had to secede.[56]

On another level, however, the conflict broke out even earlier in Germany. The primacy of industrial unions over political united organizations was not merely wrested from the union leadership by the military government and the TUC. From the outset it found support—

most clearly in Hamburg [57]—among the old industrial union leadership of the Weimar era who feared that a centralized united union would replace the old labor functionaries with communist politicians and neglect wage contracts in order to pursue political tasks with murky goals. Had the Anglo-American influence not found a willing reservoir of experienced trade-union organizers, the Allies' injunctions against the centralized political union could have been treated as mere formalism and easily circumvented. In fact, they amounted to deciding between two German groups, one of which might call for unity from the base up [58] while the other—the noncommunist—was able to build largely independent industrial unions with a quiet efficiency. In France and Italy, on the other hand, the noncommunist secessionists lamented their lack of organization because the syndicalist tradition and the extreme breadth of the postwar unions worked against the German pattern.

Party disputes partially strengthened, partially overshadowed this conflict. In the united union organization social democratic or Catholic officials competed directly with communists in terms of tactical and propaganda skills and dynamism. Until 1947 the communists made rapid progress in this competition everywhere that the occupying powers did not exert counterpressure; nor could anyone demonstrate their disloyalty. This was the case not only within the CGT, the CGIL, and the TUC—leading to a clear communist preponderance in the first two—but also in Germany, for example, in the FDGB of Greater Berlin or the industrial unions (for example, the mine workers) in the British zone.[59] At the same time communist gains were also clear within the executive organs of the World Federation of Trade Unions.[60]

Yet after the experience of Stalinist reversals on the question of unity, competitors still suspected that the communists' tactical adroitness far outstripped their credibility. The forced unification of communists and social democrats in the Soviet zone of Germany certainly strengthened this conviction. Yet to help those who had been outmaneuvered reconquer their mass base and their majorities required the effective public-relations tactic of exposing the communist advance as one of subversion carried out with sordid methods such as electoral fraud, organized tricks, political disloyalty (e.g., contrivance of "spontaneous" strikes), or as a misappropriation of the workers' interest groups for partisan ends. Events that could be interpreted in this sense were not lacking, and between 1946 and 1948, especially in the communist-dominated organizations, they were exposed with increasing propagandistic effectiveness (made possible in part through AFL assistance). In Germany the formation of the Berlin Independent Union

Opposition (UGO) against the FDGB was the most spectacular expression of this widespread trend.[61]

*Reasons in International Politics.* What proved finally decisive in triggering the potential for conflict within the united union was the social crisis of 1947, which took place in most of those European countries where the working class governed in alliance with bourgeois forces. For the bourgeois and some of the socialist representatives in these governments reacted overwhelmingly to the economic collapse of the winter and spring of 1947 with a desire for foreign economic aid.

The calculation of the liberal [i.e., laissez-faire] economists who directed economic and financial policy (including the West German Bizone * since mid-1947) looked toward the reestablishment of capitalist relations of production by replacing the political pact for growth with market mechanisms.[62] Economic stabilization was expected from elimination of the excess money supply left from the war and deregulation of the economy. This would raise the value of landed and industrial property, compel rationalization [i.e., higher efficiency and concentration of enterprises], lower the price of labor and bring the concealed unemployed into the labor force, attract investment, and draw goods to market. Capital assistance from abroad could thus help to prevent the collapse of state revenues and of the balance of payments, and the additional investment might provide a spur to growth that could at least partially limit the expected decline in wages and increased unemployment.

Given the fact that the Marshall Plan, whose capital grants made possible these [neo-liberal] reforms, divided the parties in the unions, it must be noted that American capital assistance was an economic prerequisite only within the framework of this program for liberalization. In most respects the collapse of early 1947 could be attributed to an infrastructural crisis of growth and of distribution within and between the European countries—for example, a breakdown of transportation in the Bizone at the end of 1946.[63] In this respect the collapse could also have been overcome by greater reliance on, and coordination of state control mechanisms—especially if coupled with an easing of restrictions on German production and foreign trade on the part of the occupying powers—along lines of elaborating the structural reforms already introduced.

* Ed. Note: The Bizone referred to the 1947 joining of the British and American zones into a common economic and administrative unit. Once French resistance was overcome a year later, this became the basis for a West German state.

The agreement of the West German unions to United States credits was a key decision because the food problem of the Bizone was the immediate spur to the American project and because the communists in many other united unions campaigned against American assistance. So far as we can tell, the German union leaders felt themselves under duress, given the need to finance food imports under the discriminatory foreign-trade constraints imposed by the Allied powers. Nonetheless they recognized the dangers of accelerating the division of Germany and of increasing the American influence hostile to structural reforms, especially to nationalization in the Ruhr. But since a direct conflict with the occupying power seemed hopeless, they could only attempt to at least hold open the option for structural reforms while advocating the credits. Hans Böckler coined the effective public slogan: If necessary it was better to postpone socialization than to starve.[64]

The Americans, who were obviously interested in the productive employment of their European aid, seized their opportunity. Their capital exports gave them a strategic position in the affected European economies, and at the same time allowed them to integrate these economies into a political order.[65] Even in the preliminary phase of the Marshall Plan they made it clear, not only by military government interventions in Germany but through loan negotiations with France and Italy as well, that as complementary measures they expected security against any revolutionary reaction by the labor movement, including containment of its influence and of anticapitalist structural reforms. Dissolving the ties with the communists in the governments and the unions thus had fundamental importance. The dismissal of the communists from the French government and the secession of a Christian union in Italy created the preconditions for economic aid.[66]

In Western Germany the Americans could be active in their own right once the British had conceded the American leadership role in Germany as a consequence of their own credits from the United States. They could delay decartelization, suspend nationalization in Hessia and North Rhine Westphalia, break the social democratic majority in the Bizone by setting up a second level of institutions, favor the Berlin noncommunist unions, keep in force a wage freeze and a prohibition on strikes, and undertake their own currency reform.[67] Military government looked on approvingly as the communists left the state governments and as the interzonal trade-union conferences ran into increasing difficulty and finally ended. Clay also recommended to union leaders that they give up structural reforms and tend more to the immediate interests of their members (although he interpreted even these interests very narrowly, in accordance with a preconception of class collaboration).[68] Not without reason, the Soviet Union saw the

Marshall Plan as an effort to undercut the economic and political basis
of the communist strategy of an "antifascist-democratic" transition to
socialism. This was to have been directed after all by means of communist participation in the European governments and mass organizations, especially the united unions. From the second half of 1947
the Communist parties of Western Europe thus threw their entire weight
into demonstrations against the U.S. initiative. But just this focusing
of an economic into a political crisis had to end up serving American
purposes. For the middle-class Left and the social democratic doubters
who saw the Marshall Plan as essentially a welcome injection of capital could only recognize that the communists were seeking to make the
unions the transmission belt of their political defensive and were
dropping their moderation in this conflict with their previous government partners. The Soviet trade-union newspaper [Trud] demanded
that the reformist advocates of the Marshall Plan be expelled from the
leadership of the WFTU. The TUC responded with the counterthrust
that ended with the schism of the WFTU.[69]

Secondly, the Soviet Union saw the Marshall Plan as an attack on the
integrity of its Eastern European sphere of influence. The desire of
the Czech government to receive Marshall Plan funds was an index
that American containment policy already possessed implications of
"rollback." But as an unoccupied country, Czechoslovakia was the
classic model of an "antifascist-democratic" transition to socialism in
the garb of a bourgeois republic. Were she to vote for the U.S. credits
the issue would immediately arise whether to repress similar desires
in other peoples' democracies by military force or to accept political
reversals as a consequence of American capital exports. For that reason the communists had to act preemptively in the Czechoslovak Republic. First the Czech government was threatened into withdrawing its
assent to the Marshall Plan conference, which also blocked in advance
any similar inclinations elsewhere, as, for example, in Poland. Developments in Czechoslovakia were then forced apace, especially by
means of the communist-dominated factory groups and unions; the
coalition was ended by the thoroughly organized Prague coup, and
finally a Stalinist dictatorship was instituted.[70]

The Prague coup, for which the ground at least was prepared by a
hysterically defensive reaction on the part of the Soviet Union, was a
political folly of the first order insofar as Western Europe was concerned. Comparable to the foundation of the Socialist Unity Party two
years earlier [which forced East German social democrats into a
communist-dominated structure] and to the later Berlin blockade, the
Prague coup became a psychologically pivotal event that led to the far-
reaching isolation of the communists in Western Europe and de-

stroyed all their postwar labors. More effectively than any American propaganda or pressure, the Prague coup cost the communists their credibility among their trade-union allies. The communist reaction to the announcement of the Marshall Plan made the noncommunist working class's adjustment to the political order entailed by American policies of economic restoration far easier. The reorientation began with the hitherto contained conflicts in the WFTU finally coming to a head and ending in schism. Then, according to the different balance of political forces from place to place, came the secession of the noncommunist unions (in France, Italy, Berlin) or the imposition of clear anticommunist limits by the predominantly social-democratic unions (in England and West Germany).[71]

The AFL, which had remained distant from the international union movement even in 1945 because of its uncompromising hostility to communism, abetted this process of secession by sending several missions to Europe with moral and material support. After early successes these initiatives for isolating the communists in the European unions—which complemented those of the Marshall Plan—won CIA support.[72] In France they certainly created the preconditions for the secession of the social-democratic Force Ouvrière but could hardly prevail upon the mass working-class base to switch loyalties. Nonetheless, the inner dynamic of the CGT was broken, especially since industrialists further sabotaged the union in the area of wage contracts. Even the proposal that businessmen negotiate with the noncommunist unions and thus leave the communists economically functionless corresponded to an American suggestion. What was left of the CGT, however, was too strong simply to be circumvented. The upshot of the tactics followed after the breakup of the united union was simply to weaken the entire French labor movement for more than a decade.[73]

In Western Germany the AFL was not content merely with strengthening a sympathetic union potential by sending CARE packages to tried-and-true officials, providing newsprint and money for anticommunist propaganda (e.g., for the Berlin UGO), and exerting influence on behalf of independent bread-and-butter unions. Above all the AFL was able to exert pressure on the American government so that it would no longer impede the reconstruction of union organizations at the bizonal or trizonal levels. For delay only weakened the position of the old union leadership vis-à-vis the integrated organization of the FDGB.[74]

This meant that major union officials faced an especially painful decision in view of the whole labor movement's (CDU members included) post-1945 commitment to all-German goals. Either they could discontinue organizing the unions at the new [West

German] levels of political decision-making; or, in cooperation with the occupying authorities, they have to accept the political order implicit in the move toward a West German state. With the collapse of the interzonal trade union conference over the issue of the Berlin UGO in mid-1948, priority would be given to developing a cartel of industrial unions in the three western zones rather than to the long-term goal of political, all-German organizational unity. Nonetheless, this meant more than just retaining the bird in the hand. Admittedly the provisional character of the Basic Law [the constitutional instrument of the Bonn Republic] made it easier to agree to a Western state and to renounce a constitutional framework that would have established the structural reforms inherent in the basic union demands. Nevertheless, the fact that the same concepts of Economic Democracy still shaped the DGB's platform of 1949 [75] demonstrated that despite all the constraints and defeats of the occupation period, union leaders still believed they could yet bring about the program of the united union. For now the unions were organized at the highest levels of the political order, and labor's claims could no longer be countered by military demands.

After the international union schism, the labor movement in most European countries went on the defensive for a good decade. In the period of Cold War reaction the collapse of the political united union made it possible not only for businessmen to play off the unions against each other, but also led to a smouldering crisis of function and identity among the competing unions, especially in France and Italy. The structural reforms of the postwar years were partially reversed (e.g., some of the British nationalizations), or completely changed their social function under conditions of capitalist restoration—as in the case, perhaps, of planning and control of investment in France. For most unions the given way to overcome this identity crisis was to resume an aggressive wage policy, whether with longer-term objectives of class conflict or social partnership, and this generally led to a relatively high level of pay within limited national rates of economic growth. (Where bourgeois monetary reform redisclosed structural unemployment as in Italy, even wage possibilities remained very limited.) At the same time, though, wide circles of workers and especially white-collar employees assimilated the values of efficient performance and consumption that characterized capitalist society. . . .

## Notes

1. Horst Lademacher, *et al.*, will be publishing a long essay on the WFTU

in the 1978 *Archiv für Sozialgeschichte*. For now, see Julius Braunthal, *Geschichte der Internationale*, vol. 3 (Hanover, 1971), pp. 23ff., Hans Gottfurcht, *Die internationale Gewerkschaftsbewegung im Weltgeschehen* (Cologne, 1962), pp. 169ff.; W. Z. Foster, *Abriss der Geschichte der Weltgewerkschaftsbewegung von den Anfängen bis 1955* (East Berlin, 1960), pp. 524ff., 593ff. Some important documentation in FDGB (Freier Deutscher Gewerkschaftsbund), ed., *Zwanzig Jahre Weltgewerkschaftsbund*, vol. I (East Berlin), 1965. For the Communist Party concept of the "antifascist-democratic" stage in Europe, cf. the survey in M. Einaudi, J.-M. Domenach, A. Garosci, *Communism in Western Europe* (Ithaca, N.Y., 1951); F. Claudin, *La crise du mouvement communiste*, vol. 2 (Paris, 1972), pp. 361ff.; F. Fejtö, *Geschichte der Volksdemokratien*, vol. 1 (Graz, 1972); E. Seeber, "Die volksdemokratischen Staaten Mittel- und Sudeuropas in der interationlen Klassenauseinandersetzung zwischen Imperialismus und Sozialismus (1944–1947)" in *Jahrbuch für Geschichte der sozialistischen Länder Europas*, vol. 16, 2 (1972), pp. 39ff.; W. Diepenthal, *Drei Volksdemokratien* (on Poland, Czechoslovakia, and East Germany, 1944–48), Cologne, 1974; and for country studies especially A. J. Rieber, *Stalin and the French Communist Party 1941–1947* (New York, 1962); A. Sywottek, *Deutsche Volksdemokratie* (Düsseldorf, 1971). Of documentary value for the German case: G. Mannschatz, J. Seider, *Zum Kampf der KPD im Ruhrgebiet für die Einigung der Arbeiterklasse und die Entmachtung der Monopolherren 1945–1947* (East Berlin, 1962); H. Laschitz, *Kämpferische Demokratie gegen Faschismus* (East Berlin, 1969).

2. On the results of structural reform, cf. the stock-taking in W. Weber, ed., *Gemeinwirtschaft in Westeuropa* (Göttingen, 1962); R. Krisam, *Die Beteiligung der Arbeitnehmer an der öffentlichen Gewalt* (Leiden, 1963); G. Leminsky, *Der Arbeitnehmereinfluss in englischen und französischen Unternehmen* (Cologne, 1965).

3. The economic history of the immediate postwar phase is still largely unresearched, and just reconstructing the statistical basis for this period of great fluctuations presents special difficulties. For a survey see M. M. Postan, *An Economic History of Western Europe 1945–1964* (London, 1967); for an American estimate of the political economy of Western Europe in 1945–46, Gabriel and Joyce Kolko, *The Limits of Power* (New York, 1972), pp. 146ff. For a basic model of reconstruction, F Jánossy, *Das Ende der Wirtschaftswunder* (Frankfurt, n.d. [1969]), and for the period at the end of the phase see the comparative analysis of labor force potential in Charles P. Kindleberger, *Europe's Postwar Growth* (Cambridge, Mass., 1967). The economic crisis at the end of the war concealed a largely preserved stock of industrial capital and a still highly qualified labor force, which could quickly bring high growth rates to all European countries. In the German case the expansion of the war economy, which exceeded the toll of destruction, was balanced out by the postwar immigration. The economic upswing was delayed because of a longer aftereffect of the postwar crisis (e.g., collapse of raw materials and intermediate product supplies, effects of the occupation regime); but it did not begin merely because of

liberalization and the Marshall Plan. Cf. W. Abelshauser, *Die Wachstumsbedingungen im britisch-amerikanischen Besatzungsgebiet 1945–1948* (Stuttgart, 1975); M. Manz, *Stagnation und Aufschwung in der französischen
Besatzungszone von 1945 bis 1948* (Dissertation: Mannheim, 1968).

4. In this respect little has changed since Walter Ulbricht informed
German Communist Party functionaries in East Berlin on June 25, 1945,
that the "ideological devastation . . . has penetrated deep into the ranks of
the working class." Walter Ulbricht, *Zur Geschichte der deutschen Arbeiterbewegung,* vol. 2 (East Berlin, 1963), p. 437. Justification of the coalition
policy despite a "revolutionary wave in all of Europe," in Institut für
Marxismus-Leninismus beim Zentralkommittee der Sozialistische Einheits
Partei, ed., *Geschichte der deutschen Arbeiterbewegung,* (East Berlin, 1968),
chap. 12, pp. 28ff.; Jean Duclos, et. al., *Histoire du Parti Communiste
Francais (Manuel)* (Paris, 1964), pp. 439ff.

5. The policy of the U.S. armed forces in respect to the civilian popula-
tion in the liberated areas is documented by H. L. Coles and A. K.
Weinberg, *Civil Affairs: Soldiers Become Governors* (Washington, 1964).
For contemporaries the British intervention in Greece had special impact.
See Heinz Richter, *Griechenland zwischen Revolution und Konterrevolution
(1936–1946)* (Frankfurt, 1973), pp. 495ff. On the American attitude to the
European Left, Gabriel Kolko, *The Politics of War* (New York, 1970), pp.
31ff., 428ff. Even in 1946, the U.S. wanted to intervene militarily in France
and Italy in case of a communist electoral victory or attempted coup: see
J. and G. Kolko, *Limits of Power,* pp. 149f., 156f.

6. On union development in postwar Italy, B. Salvati, "The Rebirth of
Italian Trade Unionism, 1943–1954," in S. J. Woolf, *The Rebirth of Italy,
1943–1950* (London, 1972), pp. 181ff.; D. Albers, "Von der Einheit zum
Kampf um die Einheit," in *Das Argument* AS 2 (1974), pp. 120ff.; D. L.
Horowitz, *The Italian Labor Movement* (Cambridge, Mass., 1963), pp.
181ff.; on the political connections the essays by Quazza and Catalano in
Woolf, *Rebirth,* pp. 1ff., 57ff.; Braunthal, *Internationale,* vol. 3, pp. 69ff.;
Federico Chabod, *Die Entstehung des neuen Italien* (Reinbek, 1965). On
the resistance movement and the strikes of March 1943 in North Italy,
R. Battaglia and G. Garritano, *Der italienische Widerstandkampf 1943 bis
1945* (East Berlin, 1970), pp. 16f.; Charles F. Delzell, *Mussolini's Enemies*
(Princeton, 1961), pp. 207ff. On self-government in the liberated area
there is only one pioneering study in German: H. Bergwitz, *Die Partisan-
enrepublik Ossola* (Hanover, 1972), pp. 64–66 on its unions.

7. E. Rosen, "Victor Emanuel III und die Innenpolitik des ersten
Kabinetts Badoglio im Sommer 1943," in *Vierteljahrshefte für Zeitgeschichte*
12 (1964), pp. 44ff., especially 81ff. Text of the Buozzi-Mazzini agreement
on factory councils in M. F. Neufeld, *Labor Unions and National Politics
in Italian Industrial Plants* (Ithaca, N.Y., 1954), appendix A. For the
German parallel, Fritz Tarnow, "Labor and Trade Unions in Germany," in
*The Annals,* 260 (1948), pp. 90ff.: "Great eagerness to arrange a May 2nd
in reverse and to take over the German Labor Front." (p. 92).

8. For the developments under German occupation in the North, see

Salvati, in Woolf, *Rebirth*, pp. 189ff.; for the Allied attitude in the South, C. R. S. Harris, *Allied Military Administration of Italy 1943–1945* (London, 1957), pp. 445ff.

9. Salvati, in Woolf, *Rebirth*, pp. 185ff.; Horowitz, *Italian Labor Movement*, pp. 186ff.; M. F. Neufeld, *Italy: School for Awakening Nations* (New York, 1961), pp. 451ff.

10. On Togliatti's *"svolta"* (his change from antifascist opposition to Badoglio to joining the royal government), cf. Delzell, *Mussolini's Enemies*, pp. 336ff.; Claudin, *La crise*, vol. 2, pp. 403ff. For the CP influence on the CGIL and the affiliated socialists, Braunthal, *Internationale*, pp. 79ff., and in detail in Horowitz, *Italian Labor Movement*, pp. 202ff., 244ff. Nationalization in Italy did not derive from communist influence, but rather was initiated by Mussolini, then De Gasperi, to protect the private economy by taking over firms threatened by the depression. Cf. R. Jochimsen, "Die öffentlichen bzw. öffentlich beherrschten Wirtschaftsunternehmen im Italian," in Weber, ed., *Gemeinwirtschaft*, pp. 229ff., esp. 245; and M. Einaudi et al., *Nationalization in France and Italy* (Ithaca, N.Y., 1955), pp. 196ff.

11. Marcello De Cecco, "Economic Policy in the Reconstruction Period, 1945–1951," in Woolf, *Rebirth of Italy*, pp. 156ff.

12. Salvati, in Woolf, *Rebirth*, pp. 189, 195ff. Admittedly agreement was reached on wage escalator clauses (Albers, in *Das Argument*, pp. 128ff.), and mass dismissals were prevented at first. Nonetheless, the pay level had barely reached the austere prewar levels when prices had already doubled.

13. Albers, in *Das Argument*, pp. 132ff.; Horowitz, *Italian Labor Movement*, pp. 208ff.

14. See note 1; also W. Goldschmidt, "Ökonomische und politische Aspekte des gewerkschaftlichen Kampfes in Frankreich seit dem Zweiten Weltkrieg," in *Das Argument*, AS 2 (1974); Val R. Lorwin, *The French Labor Movement* (Cambridge, Mass., 1966), pp. 99ff.; Georges Lefranc, *Le mouvement syndical de la libération aux événements de mai-juin 1968* (Paris, 1969), pp. 11–40; J. Bruhat, M. Piolot, *Aus der Geschichte der CGT* (East Berlin, 1961), pp. 169ff.; A. Barjonet, *La C.G.T.* (Paris, 1968). For communist policy, R. Tiersky, *Le mouvement communiste en France (1920–1972)* (Paris, 1973), pp. 94ff.; J. Fauvet, *Histoire du Parti Communiste Français*, vol. 2 (Paris, 1965), pp. 139ff., 159ff., and local studies such as P. Guiral, *Libération de Marseille* (Paris, 1974), pp. 111ff.; Etienne Dejonghe and D. Laurent, *Libération du Nord et du Pas de Calais* (Paris, 1974), pp. 157ff., 217ff. For the communist stance on purging the CGT of collaborationist socialists see Rieber, *Stalin and the French Communist Party*, pp. 177ff.; Peter Novick, *The Resistance versus Vichy* (New York, 1968), pp. 131ff.

15. Henry W. Ehrmann, *French Labor from Popular Front to Liberation* (New York, 1947); anon. *La C.F.D.T.* (Paris, 1971), pp. 32ff.; G. Adam, *La C.F.T.C. 1940–1958* (Paris, 1964), pp. 37ff.

16. Text in Lorwin, *French Labor Movement*, pp. 315ff.

17. Ehrmann, *French Labor*, pp. 262ff.

18. Program of the CNR and CGT proposals for it, in Henri Michel

237    Charles S. Maier

and B. Mirkine-Guetzevitch, eds., *Les idées politiques et sociales de la Résistance* (Paris, 1954), pp. 199ff., 215ff. To the CGT proposal were appended communist and socialist amendments that indicated that the communists sought the renewal of the Popular Front's social legislation while the socialists wanted a large sphere of uncompensated nationalizations. On the CFTC attitude, Adam, *La C.F.T.C.*, pp. 93ff.; Lefranc, *Le mouvement syndical*, pp. 16ff. In addition, the CGT (like the German Federation) was impaired by the foundation of employee unions, especially the Confédération des Cadres. See H. Lange, *Wissenschaftlich-technische Intelligenz—Neue Bourgeoisie oder neue Arbeiterklasse?* (Cologne, 1972), pp. 113ff.

19. B. D. Graham, *The French Socialists and Tripartisme 1944–1947* (London, 1965), pp. 184ff.

20. On the nationalizations, H. Raidl, "Unternehmen und Institutionen der öffentlichen Wirtschaft in Frankreich," in Weber, ed., *Gemeinwirtschaft*, pp. 97ff.; M. Byé, "Nationalization in France," in Einaudi, ed., *Nationalization*, pp. 238ff.; a comparison with England in W. A. Robson, ed., *Problems of Nationalized Industry* (London, 1952), pp. 238ff. On participation, Leminsky, *Arbeitnehmereinfluss*, pp. 70ff.; P. Durand, *Die Beteiligung der Arbeitnehmer an der Gestaltung des wirtschaftlichen und sozialen Lebens in Frankreich* (Luxembourg, 1962). On planning and its transformation, P. Bauchet, *La planification française* (Paris, 1966).

21. On the PCF's campaign for production and on the strikes up to its dismissal from the government, Lefranc, *Le mouvement syndical*, pp. 29ff., 42ff.; Braunthal, *Internationale*, vol. 3, pp. 61–65; Lorwin, *The French Labor Movement*, pp. 105ff. Graham, *French Socialists*, pp. 252ff.; Rieber, *Stalin and the French Communist Party*, pp. 310ff., 347ff.; Duclos, *Parti Communiste (manuel)*, pp. 469ff.

22. On the schism and the preceding so-called Molotov strike, Lefranc, *Le mouvement syndical*, pp. 52ff.; Lorwin, *French Labor Movement*, pp. 119ff.; Barjonet, *C.G.T.*, pp. 49ff., who emphasizes CIA involvement in the formation of FO. From a syndicalist viewpoint, P. Monatte, *Trois Scissions syndicales* (Paris, 1958), pp. 176ff.; communist viewpoint in Duclos, *Manuel*, pp. 507ff.; and especially Bruhat and Piolot, *Geschichte der CGT*, pp. 193ff:; FO viewpoint itself in G. Vidalenc, *Die französische Gewerkschaftsbewegung* (Cologne, 1953), pp. 60ff.; A. Bergeron, *F.O.* (2nd ed.: Paris, 1972), pp. 24ff.

23. Braunthal, *Internationale*, vol. 3, pp. 24ff.; Henry Pelling, *The British Communist Party* (London, 1958).

24. See note 1 above.

25. On the influence of the labor movement on the government, H. Pelling, *A History of British Trade Unionism* (2nd ed.: Harmondsworth, 1971), pp. 210ff.; P. Oehlke, "Grundzüge der Entwicklung der britischen Gewerkschaftsbewegung," in *Das Argument* AS 2 (1974), pp. 65ff., esp. 91ff.; E. Bandholz, *Die englischen Gewerkschaften* (Cologne, 1961), pp. 41ff.; and on the two most important union leaders, W. Citrine, *Two Careers* (London, 1967), and Alan Bullock, *The Life and Times of Ernest Bevin*, vol. 2 (London, 1967).

26. P. E. P., ed., *British Trade Unionism* (London, 1948), pp. 5ff.; Tables also in Pelling, *Trade Unionism,* pp. 280ff.; cf. A. Villiger, *Aufbau und Verfassung der britischen und amerikanischen Gewerkschaften* (West Berlin, 1966), pp. 76ff., 105ff.

27. To avoid a wage freeze or similar government controls Bevin instituted compulsory arbitration for wage negotiations and prohibited strikes and lockouts with his Order 1305 of June 10, 1940. J. Lovell and B. C. Roberts, *A Short History of the T.U.C.* (London, 1968), pp. 146ff. On the institutions, P. E. P., *Trade Unionism,* pp. 35ff.; on resistance to the restraint policies of the government, Pelling, *Trade Unionism,* pp. 216f., 224ff.; Oehlke, "Grundzüge," p. 92.

28. For the government attempts to ease the balance of payments crisis, which led to a wage-freeze agreement with the TUC from 1948 to 1951, see G. A. Dorfman, *Wage Politics in Britain, 1945–1967* (London, 1974), esp. pp. 51ff.; criticism from the communist perspective in Oehlke, "Grundzüge," pp. 97ff.

29. Pelling, *Trade Unionism,* pp. 282f.

30. Among the discussions of British nationalization see: E. F. Schumacher, "Die Sozialisierung in Grossbritannien," in Weber, *Gemeinwirtschaft;* the survey in W. A. Robsen, ed., *Problems;* B. W. Lewis, *British Planning and Nationalization* (New York and London, 1952); D. Goldschmidt, *Stahl und Staat* (Stuttgart and Düsseldorf, 1956)—which also treats denationalization; and for a critique of the mixed economy from a Marxist perspective, B. A. Glynn and B. Sutcliffe, *British Capitalism, Workers and the Profits Squeeze* (Harmondsworth, 1972), pp. 162ff.

31. H. A. Clegg, *Industrial Democracy and Nationalization* (Oxford, 1955); for the opposition from within the unions, the opposed treatment of K. Coates and T. Topham, *The New Unionism—The Case for Workers' Control* (London, 1972), pp. 109ff.; Rudolf Kuda, *Arbeiterkontrolle in Grossbritannien* (Frankfurt, 1970), esp. pp. 139ff. Cf. Leminsky, *Arbeitnehmereinfluss,* pp. 21ff.; W. W. Haynes, *Nationalization in Practice: The British Coal Industry* (London, 1953), chap. 9ff.

32. G. Beier, "Einheitsgewerkschaft," in *Archiv für Sozialgeschichte,* 13 (1973), p. 230.

33. Admittedly many trade union leaders were politically persecuted by the Nazis, and one can demonstrate their general effort to keep in touch with each other, discussions about reconstruction plans for after fascism, and even individual acts of heroism. But neither an active mass resistance nor efforts at organizing a coup emanated from the labor movement. H. G. Schumann, *Nationalsozialismus und Gerwerkschaftsbewegung* (Hanover, 1958); H. Bednareck, *Gewerkschafter im Kampf gegen die Todfeinde der Arbeiterklasse und des deutschen Volkes 1933–1945* (East Berlin, 1966); H. Esters and H. Pelger, *Gewerkschafter im Widerstand* (Hanover, 1967); L. Reichhold, *Arbeiterbewegung jenseits des totalen Staates—Die Gewerkschaften und der 20. Juli 1944* (Cologne, Stuttgart, and Vienna, 1965).

34. Cf. Ulrich Borsdorf, "Der Weg zur Einheitsgewerkschaft," in J. Reulecke, ed., *Arbeiterbewegung an Rhein und Ruhr* (Wuppertal, 1974),

pp. 394ff., which also considers the temporary communist tactic of trying
to penetrate the German Labor Front. Cf. note 7 and the essay by Hans
Mommsen in the Reulecke volume.

35. On the foundation of the Berlin FDGB, J. Klein, *Vereint sind sie
alles?* (Hamburg, 1972); Werner Conze, *Jakob Kaiser. Politiker zwischen
Ost und West* (Stuttgart, 1969), pp. 11ff.; also K. Blank, *Beiträge zum
innerdeutschen Gewerkschaftsdialog* (Bonn, 1971), vol. 1, pp. 15ff.; G.
Griep and Ch. Steinbrecher, *Die Herausbildung des Freien Deutschen Ge-
werkschaftsbundes* (East Berlin, 1968); K. Fugger, *Geschichte der deutschen
Gewerkschaftsbewegung* (East Berlin, 1949; reprinted West Berlin, 1971),
pp. 251ff. The significance of the CGT in the formation of the Comintern
and for the German Communist Party concept of the trade unions is
stressed by H. Bednareck, *Die Gewerkschaftspolitik der KPD 1935–1939*
(East Berlin, 1969), pp. 121ff.; experiences of the other Communist parties
(especially the Italian) after 1943 as they influenced the Central Committee
of the KPD in Laschitza, *Kämpferische Demokratie*, p. 125. Cf. note 37.

36. Klein, *Vereint sind sie alles?*, pp. 108ff.; Borsdorf, "Weg zur
Einheitsgewerkschaft," p. 398.

37. On the National Committee for a Free Germany in the West and
on the German-language groups in the CGT, see Klein, pp. 11ff,; K. Pech,
*An der Seite der Résistance* (Frankfurt, 1974), pp. 263ff.; H. Duhnke, *Die
KPD von 1933 bis 1945* (Cologne, 1972), pp. 407ff.; on the cooperation
of the OSS Labor Desk in London with the International Federation of
Trade Unions (IGB), see P. H. Smith, *OSS* (Berkeley, 1972), pp. 204ff.

38. On the formation of the unions within the limits set by the occupy-
ing powers, see the Beier, Klein, Conze, Borsdorf titles above and: B. A.
Enderle and B. Heise, *Die Einheitsgewerkschaften,* 3 vols., mimeographed
(but not edited) by the DGB (Düsseldorf, 1959); Eberhard
Schmidt, *Die verhinderte Neuordnung 1945–1952* (Frankfurt, 1970); U.
Schmidt and T. Fichter, *Der erzwungene Kapitalismus* (West Berlin, 1971);
J. Kolb, *Metallgewerkschaften in der Nachkriegszeit* (Frankfurt, 1970), and
regional studies such as F. Hartmann, *Geschichte der Gewerkschaftsbewegung nach 1945 in Niedersachsen* (Hanover, 1972); P. Brandt, "Antifaschistische Einheitsbewegung. Parteien und Gewerkschaften," (dissertation,
Berlin, 1972) and now published as *Antifaschismus und Arbeiterbewegung*
(Hamburg: Christians, 1976); H. Christier, *Die Hamburger Arbeiterbewegung 1945–1949* (dissertation, Hamburg, 1974); and such union
accounts as I. G. Metall, eds., *75 Jahre Industriegewerkschaft 1891–
1966* (Frankfurt, 1966); K. Anders, *Stein für Stein* (Frankfurt, 1969);
Hans Mommsen et al., *Bergarbeiter* (exhibit catalogue, Bochum, 1969),
pp. 32ff.; DGB Landesbezirk Berlin, ed., *Berliner Gewerkschaftsgeschichte
von 1945–1950* (Berlin, 1971). Not generally realized is that the French
government—supported at home by communists and socialists—began its
policy of obstructing all-German union development in the ninth session
of the Allied Control Council on October 20, 1945, in opposition to the
wishes of the other three powers. See *Foreign Relations of the United
States,* 1945, III, 846–852.

240    The Origins of the Cold War and Contemporary Europe

39. G. Beier, *Probleme der Gründung und des Aufbaus westdeutscher Gewerkschaften unter dem Primat der Aussenpolitik* (Kronberg, 1972); also R. Radosh, *American Labor and United States Foreign Policy* (New York, 1969), pp. 325ff., and G. S. Wheeler, *Die amerikanische Deutschlandspolitik* (East Berlin, 1958), part 2. For the relations of the WFTU to Germany see the survey from the FDGB perspective in A. Behrendt, *Der Weltgewerkschaftsbund und die deutschen Gewerkschaften* (East Berlin, n.d. [1965]), chaps. 2–6.

40. Cf. th. R. Fisher, "Allied Military Government in Italy," in *The Annals*, 267 (1950), pp. 114ff., especially 117ff.

41. A few exceptions such as Kurt Schumacher aside, most of the activity of the labor movement in the days after liberation or surrender consisted of forming non-party Action Committees and unions, or preliminary factory councils and shop-steward movements, since unity in these areas seemed undisputed. (See notes 43 and 58.) Furthermore the American military government attitude, which allowed union but not political activity, made union work all the more significant. On union policies see Klein, *Vereint sind sie alles?*, pp. 135ff.; and for the licensing of political activity, Lutz Niethammer, *Entnazifierung in Bayern* (Frankfurt/M., 1972), pp. 126ff., 198ff.

42. Many examples of this in Brandt, *Antifaschismus;* Hartmann, *Gewerkschaftsbewegung;* Klein, *Vereint sind sie alles?;* and E. Schmidt, *Verhinderte Neuordnung.*

43. On the Action Committees, Niethammer, *Entnazifierung,* pp. 124ff.; Brandt, *Antifaschismus;* Hartmann, *Gewerkschaftsbewegung;* and Walter L. Dorn, *Inspektionsreisen in der U.S.-Zone,* L. Niethammer, tran. (Stuttgart, 1973), pp. 34ff. The difference from the radicalism of many partisan movements is perhaps clearest by comparison with the Greeks: see D. Eudes, *Les Kapitanios* (Paris, 1970). See also the documentary collection of Borsdorf, Brandt, Niethammer, *Arbeiterinitiative 1945* (Wuppertal, 1976).

44. U. Schmidt and Fichter used this subtitle (for *Der erzwungene Kapitalismus*) to suggest a radical potential. On the unions, G. Beier, "Zum Einfluss der Gewerkschaften," p. 40, I believe, also errs in overemphasizing the unions as "the strongest power in the interregnum."

45. On this combination in Ruhr in 1947 see E. Potthoff, *Der Kampf um die Montanmitbestimmung* (Cologne, 1957), pp. 34ff.; E. Schmidt, *Verhinderte Neuordnung,* pp. 75ff., 134ff.; Schmidt and Fichter, *Der erzwungene Kapitalismus,* pp. 23ff.; F. Deppe et al., *Kritik der Mitbestimmung* (Frankfurt, 1969), pp. 58ff.; Mommsen et al., *Bergarbeiter,* chap. 36ff.; Peter Hüttenberger, *Nordrhein-Westfalen und die Entstehung seiner parlamentarischen Demokratie* (Siegburg, 1973), pp. 410ff.; John Gimbel, *Amerikanische Besatzungspolitik in Deutschland 1945–1949* (Frankfurt, 1971), pp. 159ff., 225ff.; Mannschatz and Seider, *Zum Kampf der KPD,* pp. 195ff.; R. Badstübner, *Restauration in Westdeutschland 1945–1949* (East Berlin, 1965), pp. 233ff.

46. "Capitalism is at its last gasp," Hans Böckler, for example, declared in 1946 (E. Schmidt, *Verhinderte Neuordnung,* p. 68).

47. Said at the Nuremberg Party Congress of the SPD in 1947 (Beier, *Probleme der Gründung,* p. 43): the expression referred most immediately to acceptance of the Marshall Plan but still describes prior party practice.

48. On the further development of the tradition of Economic Democracy among the unions and the SPD see E. Schmidt, *Verhinderte Neuordnung,* pp. 61ff.; H. P. Ehni, "Sozialistische Neubauforderung und Proklamation des 'Dritten Wegs,' " in *Archiv für Sozialgeschichte,* 13 (1973), pp. 131ff.; R. Blum, *Soziale Marktwirtschaft* (Tübingen, 1969), pp. 13ff.; W. Weddingen, ed., *Untersuchungen zur sozialen Gestaltung der Wirtschaftsordnung* (West Berlin, 1950).

49. Cf. note 35. Like the CGIL and the united CGT, the FDGB was constructed from a central executive for the entire Soviet zone of occupation. West German union leaders were forced to renounce this model and work on the regional level by their occupation authorities.

50. E. Schmidt, *Verhinderte Neuordnung,* pp. 120ff.; Mommsen et al., *Bergarbeiter,* chaps. 35 and 38.

51. T. Fichter and E. Eberle, *Kampf um Bosch* (West Berlin, 1974), pp. 26ff. Similiar dissident communist criticism is found in U. Schmidt and Fichter, *Der erzwungene Kapitalismus,* pp. 43ff.; E. U. Huster et al., *Determinanten der westdeutschen Restauration 1945–1949* (Frankfurt, 1972), pp. 175ff. Since this chapter was written a new book on these strikes has appeared: Christoph Klessmann and Peter Friedemann, *Streiks und Hungermarsche im Ruhrgebiet 1946–1948* (Frankfurt and New York, 1977).

52. Only two polemically edited documentary collections are now available on this matter: A. Behrendt, *Die Interzonenkonferenzen der deutschen Gewerkschaften* (East Berlin, 2nd ed., 1960); DGB-Bundesvorstand, ed., Versprochen-gebrochen. *Die Interzonenkonferenz der deutschen Gewerkschaften von 1946–1948* (Düsseldorf, n.d. [1961]). Communist willingness to compromise was expressed in the willingness to keep the Marshall Plan issue out of the WFTU.

53. TUC, ed., *Die unabhängigen Gewerkschaften verlassen den Weltgewerkschaftsbund* (London, 1949).

54. J. and G. Kolko, *Limits of Power,* chap. 12; for the unions see also note 39.

55. This is suggested by G. S. Wheeler, *Politik mit dem Dollar* (East Berlin, 1958), an edition of parts I and II of Wheeler, *Amerikanische Politik,* published by the FDGB.

56. Radosh, *American Labor and U.S. Foreign Policy,* pp. 316ff.

57. Klein, *Vereint sind sie alles?,* pp. 192ff.; Christier, *Hamburger Arbeiterbewegung,* pp. 103ff.

58. This willingness for unity is often interpreted one-sidedly as an innovation of a new class consciousness without its authoritarian and traditional elements being taken into account. Cf. F. Moraw, *Die Parole der 'Einheit' und die Sozialdemokratie* (Bonn, 1973), pp. 60ff.

59. See note 10 and 50; Lorwin, *French Labor Movement,* pp. 107ff.

60. See note 53; Gottfurcht, *Die internationale Gewerkschaftsbewegung,* pp. 185ff.

242    The Origins of the Cold War and Contemporary Europe

61. Radosh, *American Labor and U.S. Foreign Policy*, pp. 310ff., esp. 331ff.; J. Fijalkowski et al., *Berlin–Hauptstadtanspruch und Westintegration* (Cologne and Opladen, 1967), pp. 41ff.

62. The Italian example of this position is analyzed by De Cecco, "Economic Policy in the Reconstruction Period," in Woolf, *Rebirth*, pp. 160ff.; for the German western zones see Blum, *Soziale Marktwirtschaft*, pp. 38ff., 207ff., where the currency reform is seen as the high point of American liberalizing intervention. For the European complex of events, J. and G. Kolko, *Limits of Power*, pp. 428ff.

63. *Ibid.*, pp. 346ff.; for the Bizone, Abelshauser, *Die Wachstumsbedingungen*, pp. 212ff.

64. On Böckler's stance see Ulrich Borsdorff, "Hans Böckler–Repräsentant eines Jahrhunderts gewerkschaftlicher Politik," in H. O. Vetter, ed., *Vom Sozialistengesetz zur Mitbestimmung. Zum 100. Geburtstag von Hans Böckler* (Cologne, 1975). In general on the union stance, Beier, *Probleme der Gründung*, pp. 42ff.,; E. Schmidt, *Verhinderte Neuordnung*, pp. 114ff.; Theodor Pirker, *Die blinde Macht* (2 vols.: Munich, 1960); V. Schmidt and Fichter, *Der erzwungene Kapitalismus*, pp. 37ff. That the political and economic problems of the western zones of Germany were the immediate spur to the Marshall Plan–and that the Americans developed the institutional models for carrying it out in Germany (JEIA, GARIOA)–is undisputed in the literature. See J. and G. Kolko, *Limits of Power*, pp. 349ff.; Gimbel, *Amerikanische Besatzungspolitik*, pp. 196ff., 216ff.; Hadley Arkes, *Bureaucracy, the Marshall Plan, and the National Interest* (Princeton, 1972), pp. 19ff.; J. H. Backer, *Priming the German Economy* (Durham, N.C., 1971), pp. 157ff.; A. Piettre, *L'économie allemande contemporaine* (Paris, n.d. [1952]), pp. 469ff. The most specific such argument is now in John Gimbel, *The Origins of the Marshall Plan* (Stanford, 1976).

65. That U.S. and West European economic stabilization was a motive is shown (besides by Kolko and Gimbel) by J. M. Jones, *The Fifteen Weeks* (New York, 1953), p. 205; H. B. Price, *The Marshall Plan and its Meaning* (Ithaca, 1955), pp. 29ff.; E.-O. Czempiel, *Das amerikanische Sicherheitssystem 1945–1949* (Berlin, 1966), part 3; Arkes, *Bureaucracy*, pp. 43ff., 153ff. In contrast, the anticommunist containment ideology, which grew more intense during the preparation of the aid program, both inside and outside the U.S., was geared more toward creating the public atmosphere and willingness to approve the funds. On this see, R. M. Freeland, *The Truman Doctrine and the Origins of McCarthyism* (New York, 1972).

66. Cf. note 71.

67. The best survey is in Gimbel, *Amerikanische Besatzungspolitik*, passim; for the economic aspect, Blum, *Marktwirtschaft*, pp. 182ff.; H.-H. Hartwhich, *Sozialstaatspostulat und gesellschaftlicher status quo* (Cologne and Opladen, 1970), pp. 61ff.

68. Beier, *Probleme der Gründung*, pp. 33ff., 46ff.; also Beier, "*Gründung*," pp. 47f. for specially clear examples. Documentary material also in Wheeler, *Politik mit dem Dollar*, passim.

69. For an overview, J. and G. Kolko, *Limits of Power*, pp. 361ff.; Her-

bert Feis, *From Trust to Terror* (New York, 1970), pp. 260ff.; Foster, *Abriss*, pp. 606ff.; Gottfurcht, *Die internationale Gewerkschaftsbewegung*, pp. 189ff.

70. Braunthal, *Internationale*, vol. 3, pp. 179ff.; J. and G. Kolko, *Limits of Power*, pp. 384ff.; Claudin, *La crise*, vol. 2, pp. 525ff. for surveys. For the end of the Czech coalition as connected to the collapse of the "third way" in France as a result of the Marshall Plan: R. Künstlinger, *Parteidiktatur oder demokratischer Sozialismus* (Starnberg, 1972), pp. 78ff.; also J. K. Hoensch, *Geschichte der Tschechoslovakischen Republik* (Stuttgart, 1966), pp. 136ff; as a purely internal revolution in the Czech people's own self-conception: Gewerkschaften Prace, ed., *Menschen, Arbeit, Gewerkschaften in der Tschechoslovakei* (Prague, 1959), pp. 55ff.; on the role of the unions, Diepenthal, *Drei Volksdemokratien*, pp. 122ff.

71. For the Italian schism, Salvati, in Woolf, *Rebirth*, pp. 201ff.; Horowitz, *Italian Labor Movement*, pp. 215ff.; in France, Lorwin, *French Labor Movement*, pp. 125ff.; Lefranc, *Le mouvement syndical*, pp. 65ff.; for Berlin, see note 61; for the collapse of the planned Interzonal Congress in Germany, E. Schmidt, *Verhinderte Neuordnung*, p. 118; Behrend, *Interzonenkonferenzen*, pp. 172ff.; cf. note 50. On the anticommunist campaign in the TUC, which was particularly disturbed by the communist agitation against its wage-freeze agreement, see Pelling, *Communist Party*, pp. 153ff.

72. Barjonet, *C.G.T.*, p. 51; Radosh, *American Labor and U.S. Foreign Policy*, p. 323.

73. Goldschmidt, "Ökonomische und politische Aspekte," pp. 22ff., Lefranc, *Le mouvement syndical*, pp. 77ff.

74. Besides Beier, "Probleme der Gründung," pp. 33ff., see the documentation of the Free Trade Union Committee of the AFL, ed., *Die A.F. of L. und die deutsche Arbeiterbewegung* (New York, 1950), and the contemporary critique of Viktor Agartz, *Gewerkschaft und Arbeiterklasse* (2nd ed.: Munich, 1973), pp. 97ff. ("Der Gewerkschaftliche Marshallplan").

75. For union leaders such as Böckler the connection between the Marshall Plan and the division of Germany was clear, but there is no treatment of the union stance during 1947–48 comparable to Hans Peter Schwarz, *Von Reich zur Bundesrepublik* (Neuwied and Berlin, 1966), pp. 299ff. and 483ff., who has analyzed Jakob Kaiser and Kurt Schumacher as representatives of the national labor movement forced into a decision between Marshall Plan and the communists. On the union policy in the constitutional debate see Beier, *Gründung*, pp. 53ff.; W. Sörgel, *Konsensus und Interessen* (Stuttgart, 1969), pp. 201–213.

# Bibliographical Note

English-language publications have generally been cited in the Introduction to this volume, in my own essay reprinted here as chapter 1, and in the brief prefaces to the various selections. A few more works also merit citation: John W. Wheeler-Bennett and Anthony Nicholls, *The Semblance of Peace* (New York: St. Martin's Press, 1972); Lisle A. Rose, *Dubious Victory: The United States and the End of World War II,* vol. I of *The Coming of the American Age, 1945–1946* (Kent, Ohio: Kent State University Press, 1973); on historiography: Robert W. Tucker, *The Radical Left and American Foreign Policy* (Baltimore: Johns Hopkins Press, 1971). Robert James Maddox, *The New Left and the Origins of the Cold War* (Princeton: Princeton University Press, 1973) is in my opinion a flawed critique. On the uses made of history during the Cold War see Ernest May, *"Lessons" of the Past* (New York: Oxford University Press, 1973).

Special country studies could be cited at great length. I have not included a selection on Greece, where President Truman claimed to see a direct Soviet challenge but more likely misinterpreted a native communist uprising, provoked in part by British policies in 1944–45 and later encouraged by the Yugoslavs. The interested reader can turn to John Iatrides, *Revolt in Athens: The Greek Communist "Second-Round," 1944–1945* (Princeton: Princeton University Press, 1972). Iatrides is now carrying forward his research into the civil war of the 1946–48 period. Among the foreign-language studies of European countries in the Cold War period, students should be aware of Hans-Peter Schwarz, *Vom Reich zur Bundesrepublik. Deutschland im Widerstreit der aussenpolitischen Konzeptionen in den Jahren der Besatzungsherrschaft 1945–1949* (Neuwied and Berlin: Luchterhand, 1966), an authoritative effort to describe the revival of West German political life within the options left by great-power rivalry. Ernst Nolte's equally massive, *Deutschland und der Kalte Krieg* (Munich: Piper, 1974) is almost a philosophical reflection, provocative but idiosyncratic and taking its departure point more from the student revolt in the German Federal Republic than from the Cold War itself. Some Italian studies have already been cited; for a synthesis from the perspective of the Left see Franco Catalano, *Europa e Stati Uniti negli anni della guerra fredda. Economia e politica* (Milan, 1972). On the general conditions of Europe see Richard Mayne, *The Recovery of Europe 1945–73* (rev. ed., New York: Anchor Books, 1973).

I have not included a selection on the problem of nuclear weapon rivalry, but the student who wishes to explore this important area can well begin with Martin J. Sherwin, *A World Destroyed: The Atomic Bomb and the Grand Alliance* (New York: Knopf, 1975), and Barton J. Bernstein, "The Question for Security: American Foreign Policy and International Control of Atomic Energy, 1942–1946," *Journal of American History*, LX, 4 (March 1974), 1003–1044, or his "Roosevelt, Truman and the Atomic Bomb: A Reinterpretation," *Political Science Quarterly*, 90 (1975–76), 23–69.

References to social and economic issues in the Cold War era are available in the Niethammer piece above, Thomas Paterson's *Soviet-American Confrontation* (Baltimore, Md.: Johns Hopkins, 1973), and my own essay "The Politics of Productivity: Foundations of American International Economic Policy after World War II," *International Organization*, vol. XXXI (Fall 1977), published also as: Peter Katzenstein, ed., *Between Power and Plenty* (Madison: University of Wisconsin Press, 1978). Labor history for the period has become a specialty in itself and the student can best keep up with literature and documentation for this and earlier periods by following two journals: *Le Mouvement Social* and the IWK (*Internationale Wissenschaftliche Korrespondenz zur Geschichte der deutschen Arbeiterbewegung*). *Le Mouvement Social* has featured discussions of the great strikes and workers' protests of 1947–48. See also the annual *Archiv für Sozialgeschichte,* published by the Friedrich-Ebert Stiftung.

Other major journals that specialize in the contemporary era and the Cold War years include: *Revue d'Histoire de la Deuxième Guerre Mondiale* (with themes that spill over into the eary postwar years); *Revue d'Histoire Moderne et Contemporaine,* and *Rélations Internationales* (both covering a broad period); the *Journal of Contemporary History* (London); *Italia Contemporanea* (formerly *Il Movimento di Liberazione in Italia*)—see, especially, "Il secondo dopoguerra in Italia: orientamenti della storiografia," no. 116 (July–Sept. 1974), 3–96; and *Storia Contemporanea*—with occasional important contributions to the period in *Il Mulino* and *Studi Storici.* The Munich Institut für Zeitgeschichte, which specializes in German history and documentation for the era since 1933, publishes the important *Vierteljahrshefte für Zeitgeschichte.* For ongoing United States contributions and bibliography check the *Journal of American History* and also *Diplomatic History* (along with the *Newsletter* of the Society for Historians of American Foreign Relations).

*Primary Source Material:* While archival investigation is essential for publishable work, students have the opportunity for exciting and genuinely fruitful research in published documentation. The United States Department of

State's *Foreign Relations of the United States* is edited at a stately pace and volumes presently extend up to 1949 and 1950. Those who have worked with both the printed *FRUS* and the State Department files on which they are based testify to the fairness and cogency of the selections made for publication. The underlying files are ordinarily closed for research until the corresponding volumes are published, hence the *FRUS* material is new; and even the volumes of earlier years offer much that has not been systematically thought about and written on. Within each year's issue of documentation, the first volume or two takes up U.N. or security issues and is followed by regional and country collections. For the period during and after World War II, materials on the major international conferences and the postwar Council of Foreign Ministers have been assembled in special volumes. After the publication of upcoming volumes, the State Department will switch to a three-year format so that documents of the 1950's will be selected and published in triennial units. This may diminish coverage and slow up release of the files for the years involved.

No other country currently offers an equivalent series for the post-1945 era, although the British, French, or Russians occasionally publish special collections of documentation relating to treaties and other international matters. As noted above, British cabinet papers, including summaries of cabinet meetings and special papers or studies made for cabinet consideration, are opened up through the last calendar year less thirty. French Foreign Office archives (the Quai d'Orsay) appear to be generally inaccessible for the post-1945 era, but some of the other ministerial collections may slowly be opening up for advanced students. The West German archives for the period of the Occupation reveal the faltering rebirth of political debate within very circumscribed limits. The various files collected at the Federal Archive in Koblenz require permission from the later ministries of the Federal Republic that inherited their functions. The student interested in the German situation in the Cold War can valuably consult the continuing series: *Akten zur Vorgeschichte der Bundesrepublik Deutschland 1945-1949,* issued by the Bundesarchiv and the Institut für Zeitgeschichte and published by R. Oldenbourg in Munich.

Legislative debate can often be frustratingly wordy and imprecise. Still, the student can find important rationales for policy in the U.S. *Congressional Record* and *Hansard's Parliamentary Debates.* The then-important Senate Foreign Relations Committee has also published a Historical Series (1973) of *Hearings Held in Executive Session* on important bills: *Foreign Relief Aid: 1947. Hearings . . . on S. 1774.* 80th Congress, 1st Sess., 1947; *Foreign Relief Assistance Act of 1948. Hearings . . .* 80th Congress, 2nd Sess., 1948; *Legislative Origins of the Truman Doctrine. Hearings . . . on S. 938.* 80th Congress, 1st Sess., 1947; *The Vandenburg Resolution and the North Atlantic Treaty. Hearings . . . on S. Res. 239 and on Executive L.* 80th Congress, 2nd Sess., 1948 and 81st Congress, 1st Sess., 1949.

Major repositories in the United States for unpublished collections include: the National Archives in Washington (with the State Department papers up through the publication date of FRUS) and the Modern Military

Records; the Federal Records Center in Suitlands, Md. (contiguous to Washington) with embassy files and the massive OMGUS papers; the Library of Congress; the Franklin D. Roosevelt Presidential Library at Hyde Park, N.Y.; the Harry S. Truman Presidential Library in Independence, Mo., all with important personal Manuscript collections, and in the case of the Presidential Libraries with the diverse official White House files as well. Princeton University houses the massive James Forrestal diary and papers as well as the John Foster Dulles papers and the partially accessible George Kennan collection.

Published memoirs abound but must, of course, be used with caution. As a beginning, students might consult the following: Dean Acheson, *Present at the Creation. My Years in the State Department* (New York: Norton, 1970)—superbly styled and self-assured and, in a way, representative of two whole Yale University generations of believers in beneficent American power; Konrad Adenauer, *Memoirs 1945–1953*. Beata Ruhm von Oppen, trans. (Chicago: Henry Regnery, 1965); James F. Byrnes, *Speaking Frankly* (New York: Harper & Row, 1947); Lucius D. Clay, *Decision in Germany* (Garden City: Doubleday, 1950)—see the note to the papers below: Milovan Djilas, *Conversations with Stalin*, Michael Petrovich, trans. (London: Pelican Books, 1969); W. Averell Harriman and Elie Abel, *Special Envoy to Churchill and Stalin, 1941–1946* (New York: Random House, 1975); George Kennan, *Memoirs 1925–50* and *Memoirs 1950–63* (Boston: Little, Brown, 1967, 1972); Paul-Henri Spaak, *The Continuing Battle: Memoirs of a European*, Henry Fox, trans. (Boston: Little, Brown, 1972); Harry S. Truman, *Memoirs*: vol. I, *Year of Decisions*, and vol. II, *Years of Trial and Hope* (Garden City: Doubleday, 1955, 1956).

More rewarding than the memoirs are certain journals and diaries, especially John Morton Blum's edition *From the Morgenthau Diaries*, of which vol. III, *Years of War, 1941–1945* (Boston: Houghton Mifflin, 1967) introduces postwar problems; also Blum's edition, *The Price of Vision: The Dairy of Henry A. Wallace* (Boston: Houghton Mifflin, 1973); David Lilienthal's *Journals. The Atomic Energy Years 1945–50;* Jean Edward Smith's edition of *The Papers of General Lucius D. Clay: Germany, 1945–49*, 2 vols. (Bloomington: The Indiana University Press, 1974). Former French President Vincent Auriol's *Journal du Septennat 1947–1954*, Pierre Nora and Jacques Ozouf, eds., 7 vols. (Paris: Armand Colin, 1970– ) has a wealth of material on French politics during the height of the Cold War in Europe.

# Index